I0888574

Prioritizing Employee Mental Health and Well-Being for Organizational Success

Kittisak Wongmahesak
North Bangkok University, Thailand

Roy Rillera Marzo
Curtin University, Malaysia

Uday Kumar Ghosh
Lincoln University, USA

IGI Global
Scientific Publishing
Publishing Tomorrow's Research Today

Vice President of Editorial | Melissa Wagner
Director of Acquisitions | Mikaela Felty
Director of Book Development | Jocelynn Hessler
Production Manager | Mike Brehm
Cover Design | Phillip Shickler

Published in the United States of America by
IGI Global Scientific Publishing
701 East Chocolate Avenue
Hershey, PA, 17033, USA
Tel: 717-533-8845
Fax: 717-533-7115
Website: https://www.igi-global.com E-mail: cust@igi-global.com

Copyright © 2025 by IGI Global Scientific Publishing. All rights reserved. No part of this publication may be reproduced, stored or distributed in any form or by any means, electronic or mechanical, including photocopying, without written permission from the publisher.

Product or company names used in this set are for identification purposes only. Inclusion of the names of the products or companies does not indicate a claim of ownership by IGI Global Scientific Publishing of the trademark or registered trademark.

Library of Congress Cataloging-in-Publication Data

Names: Wongmahesak, Kittisak, 1985- editor | Marzo, Roy Rillera editor | Ghosh, Uday Kumar, 1959- editor
Title: Prioritizing employee mental health and well-being for organizational success / [edited by] Kittisak Wongmahesak, Roy Rillera Marzo, Uday Kumar Ghosh.
Description: Hershey, PA : IGI Gloabl Scientific Publishing, [2025] | Includes bibliographical references and index. | Summary: "The book aims to talk about the impacts the research community by providing empirical evidence supporting the business case for investing in employee well-being"-- Provided by publisher.
Identifiers: LCCN 2025012294 (print) | LCCN 2025012295 (ebook) | ISBN 9798337322100 hardcover | ISBN 9798337322117 paperback | ISBN 9798337322124 ebook
Subjects: LCSH: Employee health promotion | Employees--Mental health | Organizational sociology | Organizational effectiveness
Classification: LCC RC969.H43 P746 2026 (print) | LCC RC969.H43 (ebook) | DDC 658.3/82--dc23/eng/20250606
LC record available at https://lccn.loc.gov/2025012294
LC ebook record available at https://lccn.loc.gov/2025012295

British Cataloguing in Publication Data
A Cataloguing in Publication record for this book is available from the British Library.

All work contributed to this book is new, previously-unpublished material.
The views expressed in this book are those of the authors, but not necessarily of the publisher.
This book contains information sourced from authentic and highly regarded references, with reasonable efforts made to ensure the reliability of the data and information presented. The authors, editors, and publisher believe the information in this book to be accurate and true as of the date of publication. Every effort has been made to trace and credit the copyright holders of all materials included. However, the authors, editors, and publisher cannot assume responsibility for the validity of all materials or the consequences of their use. Should any copyright material be found unacknowledged, please inform the publisher so that corrections may be made in future reprints.

Table of Contents

Detailed Table of Contents

Organizations are becoming more aware of the critical role mental health plays in the general performance of their operations as well as the well-being of their employees in the fast-paced, cutthroat business world of today. It is now commonly acknowledged that an organization's overall performance is greatly impacted by the mental health of its employees. Numerous consequences arise as a result of the employee's mental health. Respectful employment can promote social functioning, self-confidence, and healing for people with mental health problems. Individuals with mental health disorders are more likely to face discrimination at work and be excluded from employment altogether. Mental health is also at stake when someone is unemployed. There is no denying that the mental health of employees has an impact on businesses. Prioritizing mental health at work ethically is also a sensible business move.

This review shows a strong link between employee mental health and well-being, and organizational success. Positive mental health boosts well-being, leading to better organizational outcomes like productivity and retention. Supportive work environments, including work-life balance and social support, are crucial. Interventions improving mental health and well-being directly correlate with better organizational performance (e.g., increased productivity, lower healthcare costs). Investing in employee well-being provides a strong return on investment. Future research should focus on longitudinal studies, contextual factors, diversity and inclusion, and technological interventions. A holistic approach to supporting both mental health and well-being fosters a thriving workforce and sustainable organizational success.

Promoting the psychological health of workers is now a critical global public health priority impacting groups and societies with implications for organizational sustainability and societal advancement. In the wake of heightened workplace stress, burnout and mental health illness, workplace mental health promotion is essential. Organizations need to take a fragmented approach and incorporate mental health, flexible hours and inclusive culture, and regular wellness metrics as part of its approach. With providing employees with access to programs that promote mental resilience, creating open communication channels, and ensuring a fair distribution of workloads, organizations can bolster morale, productivity, and retention. Mental health investment contributes to not only a healthy workforce but also organizational performance, innovation and sustainability in the long run. A workplace that is psychologically healthy lays the groundwork for a more resilient, adaptive, and socially conscious global workforce.

A thriving, sustainable workplace must consider the intersection of Diversity, Equity and Inclusion (DE&I) and employee mental health. Workplaces that are committed to DE&I foster representation and belonging, which benefit employees' psychological well-being. Those organizations that connect DE&I with mental health initiatives tackle systemic inequities and address workplace stressors while creating empathetic cultures where all employees feel seen and heard. Signature strategies include having mentally healthy workplace policies that reflect the diverse needs of the employees, culturally and linguistically competent stigma-reduction programs, and equitable access to well-being resources. The leaders have a critical role to play ensuring psychological safety, driving empathy-led leadership and normalizing

Symbiotic necessities emerging changing corporate dynamic necessitates incorporating employee well-being in sustainable business practices as a means of fostering long term organizational success now and in the future. A diverse workforce increases productivity, lowers turnover and builds corporate resilience. This chapter explores the relationship between employee wellness and sustainability, discussing ways to integrate wellness efforts with business objectives. Some include mental health programs, flexible work policies and workplace ergonomics which lead to increased engagement and job satisfaction. The organizations fostering holistic well-being cultivate an environment of innovation and inclusion, leading to economic and social sustainability. Sustainable business model realizes humans are assets that require investment and collaborative uplift in a healthy work culture creates efficiencies and reduces burnout. It also features successfully integrated well-being into their sustainability frameworks and its impact on profitability and employee retention.

Flexible work policies have become foundational to contemporary organizational strategy, particularly in light of the transformative shifts triggered by the COVID-19 pandemic. This chapter investigates the multifaceted impact of such policies on employee well-being and organizational retention. Drawing from an integrative lens, it incorporates four major theoretical frameworks—Job Demands-Resources (JD-R), Self-Determination Theory (SDT), Conservation of Resources (COR), and Social Exchange Theory (SET)—to provide a comprehensive understanding of how flexible work arrangements influence employee engagement, satisfaction, and organizational loyalty. In addition to synthesizing existing scholarship, this chapter contributes a novel cross-theoretical model that bridges motivational psychology and organizational behavior. It also proposes a suite of policy evaluation tools that blend qualitative and quantitative metrics, enabling organizations to monitor and enhance the effectiveness of flexibility initiatives.

In an increasingly demanding work environment, burnout has emerged as a critical challenge for organizations and their workforce. This chapter will delve into the multifaceted nature of burnout, explore its causes, and present actionable strategies for prevention that can pave the way for a healthier, more sustainable workforce. By applying a holistic approach that encompasses individual, organizational, and societal dimensions, this chapter aims to provide readers with practical insights and tools to mitigate burnout effectively.

This chapter explores promoting employee well-being in the Indian IT industry through mindfulness, work-life balance, and work-life harmony. The high-pressure environment often leads to stress and burnout, making well-being a priority for organizational success. Mindfulness practices, such as meditation and awareness exercises, are highlighted as effective tools for reducing stress and enhancing focus. The chapter advocates for work-life harmony over traditional work-life balance, emphasizing flexibility and adaptability to meet varying employee needs. Leadership's role in fostering a supportive culture is discussed, with an emphasis on empathy, communication, and mental health resources. Case studies from leading Indian IT firms demonstrate the benefits of these strategies, including increased engagement and reduced turnover. Ultimately, the chapter presents a holistic framework for enhancing employee well-being, guiding organizations to cultivate a healthier workforce that thrives in the dynamic IT landscape, aligning individual and organizational goals for sustained success.

Chronobiology, the study of biological rhythms, plays a crucial role in workplace well-being, influencing sleep, cognitive performance, and overall health. In a 24/7 work culture, misalignment between work schedules and circadian rhythms leads to fatigue, reduced productivity, and health risks. Understanding chronotypes—morning,

transparency in AI systems could damage the relationship between patients and clinicians, with decisions based on biased datasets having the potential to reinforce inequities within society. These endeavors would allow the development of new, but still ethically sound, psychiatric practices that would restore public trust in mental healthcare and deliver better outcomes.

Cloud Computing and the Internet of Things have transformed the healthcare landscape in the digital age by improving quality of care and increasing operational efficiency. However, these technologies also entail significant employee data privacy and security risks. The current paper critically explores how the existing legislative measures successfully secure employees' data in the context of such technologies. In particular, a doctrinal research method was adopted to investigate the state of the law in the field and to identify the gaps and weaknesses. The results indicate that the existing rules, namely, the European Union General Data Protection Regulation and Digital Economy Act 2017 are insufficient to protect employee data ownership and access and ensure informed employee consent. In response, the current paper suggests reforming the laws to maintain their effectiveness in the face of rapidly developing technologies.

Health data digitalisation poses privacy and security concerns. Employee data, which we have never been able to access before, is rising with digital health. The strongest laws for the protection of employee data and privacy are actual. Consent, data collection, and third-party use agreements are mandatory for sensitive medical records. This chapter evaluates the state of data privacy due to existing legislative and regulatory measures that control the digital delivery of healthcare. The chapter initially addresses data protection laws and how they measure up against those of other countries. Assessing the results of present measures is best done by comparing them with judicial override and infringement. The findings suggest a need for improved data privacy knowledge and compliance, particularly within digital health.

Preface

INTRODUCTION

In the modern workplace, the conversation around success is no longer just about profit margins, market share, or innovation—it's about people. At the heart of any thriving organization are the individuals who make its vision a reality. Yet, the mental health and well-being of these individuals have long been overlooked in organizational strategies. The ongoing global crises, digital transformation, and fast-paced corporate environments have pushed mental health into the spotlight, demanding a paradigm shift in how organizations think about and support their employees.

This edited volume, *Prioritizing Employee Mental Health and Well-Being for Organizational Success*, brings together an interdisciplinary group of scholars and practitioners from around the globe to explore the critical intersection between employee wellness and organizational performance. Collectively, the chapters offer not only empirical insights and theoretical frameworks but also practical strategies and forward-looking innovations to cultivate mentally healthy, inclusive, and sustainable workplaces.

Each chapter reflects the growing recognition that mental health is not a personal issue to be dealt with outside the office—but a collective responsibility, integral to workplace culture, leadership, policy, and even technology. Our goal with this volume is to offer organizations, HR professionals, leaders, and researchers a comprehensive and actionable roadmap to embed well-being at the core of business success.

CHAPTER OVERVIEW

Chapter 1 by *Deepa Sharma* lays the foundation by illustrating how employee mental health significantly impacts organizational outcomes. It highlights the dual importance of ethical responsibility and business sensibility in nurturing mental health.

Chapter 2 presents a decade-long review by *Namdech, Siriatakkul, Jindachote, and Maneechai*, synthesizing research linking well-being and organizational success. A conceptual framework is proposed to guide future inquiries into this dynamic relationship.

Chapter 3 by *Singh, Chandra, and Wongmahesak* delves into practical interventions for psychological well-being, positioning it as a key to sustainability and workforce retention, while emphasizing inclusive culture and leadership.

Chapter 4 explores how Diversity, Equity, and Inclusion (DE&I) efforts intersect with mental health. *Singh, Wongmahesak, Sonkla, and Chandra* offer practical strategies for creating empathetic and mind-supportive workplaces.

Chapter 5 by *Handa and Sangal* examines leadership's role in shaping well-being, identifying leadership styles and emotional intelligence as critical levers for cultivating resilient, satisfied teams.

Chapter 6 by *Mandhyan and Sybol* introduces the idea of environmental leadership, connecting sustainability practices with employee development and organizational culture transformation.

Chapter 7 by *Bhupinder Singh* reaffirms the need to integrate wellness into business practices, advocating for employee-centric models that yield long-term growth, resilience, and innovation.

Chapter 8 by *Gupta and Nagariya* investigates the impact of flexible work arrangements on well-being and retention. It offers a unique cross-theoretical model and tools for assessing policy effectiveness.

Chapter 9 by *Prerna Mehta* takes a multi-level approach to burnout prevention, blending individual and organizational strategies to build a more sustainable and thriving workforce.

Chapter 10 by *Venkatesh Ganapathy* provides a case-based look at how the Indian IT sector is navigating well-being, mindfulness, and leadership to counteract the pressures of a fast-evolving digital landscape.

Chapter 11 by *Kalra and Kour* introduces the novel application of chronobiology in workplace scheduling, encouraging evidence-based approaches to improve performance and health through rhythm-aligned work design.

Chapter 12 by *Singh and Wongmahesak* explores biomedical innovations using deep learning and digital twins, offering futuristic and data-driven pathways to proactive employee health monitoring.

Chapter 13 by *Chandra, Singh, Wongmahesak, and Kumar* engages with the ethics of AI in psychiatric care. It balances the promise of computational intelligence with the pressing need for transparency, fairness, and trust.

Chapter 14 by *Sahu, Mallick, Singh, Wongmahesak, and Chandra* discusses data privacy in the context of cloud and IoT technologies, addressing legal gaps and proposing reforms for employee data protection.

Chapter 15 by *Mallick, Sahu, Singh, and Wongmahesak* deepens this conversation, emphasizing the unresolved challenges of digital health privacy and urging stronger compliance and awareness to protect employee rights in a data-driven era.

CONCLUSION

This collection reflects a growing understanding that mental health is not a marginal concern, but a strategic imperative. We invite readers to engage deeply with the ideas presented here, adapt them to their unique organizational contexts, and contribute to a future where work not only demands the best from people—but brings out the best in them.

Chapter 1
The Impact of Employee Mental Health on the Success of the Organization

Deepa Sharma
https://orcid.org/0000-0003-4374-917X
Maharishi Markandeshwar University, India

ABSTRACT

Organizations are becoming more aware of the critical role mental health plays in the general performance of their operations as well as the well-being of their employees in the fast-paced, cutthroat business world of today. It is now commonly acknowledged that an organization's overall performance is greatly impacted by the mental health of its employees. Numerous consequences arise as a result of the employee's mental health. Respectful employment can promote social functioning, self-confidence, and healing for people with mental health problems. Individuals with mental health disorders are more likely to face discrimination at work and be excluded from employment altogether. Mental health is also at stake when someone is unemployed. There is no denying that the mental health of employees has an impact on businesses. Prioritizing mental health at work ethically is also a sensible business move.

DOI: 10.4018/979-8-3373-2210-0.ch001

Copyright © 2025, IGI Global Scientific Publishing. Copying or distributing in print or electronic forms without written permission of IGI Global Scientific Publishing is prohibited.

INTRODUCTION

In today's world, mental health has grown in importance, and its effects on the workplace should not be undervalued. The general job performance, productivity, and satisfaction of employees are all significantly impacted by their mental health. Businesses that recognize the value of mental health in the workplace foster a welcoming and inclusive atmosphere where workers can flourish (Aarons et. al, 2006). Employers can take proactive measures to prioritize the welfare of their employees by being aware to mental health in the workplace. Employee well-being and mental health have emerged as crucial elements of organizational performance in the fast-paced, fiercely competitive corporate world of today. Maintaining the mental health and well-being of staff members not only promotes a positive work environment but also boosts output, creativity, and overall company performance (Adane et. al, 2017). This study explains the importance of concentrating on the mental health and well-being of employees as well as how companies can foster supportive work environments. Employee mental health significantly impacts organizational success by affecting productivity, engagement, and overall workplace culture. Prioritizing employee well-being leads to a more engaged and productive workforce, contributing to improved performance and reduced turnover. Conversely, poor mental health can lead to decreased productivity, absenteeism, and increased turnover, impacting the bottom line (Andrew et. al, 2010).

Actually there is a close relationship between work and mental health. Mental health is supported by a secure and healthy workplace, and mental wellness allows individuals to work efficiently. Mental health can be weakened by a dangerous or toxic work environment, and if left untreated, poor mental health can make it difficult for a person to function (Arnetz et. al, 2011). Using personal or sick days, or taking some vacation time, might help you decompress and prevent burnout when you're feeling overburdened by the responsibilities of your job. You will require more than a few days off, though, if you suffer from a chronic mental health condition like anxiety or depression. Additionally, taking care of your mental health at work involves more than just addressing current issues. If your emotional state is affecting your performance at work, you may want to take the time to talk to your employer, especially if the problem is related to your workplace (Bella et. al, 2023). However, it is understandable that many of us are reluctant to talk about our mental health with others, especially with your employer or boss. You may worry about receiving a bad review, tarnishing your reputation or harming your career. Additionally, there is still a stigma attached to mental health, which can make it as challenging to talk about openly as a physical health condition. Some people believe that experiencing stress, depression, anxiety or trauma is a sign of weakness and that it is shameful

(Charles et. al, 2005). However, the reality is that 80% of us experience a diagnosable mental health problem at some point in our lives.

So workplaces can either improve or worsen mental health for everyone, regardless of whether they have a mental health illness. On the one hand, good jobs are recognized to have a positive impact on mental health. It offers a platform for organized routines, wholesome relationships, and the development of a sense of accomplishment and purpose in addition to the ability to earn money (Dekker et. al, 1995). Employment can aid in the healing of those with severe mental health issues and is linked to enhanced social functioning and self-esteem. In addition to being a fundamental right, safe and healthy working conditions are also more likely to increase productivity and work performance, enhance employee retention, and reduce stress and conflict for all employees (Elaine et. al, 2010).

On the other side, stressors that can jeopardize mental health include unemployment, precarious or unpredictable employment, workplace discrimination, and unfavorable working conditions. Suicide attempt risk factors include unemployment, financial and job insecurity, and recent job loss. Inequity in pay, opportunities, or respect at work is some examples of inequality and unequal treatment (Finn et. al, 2012). Due to their color, sex, gender identity or expression, handicap, sexual orientation, or social status, some persons may experience discrimination at work. And origin such like as caste or class, immigration status, religion, age, or any other social trait, making individuals more vulnerable to stress at work or exacerbating pre-existing mental health issues. For those with serious mental health disorders, who are also more likely to be underpaid than the general population, the right to work is one of the most frequently violated rights (Foster et. al, 2021).

In the last we say that mental health affects our thoughts, feelings, and behaviors, it is a crucial aspect of overall wellbeing. Workplace mental health issues are prevalent and can have detrimental effects on both individuals and businesses (Gedecho et. al, 2025). Lower productivity, increased absenteeism, high turnover rates, legal issues, and ultimately a decline in revenue and profits are all possible outcomes. Employers must recognize the importance of mental health in the workplace and provide employees with the support and resources they need to manage and improve their mental health. This will lead to a more engaged, devoted and productive workforce that helps the business succeeds (Giorgi et. al, 2015). Work performance, Presenteeism, and employee absenteeism can all be significantly impacted by mental health. Encourage candid dialogue, offer resources for mental health, and support work-life balance. Strategies for promoting mental health in the workplace include finding balance, creating a happy work atmosphere, addressing mental health in employee development, promoting physical exercise, holding frequent check-ins, forming a wellness committee, reviewing organizational policies and procedures, and setting an example. A key component of any company or organization is employee productivity. It is a gauge of how successfully and economically workers are attempting to meet the company's aims and objectives. Increased productivity among employee's results in income, increased earnings, and overall success for the company (Helen et. al, 2017). The potential for higher revenue is among the most important advantages of high staff productivity. Employee productivity allows them to finish tasks faster and more effectively, which can improve the bottom line. This extra money can be utilized to reward staff for their efforts, grow the company, or invest in new initiatives.

BACKGROUND

Mental health refers to a person's psychological and emotional health, which is important for our thoughts, feelings, and actions. When we are in good mental health we can live happy lives, build and maintain healthy relationships, as well as manage the pressures of everyday life. Mental illness, on the other hand, is a condition that alters a person's mood, behavior, thoughts, or feelings. Mental illness cannot be overcome by determination alone, nor is it a sign of personal weakness (Nelson et. al, 2000). A vital component of overall well-being, mental health has historically been underestimated and frequently disregarded. But we now see how important it is, especially in the workplace. Employees must be given the tools and support they require in order to successfully manage mental health issues. By putting their mental health first, we not only improve their output and performance but also foster a more positive, healthy work atmosphere. For people to prosper in both their personal and professional life and to tackle daily obstacles with fortitude, they must have healthy mental function. The World Health Organization (WHO) acknowledges the significance of mental health and stresses that it encompasses more than just the lack of a mental illness. It affects all facets of a person's life and includes social, psychological, and emotional well-being. A number of factors influence healthy mental function, including:

a. Promoting introspection and self-awareness
b. Fostering wholesome connections with others
c. Encouraging self-control
d. Encouraging the control of emotions

Mental illnesses can impact our thoughts, emotions, and actions. The World Health Organization (WHO) lists a few typical ones as follows:

a. **Anxiety disorders:** Anxiety disorders include panic disorder, obsessive compulsive disorder, and post-traumatic stress disorder.
b. **Mood disorders:** Mood disorders include depression and bipolar disorder, which are characterized by persistently depressing or low moods that interfere with day-to-day functioning.
c. **Schizophrenia:** Hallucinations, delusions, and disordered speech or behavior brought on by an imbalance in brain chemicals are symptoms of schizophrenia.
d. **PTSD:** Uncontrollable thoughts, flashbacks, and acute anxiety brought on by a traumatic event.
e. **Eating disorders:** Anorexia nervosa, bulimia nervosa, and binge-eating disorder are examples of unhealthy eating patterns that have an impact on one's emotions and health.

Indicators of a Workplace Mental Health Problem

Everybody occasionally has awful days at work, when nothing appears to go as planned. You can find it hard to concentrate, feel too worried, agitated, or undervalued, or you might not have the energy or drive to do even the simplest work. However, if you have this feeling every day, it may be a warning sign that something is off. A lot of mental health issues can develop gradually. It's possible to become so accustomed to feeling stressed, nervous, and depressed at work that it becomes normal. However, ignoring the early warning signals of a problem won't make it go away; instead, it will only get worse over time, making you more susceptible to diseases and other health issues, leading to burnout, and negatively impacting your relationships, home life, and performance at work. It's crucial to pay attention to any changes in your thoughts, feelings, and behavior, even if the signs of mental health issues can differ greatly depending on the ailment and the individual (Martin et. al, 2019). If you or a coworker or employee exhibits multiple signs listed below, it may be time to seek assistance immediately.

a. **Deterioration in employee job performance**: You find it difficult to carry out your everyday responsibilities at work as well as at home or in your social life.
b. **Difficulty focusing and thinking:** Your memory, reasoning, or even your speaking patterns are affected, and you have trouble concentrating on tasks.
c. **Alterations in your sleeping or eating habits**: Insomnia, excessive sleep, abrupt dietary changes, or an increasing dependence on drugs and alcohol as a coping mechanism.
d. **Decline in enthusiasm for activities:** You give up pastimes you once loved, stop participating in social events and friendships, or lose interest in parts of your job that you once loved. Profound indifference may accompany this.

e. **Anxiety or fear:** You suddenly feel anxious and afraid in specific situations, or you have an excessive amount of suspicion toward people at work or in social settings.
f. **Heightened awareness:** You attempt to stay away from overly exciting events since you are more sensitive to sights and sounds. You act strangely, unusually, or uncontrollably, feel disengaged from your environment, or see or hear unreal things. Muscle soreness, headaches, and gastrointestinal problems are examples of unexplained aches and pains.

What Leads to Poor Workplace Mental Health?

Mental health issues are common in the workplace and can significantly affect both employers and employees. The World Health Organization estimates that one in four people worldwide may experience neurological or mental illnesses at some point in their lives. This means that a large portion of the workforce suffers from mental health problems at some point in their professional lives. Stress is one of the most prevalent mental health conditions in the workplace. Many things such as excessive workloads, long hours and unstable employment can cause stress. Stress can lead to anxiety and other mental health problems.

It can also have a detrimental effect on an employee's general well-being and productivity, as well as cause physical health problems such as heart disease. Burnout is another prevalent mental health problem in the job. Prolonged stress can lead to a state of mental, physical and emotional exhaustion known as burnout. It is characterized by a feeling of overload, a lack of drive and low vitality. Higher turnover rates, greater absenteeism and reduced productivity can all result from burnout. It's shocking to learn that almost half of people will experience mental health issues at some point in their lives (Montano et. al, 2014). A noteworthy 57.9% of employees agree that their work environment has a moderate to large impact on their mental health. Mental health can be negatively impacted by a wide range of job issues. It can be exhausting to accumulate stress and frustration from toxic interpersonal dynamics, inept management, and unclear communication. Uncertain job duties, strict or long work schedules, unrealistic expectations, and a lack of employee support can all contribute to employees feeling unhappy, depressed, and exhausted. The following factors make the issue even worse:

a. An abundance of tedious or unpleasant jobs.
b. Lack of a spirit of cooperation
c. Being exposed to discriminatory practices
d. Seeing coworkers given preferential treatment
e. Putting up with intimidation or harassment

Let's examine the root causes of mental health issues in workplaces. When considering an employee as a whole, personal or organizational factors may be linked to mental health problems. According to current research, the following are some of the organizations' contributing factors:

- **Work-Life Balance:** The lines separating personal and professional lives are blurred.
- **Workload and Pressure:** Too much work, deadlines, and high standards for performance.
- **Lack of Autonomy and Control:** restricted decision-making and micromanagement.
- **Social Support:** Insufficient assistance from coworkers, supervisors, and the company.
- **Organizational Change:** Lack of communication, reorganization, and uncertainty.

The job becomes a ray of hope when mental health issues arise. Employers are essential in fostering employee well-being because of their supportive behaviors and dedication to safety. In addition to protecting worker's rights, this improves company health by lowering expenses and increasing loyalty and productivity. A vibrant, long-lasting workplace culture is fostered by a strong dedication to employee care. Never undervalue the profound effects that mental health has on the workplace. Employees struggle to manage the burden of financial demands while juggling their personal and professional obligations. For everyone's wellbeing, these issues must be acknowledged and resolved.

How can Companies Encourage Mental Health at Work?

Employers can improve worker well-being in a number of ways, such as:

1. **All-inclusive Benefits:** Provide retirement plans and reasonably priced health insurance, along with programs specifically designed to help mental health.
2. **Work Flexibility:** To assist staff in managing their work-life balance, offer remote work and flexible scheduling choices.
3. **Managerial Engagement:** Frequent check-ins with managers allow for the discussion of solutions, career goal-setting, and employee concerns.
4. **Channels of Private Communication:** For management or HR inquiries, a private online method guarantees secrecy and prompt response.
5. **Workplace Benefits:** Improve the workplace via wellness programs, praise for outstanding performance, and assistance during trying times.

6. **Employee Assistance Program (EAP):** Through an extensive EAP, staff members can access resources like childcare and counseling. For workers facing emotional or professional difficulties, EAPs offer private evaluations, brief counseling, referrals, and follow-up services.
7. **Availability of Therapy and Counseling:** Offering private counseling services enables staff members to deal with challenges from their personal and professional lives in a safe setting.
8. **Programs for Wellbeing:** Programs like yoga courses, exercise memberships, and mindfulness workshops encourage mental and physical health, lowering stress levels and improving general health.
9. **Flexible Work Schedules:** Providing remote work choices or flexible work hours promotes work-life balance, lowers burnout, and raises job satisfaction.

Best Practices for Putting Mental Health Benefits Into Practice

A strategic approach that is adapted to the particular culture and workforce demographics of the company is necessary for the successful implementation of comprehensive mental health benefits. Important things to think about are:

1. **Assessment and Feedback:** Regularly conducting focus groups or surveys to learn about the preferences and needs of employees with regard to their mental health.
2. **Integration with Current Benefits:** Creating a unified support system by coordinating mental health programs with other benefits, such as wellness and healthcare efforts.
3. **Education and Training:** Educating managers and staff on resilience-building, mental health awareness, and de-stigmatization.
4. **Measuring Impact:** Developing measurements to assess how successfully mental health programs enhance company results and employee well-being. Prioritizing comprehensive mental health benefits is a calculated decision that demonstrates a dedication to developing a staff that is engaged, healthy, and productive. Organizations may improve employee retention rates, draw in top talent, and create a resilient workplace culture by taking proactive measures to address mental health. One characteristic that sets forward-thinking companies apart in the recruitment and retention of talent is the provision of mental health benefits. Adopting this trend puts businesses in a leadership position for employee well-being in addition to being in line with ethical obligations. As you continue to improve your workforce initiatives, think about how putting mental health first will affect your employee's lives and futures outside of the workplace.

The Link Between Work and Mental Health

The workplace has a huge impact on an employee's general health and well-being. Your job can give structure, meaning and purpose to your life in addition to monetary benefits. Additionally, it can give you self-realization, boost your confidence and serve as an important social outlet. However, working in a poor environment can have the opposite effect and seriously harm your emotional well-being. Workplace harassment, understaffing, long hours and a lack of support can all increase stress levels and exacerbate mental health problems such as substance abuse, anxiety and depression (Nicholas et. al, 2017). The pandemic and the significant changes to our work habits over the past few years have made these issues even worse. For example, many of us have spent months adjusting to the new pressures of working remotely, only to have to retrain and train ourselves to work on-site once again. As a result we are now stressed, restless and anxious about the future and our daily routines. Employee mental health can influence your work, which in turn can influence your productivity and job performance, just as work can influence your mental health. Indeed, according to current estimates, mental health problems cost the world economy $1 trillion a year in lost productivity, employee turnover, and absenteeism. For the majority of us, we have little control over the conditions at work (Salzer et. al, 2002). Those in senior positions above us shape the culture at work, and we frequently feel unable to voice our opinions for fear of criticism or jeopardizing our employment. There are things you can do to take care of yourself and safeguard your wellbeing, regardless of whether your mental health problems are brought on by your job or originate elsewhere and are impairing your performance at work. With these suggestions, you may learn how to discuss mental health with your boss, deal with typical workplace issues, build resilience, and better work toward reaching your full potential both at work and outside of it.

LITERATURE REVIEW

Employee mental health and organizational success are positively correlated, according to numerous researches. According to Hamouche (2023) this study examined how the corona virus COVID-19 outbreak has affected the mental health of workers, specifically their mental health and psychological distress. The results suggest that COVID-19 had a detrimental effect on people's mental health. Anxiety versus the unknown, quarantine and confinement, stigma and social isolation, financial loss and employment insecurity, and a sense of security are all examples of stressors. Additionally, three types of mediating factors individual, institutional, and organizational have been identified. Additionally, from a human resource management perspective, some suggestions are made to reduce the impact of COVID-19 on worker's mental health, during and after the pandemic. According to Monteiro (2023) the purpose of this review paper was to examine the relationship between workplace culture and employee mental health and well-being outcomes. The results suggest that employee mental health and well-being are significantly influenced by organizational culture. By creating social support, work-life balance, fair job expectations, supportive leadership, and efficient regulations, it is possible to enhance healthy workplace cultures that support workers' mental health and well-being. However, unfavorable workplace cultures including unsupportive leadership, lack of social support, high job demands, lack of work-life balance, and inadequate policies can have a detrimental effect on employees' mental health and well-being. Future research options were also included in this paper, including the need to investigate the moderating effects of individual characteristics and the potential effects of workplace culture on specific mental illnesses. According to Davenport (2016) examined how positive mental health provides benefits in both the job and non-work areas. People with good mental health perform better at work, have better social connections and are in better physical health. Positive work settings can also improve the mental health of employees. The goal of this paper was to build expert consensus on practical, realistic tips that businesses can use to encourage good mental health in the workplace. Overall, at least 80% of the two panelists rated 220 of the 278 initiatives as important or essential. Work-life balance, positive mental health and wellness initiatives, positive leadership styles, effective communication, designing jobs for positive mental health, recruitment and selection, work-life balance and mental health and wellness strategies were among the topics covered by the strategies. According to Shahzad (2024) the purpose of this study was to explore the reasons behind the mental health problems faced by university librarians and to see how these problems affect their ability to work, and what health activities university librarians can engage in to keep their bodies and minds healthy. The research methodology used was a systematic literature review. To carry out the investigation, 43 research articles were selected from peer-reviewed publications. According to the findings of the study, several factors contribute to mental health issues among library professionals, including socio-economic conditions, work-related stress, stigma, ongoing fear, lack of self-efficacy, negative thinking, job security issues, a rigid organizational climate, poor interpersonal relationships, and lack of necessary job skills, chronic diseases, and worldwide pandemics. Librarians' job performance is negatively affected by mental health concerns. The sustainability of librarians' physical and mental fitness is supported by a variety of activities, such as self-care training, continuing professional development, social connections, mental health center membership, emotional health training sessions, and physical and mental exercises, *etc*. According to Wyatt (2023) estimating that 20% of people suffer from mental illness and most employees reporting at least one symptom of poor mental health, mental health issues are a common workplace concern. However, research on issues related to jobs and mental health is still sparse and scattered. We provide a historical summary of how workplaces have addressed mental health versus physical health, highlighting instances in which companies' approach to physical health can be used as a template for addressing mental health. Findings from an interdisciplinary evaluation of 556 studies on mental health issues and work are then presented. The analysis integrates themes into three main categories: interventions, consequences, and antecedents to mental health issues. We offer recommendations for important future research topics based on these findings, such as a greater focus on proactive workplace interventions and studies that examine the intersections and relationships between mental health and mental illness at work. We intend to advance future research on the prevention and support of employees with mental health issues by clarifying the complex relationships between employment and mental health. According to Ruth (2007) this study looked at how work-related pressures affect the mental health of self-employed and organizationally employed workers. Participants were selected from those already involved in Australia's Path through Life project. 2275 men and women between the ages of 40 and 44 who were employed at the time of the interview took part in a community survey. Under the guidance of the interviewer, participants entered their answers into a portable computer. Results showed that both men and women working for themselves reported having more decision-making power than those working for an organization, and women working for themselves also reported having more manageable job demands. Men working for them did not experience any health benefits. However, compared to their colleagues working for organizations, women working for themselves reported poorer physical health. The use of GP services by self-employed men was most strongly associated with work stress factors, but the use of those services by women was more strongly linked to their experiences of stress in organizational employment. In general, it was found that self-employment was associated with comparatively few benefits to mental health. According to Sharma (2020) the purpose of this study was to explore the relationship between mental health and workplace spirituality in which employee engagement acts as a mediating factor. This study also looks at how employee engagement may act as a mediator in the relationship between mental health and organizational justice. 344 Indian information technology professionals provided data. The model fit of workplace spirituality and its relationships to mental health, organizational justice, and employee engagement was assessed using structural equation modeling. The findings showed that organizational justice and workplace spirituality significantly and favorably influence employee engagement, which is strongly correlated with employee mental health. The findings also showed that the relationship between organizational justice and mental health and the relationship between workplace spirituality and mental health are both mediated to some extent by employee engagement. According to Provencher (2011) the purpose of this research was to suggest that adopting a paradigm of mental health as a holistic condition can enhance the study and promotion of recovery. After an evaluation of the literature over the past 20 years, pathways to full mental health in recovery are suggested. With the goal of promoting positive mental health in recovery, more effort is needed to develop interventions focused on improving positive feelings toward life and a sense of fulfillment in both private and social life. More studies on positive mental health are also needed to evaluate the full spectrum of recovery outcomes associated with adaptation and restoration processes. It is also necessary to have a deeper understanding of the environmental and personal elements that support or hinder the attainment of full mental health during recovery. According to Funk (2012) this paper based on the findings of the WHO report on mental health and development, seeks to highlight the negative impacts of untreated mental disorders on human rights, health, society and the economy in low and middle-income countries (LMICs) and to suggest practical ways to address mental disorders and their impacts as part of a comprehensive development strategy. The idea that mental problems should be a major priority for development plans is supported by evidence of the close links between poverty and mental disorders. Homelessness, rates of imprisonment, poor educational opportunities and outcomes, unemployment and low income are just a few of the many and far-reaching social impacts of mental illness. To end the cycle of poverty and mental illness, targeted programmes to reduce poverty are needed. Enforcing human rights protection, facilitating education, employment and housing opportunities and providing readily available and efficient services and support are all examples of actions that should be taken to specifically meet the needs of people with mental health disorders. According to Bovopoulos (2018) found that appointing staff with mental health first aid training as mental health first aid officers (MHFAO) and similar to physical first aid officers (PFAO) who handle physical health emergencies was a new trend in Australian organizations. The goal of this research was to better understand the nature of mental health first aid officer's roles in businesses and to formulate recommendations for other workplaces. The findings showed that depending on their degree of experience, organizations tended to choose different approaches to implementation. Organizations mostly agreed about the advantages and difficulties of the position. According to Codinhoto (2009) the purpose of this article was to present a conceptual framework categorizing the characteristics and qualities of the built environment that influence health outcomes. A thorough evaluation of the literature was conducted and 1,163 abstracts evaluated, 92 papers were reviewed. Despite the lack of clarity about cause-and-effect relationships, there is a significant amount of research that links the healthcare environment to patients' health outcomes.

Reasons for Poor Mental Health in the Workplace

Workplaces are intricate networks of relationships, demands, and pressures that, if not properly managed, can serve as fertile ground for mental health problems. The following elements are highlighted by the World Health Organization as crucial causes of poor mental health at work:

1. **Workload**: Employees may suffer from stress, burnout, tiredness, and exhaustion if they have too much work to accomplish, not enough time to complete it, or too many expectations to meet. Employees' work-life balance may also be impacted by their workload since they may require extra time and effort to attend to their personal and family requirements.
2. **Control**: Workers may feel helpless, irritated, and demotivated if they have little to no control over their work duties, procedures, or results. Employee autonomy and creativity may also be impacted by control since they may have fewer opportunities to voice their opinions or make decisions.
3. **Support**: Workers may feel alone, abandoned, and underappreciated if they don't receive enough assistance from their supervisors, coworkers, or company. Because they could be less likely to receive direction or gratitude, support might also have an impact on employee feedback and recognition.
4. **Role**: Employees may suffer from uncertainty, anxiety, and role strain if their roles, obligations, or expectations are unclear or contradictory. Employee identity and purpose may also be impacted by the function since they may require greater clarification or alignment with their values or work goals.
5. **Relationships**: Employees may experience conflict, harassment, bullying, or discrimination if they have unfavorable or antagonistic relationships with their superiors, coworkers, clients, or stakeholders. Employee trust and cooperation can also be impacted by connections since they may treat others with less respect or cooperation.
6. **Change**: Employees may feel uneasy, insecure, and afraid when they encounter frequent or unanticipated changes to their jobs, policies, procedures, or work environment. Employees may experience less stability or predictability in their work as a result of change, which can also impact their capacity to adapt and learn.

Factors Leads the Mental Health in Workplace

Several factors can have a detrimental impact on workers' mental health at work, including:

1. **Ineffective management and communication techniques:** A good manager-employee relationship is characterized by engaging and kind management methods and communication. On the other hand, inadequate communication and procedures result in strained relationships, poor mental health, and elevated stress levels at work. Mental health can be adversely affected by inadequate leadership, supervisor's lack of support, and a lack of acknowledgment or feedback. Stress levels may rise and job satisfaction may decline for workers who don't feel appreciated or supported.
2. **Low levels of employee support:** Employees may feel overburdened and demotivated if managers fail to share resources or assist in removing barriers. Managers should show staff members how to complete jobs they are unsure of and be ready to answer inquiries rather than relying on them to figure it out on their own.
3. **Pressure to perform:** Employees are subjected to unwarranted pressure to perform at their best all the time. Employees may experience stress, burnout, and anxiety as a result of an excessive workload, lengthy workdays, arbitrary deadlines, and high job demands. Mental health can suffer when one feels overburdened and incapable of handling the workload.
4. **Work-life balance:** Mental health problems may be exacerbated by an unbalanced work-life balance. Employees may experience stress, fatigue, and a decline in general well-being if they are unable to set aside adequate time for hobbies, relationships, and leisure activities outside of work.
5. **Organizational Culture:** An organization's culture has a big influence on mental health. Anxiety, sadness, and other mental health issues can be exacerbated by a toxic workplace that is marked by bullying, harassment, discrimination, or a lack of support from manager and coworkers.
6. **Job Insecurity:** In 2020, workers experienced significant stress from losing their jobs as a result of the COVID-19 outbreak. The dread of not being able to support one's family or pay expenses can have a negative impact on one's mental health. Uncertainty about job security, fear of layoffs, and ongoing pressure to perform well can all contribute to stress and anxiety. When you are emotionally and psychologically healthy, employees come to your work with good mental health, which can affect employee productivity and well-being. Being flexible, resilient, and adaptable comes natural to you. You are able to handle the difficulties you face. You thrive both emotionally and professionally,

and you make a significant contribution to your team. Even if it is not serious, poor mental health at work has many detrimental effects on your career.

Effects of Employee Wellness on Organization Success

Every element of our life is impacted by mental health, which is a crucial component of total wellbeing. It has a significant impact on our thoughts, emotions, and actions. Being in good mental health allows us to live happy lives, build and preserve wholesome relationships, and manage the pressures of everyday life. Contrarily, mental illness is a disorder that impacts a person's thoughts, feelings, behavior, or mood and necessitates support and treatment from a professional. Another crucial element of any company or organization is employee productivity. It gauges how successfully and economically workers are attempting to meet the company's aims and objectives. High staff levels increased revenue, earnings, and overall business performance are all correlated with productivity (Timothy et. al, 2003) . Workplace mental health problems are common and can significantly affect both employers and employees. They may result in high turnover rates, higher absenteeism, lower productivity, and legal problems.

Wellness among employees is becoming a key component of prosperous businesses all around the world. Building a culture that values physical, mental, and emotional well-being is not only advantageous in today's cutthroat business environment, but also essential. Businesses that fund wellness initiatives frequently experience observable results, such as improved employee engagement, less absenteeism, increased productivity, and fewer medical expenses. Every element of our life is impacted by mental health, particularly how well we function at work. When an employee's mental health deteriorates, it can negatively impact key performance indicators including creativity, productivity, and social engagement. Businesses need their employees to prosper and realize their full potential, and a workplace that prioritizes mental health can help them do just that (Tisu et. al, 2020). Companies put a lot of effort into creating a healthy work environment since employee happiness and satisfaction are crucial in today's industries. Employees have potential if the working environment is good. Employees' physical and mental well-being should be in harmony to enable them to concentrate on their work without interruption. Below the effects of employee wellbeing on an organization and the reasons why businesses should place a high premium on it.

1. **Improving Performance and Productivity:** Employee well-being has the most direct effect on output. Employees may concentrate better, perform more productively, and contribute more successfully to the objectives of the company when they are in good physical and mental health. Organizations may be significantly

impacted by workplace mental health issues. Productivity loss is among the most notable effects. Employees who are experiencing mental health problems could find it challenging to concentrate and finish tasks. In the end, this may cause the company to lose money and earnings. Increased absenteeism is another possible effect of mental health problems at work. Workers may be more prone to take time off for medical or mental health-related reasons if they are dealing with mental health concerns. This can generate interruptions at work and raise absenteeism, all of which can have a detrimental effect on the organization's performance as a whole (Veage et. al, 2014). High turnover rates are another effect of mental health problems in the job. Employees may be more prone to quit their jobs if they are experiencing mental health problems. High employee turnover rates can be expensive for businesses because they may need to invest in hiring and on boarding new staff.

a. **Physical Health:** To sustain high energy levels and stamina during the workday, regular exercise, a healthy diet, and adequate sleep are essential. Employees who participate in wellness initiatives that encourage physical exercise, such walking meetings, on-site fitness classes, or gym memberships, stay more physically fit and are more productive.
b. **Mental Health:** One of the main factors reducing productivity is stress. Employee wellness initiatives that incorporate mental health services, such mindfulness training, stress management seminars, or counseling, assist staff in reducing stress, enhancing concentration, and preserving emotional equilibrium. Employees perform far better when they feel emotionally and cognitively supported.

2. **Reducing on Presenteeism and Absenteeism**: Presenteeism i.e. being at work but not performing fully due to health issues and absenteeism i.e. taking time off due to illness are directly correlated with employee wellness. These problems can be considerably decreased by wellness initiatives that focus on early detection and prevention.
   a. **Absenteeism:** Employees in good health are less prone to get sick. Absenteeism rates are lower in organizations that offer access to preventative health services such routine health screenings, immunizations, and exercise programs. The workflow is less disrupted and overall productivity is increased when sick days are reduced.
   b. **Presenteeism:** Health problems such as chronic pain, exhaustion, or stress might keep workers from giving their best effort even when they show up for work. Programs for wellness that focus on mental health, chronic diseases, and ergonomics assist workers remain completely focused on their task, which lowers the productivity loss brought on by Presenteeism.

Because they might have to cover for their absent coworkers, other employees' morale and productivity may suffer as a result of absenteeism. Increased stress and burnout may result from this, which may exacerbate mental health conditions. Furthermore, frequent absences might cause an employee to struggle to keep up with their workload, which can result in subpar work and make it harder to fulfill deadlines. Presenteeism, which occurs when an employee is physically present at work but is not completely engaged or productive because of mental health concerns, can also result from mental health issues. Additionally, the organization may suffer from lower morale and productivity as a result of this. Organizations must acknowledge the influence of mental health issues on employee absenteeism and offer assistance to employees who are experiencing difficulties. This could be granting access to mental health resources, establishing Employee Assistance Programs (EAP) and fostering an environment that promotes candid conversations about mental health. Employers can lessen the effects of absence and assist staff in managing their mental health by offering support (Wendy et. al, 2010). To sum up, mental health conditions can significantly affect employee absenteeism, which can lower morale and productivity among coworkers. Organizations must acknowledge the significance of mental health. And on employee absenteeism and to offer assistance to workers who are having difficulties. This will lessen the effect of absenteeism on the company and assist guarantee that workers can manage their mental health.

3. **Improving Morale and Employee Engagement**: Employee engagement and morale can be considerably raised by a well-executed wellness program. Employees are more likely to feel appreciated and inspired to help the business succeed when they perceive that their employer actually cares about their welfare.
    a. **Workplace Contentment:** Wellness initiatives foster a supportive workplace where staff members feel encouraged to pursue their personal and professional goals. Increased drive, a sense of belonging, and a willingness to go above and beyond in their roles are all results of this satisfaction.
    b. **Employee Retention:** Motivated workers are less likely to quit their jobs. Strong wellness programs increase employee retention because workers value the support and perks they receive. Reduced turnover rates improve the company's financial health by lowering the costs of hiring and training new employees.
4. **Strengthening Communication and Teamwork**: Employee relationships can be strengthened through health initiatives that incorporate team-building exercises, group fitness competitions, or wellness seminars. These initiatives foster friendship, enhance communication, and promote teamwork.

a. **Team Spirit:** Employees connect over common objectives when they take part in wellness initiatives or activities together. This encourages cooperation and a sense of teamwork, which improves workplace collaboration. A more cohesive group can collaborate more successfully and handle issues more skillfully.
b. **Open Communication:** Wellness initiatives that emphasize emotional intelligence, stress reduction, or mental health promote employees to talk more candidly about their wants and difficulties. This fosters a positive work environment where staff members feel comfortable talking about their health, which improves communication throughout the company.

5. **Cutting Medical Expenses**: Employers and employees may both save a lot of money on healthcare by investing in employee wellness. Wellness programs reduce the risk of mental health disorders, chronic diseases, and other long-term health challenges by encouraging healthy lives and preventive care.
   a. **Prevention of Chronic Disease:** Wellness initiatives that emphasize lifestyle modifications, such as eating better, exercising more, and getting regular checkups, can aid in the prevention of chronic diseases including diabetes, heart disease, and obesity. This lessens the need for expensive hospital stays and medical procedures.
   b. **Mental Health Support:** Burnout, sadness, and anxiety are just a few of the mental health conditions that have a major impact on healthcare expenses. Organizations can lessen the cost of addressing mental health issues by providing support through employee assistance programs (EAPs), therapy sessions, or mindfulness training.
6. **Fostering a Positive Workplace Environment**: Programs for employee wellness help create a healthy workplace culture where work-life balance, health, and well-being are valued. Employees gain from this cultural change, as does the company's reputation and public image.
   a. **Attracting Top Talent:** One of the most important selling points for luring top talent is a robust corporate culture that places a high priority on well-being. More and more job applicants are searching for employers who care about their personal well-being in addition to competitive pay.
   b. **Employer branding:** Businesses that implement wellness initiatives successfully establish a reputation for being socially conscious and employee-friendly. This improves their employer branding, increasing their attractiveness to stakeholders, consumers, and potential employees.
7. **Fostering Innovation and Creativity:** Creativity and inventiveness depend on a healthy body and mind. Workers who are in good physical and mental health are more likely to think creatively, approach challenges objectively, and generate new ideas.

a. **Mental Clarity:** Wellness initiatives that incorporate stress-reduction methods, mindfulness training, or meditation assist staff members in purging their thoughts of outside distractions. Greater creativity and problem-solving skills result from more focused thinking brought on by this mental clarity.
b. **Work-Life Balance:** Encouraging work-life balance through wellness programs provides employees with the time and space they require to rejuvenate away from the office. Employees who are well-rested and less stressed are more inclined to approach their work with new ideas and a different viewpoint.

8. **Increasing Employee Advocacy and Loyalty:** Workers are more likely to remain devoted to the organization if they believe their boss truly cares about their well-being. Additionally, they start advocating for the organization by telling their friends, family, and professional networks about it.
   a. **Loyalty:** Knowing that their health and well-being are taken care of makes workers who gain from wellness initiatives feel more devoted to their company. This loyalty increases organizational stability and lowers turnover.
   b. **Word-of-Mouth Advocacy:** Workers who are happy with their workplace and wellness perks frequently tell others about their good experiences. Word-of-mouth advertising may result from this, increasing the company's appeal to both clients and prospective employees.
9. **Fulfilling Legal and Ethical Requirements:** Workplace wellness is subject to legal and ethical requirements in many nations. Providing a thorough wellness program enables businesses to meet both their ethical obligation to look out for their employees and these rules.
   a. **Observance:** Businesses may stay in compliance with labor regulations and lower their risk of legal problems by making sure workers have access to work-life balance programs, mental health support, and health and safety safeguards.
   b. **Moral Obligation:** Setting wellbeing as a top priority shows that the company loves its people as individuals as well as employees. This moral strategy promotes long-term success and enhances the organization's reputation.
10. **Supporting Leadership Development:** Wellness initiatives that emphasize mental and emotional health, such workshops on emotional intelligence or leadership coaching, can make a big difference in the growth of the organization's future leaders.
    a. **Emotional Intelligence:** Emotionally intelligent leaders are better able to motivate people, manage teams, and settle disputes. Wellness initiatives that foster emotional intelligence via coaching and training produce leaders capable of enacting constructive organizational change.

b. **Resilience:** Wellness programs that teach stress management and resilience give leaders the tools they need to overcome obstacles, set a good example, and remain composed under duress.

Strategies Adopted by an Organization for Employee Well-Being and Mental Health

Employee mental health has a significant impact on their cognitive wellbeing, engagement, productivity, and retention. The success of the organization is significantly impacted by this. This study explores potential interventions and highlights elements that contribute to mental health issues in order to analyze the relationship between employee mental health and organizational success.

1. **Put Mental Health Programs into Action:** Create all-encompassing mental health initiatives that incorporate tools like stress management classes, mental health days, and counseling services. Encourage staff members to make use of these resources without worrying about criticism or shame.
2. **Encourage Open Communication:** Establish a setting where workers are at ease talking about their mental health. Promote mental health awareness initiatives inside the company and train managers on how to assist staff members who are struggling with mental health concerns to foster open communication. Encouraging mental health in the workplace is crucial for both the organization's success and the welfare of its personnel. Organizations can use a variety of tactics to support mental health in the workplace. **Promote candid communication:** The stigma attached to mental health problems can be lessened by fostering an environment where workers feel free to talk about their mental health. Promoting candid conversations about mental health among staff members can also make it easier for supervisors and coworkers to spot potential problems and offer support.
3. **Encourage a healthy Work-Life Balance**: By providing flexible work arrangements like remote work choices and adjustable hours, employers may assist staff in striking a healthy work-life balance. To avoid burnout, encourage staff members to take regular holidays and breaks.
4. **Offer instruction and training**: Use seminars, workshops, and educational materials to teach staff members the value of mental health and wellness. Managers should also receive training so they can identify the warning indications of mental health problems and react properly.
5. **Establish a Helpful Environment:** Create an environment at work that promotes mental health by making sure it is secure and cozy. This can include ergonomic workspaces, peaceful areas for rest, and availability of wholesome snacks

and drinks. Giving staff members access to counseling services or Employee Assistance Programs can help them manage their mental health and lessen the effects of mental health conditions on their work output. Fostering a supportive workplace culture where staff members feel appreciated and respected can support mental health. This can involve rewarding and recognizing hard effort, encouraging collaboration, and cooperation as well as resolving any harassment or discrimination concerns. Address mental health in employee development: Including instruction and training on mental health in employee development programs can assist staff members in supporting their coworkers and comprehending and managing their own mental health.

6. **Encourage Work-Life Balance:** Stress and burnout can be decreased by encouraging employees to take breaks and by fostering a positive work-life balance. This can involve providing flexible work schedules, motivating staff to take breaks when necessary, and encouraging vacation time utilization.
7. **Evaluate and Enhance Frequently**: Evaluate the success of mental health programs on a regular basis using employee feedback and questionnaires. Utilize this data to continuously enhance and modify programs to satisfy changing labor demands.
8. **Promote Physical Activity:** Promoting physical activity among staff members, such as yoga or exercise, can help lower stress and enhance mental health in general. Frequent check-ins: Frequent check-ins with staff members can assist supervisors and coworkers in recognizing signs of distress and offering assistance. Make a committee for wellness and establish a wellness committee composed of staff members to recognize and handle workplace mental health concerns. Examine the policies and processes of the organization and examine company policies and practices to make sure they support and include workers with mental health concerns. Set an example: Senior executives need to set an example by speaking out about the value of mental health and fostering a culture of support. Organizations can use a variety of tactics to encourage mental wellness in the workplace (Zaka et. al, 2020). These tactics include fostering open communication, offering tools for mental health, supporting work-life balance, establishing a wellness committee, addressing mental health in employee development, promoting physical activity, doing frequent check-ins, establishing a positive work atmosphere, examining organizational policies and procedures, and setting an example. Employers may foster a positive work environment that supports mental health and assists staff in managing their mental health by putting these measures into practice.

RECOMMENDATIONS

Implementing flexible work schedules, creating a positive workplace culture, offering mental health services, and fostering open communication are all ways to promote employee mental health and boost company effectiveness. Prioritizing these areas can improve worker well-being, which will raise engagement and productivity and have a beneficial effect on the company as a whole. Understanding the current state of affairs, determining the gaps and needs, assessing the effects and results, and enhancing the policies and procedures all depend on conducting a workplace mental health risk assessment. However, there is no one easy approach to measure mental health in the workplace, so it might be difficult. As a result, we give some suggestions regarding this:

1. **Adjustable Work Schedules:** Employers have to encourage flexible work arrangements, wellness programs, and healthy lifestyles. This can reduce workplace stress while improving employees' mental health and wellbeing.
   a. Flexible schedules: Allow workers to select their own working hours, which may lessen the stress that comes with strict schedules.
   b. Remote work: Enabling workers to work from home can enhance work-life balance and reduce stress associated with commuting.
   c. Unambiguous expectations: Make sure that flexible scheduling doesn't impair output or lead to more stress.
2. **Foster a Culture of Support at Work:** Employers should routinely evaluate workplace culture in order to identify areas that require improvement and track progress over time. This can guarantee the success of organizational initiatives to alter workplace culture and the creation of a productive and encouraging work atmosphere.
   a. Promote candid communication: Establish a setting where workers are at ease talking about mental health issues. Encourage managers to inquire about their staff members' well-being on a frequent basis.
   b. Empathetic leadership: Teach executives to actively listen to staff concerns and react to them with empathy.
   c. Anonymous comments: Establish anonymous avenues for staff members to provide input on enhancing the workplace. Encourage a feeling of community and camaraderie by organizing social gatherings and team-building exercises.
3. **Resources for Mental Health:**
   a. Employee Assistance Programs (EAPs): Make counseling, support services, and other resources available to staff members.

b. Wellness initiatives: Provide activities like yoga sessions, meditation spaces, or fitness competitions that support both mental and physical health.
c. Benefits offered at work: Promote wellness programs, honor outstanding performance, and offer assistance during trying times to improve the working environment.
d. Benefits related to mental health: Provide full health coverage together with services specifically designed to help mental health.
e. Education and training: Teach managers and staff how to identify the warning signs of mental health problems and how to properly handle stress.

Discussions: This study discusses how employee mental health at workplace hinders organizational growth. Also, mental health problems lead to a significant increase in employee dissatisfaction, reduced productivity, work-life imbalance, excessive workload and pressure, workplace interactions, lack of cooperation and lack of engagement. The strategies adopted by the organization for employee well-being and mental health are also discussed and some recommendations are also made to prevent and manage employee-related mental health problems.

FINDINGS

The finding showed that the impact that employee's mental health has on businesses cannot be denied. In addition to being ethically imperative, prioritizing mental health at work is also a wise business move. Organizations can establish a productive and enjoyable workplace culture by funding mental health initiatives, creating a caring environment, and encouraging frank conversations about mental health. In addition to helping individual employees, identifying and addressing mental health issues will ultimately enhance organizational success by increasing employee retention, productivity, and absenteeism. Businesses that prioritize the mental health of their employees are more likely to attract and retain top talent, encourage creativity and teamwork, and develop a strong and resilient workforce. The findings further observed that employees' mental health and well-being are significantly impacted by their workplace culture. Research shows that constructive and healthy company cultures can enhance employee well-being, while toxic workplace cultures can lead to negative outcomes such as depression, burnout, and stress. To address this issue, organizations should prioritize developing a supportive workplace culture that promotes employee well-being as well as a sense of belonging and support. This can be achieved through a number of strategies, such as providing mental health resources, promoting work-life balance, and requesting employee opinions and involvement in decision-making for the company and individual workers, *etc.*

Scope of Future Research

The study has determined the impact of employee mental health on the success of the organization. Employees are assets to the organization, so the factors influencing their mental health can also be investigated in the future in the education sector and its impact on the mental health of students, banking sector, medical sector and other sectors.

CONCLUSION

The mental health and well-being of employees are essential to any company's performance. Businesses can improve employee satisfaction, productivity, and retention by putting in place efficient mental health programs, encouraging open communication, advocating for work-life balance, and developing a positive work environment. In the end, making investments in the mental health of employees is not just the right thing to do, but also a wise business move that promotes long-term success. There is no denying the impact that employees' mental health has on businesses. In addition to being morally required, putting mental health first at work is also a wise business move. Organizations can establish a productive and pleasant workplace culture by funding mental health initiatives, cultivating a caring atmosphere, and encouraging candid conversations about mental health. In addition to helping individual workers, identifying and resolving mental health issues will eventually increase organizational success by boosting employee retention, productivity, and absenteeism. Businesses that put their workers' mental health first are more likely to draw and keep top talent, encourage creativity and teamwork, and develop a robust and resilient staff. As result, workplace mental health problems can significantly affect organizations. They may result in high turnover rates, higher absenteeism, lower productivity, and legal problems. Employers need to understand the value of mental health in the workplace, and they ought to give staff members the tools and assistance they need to control and enhance their mental health. This can result in a more devoted, engaged, and productive workforce, which will eventually help the business succeed.

REFERENCES

Aarons, G. A., & Sawitzky, A. C. (2006). Organizational culture and climate and mental health provider attitudes toward evidence-based practice. *Psychological Services*, *3*(1), 61–72. DOI: 10.1037/1541-1559.3.1.61

Adane, A. A., & Jemal, K. (2017). Mental health training for primary health care workers and implication for success of integration of mental health into primary care: Evaluation of effect on knowledge, attitude and practices (KAP). *International Journal of Mental Health Systems*, *11*(1), 63–69. DOI: 10.1186/s13033-017-0169-8

Szeto, A. C., & Dobson, K. S. (2010). Reducing the stigma of mental disorders at work: A review of current workplace anti-stigma intervention programs. *Applied & Preventive Psychology*, *14*(1-4), 41–56.

Arnetz, B. B., & Arnetz, J. E. (2011). Organizational Climate, Occupational Stress, and Employee Mental Health. *Journal of Occupational and Environmental Medicine*, *53*(1), 34–42. DOI: 10.1097/JOM.0b013e3181ffo5b

Bella, K. M. J. (2023). The power of employee well-being: A catalyst for organizational success. *International Journal of Scientific Research in Modern Science and Technology*, *2*(4), 20–26.

Bovopoulos, N., & Jorm, A. (2018). Exploring the role of mental health first aid officers in workplaces: A qualitative study using case study methodology. *International Journal of Workplace Health Management*, *11*(6), 366–381. DOI: 10.1108/IJWHM-06-2018-0082

Brohan, E., & Thornicroft, G. (2010). Employees with mental health problems: Survey of UK employers' knowledge, attitudes and workplace practices. *Epidemiologia e Psichiatria Sociale*, *19*(4), 326–332. DOI: 10.1017/S1121189X0000066X

Codinhoto, R., & Cooper, R. (2009). The impacts of the built environment on health outcomes. *Facilities*, *27*(3/4), 138–151. DOI: 10.1108/02632770910933152

Davenport, L. J., & Reavley, N. J. (2016). How can organizations help employees thrive? The development of guidelines for promoting positive mental health at work. *International Journal of Workplace Health Management*, *9*(4), 411–427. DOI: 10.1108/IJWHM-01-2016-0001

Dekker, S. W., & Schaufeli, W. B. (1995). The Effects of Job Insecurity on Psychological Health and Withdrawal: A Longitudinal Study. *Australian Psychologist*, *30*(1), 57–63. DOI: 10.1080/00050069508259607

Nielsen, M. B. D., Bültmann, U., Madsen, I. E. H., Martin, M., Christensen, U., Diderichsen, F., & Rugulies, R. (2011). Health, work, and personal-related predictors of time to return to work among employees with mental health problems. *Disability and Rehabilitation*, *34*(15), 1311–1316. DOI: 10.3109/09638288.2011.641664

Foster, K., Roche, M., Giandinoto, J.-A., Platania-Phung, C., & Furness, T. (2021). Mental health matters: A cross-sectional study of mental health nurses' health-related quality of life and work-related stressors. *International Journal of Mental Health Nursing*, *30*(3), 624–634. DOI: 10.1111/inm.12823

Funk, M., Drew, N., & Knapp, M. (2012). Mental health, poverty and development. *Journal of Public Mental Health*, *11*(4), 166–185. DOI: 10.1108/17465721211289356

Gedecho, E. K., & Kim, S. (2025). Mental health and well-being in tourism scholarship: A Horizon 2050 paper. *Tourism Review*, *80*(1), 108–120. https://doi.org/ DOI: 10.1108/TR-12-2023-0842

Giorgi, G., & Cupelli, V. (2015). Economic stress in the workplace: The impact of fear of the crisis on mental health. *Work (Reading, Mass.)*, *51*(1), 135–142. DOI: 10.3233/WOR-141844

Glisson, C., & Schoenwald, S. K. (2005). The ARC Organizational and Community Intervention Strategy for Implementing Evidence-Based Children's Mental Health Treatments. *Mental Health Services Research*, *7*(4), 243–259. DOI: 10.1007/s11020-005-7456-1

Goetzel, R. Z., Ozminkowski, R. J., Sederer, L. I., & Mark, T. L. (2002, April). The Business Case for Quality Mental Health Services: Why Employers Should Care About the Mental Health and Well-Being of Their Employees. *Journal of Occupational and Environmental Medicine*, *44*(4), 320–330.

Hamouche, S. (2023). COVID-19 and employees' mental health: Stressors, moderators and agenda for organizational actions. *Emerald Open Research*, *1*(2). Advance online publication. DOI: 10.1108/EOR-02-2023-0004

Harvey, S. B., Modini, M., Joyce, S., Milligan-Saville, J. S., Tan, L., Mykletun, A., & Mitchell, P. B. (2017). Can work make you mentally ill? A systematic meta-review of work-related risk factors for common mental health problems. *Occupational and Environmental Medicine*, *74*(4), 301–310.

Janssen, M., & Engels, J. (2018). Effects of Mindfulness-Based Stress Reduction on employees' mental health: A systematic review. *PLoS One*, *13*(1), e0191332. DOI: 10.1371/journal.pone.0191332

Lee, W., & Cronin, M. A. (2023). Mental Health and Mental Illness in Organizations: A Review, Comparison, and Extension. *The Academy of Management Annals, 17*(2), 751–797. Advance online publication. DOI: 10.5465/annals.2021.0211

Reece, A., Yaden, D., Kellerman, G., Robichaux, A., Goldstein, R., Schwartz, B., & Baumeister, R. (2021). Mattering is an indicator of organizational health and employee success. *The Journal of Positive Psychology, 16*(2), 228–248.

Montano, D., & Siegrist, J. (2014). Effects of organisational-level interventions at work on employees' health: A systematic review. *BMC Public Health, 14*(1), 135–144. DOI: 10.1186/1471-2458-14-135

Monteiro, E., & Joseph, J. (2023). A Review on the Impact of Workplace Culture on Employee Mental Health and Well-Being [IJCSBE]. *International Journal of Case Studies in Business, IT, and Education, 7*(2), 291–317. DOI: 10.47992/IJCSBE.2581.6942.0274

Nelson, D. L., & Burke, R. J. (2000). Women executives: Health, stress, and success. *The Academy of Management Perspectives, 14*(2), 107–121. DOI: 10.5465/ame.2000.3819310

Stratton, E., Lampit, A., Choi, I., Calvo, R. A., Harvey, S. B., & Glozier, N. (2017). Effectiveness of eHealth interventions for reducing mental health conditions in employees: A systematic review and meta-analysis. *PLoS One, 12*(12), e0189904.

Provencher, H. L., & Keyes, C. L. M. (2011). Complete mental health recovery: Bridging mental illness with positive mental health. *Journal of Public Mental Health, 10*(1), 57–69. DOI: 10.1108/17465721111134556

Quilitch, H. R. (1978). Using a simple feedback procedure to reinforce the submission of written suggestions by mental health employees. *Journal of Organizational Behavior Management, 1*(2), 155–163. DOI: 10.1300/J075v01n02_07

Parslow, R. A., Jorm, A. F., Christensen, H., Rodgers, B., Strazdins, L., & D'Souza, R. M. (2004). The associations between work stress and mental health: A comparison of organizationally employed and self-employed workers. *Work and Stress, 18*(3), 231–244.

Salzer, M. S. (2002). Consumer-delivered services as a best practice in mental health care delivery and the development of practice guidelines. *Psychiatric Rehabilitation Skills, 6*(3), 355–382. DOI: 10.1080/10973430208408443

Shahzad, K., Khan, S. A., & Iqbal, A. (2024). Mental health issues of university librarians: A systematic literature review. *Global Knowledge, Memory and Communication*. Advance online publication. DOI: 10.1108/GKMC-07-2023-0261

Sharma, P. K., & Kumra, R. (2020). Relationship between workplace spirituality, organizational justice and mental health: Mediation role of employee engagement. *Journal of Advances in Management Research*, *17*(5), 627–650. DOI: 10.1108/JAMR-01-2020-0007

DeGroot, T., & Kiker, D. S. (2003). A meta-analysis of the non-monetary effects of employee health management programs. Human Resource Management: Published in Cooperation with the School of Business Administration, The University of Michigan and in alliance with the Society of Human Resources Management, 42(1), 53-69.

Tisu, L., Lup a, D., Vîrgă, D., & Rusu, A. (2020). Personality characteristics, job performance and mental health: The mediating role of work engagement. *Personality and Individual Differences*, *153*, 109644.

Veage, S., Ciarrochi, J., Deane, F. P., Andresen, R., Oades, L. G., & Crowe, T. P. (2014). Value congruence, importance and success and in the workplace: Links with well-being and burnout amongst mental health practitioners. *Journal of Contextual Behavioral Science*, *3*(4), 258–264. DOI: 10.1016/j.jcbs.2014.06.004

Loretto, W., Platt, S., & Popham, F. (2010). Workplace change and employee mental health: Results from a longitudinal study. *British Journal of Management*, *21*(2), 526–540.

Ahmed, K. A. (2020). Employees' mental health and productivity and its impact on contextual and task performance in organizations. *Journal of Advanced Research in Dynamical and Control System*, *12*(8).

Chapter 2

Exploring the Interconnection Between Employee Mental Health, Well-Being, and Organizational Success: A Decadal Review and Conceptual Framework for Future Research

Puthisat Namdech
https://orcid.org/0009-0001-3405-6497
North Bangkok University, Thailand

Parinya Siriatakkul
North Bangkok University, Thailand

Piyawadee Jindachote
Suan Sunandha Rajabhat University, Thailand

Samneang Maneechai
Suan Sunandha Rajabhat University, Thailand

ABSTRACT

This review shows a strong link between employee mental health and well-being, and organizational success. Positive mental health boosts well-being, leading to better organizational outcomes like productivity and retention. Supportive work environments, including work-life balance and social support, are crucial. Interventions

DOI: 10.4018/979-8-3373-2210-0.ch002

Copyright © 2025, IGI Global Scientific Publishing. Copying or distributing in print or electronic forms without written permission of IGI Global Scientific Publishing is prohibited.

improving mental health and well-being directly correlate with better organizational performance (e.g., increased productivity, lower healthcare costs). Investing in employee well-being provides a strong return on investment. Future research should focus on longitudinal studies, contextual factors, diversity and inclusion, and technological interventions. A holistic approach to supporting both mental health and well-being fosters a thriving workforce and sustainable organizational success.

INTRODUCTION

In recent years, the acknowledgment of employee mental health and well-being has emerged as a critical factor influencing organizational success (Watthanabut & Manasabutr, 2017; Rattanasirivilai, 2024). The complex interplay between these factors has garnered attention from researchers, policymakers, and organizational leaders alike, particularly in the context of the dramatic shifts provoked by the COVID-19 pandemic. During this unprecedented crisis, mental health issues became more pronounced, affecting employees' ability to perform, engage, and thrive (Hamouche, 2020; Somani, 2022). As such, understanding the relationship between employee mental health, well-being, and organizational success has become paramount for creating resilient and thriving workplaces.

The World Health Organization (WHO) defines mental health as "a state of well-being in which every individual realizes his or her potential, can cope with the normal stresses of life, can work productively and fruitfully, and is able to make a contribution to his or her community" (Mei et al., 2023). This definition underscores the importance of creating supportive work environments that nurture mental well-being among employees. However, mental health challenges, such as anxiety and depression, have increasingly surfaced in organizations worldwide. Research indicates that untreated mental health conditions can lead to declining productivity, increased absenteeism, and higher turnover rates (Fujimoto et al., 2024; Vaidyanathan & Mahapatra, 2020; Khan et al., 2022). Thus, organizations face a pressing need to address mental health concerns proactively to foster an engaged and productive workforce.

Equally, employee well-being is a multifaceted construct that encompasses not only mental health but also physical, emotional, and social dimensions (Pandya et al., 2022). The relationship between these facets and organizational success is supported by empirical evidence revealing that well-being initiatives often correlate with improved job performance, employee loyalty, and overall organizational effectiveness (Elshaer & Azazz, 2023; Elufioye et al., 2024). Employees who report high levels of well-being tend to exhibit greater job satisfaction, creativity, and productivity, which collectively contribute to enhanced organizational performance. For instance, researchers have indicated that comprehensive employee well-being programs can lead to substantial increases in productivity; estimates suggest that for every dollar invested in employee well-being, organizations can save anywhere between three to fifteen dollars in return on investment (Pandya et al., 2022).

Moreover, organizational culture significantly influences employee mental health and well-being. A positive organizational culture characterized by supportive leadership, open communication, and community care can act as a protective factor, mitigating the impact of work-related challenges on mental health (Monteiro & Joseph, 2023). Studies show that organizations prioritizing mental health and well-being measures often experience lower levels of stress and burnout among employees, leading to better retention rates and reduced healthcare costs (Gayed et al., 2018). Conversely, toxic workplace cultures, characterized by hierarchical management structures, high levels of competition, and lack of support, can exacerbate mental health issues and lead to detrimental outcomes for both employees and organizations (Alsomaidaee et al., 2023).

Furthermore, the COVID-19 pandemic highlighted the need for organizations to re-evaluate their approach toward employee mental health and well-being. Remote work, isolation, and uncertainty triggered new stressors that compound existing mental health challenges, making it imperative for organizations to implement strategies that enhance both the mental health of employees and overall workplace dynamics (AlAmeri, 2023). During this period, organizations that were quick to adapt and provide mental health resources, such as Employee Assistance Programs (EAPs), also demonstrated improved employee satisfaction, engagement, and performance (Dongarwar et al., 2020; Irvine & Suter, 2023). These resources fostered supportive networks that enabled employees to cope with immense stress and uncertainties, emphasizing that proactive mental health policies are essential for organizations navigating turbulent times.

As organizations strive for success in an increasingly volatile business environment, the significance of fostering mental health and well-being cannot be overstated. Leadership plays a crucial role in creating a culture that prioritizes mental health. Leaders trained in mental health awareness and supportive practices can substantially enhance employees' experiences, increase trust, and cultivate an environment conducive to well-being (Dimoff & Kelloway, 2019; Hanisch et al., 2017). The effectiveness of such leadership training programs has been demonstrated in studies showing improved utilization of mental health resources and enhanced employee-resource interaction (Shanker, 2024; Kotera et al., 2021). Furthermore, organizations should recognize the potential return on investment derived from committed mental health strategies, which not only support employees personally but also elevate overall organizational performance metrics (Ghazali et al., 2023).

To construct effective future interventions, it is critical to disentangle the complex relationships involving employee mental health, well-being, and organizational success. Established frameworks and empirical studies provide a foundational basis for understanding these correlations, yet there remains an urgent need for systematic quantitative research to validate these relationships further. Such research can quantitatively assess how varying levels of employee mental health and well-being impact key performance indicators, thereby enabling organizations to optimize their approaches and develop targeted strategies. For example, measuring the correlation between specific mental health interventions and quantifiable organizational performance metrics, such as productivity, employee retention, and healthcare cost reduction, would establish a clearer nexus between these constructs (Srivastava, 2023; Hasanudin et al., 2022).

Moreover, understanding the two-way relationship between mental health and well-being is essential for businesses seeking sustainable success. Mental health cannot be viewed in isolation; instead, it interacts dynamically with well-being dimensions such as stress management, employee support systems, and work-life balance initiatives. Positive mental health bolsters overall well-being, while high levels of well-being facilitate better mental health (Ward et al., 2023; Lee & Kim, 2023). An integrative approach to enhance both constructs can lead to synergistic effects benefiting all organizational aspects, ultimately driving sustained improvements in performance and success.

In conclusion, the growing literature on the relationship between employee mental health, well-being, and organizational success underscores the importance of adopting a comprehensive view of employee management practices. Organizations must prioritize mental health and cultivate environments that support employee well-being for lasting success. Future quantitative research should focus on formally validating the relationships between these variables. Investigations involving interconnected variables could also illuminate the pathways that promote flourishing workplaces. By embracing these principles, organizations can foster a proactive culture that encompasses mental health promotion, employee well-being, and enhanced organizational success.

THE CONCEPT AND IMPLICATIONS OF EMPLOYEE MENTAL HEALTH FOR ORGANIZATIONAL SUCCESS

Definition of Employee Mental Health

Employee mental health is a multifaceted and dynamic construct that encompasses the psychological, emotional, and social well-being of individuals in the workplace. According to the World Health Organization (WHO), mental health is defined as a state of well-being wherein individuals realize their abilities, cope with the normal stresses of life, work productively, and contribute to their communities (AlAmeri, 2023). This definition underscores the premise that mental health is not merely the absence of mental disorders but includes a spectrum of positive psychological functioning. In the workplace context, employee mental health encompasses several important facets, including job satisfaction, stress management, emotional regulation, and resilience. Collectively, these aspects create an environment conducive to productivity, creativity, and overall organizational success.

Within this conceptual framework, employee mental health is influenced by the interplay of individual traits and external factors, such as organizational culture, job demands, and the availability of support systems. Research indicates that organizations that prioritize employee mental health are likely to experience lower rates of attrition, absenteeism, and presenteeism, resulting in increased operational efficiency and profitability (Amponsah-Tawiah et al., 2023; Hauff et al., 2022).

Key Components of Employee Mental Health

1. Psychological Well Being: Psychological well-being represents a core aspect of employee mental health and encompasses various factors, including emotional balance, life satisfaction, and the absence of psychological distress. This aspect is reflected in the dual continuum model, which posits that mental health exists along a continuum where individuals may experience high levels of mental well-being alongside mental illness (Kinman, 2016; Harding et al., 2019). Research demonstrates that employees with healthy psychological well-being perform better and engage more deeply with their roles, thereby enhancing overall workplace productivity (Jnaneswar & Sulphey, 2021).
2. Emotional Regulation: Emotional regulation refers to the ability to manage and respond to one's emotions appropriately in different situations. Studies indicate that employees proficient in emotional regulation tend to exhibit lower levels of stress and burnout, leading to improved job satisfaction and performance (Martín et al., 2018; Zheng et al., 2015). Organizations that provide training in emotional intelligence and regulation contribute positively to their employee's

mental health, facilitating healthier workplace interactions and better coping mechanisms for stress (Lorber & Dobnik, 2022).

3. Resilience: Resilience, defined as the ability to bounce back from adversity, is a fundamental component of mental health. Research illustrates that resilient employees not only recover from setbacks more effectively but also foster a more positive workplace environment. Organizations that implement resilience-building programs observe higher employee retention rates and increased job satisfaction (Agteren et al., 2018; Martín et al., 2018). Resilience can be cultivated through supportive leadership, appropriate training programs, and the development of a strong organizational culture that encourages adaptability and growth.
4. Work-Life Balance: Achieving a balance between work responsibilities and personal life is crucial for maintaining mental health. Research has shown that employees overwhelmed by work demands and lacking adequate support for personal commitments are more prone to stress and mental health issues (Cerdeira et al., 2023; Dutta & Mishra, 2023). Organizations that actively promote work-life balance through flexible work arrangements and comprehensive leave policies contribute significantly to their employees' mental health. Such measures not only enhance employees' overall well-being but also their productivity and engagement.
5. Workplace Environment: The organizational environment shapes employee mental health significantly. Positive workplace cultures characterized by inclusivity, transparency, and support tend to enhance mental well-being, while toxic environments marked by high stress, competition, and poor communication can severely undermine mental health (Laidlaw et al., 2015; Görgényi-Hegyes et al., 2021). By cultivating a supportive workplace culture, organizations can foster better mental health outcomes for their employees.
6. Social Support: The presence of supportive relationships within the workplace acts as a buffer against stress and enhances employees' mental health. Studies have repeatedly demonstrated that employees who experience social support from colleagues and supervisors report lower incidences of mental health issues and higher job satisfaction (Chetty, 2017; Amponsah-Tawiah et al., 2023). Organizations should prioritize initiatives that strengthen interpersonal relationships, such as team-building activities, mentoring programs, and open communication channels, as these can considerably improve both employee morale and productivity.

Implications For Organizational Success

The implications of prioritizing employee mental health extend far beyond individual well-being; they have pivotal consequences for organizational success and sustainability. When organizations create an environment that supports mental health, they position themselves to benefit from numerous positive outcomes.

1. Increased Productivity: Research consistently shows that a positive mental health environment contributes significantly to employee engagement and productivity. When employees feel supported and mentally well, they are more likely to put forth discretionary effort and creativity in their roles, leading to innovation and high performance (Hauff et al., 2022; Deka et al., 2024). Studies have noted that organizations investing in comprehensive mental health initiatives can achieve up to a 12% increase in productivity attributable to enhanced workforce engagement and morale (Young et al., 2024).
2. Reduced Absenteeism and Turnover: Fostering a mentally healthy workplace can lead to significantly decreased rates of absenteeism and turnover. Studies indicate that organizations with robust mental health support systems experience lower employee attrition (Yulianti & Fitdiarini, 2023). For instance, one meta-analysis found that organizations promoting mental health saw a reduction in turnover rates by as much as 25% when compared to those without similar initiatives (Nielsen et al., 2022). Reduced turnover not only lowers recruitment and training costs but also enhances organizational stability and preserves institutional knowledge.
3. Enhanced Employee Loyalty and Job Satisfaction: Investing in employee mental health is strongly associated with increased loyalty and job satisfaction among staff members. Employees who perceive organizational investments in their well-being are likely to feel valued, leading to increased commitment and organizational loyalty (Dougall et al., 2023). This, in turn, fosters a positive workplace culture and reduces the likelihood of talent loss to competitors.
4. Improved Organizational Reputation: Organizations that regularly prioritize mental health initiatives enhance their reputation, positioning themselves as attractive employers within the labor market (Wel et al., 2015; Young et al., 2024). Strong organizational ethics concerning mental health can enhance a company's image, attracting top talent and fostering a diverse, competent workforce that aligns with modern workforce expectations.
5. Long-Term Health Care Savings: Organizations that attend to the mental health needs of their employees potentially realize long-term cost savings in health care. A study by the Integrated Benefits Institute reported that mental health-related absenteeism can cost organizations up to $400 billion annually in lost

productivity and healthcare expenses. By implementing effective mental health strategies, organizations can reduce healthcare costs significantly, thereby reallocating resources towards initiatives that drive growth and innovation.

6. Fostering a Culture of Resilience and Adaptability: Cultivating a strong foundation of mental health resilience equips employees and organizations to adapt efficiently to challenges such as economic downturns or crises, including the unprecedented challenges posed by the COVID-19 pandemic. Resilient organizations are more adept at navigating change and uncertainty, which positions them favorably for sustainable success in today's ever-evolving business landscape.

In conclusion, employee mental health is a multidimensional construct that is crucial for individual and organizational success. By prioritizing mental health through comprehensive support systems, work-life balance initiatives, and cultivating a positive workplace environment, organizations can enhance productivity, reduce turnover, and establish long-term financial viability. As research continues to elucidate the strong links between employee mental well-being and organizational effectiveness, leaders must remain committed to investing in their workforce to unlock the potential benefits of a mentally healthy workplace.

THE CONCEPT AND IMPLICATIONS OF EMPLOYEE WELL-BEING FOR ORGANIZATIONAL SUCCESS

Definition of Employee Well-Being

Employee well-being refers to the overall mental, physical, emotional, and social health of individuals in the workplace. It encompasses how workers experience their jobs, their level of satisfaction with their roles, and how these factors affect their quality of life both inside and outside the work environment (Bryson et al., 2017; Khoreva & Wechtler, 2018). The construct has evolved to include not only the absence of stressors and mental health issues but also positive dimensions of happiness and fulfillment derived from work situations. Extensive literature suggests that employee well-being is a key indicator of organizational effectiveness, as healthy and satisfied employees tend to be more productive, engaged, and loyal to their organizations (Ahmed et al., 2020; Tu n, 2019). Additionally, well-being reflects a holistic view of employees as individuals who require attention and support in multiple life domains, making it a priority for companies aspiring to enhance their workplace culture.

Key Components of Employee Well-Being

1. Physical Well-Being: This component encompasses all aspects of health that are directly related to physical fitness, nutrition, and the absence of chronic illness. Research highlights that a positive correlation exists between physical health and productivity. Employees who engage in regular physical activity are reported to have lower absenteeism rates and improved performance (Schultz & Burton, 2018; Marín-García & Bonavía, 2021). Organizations can foster physical well-being by encouraging fitness programs, providing access to healthy food choices, and supporting initiatives such as health check-ups and wellness challenges.
2. Psychological Well-Being: Psychological well-being refers to the emotional, mental, and psychological state of an employee. It includes components such as stress, anxiety, overall mood, and job satisfaction. Researchers emphasize that organizations investing in mental health resources see reductions in mental wellness issues, which correlate with improvements in productivity and engagement (Garg, 2017; Hendriks et al., 2020). Organizations that foster an atmosphere of open communication about mental health provide access to mental health resources, train managers to recognize signs of mental distress and invest significantly in employee psychological well-being.
3. Social Well-Being: Social well-being pertains to an employee's ability to interact positively with colleagues and maintain healthy relationships within the workplace. The quality of interpersonal relationships can significantly affect morale and job satisfaction (Wardani et al., 2023; Wiencke et al., 2019). Organizations can enhance social well-being by promoting teamwork, collaboration, and opportunities for workers to build rapport through team-building exercises, mentorship programs, and social events. Studies suggest that a supportive work environment offering a strong sense of community increases employees' commitment to their organization and enhances their overall experience at work (Pawar, 2016).
4. Financial Well-Being: Financial well-being is increasingly recognized as a vital aspect of overall employee well-being. Employees with financial security are reported to have lower stress levels, higher job satisfaction, and enhanced productivity (Khoreva & Wechtler, 2018). Organizations can help employees improve their financial well-being by providing resources such as financial literacy programs, retirement planning services, and access to counseling for financial management. Such initiatives not only reduce financial stress but reinforce trust between employees and employers.

5. Engagement and Job Satisfaction: Employee engagement refers to the emotional commitment employees have towards their jobs, which affects their willingness to invest effort into their work. High levels of engagement are strongly linked to job satisfaction, which affects retention rates and productivity (Rurkkhum, 2023; Edwards & Marcus, 2018). Organizations can drive engagement by recognizing accomplishments, involving employees in decision-making, and offering career development opportunities. Research demonstrates that engaged employees express higher levels of commitment to their organizations, fostering an environment of positivity and productivity (Ahmed et al., 2020; Hsu et al., 2019).
6. Work-Life Balance: A component of overall well-being, work-life balance involves managing work demands alongside personal life responsibilities. An imbalance can lead to stress burnout and a decline in health (Pradhan & Hati, 2019; Azizah et al., 2023). Companies that prioritize work-life balance by offering flexible working arrangements, parental leave, and remote work options foster employee satisfaction and loyalty. Studies indicate that effective work-life balance initiatives can improve both retention and employee productivity as workers feel more supported and valued (Bryson et al., 2017; Hsu et al., 2019).

Implications for Organizational Success

The implications of prioritizing employee well-being for organizational success are substantial and multifaceted. Companies that invest in fostering employee well-being experience several benefits, many of which translate to improved performance metrics and sustainable growth.

1. Increased Productivity: Organizations that promote well-being typically witness enhanced productivity levels. Research indicates that well-being programs lead to higher employee engagement and reduce instances of absenteeism and presenteeism (Bryson et al., 2017; Khoreva & Wechtler, 2018). Findings suggest that employees who feel supported in their well-being outperform their counterparts (Garg, 2017; Hendriks et al., 2020).
2. Enhanced Employee Engagement: Higher levels of employee well-being have a direct positive correlation with engagement levels (Suwannapirom & Pranee, 2023). Engaged employees exhibit greater enthusiasm for their roles, leading to creativity and innovation in work practices. They contribute actively to the organization's goals and demonstrate lower turnover rates (Rurkkhum, 2023). Companies can benefit significantly by fostering a positive workplace culture that supports and nurtures employees' overall well-being.

3. Retention of Talent: Employee well-being initiatives often lead to significant improvements in employee loyalty and satisfaction. When employees feel their well-being is prioritized, they are less likely to seek employment elsewhere (Mäkikangas et al., 2016). Organizations that focus on employee well-being can reduce turnover costs, which can reach significant percentages of an individual's salary in recruitment and training expenses (Ahmed et al., 2020).
4. Improved Organizational Culture: Fostering a culture of well-being enhances workplace morale and promotes camaraderie among employees. Positive organizational culture is linked with higher employee satisfaction and loyalty. Organizations adept at nurturing a supportive culture can expect not only higher employee retention rates but also positive employer branding, which attracts new talent (Khoreva & Wechsler, 2018; Garg, 2017).
5. Healthier Work Environment: Prioritizing employee well-being correlates with a healthier workplace environment, ultimately resulting in decreased healthcare costs for organizations. Companies that support health-promoting initiatives potentially save on healthcare claims related to stress, mental health concerns, and chronic diseases associated with unhealthy work environments (Schultz & Burton, 2018; Marín-García & Bonavía, 2021).
6. Positive Impact on Customer Experience: Employees who are mentally and physically well are more likely to engage positively with customers, fostering an improved customer experience and loyalty (Oja et al., 2019). Studies indicate that employee satisfaction and well-being directly impact customer satisfaction scores, highlighting the intricate relationship between employee and customer experiences (Wieneke et al., 2019).
7. Long-Term Sustainability: Organizations that prioritize employee well-being position themselves to navigate market fluctuations and crises effectively. Employees with high levels of well-being demonstrate resilience and adaptability, which are essential attributes during challenging times (Pawar, 2016). The COVID-19 pandemic underscored the necessity of investing in employee well-being, as organizations that had established strong well-being frameworks adapted more readily and maintained business continuity (Schultz & Burton, 2018).

In conclusion, employee well-being is a crucial construct that significantly affects organizational success. Through its multifaceted components—physical, psychological, social, and financial well-being, engagement, and work-life balance—organizations can cultivate a productive, loyal, and satisfied workforce. As research continually reinforces the positive relationship between well-being and organizational performance, leaders must recognize the imperative to prioritize employee well-being through comprehensive support systems and active engagement strategies.

THE INTERRELATIONSHIP BETWEEN EMPLOYEE MENTAL HEALTH AND EMPLOYEE WELL-BEING

The interplay between employee mental health and employee well-being is an essential aspect of organizational behavior, significantly influencing individual performance and overall organizational success. Understanding this relationship requires an examination of how one factor can affect the other and vice versa. The following sections synthesize research findings that highlight the causal directions between these two constructs while underscoring the importance of their interdependence.

Employee Mental Health as a Predictor of Employee Well-Being

A robust body of research indicates a compelling relationship where employee mental health directly influences employee well-being. Positive mental health, characterized by resilience, emotional regulation, and the absence of psychological disorders, is foundational to fostering a sense of well-being among employees. For instance, Dimoff and Kelloway, 2019 explored how managerial support and mental health training positively affected employees' resource utilization, leading to improved well-being outcomes. The study revealed that employees with better mental health reported enhanced job satisfaction and fewer behavioral issues.

Additionally, a study by Lu et al. (2022) established that mental health directly mediates job performance through work engagement. Employees struggling with mental health issues were more likely to experience absenteeism and presenteeism, leading to decreased overall well-being. In contrast, those who maintained good mental health reported elevated levels of engagement and satisfaction, indicating that mental health is critical for fostering a positive perception of one's work life.

Moreover, psychological stress stemming from work-related factors negatively impacts mental health and subsequently affects employee well-being. Liu et al. (2021) highlighted that deficiencies in workplace support can exacerbate mental health challenges, leading to adverse outcomes such as stress, anxiety, and lowered well-being. As such, employees facing high levels of psychological demands are further at risk of deteriorating mental health, which can create a spiraling effect detrimental to both personal and organizational outcomes.

Research by Sharma and Kumra (2020) also elucidated this relationship, indicating that workplace spirituality—integral in developing a supportive work culture—enhances mental health, which, in turn, fosters employee well-being. Their model suggests that when employees are spiritually fulfilled, they are more resilient against mental health challenges, leading to greater overall satisfaction and a sense of purpose in their roles.

Employee Well-Being as a Predictor of Employee Mental Health

Conversely, research highlights that employee well-being significantly affects mental health outcomes, illustrating a reciprocal relationship. Well-being, encompassing emotional, physical, and social dimensions, bolsters employees' mental resilience. For instance, Mathibe and Chinyamurindi (2021) found that employees with higher levels of well-being demonstrated increased capacity to cope with workplace stressors, leading to better overall mental health. This suggests that organizations prioritizing well-being initiatives can create environments where employees experience lower instances of mental distress.

Furthermore, studies indicate that fostering a supportive workplace culture enhances employee well-being, which subsequently leads to improvements in mental health. A comprehensive study by Khan et al. (2021) examined how fear of economic uncertainty during the COVID-19 pandemic impacted employees' well-being and mental health, concluding that perceived job insecurity directly correlated with declines in both constructs. Providing employees with job security and psychological support created circumstances that improved well-being, leading to enhanced mental health outcomes.

The role of job satisfaction in moderating the relationship between well-being and mental health is also documented. Nguyen et al. (2023) emphasize that job satisfaction serves as a mediator; employees with high job satisfaction experience fewer mental health challenges, demonstrating that positive work environments with high well-being levels directly contribute to mental health improvement.

Additionally, research indicates that enhancing employee engagement, a critical element linked to well-being, significantly mitigated the effects of stress and anxiety on mental health outcomes, exemplifying that prioritized employee well-being contributes positively to mental health (Falcon et al., 2021).

The Interrelationship of Employee Mental Health and Well-Being

The intricate relationship between employee mental health and employee well-being is reciprocal, with each construct influencing the other in significant ways. Research consistently demonstrates that positive mental health fosters enhanced employee well-being, leading to increased satisfaction and productivity. Similarly, higher levels of well-being contribute to better mental health by providing individuals with the resources necessary to cope with stress and adversity.

Furthermore, effective workplace practices that promote both mental health and well-being yield considerable benefits for organizations, including reduced turnover, decreased absenteeism, and enhanced performance metrics. For instance, organizations that prioritize comprehensive mental health programs and well-being initiatives not only improve employees' mental and emotional states but also cultivate an environment where organizational success is borne out of a healthy and engaged workforce (Oh et al., 2017; Hossain et al., 2021).

Additionally, the influence of leadership styles, social support, and workplace culture plays a crucial role in shaping this dynamic interrelationship. As organizations continue to evolve in increasingly complex landscapes, understanding and harnessing the synergies between employee mental health and well-being can prove invaluable for cultivating a resilient and high-performing workforce.

In conclusion, the reciprocal relationship between employee mental health and employee well-being should inform organizational practices aimed at enhancing workplace culture and performance. By recognizing the importance of this interrelationship and adopting integrated approaches to support both constructs, organizations can position themselves for sustained success.

CONCLUSION AND DIRECTIONS FOR FUTURE RESEARCH

The relationship between employee mental health and employee well-being is a fundamental area of interest for both organizational leaders and researchers. As workplaces continue to evolve in complexity, understanding the interconnectedness of these two constructs is crucial for fostering a healthy, productive workforce. This article has synthesized existing research on the relationship, revealing that employee mental health significantly influences well-being and vice versa.

The current findings emphasize the necessity of approaching mental health and well-being as a unified construct rather than disparate elements. Organizations that successfully integrate these components into their workplace culture not only enhance individual employee experiences but also contribute to broader organizational effectiveness. Positive mental health serves as a foundation for overall employee well-being, while improved well-being promotes better mental health outcomes.

Importance of Mental Health Support and Well-Being Initiatives

The findings indicate that workplaces that prioritize mental health through comprehensive support systems yield beneficial effects. Organizations offering mental health training, resources like Employee Assistance Programs (EAPs), and cultivating a supportive culture see increased productivity and lower turnover rates (Dimoff & Kelloway, 2019; Shimazu et al., 2016). Importantly, organizations should not only focus on reactive strategies but also proactively promote mental health through preventive measures such as stress management programs, resilience training, and fostering a positive workplace environment to enhance the overall well-being of employees (Dimoff & Kelloway, 2019; Sharma & Kumra, 2020; Reimann & Guzy, 2017).

Moreover, the studies reviewed suggest that leadership plays a crucial role in this dynamic. Effective leaders who prioritize mental health and encourage open communication can cultivate an environment that fosters both employee mental health and well-being (Kotera et al., 2021; Vonderlin et al., 2021). This leadership involvement can enhance psychological safety within organizations, allowing employees to feel safe in discussing their mental health challenges without fear of stigma or reprisal (Mathibe & Chinyamurindi, 2021; Lu et al., 2022).

Directions for Future Research

To further elucidate the interrelationship between employee mental health and well-being, future quantitative research should aim to explore several key areas.

1. Causality and Longitudinal Studies: Most existing research has focused on correlational data, leaving gaps in understanding the causal relationships between mental health and well-being. Longitudinal studies could help ascertain whether improvements in one aspect reliably lead to improvements in the other over time. This would allow organizations to determine the effectiveness of their interventions and adapt them accordingly for optimal results (Martín et al., 2018; Davenport et al., 2016).
2. Diverse Work Environments: Future research should consider the varying contexts in which employees operate. The effects of mental health and well-being can differ across industries, cultures, and organizational structures. For instance, the hospitality industry has unique mental health challenges and requires customized interventions that address the distinctive needs of specific sectors (Khan et al., 2021; Liu et al., 2021).
3. Employee Demographics and Mental Health Literacy: Research into how demographic factors (e.g., age, gender, ethnicity) impact employees' perceptions of mental health and well-being is critical. Understanding these relationships can inform tailored organizational strategies that accommodate diverse employee experiences (Bondar et al., 2022). Additionally, increasing mental health literacy among employees can reduce stigma and improve the utilization of mental health resources, further enhancing organizational well-being (Rai, 2015; Cao et al., 2022).
4. Integration of Technology and Mental Health: As digital mental health solutions gain traction, future research should assess the effectiveness of technology-based interventions in supporting employee mental health and well-being.

Understanding how apps, telehealth services, and other digital tools might enhance or detract from employee support can provide insightful avenues for enhancing workplace mental health initiatives (Somani, 2022; Falcon et al., 2021).

5. Impact of Remote Work: Given the shifting dynamics towards flexible working arrangements post-pandemic, exploring how remote work influences employee mental health and well-being is timely. Research should focus on understanding how virtual team interactions, social isolation, and changes in job demands affect mental health outcomes (Nizam et al., 2024; Dutraj & Sengupta, 2024).
6. Workplace Policy Evaluations: Future studies should evaluate the efficacy of workplace policies related to mental health. Assessing the impact of policies like mental health days, flexible working hours, and comprehensive wellness programs will be critical in determining effective organizational strategies (Zhu et al., 2016; Fløvik et al., 2018). Identifying best practices across organizations will help craft effective models that can be adapted to various institutional contexts.

The dialogue surrounding employee mental health and well-being continues to evolve, but the evidence is clear: supporting both constructs is imperative to fostering a thriving workforce. Organizations that invest strategically in such initiatives can expect a myriad of benefits, including improved productivity, enhanced employee engagement, lower turnover, and increased overall satisfaction (Majcherek et al., 2022; Strudwick et al., 2023).

As the contemporary workforce navigates unprecedented challenges shaped by the evolving economic and social landscapes, embracing a holistic understanding of employee mental health and well-being must be paramount in organizational policies and practices. Future research must bridge existing gaps and continue examining the intricacies of these constructs to guide organizations in their efforts to create healthier work environments conducive to individual and collective success.

REFERENCES

Agteren, J., Iasiello, M., & Lo, L. (2018). Improving the well-being and resilience of health services staff via psychological skills training. *BMC Research Notes*, *11*(1), 924. Advance online publication. DOI: 10.1186/s13104-018-4034-x PMID: 30577884

Ahmed, M., Zehou, S., Raza, S., Qureshi, M., & Yousufi, S. (2020). Impact ofcsrand environmental triggers on employee green behavior: The mediating effect of employeewell-being. *Corporate Social Responsibility and Environmental Management*, *27*(5), 2225–2239. DOI: 10.1002/csr.1960

AlAmeri, A. (2023). Covid-19 impact on employees behavior and mental well-being in uae (abu dhabi emirates). *Journal of Human Resource and Leadership*, *8*(2), 20–34. DOI: 10.47604/jhrl.1975

Alsomaidaee, M., Joumaa, B., & Khalid, K. (2023). Toxic workplace, mental health and employee well-being, the moderator role of paternalistic leadership, an empirical study. *Journal of Applied Business and Technology*, *4*(2), 114–129. DOI: 10.35145/jabt.v4i2.126

Amponsah-Tawiah, K., Mensah, J., Boakyewaa, R., & Asare, G. (2023). From muddiness to madness: An examination of decent work and mental health in the ghanaian mining industry. *International Journal of Law and Management*, *65*(4), 289–299. DOI: 10.1108/IJLMA-01-2022-0001

Azizah, S., Raharjo, A., & Kristiana, I. (2023). Humility and psychological well-being of hospital employees. Proc. Int. Conf. of Psy. Stu., 4, 280-286. DOI: 10.58959/icpsychc.v4i1.45

Bondar, J., Morrow, C., Gueorguieva, R., Brown, M., Hawrilenko, M., Krystal, J., & Chekroud, A. (2022). Clinical and financial outcomes associated with a workplace mental health program before and during the covid-19 pandemic. *JAMA Network Open*, *5*(6), e2216349. DOI: 10.1001/jamanetworkopen.2022.16349 PMID: 35679044

Bryson, A., Forth, J., & Stokes, L. (2017). Does employees' subjective well-being affect workplace performance? *Human Relations*, *70*(8), 1017–1037. DOI: 10.1177/0018726717693073

Cao, X., Zhang, H., Li, P., & Huang, X. (2022). The influence of mental health on job satisfaction: Mediating effect of psychological capital and social capital. *Frontiers in Public Health*, *10*, 797274. Advance online publication. DOI: 10.3389/fpubh.2022.797274 PMID: 35211441

Cerdeira, J., Cakirpaloglu, S., & Cakirpaloglu, P. (2023). Crushing the spirit: Unmasking the impact of workplace bullying on psychological well-being among portuguese employees. *Administrative Sciences*, *13*(11), 244. DOI: 10.3390/admsci13110244

Chetty, L. (2017). An evaluation of the health and well-being needs of employees: An organizational case study. *Journal of Occupational Health*, *59*(1), 88–90. DOI: 10.1539/joh.16-0197-BR PMID: 27853056

Davenport, L., Allisey, A., Page, K., LaMontagne, A., & Reavley, N. (2016). How can organisations help employees thrive? the development of guidelines for promoting positive mental health at work. *International Journal of Workplace Health Management*, *9*(4), 411–427. DOI: 10.1108/IJWHM-01-2016-0001

Deka, P., Singh, G., Sharma, C., Verma, P., & Kapoor, S. (2024). The interplay of resilience, stress, mental well-being and task performance: Implications for sustainable workplaces. *Model Assisted Statistics and Applications : An International Journal*, *19*(3), 265–274. DOI: 10.3233/MAS-241933

Dimoff, J., & Kelloway, E. (2019). With a little help from my boss: The impact of workplace mental health training on leader behaviors and employee resource utilization. *Journal of Occupational Health Psychology*, *24*(1), 4–19. DOI: 10.1037/ocp0000126 PMID: 29939045

Dongarwar, D., Yusuf, K., Maiyegun, S., Ibrahimi, S., Ikedionwu, C., & Salihu, H. (2020). Covid-19 and neuro-behavioral economics: A conceptual framework to improve physical and mental health among remote workers. *International Journal of MCH and AIDS*, *9*(3), 360–363. DOI: 10.21106/ijma.399 PMID: 33014623

Dougall, I., Vasiljevic, M., Kutlaca, M., & Weick, M. (2023). Socioeconomic inequalities in mental health and well-being among uk students during the covid-19 pandemic: Clarifying underlying mechanisms. *PLoS One*, *18*(11), e0292842. DOI: 10.1371/journal.pone.0292842 PMID: 37910542

Dutraj, R. and Sengupta, P. (2024). Investigation into the nexus between workplace spirituality and employee performance in Indian banks: the interplay with mental health as a mediating factor in the context of West Bengal, India. Journal of Human Resource Management – HR Advances and Developments, 2024(1), 109-127. DOI: 10.46287/KLSN5929

Dutta, D., & Mishra, S. (2023). Bots for mental health: The boundaries of human and technology agencies for enabling mental well-being within organizations. *Personnel Review*, *53*(5), 1129–1156. DOI: 10.1108/PR-11-2022-0832

Edwards, A., & Marcus, S. (2018). Employee perceptions of well-being programs. *Journal of Social, Behavioral and Health Sciences*, *12*(1). Advance online publication. DOI: 10.5590/JSBHS.2018.12.1.07

Elshaer, I., & Azazz, A. (2023). Mental health of tourism employees post covid-19 pandemic: A test of antecedents and moderators. *European Journal of Investigation in Health, Psychology and Education*, *13*(3), 626–641. DOI: 10.3390/ejihpe13030048 PMID: 36975400

Elufioye, O., Ndubuisi, N., Daraojimba, R., Awonuga, K., Ayanponle, L., & Asuzu, O.Oluwafunmi Adijat ElufioyeNdubuisi Leonard NdubuisiRosita Ebere Daraojimba Kehinde Feranmi AwonugaLatifat Omolara AyanponleOnyeka Franca Asuzu. (2024). Reviewing employee well-being and mental health initiatives in contemporary hr practices. *International Journal of Science and Research Archive*, *11*(1), 828–840. DOI: 10.30574/ijsra.2024.11.1.0153

Falcon, M., Chen, C., Bandari, R., Kocher, B., & Shah, N. (2021). Impact of evidence-based psychotherapy on employee retention. *Medical Research Archives*, *9*(11). Advance online publication. DOI: 10.18103/mra.v9i11.2574

Fløvik, L., Knardahl, S., & Christensen, J. (2018). Organizational change and employee mental health: A prospective multilevel study of the associations between organizational changes and clinically relevant mental distress. *Scandinavian Journal of Work, Environment & Health*, *45*(2), 134–145. DOI: 10.5271/sjweh.3777 PMID: 30334062

Fujimoto, A., Kanegae, H., Kitaoka, K., Ohashi, M., Okada, K., Node, K., Takase, K., Fukuda, H., Miyazaki, T., & Yano, Y. (2024). The association between employee lifestyles and the rates of mental health-related absenteeism and turnover in japanese companies. *Epidemiology and Health*, *46*, e2024068. DOI: 10.4178/epih.e2024068 PMID: 39118545

Garg, N. (2017). Workplace spirituality and employee well-being: An empirical exploration. *Journal of Human Values*, *23*(2), 129–147. DOI: 10.1177/0971685816689741

Ghazali, H., Rahim, N., Ismail, N., Othman, M., & Ishak, M. (2023). Covid-19 related mental health effects in the workplace: A case of fast-food industry in malaysia. *International Journal of Human Resource Studies*, *13*(1), 21. DOI: 10.5296/ijhrs.v13i1.20441

Görgényi-Hegyes, É., Nathan, R., & Fekete-Farkas, M. (2021). Workplace health promotion, employee well-being and loyalty during covid-19 pandemic—Large scale empirical evidence from hungary. *Economies*, *9*(2), 55. DOI: 10.3390/economies9020055

Hamouche, S. (2020). Covid-19 and employees' mental health: Stressors, moderators and agenda for organizational actions. *Emerald Open Research*, *2*(2), 15. DOI: 10.1108/EOR-02-2023-0004

Hanisch, S., Birner, U., Oberhauser, C., Nowak, D., & Sabariego, C. (2017). Development and evaluation of digital game-based training for managers to promote employee mental health and reduce mental illness stigma at work: Quasi-experimental study of program effectiveness. *JMIR Mental Health*, *4*(3), e31. DOI: 10.2196/mental.7600 PMID: 28778839

Harding, S., Morris, R., Gunnell, D., Ford, T., Hollingworth, W., Tilling, K., Evans, R., Bell, S., Grey, J., Brockman, R., Campbell, R., Araya, R., Murphy, S., & Kidger, J. (2019). Is teachers' mental health and well-being associated with students' mental health and well-being? *Journal of Affective Disorders*, *253*, 460–466. DOI: 10.1016/j.jad.2019.03.046 PMID: 30189355

Hasanudin, S., Safar, F., Saaidun, N., & Abdullah, N. (2022). A survey on occupational mental health at a private college in northern region of peninsular malaysia. *Advances in Business Research International Journal*, *8*(1), 1–9. DOI: 10.24191/abrij.v8i1.17679

Hauff, S., Krick, A., Klebe, L., & Felfe, J. (2022). High-performance work practices and employee well-being—Does health-oriented leadership make a difference? *Frontiers in Psychology*, *13*, 833028. Advance online publication. DOI: 10.3389/fpsyg.2022.833028 PMID: 35310243

Hendriks, M., Burger, M., Rijsenbilt, A., Pleeging, E., & Commandeur, H. (2020). Virtuous leadership: A source of employee well-being and trust. *Management Research Review*, *43*(8), 951–970. DOI: 10.1108/MRR-07-2019-0326

Hossain, S., Moll, S., Tompa, E., & Gewurtz, R. (2021). The interactive process of negotiating workplace accommodations for employees with mental health conditions. *Work (Reading, Mass.)*, *69*(1), 75–90. DOI: 10.3233/WOR-213459 PMID: 33998573

Hsu, F., Liu, Y., & Tsaur, S. (2019). The impact of workplace bullying on hotel employees' well-being. *International Journal of Contemporary Hospitality Management*, *31*(4), 1702–1719. DOI: 10.1108/IJCHM-04-2018-0330

Irvine, A., & Suter, J. (2023). Managing mental health problems in the workplace: Are small businesses different? *Employee Relations*, *45*(5), 1161–1179. DOI: 10.1108/ER-09-2022-0451

Jnaneswar, K., & Sulphey, M. (2021). Workplace spirituality, self-compassion and mindfulness as antecedents of employee mental well-being. *South Asian Journal of Business Studies*, *12*(2), 269–292. DOI: 10.1108/SAJBS-07-2020-0258

Khan, K., e-Habiba, U., Sabeen, Z., & Waseem, M. (2022). Occupational mental health of non-family members in family firms: Evidence from pakistan. *Frontiers in Public Health*, *10*, 961553. Advance online publication. DOI: 10.3389/fpubh.2022.961553 PMID: 36225765

Khan, K., Niazi, A., Nasir, A., Hussain, M., & Khan, M. (2021). The effect of covid-19 on the hospitality industry: The implication for open innovation. *Journal of Open Innovation*, *7*(1), 30. DOI: 10.3390/joitmc7010030

Khoreva, V., & Wechtler, H. (2018). HR practices and employee performance: The mediating role of well-being. *Employee Relations*, *40*(2), 227–243. DOI: 10.1108/ER-08-2017-0191

Kinman, G. (2016). Effort–reward imbalance and overcommitment in uk academics: Implications for mental health, satisfaction and retention. *Journal of Higher Education Policy and Management*, *38*(5), 504–518. DOI: 10.1080/1360080X.2016.1181884

Kotera, Y., Mayer, C., & Vanderheiden, E. (2021). Cross-cultural comparison of mental health between german and south african employees: Shame, self-compassion, work engagement, and work motivation. *Frontiers in Psychology*, *12*, 627851. Advance online publication. DOI: 10.3389/fpsyg.2021.627851 PMID: 34239473

Laidlaw, A., McLellan, J., & Özakinci, G. (2015). Understanding undergraduate student perceptions of mental health, mental well-being and help-seeking behaviour. *Studies in Higher Education*, *41*(12), 2156–2168. DOI: 10.1080/03075079.2015.1026890

Lee, M., & Kim, B. (2023). Effect of the employees' mental toughness on organizational commitment and job satisfaction: Mediating psychological well-being. *Administrative Sciences*, *13*(5), 133. DOI: 10.3390/admsci13050133

Liu, W., Xu, Y., & Ma, D. (2021). Work-related mental health under covid-19 restrictions: A mini literature review. *Frontiers in Public Health*, *9*, 788370. Advance online publication. DOI: 10.3389/fpubh.2021.788370 PMID: 34900925

Lorber, M., & Dobnik, M. (2022). The importance of monitoring the psychological well-being and mental health of nursing staff for sustainable management. *Sustainability (Basel)*, *14*(14), 8300. DOI: 10.3390/su14148300

Lu, X., Yu, H., & Shan, B. (2022). Relationship between employee mental health and job performance: Mediation role of innovative behavior and work engagement. *International Journal of Environmental Research and Public Health, 19*(11), 6599. DOI: 10.3390/ijerph19116599 PMID: 35682185

Majcherek, D., Kowalski, A., & Lewandowska, M. (2022). Lifestyle, demographic and socio-economic determinants of mental health disorders of employees in the european countries. *International Journal of Environmental Research and Public Health, 19*(19), 11913. DOI: 10.3390/ijerph191911913 PMID: 36231214

Mäkikangas, A., Kinnunen, U., Feldt, T., & Schaufeli, W. (2016). The longitudinal development of employee well-being: A systematic review. *Work and Stress, 30*(1), 46–70. DOI: 10.1080/02678373.2015.1126870

Marín-García, J., & Bonavía, T. (2021). Empowerment and employee well-being: A mediation analysis study. *International Journal of Environmental Research and Public Health, 18*(11), 5822. DOI: 10.3390/ijerph18115822 PMID: 34071574

Martín, À., Woods, M., & Dawkins, S. (2018). How managers experience situations involving employee mental ill-health. *International Journal of Workplace Health Management, 11*(6), 442–463. DOI: 10.1108/IJWHM-09-2017-0069

Mathibe, M., & Chinyamurindi, W. (2021). Determinants of employee mental health in the south african public service: The role of organizational citizenship behaviours and workplace social support. *Advances in Mental Health, 19*(3), 306–316. DOI: 10.1080/18387357.2021.1938153

Mei, W., Wu, J., Zoghbi-Manrique-de-Lara, P., Liu, L., He, Y., & Song, M. (2023). Lose at sunrise, but gain at sunset: Linking social cyberloafing to psychological detachment, personal life enhancement of work, and mental health. *Work (Reading, Mass.), 75*(1), 339–348. DOI: 10.3233/WOR-220126 PMID: 36591686

Monteiro, E. and Joseph, J. (2023). A review on the impact of workplace culture on employee mental health and well-being. International Journal of Case Studies in Business It and Education, 291-317. DOI: 10.47992/IJCSBE.2581.6942.0274

Nguyen, M., Rundle-Thiele, S., Malik, A., & Budhwar, P. (2023). Impact of technology-based knowledge sharing on employee outcomes: Moderation effects of training, support and leadership. *Journal of Knowledge Management, 27*(8), 2283–2301. DOI: 10.1108/JKM-07-2022-0552

Nielsen, M., Ekholm, O., Møller, S., Ersbøll, A., Santini, Z., Grønbæk, M., & Thygesen, L. (2022). Mental well-being among danish employees during the covid-19 pandemic: Results from a longitudinal study on the role of industry and working environment. *European Journal of Public Health*, *32*(6), 871–876. DOI: 10.1093/eurpub/ckac150 PMID: 36228122

Nizam, N., Mokhtar, U., Dahlan, N., Bakri, N., Ahmad, M., & Safwan, N. (2024). Exploring the correlation between physical activity levels and mental health among employees at majlis sukan negeri johor. *International Journal of Academic Research in Business & Social Sciences*, *14*(3). Advance online publication. DOI: 10.6007/IJARBSS/v14-i3/20818

Oh, H., Park, H., & Boo, S. (2017). Mental health status and its predictors among call center employees: A cross-sectional study. *Nursing & Health Sciences*, *19*(2), 228–236. DOI: 10.1111/nhs.12334 PMID: 28295980

Oja, B., Kim, M., Perrewé, P., & Anagnostopoulos, C. (2019). Conceptualizing a-hero for sport employees' well-being. *Sport, Business and Management*, *9*(4), 363–380. DOI: 10.1108/SBM-10-2018-0084

Pandya, A., Khanal, N., & Upadhyaya, M. (2022). Workplace mental health interventions in india: A rapid systematic scoping review. *Frontiers in Public Health*, *10*, 800880. Advance online publication. DOI: 10.3389/fpubh.2022.800880 PMID: 35592077

Pawar, B. (2016). Workplace spirituality and employee well-being: An empirical examination. *Employee Relations*, *38*(6), 975–994. DOI: 10.1108/ER-11-2015-0215

Pradhan, R., & Hati, L. (2019). The measurement of employee well-being: Development and validation of a scale. *Global Business Review*, *23*(2), 385–407. DOI: 10.1177/0972150919859101

Rai, S. (2015). Organizational justice and employee mental health's moderating roles in organizational identification. *South Asian Journal of Global Business Research*, *4*(1), 68–84. DOI: 10.1108/SAJGBR-01-2014-0006

Rattanasirivilai, S. (2024). Happiness Based on the Happy Workplace Concept of Military Officials: Evidence in Thailand. *Asian Political Science Review*, *8*(2), 8–16.

Reimann, M., & Guzy, J. (2017). Psychological contract breach and employee health: The relevance of unmet obligations for mental and physical health. *Journal of Work and Organizational Psychology*, *33*(1), 1–11. DOI: 10.1016/j.rpto.2016.11.001

Rurkkhum, S. (2023). A bundle of human resource practices and employee resilience: The role of employee well-being. *Asia-Pacific Journal of Business Administration, 16*(3), 716–731. DOI: 10.1108/APJBA-01-2022-0050

Schultz, A., & Burton, W. (2018). Sleep: An integral component of employee well-being programs. *American Journal of Health Promotion, 32*(7), 1639–1641. DOI: 10.1177/0890117118790621c PMID: 30099898

Shanker, M. (2024). Impact of social media usage & social engagement on physical- mental health of young employees. *International Journal of Social Science and Human Research, 7*(04). Advance online publication. DOI: 10.47191/ijsshr/v7-i04-69

Sharma, P., & Kumra, R. (2020). Relationship between workplace spirituality, organizational justice and mental health: Mediation role of employee engagement. *Journal of Advances in Management Research, 17*(5), 627–650. DOI: 10.1108/JAMR-01-2020-0007

Shimazu, A., Matsudaira, K., Jonge, J., Tosaka, N., Watanabe, K., & Takahashi, M. (2016). Psychological detachment from work during non-work time: Linear or curvilinear relations with mental health and work engagement? *Industrial Health, 54*(3), 282–292. DOI: 10.2486/indhealth.2015-0097 PMID: 26829972

Somani, P. (2022). Managing mental health at work during periods of uncertainty. *Journal of Economics Finance and Management Studies, 05*(04). Advance online publication. DOI: 10.47191/jefms/v5-i4-13

Srivastava, H. (2023). How motivational leadership can positively affect the mental health of employees, leading to better productivity. *Russian Law Journal, 11*(3). Advance online publication. DOI: 10.52783/rlj.v11i3.2050

Strudwick, J., Gayed, A., Deady, M., Haffar, S., Mobbs, S., Malik, A., Akhtar, A., Braund, T., Bryant, R. A., & Harvey, S. (2023). Workplace mental health screening: A systematic review and meta-analysis. *Occupational and Environmental Medicine, 80*(8), 469–484. DOI: 10.1136/oemed-2022-108608 PMID: 37321849

Suwannapirom, P., & Pranee, S. (2023). A Model of Enhancing Innovative Work Behavior of Airports of Thailand. *Asian Administration and Management Review, 6*(2), 12–22.

Tu n, L. (2019). Discretionary hr practices and employee well-being. *Personnel Review, 49*(1), 43–66. DOI: 10.1108/PR-05-2018-0162

Vaidyanathan, S., & Mahapatra, G. (2020). Enhancing employee stress resilience (wellness): A study of women leaders in asia pacific. *NHRD Network Journal*, *14*(1), 144–154. DOI: 10.1177/2631454120973513

Vonderlin, R., Schmidt, B., Müller, G., Biermann, M., Kleindienst, N., Bohus, M., & Lyssenko, L. (2021). Health-oriented leadership and mental health from supervisor and employee perspectives: A multilevel and multisource approach. *Frontiers in Psychology*, *11*, 614803. Advance online publication. DOI: 10.3389/fpsyg.2020.614803 PMID: 33536980

Ward, E., Fragala, M., Birse, C., Hawrilenko, M., Smolka, C., Ambwani, G., Brown, M., Krystal, J. H., Corlett, P. R., & Chekroud, A. (2023). Assessing the impact of a comprehensive mental health program on frontline health service workers. *PLoS One*, *18*(11), e0294414. DOI: 10.1371/journal.pone.0294414 PMID: 37988363

Wardani, L., Apriliani, A., Riskinanti, K., Dearly, D., & Sharif, S. (2023). The role of employee well-being as a moderator: Job crafting and work engagement. *Indigenous Jurnal Ilmiah Psikologi*, *8*(1), 22–38. DOI: 10.23917/indigenous.v8i1.19903

Watthanabut, B., & Manasabutr, S. (2017). Happy Workplace according to Buddhist Way. *PSAKU International Journal of Interdisciplinary Research*, *6*(1), 21–28. DOI: 10.12778/235108618X15452373185949

Wel, K., Bambra, C., Dragano, N., Eikemo, T., & Lunau, T. (2015). Risk and resilience: health inequalities, working conditions and sickness benefit arrangements: an analysis of the 2010 european working conditions survey. *Sociology of Health & Illness*, *37*(8), 1157–1172. DOI: 10.1111/1467-9566.12293 PMID: 26094941

Wieneke, K., Egginton, J., Jenkins, S., Kruse, G., López-Jiménez, F., Mungo, M., Riley, B. A., & Limburg, P. (2019). Well-being champion impact on employee engagement, staff satisfaction, and employee well-being. *Mayo Clinic Proceedings. Innovations, Quality & Outcomes*, *3*(2), 106–115. DOI: 10.1016/j.mayocpiqo.2019.04.001 PMID: 31193868

Young, A., Bourke, A., Foley, S., & Blasi, Z. (2024). Effects of time management interventions on mental health and well-being factors: A protocol for a systematic review. *PLoS One*, *19*(3), e0288887. DOI: 10.1371/journal.pone.0288887 PMID: 38466711

Yulianti, P., & Fitdiarini, N. (2023). Job insecurity and psychological well-being: Is it necessary to foster employee performance. *International Journal of Current Science Research and Review*, *06*(06). Advance online publication. DOI: 10.47191/ijcsrr/V6-i6-14

Zheng, C., Molineux, J., Mirshekary, S., & Scarparo, S. (2015). Developing individual and organisational work-life balance strategies to improve employee health and well-being. *Employee Relations*, *37*(3), 354–379. DOI: 10.1108/ER-10-2013-0142

Zhu, S., Tse, S., Goodyear-Smith, F., Yuen, W., & Wong, P. (2016). Health-related behaviours and mental health in hong kong employees. *Occupational Medicine*, *67*(1), 26–32. DOI: 10.1093/occmed/kqw137 PMID: 27707896

Chapter 3
Prioritizing Employee Psychological Well-Being: A Practical Guide to Organizational Sustainability

Bhupinder Singh
https://orcid.org/0009-0006-4779-2553
Sharda University, India

Saurabh Chandra
https://orcid.org/0000-0003-4172-9968
Bennett University, Greater Noida, India

Kittisak Wongmahesak
https://orcid.org/0009-0000-2129-4691
North Bangkok University, Thailand

ABSTRACT

Promoting the psychological health of workers is now a critical global public health priority impacting groups and societies with implications for organizational sustainability and societal advancement. In the wake of heightened workplace stress, burnout and mental health illness, workplace mental health promotion is essential. Organizations need to take a fragmented approach and incorporate mental health, flexible hours and inclusive culture, and regular wellness metrics as part of its approach. With providing employees with access to programs that promote mental resilience, creating open communication channels, and ensuring a fair distribution of workloads, organizations can bolster morale, productivity, and retention. Mental health investment contributes to not only a healthy workforce but also organizational performance, innovation and sustainability in the long run. A

DOI: 10.4018/979-8-3373-2210-0.ch003

opyright © 2025, IGI Global Scientific Publishing. Copying or distributing in print or electronic forms without written permission of IGI Global Scientific Publishing is prohibited.

workplace that is psychologically healthy lays the groundwork for a more resilient, adaptive, and socially conscious global workforce.

1. INTRODUCTION

Improving employee psychological health is no longer an optional add-on but a key pillar of world public health and business sustainability. Mental wellness needs recognition and support as a basic labor right, from governments and from global health agencies as well. Workplaces are fast evolving, with rapid technological advancements, economic uncertainties, and growing demands, leading to the mental wellness of employees being under strain more than ever (Momin & Rolla, 2025). These include workplace burnout, chronic stress, depression, and anxiety, which have become a significant global health crisis; lower productivity, absenteeism, high turnover, and soaring healthcare expense. For example, the World Health Organization (WHO) and International Labour Organization (ILO) (see attached) underscore the need to promote psychological well-being in workplaces, and note that mental health is an integral part of overall public health and is crucial for sustainable development and economic growth. Workplaces are microcosms of society, and the psychological health of their members influences families, communities and even nations. Thus, supporting a mentally healthy workforce is not only an employer responsibility but a public health priority as well (Amoadu et al., 2025). By embedding psychological wellness in the organizational DNA, institutions can create inclusive, equitable, and resilient work environments that align with the principles of sustainability and human rights.

Worldwide companies are waking up to the idea that good mental health gets the basis for long term success. When employees' psychological well-being is optimal, their performance is marked by engagement, creativity, and commitment (de Silva, 2025). They have higher emotional quotient, cope with change better and develop better interpersonal relations all of which are essential for a collaborative and innovative work culture. The consequences are gripping and far-reaching however when mental well-being is ignored. Burnout, WHO recently classified as an occupational phenomenon, is described as a decrease in performance, emotional exhaustion, and cynicism. Recent evidence from around the world shows that global lost productivity due to poor mental health costs the world economy over $1 trillion each year. These statistics highlight the critical need for organizations to take action now. Sustainable organizations cannot expect worklife balance and employee benefits to suffice; they need to cultivate psychological safety, so workers feel seen, heard, valued and supported in their emotional journeys.

TO boost psychological well-being in the workplace, we must develop multi-layered interventions that take individual, group, and organizational dynamics into account. Implementing such initiatives at the individual level, while promoting self-care, emotional literacy and work-life balance through programs and policies, can empower employees to take ownership of their own mental health. Team-level interventions like fostering supportive leadership and peer relationships create belonging and mutual accountability. Organizationally, embedding mental wellness into policies, performance reviews, onboarding, and training serve to solidify a pre-culture of care.

Metrics that are directly related to psychological well-being, such as mental health surveys, engagement indices, and burnout risk assessments, should be continuously tracked so that data-informed changes can be made. AI-powered technological tools can be employed to recognize early signs of psychological distress and curate interventions based on these signs while also prioritizing the privacy of all employees. To sum up, improving psychological well-being is a global priority that knows no boundaries and is applicable in various domains. Investing into development of employee minds not just ensures a healthier workforce but also helps in building a culture of innovation, equity and sustainability. The future of work must be anchored in psychological health, then it can make progress that can be called sustainable and humane (Begum, 2025).

1.1 Significance of Psychological Health in the Workplace

This combined with the isolation of remote working, fear of getting ill, financial stress, and increasingly blurred work-life boundaries caused cases of mental health disorders to spike around the world. Such a crisis acted as an awakening, bringing home the realization that psychological health is an important part of the organizational continuity and disaster preparedness. Some more progressive companies developed flexible work policies, mental wellness apps, online therapy sessions, mindfulness training and peer support circles to help their workforce navigate pandemic-fueled stress. These practices need to be institutionalized and scaled up, as long-term strategies rather than stopgap solutions. Governments also play an important role in protecting mental health in the workplace by supporting strong legal frameworks and public-private partnerships that help empower employers to support workers' mental health rights. Integrate mental health policies into occupational health and safety laws, and bolster a culture of transparency, zero tolerance of stigma and discrimination.

Psychological well-being is a critical component of holistic employee development in an organization and is a key factor for long-term sustainability. Two Sustainable Development Goals (SDGs), specifically, SDG 3 (Good Health and

Well-being) and SDG 8 (Decent Work and Economic Growth), emphasize the need for inclusive and supportive work environments that prioritize mental health. Investing in psychological well-being drives organizational resilience, enabling companies to navigate market disruption, innovate responsibly, and attract and retain top talent. Also, visibly supporting mental health not only generates trust within the organization, but also leads to enhanced company reputation and social goodwill. It also fits into Environmental, Social and Governance (ESG) measures that are becoming a common means to gauge a company's long-term viability. Hence mental wellness programs should not only be viewed as legal and moral responsibilities but as practical compulsion driving organizational productivity and societal interest (Lindencrona, 2025).

2. PSYCHOLOGICAL WELL-BEING IN THE WORKPLACE: INDICATORS OF MENTAL HEALTH AT WORK

Psychological well-being at work has become one of the key factors for organizational effectiveness, employee satisfaction and sustainable development. It refers to the mental, emotional and cognitive well-being of employees as a whole, including their capacity to manage stress, work productively, form meaningful relationships and contribute to the environment in the organization. In contemporary work environments which are often marked by high pressure, digitalization and socio-economic uncertainty, the need to understand and measure key mental health indicators at work is increasingly salient. The workplace psychological well-being indicators act as diagnostic screens for organizations to identify stress exposures, offer preventive solutions, and create a culture of psychological safety and resilience. These indicators are multi-dimensional and include emotional, behavioral, cognitive, physiological, and social factors. They illustrate individuals' immediate mental state as well as hint at underlying systemic and cultural forces at play within organizations. Thus, strong stewardship of these indicators paves the way for prevention, prudent management practices, and investment in human capital.

Employee engagement has been regarded as one of the best proxies for mental health at work, demonstrating the degree to which employees feel both emotionally attached and passionately engaged with their profession and workplace. Vigoris, dedicated, and acts with sense of purpose - such are the traits for the highly engaged employees helping to yield positive contributions to the organizational outcomes. In contrast, disengagement or detachment may be a sign of psychological strain, burnout or dissatisfaction, which can tell if employees are mentally detached and potentially dealing with stress or anxiety. Companies that monitor engagement through ongoing surveys, one-on-one feedback, and performance analytics can note drops that may correlate with mental health issues. A nearby measure is job satisfaction, which refers to how satisfied workers are with their role, work-life balance, compensation, and the relationships they build there. In fact, persistent dissatisfaction is closely associated with emotional exhaustion, reduced motivation, and increased turnover intentions all of which serve as red flags for diminished psychological well-being (Lindencrona, 2025).

Absenteeism and presenteeism figure as useful markers of workplace mental health too. Absenteeism is when employees are repeatedly absent from work due to illness and stress, and presenteeism is when employees are present in body but not in mind, because their mental health is failing, leading to reduced productivity. Stan in particular flagged mental health issues such as depression, anxiety disorders or chronic fatigue as the most likely reasons for multiple absences without substantive medical justification, particularly in high-pressure roles. Presenteeism being present but dysfunctional is less visible but potentially more dangerous, as it can happen without anyone noticing and can stealthily deplete productivity and morale (Paudyal et al., 2025). By monitoring attendance patterns, workflow metrics and behavioral cues, organizations can detect these trends and design support systems that emphasize mental well-being.

2.1 Link between Employee Wellness and Organizational Performance

Stress levels and coping mechanisms are another major cluster of indicators. Job stress can arise from excessive workload, absence of clear job expectations, absence of autonomy, or toxic workplace cultures. Over time, not only does stress impact our mental functioning, but it also has the potential to lead to physical problems including high blood pressure, insomnia or digestive diseases. Chronic stress changes the chemistry of the brain, making it harder to focus and governing emotion (Wang et al., 2025). Stressed employees may be short with their colleagues, isolate themselves, or be overly reactive to constructive feedback; all of these things impact on team dynamics and working together on collaborative projects. Organizations can measure stress using anonymous wellness surveys, open-door HR policies and routine well-being check-ins. In addition, assessing how workers deal with stress positively, with problem-solving and mindfulness, or negatively, with substance use or isolation can help inform specific efforts to improve mental health.

Interpersonal relationships and the ways team members communicate with each other are telling of mental health within teams. Healthy interactions between peers attest to constructive communication and mutual respect, two elements of positive psychological well-being. In contrast, if someone engages in regular arguments, backs out of team pursuits, demonstrates passive-aggressive reactions, or communicates poorly, chances are he or she is struggling emotionally or psychologically (Papageorgiou et al., 2025). A hallmark of psychological wellness is the ability to maintain healthy work relationships, ask for help when needed, and positive contribute to others' group efforts all of which require resilience and social adaptability. Watching these relational markers over time with team diagnostics, leadership observations, and org-network analysis can provide useful insights into the workplace mental health climate.

Creativity, decision-making ability, attention span, memory and other cognitive indicators are often overlooked, even though they are tightly coupled with mental well-being. Psychological distress can affect cognitive functioning, making it difficult for employees to concentrate, think clearly, or solve problems effectively. Frequent errors, indecision, forgetfulness, or declining output quality may not merely be performance issues but the effects of deeper mental fatigue or burn-out. In contrast, employees with good psychological well-being tend to be agile thinkers and flexible, and demonstrate a high degree of initiative. Workplace strategies (such as incorporating cognitive assessments as part of professional development programs or performance review) could also help to detect when support may be necessary.

2.2 Emerging Trends in Work-Related Mental Health Issues

Changes in behavior and mood are among the clearest signs of psychological distress. The changes in an employee's behavior that are usually most evident becoming more irritable, withdrawn, aggressive or unmotivated are often the telltale signs that something is wrong. Though we all have ups and downs, persistent or extreme mood fluctuations can indicate anxiety, depression or other psychological conditions. It is a 'must' to design a workplace atmosphere that recognises such changes with empathy instead of judgement as early intervention can mean the difference between recovery and serious long-term mental health issues. Message Boards Managers and HR professionals should be trained to spot such behavioral cues and respond appropriately without breaching confidentiality or triggering stigma.

The ability to maintain work-life balance and set boundaries is seen as a marker of psychological health. Employees who are able to navigate and balance their personal and professional lives without ongoing conflict or compromise tend to enjoy mental-health benefits (Wieneke et al., 2025). By contrast, people who feel pressured to be "always on," those who feel guilty for taking breaks, or those who neglect personal time chronically are highly prone to burnout. This is an increasingly relevant marker as the rise of remote work and computerized workplace communication tools breaks down traditional lines between personal life and work. Asked to set boundaries and avoid judgement whilst feeling empowered to work flexible hours, can go a long way in promoting mental wellness in the workplace.

They shape and reflect mental health conditions, and organizational culture and leadership styles are another way in which this is done. Such a culture of openness, inclusion and psychological safety empowers employees to raise issues, ask for help and innovate without the fear of being punished. In contrast, punitive workplaces with inflexible hierarchies and micromanagement can squash morale and worsen mental health issues. Leaders who demonstrate empathy, emotional intelligence, and vulnerability help create a positive workspace. Regular organizational health assessments, 360-degree feedback, and culture audits can quantify collective mental well-being and reveal areas for systemic change.

The feedback loops and psychological empowerment matter. Regular, constructive feedback, coupled with the ability to make decisions and contribute to organizational goals, is more likely to lead to a sense of purpose, competence and psychological wellbeing for employees (Peethambaran & Naim, 2025). On the other hand, hinder feedback, acknowledgment, or independence can create a sensation of powerlessness or dissipation. From a mentally wholesome workplace experience, participatory leadership, continuous learning opportunities, and career growth pathways will strengthen it.

At the workplace we have multiple interconnected and embedded aspects to mental well–being. When considered together, the emotional, cognitive, behavioral, relational, and structural indicators they self-report create a holistic view of employee psychological health. Whether the workplace is physical or remote, learning to notice the signs early on, your own, of your organization, and those of your team members is an urgent need and necessary to create a culture of well-being. Psychological well-being is not a luxury or a nice-to-have it is the bedrock of a healthy, robust, future-ready workforce.

3. PSYCHOLOGICAL WELL-BEING AS A GLOBAL PUBLIC HEALTH PRIORITY

Psychological well-being increasingly has become a fundamental global public health priority of the 21st century, surpassing traditional understandings of health in individualistic terms to include economic, social, and political dimensions of global sustainability. As mental health is increasingly recognized as integral to overall health, productivity, and socioeconomic development, there is growing recognition that psychological well-being is no longer a health issue only, but a prerequisite to achieving the United Nations' Sustainable Development Goals (SDGs) with SDG 3 (Good Health and Well-being) being at the forefront (Kock et al., 2025). The projections for the rapidly growing burden of mental health disorders globally namely depression, anxiety and stress-related disorders call upon nation states to tackle the psychological health of populations as a key issue on the public health agenda. The governments, international organizations, and civil society are growing aware of the need to support the psychological well-being of people in order to build resilient health systems, equitable societies, and inclusive growth.

The importance of mental health disorders constitutes the leading cause of global burden of disease and disability. According to the World Health Organization (WHO), approximately one person out of eight lives with a mental disorder, and depression alone affects more than 280 million people. Mental health disorders are among the top 5 or 10 causes of disability, numbering one in six across the globe, costing the world trillions of dollars in productivity lost. Mental health disorders are the most common cause of disability worldwide; however, they continue to be underdiagnosed, underfunded, and stigmatized. Treatment for these conditions is severely lacking: in low- and middle-income countries as many as 85 per cent of people with mental health conditions receive no treatment whatsoever. The implications of this neglect are significant untreated mental health disorders not only decrease health-related quality of life and increase morbidity, but also worsen other health conditions, including cardiovascular diseases, diabetes and substance use disorders. Further, low psychological well-being is associated with social determinants of health such as poverty, unemployment, discrimination, and violence. We must address these underlying social, economic, and environmental determinants through integrated public health approaches as the only viable means of providing holistic mental health care (Nguyen et al., 2025).

Psychological well-being is a multi-faceted concept covering emotional resilience, life satisfaction, cognitive functioning, sense of purpose, self-acceptance, and the cultivation of significant connections. Mental health also includes how we handle stress, relate to others, and make choices. Mental health is not just the absence of mental illness, but also the presence of mental wellness and positive mental states that allow people to manage hardship and contribute to society. Hence public health efforts should move away from solely curative approaches to preventive and promotive interventions across the life-course to enhance mental well-being from early childhood to old age. Scalable solutions embedded in broader health and social systems include school-based mental health programs, workplace well-being initiatives, community resilience-building work and digital mental health approaches. For example, we have primary health care in the country, now if mental health services were integrated into the primary health care then services would be accessible and stigma would be reduced and along with that if we start with universal mental health education there will be a culture of empathy, support and early intervention.

3.1 Global Mental Health Crisis and Workplace Impact

It emphasizes the need for comprehensive policies, legal safeguards, and global collaboration in the pursuit of psychological health. The WHO's Comprehensive Mental Health Action Plan outlines a roadmap for countries to create inclusive mental health systems, strengthen governance, and deliver rights-based care. But the implementation of policy is frequently delayed due to time loss in funding, scarcity of mental health practitioners, insufficient knowledge regarding mental health and absence of political will. Achieving this will require ongoing investment, capacity-building, and cross-sector collaboration to bridge the mental health policy-practice gap. Ensuring that mental health budgets reflect its status as a significant public health issuc and promoting mental health equity by prioritizing marginalized and vulnerable populations such as refugees, minorities, persons with disabilities (PWD), and LGBTQ+ individuals who tend to experience increased (and compounded) mental health risk in the wake of systemic discrimination is therefore critical and should be the responsibility of governments (Bolatov et al., 2025).

That of technology and innovation in fostering psychological well-being as a public health priority is equally transformative. However, the emergence of digital mental health services, teletherapy, AI-hosted mental health assessments and mobile health (mHealth) applications has transformed the method of accessing psychological support, especially in areas with fewer resources. Such innovations not only fill the gaps that geographical and wider resource factors present, but provide personalized, scalable mental health monitoring, self-care and professional interventions. Yet digital health solutions must be developed and deployed with ethical safeguards, data privacy protections, and cultural sensitivity to ensure inclusivity and effectiveness. With countless innovations coming out, there's a health risk attached to unregulated and untrusted technology, as well as a quality assurance problem, so governments and global agencies can also step in and demand regulation and responsibility for the same.

In the global landscape, psychological well-being intersects with a myriad of challenges; humanitarian crises, climate change, pandemics, socioeconomic inequalities rendering its relevance cross-cutting to the entirety of international development and diplomacy (Fung et al., 2025). Natural disasters and forced migration and climate-induced displacement include conflict zones and trigger wide-scale psychological trauma, and mental health and psychosocial support (MHPSS) need to be included as part of various frameworks of emergency response and recovery. The mental health consequences of climate change, from eco-anxiety to post-disaster stress, underscore the need to integrate psychological considerations into climate and disaster planning and preparedness strategies. Global aid and development partners: International agencies such as the United Nations, the World Bank and

UNICEF, must prioritize psychological resilience in their global aid and development programs, treating mental well-being as a right and as an enabler of peace, sustainability and inclusive recovery.

3.2 Role of WHO, ILO, and UN SDG 3 (Good Health and Well-Being)

The psychological well-being is on the top of global public health agenda of the 21st century. It is vibrant, inclusive, and an integral part of human development, economic vibrancy and social progress. Elevating psychological well-being transforms the paradigm from reactive, disease-oriented strategies toward proactive, people-oriented approaches that integrate mental health into the full spectrum of public policy, governance, education, labour, and health care (Sethumadhavan, 2025). With political commitment, community engagement, scientific innovation and equitable resource allocation, the global community can advance mental well-being as a universal right and key pillar of sustainable development. When they come together to elevate mental health to a priority of the public health agenda, we open doors to a more humane, efficient and robust world.

3.3 Public Health Implications of Workplace Mental Distress

The importance of psychological well-being as a global public health priority has another dimension: that of workplace relevance and organizational sustainability. Employee mental health drives productivity, job satisfaction, innovation and retention, while poor mental health is correlated with absenteeism, burnout and turnover. The WHO and ILO have stated the significance of our workplaces being mental health-friendly through promoting psychological safety, work-life balance, and stress management. Governments can facilitate this with occupational health policies, the adoption of incentives to increase access to mental health programs, and public-private partnerships that create mentally healthy work environments. Investing in workplace mental health is not only a moral imperative but an economic one, as studies show that the return of every dollar spent on mental health promotion and prevention is of four to one.

Culturally appropriate approaches are needed to raise the profile of psychological health as a global PHI. Mental health is intricately shaped by cultural frameworks: the societal norms, values, and expressions that dictate how distress is perceived, expressed, and treated. They need to involve local communities and traditional health systems and knowledge, so that mental health practice is relevant and culturally respectful in the context of vibrant cultural diversity. In their diverse cultural contexts, community-based mental health care, peer support networks, and participatory health promotion models can empower individuals and de-stigmatize mental health (Ongel et al., 2025). The local languages and culturally relevant media campaigns will enhance mental health literacy and silence-breaking, which will promote help-seeking behavior and change social attitudes in this regard.

4. ORGANIZATIONAL APPROACHES TO PROMOTE EMPLOYEE MENTAL WELLNESS

Mental wellness at the organizational level has now transitioned to become one of the key pillars that need to be instilled in order to keep up a resilient, productive and sustainable workforce within the evolved work environments of today. As employees in all industries experience rising incidences of mental health challenges such as stress, anxiety, burnout, and depression, more and more organizations are embedding mental wellness strategies into the heart of their operating models. Such nurturing of mental well-being at work must stem from a pro-organizational culture valuing psychological safety, transparency in communication, and empathy. The most effective strategies consists in using leadership commitment to create a supportive work environment (Gkliati et al., 2025). When leaders engage in healthy behaviors, value work-life balance, and listen to employee concerns, that behavior becomes normalized and conversations about mental health happen more and stigma gets dissipated. Adapted human resource policies, including flexible work arrangements hybrid models, job sharing, compressed workweeks can mitigate work-related stressors significantly and give employees increased autonomy and control over their schedules.

Embedding mental health resources within the organization is also key. Employee Assistance Programs (EAPs), counseling services, therapists on sites and mental health helplines can help employees who are going through psychological distress with timely and confidential support. Also, training managers and team leaders to identify early signs of mental health issues is an important investment in enabling early intervention as well as creating a culture of responsiveness and empathy in the workplace. Organizational mental health literacy programs and workshops on emotional resilience, mindfulness, and stress management provide additional empowerment by equipping employees with the tools to effectively handle challenges. Fostering peer-support groups and internal mental health champions can help develop a sense of community and shared responsibility. And, organizations that foster fair workloads, realistic expectations and open communication reduce anxiety and increase job satisfaction.

Such recognition and reward systems that acknowledge employee efforts not only improve morale but also strengthen positive mental states and inherent motivation. Also vital is the physical design of the workplace well-ventilated, ergonomically structured spaces with quiet or relaxation rooms can make a big difference in psychological comfort and sensory overload. Routine mental wellness checkups, surveys, and feedback loops help organizations track well-being trends and tailor strategies accordingly (Alfaraby & Sinambela, 2025). Above all, inclusive practices of diversity, equity, and belonging contribute to mental wellness since they make sure all employees feel valued, respected, and psychologically safe. In a life after a pandemic, when hybrid and remote work models are on the rise, digital well-being, including measuring screen time, virtual meeting fatigue and digital disconnection, are also being recognized. Companies that integrate mental wellness with other policies, practices, and culture, not only protect their employees' well-being, but also release higher levels of creativity, loyalty, and engagement and build long-term organizational sustainability.

5. STRESS MANAGEMENT AND RESILIENCE BUILDING PROGRAMS

The complexities of modern workplaces, stress management and resilience building programs are increasingly indispensable parts of holistic employee wellness programs. As employees contend with increasing workloads, rapid technological advances, job insecurity and the spillage of work into personal life, stress has emerged as a top-of-mind issue with physiology-altering consequences on mental and physical health. The other aspect of combating burnout is the establishment of structured stress management programs within the organization (McGlinchey et al., 2025). These programs usually emphasize recognising stressors, teaching coping responses and developing emotional intelligence. These workshops also provide practical tools (mindfulness, meditation, time management, cognitive behavioral techniques, relaxation and breathing exercises, etc.) to help employees deal with pressure. The resilience training allows individuals to positively adapt to change and recover from setbacks, while maintaining psychological stability in times of adversity. Such strategies are preventative and proactive in nature unlike reactive interventions that seek to address stress after it has already taken a toll on performance and help to build mental fortitude and emotional flexibility before the challenges are faced.

Resilience programs also emphasize developing a growth mindset helping employees see failures as chances to learn rather than as threats. With this shift in perspective, a student must now believe they are responsible for what they make, which helps instill self-efficacy while encouraging persistence, and finding new ways to solve problems. Facilitated reflection sessions, peer-to-peer support groups and storytelling practices allow employees to offer and share experiences, normalize emotions, and take strength from collective narratives. Also, personalized coaching, mentoring, and psychological counseling can be integrated into a resilience program to provide individualized support. These interventions serve to foster greater awareness of an employee's emotional triggers, behavioural patterns and coping resources. A key factor to mention here is leadership, which is essential for ensuring the success of stress management and resilience programs (Bakri et al., 2025). By fostering empathy, encouraging vulnerability, and emphasizing work-life balance, managers naturally create psychological safety, which in turn promotes emotional well-being.

For organizations that embed these programs into their workplace culture, they also often integrate with digital platforms and mobile apps to allow employees continuous access to stress-relief resources, breathing techniques and guided meditations. Virtual resilience workshops and stress-reduction webinars can also be particularly effective with remote or hybrid teams. The constant evaluations of the programs, preferably using feedback channels like employee surveys, pulse checkers, and focus groups make sure that they can adapt to growing employee needs. Acknowledging and rewarding participation in wellness programs strengthens their significance and fosters sustainable involvement. All in all, stress management and resilience-building initiatives mitigate absenteeism and healthcare costs and foster a thriving, agile, emotionally intelligent workforce progressing the organization toward sustainable success in an increasingly complex, rapidly changing world.

6. SUSTAINABLE WORK CULTURE AND CORPORATE LONGEVITY

Building a healthier work culture is an essential foundation for the long-term survival of any business, and one that rests upon sustainable practices that foster employee well-being, social responsibility, good governance, and inclusivity within the organization (Dhand, 2025). Companies that take an inclusive approach towards sustainable values are thus able to maintain not only short-term productivity, but also long-term resilience and relevance in the face of an ever-growing list of challenges for the future. A workplace of the future must integrate performance expectations with human-centric values, precisely because employee satisfaction, mental health, and engagement are now more critical to lasting success than ever before. Companies that develop trust, safety and cooperative environments tend to retain talent, mitigate burnout, and promote innovation. This type of culture is grounded in open communication, diversity and inclusion, work-life integration, and ongoing learning opportunities. Team members are more motivated to commit to the company, contributing to corporate health and growth over the long haul.

From an operational perspective, sustainable work cultures promote responsible energy consumption, green policies, and ethical supply chains. Companies adopting environmental and social governance (ESG) principles as part of their core strategy become increasingly attractive for investors, customers, and employees alike. Integrating sustainability into workplace practices such as limiting carbon footprints through remote working opportunities, encouraging digital transformation, decreasing waste, and fostering community involvement enhances an organization's reputation and future sustainability. In addition, leadership is instrumental in modeling sustainable behavior and creating a culture of accountability (Bai et al., 2025). When executives connect organizational goals to larger societal value whether equity, climate action, or social justice they create a workforce that shares a sense of purpose aligned with the company's mission.

Longevity in the corporate world is not no longer defined solely by financial performance but by how an organization can consistently evolve, innovate and respond ethically to the needs of the stakeholders. Organizations that prioritize workforce development, encourage cross-generational collaboration, and be flexible are more resilient in the wake of economic shocks, technological disruptions, and global crises. Sustainable work cultures further enhance mental and physical wellness through policies that promote flexible work, access to mental health resources, equitable compensation, and mechanisms for regular feedback. They consistently capture and enhance their cultural wellbeing with engagement surveys, transparency dashboards, and wellness indices. So, ultimately, sustainable work culture is not a pixelated plan but an evolving ecosystem of values, practices and relationships that nurture people and the planet. Companies that understand this interfacility link are likely to survive through decades, economic relevance aside, they still need to maintain societal and environmental legitimacy as the global landscape is driven increasingly by values over profits (Andersen et al., 2025).

7. CONCLUSION AND FUTURE DIRECTIONS

Improvement of psychological well-being at work is no more a secondary requirement but a primary requirement for developing a sustainable, resilient and high-performing culture at work. In light of the rising tide of mental health problems of workers, it is imperative to embed mental wellness within the corporate agenda not as a check-in-the-box compliance formality but as a value driver underpinning human capital investment. Such organizations that create a psychologically safe and inclusive work environment, encourage stress management and work-life balance enjoy having a more engaged, loyal and innovative workforce. In fact, a sustainable work culture based on empathy, fairness, and ethical practices are crucial to the long-term sustainability of companies. The global workforce under the impact of digital transformation, socio-economic changes, and post-pandemic recovery continues to evolve, and businesses need to recalibrate their approach to employee well-being with even greater agility and intentionality.

Data-driven approaches to mental health are the future, as we integrate artificial intelligence, predictive analytics, and real-time evaluation to personalize mental fitness and mental health interventions. Appropriate safeguards should also provide for continuous education, leadership development, and psychological literacy to equip both management and employees to recognize early and address mental health challenges. In a world where mental health metrics will also contribute to ESG (Environmental, Social and Governance) reporting and sustainability objectives, we will also see such well-being indicators becoming institutionalized performance criteria. Multi-sector collaborations across governments, employers, mental health professionals, and technology providers will be essential to building scalable, inclusive, and culturally appropriate solutions. The way forward is one in which mental health is a pervasive and practical element of every aspect of organizational activity, creating workplaces that not only work well but thrive in the context of their organizational mission, purpose and values. Organizations that make the choice to focus corporate priorities on the people and planet to understand how people problems are everyone's business will ultimately create a workforce that helps change the world and make us all more sustainable in the process.

REFERENCES

Alfaraby, A., & Sinambela, L. P. (2025). Human Capital Development Strategies in Improving the Performance of The General and Financial Bureaus of The Indonesian Quarantine Agency. *International Journal of Management Science and Information Technology*, *5*(1), 20–26. DOI: 10.35870/ijmsit.v5i1.3619

Amoadu, M., Agyare, D. F., Doe, P. F., & Abraham, S. A. (2025). Examining the impact of psychosocial safety climate on working conditions, well-being and safety of healthcare providers: A scoping review. *BMC Health Services Research*, *25*(1), 90. DOI: 10.1186/s12913-025-12254-2 PMID: 39819783

Andersen, L. P., Andersen, D. R., & Pihl-Thingvad, J. (2025). Psychosocial Climate as Antecedent for Resources to Manage Emotional Demands at Work. *International Journal of Environmental Research and Public Health*, *22*(1), 64. DOI: 10.3390/ijerph22010064 PMID: 39857517

Bai, Z., Zhang, S., & He, H. (2025). Extraordinary nature and human recovery: Psychological and physiological perspectives. *Journal of Environmental Management*, *373*, 123661. DOI: 10.1016/j.jenvman.2024.123661 PMID: 39673850

Bakri, N. N., Thomson, W. M., Broadbent, J. M., & Smith, M. B. (2025). Key informants' views on the benefits, planning and implementation of workplace oral health promotion programme. *Health Promotion International*, *40*(1), daae198. DOI: 10.1093/heapro/daae198 PMID: 39883052

Begum, G. T. (2025). Achieving sustainable development goals for mental health and gender equality through work-life balance and emotional intelligence. *Gender in Management*, *40*(1), 134–150. DOI: 10.1108/GM-04-2023-0149

Bolatov, A., Baikanova, R., Igenbayeva, B., & Seisembekov, T. (2025). Health care providers have faced the pandemic altruistically, but financial support is important for their well-being and motivation to work. *Public Health*, *240*, 119–124. DOI: 10.1016/j.puhe.2025.01.023 PMID: 39904063

da Silva, T. M. H. R. (2025). The Role of Emotional Intelligence in Promoting Mental Peace, Healthy Work Environments, and Emotional Well-Being Among Entrepreneurs. In *Supporting Psychological and Emotional Wellbeing Among Entrepreneurs* (pp. 401–426). IGI Global.

Dhand, S. (2025). Theories and Concepts of Well-being and Happiness in the Workplace: Foundations and Practical Applications. In *Insights on Wellbeing and Happiness in the Workplace* (pp. 283-304). IGI Global Scientific Publishing.

Fung, H. Y., Sha, E. S., Chiu, W. K., & Fong, B. Y. F. (2025). Community Health Models. In *The Handbook of Primary Healthcare: The Case of Hong Kong* (pp. 19–33). Springer Nature Singapore. DOI: 10.1007/978-981-96-0817-1_2

Gkliati, A., Saiti, A., Chletsos, M., & Bechlioulis, A. P. (2025). The relationship of Minimum Wage on Employees' Well–being, Job satisfaction and Work–life balance. *The International Journal of Organizational Analysis*. Advance online publication. DOI: 10.1108/IJOA-05-2024-4520

Kock, R., Graupner, L. I., & Baloyi, S. (2025). Cultivating a culture of mental health in organisations: Reading the room. *SA Journal of Industrial Psychology*, *51*, 2233. DOI: 10.4102/sajip.v51i0.2233

Lindencrona, F. (2025). Eudaimonic well-being: A foundation for public administration systems fit to build a sustainable future. In *Sustainable Transformation and Well-being: The Role of Business for Individual and Collective Flourishing* (pp. 219–241). Springer Nature Switzerland. DOI: 10.1007/978-3-031-75566-8_14

McGlinchey, D., Roebuck, B. S., Sakauye, P., Lalonde, C., Ferns, A., & Killian, K. (2025). "Increasing Demands and Competing Priorities": How Organizational Structure Affects Worker Well-Being in the Victim Services Field. *Human Service Organizations, Management, Leadership & Governance*, *49*(2), 152–169.

Momin, M. M., & Rolla, K. P. (2025). Narratives of Workplace Well-Being: Foundations, Constructs, and UN-SDGs. In *Insights on Wellbeing and Happiness in the Workplace* (pp. 317–352). IGI Global Scientific Publishing. DOI: 10.4018/979-8-3693-2939-9.ch016

Nguyen, M. V., Khanh, H. D., Phan, C. T., & Thuc, L. D. (2025). Investigating the impacts of psychological safety climate on mental ill health in the Vietnamese construction industry. *Engineering, Construction, and Architectural Management*. Advance online publication. DOI: 10.1108/ECAM-11-2024-1576

Öngel, G., Taşkıran, E., & Çelik, G. G. (2025). Perspective Chapter: The Role of Human Resources Management in Employee Well-Being.

Papageorgiou, G., Athanasiadou, P., Tsappi, E., Xergia, S. A., Maimaris, A., & Efstathiades, A. (2025). Organizational Work, Well-Being, and Quality of Life at an Elderly Age: The Case of Cyprus. *Journal of Aging Research*, *2025*(1), 7194723. DOI: 10.1155/jare/7194723 PMID: 40017702

Paudyal, P., Wasti, S. P., Neupane, P., Sapkota, J. L., Watts, C., Kulasabanathan, K., Silwal, R., Memon, A., Shukla, P., Pathak, R. S., Michelson, D., Berry, C., Moult, A., Simkhada, P., van Teijlingen, E. R., & Cassell, J. (2025). Coproducing a culturally sensitive storytelling video intervention to improve psychosocial well-being: A multimethods participatory study with Nepalese migrant workers. *BMJ Open*, *15*(2), e086280. DOI: 10.1136/bmjopen-2024-086280 PMID: 39961714

Peethambaran, M., & Naim, M. F. (2025). Employee flourishing-at-work: A review and research agenda. *The International Journal of Organizational Analysis*. Advance online publication. DOI: 10.1108/IJOA-04-2024-4455

Sethumadhavan, R. (2025). Creating a Positive Workplace for the Employee Well-being. In *Harnessing Happiness and Wisdom for Organizational Well-Being* (pp. 131–150). IGI Global Scientific Publishing. DOI: 10.4018/979-8-3693-8457-2.ch005

Wang, Y., Ummar, R., Qureshi, T. M., Ul Haq, J., & Bonn, M. A. (2025). Employee Sustainability: How Green Practices Drive Employee Well-Being and Citizenship Behavior. *Sustainability (Basel)*, *17*(3), 936. DOI: 10.3390/su17030936

Wieneke, K. C., Berkland, B. E., Kruse, G. C., Priestley, M. R., Teal, D. M., & West, C. P. (2025, March). Charting a new path forward in addressing employee well-being in health care. []). Elsevier.]. *Mayo Clinic Proceedings*, *100*(3), 501–513. DOI: 10.1016/j.mayocp.2024.11.018 PMID: 40044362

Chapter 4

Building a Mind-Supportive Workplace: Practical DE&I Strategies for Prioritizing Employee Mental Health

Bhupinder Singh
https://orcid.org/0009-0006-4779-2553
Sharda University, India

Kittisak Wongmahesak
https://orcid.org/0009-0000-2129-4691
North Bangkok University, Thailand

Thanarat Sonkla
Royal Thai Police, Thailand

Saurabh Chandra
https://orcid.org/0000-0003-4172-9968
Bennett University, Greater Noida, India

ABSTRACT

A thriving, sustainable workplace must consider the intersection of Diversity, Equity and Inclusion (DE&I) and employee mental health. Workplaces that are committed to DE&I foster representation and belonging, which benefit employees' psychological well-being. Those organizations that connect DE&I with mental health initiatives tackle systemic inequities and address workplace stressors while creating empathetic cultures where all employees feel seen and heard. Signature strategies include having mentally healthy workplace policies that reflect the diverse needs of the employees,

DOI: 10.4018/979-8-3373-2210-0.ch004

Copyright © 2025, IGI Global Scientific Publishing. Copying or distributing in print or electronic forms without written permission of IGI Global Scientific Publishing is prohibited.

culturally and linguistically competent stigma-reduction programs, and equitable access to well-being resources. The leaders have a critical role to play ensuring psychological safety, driving empathy-led leadership and normalizing conversations around mental health. This chapter discusses ways towards building an inclusive and mind supportive workplace through DE&I focused initiatives.

1. INTRODUCTION

As it move through an age of accelerated globalization, technological disruption, and shifting societal needs, the workplace is in a state of profound evolution. As businesses see that DE&I and employee well-being are so interlinked, a more holistic approach is needed that will drive engagement, productivity and long-term success. Some of these changes include the increased focus on Diversity, Equity and Inclusion (DE&I) initiatives, as well as the growing acknowledgement of employee mental health as an organizational imperative (Mosley et al., 2025). These two, fringe domains previously treated in silos are becoming better understood as inseparable. DE&I and employee mental health align on the same mission mutually powerful to transform organizational cultures, promote social justice, and instigate holistic well-being among a diverse employee base.

Diversity, Equity & Inclusion are foundational, not aspirational, for fair, humane high-performance workplaces. When practiced authentically, DE&I frameworks help guarantee that all employees irrespective of race, gender, age, ability, sexual orientation, religion and socio-economic standing are treated equitably and feel valued, respected and supported. But having a department that is diverse and inclusive is not only about representation or doing the right thing, it has major implications for mental health. There's growing evidence that creating inclusive cultures fosters psychological safety, lowering stress and preventing burnout and alienation, especially for individuals from marginalized or underrepresented groups.

The workplace mental health issue, a newer top 10 issue, arose after the COVID-19 pandemic, among economic uncertainties and workplace model changes – notably remote and hybrid work solutions. Depression, anxiety, burnout and emotional exhaustion have spiked among employees worldwide, leading to both human and economic costs. But the experience of mental health is anything but uniform. Structural inequities, implicit bias, micro-aggressions and discrimination can compound psychological distress for many people, especially those who intersect various identities, including LGBTQ+, people of color, disabled and neuro-divergent. Because of this, mental health cannot be fully addressed without a DE&I lens.

It strives here to examine the intersection of DE&I with employee mental health as how can organizations leverage inclusive leadership, culturally informed mental health interventions, and systemic equity systems to achieve their aims of workplace well-being. It examines how organisational culture, representation and psychological safety affect the mental health of marginalised workers. Through assessing policies and programmes and drawing from real-world examples, this research urges a transformative shift to embed mental health equity within DE&I strategies to create genuinely inclusive and flourishing workplaces. Viewed through this intersectional lens, organizations can enhance their support for their employees' mental well-being and recognize that sustainable growth must be founded on empathy, equity, and human-centered values (Nittrouer et al., 2025).

2. DIVERSITY, EQUITY AND INCLUSION IN CONTEMPORARY WORKPLACES

Globally connected, socially conscious business world where the tenets of Diversity, Equity and Inclusion (DE&I) have shifted from peripheral to predecessor considerations on modern workplaces. DEI is an all-encompassing approach to human capital that recognizes, values, and intentionally fosters difference among employees, and continues to ensure these difference(s) is/are backed by equitable access and participation. Diversity custodians is the community with different identities that include but are not limited to race, gender, age, disability, sexual orientation, religion, ethnicity, socioeconomic status. Equity advocates that systems and processes are fair, so that everyone has access, given that not everyone has access to the same systems or would use the same systems in the same way to achieve the same outcome, therefore likely needing different resourcing and support. Inclusion, on the other hand, is about building an organizational culture where everyone feels welcome, respected, heard and able to participate in their entirety.

Today's workplaces are realizing that while it is vital to build a diverse workforce, it is equally important to create a workplace that is fair and equitable and cultivates diverse talent to flourish. It is the interplay of those three pillars that is critical: a workplace can share a demographic diversity as its broader community but still be inequitable in access or exclusive in culture. For example, businesses may tout gender diversity numbers while neglecting to ensure women are equally represented in leadership positions or sufficiently protected against bias and harassment. And so, DE&I work needs to be intersectional, nuanced, and embedded in the full employee experience from recruiting and onboarding to performance review, career development, and leadership succession planning. It needs intentional strategies inclusive job descriptions, training on unconscious bias, mentorship for underrepresented groups, equitable promotion policies and transparent pay practices, among them.

These benefits are twofold; focusing on integrating DE&I into the core operations of an organization has broad implications. Data consistently supports that diverse and inclusive teams lead to more creativity, innovation and problem-solving capabilities because of the diversity of perspectives. In addition, organizations that focus on DE&I report higher levels of employee engagement, lower turnover rates, improved brand image, and enhanced financial performance. Workers who believe they're being respected and valued will contribute authentically, collaborate more effectively and stay with an organization longer. Diverse teams bring a range of perspectives and problem-solving approaches that drive innovation, while inclusive workplaces mirror the broad clientele and communities they serve, adding to their cultural competence and global market savviness. But these benefits won't happen automatically — they require sustained commitment, resources, and accountability from leadership to work against structural barriers in order to create cultures of belonging.

Challenges in the intersection of DE&I are not uncommon. Resistance to change, established power dynamics, performative ally ship and insufficient tracking and metrics can all get in the way of real advancement. The intersectionality of identities race, gender identity, sexual orientation, age, disability, etc. often means that experiences of discrimination and exclusion are layered and complex, further complicating one-dimensional DE&I approaches. By understanding the unique experiences of employees who hold multiple marginalized identities, organizations can begin to apply the specific actions needed to address them. This includes gathering disaggregated data to highlight disparities, ensuring underrepresented voices are included in decision-making discussions and co-developing policies that account for the lived realities of various employee groups.

External societal movements and generational shifts in workplace expectations are also transforming contemporary DE&I practices. Both millennials and Gen Z which represent an ever-increasing portion of the workforce, care deeply about authenticity, inclusion and social impact, demanding employers to adhere to more than the client's tokenism but rather to truly commit to inclusion and equity. This has resulted in the proliferation of employee resource groups (ERGs), diversity councils, CDO (Chief Diversity Officer) roles and the inclusion of DE&I metrics in ESG (Environmental, Social and Governance) reporting. Also playing a role in advancing DE&I are technology and data analytics, which help organizations track representation, survey inclusion sentiment, and pinpoint pipeline inequities in recruitment or promotion (Johnson et al., 2025).

The intersection of Diversity, Equity and Inclusion in the modern workplace is a moral imperative as well as a strong business case. DE&I is not merely a buzzword; it is a philosophy that organizations must adopt to sustain their competitive advantage in an ever-evolving marketplace and a prerequisite for nurturing a workplace that is resilient, adaptive, and humane as it collectively build the future of work. However, real DE&I work requires more than platitudes; it requires systemic change, courageous leadership, and a steadfast commitment to justice. Emphasizing equity and inclusion in addition to diversity allows organizations to realize the full potential of their human capital, create psychological safety and belonging, and set the example for the society we all want to build together.

3. EMPLOYEE MENTAL HEALTH: THE MODERN CORPORATE DILEMMA

As the corporate world becomes progressively fast-moving and hyper-connected, employee mental health has come forth as an urgent yet, at times, neglected issue that companies need to address; one of the modern dilemmas of organizations to address urgently. Productivity, deadlines, and performance metrics have been the priority for so long that we neglected the mental well-being of our workforce and industrial scandals have snowballed into burnout, anxiety, depression and emotional exhaustion (April & Daya, 2025).

As boundaries between the personal and professional worlds become less and less defined, and especially postpandemic, as remote and hybrid models of work become the norm, employees are facing unprecedented levels of stress and isolation. Contributing to mental health challenges are toxic workplace cultures, unreasonable demands, absence of psychological safety, and insufficient systems of support which in sum serve as petri dishes of working environments in which individuals feel unappreciated, overworked, and disposable. There, this crumbling mental health landscape doesn't just reduce people's quality of life, but also significantly affects whole-organizational metrics like employee engagement, creativity, retention, and productivity. Even with increasing awareness, a strong stigma still surrounds mental health issues within corporate environments meaning that many employees may be unwilling to seek help or speak out.

Many organizations still address mental wellness at surface level providing half-hearted wellness programs but failing to resolve deeper systemic concerns. The challenge for modern corporations is to enable high performance but also to lead with kindness and empathy so that mental wellbeing can be upheld. Now, organizations must pivot from reactive to proactive mental health solutions, which includes building inclusive and supportive company environments, cultivating the ability to have difficult or open-ended conversations with workers, hyper-focused flexibility, personalized work-life integration, and access to moments of mental health care. Are leadership training on emotional intelligence, peer support initiatives, and personalized wellness plans permanently designed into our systems (rather than an optional perk)? In addition, placing mental health as a foundational pillar of corporate sustainability and responsibility is pivotal to reshaping success not just in profitability, but in people's lives. Mental wellness should not be regarded as an individual responsibility, but an organizational commitment.

The future of work is changing rapidly as digital transformation and global uncertainty converge, and safeguarding employee mental health is no longer a cosmetic concern but rather a business necessity. By approaching this conundrum with genuine care, and a little innovative thinking, we can create healthier workplace environments, stronger teams, and resilient organizations able to withstand complex times. How businesses address employee mental health will ultimately determine not only their internal culture but also their external reputation, their social impact, and their long-term viability in a purpose-driven economy.

3.1 Context and Challenges of Mental Health in Workplace

Workplace mental health consists of a broad range of emotional, psychological, and social well-being concerns that impacts how an individual thinks, feels and behaves in the workplace. This ranges from stress management and relieving anxiety to suppressing depression and enhancing wellness. Despite increasing awareness, mental health continues to be stigmatized in many organizations, which results in underreporting and untreated conditions. The main factors contributing to this are high job demands, low control, job insecurity and low organizational support. Remote work has exacerbated feelings of isolation and disconnection. Few workplaces have implemented strong mental health policies, trained leaders or the infrastructure to provide long-term support (Gray, 2025). Employees may worry about being evaluated or penalized in their careers if they admit to mental health issues. Tackling these hurdles calls for a multi-faceted and pre-emptive response embedding mental health into the organizational doctrine, providing easily-accessible tools, and cultivating an environment in which individuals feel safe, respected and valued for their well-being as a whole.

3.2 Influence of Environment on Psychological Wellness

The culture of the workplace has an deep impact on employee mental health because it can inform how a person perceives their surroundings, the people they work with, and how they react to stress on the job. Trust, inclusion, transparency and empathy can create a culture that increases well-being, improves job satisfaction and improves morale. Toxic cultures characterized by discrimination, micromanagement, lack of recognition, and impossible expectations can ward chronic stress, burnout, and anxiety in employees. People in aggressive, unhelpful locations, do not feel valued, that leads them to disassociate from their work and have psychological issues.

The organizational silence regarding mental health also contributes to the stigmatization of mental health conditions, so conversations are discouraged, and help-seeking behavior is discouraged. In that vein, leadership is essential to encourage healthy behaviors as well as psychological safety (Cavusoglu & Demirbag-Kaplan, 2025). Mental health makes that difference: a healthy organisational culture promotes resilience, facilitates innovation and builds sustainable loyalty. In an era where the demands of work are ever-increasing, embedding mental wellness in the intrinsic structures and processes of an organization is the path to create nurturing workplaces that can support individuals not just to flourish in work but also in life, that is so intricately tied to success for the organizations themselves.

3.3 Psychological Safety and Burnout and Emotional Well-Being

Psychological safety being confident that you can speak, make mistakes or show vulnerability without fear of punishment is the key to building emotional well-being and avoiding burnout. Psychological safety allows employees to share ideas, express concerns, and collaborate without fear. In stark contrast, hostile, closed environments produce emotional repression, gradually layer in stress and eventually lead to burnout, defined as a state of physical and emotional exhaustion caused by chronic workplace stress (Owens & Mills, 2025). Burnout chip away at motivation, productivity and overall health, with symptoms such as fatigue, cynicism and disengagement becoming normal. The emotional strain of being constantly on edge with no support can manifest as anxiety and depression. To promote emotional well-being, organizations should take the initiative: help de-stigmatize personal issues, be transparent and supportive, offer to help, provide mental health resources, flexible schedules, and recognition. Leaders will need to focus on compassion, and practice trauma-informed management. All in all, building psychological safety and emotional care is not just humane, it is must-have for sustainable business results.

Figure 1. Shares the points on employee mental health: The modern corporate dilemma (Source- Self Prepared- Original)

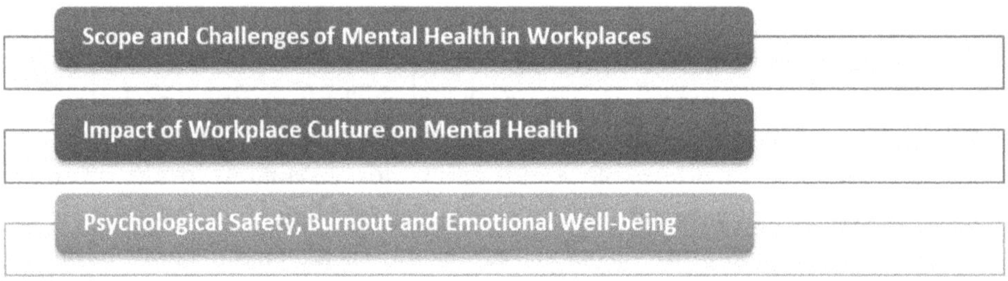

4. INTERSECTING DIVERSITY, EQUITY AND INCLUSION WITH MENTAL HEALTH STRATEGIES

The integration of Diversity, Equity, and Inclusion (DEI) and mental health strategies is the challenge of all modern workplace: it is a progressive one, not a trend but the axis for holistic organization health and sustainability. The intersection of mental health and DEI cannot be understated marginalized communities face compounded stressors and unique mental health challenges that are often dismissed with a cookie cutter approach (Correia et al., 2025). Workers from a variety of backgrounds including but not limited to race or ethnicity, gender identity, sexual orientation, socioeconomic status, disability status or cultural heritage routinely face microaggressions, discrimination, exclusion and systemic inequalities that have a direct impact on their psychological well-being. These experiences contribute to chronic stress, decreased job satisfaction and engagement, and feeling alienated in the workplace. So, a stronger and effective mental health strategy should be intersectional, acknowledging the multidimensional realities at play in peoples lives and ensuring support systems are responsive to those needs. Neglecting DEI considerations in mental health programs may also reinforce structural inequities and perpetuate the very conditions for e.g., toxic work environments, bias in leadership that contribute to mental distress among the underrepresented or marginalized employee segments.

DEI Framework for Mental Health Data around mental health supports that not all groups have equal access to care, psychological support, and representational structures within the existing systems. For example, barriers to accessing mental health services faced by racial and ethnic minorities include lack of culturally competent care, language barriers, mistrust of mental health services due to historical abuses, and stigma within their communities. Likewise, LGBTQ+ employees may battle coming out in non-inclusivity workplace, identity based discrimination, or the invalidation of their lived or work experience (Daruwalla & Ley, 2025).

These factors highlight that mental health policies should be universally accessible as well as culturally sensitive, affirming, and inclusive. So workplace interventions should do more than offer generic wellness programs, providing more granular resources, such as affinity group therapy, diverse therapist networks, inclusive employee assistance programs (EAPs) and DEI training centered on emotional intelligence and literacy about mental health. Focusing on mental health without considering systemic oppression, privilege or identity-based stressors is a disservice to those most in need and undermines the work being done to support people living with mental health conditions.

To build inclusive mental health strategies, leadership accountability and commitment to transformative change must come first. Leaders and HR professionals should understand the impact that unconscious bias, inequitable power structures, and exclusionary policies have on employees' mental health and career trajectories. Leadership from diverse backgrounds who actively advocates for equity in mental health sends a powerful message of belonging and validation (Fish et al., 2025). Building trust requires equipping leaders with tools for culturally responsive dialogue, practicing empathy, and recognizing signs of mental health distress. Collecting inclusive data on employee well-being with results disaggregated by factors like gender, race, disability or sexual orientation can also reveal disparities and guide tailored interventions. Anonymous pulse surveys, focus groups with a filter of diverse voices and psychological safety audits can help uncover mental health risks that are hidden from view with the traditional metrics. If policies are to promote flexibility, accommodation, and the integration of work into our lives, organizations must also ensure that they do so equitably across communities, recognizing that these may hold different caregiving roles, financial stressors, and systemic burdens.

Embedding DEI within the mental health strategy needs commitment to a culture of belonging where employees feel seen, heard and empowered. Representation is tremendously important people are more likely to buy into the system and participate in it when they can see people like them in leadership, mental health roles, or communication campaigns. In addition, workplace storytelling that highlights a variety of mental health experiences can help normalize struggling, break down stigma and create openness. For example, sharing the mental health journeys of employees from different backgrounds can bridge empathy between departments and lessen the solitude of those going through struggles. The organizations should be cautious not to evaluate DEI or wellness activities through a commodified lens as mere performative checkbox compliance. DEI and mental health without fighting the root causes of exclusion if not dismantling prejudices and building equitable anti-racist policies, infrastructure, benefits and growth opportunities while also iterating and evolving upon feedback and lived experience from employees (Goodman-Scott et al., 2025).

The other critical piece of the DEI-mental health intersection is recognizing how social justice movements, global crises and political events affect employee well-being. Racial injustices, gender-based violence, immigration anxieties or anti-LGBTQ+ legislation often follow us into the workplace, where these factors can spark trauma and emotional fatigue. Such companies know that they must respond to these realities by creating space for reflection, validating emotional impulses, and providing total support during such circumstances. In the face of sociopolitical upheaval, silence or neutrality from employers can corrode trust and amplify distress for impacted employees. So it needed to be approached with a trauma-informed, justice-oriented lens that recognizes mental health cannot be separated from the systems and society that shape it, which is interwoven with identity, history and power. There are practices such as mental health days, culturally relevant leave policies, healing circles and safe spaces for meetings that reflect this idea. Access to care can be furthered via partnerships with a variety of community-based mental health organizations, which may also legitimize corporate mental health programming.

Digital transformation can also bring inclusion to mental health, for example through teletherapy platforms, AI-powered support tools and virtual well-being apps. But equity must be a guiding principle (Hawke et al., 2025). The limited focus on U.S. citizens means many digital mental health tools lack cultural context, language options, or accessibility features for people with disabilities. Therefore, technology needs to be designed with inclusivity in mind, where marginalized users are not left behind when it comes to seeking care for a mental condition related to design bias or cost Inaccessibility. Incorporating employee input in the development, selection, and evaluation of mental health tech can lessen these problems and build user trust. Moreover, aggregated usage data from such platforms can provide unique insights into shifting mental health trends among various employee categories, allowing for nimble and inclusive responses.

The bottom line is that weaving Diversity, Equity, and Inclusion into mental health strategies is not simply an isolated initiative, but rather a holistic approach to growing thriving, just, and resilient workplaces. It expresses a commitment to viewing employees in their full humanity to recognizing that mental health can't be divorced from the lived experiences of race, gender, ability, sexuality and socioeconomic status. Integrating intersectionality into mental health policies sends a clear message that every voice, every mind, and every obstacle to well-being is worthy of care. Such alignment reduces disparities while embedding purpose in culture, where innovation, trust and employee loyalty flourish in an increasingly diverse and socially-aware world. As we advance into the future of work, mental health equity grounded in DEI must be a standard of excellence for all leaders and a cornerstone for sustainable business success (Schultz et al., 2025).

5. MARGINALIZED IDENTITIES AND DISPROPORTIONATE MENTAL HEALTH BURDENS

Systemic inequities, social exclusion, and structural discrimination contribute to greater mental health burden on marginalized identities people from historically oppressed or marginalized groups including racial and ethnic minorities, LGBTQ+ individuals, people with disabilities, immigrants, and individuals from lower socio-economic backgrounds. The mental health of these groups is significantly affected not only by personal experience but also by social determinants including unequal access to healthcare, education, jobs, housing, and legal protections. These intersecting layers of disadvantage lead to chronic stress, identity-based trauma, and feelings of invisibility or hyper-visibility in social and workplace contexts (Higgins & Wilson, 2025). BIPOC often experience racial microaggressions, cultural erasure, and the cognitive burden of occupying spaces that were historically and in some cases, virulently not intended for their presence. In the same context, individuals within the LGBTQ+ community may experience internalized stigma, rejection from society and prejudice from workplace environments, which only serve to increase the risk of anxiety, depression and suicidal ideation.

Individuals who belong to more than one oppressed group such as black Latina women or queer disabled persons experience this compounded trauma, what is often referred to as an intersectionality of marginalized identities. For example, a disabled queer person of color will face multiple and overlapping forms of exclusion that will significantly heighten their mental health vulnerabilities. Access to culturally competent and inclusive mental health resources is still limited for marginalized groups, despite an increased need. The unique history, culture, and identity that inform how these individuals conceptualize and pursue mental health care have been largely ignored or overlooked within mainstream healthcare models. Language barriers, under-representation of people with traumatic backgrounds among mental health professionals, financial pressures and a deep-seated mistrust of institutions born of historical or ongoing discrimination are deterrents in the way of timely and adequate care (Einwiller et al., 2025). As a result, mental health problems within marginalised groups are often overlooked, misdiagnosed, left untreated, or misconceived, resulting in deteriorating health outcomes and wider social inequalities.

In the workplace, these burdens transpire in the form of increased emotional labor, code-switching, imposter syndrome and isolation. Marginalized employees may be incentivized to downplay these identities either to fit in to dominant, work cultures or to avoid retaliation for speaking out about discrimination or bias. This only makes the feelings of alienation stronger and makes support mechanisms within organizations through which access can be utilized to build mental resilience unavailable. Organizations and institutions must treat the mental health struggles of marginalized identities not as individual personal struggles, but rather as systemic matters in need of structural change. This encompasses everything from cultivating inclusive cultures to offering targeted mental health support, to partnering with diverse community organizations and addressing the systems that hinder equitable access to care. Having engaging leadership opportunities, representation, and affirming policies that empower marginalized voices can help ease mental health burdens and improve long-term well-being. A focus on the mental well-being of marginalized segments is ultimately a moral and strategic imperative, one that lies at the heart of structural equity, justice and sustainable inclusion across all social spheres.

6. ORGANIZATIONAL INTERVENTIONS INTEGRATING DE&I AND MENTAL HEALTH

If organizations truly want to create inclusive and psychologically safe workplaces, they have to integrate Diversity, Equity and Inclusion (DE&I) with mental health support in philosophy and practice (Bisht & Riach, 2025). That kind of integration does not mean siloed policies or a few wellness offerings here and there it is a strategic, culturally responsive, and systems-level approach that acknowledges how identity, systemic bias, and structural inequalities shape mental health directly. Here's one of the most impactful interventions: embed inclusive values into company culture, emphasize leadership accountability and make psychological safety a priority as part of the employee experience. Executives and managers that lead with empathy, model vulnerability and advocate for equitable mental health practices set off a ripple effect that normalizes mental health conversations, reduces stigma and establish trust among diverse employee groups.

The development of culturally sensitive EAPs, which provide access to culturally competent mental health professionals and resources is an important organizational intervention as well. Providing multilingual services, gender-affirming care, trauma-informed therapy, and diverse therapist directories helps employees who are underrepresented feel seen and supported (Anderson et al., 2025). Simultaneously, DE&I training should continue to grow to include mental health literacy teaching employees how micro-aggressions, unconscious bias and identity-based stressors affect psychological health. Intersectional mental health programming BIPOC mental health workshops, LGBTQ+ support circles, disability-inclusive wellness sessions can provide safe spaces for community building and collective healing. Such spaces allow employees to discuss identity-specific issues without fear of being marginalized or tokenized.

The other equitable workplace practices such as flexible scheduling, paid mental health days, remote work accommodations and inclusive leave policy can really alleviate the emotional burden placed on marginalized employees who are often juggling caregiving, financial difficulty or cultural expectations." Organizations can more fully support inclusion by conducting pulse surveys and mental health audits that gather anonymized, disaggregated data helping companies understand where disparities exist and identify which groups may experience fewer benefits (Stafford et al., 2025). Consolidation of professional development threads with additional external ones such as partnership with community mental health organizations and advocacy groups can boost not only credibility but also widen reach and impact. Making certain that mental health support is responsive to global events and socio-political stressors like racial injustice, war or gender-based violence is also crucial to showing allyship and care.

Ultimately, organizations that truly embrace DE&I and mental health are organizations willing to invest at every level to create equity and health among all of its employees (Singh et al., 2025). Such integration builds resilience, loyalty and a shared sense of belonging, as well as increasing productivity, creativity and retention (Curry et al., 2025). In the increasingly complex and socially conscientious world of work, addressing mental health through a DE&I lens isn't optional; it's essential to sustainable success and ethical leadership.

7. CONCLUSION AND FUTURE SCOPE

As the nation gets back to business as usual, and for most of us, that means returning to the workplace, the issue of employee mental health has taken center stage: a DE&I issue that is not just a moral obligation, it's a strategic necessity. In an increasingly culturally and demographically diverse workplace, attention must be given to the identity-based challenges and systemic inequities in terms of the psychological well-being of workers. Mental health issues can no longer be addressed in a vacuum from the organizational culture, power dynamics or social constructs influencing the employee experience. Organizations can create inclusive, supportive, psychological safe environments that empower all employees, especially those who are part of marginalized or underrepresented groups, by integrating DE&I principles with strategies for mental health. This comprehensive strategy not only strengthens employee engagement but also cultivates an environment of compassion, ultimately building a resilient organization.

The future of it is so promising and exciting. Things like data analytics, artificial intelligence and organizational psychology could empower made-to-measure interventions that reflect different mental health needs across dissimilar identity spectrums. The rise will see growing pressure for ethical leadership and social accountability that will require businesses to adopt comprehensive well-being frameworks as their default corporate role. Working alongside mental health advocates, culturally competent service providers and DE&I experts will be taming the policy landscape into empathy and impact. The future studies need to also examine the long-term impacts of such initiatives, measuring not just the happiness of employees but also the larger social outcomes, including equity, access and justice. In the end, a mentally healthy, inclusive workforce is a moving target of commitment, action toward systemic reform, and collective accountability. The organizations that adopt this paradigm shift will more than reap healthier individuals; they will do well as caring, progressive and future-ready organizations.

REFERENCES

Anderson, L. A., Notice, M., Armstrong, J., & Smith, K. R. (2025). The unspoken experiences of systemic supervisors of color: A modified Delphi study. *Journal of Marital and Family Therapy*, *51*(1), e12749. DOI: 10.1111/jmft.12749 PMID: 39533407

April, K., & Daya, P. (2025). The Use of AI in HRM and Management Processes: The Promise of Diversity, Equity, and Inclusion. In *AI and Diversity in a Datafied World of Work: Will the Future of Work be Inclusive?* (Vol. 12, pp. 97–123). Emerald Publishing Limited. DOI: 10.1108/S2051-233320250000012012

Bisht, R., & Riach, K. (2025). Going loca: Depression at work as a public feeling in Peru. *Gender, Work and Organization*, *32*(2), 634–652. DOI: 10.1111/gwao.13170

Cavusoglu, L., & Demirbag-Kaplan, M. (2025). Unraveling the Threads of Marketplace Diversity. *The Journal of Consumer Affairs*, *59*(1), e70006. DOI: 10.1111/joca.70006

Correia, T., Kuhlmann, E., Lotta, G., Beja, A., Morais, R., Zapata, T., & Campbell, J. (2025). Turning the global health and care workforce crisis into action: The pathway to effective evidence-based policy and implementation. *The International Journal of Health Planning and Management*, *40*(1), 224–233. DOI: 10.1002/hpm.3860 PMID: 39396240

Curry, T., Lovecraft, A., & Quintyne, A. (2025). Exploration of Racial Dynamics and Climate Change Experience: Insights from Underrepresented Communities in Interior Alaska. *Weather, Climate, and Society*. Advance online publication. DOI: 10.1175/WCAS-D-24-0087.1

Daruwalla, S., & Ley, S. (2025). Friendship as a lifeline: Navigating the precarious landscape of the US employment-based immigration as women of color psychologists. *Family Process*, *64*(1), e13078. DOI: 10.1111/famp.13078 PMID: 39551484

Einwiller, S. A., Wolfgruber, D., & Leitner, A. K. (2025). Addressing backlash? Corporate DEI communication and user complaints on social media. *Journal of Marketing Communications*, •••, 1–19. DOI: 10.1080/13527266.2025.2471954

Fish, J. N., Paceley, M. S., Evans, S., Kosi-Huber, J. A., Phillips, D. R., & Levine, D. S. (2025). Community Efforts to Support LGBTQ+ Youth Mental Health: Programs Objectives, Development, and Delivery. *Journal of Community Psychology*, *53*(2), e70002. DOI: 10.1002/jcop.70002 PMID: 39985818

Goodman-Scott, E., Sampson, D. J., Johnson, K. F., & Sawyer-Mays, D. (2025). School counseling district leaders' experiences with anti–DEI laws and policies: A phenomenological investigation. *Journal of Counseling and Development, 103*(2), 185–200. DOI: 10.1002/jcad.12551

Gray, E. (2025). *Equity, Diversity, and Inclusion in Canadian National Sport Organizations* (Doctoral dissertation, Université d'Ottawa/University of Ottawa).

Hawke, L. D., Dada-Phillips, W., Seiyad, H., Orson, J., Goldsmith, L., Conway, S., Jordan, A., Sheikhan, N. Y., Hiebert, M., Kidd, S., & Kuluski, K. (2025). Best Practices Guidelines for the Engagement of People With Lived Experience and Family Members in Mental Health and Substance Use Health Research: A Modified Delphi Consensus Study. *Health Expectations, 28*(1), e70152. DOI: 10.1111/hex.70152 PMID: 39832210

Higgins, O., & Wilson, R. L. (2025). Integrating Artificial Intelligence (AI) With Workforce Solutions for Sustainable Care: A Follow Up to Artificial Intelligence and Machine Learning (ML) Based Decision Support Systems in Mental Health. *International Journal of Mental Health Nursing, 34*(2), e70019. DOI: 10.1111/inm.70019 PMID: 40055746

Johnson, R. M., DeCuir-Gunby, J. T., Kenney, A. J., & Lyons, T. V. (2025). Black Student Belonging in K12 Schools: Implications for Policy and Practice Amid Attacks on Diversity, Equity, and Inclusion. *Social Issues and Policy Review, 19*(1), e70002. DOI: 10.1111/sipr.70002

Mosley, T. J., Zajdel, R. A., Alderete, E., Clayton, J. A., Heidari, S., Pérez-Stable, E. J., Salt, K., & Bernard, M. A. (2025). Intersectionality and diversity, equity, and inclusion in the healthcare and scientific workforces. *Lancet Regional Health. Americas, 41*, 41. DOI: 10.1016/j.lana.2024.100973

Nittrouer, C. L., Arena, D.Jr, Silver, E. R., Avery, D. R., & Hebl, M. R. (2025). Despite the haters: The immense promise and progress of diversity, equity, and inclusion initiatives. *Journal of Organizational Behavior, 46*(1), 188–201. DOI: 10.1002/job.2835

Owens, B., & Mills, S. (2025). Conceptualizing discrimination against LGBTQ+ workers in the unbounded workplace. *The Canadian Geographer. Geographe Canadien, 69*(1), e12971. DOI: 10.1111/cag.12971

Schultz, T. R., Edemba, D., Lecuyer, M. E., Garzone, A., Henise, S., Liljestrand, A., Hinds, P. S., & King, S. (2025). LGBTQ+ Population Well-Being: Health Equity Implementation Science in Action. *Public Health Nursing (Boston, Mass.), 42*(2), 957–965. DOI: 10.1111/phn.13480 PMID: 39623732

Singh, B., Kaunert, C., & Jermsittiparsert, K. (2025). Advocating Medical Tourism and Healthcare in Global Health Market Places: Promoting Sustainability and Technological Advancements. In Jermsittiparsert, K., & Marzo, R. (Eds.), *AI Technologies and Advancements for Psychological Well-Being and Healthcare* (pp. 327–350). IGI Global., DOI: 10.4018/979-8-3693-9158-7.ch012

Stafford, A. M., Pulgar, C. A., & Villarreal-Otálora, T. (2025). Strategies to Improve Engagement of Latino Adolescents in Mental Health Research. *Mental Health Science*, *3*(1), e70005. DOI: 10.1002/mhs2.70005

Chapter 5
Exploring the Relationship Between Leadership and Well-Being

Aneesh Handa
https://orcid.org/0009-0009-4450-3252
Christ University, India

Surabhi Sangal
Christ University, India

ABSTRACT

Leadership and well-being are deeply intertwined, influencing individuals and organizational dynamics in profound ways. This study explores the bidirectional relationship between leadership styles, emotional intelligence, organizational culture, and well-being. By examining frameworks such as transformational, democratic, and ethical leadership, the research highlights the importance of adaptive, inclusive, and emotionally intelligent leadership in fostering employee satisfaction, mental health, and work-life balance. Additionally, the role of positive organizational culture and the evolving challenges of remote and hybrid leadership are analyzed. Findings suggest that leaders who emphasize empathy, ethics, and inclusivity create environments conducive to personal and collective growth. This comprehensive review provides actionable insights for leaders, policymakers, and organizations striving for effective leadership and enhanced employee well-being.

DOI: 10.4018/979-8-3373-2210-0.ch005

Copyright © 2025, IGI Global Scientific Publishing. Copying or distributing in print or electronic forms without written permission of IGI Global Scientific Publishing is prohibited.

1. INTRODUCTION TO LEADERSHIP AND WELL-BEING

In the public sector, where job demands, stress, and burnout levels are notably high, employee well-being is a crucial driver of organizational performance. According to research, reduced productivity from low employee well-being costs the world economy about $1 trillion a year (WHO, 2020). Stress at work causes absenteeism, decreased productivity, and a decline in service quality in the public sector (Cooper & Quick, 2017). Despite this, little is known about how leadership shapes well-being; most studies concentrate on how leaders affect others rather than how leadership itself affects well-being on both an individual and organizational level.

Existing research has looked at how leadership styles affect employee motivation and job satisfaction, but there is still a lack of understanding of how ethical leadership and well-being work together to generate organizational success (Avolio & Gardner, 2005). In order to close this gap, this chapter examines the reciprocal relationship between leadership and well-being, arguing that it both influences and is influenced by employee well-being. A high-performing, mentally healthy workforce is more successfully fostered by leaders who develop their own psychological resilience and ethical awareness (Søvold et al., 2021).

The primary aim of this chapter is to develop a practical framework that links leadership styles and ethical practices to employee well-being and overall organizational performance in the public sector. By integrating insights from positive psychology, transformational leadership theory, and well-being interventions, we propose strategies that can enhance both leader and employee well-being, ultimately driving sustainable organizational success.

2. THEORETICAL FRAMEWORKS IN LEADERSHIP AND WELL-BEING

Over the past couple of decades, various theories and models exploring the dynamics of leadership and well-being have been articulated in the literature. In conventional leadership literature, leadership is concerned with organizational goals, mission, and vision; leaders are expected to be enthusiastic, self-assured, collaborative, and open; and followers are meant to be invitees who follow direction willingly. In comparison, the lens of leadership well-being suggests that well-being is not a peripheral activity or an add-on, but a core enabler for successful, meaningful, and effective leadership. This suggests that the integration of leadership and well-being is not simply attitudinal, an endorsement of well-being programs and services, but is systemic, focusing on the nature of the organization and transforming what organizations and their members do and how they do things. Traditional perspectives suggest that leadership's chief task is to help followers identify and commit to the organization's mission, to be motivated to work competently toward its attainment, and to accomplish useful work for the benefit of the entity. However, this perspective is rather narrow and untenable. Leadership is symbolic and rhetorical. It is laden with meaning and constructs identities and values through imaginative rhetoric and myth-making. As an indistinct social process, it is influenced by the subjective, personal, and interpretative factors associated with the personalities, values, and inherent characteristics of particular individuals interacting with the socio-cultural and political context. Leaders activate theoretical alignment across a range of congruence-based frameworks. This refers to the intertwining of the organization, leader, follower, and stakeholder paradox, which calls for a mix of flexible and adaptive theories in response to complex questions and applied problems (Cann et al.2021)(Oleksa-Marewska and Tokar2022).

2.1. Transformational Leadership Theory

Our understanding of the contribution of leadership to employee well-being is currently shaped by a limited number of leadership theories. The range of leadership behaviors or activities associated with employee well-being appears to be quite narrow. In this paper, we describe the relationships that have been reported between contemporary leadership theories and employee well-being, and some of the gaps in the research. In order to accomplish this, we first give a summary of how leadership affects worker well-being. After defining leadership and employee well-being, we provide an overview of some important modern leadership theories. Leadership theories that have documented positive leadership practices for employee well-being are of special relevance to us.

Our summaries are brief because we introduce the wide range of theories related to leadership. These leadership theories serve as a framework for leadership research and practice in the fields of psychology, sociology, and business and organizational management. They seem to have arisen from the need to close gaps in earlier theories of leadership and offer more information on the kinds of actions that leaders might do to benefit their followers even more. 'Entropy' is left out of most of these theories. Only transformational and authentic leadership theories address employee well-being directly (Baquero, 2023)(Ortiz-Gómez et al.2022).

Table 1. Summarizing the key characteristics and well-being implications of transactional and transformational leadership:

Aspect	Transactional Leadership	Transformational Leadership
Definition	Focuses on structured tasks, rewards, and penalties based on performance.	Focuses on inspiring and motivating employees to achieve higher goals and personal development.
Leadership Style	Directive, goal-oriented, and emphasizes short-term tasks and rewards.	Inspirational, visionary, and focuses on long-term goals and personal growth.
Focus	Maintaining stability, efficiency, and compliance with set rules.	Encouraging innovation, change, and personal development.
Employee Motivation	Motivation through rewards and punishments based on performance.	Motivation through inspiring a shared vision and personal development opportunities.
Relationship with Employees	Limited interpersonal interaction; primarily focused on task achievement.	Strong interpersonal relationships; emphasizes trust, respect, and personal growth.
Employee Well-Being	Limited focus on well-being; may lead to stress due to pressure to meet targets.	High focus on well-being; fosters emotional support, engagement, and personal fulfillment.
Strengths	- Clear expectations and structure - Effective in achieving short-term goals - Maintains discipline and order	- Encourages creativity and innovation - Fosters job satisfaction and personal growth - Promotes work-life balance
Weaknesses	- May lead to burnout due to focus on targets - Lack of personal development focus - Can create feelings of dissatisfaction if goals aren't met	- Can be demanding and lead to high expectations - May require significant time and effort to implement effectively - Risk of leader burnout from constant focus on motivation
Impact on Employee Well-Being	Can be negative if employees feel overworked or undervalued due to strict focus on performance.	Positive impact through personal growth, emotional support, and fostering a sense of purpose.
Long-Term Effects on Employees	May cause disengagement, stress, and dissatisfaction in the long run.	Employees are likely to feel more empowered, engaged, and aligned with organizational goals in the long run.

2.2. Positive Psychology Theory

Positive Personal Traits in Leadership

Positive personal traits of leaders are central to various leadership theories, including transformational leadership and authentic leadership. These traits include personal integrity, a positive outlook, leadership skills, and personality strengths that contribute to a leader's effectiveness.

An authentic leader is consistent and transparent with their subordinates, builds relationships based on trust, promotes innovation, engages in participatory decision-making, and effectively manages teams. Such a leader, seen as a respectable and empowering role model, safeguards the well-being of their followers.

Similarly, transformational leaders utilize their influence responsibly, differentiating themselves from charismatic leaders through their ethical energy, humility, and balanced lifestyle. These leadership strengths can be considered an organizational virtue, impacting workplace behavior, psychological wellness, job satisfaction, and overall organizational success.

The Role of Positive Psychology in the Workplace

In modern work environments, positive psychological theory has gained traction, integrating psychological assessments into business practices. The theory appeals to the corporate world due to its emphasis on elements that contribute to desirable personal and professional functioning—beyond income, success, and wealth.

Businesses increasingly recognize the significance of positive psychological factors in fostering a healthy workplace. This approach focuses on human nature, character strengths, and the overall well-being of employees, helping organizations develop open and communicative cultures.

The Evolution of Well-Being Approaches

The well-being approach within positive psychology moves away from a deficit-based model—which focuses on problems—and instead adopts a strength-based model that enhances personal and professional fulfillment.

Well-being is a cornerstone of positive psychology, offering three distinct dimensions that influence subjective and personal global assessments. This shift in perspective transforms problem-based interpretations into a reason-enhancement approach, helping individuals achieve balanced and fulfilling lives (Kleynhans et al., 2021).

3. LEADERSHIP STYLES AND THEIR IMPACT ON WELL-BEING

Leaders can cause either satisfaction or dissatisfaction among followers. Thus, advice to change leadership in organizations is counterproductive when it is related to dissatisfaction and is appropriate if it is related to well-being. Although a wide variety of leadership theories and models exist, there is no current system for comparing the similarities and differences of these numerous models. The goal of this chapter is to describe the numerous ways in which leaders have a direct and indirect impact on followers' well-being. One common way to classify leadership style is by the degree of concern for people and production as described by the leader. The managerial grid uses a two-dimensional model that describes leadership patterns based on both of these dimensions of behavior.

Several new models have been developed that take the idea of a leadership continuum further by specifying that the leader's primary role is to establish and maintain the group's well-being. Transactional leadership is characterized by a focus on exchange: 'The leader gives something to the follower, and in return the follower owes the leader.' It may take the form of rewarding behavior that is positive or punishing behavior that is negative. Transformational leadership gets its name from the process that takes place through leadership, and it can lead to significant individual and group development. In transactional leadership, the focus is on managing, changing, improving, and shaping behavior (Kaluza et al.2022)(Huang et al.2021).

3.1. Autocratic Leadership

Autocratic Leadership and Decision-Making

Autocratic leaders are considered to be single-minded in their decision-making, relying little on group input or democratic involvement. They tend to use personal intuition to guide their actions, thereby ignoring situational and follower information that contradicts their personal beliefs and thoughts.

Impact on Employee Well-Being

Autocratic leaders care less about subordinates' well-being, thus contributing to the poor intervention of the social cohesive climate in groups. Employees, as a result, meet autocratic leaders with a negative attitude, which then develops into:

- Reduction in well-being
- Frustration of psychological needs
- Cognitive dissonance

- Counterproductive work behavior

Theories Linking Autocratic Leadership to Negative Outcomes

The relationship between autocratic behavior and negative outcomes at the individual level is also emphasized in leadership theories. Studies have traditionally highlighted negative leadership traits while ignoring the impacts on followers. Autocratic leaders are seen to make decisions with little regard for democratic participation or group input.

They frequently rely on their own intuition to direct their behavior, disregarding situational and follower information that goes against their own opinions and convictions. They are less concerned with the welfare of their subordinates, which leads to a poor intervention of the social cohesive atmosphere in groups.

Consequences of Autocratic Leadership

As a result, employees have a bad attitude when they encounter autocratic leaders, leading to:

- A decline in well-being
- Unmet psychological needs
- Cognitive dissonance
- Unproductive job behavior

Evolution of Leadership Theories

The theories of leadership also highlight the connection between authoritarian conduct and detrimental results at the individual level. Research has historically focused on bad leaders while ignoring the effects on followers.

These studies suggested that leaders should take into account both initiating structure and consideration behaviors, but they disregarded the influence of followers' feelings or any shift in positive or negative states.

Later, transactional leadership theory was introduced, which ignored the effects on followers' psychological statesand instead viewed both good and bad leaders as simply providers of rewards and punishment.

Situational and Contingency Theories

Over time, the main issues in leadership studies have evolved. While other situational theories focused on contingency factors that determine the relationship between leadership styles and subordinate outcomes, these studies excelled in expanding antecedents affecting leader behaviors. However, they still primarily focused on the effects rather than the causes of leader outcomes (Metin-Orta, 2021) (Briker et al., 2021).

3.2. Democratic Leadership

Democratic Leadership and Shared Decision-Making

Democratic leadership is notable for facilitating shared decision-making and promoting active involvement of group members. It is regularly suggested that democratic leadership is a form of group leadership. People working in trusted organizational contexts where self-governance is privileged are seen as assuming pinnacles of self-leadership, thus minimizing the need for their supervisors to exhibit traditional leadership responsibilities.

Advantages of Democratic Leadership

Enhancing role status, gaining knowledge, reversing burnout tendencies, and improving job happiness, dedication, and role innovation are all examples of these supposed continuous advantages. As a result, democratic leadership is frequently associated with shared and facilitative leadership styles as a leadership approach allegedly beneficial to promoting both individual and group flourishing.

Impact on Employee Well-Being

Democratic leadership has the capacity to improve people's well-being by encouraging a sense of personal agency. A strength-based paradigm of authentic leadership is linked to the difference between feeling vigorous, experiencing burnout, and paying attentive attention to the requirements of employees.

Democratic leadership prioritizes fostering individual development and job satisfaction. This hypothesis's rationale is based on the idea that a nondirective leadership style helps to encourage autonomy, which in turn helps to meet fundamental cognitive demands.

Psychological Benefits of Democratic Leadership

Accordingly, employees receiving autonomy support also feel:

- Valued
- Engaged in meaningful work
- Competent in their work
- Deserving of reward

This, in turn, fosters improved psychological well-being.

Social Information Processing and Trust Building

An additional theory that points to democratic leadership engendering positive employee attitudes is social information processing. Its argument is couched in terms of other enhancement occurring when democracy is operational, and therefore, trust increases, and a shared understanding further develops the psychological contract.

With democracy in action, employees then attest to being:

- More committed
- More loyal
- More involved in the organization's activities

(Devi and Subiyantoro, 2021; Oussible and Tinaztepe, 2022).

3.3. Laissez-Faire Leadership

Laissez-faire or laissez-passer is a French expression by which a political doctrine of freedom from governmental intervention is promoted, principally with respect to industry or trade. In terms of leadership, laissez-faire leadership is the absence of a leadership style and behavior. There is a lack of involvement from the supervisor in the units. The advantage of this leadership style is that the employees are given a high degree of freedom and autonomy to work on the tasks, which leads to increased job satisfaction. On the downside, subordinates are left on their own, which may lead to lower productivity as they are left uninformed, unguided, and uncorrected. The absence of leadership may also lead to an atmosphere of low retention. It has been hypothesized that the emotional role of the supervisor is concentrated with the high performer, and if this is true, it may lead to high competition for the high performer role (Marufu et al.2021).

Table 2. Summarizing the key characteristics and well-being implications of each leadership style:

Aspect	Autocratic Leadership	Democratic Leadership	Laissez-Faire Leadership
Definition	Centralized decision-making with the leader having full control.	Collaborative decision-making, considering employee input.	Minimal supervision, employees have complete freedom.
Leadership Style	Authoritative, directive, and highly structured.	Participative, consultative, and inclusive.	Hands-off, allowing employees to make decisions independently.
Decision-Making	Leader makes all decisions with little or no employee input.	Employees are encouraged to contribute ideas and decisions.	Employees make their own decisions with little leader involvement.
Employee Autonomy	Low—strict control and supervision.	Moderate—leader provides guidance but allows employee input.	High—employees have full autonomy with minimal interference.
Motivation Approach	Motivation through fear, discipline, and extrinsic rewards.	Motivation through engagement, recognition, and teamwork.	Motivation through self-direction and independence.
Communication	Top-down, one-way communication.	Open, two-way communication.	Minimal communication; only when necessary.
Creativity and Innovation	Low—discouraged due to rigid control.	High—encouraged through collaboration and brainstorming.	Very high—employees are free to explore ideas independently.
Work Environment	Tense, rule-based, and structured.	Supportive, inclusive, and engaging.	Unstructured, potentially chaotic.
Impact on Employee Well-Being	Often negative—leads to stress, anxiety, and lack of job satisfaction.	Positive—enhances job satisfaction, engagement, and well-being.	Mixed—some thrive with autonomy, while others feel lost or unsupported.
Strengths	- Ensures efficiency and discipline. - Effective in crisis situations requiring quick decisions.	- Encourages teamwork, creativity, and morale. - Employees feel valued and motivated.	- Provides freedom for innovation. - Encourages self-motivation and leadership development.
Weaknesses	- High stress and burnout risk. - Reduces employee engagement and motivation. - Low job satisfaction.	- Decision-making can be slow. - May not work well in situations requiring fast actions.	- Can lead to lack of structure and accountability. - Employees may feel directionless.

4. EMOTIONAL INTELLIGENCE IN LEADERSHIP

In the last twenty-five years, business, leadership, psychology, education, social sciences, and organizational sciences have all paid close attention to emotional intelligence. The majority of these disciplines have studied and described the various ways that the ability referred to as "emotional intelligence" influences a wide range of actions, choices, and leadership. The ability to recognize emotions in oneself and others, comprehend their significance, and control one's emotions to improve individual and/or group functioning is known as emotional intelligence. It entails being aware of one's own advantages and disadvantages, being able to interact and work with a wide variety of personalities, being able to control one's emotions—even in the face of stress or conflict—and being able to listen to and interact with team members and other stakeholders. Each of these skills has the potential to significantly enhance the quality of relationships at work and help the company achieve high performance.

Intelligence and leadership effectiveness are strongly correlated, according to all the implications highlighted in the existing literature. It is also generally acknowledged that emotional intelligence traits including self-awareness, self-regulation, motivation, empathy, and social skills are associated with effective leadership actions. Furthermore, the development of such leadership styles in a variety of circumstances is significantly influenced by emotional intelligence. These findings are significant in the backdrop of intense pressure to treat and manage "human capital" in a manner that will derive maximum advantage from their productivity (Gómez-Leal et al.2022).

4.1. Definition and Components of Emotional Intelligence

Extensive research has gone into exploring the relationship between leadership and well-being. Emotionally intelligent and transformational leaders have been found to score higher on measures of social and emotional well-being. They show a greater ability to understand and manage their own emotions, whether in the workplace or otherwise. Employees who work under emotionally intelligent transformational leaders report higher levels of well-being than those working with transactional or laissez-faire leaders.It is obvious that effective leaders must possess a basic awareness of and ability to control their emotions. In order to identify the precise aspect of emotional intelligence that contributes to better well-being, the current study investigates this phenomena in greater detail.

Emotional intelligence was not recognized as a critical component of successful leadership until the late 20th and early 21st century. Many definitions of emotional intelligence were developed, but the model that focused on motivation and emotional regulation most likely made its way into the literature first. Subsequently, theorists broadened the encyclopedic scope of emotional intelligence to encompass a person's ability to understand and value their own emotions when making decisions, comprehend the sentiments of others, and implement appropriate emotional management techniques. Even though there are many different models of emotional intelligence, they all include a set of skills that are drawn from various theoretical frameworks.

This definition is expanded in this study to include emotional skills, affective traits, and typology (Görgens-Ekermans and Roux2021)(Frias et al.2021).

4.2. Importance of Emotional Intelligence for Leaders

It's likely that leaders who are able to control their own emotions would support their staff more often. Furthermore, people who possess emotional intelligence are able to recognize, comprehend, and typically consider the mental state of others. Those who possess strong emotional intelligence are particularly adept at identifying even the smallest shifts in facial expressions that convey emotions. They are therefore able to modify their leadership style by demonstrating increased empathy and being more capable of offering their team members emotional assistance. Additionally, workers under the direction of emotionally intelligent leaders report lower levels of stress and greater job satisfaction. More precisely, individuals who operate in such an atmosphere are free to be open with their leader and are empowered to express their thoughts, emotions, and aspirations. In turn, this fosters an atmosphere where each team member feels valued and heard, which improves their wellbeing as well. Additionally, followers view leaders with strong emotional intelligence as being more encouraging. They understand that all followers require validation and have emotional needs. Thus, emotional intelligence may be seen as a facilitator of positive leader behaviors, which is in turn a driver of employee well-being (Drigas et al., 2023)(Karimi et al.2021).

5. WORK-LIFE BALANCE AND WELL-BEING

The Need for Work-Life Balance

The well-known saying, “Slow down a little in order to go faster later,” recognizes the need to take some time for oneself amidst the hectic pace of modern life. The way people live, work, and function has been completely transformed by 21st-century technology advancements. Employees now have to make judgments all the time about how to respond to job-related demands in many different aspects of their lives because most firms have extended the working day.

Challenges in Maintaining Work-Life Balance

Maintaining a healthy work-life balance is becoming increasingly difficult as employees' attempts to juggle professional and personal commitments may deplete their resources and jeopardize their well-being, happiness, and productivity. While work-related stress can sometimes serve as a source of positive energy, excessive strain can have negative consequences—not only affecting an employee's work performance but also creating stress reactions at home, which can further exacerbate job-related pressure.

Benefits of a Healthy Work-Life Balance

Achieving an optimal balance between work and personal life is beneficial for both individuals and organizations. Being productive at work while also having time for family, friends, and leisure activities is essential for maintaining a fulfilling lifestyle. A well-balanced life enables individuals to be more engaged, energetic, and satisfied, ultimately enhancing both their personal and professional experiences.

Impact on Individual Well-Being

For individuals, work-life balance is crucial as it allows them to develop to their fullest potential and improves their welfare, productivity, performance, and peace of mind. Employees who can effectively manage their schedules and allocate sufficient time and energy to their personal, family, recreational, and health objectives are more likely to experience physical well-being, mental stability, inner serenity, and emotional resilience.

Impact on Organizational Performance

At an organizational level, fostering a healthy work-life balance leads to increased job satisfaction, happiness, safety, and quality of life. It also reduces stress and tension, enhances motivation and commitment, and improves an organization's ability to attract and retain talented and dedicated employees.

The Key to a Sustainable Future

Ultimately, work-life balance plays a critical role in enhancing mental and physical well-being, contributing to greater energy, relaxation, emotional stability, and overall happiness. By prioritizing a balanced approach to work and personal life, individuals and organizations can create a more sustainable, productive, and fulfilling future. (Haider and Dasti, 2022; Cvenkel, 2021).

5.1. Challenges and Strategies for Achieving Work-Life Balance

Finding the time to connect with friends, pursue a meaningful relationship, or engage in self-reflection and self-awareness is one issue. In a time when people feel pressured to be active all the time, stay in shape, lead healthy lives, or just be able to unwind at home with a good book or a glass of wine, relaxation is another issue. Last but not least, balancing the circle of great success and lofty objectives in one's personal and professional life is necessary to manage the minute details that come with running any organization. Faculty members should ideally become proficient in all three areas of mentoring: team building, conflict resolution, stress management, setting short- and long-term personal and professional goals, organizational effectiveness, and, most crucially for leadership and wellbeing, delegation. The phrase "being overburdened with excessive demand, pressure, or fatigue" is commonly associated with a dysfunctional power dynamic. Aspiring leaders aim for a more flexible definition, ideally as the desire to better balance their personal and professional lives. Building a solid and constructive relationship with the organization is the main obstacle facing the person who rises to the position of leader at a certain work. Without making long-range plans to build the necessary caring and supportive relationships, work satisfaction, and perceived power in important domains, we will not experience happier or more fulfilling jobs (Pilbeam, 2024).

6. ORGANIZATIONAL CULTURE AND WELL-BEING

The Growing Emphasis on Work-Life Balance Policies

An increasing number of nations have developed national policies or action plans to encourage firms to implement work-life balance and employee well-being practices. Furthermore, a wide range of stakeholders, including governments, social partners, employers' associations, and non-governmental organizations, have developed initiatives to support policies that integrate work and family life.

Employer Initiatives for Work-Life Balance

In response to these policies, numerous public and private sector employers have launched programs to support work-life balance, including job sharing, teleworking, flexible scheduling, and other strategies. These initiatives provide greater flexibility for employees to juggle work and family obligations, such as long-term dependent care and high-quality childcare. At the same time, organizations implementing these strategies benefit from enhanced productivity and an improved organizational culture.

Leadership and Organizational Culture in Employee Well-Being

Although still relatively uncommon, there is growing interest in leadership techniques and organizational culture as a means to support health and prevent work-related stress. Some studies highlight the role of leaders in fostering a positive workplace environment by modeling healthy and ethical behavior, communicating health-enhancing values, being caring and empowering, setting high-performance expectations, and creating a supportive and enabling environment where employees can thrive.

The Role of Healthy Leadership in Workplace Well-Being

Healthy leaders are expected to lead with emotional intelligence, be self-aware, create collaborative relationships, and foster work-life balance. The adoption of positive and transformational leadership styles to promote health and well-being is gaining momentum. Many organizations that implement these leadership approaches report notable success stories.

The Impact of Leadership on Employee Engagement and Productivity

Cross-sectional and experimental research has demonstrated that employees working under transformational leadership or cooperative workplace practices experience greater well-being and higher productivity. While stress can lead to counterproductive work behaviors, fostering sympathetic employment relations can yield the opposite effect.

Support Systems to Enhance Employee Well-Being

The implementation of congratulatory practices, supportive models, and assistance mechanisms can help mitigate stress-related negative behaviors and even increase employee engagement. By prioritizing organizational culture and leadership strategies, companies can create a healthier, more engaged, and more productive workforce. *(Søvold et al., 2021;Tuzovic & Kabadayi, 2021).*

6.1. Creating a Positive Organizational Culture

The Role of Positive Leaders in Shaping Organizational Culture

A positive psychological environment fostered by positive leaders produces positive behaviors, which, in turn, lead to positive relationships and outcomes. A positive company culture forms the foundation of this positive psychological climate. Culture is defined as a set of shared fundamental beliefs that a group develops while addressing its internal integration and external adaptation challenges. These beliefs are proven to be effective enough to be accepted as legitimate, thus becoming part of the teaching process for new members, guiding them on the correct way to perceive, think, and feel about these issues.

Core Beliefs and Values in Organizational Culture

Strong beliefs, values, and underlying assumptions embedded in an organization's members' thoughts and behaviors form the foundation of a strong organizational culture. This type of culture promotes accountability, effort, integrity, and respect for output. The set of core values at the heart of any distinct culture is critical in shaping how the organization operates and behaves. In excellent organizations, these values include respect for employees at all levels, a focus on customer needs, the delivery of high-quality products and services, and an unwavering commitment to employees.

The Importance of Core Values and Leadership in Organizational Success

The core values of an organization drive its pursuit of superior, long-term results. These values, which encompass respect, commitment, innovation, and leadership, are embodied by strong leadership and contribute to a thriving organizational environment. In this sense, a positive culture is not just about internal harmony but also about achieving bottom-line performance in service to employees, customers, stakeholders, and the wider environment. Organizations with a strong, positive culture understand that their success depends on engaged employees, satisfied customers, and connected communities.

The Need for Positive Culture in Challenging Times

The importance of a strong, positive organizational culture becomes even more apparent during challenging times, such as technological changes, intense competition, economic fluctuations, corporate crises, and economic downturns. During such periods, a positive culture helps maintain stability, engagement, and motivation, ensuring the organization's resilience in the face of adversity.

Benefits of a Positive Organizational Culture

The benefits of cultivating a positive culture are substantial, including high employee engagement, organizational commitment, job satisfaction, and enhanced individual and team performance. A strong culture fosters an environment where employees are motivated and aligned with the organization's goals, driving overall success. (Kawiana et al., 2021; Karimi et al., 2023)

7. GENDER AND LEADERSHIP WELL-BEING

This chapter addresses the much-neglected area of performance impairments experienced by individuals in leadership roles as a result of the often acute pressures that apprehensive organizations place on them. It introduces a Gender-Leadership-Well-Being model that offers a more holistic and balanced perspective by examining three factors that influence the nature of these appraisals and associations: the gender of both leaders and subordinates, the style of leadership practiced, and what is questioned about the quality of life in the workplace. To assess the rival predictions made by these gender-stereotyping, role congruity, and transformational leadership approaches, a fresh operational definition is proposed that differentiates between despised super-critics, dazzled devotees, and moderate manipulators.

Both sides of the conversation are only partially correct. Gender appears to be unrelated to well-being issues for most employees, but the consensus is that leaders can experience greater work satisfaction and low levels of well-being, particularly if they are female or have entered roles that are stereotypic to their gender (Krug et al., 2021; Niinihuhta and Häggman-Laitila2022).

7.1. Gender Differences in Leadership Styles

The majority of leadership study to date has concentrated on the traits of leaders rather than taking their styles into account. Understanding how various styles might impact an individual's views of their health and well-being is crucial since it can be used to pinpoint risk factors and possible remedies. In order to determine if holding a leadership role is beneficial or detrimental to the leader, style is crucial. Even though leadership positions are typically viewed as beneficial and enhancing well-being, they can also be stressful for those who are in charge of them if they don't think they are capable or willing to carry out these responsibilities. However, to see if and how leadership tasks really are interpreted as challenges or hindrances, different styles of leadership have to be taken into account and precisely examined.

Research on gender and leadership has shown that women continue to appear to be underrepresented in some key leadership fields, although it is unclear if men and women actually have different leadership philosophies. Even when they must operate in less conventional settings, female leaders have been proven to be more cooperative and thoughtful than male leaders, despite certain parallels between the two sexes. Additionally, female leaders have been described as more people-oriented, emphasizing the welfare of their subordinates, and bolstering social ideals. It has been said that women's leadership styles are more transformational and democratic, which benefits their employees' status, recognition, and contentment. Given that similar stylistic preferences are commonly found when comparing male and female non-leaders, some gender differences in leadership might stem from selection processes (Mulawarman & Komariyah, 2021; Furtner et al.2021).

8. ETHICAL LEADERSHIP AND WELL-BEING

Ethical leadership serves as an excellent model for preserving and promoting both personal and others' well-being. These leaders recognize that employee well-being holds intrinsic value, independent of any practical or financial benefits. Ethical leaders hold themselves to high standards of ethics, striving to create a fair, hygienic, and compassionate organization. They embody high moral character by being truthful, reliable, equitable, and showing respect and consideration for their followers and other stakeholders. Their actions reflect a commitment to serving others and the greater good of society, rather than using power or organizational resources for personal gratification.

The Impact of Ethical Leadership on Emotional Well-Being

Experiments have demonstrated the beneficial effects of moral leadership on the emotional well-being of followers. Moral leaders convey the message that the safety and well-being of their followers come first, and that they are less concerned with advancing their own personal interests. As a result, when followers work under leaders who value honesty and fair treatment, they feel safer and report higher emotional well-being. Ethical leadership highlights the moral aspects of leadership, focusing on how leaders should act and demonstrating that individuals matter. This kind of role modeling helps prevent leaders from exploiting their followers.

Compassionate Leadership and Employee Well-Being

Compassion, empathy, and sympathy are at the core of human social relationships. These emotions are elicited by distress states or the perception of suffering in oneself or others. Compassion, specifically, involves not only the willingness to show concern for others but also to take action to help those in need. These emotions promote positive social behavior, and are associated with clear benefits for both social and health outcomes. Compassionate behavior contributes to enhanced well-being, as it fosters a supportive environment where individuals actively seek to help others in distress. Additionally, happiness and life satisfaction are positively linked to greater compassion and tenderness.(Ilyas et al., 2023; Jia et al., 2022)

8.1. Importance of Ethics in Leadership

The Impact of Stress on Employee Well-Being

The working environment in organizations is increasingly becoming more stressful. This stress compromises both the well-being and work performance of employees, which in turn proves costly to the organization. The literature highlights the potential for management and leadership to have a positive influence that counters stress-related negativity at work. Despite the growing recognition of this issue, the exact relationship between ethical leadership and employee well-being remains unclear.

The Role of Ethical Leadership in Promoting Employee Well-Being

This examination delves into theoretical models that may explain how ethical leadership influences employee well-being. It discusses the mechanisms through which ethical leadership can be used as a resource to promote well-being in the workplace. The conclusion emphasizes that ethical leadership plays a significant role in fostering well-being within organizations, thereby benefiting both individuals and the organization as a whole.

Ethical Leadership and Business Education

For many years, business institutes have emphasized ethical issues in their curricula, and researchers, practitioners, policymakers, and managers have given considerable attention to them. Despite the overarching goal of maximizing profits, organizations often face unethical behavior from employees, stemming from factors like greed and opportunistic tendencies. Employers play a critical role in influencing the attitudes and conduct of their workforce. Leadership is recognized as a key factor in determining a company's ethical behavior.

Strategies for Promoting Ethical Behavior

Several strategies have been proposed to help managers promote honesty and integrity among their staff. These include implementing the social cognitive theory of integrity in management education and fostering an ethical corporate culture. It is emphasized that cultivating and applying ethical leadership is crucial in avoiding the detrimental effects of unethical actions. Ethical leadership encompasses several important functions, including being a moral individual, an ethical manager, and establishing ethical standards for decision-making that prioritize employee well-being.(Huang et al., 2021; Jia et al., 2022; Schwepker et al., 2021)

9. TEAM DYNAMICS AND WELL-BEING

Teams are another important and interesting idea that has not been covered, but it is not difficult to extend thinking from individuals to the team level. After all, it might be argued that no individual works for long in isolation, and thus there are likely to be direct and indirect impacts from teams on the well-being of people working in them. Organizations get the work done through teams, and now they feature in virtually every part of the employment lifecycle: in recruitment and selection since companies look at teamwork skills and experiences; in setting tasks and projects; in the fixed-term contracts that people often now work, sometimes on secondment to different teams; and in relentless change, which is typically achieved through a project-based approach. At the most basic level, a team could be considered as a group of people who are typically more than a single level in the hierarchy who work more or less closely together in order to achieve a common goal. Some may not choose to cooperate at all, for example, a production line. However, it could be argued that the one goal of such groups might more realistically be the paycheck that they get at the end of the week. A more complex entity is the team that has a supervisor in the form of a team leader. The effective control of people working in teams may be an increasingly important knowledge area that could impact directly on the well-being of the team members (Fox et al.2022; Jarosz, 2021).

9.1. Building High-Performing Teams

The growing complexity and environmental turbulence in business is driving organizations to search for new work models that replace inflexible work structures with employee engagement, collaboration, motivation, knowledge sharing, and trust to improve performance. Performance directly impacts any company's competitive advantage. The development of dynamic teams is essential for improving company performance. A great deal of scientific production has been focused on studying team performance and behavior, and how they affect company performance over the years. Many concepts are associated with “working together”: collaborate, develop, share, create, and innovate, for example. All of these, combined, have a major impact on business results. When employees seek to work together, the benefits extend to employees who feel more engaged, happier, and have more positive attitudes. Aim: This research addresses the theme of teamwork and high-performance teams at work. It aims to list the main characteristics of high-performance teams, reviewing scientific articles and books aimed at the themes of teamwork and high-performance teams. There is a direct relationship between high-performance teams and high-performance organizations. When work processes become flexible, focused on results, and aimed at increasing company performance and creating value for employees, the identification of these characteristics will assist in better selecting, developing, and managing the formation of these teams (Raineri and Valenzuela-Ibarra2022; Do & Mai, 2021)

10. MENTAL HEALTH AWARENESS IN LEADERSHIP

Mental health of the workforce is every bit as important to business performance as the physical health of employees. The effects of this are not just contained to employee performance and company reputation, but also have financial implications, with mental health absence now being the biggest cause of long-term workplace sickness costs, which is lost due to labor turnover. It is therefore vital for companies to have a robust mental health strategy that looks after employees, which includes interventions focused on the prevention, detection, and signposting of mental health, as well as any necessary care and support resources for employees suffering from poor or deteriorating mental health. Another important consideration that should be very high on any sensible employee health strategy is the consideration of mental health in leadership. Is it not ironic that we have sophisticated employee health programs often led by physically fit senior managers, yet even they are not equipped with any specific training on mental health, which they themselves may unknowingly be suffering from. It is time for leadership to take full responsibility for managing mental health with employees, demonstrating to the wider business world and society as a whole that they value their employees as much as their turnover and profits. This responsibility extends beyond the leaders themselves to the bosses and junior top managers. These leaders need to understand how technical capability can impact mental health and how they can work through departmental teams to support the mental health of their departments (Joosen et al.2021; Bryan et al.2021).

10.1. Stress Management Techniques for Leaders

Techniques for managing stress are essential to the process of wellbeing. Little is known about stress management techniques for lowering leaders' stress levels, despite prior studies confirming the presence of management practices to lower staff stress. There is currently little data to support the idea that leaders can benefit from the same one-size-fits-all strategies that are recommended for subordinates. Conflict between work and family has long been acknowledged as a serious worry for all workers. Nevertheless, the concept of work-family balance is still ill-defined, much like leadership.

Working leaders with young families must somehow strike a balance between work and home because of the significant amount of work and the high levels of dedication required. Work-family literature currently emphasizes reducing friction between work and family or providing leaders with family support. The problem areas, concerns, and best practices for work-family assistance for working leaders are examined in this study. Stress is ubiquitous and is closely linked to negative consequences that will harm not just leaders but also staff members and financial performance. Consequently, stress management programs have gained popularity as a way to deal with stress. Stress management practices are categorized into types of 'people' and types of 'organizational' techniques (Donato et al.2021; Katajavuori et al., 2023).

11. THE ROLE OF COACHING AND MENTORING IN LEADERSHIP DEVELOPMENT

Coaching and Mentoring in Leadership Development

Coaching and mentoring have emerged in recent years as integral components of leadership and management development. Both aim to improve a leader's performance, yet they differ in many aspects and should not be confused. While both focus on enhancing leadership capabilities, they also contribute to the well-being and career development of the leader. This section explores the distinct roles coaching and mentoring play in leadership development.

The Role of Mentoring in Leadership and Career Development

A specific type of mentoring that blends traditional mentoring goals with the objectives of coaching is discussed here. This type of mentoring focuses on the leader's career development while also addressing their personal growth, balancing attention between business goals and individual well-being. This combination contributes to the leader's psychological well-being, promoting both career advancement and personal fulfillment.

Leadership, Effectiveness, and Well-Being

The association between leadership, effectiveness, and well-being is explored, emphasizing the leader's role in creating productive and human-friendly organizations. A balanced approach to leadership contributes to achieving sustainable development, benefiting both organizational goals and the well-being of employees. This section addresses how leaders can influence the well-being of their followers, promoting a healthier balance between personal life and work.

Emotional Intelligence and Transformational Leadership

At the heart of effective leadership lies emotional intelligence and transformational leadership. Emotional intelligence is recognized as crucial for leadership effectiveness, particularly in relationships with others and maintaining one's own well-being. Transformational leadership, which focuses on inspiring, motivating, and innovating, reflects a leader's ability to create a compelling vision for the future and drive the development and welfare of their team members. (Jarosz, 2021; Wang et al., 2021)

11.1. Benefits of Coaching and Mentoring Programs

The leaders developed their coaching skills and reflected upon their leadership role. The coach was present at the majority of sessions conducted in Russian and at all of those conducted in English. Therefore, she was able to evaluate the extent to which the participants had developed over time. Before the last session with the director general, the coach had a focus group with the mentors. This was both to ascertain the extent of the mentors' commitment to the program and its overall success.

The focus group took place at a regional retreat at which all top-level leadership were present. The mentors appreciated being involved, and they had already experienced the program as providing both direction and practical implications for the process. The coach observed the departmental meetings at which the four mentors were present to ensure that they were actually taking place. She also listened to the physical process behind the meetings, both before and after the reflections of each session. She did this while the participants were working in Russian and English (Connery & Frick, 2021; Mullen and Klimaitis2021).

12. INCLUSIVE LEADERSHIP AND WELL-BEING

Inclusive leadership entails involving, empowering, and valuing different people and different perspectives, achieving a common purpose, and creating a sense of belonging. It enhances team innovation and performance and also facilitates the well-being of team members. It is likely to do so by fostering a climate where all team members feel appreciated and valued for their unique contributions. They can be themselves and interact without fear. Perceived discrimination in the team becomes the exception rather than the rule, and therefore stress and other negative well-being outcomes related to victimization are reduced. Not surprisingly, people with relatively strong self-concepts and positive affect are more satisfied with leaders who behave in an interpersonally fair manner, providing a conducive climate for effective supportive teamwork.

Research has generally been overtly mindful of the pervasive negative impact of discrimination on well-being at work. Work teams that feel they work in an inclusive environment are more likely to experience higher levels of well-being. They have better mental and physical health and can contribute more to their full potential. How can leadership provoke this? In addition to the general leadership behaviors proposed here, it is suggested that team leaders show particular types of inclusive behavior. This occurs by role-modeling relatively high levels of individual consideration and treating each team member with dignity and respect (Jha et al., 2024; Ahmed et al., 2021; Clark & Kosciw, 2022).

12.1. Promoting Diversity and Inclusion in Leadership

Let's talk about leadership theories that emphasize diversity and inclusiveness. The concept of heroic leaders has been criticized by several leadership scholars, who have instead looked for other viewpoints on leadership and organization. They have created observations with a variety of organizations, concentrating on various leadership levels, and they have built leaders' approaches to their own work experience, working from various positions in organizations. Denial of the heroic leadership rhetoric may be conceivable from these different perspectives; what would ordinarily be the issue of sparse language concerning mystification could be supplemented. We should not forget that there are and have been female leaders, but female coworkers may offer a female perspective on the aspects of leadership that are typically reserved for men.

It is relatively clear that the selected concept represents an ideal of leadership as a gendered institution. Discussion of leadership roles often brings the issue of gender and leadership to the forefront, where masculinity becomes exclusively associated with "leadership" and femininity with "gender." From a feminist perspective, the basic standpoint implies that gender is about a natural understanding of the situation in question. With the application of such a perspective, we should define leadership as a gendered institution, since it is a socially created and maintained system of common knowledge. Its purpose is to attribute specific roles to members of their organizations and in specific situations in accord with normative expectations, to offer ideological justification. Such a position in research is consistent with the idea that social constructions of sex, sex differences, and sex role stereotypes can, as universalizing ideologies, operate symbolically and structurally in gender stratification and the conduct of everyday social life (Esquierdo-Leal & Houmanfar, 2021; Antonacopoulou & Georgiadou, 2021).

13. TECHNOLOGY AND REMOTE LEADERSHIP

Admittedly, we are dealing with a relatively new and rapidly changing area with the rapid growth and influence of technology on our work practices. As we mentioned at the outset, many of the traditional theories of leadership were embedded in a different era and, even within the last 100 years, working practices have changed beyond recognition with the technological revolution we have all experienced. Technology frees us from the traditional shackles of the workplace and provides us with a whole new range of opportunities that were simply not available even at the turn of the century. We should not pretend that technology always provides an improvement, but, as leaders of people exposed to both the benefits and the downsides of technology, our people will often turn to us for guidance and leadership. We may not always have the comfort of dwelling on the lessons of history or the wisdom of the ages, but we may often have to create the future with little knowledge about where our guiding principles should come from. For the moment, we will concern ourselves with remote leadership and not the impact technology has had on businesses in the way they are organized and conducted (Trenerry et al., 2021; Benitez et al., 2022).

13.1. Challenges and Opportunities of Remote Leadership

Widespread and concurrent paradigm developments that challenge conventional wisdom include digitalization, organizational agility, and the growing need for expertise. The old issues have resurfaced with fresh significance, as is often the case with paradigm shifts. The productivity of remote work, especially the remote leadership role in guaranteeing the performance and well-being of employees, is one such common difficulty. It's possible that technological advancements like increased technical automation and the broader availability of virtual presence tools have changed the potential for distant leadership. Businesses are taking advantage of remote working opportunities more and more, especially for certain positions. Furthermore, the rapid rise in ubiquitous connectivity is contributing to the misunderstanding around distant leader identities. Employees can now work across multiple time, place, and activity dimensions as members of a virtual company thanks to advancements in connectivity. Traditional conceptions of where and when specific sorts of work would be done must become more flexible as a result. The ability to work from home, from a distant city or country, or while bringing their kids skiing, however, goes against what a conventional leader would accept. Robust leadership techniques appear to be the first to be affected by the paradigm change. As a result of remote and hybrid work, it is easy to have a hazy mental image of how leadership works. The well-being of employees is interrelated with the ambiguity of distance itself – a unique favorite and fear indoors at the same time (Miron et al.2021; Glazer, 2021).

14. CONCLUSION AND FUTURE DIRECTIONS IN LEADERSHIP AND WELL-BEING

This chapter has highlighted the critical interplay between leadership and employee well-being, particularly within the public sector. We have established that leadership is not only a determinant of employee well-being but is also influenced by it, creating a bidirectional relationship that significantly impacts organizational success.

Effective leadership fosters a positive work environment, enhances job satisfaction, and reduces burnout, ultimately improving overall organizational performance.

To translate these insights into actionable strategies, public sector leaders should prioritize the following key steps:

Develop Leadership Training Programs Focused on Well-Being

- Integrate well-being into leadership development by providing training on emotional intelligence, stress management, and mindful leadership (Goleman, 2017).
- Establish mentoring and coaching programs that help leaders cultivate supportive relationships with employees (Avolio & Gardner, 2005).

Implement Workplace Flexibility Initiatives

- Introduce hybrid work models and flexible scheduling to help employees maintain a better work-life balance (Bailey & Kurland, 2002).
- Encourage "right to disconnect" policies that prevent work-related communication after office hours to reduce burnout.

Create a Recognition and Reward System

- Develop non-monetary and monetary reward systems, such as employee appreciation programs, promotions based on leadership skills, and well-being bonuses (Deci & Ryan, 2000).
- Encourage peer recognition programs where employees acknowledge each other's contributions to boost morale and job satisfaction.

Enhance Communication and Employee Engagement

- Establish open-door policies where employees feel comfortable discussing challenges and mental health concerns with leaders (Bass & Riggio, 2006).
- Conduct regular town halls and feedback sessions to foster transparency and active participation in decision-making.

Integrate Well-Being Metrics into Performance Evaluations

- Assess leaders not only on performance outcomes but also on their ability to create a supportive, inclusive, and psychologically safe workplace (Cooper & Quick, 2017).

- Encourage leaders to set well-being goals, such as reducing absenteeism, improving engagement, and enhancing team cohesion.

Invest in Mental Health and Wellness Programs

- Provide access to counseling, employee assistance programs, and stress management workshops (WHO, 2020).
- Offer wellness stipends for activities like yoga, meditation, and gym memberships to promote holistic health.

Foster a Culture of Ethical Leadership and Psychological Safety

- Promote ethical decision-making by incorporating integrity and fairness into leadership evaluations (Brown & Treviño, 2006).
- Train leaders to handle workplace conflicts constructively, ensuring employees feel safe to voice concerns without fear of retaliation.

By integrating these strategies, public sector organizations can cultivate a work environment where both leaders and employees thrive. This chapter contributes to the growing discourse on leadership and well-being by offering a practical framework that bridges the gap between leadership theory and real-world application. Future research should continue to explore innovative leadership approaches that further enhance employee well-being and organizational performance in an evolving work landscape.

REFERENCES

Ahmed, F., Zhao, F., Faraz, N. A., & Qin, Y. J. (2021). How inclusive leadership paves way for psychological well-being of employees during trauma and crisis: A three-wave longitudinal mediation study. [nih.gov]. *Journal of Advanced Nursing*, *77*(2), 819–831. DOI: 10.1111/jan.14637 PMID: 33231300

Antonacopoulou, E. P., & Georgiadou, A. (2021). Leading through social distancing: The future of work, corporations and leadership from home. [worktribe.com]. *Gender, Work and Organization*, *28*(2), 749–767. DOI: 10.1111/gwao.12533

Avolio, B. J., & Gardner, W. L. (2005). Authentic leadership development: Getting to the root of positive forms of leadership. *The Leadership Quarterly*, *16*(3), 315–338. DOI: 10.1016/j.leaqua.2005.03.001

Avolio, B. J., & Gardner, W. L. (2005). Authentic leadership development: Getting to the root of positive forms of leadership. *The Leadership Quarterly*, *16*(3), 315–338. DOI: 10.1016/j.leaqua.2005.03.001

Bailey, D. E., & Kurland, N. B. (2002). A review of telework research: Findings, new directions, and lessons for the study of modern work. *Journal of Organizational Behavior*, *23*(4), 383–400. DOI: 10.1002/job.144

Bass, B. M., & Riggio, R. E. (2006). *Transformational Leadership*. Psychology Press. DOI: 10.4324/9781410617095

Benitez, J., Arenas, A., Castillo, A., & Esteves, J. (2022). Impact of digital leadership capability on innovation performance: The role of platform digitization capability. *Information & Management*, *59*(2), 103590.

Briker, R., Walter, F., & Cole, M. S. (2021). Hurry up! The role of supervisors' time urgency and self-perceived status for autocratic leadership and subordinates' well-being. *Personnel Psychology*, *74*(1), 55–76.

Brown, M. E., & Treviño, L. K. (2006). Ethical leadership: A review and future directions. *The Leadership Quarterly*, *17*(6), 595–616. DOI: 10.1016/j.leaqua.2006.10.004

Bryan, M. L., Bryce, A. M., & Roberts, J. (2021). The effect of mental and physical health problems on sickness absence. [springer.com]. *The European Journal of Health Economics*, *22*(9), 1519–1533. DOI: 10.1007/s10198-021-01379-w PMID: 34626291

Clark, C. M., & Kosciw, J. G. (2022). Engaged or excluded: LGBTQ youth's participation in school sports and their relationship to psychological well-being. *Psychology in the Schools*, *59*(1), 95–114.

Connery, L. A., & Frick, W. C. (2021). A formal administrator mentoring program: Perceived learning benefits and insights into leadership well-being. ie. *Inquiry in Education*, *13*(1), 3.

Cooper, C. L., & Quick, J. C. (2017). *The Handbook of Stress and Health: A Guide to Research and Practice*. Wiley. DOI: 10.1002/9781118993811

Cooper, C. L., & Quick, J. C. (2017). *The Handbook of Stress and Health: A Guide to Research and Practice*. Wiley. DOI: 10.1002/9781118993811

Cvenkel, N. (2021). Work-life balance and well-being at work: Employees' perspective to promote a psychologically healthy workplace. In *The Palgrave handbook of corporate social responsibility* (pp. 429–451). Springer International Publishing.

Deci, E. L., & Ryan, R. M. (2000). The "what" and "why" of goal pursuits: Human needs and the self-determination of behavior. *Psychological Inquiry*, *11*(4), 227–268. DOI: 10.1207/S15327965PLI1104_01

Devi, A. D., & Subiyantoro, S. (2021). Implementation of democratic leadership style and transformational head of madrasah in improving the quality. *Nidhomul Haq: Jurnal Manajemen Pendidikan Islam*, *6*(1), 14–26.

Do, T. T., & Mai, N. K. (2021). A systematic review on high performance organization. [HTML]. *Management Research Review*, *44*(1), 181–208. DOI: 10.1108/MRR-11-2019-0495

Donato, S., Parise, M., Pagani, A. F., Lanz, M., Regalia, C., Rosnati, R., & Iafrate, R. (2021). Together against COVID-19 concerns: The role of the dyadic coping process for partners' psychological well-being during the pandemic. [frontiersin.org]. *Frontiers in Psychology*, *11*, 578395. DOI: 10.3389/fpsyg.2020.578395 PMID: 33488449

Drigas, A., Papoutsi, C., & Skianis, C. (2023). Being an emotionally intelligent leader through the nine-layer model of emotional intelligence—The supporting role of new technologies. *Sustainability*, *15*(10), 8103.

Esquierdo-Leal, J. L., & Houmanfar, R. A. (2021). Creating inclusive and equitable cultural practices by linking leadership to systemic change. *Behavior Analysis in Practice*, *14*(2), 499–512.

Fox, K. E., Johnson, S. T., Berkman, L. F., Sianoja, M., Soh, Y., Kubzansky, L. D., & Kelly, E. L. (2022). Organisational-and group-level workplace interventions and their effect on multiple domains of worker well-being: A systematic review. [HTML]. *Work and Stress, 36*(1), 30–59. DOI: 10.1080/02678373.2021.1969476

Frias, A., Hampton, D., Tharp-Barrie, K., & Thomas, J. (2021). The impact of an emotional intelligence training program on transformational leadership. [ceconnection.com]. *Nursing Management, 52*(2), 18–25. DOI: 10.1097/01.NUMA.0000731924.03153.df PMID: 33512880

Furtner, N. C., Kocher, M. G., Martinsson, P., Matzat, D., & Wollbrant, C. (2021). Gender and cooperative preferences. *Journal of Economic Behavior & Organization, 181*, 39–48. st-andrews.ac.uk. DOI: 10.1016/j.jebo.2020.11.030

Glazer, S. (2021). Organizational role ambiguity as a proxy for uncertainty avoidance. [HTML]. *International Journal of Intercultural Relations, 85*, 1–12. DOI: 10.1016/j.ijintrel.2021.08.011

Goleman, D. (2017). *Emotional Intelligence: Why It Can Matter More Than IQ*. Bantam.

Gómez-Leal, R., Holzer, A. A., Bradley, C., Fernández-Berrocal, P., & Patti, J. (2022). The relationship between emotional intelligence and leadership in school leaders: A systematic review. [researchgate.net]. *Cambridge Journal of Education, 52*(1), 1–21. DOI: 10.1080/0305764X.2021.1927987

Görgens-Ekermans, G., & Roux, C. (2021). Revisiting the emotional intelligence and transformational leadership debate:(How) does emotional intelligence matter to effective leadership? *SA Journal of Human Resource Management, 19*, 1279. journals.co.za. DOI: 10.4102/sajhrm.v19i0.1279

Haider, Z., & Dasti, R. (2022). Mentoring, research self-efficacy, work–life balance and psychological well-being of doctoral program students. [HTML]. *International Journal of Mentoring and Coaching in Education, 11*(2), 170–182. DOI: 10.1108/IJMCE-07-2020-0036

Ilyas, S., Abid, G., & Ashfaq, F. (2023). Enhancing the perceived organizational support, perceived ethical-philanthropic CSR and subjective well-being: The role of ethical leadership. *International Journal of Ethics and Systems, 39*(4), 713–736.

Jarosz, J. (2021). The impact of coaching on well-being and performance of managers and their teams during pandemic. *International Journal of Evidence Based Coaching and Mentoring, 19*(1), 4–27. brookes.ac.uk

Jha, I. N., Pal, D., & Sarkar, S. (2024). Unlocking the secret to happiness at work: The power of inclusive leadership, organizational justice and workplace inclusion. [HTML]. *Journal of Management Development, 43*(2), 200–221. DOI: 10.1108/JMD-04-2023-0136

Jia, K., Zhu, T., Zhang, W., Rasool, S. F., Asghar, A., & Chin, T. (2022). The linkage between ethical leadership, well-being, work engagement, and innovative work behavior: The empirical evidence from the higher education sector of China. [mdpi.com]. *International Journal of Environmental Research and Public Health, 19*(9), 5414. DOI: 10.3390/ijerph19095414 PMID: 35564809

Joosen, M. C., Lugtenberg, M., Arends, I., van Gestel, H. J., Schaapveld, B., Terluin, B., & Brouwers, E. P. (2021). Barriers and facilitators for return to work from the perspective of workers with common mental disorders with short, medium and long-term sickness absence: A longitudinal qualitative study. [springer.com]. *Journal of Occupational Rehabilitation*, •••, 1–12. PMID: 34580811

Kaluza, A. J., Junker, N. M., Schuh, S. C., Raesch, P., von Rooy, N. K., & van Dick, R. (2022). A leader in need is a leader indeed? The influence of leaders' stress mindset on their perception of employee well-being and their intended leadership behavior. [wiley.com]. *Applied Psychology, 71*(4), 1347–1384.

Huang, N., Qiu, S., Yang, S., & Deng, R. (2021). Ethical leadership and organizational citizenship behavior: Mediation of trust and psychological well-being. [tandfonline.com]. *Psychology Research and Behavior Management*, 655–664.

Karimi, L., Leggat, S. G., Bartram, T., Afshari, L., Sarkeshik, S., & Verulava, T. (2021). Emotional intelligence: Predictor of employees' wellbeing, quality of patient care, and psychological empowerment. [springer.com]. *BMC Psychology, 9*(1), 93. DOI: 10.1186/s40359-021-00593-8 PMID: 34088348

Karimi, S., Ahmadi Malek, F., Yaghoubi Farani, A., & Liobikienė, G. (2023). The role of transformational leadership in developing innovative work behaviors: The mediating role of employees' psychological capital. [mdpi.com]. *Sustainability (Basel), 15*(2), 1267. DOI: 10.3390/su15021267

Katajavuori, N., Vehkalahti, K., & Asikainen, H. (2023). Promoting university students' well-being and studying with an acceptance and commitment therapy (ACT)-based intervention. *Current Psychology (New Brunswick, N.J.), 42*(6), 4900–4912.

Kawiana, I., Dewi, L. K. C., Hartati, P. S., Setini, M., & Asih, D. (2021). Effects of leadership and psychological climate on organizational commitment in the digitization era. *The Journal of Asian Finance, Economics and Business, 8*(1), 1051–1062. triatmamulya.ac.id

Kleynhans, D. J., Heyns, M. M., & Stander, M. W. (2021). Authentic leadership and follower trust in the leader: The effect of precariousness. *SA Journal of Industrial Psychology*, *47*(1), 1–10. scielo.org.za. DOI: 10.4102/sajip.v47i0.1904

Krug, H., Haslam, S. A., Otto, K., & Steffens, N. K. (2021). Identity leadership, social identity continuity, and well-being at work during [Frontiers in psychology. frontiersin.org]. *COVID*, •••, 19. PMID: 34177738

Liu, F., Khong-Khai, S., Leelapattana, W., & Tsai, C. (2024). Analyzing the Influence of Leadership Style on Employee Engagement in Digital Economy. *Asian Administration and Management Review*, *7*(2), 31–44.

Lixia, C. (2017). The Relationship between Teachers' Leadership Styles and Teaching Quality in Lower Secondary Schools in Liang Zhou District of Wuwei, Gansu, China. *Asian Political Science Review*, *1*(1), 71–78. DOI: 10.12778/235108617X 15452339029545

Marufu, T. C., Collins, A., Vargas, L., Gillespie, L., & Almghairbi, D. (2021). Factors influencing retention among hospital nurses: Systematic review. [HTML]. *British Journal of Nursing (Mark Allen Publishing)*, *30*(5), 302–308. DOI: 10.12968/bjon.2021.30.5.302 PMID: 33733849

Metin-Orta, I. (2021). The impact of destructive leadership on followers' well-being. In Destructive Leadership and Management Hypocrisy: Advances in Theory and Practice (pp. 101-115). Emerald Publishing Limited.

Miron, D., Petcu, M. A., David-Sobolevschi, M. I., & Cojocariu, R. C. (2021). A multidimensional approach of the relationship between teleworking and employees well-being-Romania during the pandemic generated by the SARS-COV-2 virus. [econstor.eu]. *Amfiteatru Economic*, *23*(58), 586–600. DOI: 10.24818/EA/2021/58/586

Mulawarman, W. G., & Komariyah, L. (2021). Women and Leadership Style in School Management: Study of Gender Perspective. *Cypriot Journal of Educational Sciences*, *16*(2), 594–611.

Mullen, C. A., & Klimaitis, C. C. (2021). Defining mentoring: A literature review of issues, types, and applications. [HTML]. *Annals of the New York Academy of Sciences*, *1483*(1), 19–35. DOI: 10.1111/nyas.14176 PMID: 31309580

Niinihuhta, M., & Häggman-Laitila, A. (2022). A systematic review of the relationships between nurse leaders' leadership styles and nurses' work-related well-being. [wiley.com]. *International Journal of Nursing Practice*, *28*(5), e13040. DOI: 10.1111/ijn.13040 PMID: 35102648

Oussible, N., & Tinaztepe, C. I. H. A. N. (2022). The Effect of Democratic Leadership Style on Organizational Productivity by the mediating role of Employee performance in Turkey. [paperpublications.org]. *International Journal of Recent Research in Commerce Economics and Management*, *9*(1), 6–16.

Pilbeam, C. (2024). Practices and challenges of safety management in outsourced facilities management. *Journal of Safety Research*, *90*, 144–162.

Raineri, A., & Valenzuela-Ibarra, S. (2022). The role of inter-team relational coordination in the high-performance work systems–team performance linkage. [HTML]. *International Journal of Human Resource Management*, *33*(18), 3662–3702. DOI: 10.1080/09585192.2021.1928729

Schwepker, C. H.Jr, Valentine, S. R., Giacalone, R. A., & Promislo, M. (2021). Good barrels yield healthy apples: Organizational ethics as a mechanism for mitigating work-related stress and promoting employee well-being. [researchgate.net]. *Journal of Business Ethics*, *174*(1), 143–159. DOI: 10.1007/s10551-020-04562-w

Søvold, L. E., Naslund, J. A., Kousoulis, A. A., Saxena, S., Qoronfleh, M. W., Grobler, C., & Münter, L. (2021). Prioritizing the mental health and well-being of healthcare workers: An urgent global public health priority. [frontiersin.org]. *Frontiers in Public Health*, *9*, 679397.

Cann, R. F., Riedel-Prabhakar, R., & Powell, D. (2021). A model of positive school leadership to improve teacher wellbeing. [HTML]. *International Journal of Applied Positive Psychology*, *6*(2), 195–218.

Oleksa-Marewska, K., & Tokar, J. (2022). Facing the post-pandemic challenges: The role of leadership effectiveness in shaping the affective well-being of healthcare providers working in a hybrid work mode. [mdpi.com]. *International Journal of Environmental Research and Public Health*, *19*(21), 14388.

Baquero, A. (2023). Authentic leadership, employee work engagement, trust in the leader, and workplace well-being: A moderated mediation model. Psychology research and behavior management. tandfonline.com

Ortiz-Gómez, M., Molina-Sánchez, H., Ariza-Montes, A., & de Los Ríos-Berjillos, A. (2022). Servant leadership and authentic leadership as job resources for achieving workers' subjective well-being among organizations based on values. [tandfonline.com]. *Psychology Research and Behavior Management*, 2621–2638.

Trenerry, B., Chng, S., Wang, Y., Suhaila, Z. S., Lim, S. S., Lu, H. Y., & Oh, P. H. (2021). Preparing workplaces for digital transformation: An integrative review and framework of multi-level factors. [frontiersin.org]. *Frontiers in Psychology, 12*, 620766. DOI: 10.3389/fpsyg.2021.620766 PMID: 33833714

Tuzovic, S., & Kabadayi, S. (2021). The influence of social distancing on employee well-being: A conceptual framework and research agenda. *Journal of Service Management, 32*(2), 145–160.

Wang, W., Kang, S. W., & Choi, S. B. (2021). Effects of employee well-being and self-efficacy on the relationship between coaching leadership and knowledge sharing intention: A study of UK and US employees. [mdpi.com]. *International Journal of Environmental Research and Public Health, 18*(20), 10638. DOI: 10.3390/ijerph182010638 PMID: 34682385

Wei, S., & Bunchapattanasakda, C. (2024). Impact of Female Servant Leadership Style on Employee Engagement in Beijing's Public Universities. *Asian Political Science Review, 8*(2), 99–105.

World Health Organization (WHO). (2020). Mental health in the workplace. Retrieved from https://www.who.int/news-room/fact-sheets/detail/mental-health-at-work

Chapter 6
The Human Side of Sustainability:
Environmental Leadership and Its Impact on Employee Growth

Kartik Mandhyan
https://orcid.org/0009-0001-4516-168X
Christ University, Bengaluru, India

Sumin Samuel Sybol
https://orcid.org/0000-0002-4068-1635
Christ University, Bengaluru, India

ABSTRACT

This paper explores the relationship between leadership and environmental sustainability, emphasizing the evolving role of leaders in fostering sustainable development. It examines how leadership practices drive environmental change by integrating sustainability into decision-making, organizational strategy, and stakeholder engagement. As organizations face increasing environmental challenges, regulatory demands, and societal expectations, leaders must balance financial performance with long-term sustainability goals. The study highlights the importance of stakeholder collaboration, corporate social responsibility, and strategic leadership in advancing sustainability initiatives.

DOI: 10.4018/979-8-3373-2210-0.ch006

Copyright © 2025, IGI Global Scientific Publishing. Copying or distributing in print or electronic forms without written permission of IGI Global Scientific Publishing is prohibited.

1. INTRODUCTION TO LEADERSHIP IN THE CONTEXT OF ENVIRONMENTAL SUSTAINABILITY

Environmental challenges such as climate change, pollution, and resource depletion are not only threats to ecosystems but also to human well-being, particularly in the workplace. Research indicates that poor environmental conditions contribute to heightened employee stress, reduced productivity, and increased mental health concerns. A 2024 report by Mental Health America found that three-quarters of U.S. employees experience high work stress, negatively impacting their sleep, while three in five report adverse effects on their relationships. Additionally, a 2023 survey by the American Psychological Association revealed that 19% of workers consider their workplace to be very or somewhat toxic. Furthermore, studies show that environmental uncertainty in the workplace can elevate employees' work pressure, leading to increased rates of anxiety and depression. These findings emphasize the growing need for leadership that not only drives environmental responsibility but also prioritizes employee well-being.

This chapter argues that environmental leadership is not only crucial for planetary health but also a key driver of employee well-being. A company's commitment to environmental sustainability fosters a sense of purpose among employees, strengthens organizational values, and enhances workplace morale. Employees increasingly seek workplaces that align with their ethical and environmental values, and organizations that demonstrate a commitment to sustainability can attract and retain top talent. This reduces stress related to job security and career fulfillment while fostering a healthier, more engaged workforce. By embedding environmental responsibility into their corporate culture, organizations not only contribute to a more sustainable world but also create work environments that support employee mental health, collaboration, and overall job satisfaction.

Leadership plays a crucial role in shaping the actions and behaviours of individuals and organizations, particularly when addressing pressing global challenges such as environmental sustainability (Begum et al., 2022; Aftab et al., 2022). The qualities, behaviours, and decisions of leaders significantly influence the effectiveness of initiatives aimed at mitigating environmental issues. Leaders can either foster solutions that promote sustainable practices—thereby alleviating workplace stress and fostering a healthier environment—or perpetuate behaviours and systems that exacerbate environmental degradation, leading to increased anxiety and decreased morale among employees. Despite the importance of leadership in driving environmental change, the conceptualization of leadership in both popular discourse and academic research remains narrow and often limited to traditional frameworks (Begum et al., 2022; Aftab et al., 2022).

Typically, leadership is defined within the confines of hierarchical organizational structures and assessed based on personal character attributes. These attributes are frequently aggregated into broad and somewhat generic categories, such as calmness, charisma, or decisiveness. While such traits are valuable in certain contexts, this conventional approach overlooks the complexity and diversity of leadership actions, particularly in addressing multifaceted challenges like environmental sustainability and workplace well-being. Leaders must now consider how their environmental policies influence employee mental health, engagement, and overall job satisfaction. This limited perspective poses significant challenges in understanding the broader implications of leadership in fostering environmental solutions and employee well-being. It neglects the roles of various leadership actors beyond formal organizational hierarchies, including grassroots leaders, community organizers, and individuals in informal roles who often contribute significantly to environmental initiatives. Furthermore, the emphasis on individual traits and broad categorizations fails to account for the dynamic interplay between leaders, their followers, and the contexts in which they operate. These interactions are particularly critical in environmental sustainability, where success often depends on collaborative efforts, adaptability to local contexts, and the ability to mobilize diverse stakeholders. Consequently, the relevance of traditional leadership theories to the broader mix of leadership actions, particularly in the context of employee well-being, remains underexplored.

In recent years, some strands of scholarly literature have sought to expand the conceptualization of leadership beyond its traditional confines (Begum et al., 2022; Aftab et al., 2022). These efforts aim to reconceptualize leadership as a more fluid and context-dependent phenomenon that extends beyond individual leaders and formal organizational structures. This evolving perspective recognizes the significance of diverse follower groups and highlights the importance of leadership actions that are responsive to specific situational and contextual demands. Notably, such approaches are particularly pertinent in the context of environmental sustainability, where challenges are often deeply rooted in complex socio-ecological systems and require multifaceted solutions. In many cases, these challenges are most pronounced in less developed countries, where the interplay of environmental, social, and economic factors creates unique leadership contexts that are not adequately addressed by traditional theories.

A broader gap in leadership studies is the tendency to separate leadership theories from the specific content areas within which leadership unfolds. Classical and neo-classical leadership models often seek to develop content-independent theories that emphasize universal traits or behaviours, irrespective of the substantive issues at hand. However, this approach overlooks the critical ways in which leaders interact with and respond to the specific landscapes in which they operate.

In the context of environmental sustainability and employee well-being, such content-independent theories fall short of capturing the complexity of how leaders engage with environmental issues, shape sustainable workplace practices, and navigate the power dynamics that influence workplace morale and mental health. Leadership in this domain is inherently tied to the content of environmental challenges, requiring a nuanced understanding of ecological, social, and psychological dimensions. To illustrate how leadership shapes environmental sustainability efforts, this chapter examines the Indian cement industry—a sector that has undergone significant transformation through strategic leadership and sustainable innovation. By integrating green manufacturing practices, reducing carbon emissions, and prioritizing employee engagement, industry leaders have demonstrated how effective leadership can drive both environmental and organizational success. This case will be referenced throughout the chapter to highlight real-world applications of key leadership theories

Moreover, traditional leadership models, including those centered on charismatic or transformational leadership, often fail to align with the environmental sustainability agenda. These models typically emphasize individual influence and vision, which may not adequately address the collective and collaborative nature of environmental action or workplace well-being. Addressing environmental sustainability requires leadership that transcends individual influence and fosters collective action, distributed decision-making, and long-term thinking. This necessitates a shift in focus from individual traits to the broader dynamics of leadership systems, including the interactions between leaders, followers, and the specific contexts in which they operate.

This chapter proposes that organizations that prioritize environmental sustainability through effective leadership practices can create a more supportive and engaging work environment, leading to improved employee mental health, increased productivity, and enhanced organizational success. By integrating sustainability into leadership strategies, organizations foster a sense of purpose, encourage ethical decision-making, and build inclusive workplace cultures that benefit both employees and the environment.

The purpose of this chapter is to investigate the intersection between leadership, environmental sustainability, and employee well-being, with a particular focus on how leadership is conceptualized and enacted within this evolving context (Begum et al., 2022; Aftab et al., 2022). The chapter begins by introducing the fields of leadership and environmental sustainability, highlighting their respective contributions and limitations. It then employs discourse analysis to explore how leaders and leadership have been interpreted, appropriated, and applied in addressing environmental challenges while considering their impact on employee mental health.

By critically examining these intersections, the chapter aims to advance the understanding of leadership as a dynamic and context-sensitive phenomenon that is integral to fostering both sustainable environmental solutions and healthier workplaces. This analysis also seeks to illuminate the ways in which leadership can be reimagined to better align with the principles of environmental sustainability and employee well-being, offering insights for both theory and practice.

2. THE ROLE OF LEADERS IN DRIVING ENVIRONMENTAL INITIATIVES

In a recent discussion on advancing environmental sustainability within organizational roles, it became increasingly evident that leadership is not confined to formal positions of authority. Instead, impactful change can originate from any seat within an organization, reaffirming the idea that one does not need to hold a formal leadership title to influence outcomes positively. This aligns with the classic adage that "managers do things right, and leaders do the right things," which is particularly relevant when addressing the pressing challenges of environmental sustainability. In the contemporary global context, the emphasis on identifying and doing "the right things" has never been more critical. Issues such as global warming, the alarming loss of biodiversity, and the pervasive growth of plastics in the environment threaten the planet's capacity to sustain human life. These challenges demand a proactive, ethical, and innovative approach to leadership within organizations. As professionals engaged in policy creation, analysis, and the education of future leaders, it is imperative to articulate and underscore the distinctive role that organizational leaders play in tackling these global environmental issues (Yuliantini et al., 2021; Ojogiwa, 2021).

Organizational leaders occupy a unique position that allows them to influence not only the strategic objectives of their institutions but also the specific actions required to achieve those objectives. Leadership in the context of environmental sustainability involves setting clear, actionable goals and ensuring the allocation of adequate resources to address these goals. While it is often commendable for leaders to inspire and stimulate others to take action, the tangible allocation of resources remains a primary mechanism through which organizations demonstrate their intent to address environmental issues. For instance, committing financial, human, or technological resources to sustainability projects signals an organization's seriousness about tackling challenges such as carbon emissions, water conservation, or waste management. Though resource allocation does not guarantee success, it is an essential foundation for task accomplishment, as it establishes the operational capability to pursue environmental objectives effectively (Yuliantini et al., 2021).

Leaders also play a pivotal role in fostering commitment, driving action, and achieving results on environmental objectives. This begins with making a clear organizational commitment to sustainability, which often involves setting specific, measurable, and time-bound environmental goals. Such commitments not only provide a roadmap for action but also create accountability within the organization. For example, a commitment to achieve net-zero carbon emissions by a specific year can catalyse a series of organizational changes, including energy efficiency improvements, investment in renewable energy, and the redesign of supply chains. However, leadership extends beyond setting goals to actively engaging employees and stakeholders in the decision-making process. By involving individuals across the organization in discussions about environmental trade-offs, leaders can cultivate a shared sense of purpose and responsibility, thereby enhancing the likelihood of achieving meaningful outcomes (Ojogiwa, 2021).

Another critical aspect of leadership in environmental sustainability is the emphasis on measuring and communicating progress. Leaders must ensure that the organization's efforts are not only action-oriented but also results-driven. This requires the development and implementation of robust metrics to evaluate progress toward environmental objectives. Transparent reporting on these metrics not only builds credibility but also allows organizations to refine their strategies based on empirical evidence. For instance, regular reporting on energy consumption, waste reduction, or greenhouse gas emissions provides a clear baseline against which progress can be measured. Such transparency is essential for maintaining trust with stakeholders and demonstrating the organization's commitment to addressing global environmental problems.

Furthermore, effective leadership in environmental sustainability requires navigating complex trade-offs and ethical considerations. Environmental issues often involve competing priorities, such as balancing economic growth with ecological preservation or addressing immediate operational needs while planning for long-term sustainability. Leaders must approach these trade-offs with a commitment to ethical decision-making, ensuring that the chosen actions align with the broader goal of environmental stewardship. This is particularly important in fostering a culture of sustainability within the organization, where every employee feels empowered to contribute to environmental goals, regardless of their formal position (Yuliantini et al., 2021; Ojogiwa, 2021).

In conclusion, the challenges posed by environmental sustainability demand a multifaceted approach to leadership that goes beyond traditional management practices. A real-world example is Unilever's Sustainable Living Plan, which integrates environmental responsibility into corporate leadership, improving employee engagement and retention. Unilever's sustainability efforts have led to higher employee satisfaction, as over 80% of employees believe they contribute to a larger purpose.

Leaders must not only set objectives and allocate resources but also foster collaboration, measure progress, and navigate ethical complexities. By doing so, they can create a culture of sustainability that empowers individuals at all levels of the organization to take meaningful action. The commitment, action, and results demonstrated by organizational leaders serve as a foundation for addressing the urgent environmental challenges facing the global community. In this context, leadership is not simply about doing things right but about doing the right things to ensure a sustainable future for generations to come.

2.1. Setting Vision and Goals

Once a leader has effectively engaged others by ensuring their voices are heard and valued, the next crucial responsibility lies in setting a clear direction for the organization. This encompasses crafting a compelling vision and establishing ambitious yet attainable goals. Visionary leadership requires the ability to see beyond immediate challenges and recognize the potential for transformative change. Leaders must envision what is possible, setting the stage for meaningful progress and inspiring their teams to strive for excellence. This involves setting high expectations that challenge the team to make a significant difference in their sphere of influence and in the world at large (Aday et al., 2022; Kouzes & Posner, 2023). The leadership within India's cement industry aligns with transformational leadership principles, as seen in its ambitious sustainability goals. Cement companies have redefined business operations by implementing alternative fuels, energy-efficient production techniques, and aggressive carbon reduction targets. Leaders in this sector exemplify Kouzes & Posner's principle of 'Inspiring a Shared Vision' by engaging employees and stakeholders in sustainability-driven missions. These companies have not only reduced their carbon footprint but have also fostered an organizational culture where employees feel a sense of purpose in contributing to global sustainability efforts

Extraordinary outcomes stem from the collective capabilities, enthusiasm, and aspirations of the team, driven by a shared commitment to achieve something remarkable. Conversely, setting low or unambitious goals diminishes the team's potential and signals a lack of belief in their abilities. Unambitious goals convey mediocrity and fail to attract or retain top talent. Imagine an organization where the leader's mantra is: "We're an average team doing average work, and we expect no exceptional results." Such an attitude not only undermines morale but also stifles creativity and innovation.

On the other hand, a leader who sets high expectations and inspires a sense of purpose ignites a spark within the team, fostering a culture of excellence and shared achievement. Aspiring toward high goals does not mean ignoring the realities of challenges but embracing them as opportunities for growth and innovation. By setting and communicating ambitious goals, leaders pave the way for extraordinary outcomes, empowering their teams to transcend ordinary boundaries and achieve exceptional results.

3. LEADERSHIP STYLES AND APPROACHES IN ENVIRONMENTAL SUSTAINABILITY

While much has been written and researched on the topics of leadership and environmental sustainability individually, merging these two areas provides valuable and novel insights into the type of leadership required to address the pressing global environmental challenges confronting contemporary society. The integration of these concepts has given rise to the notion of sustainable leadership, an approach that applies not only to corporate, governance, and organizational contexts but also to broader societal and ecological domains. Sustainable leadership moves beyond the traditional traits of a leader as a problem solver, influencer, change catalyst, or moral example, emphasizing the leader's role as a steward of the global environment. This stewardship requires a long-term perspective, incorporating the principles of environmental sustainability into decision-making processes while balancing organizational success with ecological preservation (Haase, 2021; Khan et al., 2022). Sustainable leadership approaches are distinct in their dual focus on advancing an organization's financial performance and simultaneously guiding communities and broader societies toward sustainable environmental practices. Leaders who embrace this approach understand that profitability and environmental sustainability are not mutually exclusive but are, in fact, deeply interconnected. By embedding sustainability into their organizational strategies, such leaders drive innovation, reduce ecological footprints, and foster resilience in the face of climate-related risks. This dual mandate reflects a profound shift from conventional leadership paradigms, which often prioritize short-term gains, to more forward-looking approaches that consider the long-term health of the planet and its resources.

In recent years, the field of leadership research in relation to social and environmental issues has experienced significant growth and heightened interest. This development has encouraged more managers and organizational leaders to view environmental challenges not as peripheral concerns but as integral to their day-to-day responsibilities. This growing body of research underscores the need for leaders to engage actively with critical issues such as climate change, biodiversity loss, natural resource degradation, and environmental equity.

Recent studies have highlighted the impact of leadership on employee engagement and overall organizational success. Song and Suo (2025) examined how entrepreneurial leadership enhances start-up performance through internal social capital, which is crucial in fostering a collaborative and engaged workforce. Similarly, Liu et al. (2024) analyzed leadership styles in the digital economy, emphasizing their role in employee engagement. Sangperm and Chienwattanasook (2019) explored transformational leadership and its role in encouraging innovation, while Saetung (2017) discussed the influence of total quality management on management efficiency.

These findings suggest that leadership styles directly influence employee morale, job satisfaction, and productivity—elements that are equally relevant when considering environmental sustainability in the workplace. This chapter contributes to the expanding body of knowledge on leadership in environmental contexts by exploring key issues such as wildlife conservation and habitat protection, natural resource degradation and equity, and the establishment of environmental standards and justice. These areas represent some of the most urgent and complex challenges of our time, requiring leadership that is not only adaptive and innovative but also deeply committed to ethical and equitable practices. For instance, wildlife conservation and habitat protection often necessitate collaborative efforts among governments, non-governmental organizations, local communities, and private sectors. Leaders in these contexts must navigate competing interests, foster partnerships, and mobilize resources to achieve conservation goals while respecting the rights and needs of local populations.

Leadership models such as transformational and ethical leadership emphasize motivation and moral responsibility in decision-making. However, recent research highlights a growing focus on transcendental leadership, which integrates spirituality, ethics, and personal growth to drive sustainable change in organizations. There are many more styles of leadership that have their own type of distinction form others shown in (Table 1). Transcendental leaders go beyond traditional leadership by fostering deep employee engagement and aligning decision-making with long-term sustainability goals (Jedaman, Kenaphoom, & Udompan, 2022). This approach ensures that leadership is not only about achieving business outcomes but also about cultivating a values-driven organizational culture that supports both employees and environmental responsibility.

The chapter also delves into the role of leadership in establishing and upholding environmental standards and justice. Environmental justice emphasizes the fair treatment and meaningful involvement of all people, regardless of race, ethnicity, or socioeconomic status, in environmental decision-making processes. Leaders who champion environmental justice must address historical inequities, confront power imbalances, and advocate for policies that protect both the environment and the rights of disadvantaged groups.

These efforts are particularly relevant in the context of industrial activities, urban development, and climate adaptation strategies, where marginalized communities often bear the brunt of environmental harm. To provide a comprehensive perspective, this chapter examines leadership styles and approaches to environmental sustainability through two distinct bases: common and uncommon strategies employed by leaders.

Common approaches often include well-established practices such as regulatory compliance, corporate social responsibility initiatives, and public awareness campaigns. These strategies are widely recognized and implemented across various sectors, demonstrating their effectiveness in achieving incremental progress toward sustainability goals. Uncommon approaches, on the other hand, represent innovative and transformative practices that challenge conventional norms and push the boundaries of what is possible. These may include adopting circular economy principles, leveraging technology for environmental monitoring and conservation, or engaging in unconventional partnerships with indigenous communities to integrate traditional ecological knowledge into modern sustainability practices. By highlighting both common and uncommon approaches, this chapter aims to provide a nuanced understanding of how leaders can protect and manage the ecological dynamics that influence the global economy and society.

Importantly, this chapter adopts a global perspective, showcasing examples from diverse regions, including Africa, Asia, Latin America, and North America. These examples illustrate the varied ways in which leaders across different cultural, economic, and environmental contexts are addressing sustainability challenges. For instance, in Africa, leadership efforts in combating deforestation and promoting renewable energy have demonstrated the potential for transformative change in resource-constrained settings. In Asia, innovative urban planning initiatives and community-based conservation projects highlight the importance of localized leadership in addressing environmental issues. Similarly, in Latin America, indigenous leadership has played a critical role in preserving biodiversity and advocating for environmental justice. In North America, corporate leaders have increasingly prioritized sustainability as a core component of business strategy, reflecting the growing recognition of environmental issues as a critical driver of long-term success (Haase, 2021; Khan et al., 2022).

Sustainable leadership is essential for fostering long-term environmental and organizational success. While corporate leadership often emphasizes profit-driven sustainability models, educational institutions provide a unique framework for understanding strategic approaches to sustainability. Research suggests that educational administration plays a crucial role in embedding sustainability principles into decision-making, ensuring that future leaders prioritize environmental and ethical considerations (Atthakorn et al., 2024). By adopting these strategic approaches, organizations across various sectors can develop leadership models that are both socially responsible and environmentally sustainable.

In conclusion, this chapter underscores the importance of sustainable leadership as a vital framework for addressing the interconnected environmental, social, and economic challenges of our time. By examining diverse leadership styles and approaches within a global context, it aims to advance the understanding of how leaders can contribute to environmental sustainability and inspire collective action toward a more sustainable future.

Table 1. Traits of leadership styles

Leadership Style	Focus	Strengths	Limitations	Relevance to Sustainability
Transformational Leadership	Inspiring and motivating employees to exceed expectations	High engagement, innovation, and long-term vision	Can be overly idealistic; requires strong follow-through	Encourages employees to embrace sustainability through a shared vision
Ethical Leadership	Leading with integrity, fairness, and ethical principles	Promotes trust and organizational justice	May struggle with enforcing sustainability if it conflicts with business profits	Ensures corporate responsibility in environmental decision-making
Sustainable Leadership	Long-term environmental, social, and economic balance	Aligns business strategy with sustainability	Requires deep cultural change and commitment	Directly integrates sustainability into leadership practices
Servant Leadership	Prioritizing the needs of employees and stakeholders	Enhances employee well-being and community focus	Can lack decisiveness in high-pressure environments	Fosters sustainability by putting people and the planet first
Situational Leadership	Adapting leadership style based on circumstances	Flexible and responsive to challenges	Lacks a clear sustainability framework	Can be leveraged to address different environmental crises

3.1. Transformational Leadership

Is there a meaningful connection between leadership and environmental sustainability? Can we elevate this concept to the realm of overall leadership, thereby contributing to the development of a comprehensive leadership theory for society?

Undoubtedly, numerous studies have explored the intersection of these two domains, with many researchers emphasizing the role of socio-environmental responsibility as a critical component of leadership in transforming various areas of interest. If leadership is understood to influence and shape transformative processes, why not harness its potential to solidify and advance issues that are already recognized and legislated as collective imperatives? Transformational leadership, when aligned with a purpose as significant as environmental sustainability, has the capacity to foster dialogue, build consensus, and drive meaningful change within and across organizations. Leadership, in this sense, becomes a tool for shaping group behavior, clarifying objectives, and addressing shared challenges. The role of leadership in advancing environmental sustainability aligns closely with the concept of transformative leadership, which is often associated with championing positive change and achieving collective goals.

Transformational leaders possess the capacity to inspire, motivate, and guide others toward shared objectives, leveraging their influence to address pressing environmental concerns. The connection between leadership and environmental sustainability extends beyond the individual traits of leaders to encompass their ability to build and maintain collaborative efforts, establish a shared vision, and facilitate consensus among diverse stakeholders. By adopting such an approach, leaders can create environments that are conducive to innovation, problem-solving, and long-term planning—all of which are essential for addressing complex socio-environmental challenges (Suriyankietkaew et al., 2022; Hayat & Rehan, 2024). Additionally, the integration of environmental sustainability into leadership frameworks has significant implications for the broader field of leadership studies. It provides an opportunity to expand traditional models of leadership, which often focus on organizational performance and short-term gains, by incorporating a long-term, systems-oriented perspective. This perspective emphasizes the interdependence of economic, social, and environmental factors and challenges leaders to think beyond immediate outcomes. Leaders who prioritize sustainability not only drive progress within their organizations but also contribute to the broader societal shift toward ecological balance and equity.

This shift necessitates a redefinition of success, moving away from purely financial metrics to include measures of environmental and social well-being.

The coaching, consulting, and management models often associated with leadership development play a pivotal role in equipping leaders to embrace and implement sustainability initiatives. These approaches emphasize self-awareness, adaptability, and strategic thinking, enabling leaders to recognize and capitalize on opportunities for improvement within their environments.

By fostering these qualities, leadership development programs increase the likelihood of success in achieving organizational objectives while aligning these objectives with broader sustainability goals. Effective leadership, regardless of style, hinges on the leader's ability to navigate complex challenges, inspire others, and adapt to evolving circumstances. Transformational leadership, in particular, holds significant promise for advancing environmental sustainability. This style of leadership emphasizes innovation, entrepreneurship, and the proactive resolution of conflicts, positioning leaders as agents of change who can address diverse challenges effectively. Transformational leaders are uniquely suited to guide their organizations through the complexities of sustainability initiatives, leveraging their vision and influence to build consensus, foster collaboration, and drive action. Furthermore, transformational leadership transcends traditional management styles by focusing on the leader's ability to manage themselves, develop their capabilities, and align their actions with their values. This self-management aspect is critical in navigating the moral and ethical dimensions of sustainability, as leaders must consistently demonstrate integrity, accountability, and commitment to long-term goals (Suriyankietkaew et al., 2022; Hayat & Rehan, 2024).

By integrating environmental sustainability into leadership theories and practices, we can advance a more holistic understanding of what it means to lead in the 21st century. This integration underscores the importance of aligning leadership with global priorities, fostering a sense of collective responsibility, and enabling leaders to act as stewards of the planet. Ultimately, the connection between leadership and environmental sustainability is not only a reflection of contemporary challenges but also a pathway toward building a more equitable, resilient, and sustainable future for society as a whole.

4. BUILDING A CULTURE OF ENVIRONMENTAL RESPONSIBILITY WITHIN ORGANIZATIONS

We now turn to the concept of "greening" the firm, a foundational approach for emphasizing the importance of environmental responsibility in aligning organizational and societal outcomes. This framework highlights the need to adapt leader behavior to be consistent with environmental goals, particularly those that focus on the protection and preservation of the environment.

While recycling and general environmental responsibility serve as the entry points for environmental management, they represent just the beginning of a broader spectrum of sustainable practices.

Effective environmental management encompasses a range of activities, including (a) using environmentally friendly materials, (b) developing environmentally sustainable products, (c) designing production processes that minimize pollution, (d) installing equipment that is environmentally friendly, (e) avoiding practices that cause ecological damage, (f) reducing energy consumption, (g) conserving water resources, (h) implementing reduction, reuse, and recycling strategies across organizational operations, (i) adopting closed-loop systems, (j) minimizing waste and its environmental impact, and (k) encouraging stakeholders and partners to embrace environmentally sound practices.

Leadership plays a crucial role in embedding these principles into organizational culture and practices. For instance, we see strong evidence of CEO leadership driving environmental practices in industries that are inherently high in pollution and resource intensity, such as the chemical and petroleum sectors. These industries, often under significant public scrutiny and subject to high monitoring costs, have a visible incentive to adopt environmental initiatives. Leaders in these sectors are increasingly implementing measures to improve their environmental performance, both to meet regulatory requirements and to respond to public and stakeholder demands for greater accountability. On the other hand, less visible sectors, such as financial services, do not face the same level of public pressure. Consequently, firms in these industries often lack strong incentives to pursue visible environmental performance improvements, as their environmental efforts are less likely to be recognized or valued by the public. The role of business arrangements and external partnerships in advancing environmental leadership is also worth examining. In some cases, organizational commitments to environmental sustainability are inhibited by existing business models or market structures, particularly in domains like pollution prevention and voluntary efforts to exceed regulatory standards. For example, firms may resist implementing practices that go beyond legal requirements for managing released toxic chemicals due to cost concerns or competitive pressures. However, innovative and collaborative approaches can help overcome these barriers. Leaders who commit to partnerships with other firms and governmental bodies to develop negotiated environmental agreements have demonstrated the potential for significant progress. For instance, agreements targeting a 45% reduction in pollutants have been successfully analysed and implemented in certain sectors using collaborative business criteria. These partnerships illustrate how collective action, facilitated by visionary leadership, can drive environmental outcomes that exceed individual efforts or regulatory mandates. Another critical aspect of greening the firm is the integration of environmental considerations into planning processes and ongoing management systems.

Firms that excel in environmental performance often differentiate themselves through the systematic incorporation of sustainability principles into their strategic and operational planning.

This includes setting measurable environmental goals, monitoring progress, and continually refining practices to improve outcomes. A compelling example is Patagonia, whose environmental policies foster a deep sense of purpose among employees. Their sustainability-focused mission directly correlates with higher employee retention and workplace satisfaction. The company's paid activism time and use of recycled materials reflect a business model that prioritizes both environmental stewardship and employee well-being. Ultimately, the concept of greening the firm underscores the pivotal role of leadership in driving organizational transformation toward sustainability. Leaders must not only adopt environmentally sound practices within their organizations but also advocate for broader systemic changes that enable sustainable development. By leveraging their influence and fostering collaboration across industries and sectors, leaders can ensure that environmental goals are integrated into the core mission and operations of their organizations. This holistic approach, when consistently applied, has the potential to align organizational success with societal and environmental well-being, creating a future in which businesses act as stewards of the planet rather than contributors to its degradation (Shu et al., 2024; Ahsan, 2024).

4.1. Employee Engagement and Empowerment

This is an important topic and one that is, finally, gaining the recognition it so rightly deserves. As leaders and managers, we dedicate substantial thought, time, and resources to ensuring that our organizations are sustainable. We meticulously craft robust business strategies that address the significant, long-term challenges in our marketplaces. Yet, too often, we fail to fully integrate the human element into these strategies. The tangible outcomes of customer satisfaction and financial success are frequently viewed as separate from the individuals who make these achievements possible. This disconnect underscores the critical importance of how leaders engage their workforce. For an organization to truly thrive, its leaders must prioritize creating conditions that enable employees to flourish both personally and professionally. The role of leadership in bridging the gap between organizational goals and human needs has never been more vital. At the executive and corporate governance levels, we are witnessing stronger connections being forged between people, planet, and profit. The traditional focus on financial outcomes is expanding to include the well-being of employees and the broader community. To foster creativity, innovation, and diversity, leaders must build workplaces that go beyond meeting basic functional needs. These workplaces must nurture employees' aspirations for growth, both philosophical and professional, while also supporting a healthy work-life balance.

Several organizations have successfully integrated environmental sustainability initiatives that directly contribute to employee well-being. For instance, Patagonia, a leader in corporate environmental responsibility, provides employees with incentives for using public transport, supports environmental activism, and offers flexible work arrangements—leading to increased job satisfaction and lower stress levels. Similarly, Google has invested in green office spaces with natural lighting, air-purifying plants, and sustainable food programs, which have been shown to enhance employee productivity and mental well-being. In the manufacturing sector, Unilever has implemented sustainable sourcing and waste reduction programs, encouraging employees to engage in eco-friendly behaviors at work and at home, fostering a sense of purpose and reducing workplace anxiety about environmental concerns. These examples demonstrate that sustainability efforts do not just benefit the planet but also enhance employee engagement, well-being, and overall organizational success. Research shows that workplaces with natural light, greenery, and eco-conscious spaces enhance focus and job satisfaction, reinforcing the link between sustainability and employee engagement. On a broader scale, organizations must embrace their roles as integral parts of the communities in which they operate, rather than existing as isolated entities. Businesses hold tremendous potential to enrich local economies and improve the quality of life in surrounding areas. Some companies excel at this, channeling wealth and resources into their communities, while others lag behind, failing to recognize the reciprocal benefits of such engagement. By contributing to the social and economic fabric of their environments, organizations can generate goodwill and foster deeper connections with stakeholders. This aligns seamlessly with the aspirations of policymakers and politicians who strive to elevate the quality of life for all citizens. At an even more fundamental level, corporations bear a philosophical and moral responsibility to contribute to the prosperity of their employees and the communities they touch. This obligation goes beyond mere economic transactions; it is rooted in the recognition that businesses have a duty to enhance human well-being. Leaders must recognize that when organizations adopt this ethos, they do more than just meet their ethical obligations—they create a culture of purpose and meaning. This approach is not just common sense; it is also supported by evidence. Research consistently shows that employees are more engaged, motivated, and loyal to companies that prioritize their well-being and operate with a sense of social responsibility. Ultimately, this philosophy reflects a profound truth: businesses are not just engines of economic activity but are also communities in their own right. Leaders who embrace this perspective empower their organizations to thrive in a way that is sustainable, ethical, and deeply connected to the people and places they serve. By fostering an environment where creativity, diversity, and compassion can flourish, businesses can achieve enduring success that benefits not just their bottom lines but also their people and the planet. As we move forward, let us build organizations that are truly aligned with these principles, creating a legacy of prosperity for all (Abid et al., 2021; Joel and Oguanobi, 2024).

5. ETHICAL LEADERSHIP AND ENVIRONMENTAL DECISION MAKING

Human activity continues to leave a profound imprint on the environment, driving significant and often irreversible changes. The scale and nature of humanity's immediate and long-term impacts on ecosystems have spurred vigorous debate, particularly about the role organizations play in these changes and the ethical responsibilities they bear as a result.

In this context, leadership emerges as a pivotal factor within organizational settings, as leaders hold the capacity to shape behaviors, influence decision-making, and ultimately determine the extent of an organization's environmental footprint. Leadership decisions are often the critical juncture at which ethical considerations and organizational actions converge, making the role of ethical leadership indispensable in the broader efforts toward environmental sustainability.

As stewards of both organizational and societal outcomes, leaders bear the responsibility of fostering ethical behaviors that align with long-term ecological and social goals.

Research in this area has explored how leaders themselves become more ethically grounded and how external pressures—especially from their followers—compel them to lead from a moral and principled standpoint. However, there remains a disconnect between theoretical understandings of ethical leadership and its practical application within organizations. Too often, the decline of ethical leadership stems from a disproportionate focus on financial outcomes at the expense of social and environmental considerations. This tension between profitability and sustainability is compounded by growing societal expectations for organizations to fulfill their corporate environmental responsibilities. Navigating these complex responsibilities requires leaders to integrate principles of social and environmental sustainability into the core of their decision-making processes.

One of the most critical ways leaders can demonstrate ethical behavior is by driving group-level change within organizations. Collaborative efforts within groups are not only foundational to sound ethical decision-making but also serve as a mechanism for embedding sustainability into organizational culture. Group dynamics allow for the sharing of diverse perspectives, fostering innovative solutions to environmental challenges while reinforcing accountability. In this way, ethical leadership transcends individual decisions and becomes a collective effort rooted in long-term stewardship. High-quality decision-making processes that incorporate ethical and environmental considerations can lead to stronger relationships with stakeholders, improved governance practices, and sustained financial performance over time. By embracing these principles, organizations can align their operations with societal expectations, promoting a balance between profitability, social responsibility, and ecological preservation.

Ultimately, the integration of ethical leadership within the framework of environmental sustainability offers a pathway toward more responsible and impactful decision-making. Leaders who prioritize these values not only contribute to the resilience of their organizations but also help lay the groundwork for a more sustainable and equitable future for society at large (López-Cabarcos et al., 2022; Specchia et al., 2021).

6. THE IMPORTANCE OF COLLABORATION AND PARTNERSHIPS IN ENVIRONMENTAL LEADERSHIP

The United Nations Sustainable Development Goals (UN SDGs) underscore the importance of "partnership" and "collaboration" as critical mechanisms for achieving global goals.

These principles highlight that the complexity and interconnectedness of global challenges require collective efforts rather than isolated actions. Harnessing the global capacity for collaboration means that partnerships will increasingly serve as the foundation for addressing challenges at local, regional, and national levels.

Leaders across the spectrum must therefore possess the ability to engage with diverse groups of stakeholders, encompassing a wide range of sectors, perspectives, and organizational objectives. Addressing such multifaceted challenges requires leaders to adopt a holistic understanding of the issues at hand while fostering a culture that values inclusivity, mutual respect, and collaboration. This necessitates the ability to focus on shared goals and to cultivate partnerships that transcend traditional boundaries to find innovative and sustainable solutions. Leadership in this context involves more than simply acknowledging the value of collaboration; it demands active engagement in creating environments where diverse viewpoints are not only welcome but are seen as essential for effective problem-solving. Achieving measurable commitments by corporations toward environmental and social sustainability reflects the power of these unique collaborations. It demonstrates that leaders at all levels can, and often do, unite around shared values and the pursuit of common global and public interests. In doing so, they drive meaningful progress on sustainability indicators, fostering a balance between economic prosperity, environmental stewardship, and social equity. These actions exemplify the transformative potential of leadership rooted in collaborative and inclusive principles, highlighting the critical role leaders play in shaping organizational contributions to global sustainability goals. A particularly significant dimension of this leadership is thought leadership, which moves beyond the surface-level rhetoric frequently found in boardroom discussions and public forums. It calls for tangible action and meaningful transformation, grounded in commitments that align with broader sustainability goals. On a voluntary basis, many organizations are advancing the narrative that those who commit to sustainability reporting and continuous improvement in this area are setting themselves apart in meaningful ways.

These organizations demonstrate a genuine differentiation, not just in terms of their operational practices but also in how they engage with stakeholders and communicate their long-term vision. For industry leaders, this commitment to sustainability becomes an expectation not only for their organizations but also for others in their supply chains. The benefits of such approaches extend beyond reputational gains, with measurable financial and operational advantages. Good corporate governance, often emphasized by sustainability-oriented organizations, is increasingly valued by investors as an indicator of long-term resilience and strategic foresight. At the same time, sustainability initiatives frequently lead to lower resource consumption and waste management costs, achieved through improvements in processes, operations, and supply chain efficiency.

For example, studies reveal that organizations in North America alone have identified operating savings exceeding $100 billion through sustainability-driven initiatives. These savings are accompanied by significant environmental benefits, including the conservation of nearly ten trillion litres of water and a reduction in coal usage by approximately 55 billion tons. These achievements demonstrate the tangible outcomes that can arise from aligning corporate practices with sustainability goals, highlighting the role of innovative leadership in driving these advancements. In essence, the alignment of corporate strategies with global sustainability objectives is a testament to the potential of partnerships and collaborations to create lasting value. Leaders who champion these efforts are instrumental in fostering environments where shared purpose, inclusivity, and innovation converge to address pressing environmental and social challenges. By prioritizing sustainability and embedding it into the fabric of their organizational cultures, these leaders not only contribute to the achievement of the UN SDGs but also set a precedent for others to follow. Their work underscores the idea that true leadership is not defined solely by profit margins or short-term gains but by the ability to inspire collective action toward a sustainable future for all (Liu et al., 2022; Pless et al., 2021).

6.1. Stakeholder Engagement

Equitable resource management stands as a central pillar of sustainable development and ethical organizational practice, particularly in contexts where public or common-pool resources are at play. In exploring this theme, it becomes clear that workers, as a distinct stakeholder group, and marginalized or vulnerable populations, as broader and more diffuse categories, must each be considered as integral participants in resource allocation and governance. Workers hold both instrumental and intrinsic rights to partake in the benefits derived from economic activities, especially those reliant on resources that are shared or held in trust for the collective good. These rights are not only rooted in notions of fairness but also derive from broader ethical and practical considerations that emphasize the importance of inclusivity and shared prosperity in the management of limited and often contested resources.

However, the case studies reveal a recurring tension between the dominant narratives framing public resources as mere instruments of profit generation and alternative perspectives that advocate for their equitable use and stewardship. The stakeholders most often empowered by the dominant narrative—typically corporate actors or politically influential entities—tend to wield significant power in shaping resource governance frameworks. Their discourse, centred around maximizing profit, often marginalizes other voices, particularly those advocating for the rights of workers and vulnerable populations.

Leaders seeking to challenge this narrative rarely do so unilaterally, as the entrenched structures supporting the status quo are formidable. Instead, meaningful progress often requires the formation of collective action coalitions, such as public-private partnerships, where diverse stakeholders collaborate to redefine the terms of engagement and establish frameworks that prioritize equity and sustainability.

Even in cases where secure access rights to common-pool resources exist, particularly in nonmarket or cooperative organizations, employees may still face barriers to fully realizing the use value of these resources. In some instances, employees may advocate for rights analogous to those of shareholders, seeking to share in the economic and social benefits generated from the sustainable utilization of shared resources. This advocacy is often met with resistance, particularly when dominant stakeholders perceive such assertions as threats to their control or profitability. The mere existence of vertically integrated resource control often serves as a justification for reinforcing dominant discourses, as it allows powerful stakeholders to argue that sharing access or benefits could jeopardize future resource availability or competitiveness. This framing is frequently used to discourage resource-sharing initiatives, even when evidence suggests that equitable access could enhance overall resource sustainability and societal well-being.

The challenges of equitable resource management are further compounded by the broader implications of worker wellness and holistic economic justice. Organizations and leaders must recognize that the well-being of workers extends beyond mere income or financial gain. While equitable resource sharing may address some aspects of economic justice, it is equally important to consider the broader dimensions of wellness, including access to healthcare, education, and safe working conditions. Leaders in cooperative or nonmarket organizations, in particular, face the dual challenge of ensuring equitable resource allocation while addressing the interconnected needs of their workforce. This requires a comprehensive approach that views workers not just as economic actors but as individuals with complex and multifaceted needs.

Moreover, the resistance to equitable resource sharing is often rooted in deeper systemic issues, including power imbalances and entrenched social hierarchies. Dominant stakeholders, particularly those benefiting from vertically integrated resource control, may use anticompetitive arguments to discredit efforts at resource-sharing, framing such initiatives as threats to market stability or future resource access. These narratives are often bolstered by structural advantages that enable dominant actors to maintain their control over critical resources while limiting the ability of less powerful stakeholders, such as workers and marginalized communities, to assert their rights. Overcoming these challenges requires leaders to adopt a nuanced and strategic approach, leveraging partnerships, advocacy, and evidence-based practices to shift the discourse toward one that prioritizes equity and sustainability.

In addressing these challenges, the role of collective action becomes increasingly significant. Public-private partnerships, multi-stakeholder initiatives, and cooperative models offer promising avenues for advancing equitable resource management. By bringing together diverse perspectives and pooling resources, these coalitions can challenge dominant narratives and create alternative frameworks that prioritize shared benefits and long-term sustainability. Beyond its impact on environmental sustainability, effective environmental leadership has profound implications for employee well-being. Organizations that actively promote sustainable practices foster a workplace culture rooted in ethical responsibility, collaboration, and shared purpose. This, in turn, enhances employee morale, reduces workplace stress, and increases job satisfaction. Employees feel more engaged and fulfilled when they work for organizations that align with their values, leading to improved mental health and overall organizational success. Moving forward, businesses must recognize that sustainability is not just an environmental priority but a critical factor in building resilient, motivated, and high-performing workforce

By fostering a culture of environmental responsibility, organizations can enhance employee morale, job satisfaction, and overall mental well-being. Employees who work for environmentally conscious organizations experience greater purpose, reduced stress, and a deeper sense of alignment between personal and corporate values. Moreover, environmentally responsible companies attract and retain top talent, improving long-term organizational stability. Leaders must recognize that prioritizing sustainability is not just a corporate responsibility but a strategic investment in both human and environmental capital. By embracing environmental leadership, organizations can create a virtuous cycle of positive impact, benefiting both the planet and its people. It is time for leaders to integrate sustainability into their core strategies—not just as an ethical obligation, but as a pathway to fostering healthier, more engaged, and more productive workforces."

Ultimately, equitable resource management is about more than just redistributing economic gains—it is about fostering a culture of shared responsibility and stewardship that recognizes the intrinsic value of workers, marginalized groups, and the broader community. Leaders who embrace this perspective have the potential to drive transformative change, challenging entrenched power dynamics and advancing a vision of sustainability that is both inclusive and holistic. As highlighted by scholars such as De Haas (2021) and Fakunle (2021), the path to equitable resource management is fraught with challenges, but it also offers immense opportunities for creating more just and sustainable organizational practices. By centring the needs and rights of workers and vulnerable populations, leaders can help build systems that not only sustain resources but also empower individuals and communities to thrive.

7. MEASURING AND EVALUATING LEADERSHIP IMPACT ON ENVIRONMENTAL SUSTAINABILITY

Throughout this book, we have delved into leadership by examining the intricate relationships between leaders, followers, and the contexts in which they interact. Our exploration has been shaped by the time-bound episodes of human interaction and has sought to identify best practices across industrial, societal, and geopolitical dimensions. This work is particularly pertinent in an era defined by rapid changes, complex global challenges, and the pressing need for adaptability in leadership practices. Recent events, including economic upheavals, social transformations, and geopolitical tensions, have highlighted the significance of revisiting our central research question: Are there specific sets of leadership practices that are most likely to foster desired development and change within particular contexts? The urgency of answering this question lies in its implications for advancing both theoretical understanding and practical applications of leadership in today's world.

One of the most critical aspects of leadership lies in its ability to measure, monitor, evaluate, and report on outcomes. Leadership is not merely about envisioning change or inspiring action; it is also deeply rooted in the capacity to assess the effectiveness of interventions and strategies in achieving desired results. The process of evaluation and reporting ensures accountability and transparency, offering a window into the mechanisms that drive success or failure. For practitioners, this ability fosters continuous learning and improvement, while for researchers and observers, it provides a robust framework for assessing the value of different leadership practices. Standardization in measurement and consistency in reporting are fundamental components of this process, enabling leaders to provide meaningful insights into their actions and decisions.

By adhering to established reporting standards, organizations and leaders can ensure that their efforts are evaluated in a manner that is both objective and comparable across time and contexts.

Transparency, facilitated by rigorous evaluation and reporting, is indispensable to the work of leadership. It is through transparency that leaders can build trust with their teams, stakeholders, and the wider community. Trust, in turn, is a cornerstone of effective leadership, as it creates an environment where collaboration, innovation, and collective action can flourish. Moreover, transparency enables practitioners to identify areas of improvement, learn from both successes and failures, and adapt their strategies to meet evolving challenges. This iterative process of learning and adaptation is central to the concept of leadership as a dynamic and context-dependent practice. Leadership is not a static quality or a one-size-fits-all approach; it is a continuous journey of growth, reflection, and refinement, guided by the principles of accountability and evidence-based decision-making.

Evaluation plays a multifaceted role in leadership, encompassing cross-sectional, longitudinal, and multidimensional comparisons. Cross-sectional evaluations allow leaders to assess the effectiveness of their practices at a given point in time, providing a snapshot of performance and outcomes. Longitudinal evaluations, on the other hand, track changes and progress over time, offering valuable insights into the sustainability and long-term impact of leadership initiatives. Multidimensional evaluations consider the interplay of various factors, such as organizational capacity, external partnerships, and societal influences, to provide a holistic understanding of leadership effectiveness. Together, these forms of evaluation create a comprehensive framework for analysing and improving leadership practices, ensuring that they are responsive to the complexities and nuances of their specific contexts.

Feedback loops are a critical component of the evaluation process, serving as a bridge between assessment and action. By integrating regular feedback into their decision-making processes, leaders can identify emerging trends, anticipate potential challenges, and make informed adjustments to their strategies. Feedback loops also foster a culture of openness and collaboration, where stakeholders are encouraged to share their perspectives and contribute to the decision-making process. This participatory approach enhances the legitimacy and effectiveness of leadership, as it ensures that decisions are grounded in diverse viewpoints and are aligned with the needs and aspirations of the broader community.

Formative and summative evaluations represent two complementary approaches to assessing leadership practices. Formative evaluation focuses on identifying areas for improvement during the implementation of a policy, program, or project. It provides leaders with actionable insights that can be used to refine their strategies and enhance their effectiveness in real time. For example, a formative evaluation might reveal that a leadership initiative is facing resistance from key stakeholders due to a lack of communication or transparency.

Armed with this information, leaders can take corrective actions, such as improving stakeholder engagement or providing additional resources to address concerns. Summative evaluation, on the other hand, takes a more comprehensive view, assessing the overall impact of a leadership initiative after its completion. It integrates data from various sources to evaluate outcomes in comparison to the preexisting situation and the intended objectives. Summative evaluations are particularly valuable for generating knowledge about the long-term effects of leadership practices, as they provide a basis for understanding what works, why it works, and under what conditions it is most effective.

The integration of formative and summative evaluations into leadership practices supports a culture of evidence-based decision-making. This approach enables leaders to balance short-term priorities with long-term goals, ensuring that their actions are both effective and sustainable. It also fosters accountability, as leaders are required to demonstrate the impact of their decisions and justify their use of resources. In an era where public trust in institutions is often fragile, the ability to provide credible and transparent evidence of leadership effectiveness is more important than ever. Evaluation and reporting serve as powerful tools for building and maintaining this trust, as they offer a tangible demonstration of a leader's commitment to ethical and responsible governance.

Effective leadership in environmental sustainability must be measurable to ensure accountability and progress. Organizations use sustainability KPIs to evaluate leadership impact on both environmental (Table.2) and employee well-being. Some commonly used KPIs include:

1. Environmental Metrics
   - Carbon Emissions Reduction – Percentage decrease in CO_2 emissions per unit of production.
   - Energy Efficiency Improvement – Reduction in energy consumption per output unit (e.g., kWh per ton of cement in the cement industry).
   - Waste Diversion Rate – Percentage of waste materials reused or recycled instead of landfilled.
   - Water Usage Efficiency – Reduction in water consumption per operational cycle.
2. Employee Well-being and Engagement Metrics
   - Sustainability Participation Rate – Percentage of employees engaged in green initiatives (e.g., sustainability committees, eco-training programs).

- Job Satisfaction Scores – Surveys assessing employee morale and motivation in environmentally responsible firms.
- Workplace Stress Reduction – Reduction in reported workplace stress levels due to green work environments (e.g., biophilic office spaces, remote work policies).

3. Corporate Social Responsibility (CSR) and Sustainable Development Goals (SDGs)Alignment

Table 2. Evaluating leadership via sustainability KPIs

SDG Goal	Relevant Sustainability Leadership Action
SDG 7: Affordable & Clean Energy	Transition to renewable energy sources in operations.
SDG 12: Responsible Consumption & Production	Reduction in waste generation & circular economy adoption.
SDG 13: Climate Action	Implementation of carbon-neutral strategies & policy advocacy.

Leadership clusters—encompassing policies, programs, projects, specific leaders, internal organizational capabilities, and external partnerships—are among the key elements that can be evaluated and improved through systematic assessment. For instance, evaluating a leadership policy might involve examining its alignment with organizational goals, its responsiveness to stakeholder needs, and its impact on key performance indicators. Similarly, evaluating a leadership program or project might involve assessing its implementation, outcomes, and scalability. By applying these principles to individual leaders, organizations can identify strengths and areas for development, enabling targeted interventions that enhance leadership capacity at both individual and collective levels. Internal organizational capability and external partnerships are particularly important dimensions of leadership evaluation. Internal capability refers to the organization's capacity to support and sustain effective leadership practices, including factors such as culture, structure, and resources. External partnerships, on the other hand, highlight the importance of collaboration and collective action in addressing complex challenges. Evaluating these dimensions requires a nuanced understanding of the interdependencies and synergies that exist between organizations and their external environments. For example, a successful partnership might be characterized by mutual trust, shared goals, and effective communication, while a less effective partnership might suffer from misaligned priorities or a lack of accountability. By evaluating these factors, leaders can identify opportunities to strengthen their partnerships and enhance their overall impact.

Ultimately, the ability to measure, monitor, evaluate, and report on results is not just a technical skill; it is a fundamental aspect of effective leadership (Table 3&4). It enables leaders to navigate the complexities of their roles, respond to changing circumstances, and drive meaningful change. It also provides a framework for understanding and improving the practice of leadership itself, offering valuable insights that can inform future research and practice. As emphasized by Smith et al. (2022) and Di et al. (2022), the integration of evaluation and reporting into leadership practices is essential for achieving transparency, accountability, and sustained impact. By embracing these principles, leaders can ensure that their actions are not only effective but also ethical, equitable, and aligned with the broader goals of societal and organizational progress.

1. Sustainability Balanced Scorecard (SBSC): The Sustainability Balanced Scorecard (SBSC) extends the traditional BSC framework by adding sustainability dimensions. It evaluates leadership across four perspectives:

Table 3. Using reports in evalucation

Perspective	Key Focus	Metrics for Evaluation
Financial	Cost savings from sustainability efforts	ROI on green investments, energy cost reduction %
Customer & Stakeholder	Reputation & brand trust	CSR rankings, employee & consumer sustainability perception surveys
Internal Processes	Sustainable operations & leadership influence	Waste reduction %, carbon footprint tracking, % of employees in green initiatives
Learning & Growth	Employee engagement & sustainability innovation	Sustainability training participation, green R&D investment, leadership sustainability scores

2. GRI Standards for Sustainability Leadership Reporting

The Global Reporting Initiative (GRI) provides an internationally recognized framework for sustainability reporting. Key GRI indicators for evaluating leadership impact include:

- GRI 305 – Emissions: Leadership-driven policies to cut GHG emissions.
- GRI 403 – Occupational Health & Safety: Impact of green workspaces on employee well-being.
- GRI 404 – Training & Education: Sustainability leadership development programs.

- GRI 413 – Local Community Impact: Leadership's role in CSR & community sustainability.

3. ESG Criteria for Leadership Assessment: Organizations can evaluate leadership impact through Environmental, Social, and Governance (ESG) metrics, which investors and stakeholders widely use.

Table 4. Sustainability leadership reporting

Dimension	Evaluation Focus	Example Metrics
Environmental (E)	Carbon footprint, sustainability initiatives	CO_2 reduction %, waste management efficiency
Social (S)	Employee well-being, diversity & inclusion	Job satisfaction surveys, employee health index
Governance (G)	Ethical leadership, compliance with green regulations	Board-level sustainability policies, ESG compliance ratings

In conclusion, the journey of leadership is one of continuous learning and adaptation, guided by the principles of evaluation, accountability, and evidence-based decision-making. Through the systematic assessment of leadership practices, leaders can identify what works, why it works, and how it can be improved. This process of reflection and refinement is essential for navigating the complexities of today's world and for driving meaningful and lasting change. As we have explored throughout this book, leadership is not a static quality but a dynamic and evolving practice, rooted in the relationships between leaders, followers, and contexts. Future research should also examine the psychological and behavioral impacts of environmental leadership on employees. Studies could explore how eco-friendly workplace initiatives influence job satisfaction, stress reduction, and mental health outcomes. Additionally, longitudinal research could assess whether sustainability-driven organizations experience lower burnout rates and higher employee engagement over time. Another key area of exploration is the role of leadership communication in fostering an environmentally conscious workplace culture that enhances employee well-being. Understanding these relationships would help refine leadership strategies that maximize both sustainability and workforce well-being.

8. CASE STUDIES OF SUCCESSFUL ENVIRONMENTAL LEADERSHIP INITIATIVES

The Indian cement industry provides a compelling example of environmental leadership in action, offering valuable insights into how industrial sectors can embrace sustainable practices while maintaining competitiveness and growth. In recent years, a majority of Indian cement producers have taken significant strides toward improving their energy efficiency and reducing their environmental impact. This transformation has been driven by a combination of regulatory pressures, rising stakeholder expectations, and a growing recognition of the long-term benefits of sustainability. Indian cement companies have invested in modern, emissions-efficient kiln lines, either by upgrading their existing facilities or purchasing more advanced equipment. These efforts represent a significant commitment to reducing greenhouse gas emissions, optimizing resource use, and addressing broader environmental concerns.

A key component of this shift has been the focus on improving combustion practices, which play a critical role in determining the energy efficiency and emissions profile of cement manufacturing. By adopting best practices in combustion, many Indian cement companies have been able to reduce their fuel consumption and cut down on harmful emissions, including carbon dioxide (CO_2) and particulate matter. Additionally, several companies have embraced innovative fuel strategies, such as installing systems to utilize waste-derived or tire-derived fuels. This approach not only helps to reduce dependency on conventional fossil fuels but also addresses waste management challenges by repurposing materials that would otherwise contribute to landfill burdens. These initiatives exemplify how the cement industry is leveraging technology and innovation to achieve dual benefits: improving operational efficiency while advancing environmental sustainability.

Air pollution control technologies have also been a focal point for the industry's environmental leadership efforts. Many Indian cement producers have installed and optimized advanced air pollution control systems, such as electrostatic precipitators, baghouses, and scrubbers, to reduce emissions of particulate matter and other pollutants. These systems are designed to capture and neutralize harmful emissions, ensuring compliance with increasingly stringent environmental regulations. The adoption of such technologies not only improves air quality in the surrounding communities but also enhances the corporate social responsibility (CSR) profile of these companies. By taking proactive steps to mitigate their environmental footprint, Indian cement companies are demonstrating their commitment to sustainable development and responsible corporate behaviour.

However, the industry's leadership in environmental sustainability extends beyond these technological upgrades. Several leading cement companies in India have taken a broader and more strategic approach to sustainability by focusing on in-process demand reduction. This involves systematically reducing the utilization of raw materials, minimizing associated emissions, and improving process efficiencies throughout the production cycle. In-process demand reduction is an important environmental leadership action because it allows companies to increase their output without increasing kiln feed requirements. By optimizing resource utilization, these companies can simultaneously reduce their environmental impacts and enhance their operational flexibility. The freed-up process capacity can then be reallocated to meet growing customer demands, thereby driving profitability and competitiveness in the marketplace.

The net effect of these measures is significant. By adopting in-process demand reduction strategies, Indian cement companies are achieving a more sustainable balance between production and resource utilization. This approach reduces the extraction and consumption of finite natural resources, cuts down on waste generation, and lowers overall emissions. It also positions these companies as leaders in the global cement industry, setting benchmarks for sustainable practices that can be emulated by others. These efforts highlight the potential for industries to achieve environmental and economic goals simultaneously, demonstrating that sustainability is not a trade-off but rather a pathway to long-term success.

In addition to technological and process innovations, the Indian cement industry has also embraced grassroots-focused environmental initiatives. These industry-wide programs represent a unique and innovative model for integrated stakeholder partnerships. By collaborating with local communities, government agencies, and other stakeholders, Indian cement companies are addressing environmental challenges at the grassroots level. For example, programs aimed at afforestation, water conservation, and community-based waste management have not only provided substantial environmental benefits but also enhanced the reputation and CSR image of participating companies. Such initiatives showcase the power of collective action and multi-sector collaboration in driving meaningful change. They also provide a template for other industries seeking to align their operations with the principles of sustainability and social responsibility.

The grassroots approach to environmental leadership is particularly noteworthy for its emphasis on inclusivity and local engagement. By involving local stakeholders in the design and implementation of environmental projects, Indian cement companies are ensuring that these initiatives are responsive to the needs and priorities of the communities they serve. This participatory approach fosters a sense of ownership and accountability among stakeholders, increasing the likelihood of long-term success. Moreover, it demonstrates that environmental leadership is not limited to corporate boardrooms or high-level policy discussions; it is a shared responsibility that requires the active involvement of all sectors of society.

The pioneering efforts of the Indian cement industry are also evident in their quest for cleaner production technologies. Companies are investing in research and development to identify and implement innovative solutions that reduce environmental impacts while enhancing process efficiency. For instance, advancements in alternative cementitious materials, such as fly ash and slag, are helping to reduce the carbon footprint of cement production. Similarly, initiatives to improve the recyclability of cement constituents are opening up new opportunities for circular economy practices. These innovations not only contribute to environmental sustainability but also provide practical examples of capable corporate environmental leadership that can inspire other industries to follow suit.

Another significant aspect of the industry's environmental leadership is its focus on reducing energy consumption and optimizing resource use. Energy efficiency measures, such as waste heat recovery systems and energy-efficient motors, are helping companies to lower their energy costs and reduce greenhouse gas emissions. These measures are particularly important in the context of India's growing energy demand and the need to transition to a low-carbon economy. By demonstrating the economic and environmental benefits of energy efficiency, the cement industry is setting an example for other energy-intensive sectors to adopt similar practices.

The Indian cement industry case study highlights how sustainable leadership transforms traditional industries by implementing eco-friendly practices and reducing carbon footprints. A similar approach is evident in the high-tech sector, where leadership must balance innovation with sustainability. Research on high-tech enterprises in Guangxi Province reveals that sustainable leadership enhances long-term business resilience by integrating green strategies into core business models (Lyu, Horadal, Sawangcharoen, & Teekasap, 2024). These findings suggest that regardless of industry, leadership in sustainability is a key driver of competitive advantage, innovation, and employee commitment.

In conclusion, the Indian cement industry's environmental leadership is developing at a rapid pace, driven by a combination of regulatory pressures, stakeholder expectations, and a commitment to sustainability. By investing in modern technologies, improving process efficiencies, and adopting innovative fuel and resource strategies, Indian cement companies are setting new benchmarks for environmental stewardship. Their efforts are not only reducing environmental impacts but also enhancing manufacturing profitability and production capacity. Moreover, the industry's grassroots-focused initiatives and collaborative partnerships provide a valuable model for integrated stakeholder engagement and multi-sector collaboration. As these companies continue to push the boundaries of cleaner production technologies and sustainable practices, they are proving that environmental leadership is both an ethical imperative and a business opportunity. The Indian cement industry stands as a shining example of how industrial sectors can lead the way toward a more sustainable and equitable future, offering lessons that are relevant not only to the global cement industry but also to other sectors striving to balance economic growth with environmental responsibility.

REFERENCES

Atthakorn, S., Kaiyanan, C., Phoorisophon, T., Ludpa, Y., Seti, S., Lavong, A., & Pliankham, P. (2024). Strategic approaches in educational administration and management for advancing sustainable development. *Journal of Education and Learning Reviews*, *1*(3), 21–32. DOI: 10.60027/jelr.2024.796

Begum, S., Ashfaq, M., Xia, E., & Awan, U. (2022). Does green transformational leadership lead to green innovation? The role of green thinking and creative process engagement. [wiley.com]. *Business Strategy and the Environment*, *31*(1), 580–597.

Aftab, J., Abid, N., Sarwar, H., & Veneziani, M. (2022). Environmental ethics, green innovation, and sustainable performance: Exploring the role of environmental leadership and environmental strategy. [HTML]. *Journal of Cleaner Production*.

Jedaman, P., Kenaphoom, S., & Udompan, A. (2022). Transcendental leadership in leader's strategies management under the 21st-century dynamics era. *Interdisciplinary Academic and Research Journal*, *2*(3), 27–44.

Lyu, G., Horadal, P., Sawangcharoen, K., & Teekasap, S. (2024). Leadership for sustainable growth of high-tech enterprises in Guangxi Province. *International Journal of Sociologies and Anthropologies Science Reviews*, *4*(6), 139–150. DOI: 10.60027/ijsasr.2024.4777

Ojogiwa, O. T. (2021). The crux of strategic leadership for a transformed public sector management in Nigeria. [sobiad.org]. *International Journal of Business and Management Studies*, *13*(1), 83–96.

Aday, J. S., Heifets, B. D., Pratscher, S. D., Bradley, E., Rosen, R., & Woolley, J. D. (2022). Great Expectations: Recommendations for improving the methodological rigor of psychedelic clinical trials. [nih.gov]. *Psychopharmacology*, *239*(6), 1989–2010.

Kouzes, J. M. & Posner, B. Z. (2023). The leadership challenge: How to make extraordinary things happen in organizations. cjpl.org

Haase, D. (2021). Integrating Ecosystem Services, Green Infrastructure and Nature-Based Solutions—New Perspectives in Sustainable Urban Land Management: Combining Knowledge About Urban Nature for Action. Sustainable Land Management in a European Context: A Co-Design Approach, 305-318. oapen.org

Khan, I., Zakari, A., Zhang, J., Dagar, V., & Singh, S. (2022). … trilemma energy balance, clean energy transitions, and economic expansion in the midst of environmental sustainability: New insights from three trilemma leadership. [HTML]. *Energy*.

Sahoo, N., Kumar, A., & Samsher, . (2022). Review on energy conservation and emission reduction approaches for cement industry. [HTML]. *Environmental Development, 44*, 100767. DOI: 10.1016/j.envdev.2022.100767

Shu, Y., Zhuang, X., Ying, R., & Xu, G. (2024). … Pressure and the Integration of Corporate Environmental and Financial Performance: Empirical Evidence from Listed Companies in Heavily Polluting Industries in…. Sustainability. mdpi.com

Ahsan, M. J. (2024). Green leadership and innovation: Catalysts for environmental performance in Italian manufacturing. [HTML]. *The International Journal of Organizational Analysis.*

Abid, G., Arya, B., Arshad, A., Ahmed, S., & Farooqi, S. (2021). Positive personality traits and self-leadership in sustainable organizations: Mediating influence of thriving and moderating role of proactive personality. [HTML]. *Sustainable Production and Consumption, 25*, 299–311.

Joel, O. T., & Oguanobi, V. U. (2024). Leadership and management in high-growth environments: Effective strategies for the clean energy sector. [fepbl.com]. *International Journal of Management & Entrepreneurship Research, 6*(5), 1423–1440.

López-Cabarcos, M. Á., Vázquez-Rodríguez, P., & Quiñoá-Piñeiro, L. M. (2022). An approach to employees' job performance through work environmental variables and leadership behaviours. [sciencedirect.com]. *Journal of Business Research, 140*, 361–369.

Smith, H. A., Besunder, J. B., Betters, K. A., Johnson, P. N., Srinivasan, V., Stormorken, A., & Berkenbosch, J. W. (2022). 2022 Society of Critical Care Medicine clinical practice guidelines on prevention and management of pain, agitation, neuromuscular blockade, and delirium in critically ill pediatric patients with consideration of the ICU environment and early mobility. [stonybrookmedicine.edu]. *Pediatric Critical Care Medicine, 23*(2), e74–e110.

Di Maio, M., Basch, E., Denis, F., Fallowfield, L. J., Ganz, P. A., & Howell, D.ESMO Guidelines Committee. (2022). The role of patient-reported outcome measures in the continuum of cancer clinical care: ESMO Clinical Practice Guideline. [sciencedirect.com]. *Annals of Oncology : Official Journal of the European Society for Medical Oncology, 33*(9), 878–892.

Ahmed, M., Bashar, I., Alam, S. T., Wasi, A. I., Jerin, I., Khatun, S., & Rahman, M. (2021). An overview of Asian cement industry: Environmental impacts, research methodologies and mitigation measures. [HTML]. *Sustainable Production and Consumption, 28*, 1018–1039.

Specchia, M. L., Cozzolino, M. R., Carini, E., Di Pilla, A., Galletti, C., Ricciardi, W., & Damiani, G. (2021). Leadership styles and nurses' job satisfaction. Results of a systematic review. [mdpi.com]. *International Journal of Environmental Research and Public Health, 18*(4), 1552.

Liu, B. F., Shi, D., Lim, J. R., Islam, K., Edwards, A. L., & Seeger, M. (2022). When crises hit home: How US higher education leaders navigate values during uncertain times. [springer.com]. *Journal of Business Ethics, 179*(2), 353–368.

Pless, N. M., Sengupta, A., Wheeler, M. A., & Maak, T. (2021). Responsible Leadership and the Reflective CEO: Resolving Stakeholder Conflict by Imagining What Could be done. Journal of Business Ethics. springer.com

De Haas, H. (2021). A theory of migration: the aspirations-capabilities framework. Comparative migration studies. springer.com

Fakunle, O. (2021). Developing a framework for international students' rationales for studying abroad, beyond economic factors. Policy Futures in Education. sagepub.com

Suriyankietkaew, S., Krittayaruangroj, K., & Iamsawan, N. (2022). Sustainable Leadership practices and competencies of SMEs for sustainability and resilience: A community-based social enterprise study. Sustainability. mdpi.com

Hayat, I. & Rehan, Q. (2024). Investigating The Roles of Pakistani Private Secondary School Teachers and Principals as Environmental Sustainable Leaders. Jahan-e-Tahqeeq. jahan-e-tahqeeq.com

Yuliantini, T., Daru, A. S. I. H., Sudiro, A., Apriadi, I., Yuniarinto, A., Suryadhi, J., & Kurniawan, D. (2021, October). Online-Learning Program To Develop Leadership On Student Council Organisation. In ICCD (Vol. 3, No. 1, pp. 303-307).

Chapter 7
Assimilating Employee Well-Being Into Sustainable Business Practices for Successful Organization:
A Path to Long-Term Growth and Productivity

Bhupinder Singh
https://orcid.org/0009-0006-4779-2553
Sharda University, India

ABSTRACT

Symbiotic necessities emerging changing corporate dynamic necessitates incorporating employee well-being in sustainable business practices as a means of fostering long term organizational success now and in the future. A diverse workforce increases productivity, lowers turnover and builds corporate resilience. This chapter explores the relationship between employee wellness and sustainability, discussing ways to integrate wellness efforts with business objectives. Some include mental health programs, flexible work policies and workplace ergonomics which lead to increased engagement and job satisfaction. The organizations fostering holistic well-being cultivate an environment of innovation and inclusion, leading to economic and social sustainability. Sustainable business model realizes humans are assets that require investment and collaborative uplift in a healthy work culture creates efficiencies and reduces burnout. It also features successfully integrated well-being into their sustainability frameworks and its impact on profitability and employee retention.

DOI: 10.4018/979-8-3373-2210-0.ch007

Copyright © 2025, IGI Global Scientific Publishing. Copying or distributing in print or electronic forms without written permission of IGI Global Scientific Publishing is prohibited.

1. INTRODUCTION

Employee well-being is a crucial aspect of the social dimension of sustainability and is often overlooked. Companies that truly care about their employees embrace mental health programs like counseling services, mindfulness activities, stress management workshops (Lee et al., 2024). The addition of diversity, equity, and inclusion (DEI) initiatives by companies are creating a fair and supportive work environment that helps close the gap even more as it relates to employee satisfaction, and psychological safety. Companies that care about the overall well-being of their employees, including their physical health, mental health, and work-life balance, will see greater engagement, reduced turnover, and improved overall performance. By actively prioritizing employee well-being as a core aspect of sustainable business practices, organizations can create a culture of resilience, innovation, and collaboration that is better equipped to tackle the challenges of the modern world. Organizations that prioritize employee wellness through policies around flexible working arrangements, mental health support, ergonomic workspaces and continual professional development create a working environment that fosters employee satisfaction and retention. This subsequently strengthens the organization's brand reputation, positioning it as an employer of choice for top talent.

The financial performance of organisations is directly linked to Sustainable Businesses that place an importance on their employee's wellbeing. Successful work environments benefit from investments in employee health and engagement, leading to lower levels of absenteeism, increased productivity and improved job performance (Singh & Chandra, 2025). Research shows that organizations that foster a culture of well-being tend to have lower healthcare costs and greater profitability. Valuing, Supporting, and Engaging Employees to Achieve Organizational Goals Positive workplace culture fosters an environment that enables employees to thrive. Moreover, companies that demonstrate ethical labor practices and prioritize the welfare of their employees are more likely to earn the trust of consumers and stakeholders alike, further bolstering their over-arching corporate social responsibility (CSR) efforts.

Digital transformation and technology are both key pillars of sustainable employee well-being engine. AI-driven wellness applications can be used, along with remote work solutions and data-driven insights to help organizations shape their well-being programs to the needs of employees. Wearable technology and health monitoring systems are helping to promote preventive healthcare, which cuts long-term medical costs and provides a healthier workforce. In addition, AI-driven analytics help companies identify workplace stressors and provide proactive solutions to enhance employee engagement (Singh et al., 2025).

So, integrating employee well-being into sustainable business practices is not just a fad it's a crucial component of business success. Organisations that invest in the health and wellbeing of their workforce create a sustainable platform for long term growth, innovation and competitive advantage. A properly supported and valued workforce has increased productivity, improved morale, and a more sustainable business environment. On the corporate side, it's about digitally transforming and ensuring corporate sustainability as organizations evolve and change, making wellness a key component of all business strategies with an eye towards the well-being of the business, the employees and ultimately, society as a whole.

1.1 Significance of Employee Well-Being in Business Sustainability

Ensuring employee well-being has become a key pillar of sustainable business practices, with a direct impact on organizational success, productivity, and long-term resilience (Singh & Kaunert, 2025). Sustainability now encompasses social responsibility alongside environmental and economic factors in the changing landscape of corporate climate today, with employee well-being serving as a base pillar. Such an organization with a focus on its people is also said to drive healthy employees and help strengthen employee morale, lessen downtime, and lower turnover as well. When employees are valued and feel supported, they help propel an organization's mission through innovation and operational efficiency. On the other hand, ignoring well-being can lead to workplace stress, burnout, and lowered morale, all of which can have negative business impacts. Integrating well-being initiatives creates a win-win for businesses as it not only improves employee satisfaction but also strengthens the foundation for sustainable, long term success within the organization (Olaleye & Lekunze, 2024).

A sound organization bolsters its community with its financial and technological resources as well as its human capital. Innovation, customer satisfaction, and overall business performance all rely on employees. The approach entails taking care of their physical, mental, and emotional well-being, resulting in a resilient employee base that can respond to market shifts and industry disruptions (Karakitapoglu-Aygun et al., 2024). Wellness programs including flexible working conditions, health and wellness programs, employee assistance programs, and mental health support show an organisation's commitment to its staff. Implementing such strategies goes a long way not only in boosting employee retention but also in attracting the best of the talent that looks for organizations that offer holistic growth. Companies that prioritize well-being are more likely to earn consumer loyalty, with consumers increasingly choosing to buy from brands that reflect their values surrounding ethical labor practices and CSR.

They contribute to the financial aspect of doing good business, and employee wellbeing does play a direct role in sustainability practices. Research shows that organizations that implemented well-being initiatives are recording reduced health care costs, fewer incidents of workplace accidents, and increased productivity. Employees who feel supported both physically and mentally work better, resulting in greater efficiency and innovation. Moreover, sustainable well-being initiatives help create an inclusive workplace culture that nurtures diversity, equity, and inclusion (DEI) and a sense of belonging and engagement. With the changing tide of the corporate world comes a change in employee well being that needs to be addressed and for the organisation which do not take this into consideration, they will be left behind in this competitive world. Hence, organizations must treat employee wellness as a core building block of their sustainability strategy instead of seeing it as a cost to carry. Companies that embrace a people-first approach, ensuring the well-being of their employees, will ultimately benefit from sustainable growth, a stronger brand reputation, and a positive impact on society, paving the way for a healthier, happier future for all (Stalin et al., 2024).

1.2 Objectives of the Chapter

This chapter has the following objectives to:

- Explore how employee well-being enhances long-term organizational success.
- Examine sustainable business practices that foster a healthy workplace.
- Analyze the financial and operational benefits of prioritizing workforce well-being.

Figure 1. Shares the objectives of the chapter (Source- Self Prepared- Original)

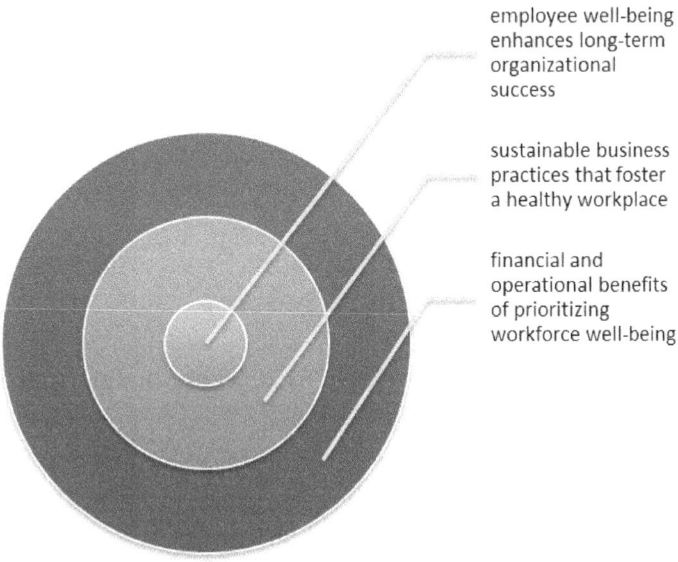

2. EMPLOYEE WELL-BEING IN THE CORPORATE LANDSCAPE: DIMENSIONS OF EMPLOYEE WELL-BEING

Employee well-being is at the forefront of the contemporary corporate landscape, as businesses increasingly leverage understanding the needs and motivations of their employees to drive success. Workplace well-being impacts more than just physical well-being; it also includes mental, emotional, financial and social well-being. All of these aspects are essential for employee experiences, job performance and the overall organizational effectiveness. Companies that ignore these dimensions suffer from high attrition, absenteeism, workplace stress, and disappointment in employee engagement.

With changing work environments, including remote and hybrid work, organizations must consider a new and expanding definition of employee well-being. A high-performance workplace that promotes employee well-being across all dimensions is both a sustainable and beneficial culture for employees and employers alike (Kong et al., 2024). Well-being of employees is a broad category involving physical, mental, financial, social, and work-life balance dimensions. This holistic approach not only supports the well-being of employees but is also key to the success of the organization, with higher engagement, productivity and retention. Business that emphasize holistic well-being attract top talent and establish a great workplace culture, resulting in competitive advantage in today's Corporate World. With the ongoing digital transformation, more companies are adopting remote work practices and dealing with economic uncertainties, investing in employee well-being is still a key strategy to drive sustainable growth. Those enterprises that effectively marry well-being with corporate sustainability will heighten employee engagement and create both healthy and high-performing teams that will ensure long-term innovation and success.

2.1 Physical Well-Being: Healthy Work Environments, Wellness Programs and Medical Support

Physical health is the cornerstone of employee wellness and productivity. It relates to employees' overall physical well-being, which includes access to healthcare, workplace ergonomics, diet and exercise. It gets a physically healthier workforce, less downtime, chronic disease, workplace fatigue or injuries which means maximum efficiency and minimum healthcare cost. Health and wellness programs with health insurance, frequent physical exercise, and workstations designed to minimize occupational risks are crucial elements of organizations that develop physical well-being (Genedy et al., 2024). The firms are investing more in preventive healthcare like on-site medical examinations, vaccination drives, and mental wellness screening. As we embrace this new era, companies harness wearable technology and AI-powered health monitoring to keep an eye on workforce health metrics and offer tailored solutions for well-being. In addition, corporate wellness programmes that provide yoga classes at work, subsidised gym memberships, and flexible working hours also encourage employees to lead an active, balanced lifestyle, which helps reduce stress and improve overall job performance.

2.2 Well-Being for Mind and Emotions: Stress Management, Psychological Safety and Emotional Resilience

Employees in the modern workplace face numerous challenges: the pressures of work, insecurity of jobs and imbalance of work and life, which inevitably affect mental and emotional well-being. Stress, anxiety, depression, and other mental health problems are becoming increasingly common in companies, affecting staff morale, productivity, and retention rates. Companies that make mental and emotional health a priority foster a workplace that is psychologically safe, where employees feel supported and valued throughout their journey. To support emotional resilience, organizations are implementing mental health initiatives like Employee Assistance

Programs (EAPs), professional counseling services, stress management workshops, and mindfulness training.

The way to combat this is through leaders and managers promoting inclusivity and empathy, noticing burnout signs among the team, and communicating this with the team and discussing also how to redistribute workload. But the hybrid- and remote-work models brought new mental health challenges with them, starting with social isolation and digital fatigue (Roberge et al., 2024). Virtual wellness programs, flexible work arrangements, and digital detox policies to deal with these issues can help employees in achieving a healthy work-life balance. Encouraging employees to take breaks, ensuring they have proper work-life balance, and fostering a supportive environment are integral parts of an organization's culture that prioritize mental well-being.

2.3 Financial Well-Being: Fair Wages/ Salary, Retirement Plans and Economic Security Programs

The key component of employee satisfaction and long-term stability is financial well-being. When employees' economic security is in question, it directly hits their stress levels, job performance, and overall quality of life. Workers experiencing financial stress (students debt, lack of savings, poor retirement planning) then to put their mind-and-persons elsewhere which translates to anxiety and disengagement from their daily work duties. Such organisations also mistake the financial literacy and offering align with monetary well-being offering adequate pay, clear pay structures, and retirement benefits.

A salary, princely bonuses, and strong incentives help employees feel appreciated and welcome to give which an excellent effort. A company can also run a financial wellness program that includes education about budgeting, savings, investments, debt management, etc. In response, employers have been including some more flexible compensation elements like student loan repayment assistance or childcare assistance or one-off grants for emergencies to help employees deal with financial stress the right way (Guhn et al., 2024). Financial stability also leads to a confident workforce that is not prone to sad changes in work.

2.4 Social Dimension: Well-Being and Relationships in the Workplace

collaboration and teamwork within an organization. All organisations can be ways in which getting to know your colleagues and being supported by your leaders are key to improved engagement and productivity. An encouraging social work environment strengthens trust, communication, and respect between all members of the team. Organizations that care about social good build inclusive workplace communities where DEI programs succeed. Solid workplace relationships are part of a healthy corporate ecosystem that lowers stress, increases job satisfaction and fosters innovation. In terms of social well-being, organizations can help nurture this by encouraging team-building activities, mentorship programs, employee resource groups, and networking (Elshaer et al., 2024).

These values therefore help with cross-functional collaboration as they encourage an inclusive culture through which employees feel heard and appreciated, boosting job satisfaction and engagement levels. In the form of CSR, social well-being isn't just my neighbor at the office, rather there is a CSR person that initiates community service projects in the office, volunteering programs, sustainability and up-skilling programs. Such activities empower employees and add meaning to their work by re-establishing their connection with the organization's mission and values.

2.5 Worker Lifestyle and Mobility Flexibility

In order for employees to feel good about their jobs, they must maintain a work/life balance. Simply put, work-life balance is the extent to which employees are able to meet work demands while still having time for personal interests, their family, and relaxation. Encouraging healthy practices Flexible working arrangements along with remote working options and paid time off additionally helps support employees' holistic well-being and work productivity. Companies that promote a good work-life balance know that employees work well when they can control their own working styles and hours. Some of these policies, like parental leave, mental health days, sabbaticals and no-email-after-hours initiatives, assist workers in remaining motivated and avoiding burnout over the long haul. As its employee empowerment approaches offer an alternative work arrangement, it not only allows them to determine how efficiently they can perform but also removing themselves from the burden of taking time off when work gets busy due to rigid plans. Employee retention: Work-life balance is correlated with employee retention, as professionals will always seek employers who support flexibility and adaptability (Gutman et al., 2024).

3. SUSTAINABLE BUSINESS PRACTICES AND EMPLOYEE WELL-BEING: ENVIRONMENTAL, SOCIAL AND GOVERNANCE (ESG) FACTORS

The development of sustainable business practices has become an essential structure for companies aiming to attain long-term development, viability, and moral duty (Khan et al., 2024). At the core of sustainability is the recognition that they have a healthy motivated and engaged employee base as the center point for operational success and sustainability of the organization. Introduced to mainstream business practices in the early 2000s, the Environmental, Social, and Governance (ESG) framework gives companies a structured way to incorporate sustainability into business practices, ensuring not just financial profitability but also environmentally sound, socially responsible, and well-governed operations. Such ESG factors are key components for workplace policy, employee health and well-being initiatives and corporate sustainability efforts. Aligning their strategic objectives with ESG principles, they promote an ethics-focused culture of leadership, social inclusion, and environmentalism, resulting in a more human-centric and sustainable workplace. Such initiatives improve employee quality of life and productivity but also fortify corporate reputation and help attract top talent and drive sustainable returns over the long term for organizations that keep their well-being measures aligned with environmental, governance and social (ESG) goals (Jose et al., 2024).

As one of the key pillars of ESG, environmental sustainability plays a direct and indirect role in the well-being of employees. By adopting eco-friendly practices, businesses create a healthier workspace, preventing environmental hazards and contributing positively to the employees' well-being. Companies that emphasize green office designs, energy efficient infrastructure, green technologies, and waste reduction give employees safer and healthier spaces. Indoor air quality, noise pollution, and exposure to hazardous chemicals at work can all individually affect the health of workers, from respiratory illness to fatigue, which may lead to poor productivity. Incorporating sustainable solutions like green buildings, air purification systems, and environmentally friendly workplace designs fosters workplace well-being by providing clean air, natural light, and ergonomic working environments.

Businesses with environmental responsibility are actively involving employees in sustainability initiatives, including corporate recycling programs, carbon footprint and climate action projects. Employees who engage in workplace sustainability activities develop a sense of purpose, resulting in more meaningful connections to the organization's values (Huang & Zhou, 2024). Another benefit is that remote work and hybrid work models contribute to a far more sustainable society through lower carbon emissions as employees reduce the amount of commuting they do each day, while continuing to enable a better work-life balance for all employees. Companies that focus on sustainable supply chain management and ethical sourcing practices also prevent employees from being placed in hazardous work environments, ultimately defending health and safety standards. Thus, environmental sustainability is a significant factor for employee well-being and fosters a healthier and more accountable corporate ecosystem.

Any sustainable strategy involves human capital, and this is where the social aspect of ESG comes into play, encompassing workplace culture, diversity, equity, and inclusion (DEI), human rights and community engagement. A socially responsible company takes care of its employees creating a diverse, supportive, and fair workplace. When successful organizations value and respect diversity and inclusion in the workplace, not only are a more diverse workforce produced, but a culture of belonging is fostered and high job satisfaction and engagement maintained (Cascio & Ehrhardt, 2024). By exercising the Public Interest Principle, companies safeguard their role as leaders by addressing issues such as pay equity, gender equality, and non-discrimination, resulting in a strong foundation of social well-being in the workplace months in advance (spilling into the moonshot) as disparities decrease and employees feel a sense of social justice.

Company practices in areas such as fair compensation, development, and work-life balance also impact employee health. Investing in employee training, mentorship programs, and career advancement opportunities are key contributors to long-term job satisfaction and retention. Additionally, businesses that align flexible work practices, paid parental leave policies, and mental health initiatives show that they care about employees' complete health and wellbeing. Social well-being goes beyond the workplace, with organizations encouraging employees to take part in corporate social responsibility (CSR) programs, volunteer work, and community engagement activities. Researchers have found that employees engaged in social impact projects enjoy increased work satisfaction, mission alignment, and sense of meaning in their work.

The other key ingredient of social sustainability is workplace safety and employee rights. When organizations maintain ethical labor practices, enforce anti-harassment policies, and create a psychologically safe work environment, they develop a culture of trust and transparency; Ignoring employee well-being or social responsibility can lead to reputational damage, lower employee morale, and possible legal ramifications (Subramony & Rosenbaum, 2024). Thus, social sustainability implementation in workplace policies improves employee loyalty, enhances collaboration and contributes overall business performance.

Corporate governance is an important aspect of ESG that can affect employee well-being through ethical leadership, good decision-making, and compliance with regulations. Strong governance frameworks help ensure that businesses are run with integrity, accountability, and fairness, providing employees with a safe and empowering workplace. This is the place where ethical business practices, anti-corruption, and equitable workplace policies mean employees are more likely to thrive, and ethical leadership plays a crucial role in building the trust necessary for these policies to be effective. Governance can also be categorized into workplace wellbeing factors that includes fair compensation, compliance with labor laws, and protection of employee rights. Making sure to communicate clearly the policies around wages, performance appraise, and promos results in a meritocratic culture that encourages employees to perform well in their roles. Moreover, organizations that prioritize data privacy and cybersecurity policies safeguard employees against digital threats, ensuring the security of both personal and professional data.

Companies implementing strong corporate governance mechanisms from whistleblower protection policies, grievance redressal systems, to employee representation in decision-making processes foster positive work culture and improve employee well-being. Providing employees with a voice with the ability to voice concerns, present insights, participate in governance structures cultivates a sense of inclusivity and empowerment (Gulzar et al., 2024). The governance structures that link executive leadership with employee interests help keep workforce wellness at the forefront of decisions made in the corporate boardroom. Employee trust improves, workplace conflicts dissipate, and brand reputation flourishes within these organizations.

With employees increasingly mindful of workplace sustainability, organizations that commit to ESG leadership become magnets for top-flight talent seeking responsible and ethical environment in which to grow their careers. Research shows that organizations where strong ESG policies are in place tended to have lower turnover rates; employees would prefer to remain committed to organizations that aligned with their values and kept their welfare in mind. In addition, companies that focus on improving the well being of workers through ESG practices also show increased rates of retained staff, innovation, and productivity, which leads to increased corporate success (Pillai et al., 2024).

Financially, ESG-harmonized clear up an opportunity lead on the competitive motive in the community because of predispose toward to activities that wed sustainable development and corporate duty. Organizations that fail to consider ESG factors put themselves at risk of reputational damage, regulatory fines, and investor loss of confidence. Integrating ESG comes as a must across workplace well-being programs that will not only append the employees morale but will also strengthen them holistically in facing the uncertain economic and environmental circumstances to come.

Well-being of employees and sustainable businesses are closely intertwined in the ESG ecosystem. Environmental factors impact workplace health and sustainability, social factors shape corporate culture and inclusivity, and governance factors ensure ethical leadership and compliance. ESG-driven well-being initiatives help businesses engender a healthier, happier and more productive workforce while at the same time elevating corporate reputation and financial stability (Ozkan et al., 2024). In a time when sustainability serves as a key differentiator for business success, businesses that strive towards ESG principles and the welfare of employees will take strong stands as leaders of ethical corporate success and will ensure long term benefits of growth and sustainability.

4. ROLE OF TECHNOLOGY IN PROMOTING EMPLOYEE WELL-BEING

Technology is evolving at an unprecedented pace and reshaping workplace dynamics, making employee well-being an imperative opportunity for digital intervention. With businesses in the modern world opting to integrate technologies in organizations, organizations are using digital innovations to focus on workplace wellness, work-life balance, and supportive environment for employees. Technology-intended wellness solutions feature tools such as artificial intelligence (AI), machine learning (ML), telehealth, digital health platforms, predictive analytics and remote work. Device алмagingo Such innovations allow corporations to enable proactive supervision of their employees' mental and physical health concerns, all while enhancing job satisfaction and productivity levels.

Organizations can also use technology to enable targeted well-being plans, real-time tracking of employee health with regular feedback to the employees, enhancing the total well-being experience and fostering inclusivity and engagement. The ability to employ AI-driven applications, wearables, and digital communication and technologies to optimize workplace wellness has given way to employees being able to access the tools and resources they need to stay healthy away from the job (Hoare & Vandenberghe, 2024). However, the usage of technology in employee well-being programs provides a comprehensive approach to mental health assistance, stress management, physical well-being, and digital inclusion.

4.1 Digital Transformation on Workplace Well-being

AI-powered well-being apps and analytics, telemedicine, and mental health-focused virtual health solutions are becoming indispensable. AI powered well-being applications analyze employee behavior, stress levels, and productivity patterns to offer personalized wellness strategies. With applications that employ sentiment analysis, machine learning algorithms and biometric data to spot indicators of stress, burnout and emotional distress. Organizations can take a proactive approach by using AI-powered insights to flag employees at risk for physical or mental health problems, and then provide interventions as needed.

Artificial intelligence (AI) chatbots and virtual mental health assistants offer employees real-time support by providing guided meditation, cognitive behavioral therapy (CBT) techniques, and stress-relief exercises. These smart tools are anonymous, so employees do not feel the stigma of seeking mental health help. Moreover, AI-based well-being platforms can also be integrated with employee assistance programs (EAPs), enabling employees to access counseling services, wellness resources, and self-care suggestions seamlessly (Cavanagh et al., 2024). AI-powered analytics allow HR departments to analyze workforce well-being at a macro level, assisting organizations in recognizing workplace stressors, and establishing policies that lead to better working conditions. That's where AI can help businesses analyze employee engagement, monitor stress level, and personalize wellness programs to suit individual needs, resulting in happy and productive employees.

4.2 Employee Telemedicine and Virtual Health Solutions

Then telemedicine has become a revolutionary solution to employee health and wellbeing offering workers with instant access to health care professionals allowing them to do virtual consultations. "As digital health platforms continue to gain traction, employees can book medical appointments, obtain diagnoses, and access treatment plans from the comfort of their workplace or home. Virtual health solutions are key in addressing not just physical health issues but also mental health care. Employees suffering from stress, anxiety or burnout can find licensed therapists and mental health professionals through telehealth platforms (Adkins et al., 2024). They are removing barriers associated with rote in-person healthcare appointments, such as time and stigma, making mental health services easier for employees to access.

Also, telemedicine simplifies preventive healthcare, as it allows employees to keep track of their health metrics through mobile applications and wearable devices. With the ability to monitor health in real time, people can identify early symptoms of health care issues and address potential issues such as high blood pressure or irregular heartbeats, and undertake medical intervention promptly. Companies that incorporate telemedicine into their welfare initiatives help employees to assume control of their health, pumming productivity and reducing absenteeism.

4.3 Using AI and Machine Learning for Workplace Stress Management

It's a considerable dilemma; it hampers employees' productivity, mental health, and job satisfaction. Workplace stress management is being revolutionized by AI and machine learning technologies, allowing the use of predictive analytics, real-time monitoring, and personalized interventions to reduce stress and improve employee well-being. AI-Powered Predictive Analytics Will Transform Employee Stress And Mental Health Management Machine learning algorithms work to process historical data, trends in the workplace, and patterns in the behavior of employees to extract potential generators of strains and risks to mental health. HR professionals can also rely on these predictive models to spot early warning signs for burnout, depression and anxiety before they become serious health issues.

Using tools for AI-based analysis of sentiment, the businesses can check on the mood of the employee and their engagement level as indicated by workplace communication, including emails, chat messages and performance reviews (Merung et al., 2024). Should an AI system identify potential distress, disengagement, etc. in an individual employee, HR teams can proactively step in with customized support, counselling services, or any support that meets their needs. AI-driven wellness dashboards also offer real-time data about your employees' holistic well-being, enabling managers to introduce stress-reduction initiatives, including flexible work hours, mindful programs, and work distribution techniques.

4.4 Wearable Technology for Employee Wellness and Health Monitoring

Wearable technology is revolutionizing workplace wellness by allowing employees to track their health metrics and lead a healthier lifestyle (smartwatches and fitness trackers). Wearable devices that monitor: heart rate, sleep quality, amount of physical activity, or stress levels in real time, are able to give immediate and real time feedback to clients on vital signs.

The use of wearables is also a natural fit for corporate wellness programs, and integrating them in workplace wellness initiatives can help corporations drive other positive outcomes as employees walk more, relieve stress and, otherwise, improve their overall wellness. Certain organizations equip their employees with wearable devices as part of corporate wellness initiatives, motivating them to engage in step challenges, mindfulness exercises, and healthy lifestyle programs. AI duty-wearable devices can monitor biometric data to identify early signs of work fatigue and job stress, letting employees know when to take breaks or conduct relaxation techniques (Aripin et al., 2024). Wearable device anonymized data can be valuable for employers seeking insight into general workforce health trends and tailoring wellness programs that align with employee needs. You should wear Wearable and it is also good for office, office Work and to be Fit.

4.5 Remote Work and Digital Inclusion

The new normal of working from home has reshaped the traditional workplace structure and highlighted the need for digital inclusion, workplace cyber security and work-life balance as essentials for employees and their overall health. Organizations that have adopted digital tools to facilitate remote work also need to "practice" psychological safety and inclusivity in virtual spaces. Digital collaboration tools have enabled remote work, which has provided employees more flexibility and autonomy in how they navigate their work-life balance. The seamless communication and collaboration offered by platforms such as Zoom, Microsoft Teams, and Slack allow employees of the business to work from wherever they choose, at their pace. But transitioning to remote work also demands clear boundaries from businesses to avoid burnout and digital fatigue.

Setting up such a work environment brings in balance and light when organizations enable remote work with working hours, breaks, mental health drive, etc. Some tools that fall under digital well -being applications focus on timers are mindfulness applications and virtual well being applications that help to manage stress and ensure productivity without being overwhelmed. Using technology to enable flexible work arrangements improves employee satisfaction, engagement, and overall well-being for businesses (Deb et al., 2024).

4.6 Drive Psychological Safety and Cybersecurity in Digital Workplaces

As digital transformation accelerates, cybersecurity and psychological safety in remote work is critical. Remote employees frequently face cybersecurity threats, including phishing attacks and data breaches, which can cause stress and anxiety. From adopting multi-factor authentication and encrypted communication to conduction cybersecurity training, organizations must implement stringent measures as safeguards to protect employees from digital threats. Psychological safety in virtual workplaces. Chemistry between team members in the physical workplace depends on social norms that develop with the organisation, but the same is not always true within virtual workplaces. Businesses need to emphasize open communication, offer virtual team-building activities and give staff assurances concerns can be raised without judgment or repercussions. Moreover, while putting in place policies around online harassment, discrimination, and digital fatigue also goes a long way toward psychologically-safe remote work environments.

Technology enhances employee well-being with AI wellness apps, telemedicine, predictive analytics, wearables, and remote work. Digital transformation allows companies to build cleaner, more inclusive, and more flexible workplaces that respond to the physical and mental well-being of team members. Why this is important: As organizations continue to adopt technological innovations, it's crucial for them to ensure that digital solutions are accessible, secure, and integrated with a holistic perspective of the employees' needs (Mahipalan & Garg, 2024). Through the strategic application of AI, machine learning, in addition to digital tools, companies can cultivate an environment of well-being, resilience, in addition to productivity, which leads to building long-term organizational success in addition to employee satisfaction.

5. CHALLENGES IN IMPLEMENTING SUSTAINABLE WELL-BEING PRACTICES

The implementation of sustainable well-being practices within the corporate environment is not without its challenges; several obstacles can limit their effectiveness and success. Finding a balance between employees, profits, and the sustainability agenda often poses problems for companies. Simply getting well-being programs to align with business objectives is complex enough, but throw in costs, resistance to change and no measurable outcome, and it becomes impossible for most organizations to maintain long-term well-being strategies.

Many organizations often struggle with budgeting for workplace wellness programs, ergonomic infrastructure, and wellness programs (especially SMEs). Developing sustainable well-being practices needs wellness technology, mental health resources, and flexible working policies, which some businesses may see as discretionary spending. In addition, firms competing in saturated sectors might focus on short-term profitability, deferring the investments required to enhance employee health well-beings or sustainability as well (Pattali et al., 2024).

Resistance to change and the limits of corporate culture present another significant roadblock. Traditional work environments prioritize productivity and efficiency over holistic employee well-being. The employees may push back against workplace wellness policies because of cultural inertia, skepticism over effectiveness or worries about added responsibilities. In some organizations, employees may be scared to engage in well-being programs for fear of perceived stigma, particularly around mental health support. Employees follow the lead of those higher up the organizational hierarchy; when they fail to support well-being programs, their employees tend to participate less.

Measuring well-being outcomes can be another challenge to organizations. It's not objective like financial performance or productivity metrics; employee well-being is subjective, and it varies from person to person. Most companies don't do a good job at creating KPIs that indicate how successful their well-being programs really are (Russell-Bennett et al., 2024). Senior management will not invest more in well-being programs without hard data that justifies the ROI of doing so. Furthermore, organizations often do not have the tools and expertise to take a measurement of employee well-being, resulting in strategies that fall short of providing meaningful results.

However, such practices are hindered by the digital divide and inclusivity concerns. Although AI-enabled wellness apps, telemedicine, and digital engagement tools have opened new avenues, employees who lack access to technology or are unable to navigate digital platforms may potentially miss the benefits of these technologies (Rathobei et al., 2024). Some remote and hybrid workers, especially those in developing countries, may not have access to the same levels of connectivity as employees in other regions, limiting their ability to participate fully in virtual wellness initiatives. A persistent challenge facing organizations working toward promoting equitable workplace wellness programs is ensuring that well-being initiatives have inclusivity and accessibility from a digital lens.

When it comes to workplace well-being initiatives, legal and ethical considerations cannot be ignored. The use of AI for predictive analytics, health monitoring through the use of wearables, and biometric tracking come with issues of privacy. If employees have to share health data, they may be wary about being surveilled or of having their information misused. Complying with data protection and workplace privacy laws. Without sacrificing employee trust and employee experience Organizations use machine learning to gather insights and information from the data collected.

However, organizations can overcome these challenges by adopting a strategic approach through committed leadership, ensuring transparency in their measurement framework, guaranteeing digital inclusion, and integrating ethical dimensions in their well-being initiatives (Pagkratis & Dobson, 2024).

6. FUTURE TRENDS AND INNOVATIONS IN EMPLOYEE WELL-BEING

The workplace, hence, is going to transform in the future around employee well-being with the help of emerging tech, changing workplace dynamics, and the focus on holistic health. More than ever, organizations are realizing that well-being encompasses much more than standard healthcare benefits; it encompasses mental resilience, financial security, harmony in work and personal life, and social ties. So, companies need to embrace state-of-the-art innovations to uplift workplace wellness programs for sustainable business ecosystems (Magalhaes et al., 2024).

AI-Driven Personalized Well-Being Programs ML and AI will assist organizations within the identification of the reasons for stress and based on the employees health data analyzed by the organization, will help them to suggest tailor made recommendations for well-being that can assist in the long term employee satisfaction. AI-enabled chatbots and virtual mental health counselors provide support when needed in real time, letting employees access discreet counseling services 24/7. A significant feature of predictive analytics is determining early symptoms of burnout so that employers can intervene before problems worsen.

The other important innovations is the integration of wearable technology and Internet of Things (IoT) devices that enable health monitoring (Tsiotsou et al., 2024). Wearable technology such as smartwatches, fitness trackers, and biosensors enables employees to track their physical activity, sleep patterns, and even their stress levels, encouraging proactive health management. Employers have the option to access aggregated, anonymised data from these devices, which can help them create programmes that address specific health concerns and foster a healthier work environment.

The future of remote and hybrid work will also reshape employee well-being strategies. Companies are increasingly allocating funds to digital wellness tools, VR-based relaxation therapies and cyber safe practices that ensure psychological safety at digital workspaces (Namdech et al., 2025). Also, workplace flexibility will evolve with four-day workweeks, asynchronous work models, and better parental leave policies to help support work-life balance becoming priorities for companies. Sustainability and inclusivity will be central to shaping the future of workplace well-being as businesses embrace a future-focused vision that ensures well-being strategies are accessible to employees in all roles, locations and socio-economic segments (Davey et al., 2024).

7. CONCLUSION

Well-being at work is the critical ingredient for sustainable business success, not just an HR responsibility Companies that make holistic well-being initiatives a priority see a more engaged, healthier working population, resulting in higher productivity, lower turnover, and more positive employer perception. Not only does sustainable well-being promote a healthy workforce but it also puts businesses in a better position for long-term business resilience by minimising workplace-related stress, enhancing employee morale and nurturing a culture of inclusiveness and support. When businesses adopt a long-term perspective, committing to total well-being through data-led programs designed for each organization, obstacles can be overcome with strong leadership commitment backed by a technology-enabled health and well-being approach. Emerging trends such as AI-based well-being analytics, health tracking through wearables, and flexible work practices will guarantee that employee well-being strategies will keep up to date with the demands of the modern workforce. In an increasingly fluid corporate environment, companies need to consider employee well-being as a strategic investment rather than an initiative of choice. As businesses build a culture of preventative health, inclusivity, and continuous development, employees will flourish in workplaces that drive sustained success for both organizations and communities.

REFERENCES

Adkins, J. A., Douglas, S., Voorhies, P., & Bickman, L. (2024). Program evaluation: The bottom line in organizational health.

Aripin, Z., Agusiady, R., & Ariyanti, M. (2024). The Importance of a Sense Of Purpose For Salespersons: More Than Just A Financial Aspect. *Journal of Economics, Accounting, Business, Management. Engineering and Society*, *1*(3), 48–62.

Aripin, Z., Matriadi, F., & Ermeila, S. (2024, February). Optimization of Worker Work Environment, Robots, and Marketing Strategy: The Impact of Digital-Based Spatiotemporal Dynamics on Human Resource Management (HRM). *Journal of Jabar Economic Society Networking Forum*, *1*(3), 33–49.

Cascio, W. F., & Ehrhardt, K. (2024). Designing recruitment programs for impact. In *Essentials of Employee Recruitment* (pp. 330–350). Routledge. DOI: 10.4324/9781003356752-20

Cavanagh, J., Bartram, T., Walker, M., Pariona-Cabrera, P., & Halvorsen, B. (2024). Health services in Australia and the impact of antiquated rostering practices on medical scientists: A case for HR analytics and evidenced-based human resource management. *Personnel Review*, *53*(1), 18–33. DOI: 10.1108/PR-09-2021-0690

Davey, J., Johns, R., & Leino, H. M. (2024). Strengths-based service solutions: mapping a way forward in marketplace vulnerabilities. In *A Research Agenda for Service Marketing* (pp. 251–280). Edward Elgar Publishing. DOI: 10.4337/9781803923178.00021

Deb, B. C., Rahman, M. M., & Haseeb, M. (2024). Unveiling the impact on corporate social responsibility through green tax and green financing: A PLS-SEM approach. *Environmental Science and Pollution Research International*, *31*(1), 1543–1561. DOI: 10.1007/s11356-023-31150-y PMID: 38041735

Elshaer, I. A., Azazz, A. M., Ghaleb, M. M., Abdulaziz, T. A., Mansour, M. A., & Fayyad, S. (2024). The impact of work-related ICT use on perceived injustice: Exploring the effects of work role overload and psychological detachment. *Journal of Open Innovation*, *10*(1), 100208. DOI: 10.1016/j.joitmc.2024.100208

Genedy, M., Hellerstedt, K., Naldi, L., & Wiklund, J. (2024). Growing pains in scale-ups: How scaling affects new venture employee burnout and job satisfaction. *Journal of Business Venturing*, *39*(2), 106367. DOI: 10.1016/j.jbusvent.2023.106367

Guhn, M., Gadermann, A., & Wu, A. D. (2024). Trends in international mathematics and science study (TIMSS). In *Encyclopedia of quality of life and well-being research* (pp. 7309–7311). Springer International Publishing.

Gulzar, S., Hussain, K., Akhlaq, A., Abbas, Z., & Ghauri, S. (2024). Exploring the psychological contract breach of nurses in healthcare: An exploratory study. *Asia-Pacific Journal of Business Administration*, *16*(1), 204–230. DOI: 10.1108/APJBA-03-2021-0102

Gutman, L. M., Younas, F., Perowne, R., & O'Hanrachtaigh, E. (2024). Lived experiences of diverse university staff during COVID-19: An examination of workplace wellbeing. *Studies in Higher Education*, *49*(2), 251–268. DOI: 10.1080/03075079.2023.2231015

Hoare, C., & Vandenberghe, C. (2024). Are they created equal? A relative weights analysis of the contributions of job demands and resources to well-being and turnover intention. *Psychological Reports*, *127*(1), 392–418. DOI: 10.1177/00332941221103536 PMID: 35707875

Huang, D., & Zhou, H. (2024). Self-sacrificial leadership, thriving at work, workplace well-being, and work–family conflict during the COVID-19 crisis: The moderating role of self-leadership. *Business Research Quarterly*, *27*(1), 10–25. DOI: 10.1177/23409444231203744

Jose, G., PM, N., & Kuriakose, V. (. (2024). HRM practices and employee engagement: Role of personal resources-a study among nurses. *International Journal of Productivity and Performance Management*, *73*(1), 1–17. DOI: 10.1108/IJPPM-04-2021-0212

Karakitapoğlu-Aygün, Z., Erdogan, B., Caughlin, D. E., & Bauer, T. N. (2024). Transformational leadership, idiosyncratic deals and employee outcomes. *Personnel Review*, *53*(2), 562–579. DOI: 10.1108/PR-07-2022-0470

Khan, M. A., Kumar, J., Shoukat, M. H., & Selem, K. M. (2024). Does injustice perception threaten organizational performance in the healthcare setting? A sequential mediation examination. *International Journal of Conflict Management*, *35*(2), 287–308. DOI: 10.1108/IJCMA-05-2023-0100

Kong, D., Liu, J., Wang, Y., & Zhu, L. (2024). Employee stock ownership plans and corporate environmental engagement. *Journal of Business Ethics*, *189*(1), 177–199. DOI: 10.1007/s10551-023-05334-y

Lee, J., Resick, C. J., Allen, J. A., Davis, A. L., & Taylor, J. A. (2024). Interplay between safety climate and emotional exhaustion: Effects on first responders' safety behavior and wellbeing over time. *Journal of Business and Psychology*, *39*(1), 209–231. DOI: 10.1007/s10869-022-09869-1 PMID: 36573129

Magalhães, A., dos Santos, N. R., & Pais, L. (2024). Human resource management practices and decent work in UN global compact: A qualitative analysis of participants' reports. *Social Sciences (Basel, Switzerland), 13*(1), 56. DOI: 10.3390/socsci13010056

Mahipalan, M., & Garg, N. (2024). Does workplace toxicity undermine psychological capital (PsyCap) of the employees? Exploring the moderating role of gratitude. *The International Journal of Organizational Analysis*, *32*(3), 476–503. DOI: 10.1108/IJOA-12-2022-3543

Merung, A. Y., Sofyan, I. R., Sudirman, N. A., & Sma, A. (2024). Do Entrepreneurial Competence and Psychological Well-Being Affect Entrepreneurial Interest among Young Entrepreneurs? *Indonesian Journal of Business and Entrepreneurship Research*, *2*(1), 63–75. DOI: 10.62794/ijober.v2i1.1445

Namdech, P., Rotjanawasuthorn, S., Singh, B., & Kaunert, C. (2025). Harnessing Artificial Intelligence for Lifelong Education: Opportunities and Challenges. *Asian Education and Learning Review*, *3*(2), 4–4.

Olaleye, B. R., & Lekunze, J. N. (2024). Emotional intelligence and psychological resilience on workplace bullying and employee performance: A moderated-mediation perspective. *Journal of Law and Sustainable Development*, *12*(1), e2159–e2159.

Ozkan, S., Tari Selcuk, K., & Kan, Z. E. (2024). Is green behaviors of health professionals related to green practices in the workplace? Multicenter study in Turkey. *International Journal of Environmental Health Research*, *34*(2), 898–910. DOI: 10.1080/09603123.2023.2185209 PMID: 36854645

Pagkratis, K., & Dobson, S. (2024). Promoting Learning Inclusion Through the Global Network of Learning Cities and Sustainable Development Goals (SDGs). In *Learning Inclusion in a Digital Age: Belonging and Finding a Voice with the Disadvantaged* (pp. 49–63). Springer Nature Singapore. DOI: 10.1007/978-981-99-7196-1_4

Pattali, S., Sankar, J. P., Al Qahtani, H., Menon, N., & Faizal, S. (2024). Effect of leadership styles on turnover intention among staff nurses in private hospitals: The moderating effect of perceived organizational support. *BMC Health Services Research*, *24*(1), 1–13. DOI: 10.1186/s12913-024-10674-0 PMID: 38355546

Pillai, R., Ghanghorkar, Y., Sivathanu, B., Algharabat, R., & Rana, N. P. (2024). Adoption of artificial intelligence (AI) based employee experience (EEX) chatbots. *Information Technology & People*, *37*(1), 449–478. DOI: 10.1108/ITP-04-2022-0287

Rathobei, K. E., Ranängen, H., & Lindman, Å. (2024). Exploring broad value creation in mining-Corporate social responsibility and stakeholder management in practice. *The Extractive Industries and Society*, *17*, 101412. DOI: 10.1016/j.exis.2024.101412

Roberge, C., Meunier, S., & Cleary, J. (2024). In Action at Work! Mental Health Self-Management Strategies for Employees Experiencing Anxiety or Depressive Symptoms. *Canadian Journal of Behavioural Science*, *56*(1), 10–19. DOI: 10.1037/cbs0000346

Russell-Bennett, R., Rosenbaum, M. S., Fisk, R. P., & Raciti, M. M. (2024). SDG editorial: Improving life on planet earth–a call to action for service research to achieve the sustainable development goals (SDGs). *Journal of Services Marketing*, *38*(2), 145–152. DOI: 10.1108/JSM-11-2023-0425

Singh, B., & Chandra, S. (2025). Augmented Reality and Virtual Reality in Health Advancements and Medical Education: Runway for Future Ready Healthcare Services. In R. R., S. Chowdhury, S. Kardy, R. Damaševičius, & R. Govindaraj (Eds.), *Digital Twins for Sustainable Healthcare in the Metaverse* (pp. 197-218). IGI Global Scientific Publishing. DOI: 10.4018/979-8-3693-4199-5.ch008

Singh, B., Hammouch, H., & Chandra, S. (2025). Innovative Wind Energy Solutions for Smart-Sustainable Communities: Vision for Intelligent Energy Management and Climate Resilience in Industry 5.0. In Mitra, D., Choudhury, T., Madan, A., Chattaraj, S., & Pellegrini, M. (Eds.), *AI Technologies for Enhancing Recycling Processes* (pp. 491–508). IGI Global Scientific Publishing., DOI: 10.4018/979-8-3693-7282-1.ch020

Singh, B., & Kaunert, C. (2025). Leveraging IoT for Patient Monitoring and Smart Healthcare: Connected Healthcare System. In Revolutionizing Healthcare Systems Through Cloud Computing and IoT (pp. 27-46). IGI Global.

Stalin, M. V., & Maheswari, M. U. (2024). The Influence of Human Resource Management Practices on Employee Work Engagement In Selected Manufacturing Companies in South India. *The Journal of Research Administration*, *6*(1).

Subramony, M., & Rosenbaum, M. S. (2024). SDG commentary: Economic services for work and growth for all humans. *Journal of Services Marketing*, *38*(2), 190–216. DOI: 10.1108/JSM-05-2023-0201

Tsiotsou, R. H., Kabadayi, S., & Fisk, R. P. (2024). Advocating human rights and Sustainable Development Goals: an ecosystem-based Transformative Service Research (TSR) approach. In *A Research Agenda for Service Marketing* (pp. 225-249). Edward Elgar Publishing.

Chapter 8
The Impact of Flexible Work Policies on Employee Well-Being and Retention in Modern Organizations

Ishani Gupta
https://orcid.org/0009-0004-2560-6188
Christ University, Bengaluru, India

Ramji Nagariya
https://orcid.org/0000-0002-2739-9838
Christ University, Bengaluru, India

ABSTRACT

Flexible work policies have become foundational to contemporary organizational strategy, particularly in light of the transformative shifts triggered by the COVID-19 pandemic. This chapter investigates the multifaceted impact of such policies on employee well-being and organizational retention. Drawing from an integrative lens, it incorporates four major theoretical frameworks—Job Demands-Resources (JD-R), Self-Determination Theory (SDT), Conservation of Resources (COR), and Social Exchange Theory (SET)—to provide a comprehensive understanding of how flexible work arrangements influence employee engagement, satisfaction, and organizational loyalty. In addition to synthesizing existing scholarship, this chapter contributes a novel cross-theoretical model that bridges motivational psychology and organizational behavior. It also proposes a suite of policy evaluation tools that blend qualitative and quantitative metrics, enabling organizations to monitor and

DOI: 10.4018/979-8-3373-2210-0.ch008

Copyright © 2025, IGI Global Scientific Publishing. Copying or distributing in print or electronic forms without written permission of IGI Global Scientific Publishing is prohibited.

enhance the effectiveness of flexibility initiatives.

INTRODUCTION

The evolution of work structures in modern organizations has been significantly influenced by the increasing need for flexibility in employment practices. The traditional nine-to-five work model, once considered the gold standard of productivity and efficiency, has undergone substantial transformation in response to technological advancements, changing workforce expectations, and global economic shifts. In recent years, the rise of flexible work policies has emerged as a defining characteristic of contemporary organizational strategy, offering employees greater autonomy while simultaneously reshaping traditional work environments. These policies encompass various arrangements, including remote work, hybrid work models, compressed workweeks, and flexible scheduling, all of which contribute to enhancing employee well-being and retention.

The significance of flexible work policies is rooted in their ability to foster work-life balance, mitigate work-related stress, and increase job satisfaction, ultimately leading to higher levels of productivity and commitment among employees. The COVID-19 pandemic served as a catalyst for the widespread adoption of flexible work arrangements, compelling organizations across industries to reassess their operational models and embrace alternative work structures. As organizations adapt to the post-pandemic era, it has become evident that flexible work policies are no longer a temporary solution but a fundamental aspect of the evolving workplace landscape.

The concept of flexible work policies has gained momentum as organizations strive to balance productivity with employee satisfaction. These policies, which include remote work options, flexible scheduling, and compressed workweeks, have been linked to enhanced job satisfaction, reduced stress, and increased employee retention. This chapter explores the significance of flexible work policies in modern organizations and their role in fostering employee well-being and loyalty.

1. BACKGROUND AND SIGNIFICANCE

In recent years as organizations worldwide strive to balance productivity with employee satisfaction. flexible work policies has gained substantial attention. As the traditional nine-to-five work model becomes increasingly outdated, businesses are adopting alternative work arrangements, such as remote work, flexible scheduling, and compressed workweeks, to accommodate the evolving needs of the workforce

(Kossek & Thompson, 2016). These policies have been linked to enhanced job satisfaction, reduced stress levels, and increased employee retention, making them a crucial element in modern organizational strategies (Bloom et al., 2015). The shift toward flexible work arrangements has been accelerated by technological advancements and global crises, most notably the COVID-19 pandemic, which necessitated the rapid adoption of remote work (Barrero, Bloom, & Davis, 2021).

Flexible work policies represent a fundamental shift in how organizations manage human resources. Instead of a rigid work environment, these policies allow employees greater autonomy in determining when and where they work, which has been shown to improve overall well-being and work-life balance (Allen et al., 2021). Organizations that have successfully integrated flexible work arrangements report higher levels of employee engagement and productivity (Gajendran & Harrison, 2007). Additionally, companies that support such policies tend to attract and retain top talent, as modern workers increasingly prioritize flexibility when choosing an employer (Global Workplace Analytics, 2020).

The growing interest in flexible work policies is driven by a combination of societal, technological, and economic factors. Historically, the concept of work flexibility dates back to the early 20th century when Henry Ford introduced the five-day workweek to enhance productivity and worker satisfaction (Hunnicutt, 2013). Since then, various forms of alternative work arrangements have emerged, including flextime, job sharing, and telecommuting, all aimed at improving employee well-being and organizational efficiency (Golden & Veiga, 2005).

The digital revolution of the late 20th and early 21st centuries further facilitated the expansion of flexible work policies. The advent of high-speed internet, cloud computing, and digital collaboration tools enabled employees to perform tasks from remote locations without compromising efficiency (Messenger & Gschwind, 2016). These technological advancements have made remote work more feasible and scalable, allowing organizations to offer greater flexibility to their workforce.

In addition to technological factors, workforce expectations have played a crucial role in shaping the demand for flexible work arrangements. Modern employees, particularly millennials and Generation Z professionals, prioritize work-life balance, autonomy, and meaningful work experiences when evaluating job opportunities (Deloitte, 2020). Organizations that fail to accommodate these preferences risk higher turnover rates and difficulties in attracting top talent. Research indicates that companies with well-structured flexible work policies experience increased employee satisfaction, lower stress levels, and enhanced loyalty (Allen et al., 2021).

Evolution of Flexible Work Policies

Flexible work policies has evolved over several decades, influenced by shifting labor market dynamics and organizational priorities. The earliest forms of workplace flexibility were introduced in the 1960s and 1970s, when telecommuting gained traction as an alternative work arrangement for professionals in the technology and knowledge sectors (Nilles, 1998). By the 1980s and 1990s, flextime and compressed workweeks became popular in various industries, allowing employees to tailor their work schedules to their personal needs while maintaining productivity (Golden & Veiga, 2005).

The 21st century witnessed a significant expansion of flexible work policies, driven by rapid advancements in digital technology and the rise of the gig economy. The proliferation of digital collaboration tools such as Slack, Zoom, and Microsoft Teams enabled seamless remote work, further solidifying the viability of flexible work arrangements (Carnevale & Hatak, 2020). Moreover, the COVID-19 pandemic accelerated the adoption of remote work policies, forcing organizations worldwide to rethink traditional work structures. Many companies realized that productivity could be maintained, or even enhanced, in remote and hybrid settings, prompting a permanent shift toward flexible work arrangements (Barrero, Bloom, & Davis, 2021).

Flexible work policies include various arrangements that balance organizational and employee needs, enhancing productivity and work-life balance. Common types include:

Remote Work: Employees work outside the office, often full-time or part-time, using digital tools (Bailey & Kurland, 2002). Benefits include reduced commuting, lower costs, and improved work-life balance. Challenges include communication issues, performance monitoring, and blurred work-life boundaries.

Flexible Scheduling: Employees choose their working hours within set limits. Types include flextime and ROWE (Rapoport et al., 2002). It boosts productivity and job satisfaction but can lead to coordination challenges and potential overwork.

Compressed Workweeks: Employees work longer hours on fewer days, like four 10-hour days (Moen et al., 2016). It offers extended time off and reduced commuting, but can cause fatigue and scheduling conflicts with clients.

Job Sharing: Two employees share one full-time job, offering work-life balance and skill diversification (Clifton & Shepard, 2004). Challenges include communication and unequal workload distribution.

Hybrid Work Models: A mix of in-office and remote work, offering flexibility and collaboration (Allen et al., 2021). Benefits include improved engagement and cost savings, but it can strain organizational culture and create inequalities in work arrangements.

Research Objectives and Questions

The primary objective of this research is to analyze the impact of flexible work policies on employee well-being and retention. The study aims to:

RQ1. Examine how flexible work arrangements influence job satisfaction, work-life balance, and psychological well-being.
RQ2. Assess the role of flexible work policies in reducing employee turnover and enhancing organizational commitment.
RQ3. Identify challenges associated with implementing flexible work arrangements and propose strategic solutions.
RQ4. Explore industry-specific applications of flexible work policies and their long-term implications for workforce productivity.

2. THEORETICAL FRAMEWORKS AND LITERATURE REVIEW

2.1 Job Demands-Resources (JD-R) Model

The Job Demands-Resources (JD-R) model is a widely recognized theoretical framework that explains the relationship between job demands, job resources, and employee well-being (Bakker & Demerouti, 2007). The model classifies workplace factors into two main categories: job demands and job resources. Job demands refer to aspects of a job that require sustained effort and are associated with psychological and physical costs, such as workload, deadlines, and emotional labor. Job resources, on the other hand, include physical, psychological, social, and organizational aspects that help employees meet job demands, reduce strain, and facilitate personal growth (Demerouti et al., 2001).

Relevance to Flexible Work Policies

Flexible work arrangements, such as remote work, flexible scheduling, and compressed workweeks, serve as crucial job resources that help employees manage work demands effectively. Research suggests that flexible work policies provide employees with autonomy, control over their schedules, and an improved work-life balance, which mitigates job-related stress and burnout (Schaufeli & Taris, 2014). Employees with greater job resources tend to be more engaged, as they can better manage their work responsibilities without experiencing excessive strain. This engagement, in turn, leads to improved job performance and reduced turnover intentions (Bakker et al., 2008).

A study by Schaufeli and Taris (2014) found that employees with higher levels of job resources reported lower burnout rates and higher productivity. By reducing job demands and enhancing resources, flexible work policies foster a work environment that promotes psychological well-being and organizational commitment.

2.2 Self-Determination Theory (SDT)

Self-Determination Theory (SDT), developed by Deci and Ryan (1985), posits that human motivation is driven by three fundamental psychological needs: autonomy, competence, and relatedness. Autonomy refers to the need to feel in control of one's actions and decisions, competence relates to the need for mastery and effectiveness in activities, and relatedness involves the need to connect with others and feel a sense of belonging (Deci & Ryan, 2000).

Impact of Flexible Work Policies

Flexible work arrangements directly address the need for autonomy by allowing employees to manage their work schedules, choose their work environments, and balance professional and personal commitments. Research indicates that when employees experience greater autonomy, they are more intrinsically motivated, which enhances job satisfaction and productivity (Gagné & Deci, 2005).

Additionally, competence is fostered through flexible work policies by enabling employees to work at their optimal times and conditions, thereby increasing efficiency and skill development. Relatedness is also supported through virtual collaboration tools that allow employees to maintain strong social connections with colleagues, despite working remotely (Deci et al., 2017).

A meta-analysis by Ryan and Deci (2017) found that organizations implementing autonomy-supportive work environments reported higher employee engagement, well-being, and retention rates. These findings highlight the importance of flexible work policies in promoting a work culture that aligns with employees' intrinsic motivation.

2.3 Conservation of Resources (COR) Theory

The Conservation of Resources (COR) theory, proposed by Hobfoll (1989), suggests that individuals strive to acquire, maintain, and protect valuable resources, such as time, energy, and social support. When individuals perceive a threat to their resources or experience resource depletion, they are more likely to experience stress and burnout. Conversely, when organizations provide employees with mechanisms to conserve their resources, such as flexible work policies, employees experience lower stress and improved job performance (Halbesleben et al., 2014).

Application to Flexible Work Arrangements

Flexible work arrangements enable employees to conserve essential resources by reducing commute times, minimizing workplace distractions, and allowing for better time management. Research by ten Brummelhuis and Bakker (2012) suggests that employees who can manage their work schedules effectively experience lower exhaustion levels and higher job satisfaction.

A study by Halbesleben et al. (2014) demonstrated that employees with access to flexible work policies reported fewer stress-related health issues and greater work engagement. By providing employees with autonomy over their schedules and reducing unnecessary job demands, organizations help employees maintain their resources, ultimately enhancing productivity and retention.

2.4 Social Exchange Theory (SET)

Social Exchange Theory (SET), developed by Blau (1964), explains workplace relationships based on the principle of reciprocity. According to SET, employees who perceive organizational support are more likely to reciprocate with increased commitment, loyalty, and productivity (Cropanzano & Mitchell, 2005).

Impact of Flexible Work Policies

Flexible work arrangements serve as a form of organizational support, signaling to employees that their well-being and personal needs are valued. When employees perceive that their employer is investing in their work-life balance, they develop a sense of loyalty and commitment to the organization (Eisenberger et al., 2001).

Research by Kossek et al. (2014) found that employees who benefited from flexible work policies exhibited higher levels of job satisfaction and organizational commitment. Moreover, these employees were more likely to engage in discretionary efforts, such as helping colleagues and contributing to organizational success beyond their formal job responsibilities.

A longitudinal study by (Wayne et al., 2020) revealed that employees who received flexible work options displayed higher retention rates and lower absenteeism, further demonstrating the reciprocal nature of social exchange in the workplace.

Table 1. Flexible work policies

Dimension	JD-R Model	SDT (Self-Determination Theory)	COR (Conservation of Resources)
Core Focus	Balance between job demands and available resources	Fulfillment of basic psychological needs: autonomy, competence, relatedness	Preservation and accumulation of valuable personal and job-related resources
Relevance to Flex Work	Flexible work reduces demands (e.g., commute, rigidity) and increases resources (e.g., autonomy, support)	Flexibility supports autonomy (choice in schedule), competence (work at peak times), relatedness (digital connection)	Reduces resource depletion (e.g., time, energy) and aids recovery via schedule control
Key Outcomes	Higher engagement, lower burnout, better performance	Intrinsic motivation, higher job satisfaction, improved well-being	Lower stress, increased resilience, improved retention
Examples in Practice	Remote work reduces time demands and enhances personal control (resource gain)	Flexible hours allow employees to self-direct and feel capable	Flextime enables better energy and time management, protecting personal resources
Implications for Retention	Employees stay where they feel resourced and not overburdened	Motivation through autonomy increases attachment to role/ organization	Retention improves when employees are not in constant "resource threat" mode
HR Strategy Alignment	Design roles that reduce non-essential demands and increase flexible resources	Foster an environment that nurtures autonomy and meaningful connection	Provide tools and freedom that allow employees to conserve and replenish resources

2.5 Boundary Theory

Boundary Theory explores how individuals manage the boundaries between work and personal life (Ashforth et al., 2000). Some individuals prefer to integrate work and personal life seamlessly, while others prefer to maintain clear distinctions between the two domains.

5 Role of Flexible Work Policies

Flexible work arrangements play a critical role in enhancing employee well-being by allowing individuals to align their work schedules and environments with personal needs and preferences. These policies reduce work-life conflict and promote a healthier integration or segmentation of work and personal life, depending on individual boundary management styles. For example, remote work supports those who prefer work-life integration, while designated hours and fixed locations benefit those who seek clear distinctions between work and home life (Ashforth et al., 2000; Kossek et al., 2012).

Psychological Benefits

A central psychological benefit of flexible work policies is stress reduction, which is driven largely by increased job autonomy. According to the Job Demand-Control Model (Karasek, 1979), autonomy serves as a buffer against the adverse effects of high job demands. Employees who control when, where, and how they work experience less psychological strain and a reduced risk of burnout (Gajendran & Harrison, 2007). This autonomy also supports intrinsic motivation and psychological resilience (Gagné & Deci, 2005), contributing to enhanced job satisfaction and emotional well-being (Shockley & Allen, 2015).

Flexible arrangements also enable psychological detachment—a critical factor in recovery from work-related stress. Employees with control over their schedules are more likely to engage in health-promoting behaviors such as mindfulness, leisure activities, and quality time with family, which reduce anxiety and prevent burnout (Sonnentag & Fritz, 2007; Grawitch et al., 2010).

Tailored Benefits Across the Employee Lifecycle

Different types of flexibility offer unique psychological benefits depending on an employee's personality, life stage, or caregiving status. For example:

- Younger employees benefit from self-paced work that supports skill development and manages early-career pressures.
- Mid-career professionals use flexible hours or compressed workweeks to balance family responsibilities.
- Older workers transitioning toward retirement may prefer part-time or remote options that reduce cognitive and physical strain (de Menezes & Kelliher, 2011).

Similarly, introverts and caregivers may benefit from reduced social stressors and greater logistical flexibility, while extraverts and early-career employees may prefer hybrid arrangements that provide structured social engagement (Brough & O'Driscoll, 2010; Kossek et al., 2012).

Physical Health Benefits

Flexible work arrangements also offer significant physical health benefits. Employees with flexible schedules avoid long commutes, maintain better sleep hygiene, and engage more frequently in physical activity, all of which contribute to lower stress and better health outcomes (Basner et al., 2014; Tavares, 2017). The ability to tailor one's work environment—such as using ergonomic setups, incorporating movement, or working in natural light—reduces musculoskeletal strain and enhances comfort (Robertson et al., 2013; Mattioli et al., 2020).

Additionally, flexible work supports preventative health behaviors, such as regular medical checkups and wellness routines, leading to long-term health improvements and decreased absenteeism (Tavares, 2017; de Menezes & Kelliher, 2011).

Risks and Mitigation Strategies

While the benefits are substantial, flexible work policies are not without challenges. Poorly designed policies can result in blurred boundaries, where employees feel the need to be constantly available, increasing stress and cognitive overload (Derks et al., 2014). Social isolation is another risk, as reduced face-to-face interaction may limit emotional support and collaboration opportunities.

To mitigate these downsides, organizations should implement strategies such as:

- Establishing digital curfews and communication norms,
- Providing boundary-setting training for employees and managers,
- Facilitating regular check-ins for social connection,
- Promoting leadership behaviors that model healthy work-life integration.

Integrating digital wellness tools and fostering autonomy-supportive leadership can further ensure that flexibility supports rather than undermines employee well-being (Ryan & Deci, 2017).

In conclusion, Flexible work policies contribute to improved psychological and physical health through mechanisms such as autonomy, job control, and personalized work conditions. These benefits are especially pronounced when flexibility is tailored to the needs of diverse employee populations across different life stages.

When designed intentionally, flexible work arrangements reduce stress, support well-being, and enhance both individual and organizational performance.

4. THE IMPACT OF FLEXIBLE WORK POLICIES ON EMPLOYEE RETENTION

4.1 Employee Commitment and Job Satisfaction

Flexible work policies significantly contribute to higher levels of employee commitment and job satisfaction, which, in turn, positively affect employee retention rates. Employees who experience autonomy in their work schedules often report increased motivation and engagement, leading to greater job satisfaction (Masuda et al., 2012). Research has demonstrated that when employees feel trusted to manage their schedules, they develop a stronger psychological attachment to their organization, reducing turnover rates (Allen et al., 2013).

Moreover, job satisfaction is closely linked to perceived organizational support. Employees who believe their organization genuinely cares about their well-being are more committed to their roles (Eisenberger et al., 1986). A study by de Menezes and Kelliher (2011) found that flexible work arrangements significantly contribute to a positive work environment, reducing absenteeism and improving overall job satisfaction. Employees who can tailor their work schedules to their needs are more likely to perform efficiently and remain engaged in their tasks (Ten Brummelhuis & Bakker, 2012).

4.2 Attraction and Retention of Talent

Flexible work policies contribute to employee retention by fostering a positive organizational culture. Employees who experience workplace flexibility are less likely to seek alternative job opportunities, as they feel a stronger connection to their employer (Kelliher & Anderson, 2010). According to a study by Bloom et al. (2015), companies that implemented remote work policies observed a significant reduction in turnover rates due to increased employee satisfaction and reduced commuting stress.

In addition to attracting new talent, flexible work arrangements help retain employees by accommodating their evolving needs. For instance, working parents and caregivers benefit greatly from telecommuting and flextime arrangements, enabling them to balance professional and personal responsibilities effectively (Hill et al., 2008). Employees who feel their employer supports their work-life balance are more likely to remain loyal to the company (Kossek & Michel, 2011).

Several multinational corporations have recognized the importance of flexible work arrangements in talent retention. For example, companies such as Google and Microsoft have adopted hybrid work models that allow employees to work remotely while maintaining in-office collaboration when necessary. Studies indicate that such policies enhance job satisfaction and reduce attrition rates, demonstrating the long-term benefits of flexible work environments (OECD, 2021).

In conclusion for Global Perspective,

A. Well-being
   - **India**: A report by the National Association of Software and Service Companies (NASSCOM) found that Indian companies that implemented flexible work options saw reduced employee turnover and improved job satisfaction. For instance, **Infosys** has provided employees with the option to work from home or adopt flexible hours, which helped alleviate the stress often associated with long commutes in large cities like Bangalore.
   - **Japan**: In Japan, where the work culture has traditionally emphasized long hours and dedication, companies like **Rakuten** have pioneered the "work from anywhere" initiative. By shifting away from rigid office hours, Rakuten has seen improvements in employee satisfaction and mental health, particularly among workers with caregiving responsibilities, who previously found it difficult to meet both work and personal demands.

B. Job Satisfaction
   - **China**: Chinese companies are starting to embrace flexible work arrangements, especially in the tech industry. **Alibaba** and **Tencent** have introduced various forms of flexible work, allowing employees to work from home or take advantage of flexible hours. This change was particularly well-received by the younger workforce, improving job satisfaction levels by promoting a better work-life balance.
   - **Brazil**: In Brazil, a growing number of companies are recognizing the importance of flexible work in fostering job satisfaction. For example, Grupo Pão de Açúcar, one of the largest retailers in Brazil, has offered flexible schedules and remote work options to its employees in response to demands for better work-life balance. This initiative has contributed to improved employee morale, particularly among those who are parents or caretakers.

C. Reduced Stress and Burnout
   - **South Korea**: South Korea has one of the longest working hours in the world, leading to high levels of work-related stress and burnout. To

combat this, companies like **Samsung** have implemented flexible work policies, including telecommuting options, to help reduce stress and improve employee well-being. These efforts are part of a broader national strategy to address "overwork culture," helping workers balance personal and professional lives.

- **United Arab Emirates (UAE)**: In the UAE, flexible work arrangements are increasingly being seen as a way to reduce the pressure of traditional office culture. **Dubai's government** implemented a four-day workweek to support mental health and reduce stress, becoming a model for other regions in the Middle East. This initiative has seen positive feedback from employees, particularly in terms of well-being and stress reduction.

D. Employee Retention

- **Mexico**: In Mexico, companies like **Bimbo** have implemented flexible work options, which have contributed to greater employee retention. The country has seen high turnover in the past, and offering flexibility has become a strategic tool for retaining workers, especially in the competitive manufacturing and retail sectors.
- **Singapore**: **DBS Bank** in Singapore has been a leader in promoting flexible work schedules as part of its broader strategy to boost employee retention. With a focus on work-life integration, the company reported lower turnover rates and greater overall satisfaction among its employees, particularly among women and millennials.

Critical Analysis of Evidence Linking Flexible Work Policies and Mental Health Outcomes

Flexible work arrangements have gained widespread recognition for their potential to improve employee well-being, yet the link between flexible work and mental health outcomes is more nuanced than often depicted. While reduced commuting times and greater autonomy over work schedules can alleviate anxiety (Fitzgerald, 2020), poorly structured remote work can create anticipatory stress due to uncertainty, unclear expectations, and reduced social interaction (Nguyen et al., 2021). Similarly, flexibility can contribute to reduced depression by enhancing autonomy and social support (Cao et al., 2021), but it may exacerbate feelings of isolation for employees who require higher levels of social engagement (Smith & Lockwood, 2020). Furthermore, flexibility alone does not shield employees from burnout; the balance between high job demands and low autonomy is a critical factor (Maslach

& Leiter, 2017). When workload expectations are not adjusted in conjunction with flexible work, employees may still face high levels of stress and emotional exhaustion.

Several factors mediate or moderate the mental health outcomes associated with flexible work. Organizational culture, characterized by psychological safety and open communication, is vital in amplifying the benefits of flexible work policies (Kirkpatrick et al., 2019). Leadership support is another key factor; autonomy-supportive leadership, which encourages independence while maintaining clear expectations, has been shown to reduce employee stress and increase job satisfaction (Deci et al., 2017). Job design is equally important, as flexibility without clear task structure and sufficient resources may lead to role ambiguity, nullifying the positive effects of flexible schedules (Rothbard et al., 2005). Moreover, the tools used for digital communication and collaboration play a significant role in mediating flexible work outcomes. Effective technology can enhance productivity and connection, especially for neurodiverse employees or those with accessibility needs (Marschark et al., 2020).

Despite the promise of flexible work arrangements, current research on the subject is not without its limitations. A major flaw in the literature is the over-reliance on self-reports for measuring mental health outcomes, which are prone to bias and lack objective validation (Bailey & Kurland, 2020). Additionally, most studies rely on cross-sectional designs, limiting causal inferences about the long-term effects of flexible work on mental health. Longitudinal and experimental research is needed to capture the trajectory of mental health outcomes over time (Greenhaus et al., 2020). Many studies also focus on high-income, white-collar populations, leaving gaps in understanding the impact of flexible work across diverse industries, socio-economic statuses, and cultural contexts (Shin et al., 2022). Furthermore, the lack of differentiation between types of flexibility (e.g., remote vs. hybrid vs. flextime) makes it difficult to assess the specific impacts of each model on mental health (Wong et al., 2021). Finally, there is a significant gap in intersectional analyses, with limited research on how race, gender identity, disability, and caregiving responsibilities influence the mental health outcomes of flexible work policies (Harris et al., 2023).

To strengthen the evidence base and inform better policy-making, future research should adopt a multi-method approach, integrating objective markers such as physiological stress measures, behavioral data, and structured clinical interviews to assess mental health more accurately (Sonnentag et al., 2020). Longitudinal studies are also needed to understand the long-term mental health trajectories of employees in flexible work arrangements (Bergström et al., 2021). Further exploration of cross-cultural and sector-specific implications is crucial, as the effects of flexible work on mental health may vary across different work environments and cultural contexts (Harrison & Willness, 2022). Additionally, there is a need for more intersectional research to examine how flexible work affects diverse groups, including those from marginalized communities, to ensure that policies do not inadvertently perpetuate inequities (Tucker & Lindsay, 2023). Finally, the development of typologies or frameworks that categorize different types of flexible work policies and their specific psychological outcomes will be crucial for future research and practice (Bakker & Demerouti, 2020).

5. STRESS MANAGEMENT PROGRAMS AND RESOURCES

Effective stress management programs can significantly contribute to employee well-being, especially in flexible or remote work environments where boundaries between work and personal life may blur. Here are some programs and resources that have been proven to support mental health:

- Employee Assistance Programs (EAPs): These programs offer confidential counseling services, mental health resources, and stress management workshops. For instance, companies like IBM and Salesforce have utilized EAPs to provide 24/7 support to their employees, offering resources ranging from therapy sessions to mindfulness training (Shallcross et al., 2019).
- Mindfulness and Meditation Workshops: Programs like Headspace for Work or Calm for Business provide employees with guided meditation sessions, mindfulness exercises, and resources for improving mental focus and reducing stress. Research has shown that mindfulness programs can lower stress levels and improve cognitive function (Zeidan et al., 2010).
- Mental Health Days and Paid Time Off (PTO): Providing dedicated time off for mental health reasons has become more widespread. For example, LinkedIn offers employees "Mental Health Days" as part of their PTO policy, recognizing the importance of mental health in overall productivity (Caldwell, 2021). This allows employees to disconnect without feeling guilty, promoting recovery from stress.
- Online Stress Management Courses: Platforms like Headspace and BetterHelp also offer online resources for managing work-related stress, providing employees with tools to develop healthy coping strategies and manage their emotional well-being effectively.

The effectiveness of stress management resources, organizations must foster a culture that actively encourages employees to utilize these programs without fear of stigma or negative consequences. This can be achieved through leadership modelling, where senior leaders openly advocate for mental health awareness, creating an environment where seeking help is normalized. Peer support programs, such as Google's "Wellness Ambassadors," can also facilitate solidarity among employees, while integrating mental health discussions into regular conversations- like team meetings and performance reviews helps normalize these topics. Additionally, confidentiality and privacy assurances ensure that employees feel secure in using mental health resources without fear of career repercussions.

Managers play a critical role in addressing stress and burnout, particularly in remote or flexible work settings where signs of distress may not be immediately apparent. Regular check-ins with active listening allow employees to express concerns about their workload and well-being in a safe space. Managers should be attentive to early signs of burnout, such as absenteeism, disengagement, or emotional exhaustion, and respond with empathy by adjusting workloads or offering support. Encouraging healthy work-life boundaries, such as regular breaks and defined office hours, further helps mitigate stress, while promoting team resilience and collaboration ensures a supportive work environment.

Finally, managers can offer tailored support to employees showing signs of stress by adjusting their schedules or workload and providing mental health resources. Encouraging peer support and group well-being through activities like virtual mindfulness sessions or stretching breaks strengthens the sense of community and reduces stress. By investing in stress management resources, cultivating a supportive culture, and equipping managers with the tools to address burnout, organizations can enhance employee well-being, improve engagement, and reduce turnover in remote or flexible work environments.

To effectively implement and manage flexible work policies that prioritize employee mental health, managers must focus on creating structures that support both flexibility and well-being. A key recommendation is to establish clear expectations and boundaries for flexible work arrangements. This includes setting up designated "office hours" and ensuring employees have the flexibility to disconnect outside of those hours. Managers should communicate the importance of maintaining work-life boundaries and encourage employees to take breaks, use vacation days, and disconnect fully during non-working hours. Additionally, managers can provide access to mental health resources such as Employee Assistance Programs (EAPs), mindfulness workshops, and stress management resources to support employees in managing the pressures that come with flexible work. Regular check-ins should be scheduled to ensure that employees feel supported and have the opportunity to discuss any challenges related to their work arrangements or mental health.

From a theoretical standpoint, the **Job Demand-Control Model** (Karasek, 1979) provides a useful framework for understanding how flexible work policies can impact employee mental health. According to this model, employees who have control over their work environment and schedule are better able to manage job demands, leading to reduced stress and improved mental health outcomes. Managers should empower employees with autonomy over when, where, and how they work, ensuring that they feel in control of their tasks and work-life balance. Additionally, the **Conservation of Resources (COR) Theory** (Hobfoll, 1989) suggests that employees who are provided with sufficient resources, such as time, support, and flexibility, are more resilient to stress. Managers can apply this theory by ensuring that employees have the resources they need to thrive in a flexible environment, such as ergonomic home office setups, flexible schedules, and adequate time for rest and recovery.

Furthermore, managers should recognize the importance of **social support** in mental health. According to **Social Support Theory**, the emotional and practical support provided by colleagues and supervisors plays a crucial role in buffering stress. In a flexible or remote work environment, where social isolation may be a concern, managers can foster a culture of connection by encouraging team-building activities, peer support programs, and regular virtual meetings. By cultivating an environment where employees feel both autonomous and supported, managers can enhance job satisfaction, engagement, and overall mental well-being, ensuring that flexible work policies contribute to long-term success for both the employees and the organization.

6. FLEXIBLE WORK POLICIES AND DEI: ENHANCING INCLUSION THROUGH EQUITABLE FLEXIBILITY

Flexible work policies offer a significant opportunity to advance Diversity, Equity, and Inclusion (DEI) goals within organizations—if designed and implemented equitably. While many flexible arrangements are intended to promote well-being and autonomy, they may inadvertently reinforce disparities if access and support are uneven across roles or demographics (Kossek & Lautsch, 2018).

There are few points to consider:

Impact on Underrepresented and Marginalized Groups- Working Parents and Caregivers: Women, particularly mothers, disproportionately bear caregiving responsibilities. Flexible scheduling and remote options can help mitigate career penalties and support continued workforce participation (Williams et al., 2016).

People with Disabilities: Remote work can eliminate physical and social barriers, increasing autonomy and accessibility for employees with disabilities (Schur et al., 2020).

Racial and Ethnic Minorities: Marginalized racial groups may benefit from reduced microaggressions and enhanced psychological safety in remote settings, although lack of in-person visibility may still impact advancement (Robinson et al., 2019).

LGBTQ+ Employees: Flexible work arrangements may foster inclusivity by enabling employees to work in environments where they feel safer and less subject to bias or identity suppression (Gates, 2022).

Risks of Unequal Access: Despite potential benefits, access to flexibility often correlates with job type or level of seniority. This dynamic may disproportionately exclude underrepresented groups in front-line or lower-wage positions, reinforcing existing inequities (Kossek et al., 2014).

Fostering Inclusion Through Equitable Design: To ensure flexible work supports DEI rather than undermining it, organizations should conduct equity audits to assess access disparities (Williams et al., 2016) and design flexibility across roles, including shift autonomy and location variety (Kossek & Lautsch, 2018). Also, they should ensure inclusive tech and tools, addressing accessibility and usability for all (Schur et al., 2020) by training managers to counteract proximity bias and fairly evaluate all work formats (Robinson et al., 2019).

Strategic DEI Outcomes: When equity is embedded in flexible policy design, organizations can achieve:

- Improved representation and retention of marginalized talent,
- Enhanced trust and engagement across diverse demographics,
- A more inclusive culture that reflects real investment in well-being and belonging.

7. POLICY EVALUATION TOOLS FOR FLEXIBLE WORK ARRANGEMENTS

Evaluating the effectiveness of flexible work policies is essential to ensure that these initiatives align with organizational goals while supporting employee well-being and retention. A comprehensive approach to evaluation combines both quantitative metrics and qualitative insights, using dashboards, surveys, and continuous feedback mechanisms to provide a holistic understanding of policy impact.

A primary tool in this evaluation is the use of outcome-based Key Performance Indicators (KPIs) tailored to specific organizational objectives. These indicators commonly include turnover and retention rates to assess changes before and after policy implementation (Tavares, 2017), absenteeism rates to determine whether flexibility reduces unplanned absences (Bloom et al., 2015), and employee satisfaction levels measured through instruments such as the Gallup Q12 or the Job Satisfaction Survey (JSS) (Grawitch et al., 2006). Productivity can be tracked through deliverables per employee, average project completion times, and self-reported productivity levels (Wang et al., 2020). Additionally, utilization rates of flexible arrangements—such as remote workdays, flex hours, and job-sharing—should be monitored across departments and demographic groups to ensure equitable access.

Employee feedback plays a crucial role in understanding the lived experiences behind the data. Regular pulse surveys can measure morale, stress levels, and perceptions of fairness on a monthly or quarterly basis (Chen & Nath, 2021). One-on-one check-ins between managers and employees provide opportunities for more in-depth conversations about the benefits and limitations of flexible work (Kossek et al., 2014), while focus groups with diverse participants can uncover challenges related to diversity, equity, and inclusion (DEI) in the accessibility of these policies.

To further ensure equity, organizations should conduct DEI audits that include access gap analyses comparing usage rates across job roles, gender, ability, and other identities (Kossek & Lautsch, 2018). Reviews of promotion and compensation data can reveal whether employees using flexible arrangements face unintended penalties in visibility or advancement opportunities (Golden & Gajendran, 2019), helping organizations detect and address potential inequities.

Technology also plays a vital role in policy evaluation. Centralized digital dashboards can track real-time data such as the frequency of flexible work option usage, well-being indicators from stress and burnout surveys, turnover trends by team, and diversity-related metrics like flexible policy adoption among underrepresented groups. These visual tools allow human resources and leadership teams to identify patterns and disparities quickly, enabling timely and informed decision-making (Brougham & Haar, 2018).

Organizations should also engage in benchmarking and external comparisons to evaluate their flexible work strategies against industry standards and competitor practices. Participating in external surveys, third-party audits such as Great Place to Work®, and referencing annual reports from organizations like SHRM or the OECD can provide valuable context for policy refinement and innovation.

Finally, policy evaluation must follow a continuous improvement model. Flexible work arrangements and their outcomes evolve alongside changes in workforce expectations, technology, and societal trends. Reviewing and updating policies at least annually ensures they remain relevant, effective, and responsive to employee needs (Spreitzer et al., 2017). A dynamic feedback loop that incorporates data analysis, employee insights, and new research findings will allow organizations to adapt and thrive in a changing work environment.

Table 2. Industry-specific implementation of flexible work policies

Industry	Flexible Work Practices	Challenges	Best Practices
Healthcare	Self-scheduling, telehealth, flexible shifts for support staff	Limited remote roles, burnout, coordination issues	Shift-bidding apps, mental health days, cross-training
IT/Tech	Fully remote roles, asynchronous work, global teams, 4-day workweeks	Time zone differences, digital fatigue, maintaining culture	Remote-first policies, digital wellness norms, outcome-based evaluations
Manufacturing	Flexible shifts, compressed weeks, remote IoT monitoring	Physical presence required, safety regulations, complex scheduling	Real-time scheduling, ergonomic shifts, remote diagnostics roles
Education	Hybrid teaching, virtual office hours, asynchronous content	Student engagement, tech disparities, curriculum constraints	Blended learning, flexible grading, ed-tech investment
Finance	Remote advisory, hybrid compliance roles, flextime	Security/compliance concerns, high coordination demands	Encrypted tools, role-based flexibility, office rotations
Retail	Shift swapping apps, part-time flexibility, remote backend roles	Limited remote roles, demand fluctuation, regulations	Dynamic scheduling, self-service HR portals, backend remote setups

- **Implementing Continuous Improvement Measures**

Based on assessment findings, organizations should refine their flexible work policies and introduce improvements. This may include updating technological infrastructure, adjusting eligibility criteria, or enhancing training programs (Spreitzer, Cameron, & Garrett, 2017). A culture of continuous improvement ensures that flexible work policies remain relevant, effective, and aligned with organizational objectives.

8. CHALLENGES IN IMPLEMENTING FLEXIBLE WORK POLICIES

Flexible work policies have gained significant traction in modern organizations, particularly in the wake of global disruptions such as the COVID-19 pandemic. These policies offer employees greater control over their work schedules, leading to improved work-life balance, increased job satisfaction, and enhanced productivity. However, despite these advantages, implementing flexible work policies presents several challenges. Organizations must address concerns related to equity and fairness, collaboration and communication barriers, and performance management and productivity tracking to ensure successful adoption. This paper explores these challenges in depth, supported by relevant literature and empirical evidence.

8.1 Equity and Fairness Concerns

Equity and fairness in flexible work policies refer to ensuring that all employees receive equal treatment and opportunities, regardless of job roles, personal circumstances, or work arrangements (Kossek et al., 2016). While these policies aim to accommodate diverse needs, they can also create disparities between employees in remote-eligible roles and those whose jobs require physical presence (Colbert et al., 2016). For instance, knowledge workers such as IT professionals and administrative staff may enjoy remote work privileges, whereas frontline workers in healthcare or manufacturing must remain on-site (Bloom et al., 2015). This discrepancy may result in perceptions of favoritism, resentment, and reduced morale among on-site employees, especially when remote workers receive additional benefits such as flexible schedules or home office stipends (Golden & Gajendran, 2019; Kossek & Lautsch, 2018). Moreover, workload imbalances may occur, with on-site workers shouldering more responsibilities while their remote counterparts experience greater autonomy (Nguyen & Armoogum, 2021).

Another pressing issue is the impact of flexible work on career development. Remote workers may have limited access to informal networking, mentorship, and leadership visibility—factors crucial to career progression (Golden & Gajendran, 2019). Research indicates that in-office employees are more likely to be promoted than their remote peers (Nguyen & Armoogum, 2021), often due to proximity bias, where managers equate physical presence with productivity and dedication (Gajendran et al., 2015). Consequently, remote employees may face systemic disadvantages, unless organizations adopt fair and objective evaluation criteria that account for these differences (Pulakos et al., 2015; Leonardi, 2021).

Additionally, maintaining equity requires adherence to legal standards and the establishment of transparent internal policies. Organizations must navigate complex labor regulations across jurisdictions concerning remote work arrangements, compensation, and working hours (Drucker, 1999). Clear frameworks outlining eligibility, performance expectations, and compensation structures are essential to ensuring fairness and avoiding legal disputes (Bailey & Kurland, 2002). Transparent communication of these policies is equally critical to foster employee trust and ensure mutual understanding (Tarafdar et al., 2019).

8.2 Collaboration and Communication Barriers

The effectiveness of flexible work models also hinges on seamless communication and collaboration. However, remote and hybrid work arrangements introduce significant barriers in these domains (Bailey & Kurland, 2002). Coordinating tasks across different time zones and schedules can lead to delays and inefficiencies, especially in asynchronous communication settings where team members respond at varying times (Gibbs et al., 2021). These challenges are particularly evident in global teams that struggle with scheduling real-time meetings and maintaining consistent communication flows (Gajendran et al., 2015; Leonardi, 2021). Although digital tools like Slack, Microsoft Teams, and Trello facilitate collaboration, they cannot fully replicate the immediacy and nuance of in-person interactions (Kossek & Lautsch, 2018).

Furthermore, the increased reliance on virtual platforms has led to concerns about digital fatigue and disengagement. Employees frequently exposed to extended virtual meetings often report decreased concentration, mental exhaustion, and lower participation levels (Nilles, 1998; Tarafdar et al., 2019). The lack of engaging, face-to-face interactions contributes to these issues and may undermine communication effectiveness (Golden & Gajendran, 2019). Compounding this is the blurring of boundaries between work and personal life in remote settings, which can lead to burnout and adversely impact work-life balance (Kossek et al., 2016).

8.3 Performance Management and Productivity Tracking

Flexible work environments also challenge traditional models of performance management. Organizations must strike a balance between granting employees' autonomy and ensuring accountability (Pulakos et al., 2015). Excessive surveillance, such as tracking keystrokes or mandating constant availability, often fosters distrust and micromanagement, which can harm employee morale and productivity (Deci et al., 2017). Instead, outcome-based performance metrics that prioritize results over physical presence are more conducive to trust and empowerment (Drucker, 1999). Transparent performance expectations, combined with support for employee self-motivation, enable better alignment with organizational goals (Nguyen & Armoogum, 2021).

Another concern is the potential for bias in evaluating remote workers. Managers may unconsciously favor employees who are physically present, associating visibility with productivity—a phenomenon known as proximity bias (Gajendran et al., 2015). This can disadvantage remote workers during performance reviews and hinder their career progression. To mitigate this, organizations should adopt objective, data-driven performance assessment methods and conduct regular check-ins to provide continuous feedback and development opportunities (Kossek & Lautsch, 2018; Leonardi, 2021).

Overcoming Resistance to Flexible Work Policies

Resistance to flexible work policies can arise from both management and employees. Managers often worry about losing control or facing productivity declines. These concerns can be mitigated by implementing clear outcome-based performance metrics and equipping managers with tools and training for remote supervision. Organizational culture change is also essential, where leaders must actively endorse and model flexible work practices to set the tone.

On the employee side, concerns may include fear of being penalized for using flexibility, lack of digital access or literacy, and reduced social interaction. Organizations can address these by ensuring transparent promotion policies, offering technology support, and maintaining structured hybrid options that balance flexibility with connection.

A broader organizational strategy should include phased implementation, employee involvement in policy design, and ongoing communication and feedback mechanisms. These approaches foster ownership and understanding, helping transform resistance into support and ensuring the long-term success of flexible work initiatives.

Long-Term Impact on Organizational Culture and Innovation

Flexible work policies can profoundly shape organizational culture over time, fostering a climate of trust, autonomy, and inclusivity. As hierarchical structures give way to more agile, decentralized models of work, employees often report stronger feelings of empowerment and ownership. These cultural shifts encourage continuous learning and psychological safety, which are essential ingredients for a resilient and adaptive workforce.

Moreover, flexibility supports innovation by enabling diverse forms of collaboration, including asynchronous teamwork and global talent integration. With greater autonomy, employees are more likely to take initiative, experiment, and share ideas. Remote and hybrid environments can also reduce cognitive load and stress, freeing up mental capacity for creative thinking. Organizations that embrace flexible work are thus more likely to evolve into learning cultures where innovation is not just permitted but expected.

To sustain this momentum, leadership must reinforce open communication, celebrate innovative efforts, and ensure inclusive access to flexible opportunities across roles. Over the long term, this alignment between flexibility, culture, and innovation can drive sustained competitive advantage.

Strategic Recommendations for Organizations

Flexible work policies have gained significant traction in modern organizations, especially following the global shift triggered by the COVID-19 pandemic. This paper explores strategic recommendations for organizations aiming to optimize the advantages of flexible work policies. It elaborates on the importance of developing clear guidelines, leveraging technology, fostering a culture of trust, providing training and support, and regularly assessing policy effectiveness. By implementing these strategies, organizations can enhance employee satisfaction, productivity, and overall organizational success.

The rise of flexible work policies has revolutionized the traditional workplace, allowing organizations to foster employee well-being, increase productivity, and improve job satisfaction. However, the successful implementation of these policies requires strategic planning and execution. This paper elaborates on five key recommendations for organizations to optimize their flexible work policies: developing clear guidelines, leveraging technology, promoting a culture of trust, providing training and support, and regularly assessing policy effectiveness.

Flexible work policies should align with organizational goals, employee needs, and industry standards. Core objectives include improving work-life balance, cutting operational costs, and attracting diverse talent. To ensure fairness, clear eligibility criteria must be established based on job roles, collaboration needs, and data security concerns.

Organizations must set performance expectations focused on outcomes, using KPIs such as task completion and quality of work. Compliance with labor laws, cybersecurity regulations, and tax requirements is critical, especially when managing a geographically dispersed workforce.

Technology plays a vital role in flexible work success. Tools like Teams, Zoom, and Asana enhance collaboration, while cloud platforms streamline access to documents. Strong cybersecurity protocols and AI-powered performance analytics improve security, efficiency, and decision-making.

Trust is essential in flexible work environments. Leaders should shift to outcome-based management, maintain transparent communication, and recognize achievements. Fostering social connection through virtual team-building and open dialogue helps reduce isolation and increase engagement.

Ongoing training and support are crucial. Managers need skills for remote leadership, while employees must be digitally literate and equipped for work-life balance. Regular feedback, productivity tracking, and benchmarking against industry standards help refine policies and ensure long-term effectiveness.

Case Studies: Real-World Implementation of Flexible Work Policies

This section examines how Microsoft, Salesforce, and Spotify have successfully implemented flexible work policies, offering insights into their distinct strategies and outcomes. Microsoft introduced a hybrid model in 2021, focusing on cultural transformation, leadership adaptation, and digital infrastructure, resulting in improved employee satisfaction and engagement (Microsoft, 2021a). Salesforce's "Success from Anywhere" initiative emphasized employee empowerment, equity, and innovation, leading to higher retention and a more diverse workforce (Salesforce, 2022). Spotify's "Work from Anywhere" program offered complete autonomy, fostering creativity, reducing stress, and enhancing employee satisfaction while expanding their talent pool (Spotify, 2021a). These case studies demonstrate that successful flexible work requires more than policy changes; it involves deep cultural, managerial, and technological shifts that align with organizational behavior theories such as JD-R, SDT, COR, and SET. Investments in well-being, autonomy, and trust helped enhance productivity, job satisfaction, and retention across these companies, offering valuable lessons for organizations adopting flexible work models.

Enhancing Cybersecurity in Flexible Work Environments

As flexible work arrangements increase, so do cybersecurity risks such as data breaches and phishing attacks. To address these challenges, companies must implement robust cybersecurity strategies. For example, the 2020 SolarWinds attack highlighted vulnerabilities in remote systems, prompting stronger security measures. Key systems like Virtual Private Networks (VPNs), Zero Trust models (e.g., Google's BeyondCorp), and Multi factor Authentication (MFA) are essential in securing remote work. Companies like Microsoft, Salesforce, and Spotify exemplify these strategies, using tools like Azure AD, encryption, and cybersecurity training to protect their remote workforces. These approaches not only enhance security but also provide valuable lessons for other organizations seeking to secure their flexible work environments.

Future Trends

In the context of flexible work arrangements, AI is poised to play a transformative role. Automation tools, powered by artificial intelligence, will streamline operations and reduce manual tasks, offering employees greater flexibility. AI-driven software will enhance remote collaboration, optimize project management, and provide personalized work experiences by adapting to individual preferences and productivity patterns.

Digital nomadism is becoming increasingly popular, driven by both technology and the desire for a better work-life balance. With tools enabling remote work from any location, employees are no longer tied to a fixed office space. This shift allows organizations to tap into a global talent pool, fostering diversity and enhancing creativity within teams. However, it also requires a robust infrastructure for seamless connectivity, security, and legal frameworks for international work.

Evolving work models are shifting toward hybrid and fully remote structures. The traditional 9-to-5 workday is being replaced by flexible schedules that focus on output rather than hours spent in the office. As companies adjust to these new paradigms, there is a growing emphasis on employee well-being, performance-based metrics, and results-oriented cultures. This transformation is not just about where work is done but also how it's done, emphasizing autonomy, trust, and collaboration.

CONCLUSION

The implementation of flexible work policies has emerged as a transformative force in modern organizational strategies, significantly impacting employee well-being and retention. As organizations continue to navigate an increasingly dynamic and competitive labor market, the emphasis on work flexibility has evolved from being a mere employee benefit to a fundamental business imperative. The findings of this research underscore the profound implications of flexible work arrangements on job satisfaction, work-life balance, psychological well-being, productivity, and overall organizational commitment.

Flexible work policies have evolved from a reactive response to global disruption into a critical component of forward-thinking organizational strategy. This chapter offers an original contribution to the literature by developing an integrative framework that brings together the Job Demands-Resources (JD-R) model, Self-Determination Theory (SDT), Conservation of Resources (COR) theory, and Social Exchange Theory (SET). By uniting these perspectives, the chapter demonstrates how flexible work policies can simultaneously reduce psychological strain, promote intrinsic motivation, safeguard employee resources, and build reciprocal trust between employers and staff. It advances beyond theoretical discussion by proposing a comprehensive evaluation toolkit, complete with KPIs, DEI audits, and digital dashboards, to assess policy effectiveness. Additionally, it presents sector-specific implementation strategies and real-world case illustrations, offering a nuanced understanding of how flexibility manifests across various industries. In synthesizing theory with practice, the chapter underscores that flexible work is not merely a benefit but a strategic necessity—critical for fostering sustainable engagement, enhancing retention, and achieving competitive advantage in the evolving landscape of work.

In conclusion, flexible work policies have redefined traditional employment paradigms, offering significant benefits for both employees and organizations. By enhancing work-life balance, reducing stress, and fostering a culture of autonomy, these policies contribute to improved employee well-being and retention. However, the successful implementation of flexible work arrangements requires careful consideration of equity, leadership adaptation, technological integration, and performance management strategies. Organizations that prioritize these factors stand to gain a competitive advantage in talent retention, employee satisfaction, and overall business performance. As the workforce continues to evolve, embracing flexibility as a core component of organizational strategy will be essential in shaping the future of work.

REFERENCES

Allen, T. D., Golden, T. D., & Shockley, K. M. (2015). How effective is telecommuting? Assessing the status of our scientific findings. *Psychological Science in the Public Interest, 16*(2), 40–68. DOI: 10.1177/1529100615593273 PMID: 26403188

Allen, T. D., Golden, T. D., & Shockley, K. M. (2021). Flexible work arrangements and work-family conflict: A meta-analysis of their effects on work-life balance. *The Journal of Applied Psychology*, *106*(6), 892–915. DOI: 10.1037/apl0000899

Allen, T. D., Johnson, R. C., Kiburz, K. M., & Shockley, K. M. (2013). Work–family conflict and flexible work arrangements: Deconstructing flexibility. *Personnel Psychology*, *66*(2), 345–376. DOI: 10.1111/peps.12012

Ashforth, B. E., Kreiner, G. E., & Fugate, M. (2000). All in a day's work: Boundaries and micro role transitions. *Academy of Management Review*, *25*(3), 472–491. DOI: 10.2307/259305

Bai, X., Li, H., & Wang, L. (2019). Work–family conflict and employee retention: A moderated mediation model. *Journal of Business Research*, *100*, 103–111. DOI: 10.1016/j.jbusres.2019.03.021

Bai, X., Li, H., & Wang, L. (2019). Work–family conflict and employee retention: A moderated mediation model. *Journal of Business Research*, *100*, 103–111. DOI: 10.1016/j.jbusres.2019.03.021

Bailey, D. E., & Kurland, N. B. (2002). A review of telework research: Findings, new directions, and lessons for the study of modern work. *Journal of Organizational Behavior*, *23*(4), 383–400. DOI: 10.1002/job.144

Bailey, D. E., & Kurland, N. B. (2020). A review of telework research: Findings and implications for the future of flexible work. *Human Resource Management Review*, *30*(4), 100692. DOI: 10.1016/j.hrmr.2020.100692

Bakker, A. B., & Demerouti, E. (2007). The Job Demands-Resources model: State of the art. *Journal of Managerial Psychology*, *22*(3), 309–328. DOI: 10.1108/02683940710733115

Barnes, C. M., Wagner, D. T., Ghumman, S., & Koopman, J. (2019). Sleep and employee performance: Advancing research and practice. *Annual Review of Organizational Psychology and Organizational Behavior*, *6*, 77–102. DOI: 10.1146/annurev-orgpsych-012218-015027

Barrero, J. M., Bloom, N., & Davis, S. J. (2021). *Why working from home will stick.* National Bureau of Economic Research., DOI: 10.3386/w28731

Beers, T. M. (2000). Flexible schedules and shift work: Replacing the '9-to-5' workday? *Monthly Labor Review*, *123*(6), 33–40.

Bergström, G., Bodin, T., & Lindh, T. (2021). Remote work and mental health: A longitudinal study of work-related factors, stress, and well-being. *Scandinavian Journal of Work, Environment & Health*, *47*(1), 8–15. DOI: 10.5271/sjweh.3938

Blau, P. M. (1964). *Exchange and power in social life.* Wiley.

Bloom, N., Liang, J., Roberts, J., & Ying, Z. J. (2015). Does working from home work? Evidence from a Chinese experiment. *The Quarterly Journal of Economics*, *130*(1), 165–218. DOI: 10.1093/qje/qju032

Bloom, N., Liang, J., Roberts, J., & Ying, Z. J. (2015). Does working from home work? Evidence from a Chinese experiment. *The Quarterly Journal of Economics*, *130*(1), 165–218. DOI: 10.1093/qje/qju032

Brough, P., & O'Driscoll, M. P. (2010). Organizational interventions for balancing work and home demands: An overview. *Work and Stress*, *24*(3), 280–297. DOI: 10.1080/02678373.2010.506808

Brougham, D., & Haar, J. M. (2018). Smart technology, artificial intelligence, robotics, and algorithms (STARA): Employees' perceptions of future workplace technology change. *International Journal of Human Resource Management*, *29*(10), 1547–1566. DOI: 10.1080/09585192.2017.1362666

Brougham, D., & Haar, J. M. (2018). Smart technology, artificial intelligence, robotics, and algorithms (STARA): Employees' perceptions of future workplace technology change. *International Journal of Human Resource Management*, *29*(10), 1547–1566. DOI: 10.1080/09585192.2017.1362666

Buxton, O. M., Lee, S., L'Hermite-Balériaux, M., Turek, F. W., & Van Cauter, E. (2016). Sleep and performance. *Nature Reviews. Neuroscience*, *17*(6), 388–399. DOI: 10.1038/nrn.2016.53 PMID: 27320790

Cao, X., Zhang, Z., & Jiang, L. (2021). The effect of flexible work arrangements on employee mental health: A systematic review and meta-analysis. *Journal of Organizational Behavior*, *42*(8), 920–944. DOI: 10.1002/job.2527

Carnevale, J. B., & Hatak, I. (2020). Employee adjustment and well-being in the era of COVID-19: Implications for human resource management. *Journal of Business Research*, *116*, 183–187. DOI: 10.1016/j.jbusres.2020.05.037 PMID: 32501303

Chatterjee, K., Clark, B., Martin, A., & Davis, A. (2020). The commuting and well-being study: Understanding the impact of commuting on people's lives. *Transportation Research Part A, Policy and Practice*, *132*, 157–173. DOI: 10.1016/j.tra.2020.06.006

Chen, C., & Nath, R. (2021). Organizational agility and digital HRM: Facilitating work flexibility through technology. *Journal of Business Research*, *124*, 293–304. DOI: 10.1016/j.jbusres.2020.11.051

Clark, S. C. (2000). Work/family border theory: A new theory of work/family balance. *Human Relations*, *53*(6), 747–770. DOI: 10.1177/0018726700536001

Deci, E. L., & Ryan, R. M. (1985). *Intrinsic motivation and self-determination in human behavior*. Springer. DOI: 10.1007/978-1-4899-2271-7

Deci, E. L., Vallerand, R. J., & Ryan, R. M. (2017). Self-determination and motivational development in work settings. *Journal of Organizational Behavior*, *38*(2), 257–271. DOI: 10.1002/job.2308

Deloitte. (2020). *2020 Global Human Capital Trends: The social enterprise at work—Paradox as a path forward*. Deloitte Insights.

Derks, D., van Mierlo, H., & Schmitz, E. B. (2014). A diary study on work-related smartphone use, psychological detachment and exhaustion: Examining the role of the perceived segmentation norm. *Journal of Occupational Health Psychology*, *19*(1), 74–84. DOI: 10.1037/a0035076 PMID: 24447222

Felstead, A., & Henseke, G. (2017). Assessing the growth of remote working and its consequences for effort, well-being, and work-life balance. *New Technology, Work and Employment*, *32*(3), 195–212. DOI: 10.1111/ntwe.12097

Felstead, A., & Henseke, G. (2017). Assessing the growth of remote working and its consequences for effort, well-being, and work-life balance. *New Technology, Work and Employment*, *32*(3), 195–212. DOI: 10.1111/ntwe.12097

Fitzgerald, L. (2020). The impact of telecommuting on employee anxiety: A mixed-methods approach. *International Journal of Stress Management*, *27*(1), 65–74. DOI: 10.1037/str0000101

Gajendran, R. S., & Harrison, D. A. (2007). The good, the bad, and the unknown about telecommuting: Meta-analysis of psychological mediators and individual consequences. *The Journal of Applied Psychology*, *92*(6), 1524–1541. DOI: 10.1037/0021-9010.92.6.1524 PMID: 18020794

Gates, G. J. (2022). LGBTQ+ employees and workplace inclusion: Current challenges and strategies. *Human Resource Management Review*, *32*(1), 100867. DOI: 10.1016/j.hrmr.2021.100867

Golden, T. D., & Gajendran, R. S. (2019). Unpacking telecommuting's effect on performance: Is it about time spent or time saved? *Human Resource Management Review*, *29*(2), 184–195. DOI: 10.1016/j.hrmr.2018.02.003

Golden, T. D., & Veiga, J. F. (2005). The impact of extent of telecommuting on job satisfaction: Resolving inconsistent findings. *Journal of Management*, *31*(2), 301–318. DOI: 10.1177/0149206304271768

Grawitch, M. J., Gottschalk, M., & Munz, D. C. (2006). The path to a healthy workplace: A critical review linking healthy workplace practices, employee well-being, and organizational improvements. *Consulting Psychology Journal*, *58*(3), 129–147. DOI: 10.1037/1065-9293.58.3.129

Greenhaus, J. H., Collins, K. M., & Shaw, J. D. (2020). The work-family interface: A review and look forward. *Journal of Vocational Behavior*, *118*, 103484. DOI: 10.1016/j.jvb.2020.103484

Harris, R., Maxwell, T., & Tate, H. (2023). A systematic review of telework, gender, and intersectionality in the modern workplace. *International Journal of Human Resource Management*, *34*(5), 1022–1045. DOI: 10.1080/09585192.2022.2105731

Harrison, R., & Willness, C. (2022). Cross-cultural differences in perceptions of flexible work: A global study of mental health outcomes. *Journal of Cross-Cultural Psychology*, *53*(4), 529–549. DOI: 10.1177/00220221221019530

Hobfoll, S. E. (1989). Conservation of resources: A new attempt at conceptualizing stress. *The American Psychologist*, *44*(3), 513–524. DOI: 10.1037/0003-066X.44.3.513 PMID: 2648906

Kirkpatrick, S. A., Verburg, R. M., & Vandewaerde, A. (2019). Organizational culture and employee well-being: A systematic review. *European Journal of Work and Organizational Psychology*, *28*(6), 738–753. DOI: 10.1080/1359432X.2019.1628665

Kossek, E. E., & Lautsch, B. A. (2018). Work-life flexibility for whom? Occupational status and work-life inequality in upper, middle, and lower level jobs. *The Academy of Management Annals*, *12*(1), 5–36. DOI: 10.5465/annals.2016.0059

Kossek, E. E., & Lautsch, B. A. (2018). Work-life flexibility for whom? Occupational status and work-life inequality in upper, middle, and lower level jobs. *The Academy of Management Annals*, *12*(1), 5–36. DOI: 10.5465/annals.2016.0059

Kossek, E. E., Ollier-Malaterre, A., Lee, M. D., Pichler, S., & Hall, D. T. (2014). Matchmaking flexibility: Organizational initiatives and individual use of formal and informal flexibility. *Journal of Vocational Behavior*, *84*(3), 377–389. DOI: 10.1016/j.jvb.2014.01.007

Marschark, M., Shaver, L. A., & Boudreau, L. (2020). The role of technology in enhancing the mental health of remote workers. *Technology in Human Services*, *38*(2), 56–72. DOI: 10.1080/15228835.2020.1833359

Maslach, C., & Leiter, M. P. (2016). Understanding the burnout experience: Recent research and its implications for psychiatry. *World Psychiatry; Official Journal of the World Psychiatric Association (WPA)*, *15*(2), 103–111. DOI: 10.1002/wps.20311 PMID: 27265691

Maslach, C., & Leiter, M. P. (2017). *The truth about burnout: How organizations cause personal stress and what to do about it*. Jossey-Bass.

Messenger, J. C., & Gschwind, L. (2016). Three generations of telework: New ICTs and the (r)evolution from home office to virtual office. *New Technology, Work and Employment*, *31*(3), 195–208. DOI: 10.1111/ntwe.12073

Microsoft. (2021a). Embracing a flexible workplace. https://blogs.microsoft.com/blog/2021/03/22/hybrid-work-is-just-work/

Microsoft. (2021b). Building digital resilience in the workplace. https://news.microsoft.com

Microsoft. (2021c). 2021 Work Trend Index: The next great disruption is hybrid work—Are we ready? https://www.microsoft.com/en-us/worklab/work-trend-index/hybrid-work

Nguyen, L. T., Chen, R., & Zhang, W. (2021). Remote work and stress in the era of COVID-19: The role of work structures and leadership practices. *The Journal of Applied Psychology*, *106*(6), 935–947. DOI: 10.1037/apl0000506

Robinson, M. A., Allen, J. A., & Staley, A. M. (2019). Remote work and inclusion: Diversity impacts of distance work arrangements. *Equality, Diversity and Inclusion*, *38*(5), 503–516. DOI: 10.1108/EDI-04-2018-0076

Rothbard, N. P., Phillips, K. W., & Dumas, T. L. (2005). Managing multiple roles: Work-family policies and individuals' organizational attachment. *Organization Science*, *16*(3), 243–267. DOI: 10.1287/orsc.1050.0124

Salesforce. (2021). How we're reopening our offices safely. https://www.salesforce.com/news

Salesforce. (2022). Success from anywhere: Our strategy for the future of work. https://www.salesforce.com/company/news-press/stories/

Schur, L., Ameri, M., & Kruse, D. (2020). Telework after COVID: A "silver lining" for workers with disabilities? *Journal of Occupational Rehabilitation*, *30*(4), 521–536. DOI: 10.1007/s10926-020-09936-5 PMID: 33156435

Shin, J., Han, H., & Ko, H. (2022). Telework and well-being: A review of empirical studies on the relationship between remote work and mental health outcomes. *Social Science & Medicine*, *277*, 113724. DOI: 10.1016/j.socscimed.2021.113724

Smith, A., & Lockwood, N. (2020). The hidden costs of remote work: Psychological effects of social isolation on mental health. *Journal of Occupational Health Psychology*, *25*(3), 135–149. DOI: 10.1037/ocp0000198

Sonnentag, S., Binnewies, C., & Mojza, E. J. (2020). Can work be fun? The role of work characteristics and individual differences in promoting work-related well-being. *Journal of Vocational Behavior*, *109*, 151–165. DOI: 10.1016/j.jvb.2018.08.008

Spotify. (2021a). Spotify announces Work From Anywhere program. https://newsroom.spotify.com/2021-02-12/introducing-work-from-anywhere/

Spotify. (2021b). How Spotify redesigned work to unlock global talent. https://hrblog.spotify.com

Spreitzer, G., Cameron, L., & Garrett, L. (2017). Alternative work arrangements: Two images of the new world of work. *Annual Review of Organizational Psychology and Organizational Behavior*, *4*(1), 473–499. DOI: 10.1146/annurev-orgpsych-032516-113332

Tavares, A. I. (2017). Telework and health effects review. *International Journal of Healthcare*, *3*(2), 30–36. DOI: 10.5430/ijh.v3n2p30

Tucker, M. A., & Lindsay, D. P. (2023). The intersectionality of flexible work policies: Implications for marginalized employees. *Journal of Business and Psychology*, *38*(2), 1015–1034. DOI: 10.1007/s10869-022-09837-9

Wang, B., Liu, Y., & Parker, S. K. (2020). How does the use of information communication technology affect individuals? A work design perspective. *The Academy of Management Annals*, *14*(2), 695–725. DOI: 10.5465/annals.2018.0127

Wang, B., Liu, Y., Qian, J., & Parker, S. K. (2020). Achieving effective remote working during the COVID-19 pandemic: A work design perspective. *Applied Psychology*, *70*(1), 16–59. DOI: 10.1111/apps.12290 PMID: 33230359

Williams, J. C., Blair-Loy, M., & Berdahl, J. L. (2016). Cultural schemas, social class, and the flexibility stigma. *The Journal of Social Issues*, *72*(2), 209–232. DOI: 10.1111/josi.12012

Wong, P., Elsbach, K. D., & Fridman, S. (2021). The mental health impact of flexible work models: A review and agenda for future research. *Journal of Organizational Behavior*, *42*(3), 330–347. DOI: 10.1002/job.2520

Chapter 9
A Multi-Level Approach to Burnout Prevention:
Strategies for a Sustainable and Thriving Workforce

Prerna Mehta
https://orcid.org/0009-0003-1300-588X
GD Rungta College of Science and Technology, India

ABSTRACT

In an increasingly demanding work environment, burnout has emerged as a critical challenge for organizations and their workforce. This chapter will delve into the multifaceted nature of burnout, explore its causes, and present actionable strategies for prevention that can pave the way for a healthier, more sustainable workforce. By applying a holistic approach that encompasses individual, organizational, and societal dimensions, this chapter aims to provide readers with practical insights and tools to mitigate burnout effectively.

1. INTRODUCTION TO BURNOUT

Burnout has emerged as an important issue in today's workforce, affecting more than 70% of employees in various fields, including healthcare, education and business (Barowes et al., 2023). This psychological 'exhaustion' is long -term work pressure and has a widespread impact, with increased turnover, reduction in job satisfaction and decrease in productivity (Maricuţoiu et al., 2016). The World Health Organization estimates that the cost of the workplace burnout costs around $ 1.5 trillion, which is annual due to lost productivity (Bianchi and Shonfeld, 2023), which highlights the immediate need for effective prevention strategies. This figure

DOI: 10.4018/979-8-3373-2210-0.ch009

Copyright © 2025, IGI Global Scientific Publishing. Copying or distributing in print or electronic forms without written permission of IGI Global Scientific Publishing is prohibited.

represents a significant increase compared to previous estimates, underscoring the escalating crisis of burnout in the workplace. The rising financial burden emphasizes the immediate need for effective prevention strategies, not only to alleviate the human toll of burnout but also to mitigate its growing economic impact on organizations and economies worldwide.

Beyond personal results, burnouts can lead to old health issues, such as fatigue, anxiety and depression, managers and policy makers to consider the burnout as an important organizational concern rather than just an HR issue. Employee assistance programs, flexible work system and reducing mental health stigma are essential steps towards addressing this crisis (Amsrud et al., 2019).

This paper aims to analyze the multifaceted nature of burnout, explore its components, and identify effective strategies for prevention and intervention in the workplace.

Figure 1. Burnout cycle

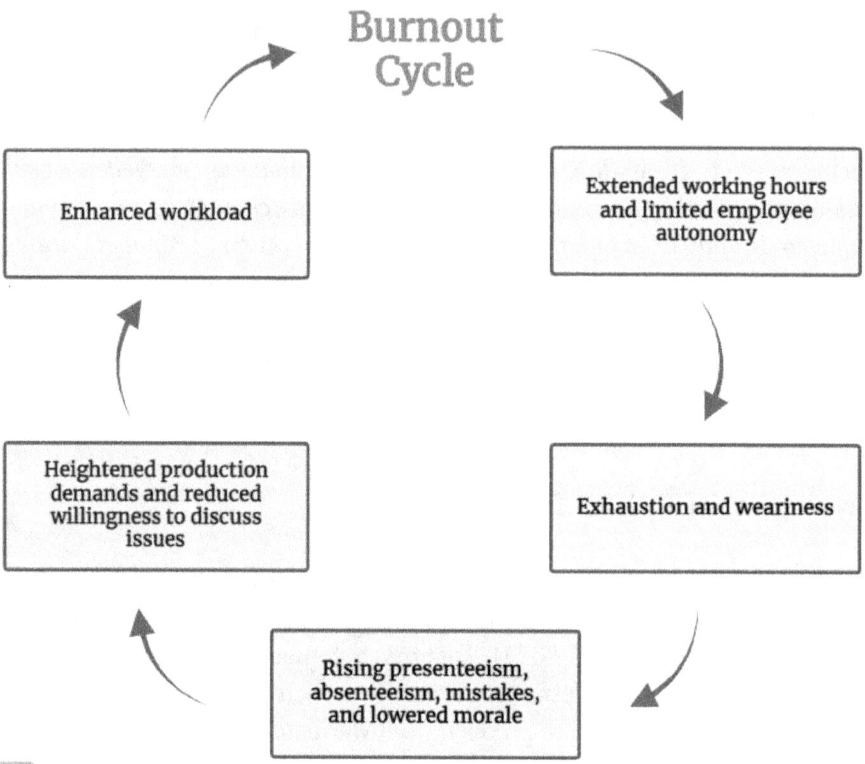

- Economic and Personal Costs Associated with Burnout

1.1 Understanding Burnout and Its Significance in the Workplace

Burnout has become a key issue in organizational psychology and HR management because it affects how employees feel and how well companies do. Unlike regular stress, burnout leaves people feeling worn out and disconnected from their work. This often happens when they face long-term stress without enough time to recover.

- The Many Sides of Burnout

Burnout has many causes such as job pressures available resources, and personal traits. The Job Demand-Resources (JD-R) model suggests that high job demands can bring on burnout, but enough resources (like help from coworkers and bosses freedom to make decisions, and chances to grow) can lessen its impact. New studies show that the link between job demands and resources isn't simple; for instance, workers who think their workloads are doable and have strong social backing are less likely to burn out (Bakker et al., 2004).

A study from 2023 in the "Journal of Occupational Health Psychology" points out that personal risk factors—like personality traits such as neuroticism—have a big impact on how likely someone is to burn out. This explains why some people do well in high-stress jobs while others have a hard time. Also, things like age, gender, and life situations can affect how people experience burnout. For example younger workers might report feeling more burned out because they're dealing with pressures from both their career growth and personal life at the same time (Villaume et al., 2024).

- The Preparedness for Psychological Safety

The evidence of burnout impacting the workplace is not just for individuals but organizational culture and staffing are equally important. The business world is increasingly awakening to the reality of the importance of fostering psychological safety with which people can speak up without consequences. This cultural change is becoming more profound as many researches have undertaken have associated psychological safety to reduced rate of burnout and high level of job satisfaction.

As a result, understanding burnout has adopted new perspectives especially with the growing advancements in working conditions such as remote working and the hybrid model. The home based employees are likely to experience quite a lot of challenges since the distinction between work related tasks and personal responsibilities is not very clear, and this leads to high levels of stress. In 2022, Microsoft research detected that remote workers experienced increased social loneliness, which is why organizations must continually provide opportunities for virtual interaction (Bareket-Bojmel et al., 2023).

- The Ripple Effect on Organizational Performance

From the business point of view, the problem of burnout is extremely important because it is tightly connected with such values as productivity, innovation, and corporate culture. According to another Gallup report in 2023, organisations that have low levels of employee burnout, meaning employees who are not disengaged, achieve 21% more profitability than organisations whose employees are disengaged. On the other hand, when burnout rates are high, the organization adopts a negative organizational culture that makes qualified talent flee and lower morale among the team .

Consequently, the study of burnout in the workplace is not only relevant to promoting employees' satisfaction and productivity but also organizational concern. As this paper has highlighted burnout is a complex phenomenon with an interrelated sense of engagement, well-being, and productivity for any organization to consider when conceptualizing burnout and designing strategy for the improvement personal and organizational burnout. These are the fundamentals for the following discussions on prevention measures as well as the cultural changes needed to promote a healthier work context.

1.2 Economic and Personal Costs Associated with Burnout

It underlines that the cost related to the burnout have become more visible from the economic and personal perspective, have an impact on employees and organizational resilience. Knowledge of these costs is crucial in order to promote politico-practical changes reducing burnout rates and its effects.

¬ Economic Costs: A Detailed Analysis

These overall costs of burnout manifest themselves at multiple levels of organizational functioning and impact of work outcomes, employee health care, and rates of staff turnover.

1. Productivity Loss: World Health Organisation recently noted workplace burnout as one of the causes of low productivity amongst employees. Another study referred to in "Occupational Health Psychology" meta-analysis shows that people experiencing burnout are actually 63% less productive than people who don't. This loss is attributed to not only the regular absenteeism but also there is

presenteeism, that means that even the employee is physically in the workplace but mentally completely checked out, which can also negatively impact group efficiency (Surana & Singh, 2013).

2. Healthcare Costs: Research has indicated that employees experiencing burnout suffer from worse physical and mental conditions thus, are likely to drain the company's healthcare systems., Research done by Gibson in the "American Journal of Public Health" shows that presenting burnout levels above normal can increase one's healthcare costs by thirty percent. Such costs are incurred on the employees and organizations since organizations bear the additional costs in the form of higher insurance costs and health resource utilization (Patzelt & Shepherd, 2024).
3. Turnover Costs: The burnout which leads to employee turnover has the following monetary consequences. The average cost of recruiting new employee as stated by the SHRM is between 50 percent and 200 percent of the employees' annual salary depending on the position of the employee in the organization. According to the study conducted in 2024, the high turnover rates driven by burnout cost an organisation $4,000 and generally requires 6 months to some other years to fill a position in the organisation, chiefly the organisations experienced fluctuations in operations and even the remaining staff also suffers from burnout (Al-Suraihi et al., 2021).
4. Impact on Innovation: Beyond operational and financial implications, burnout stifles innovation within organizations. A LinkedIn survey conducted in 2023 found that 42% of organizations identified burnout as a key reason behind decreased innovation. This stagnation results not only in reduced competitive advantage but also in a diminished capacity to adapt to market demands, impacting long-term viability (Syed Mohamad et al., 2023).

Personal Costs: Health and Well-being

The personal consequences of burnout can be profound, affecting various aspects of an individual's life, including mental, emotional, and physical health.

1. Mental Health Impact: Research indicates a significant link between burnout and the exacerbation of mental health issues. A 2023 meta-analysis highlighted that individuals with high levels of burnout have a 38% increased risk of experiencing anxiety disorders and depressive symptoms. These conditions can be debilitating, leading to lasting cognitive and emotional challenges that complicate recovery (Koutsimani et al., 2019).
2. Physical Health Consequences: The relationship between burnout and physical health issues has been examined in depth. A cohort study published in the "Journal of Psychosomatic Research" in late 2023 established that chronic burnout is

associated with a heightened risk of conditions such as hypertension, heart disease, and metabolic syndrome. The physiological stress response can lead to alterations in body systems, compromising long-term health and resilience (Honkonen et al., 2006).

3. Deterioration of Work-Life Balance: Prolonged stress can critically affect the human's ability to function productively at the workplace and in their relationships and happiness in the overall life. In the "Journal of Occupational and Environmental Medicine" it was found out that employees evidenced burnout marks had their personal fulfillment and satisfaction lowered by 45 percent. This deterioration keeps a cycle of stressed that hinders the healing process and may cause some relational difficulties in the long run (Page et al., 2014).
4. Quality of Life Decline: The quality of life of clients who are experiencing burnout is hugely impacted. Refactoring the Future's 2022 study also reveals that over two-third of burnout patients manifested hopelessness and anempathy for life activities. These affective losses in autonomy, mastery, and meaning lead to this or that decrease in subjective well-being, and most often to the deterioration of quality of life, as well as to enhanced feelings of loneliness and rejection, aggravating mental disorders (Edú-Valsania et al., 2022).

The financial implications of burnout as well as the consequences of burnout on the lives of individuals implicated that more needs to be done, in order to combat this worrysome phenomenon in organizations. Knowledge of these costs fuels the search for more information on approaches that will help prevent and mitigate burnout in the workplace.

2.1 Understanding the Causes of Burnout

Burnout is the state of physical, mental and spiritual exhaustion that results from different factors that are aligned in one way or the other. Studying these causes contributes to an understanding of how burnout progresses and may assist to prevent it.

1. Environmental Stressors: Some of the factors that have been found to lead to burnout include; noise pollution, lack of adequate lighting, and improper design of working environment. A study by Gifford and his team published in the "Journal of Environmental Psychology "in 2023, explained how poor organizational environment and designs cause stress and burn out by 25 percent among the employees (Sinkinson & Hicks, 2013).
2. Job Insecurity: This was followed by frequent economic changes and then the rise of the gig economy results in job insecurity for a lot of workers. A survey conducted by the American Psychological Association in 2022 showed that

only 60% of employees are worried about job security; something that rises with emotional exhaustion levels and decreases job satisfaction levels. There is anxiety within those who work in sectors where job insecurity is rising such as the developing economies, this leads to a burnt out society (Agrawal & Bhukya, 2022).

3. Cognitive Overload: Being challenged at the workplace is a common thing today, due to the fact that all our employees are forced to juggle multiple tasks in parallel hence resulting to cognitive overload. A research article published in the "Cognitive Science" in 2023 showed that not only are employees unable to be productive when their workload exceeds mental capacity, but they also experience more burnout. Employees disclosed that they experienced stress especially when often asked to multitask since this interferes with focus and adds a lot of pressure to the employee (Wickens, 2008).
4. Change Fatigue: Recurring organisational change, for instance through restructuring or through leaders' changes mean that change fatigue is almost inevitable. A study conducted revealed that employees that are put through change consistently without management providing them with information or support, reported higher proliferation rates of stress and burnout. This easily observable phenomena highlights the need to manage change in organizations and the health of employees during transition (de Vries & de Vries, 2023).
5. Lack of Recognition: It entails that employees are not recognised for their efforts, which results in disengagement, and emotional strain. A research that was conducted in 2023 by Gallup showed that people who complained that their work was not appreciated by their employers are coping with burnout at 50 percent more than other employees. This goes a long way into explaining why recognition and reward is very integral for the stability of employee motivation and mental health (D. L. Pandey & Risal, 2023).

2.2 Contributing Factors and At-Risk Groups

These factors cause burnout, and they may overlap in some way, placing specific populations at greater risk. Announcing these factors and groups is crucial for defining the directions for combating burnout.

1. Interpersonal Relationships: Fortunately, burnout has been found to have some predictable causes including, strained relationships with co-workers or bosses. Research also pointed out that those employees who suffered from high workplace conflict and lack of sufficient support from the colleagues, had 40% higher burnout risk. The positive aspect of planning for positive relations

in the workplace since social relations at the workplace are a source of stress, enhancing social relations becomes a major push (Gray et al., 2020).

2. Work Role Stressors: Some positions simply require the employee to be in a stressful place where they are bound to get burnt out. A study found out that workers in high-stress jobs that include direct customer interfaces, biomedical workplaces, teachers, supervisors and managers, and employees enduring emotional labor jobs are more vulnerable to burnout. These roles involve emotional demands and responsibility, and this makes them to fully exhaust the person and disengage from other duties (Tabaj et al., 2015).
3. Generational Differences: Working generations are distinct in terms of burnout because they have different expectations and work values. A study showed that whereas the Millennials and Gen Z have some burnout symptoms similar with that of the older generation employees, they have somewhat different characteristics. They value autonomic work-life balance and mental health issues, and experiencing burnout if any among them has a higher propensity than the others. This special treasury shows that there are different strategies for combating burnout that depend on age (Rani & Samuel, 2016).
4. Cultural Factors: There is a particularly strong correlation between burnout levels and an organization's culture. It is estimate that companies that cultivate institutional workaholism – that is, the organizational climate where employees – and perhaps especially knowledge workers – are encouraged to have little time or energy left for anything else but work – will experience considerably higher rates of burnout. A survey conducted in 2022 revealed that Organizational Culture with toxic characteristics had burn out 60% higher than those with healthy culture (S. Pandey & Sharma, 2016).
5. Vulnerability in Remote Work: While remote work brings flexibility and flexibility at work, it also introduces special features that can lead to burnout. A current study conducted suggest that remote employees experience emotional contagion which results in a burned-out state due to feelings of loneliness and detachment from the group/teams. It is especially important now for organizations to establish and support virtual team building processes where such structures and routines are still lacking.
6. Underrepresented Groups: Workers from different marginalised groups (racialised and sexualised minorities in particular) experience extra pressures that exposes them to risk of burnout. From studies conducted previously, prejudices and structural vulnerabilities can make the employees of these groups stress more and increase their emotional labour and emotional detachment. A report on burnout revealed that minority employees are burnt out 30% more than others making it important for companies to have inclusiveness programs and support.

In light of different possible causes and risk factors for burnout, as well as problematic groups, it is possible to start adopting measures to prevent or combat burnout, and promote well-being within an organization. Managing these challenges ensures healthy employees and organization performance improvement in difficult situations.

2.2 Consequences for Mental Health and Organizations

A safe bet to make is that burnout has a profound impact on not only the person experiencing it, but also on organizational productivity and ethos . By understanding these consequences, which as have been sourced from recent research and discovery, organizations can consider taking measures which can combat burnout and its effects.

¬ Mental Health Outcomes-reaching consequences, not only for the individual's mental health but also for organizational performance and culture. Understanding these consequences—backed by recent research and discoveries—can help organizations take proactive measures to address burnout and its effects.

¬ Consequences for Mental Health

1. Increased Anxiety and Depression: Of all possible paths, the association between burnout and anxiety or depression is one of the best substantiated. A study found that burnout raises the risk of depressive symptoms and anxiety disorders by 70 percent. This serves to shows that there is a dire need to practice early detection and intervention to avoid the above severe mental health impacts (Koutsimani et al., 2019b).
2. Cognitive Impairments: Burnout often brings out poor working and recall memory, poor judgement, and last but not least, poor concentration. Burn-out patients suffer from something called 'cognitive fog,' meaning that their minds are fogged up and they are not able to think with the appropriate clarity: this leads to decreased productivity and quality of life.
3. Physical Health Decline: Mental exhaustion of burn out can have physical symptoms which are fatigue, headache, stomach disorder or even a weakened immune system. According to the systematic review, burnout is related to higher risk of cardiovascular diseases. This implies that some of the impacts of burnout are not restricted to psychological, may also have an escalated physical health impact.
4. Reduced Self-Esteem and Identity Crisis: Staff may develop burnout, which demoralises the individual as he or she feels incompetent and questions own capability. The above 2023 qualitative study demonstrated that after experiencing burnout most people go through identity crisis because of the challenges they encounter when trying to find new roles to portray in their careers or new sources of meaning and value. Such letting go can result in the exacerbation of

symptoms which in turn lead to a further marginalisation of work and personal life.

5. Increased Risk of Substance Abuse: Many studies have identified burnout as having a positive correlation with substance use as people look for how to handle stress and pain. The study explains that participants with more severe burnout symptoms were 40% more likely to indulge in risky substance use. This goes to support why there is need for Works Mental Health interventions to counter maladaptive thinking patterns developed in the course of performing their duties.

2.2 Consequences for Organizations

A study revealed that burnout has negative impacts which affect organizations in the following ways. According to a 2024 World Health Organization's report for corporate organizations with workers experiencing employee burnout, workers productivity can decrease up to forty percent financially and timeline on various projects. Moreover, the Society for Human Resource Management revealed in a study conducted in 2022 that burnout causes organizations a 50-percent higher turnover rate than organizations with proper management, thus high recruitment and training costs . Organizational outcomes decline, such as the alarmingly low employee engagement that a 2023 Gallup report reveals shows surveyed burned-out participants to be 63% more likely to be disengaged across the company, negatively affecting organizational customer relations and interactive environments. Additionally, a study established that burn out remains a norm within workplaces, leading to a toxic organizational culture whereby stress generates more stress and low morale, more morale. It also goes to financial loss in relation to healthcare costs, for example, a study conducted in 2024 showed that companies with high reported burnout costs heath care 30% more than those with engaged staff. Last but not the least, the recruitment problem can also be influenced by a negative reputation level which also was shown in a lack of favorable employee well-being; according to a survey from 2023 job seekers pay significant attention to the organizational culture. To reduce burnout it is necessary to help the employees to become better and more satisfied with their own and their colleagues' professional lives (Khammissa et al., 2022).

3. STRATEGIES FOR PREVENTION

The prevention of burnout involves efforts that are individual as well as efforts that need to come from organizations. Mindfulness exercises, adequate exercise, access to social conditioning and material support help to achieve individual stress hardiness while organization can work on providing a supportive organizational culture, involving the workers in flexible working and making available to them stress mitigation resources. New studies confirm the efficiency of these approaches, underlining the anti-burnout and salutogenic functions of well-tempered strategies. By emphasizing such strategies, both the employees and organisations are able to develop a healthy, efficient and satisfying workplace that can generate long-term results.

Table 1. Shows the literature review.

Category	Strategy	Description	Research Findings	Reference
Individual	Mindfulness Practices	Minds being used through practices including meditation, deep breathing exercises etc included in the day to day activities.	According to a study conducted in 2023 in 'Mindfulness', this habit helped decrease burnout level by the 30percent improving the customer's emotional well-being.	(Komariah et al., 2022)
	Setting Healthy Boundaries	Creating organisational policies that separate the working life from the personal life to avoid work interference.	Similarly, a 2024 APA survey found people with strong boundaries had 40% less burnout rates than people with weak boundaries.	(Dr. K. MAJINI JES BELLA, 2023)
	Engaging in Regular Physical Activity	Taking part in exercise to improve certain basic human functions; eradicating stress and likelihood of developing fatigue.	As stated by a research in the American Journal, the level of physical activity was associated with a decrease in burn out level by 30 per cent.	(Malm et al., 2019)
	Building Social Support Networks	Exploring ways by which relationships at the workplace and and beyond can be enhanced for purposes of affection.	Another cross sectional study done showed that people who have strong social support are 25% less likely to burn out.	(Tian & Freeman, 2024)
	Pursuing Continuous Learning and Development	Professional development and carrying out of exploration activities that involves personal and career skill boosters to minimize job burnout.	An examine identified that by 20%, the development program workers mentioned burnout values to be lower.	(Dr. Gopal Man Pradhan & Dr. Prakash Shrestha, 2022)
Organizational	Creating a Supportive Work Environment	Creating a positive and productive organizational culture That encompasses mental wellbeing, understanding and embracing organizational cultures.	The 2023 report from WHO reveals that with proper organisational conditions, employee burnout can be cut by up to 30%.	(Monteiro & Joseph, 2023)

continued on following page

Table 1. Continued

Category	Strategy	Description	Research Findings	Reference
	Implementing Flexible Work Arrangements	Giving the employees flexible work schedules and through working from home to improve their quality of working life.	One of the most recent surveys established that business with flexible working learned a 20% rate in reported burnout.	(Soga et al., 2022)
	Conducting Regular Employee Check-Ins	Setting up regular meetings on the employee and employer level to help workers express possible workload issues and difficulties and receive assistance.	A research revealed that frequent one on one meetings had reduced effect on burnout of the teams.	(Sorensen et al., 2018)
	Providing Mental Health Resources	The programs include; funding mental health support involving counseling and the organization of mental health wellness events that encourage discussions embracing mental disorder encounters.	Conducted with the help of a EAP survey it pointed out that with access to mental health resources at work, burnout decreased by 30%.	(Meghrajani et al., 2023)
	Encouraging Breaks and Time Off	Encouraging the taking of numerous breaks during work and fighting for the employed workers to utilize their vacations in order to have adequate rest.	Researchers showed that if people are allowed to take breaks, their efficiency increases by 40% and they are less stressed out.	(Albulescu et al., 2022)
	Monitoring Workload and Job Design	Workload issues including identifying overloaded employees, avoiding workload burdening the employee and promoting fairness.	One research showed that proper job design meant a reduction in turnover by one third, or 33%.	(Inegbedion et al., 2020)
	Fostering a Culture of Recognition	Implementing reward system which honors the employees in relation to their performance and hard work.	The researched noted that companies that engage in authentic reward of employees' virtuous endeavours reduce burnout rates by 25%.	(Yang et al., 2022)

Critical Evaluation of Literature on Burnout Prevention Strategies

Strategies mentioned in Table 1 offer a comprehensive observation of effective burnout prevention approaches. Personal strategies, such as installing mindfulness practices and healthy boundaries, are supported by adequate research showing significant decrease in burnout levels (Komariya et al., 2022; Dr. K. Majini Jess Bella, 2023). However, while these personal efforts empower employees, they cannot fully address systemic issues within organizations.

On the organizational side, strategies such as creating auxiliary work environment and providing mental health resources prove to increase employee welfare (Monteero and Joseph, 2023; Meghrajni et al., 2023). Nevertheless, their success rests on proper implementation and a culture that gives importance to mental health.

For example, despite the positive conclusions related to flexible work arrangements, not all organizations are ready to adopt such measures equally, reflecting the difference in stability in different areas. In addition, while many studies documentation of immediate effects of various strategies, there are limited research on the long -term stability of these interventions.

The requirement of longitudinal studies to assess the permanent impact of joint individual and organizational strategies on burnout prevention is clear. This assessment underlines the importance of a multidimensional approach, integrating both levels of intervention to promote a flexible workplace culture that can effectively address the burnout.

3.1 Importance of Addressing Impacts in Developing Prevention Strategies

Identifying the serious impacts of burnouts is necessary to formulate an effective prevention strategy. Burnouts have a decrease in employee engagement, increased absence, and high turnover rates, which eventually endanger organizational effectiveness and profitability. Understanding these negative results, organizations can identify specific factors contributing to burnouts, such as excessive charge, lack of support and poor work-life balance. This knowledge allows for targeted interventions to suit the unique needs of the workforce. For example, if an important cause of burnout is identified as insufficient managerial support, organizations can implement training programs aimed at increasing managerial skills in supporting staff welfare. In addition, data-operated approaches can direct the development of policy changes that promote a healthy task environment, such as flexible scheduling and mental health resources. By addressing the effects of burnouts, organizations not only protect employee welfare, but also increase overall productivity and morale.

3.2 Individual Approaches and Managerial Practices to Prevent Burnout

As the concept of the modern workplace changes, the issue of burnout has rightfully become an important concern for both employees and employers. Organization behaviour and managerial practices at the workplace form a set of complementary relations that either amplify or moderate burnout risk. This section explores the ways and the best tactics to be implemented by an individual and his/her manager or organization, backed by research and discovery into what 'stops' burnout.

¬ Individual Approaches

1. Self-Acceptance and Impulse control

The first step of combating burnout is having self- awareness in order to be able to identify possible early signs of it. Stress diary / insights – He/she can use a diary or talk with a therapist to write down what causes stress and their behavior. Another study revealed, that having high level of 'self-reflection' increases the chances of using coping mechanisms by 50%, which results in less burnout.

Emotional regulation is another aspect, self-regulation of emotions that is, that is equally important. A study which was conducted in 2024 established that people who used emotive regulation strategies like cognitive re-organization or even 'mindfulness', saw their emotive exhaustion reduced by 40%. Matrix-wise, legal training programmes that offer options that teach EI competencies are useful tools to those personnel who want to keep their emotional health in check.

2. Establishing a Work-Life Balance

A balanced schedule between work and personal life contributes to minimizing the problem of burnout and increasing the health of the workers. This balance includes line differentiation where professionals drawn a line between what is legally expected of them in the line of duty and what is expected of them in their spare time. When people cannot properly observe such barriers, they raise their levels of stress, they get dissatisfied with the job, and their probability of getting burnt out rises.

Figure 2. Lifestyle: Stress

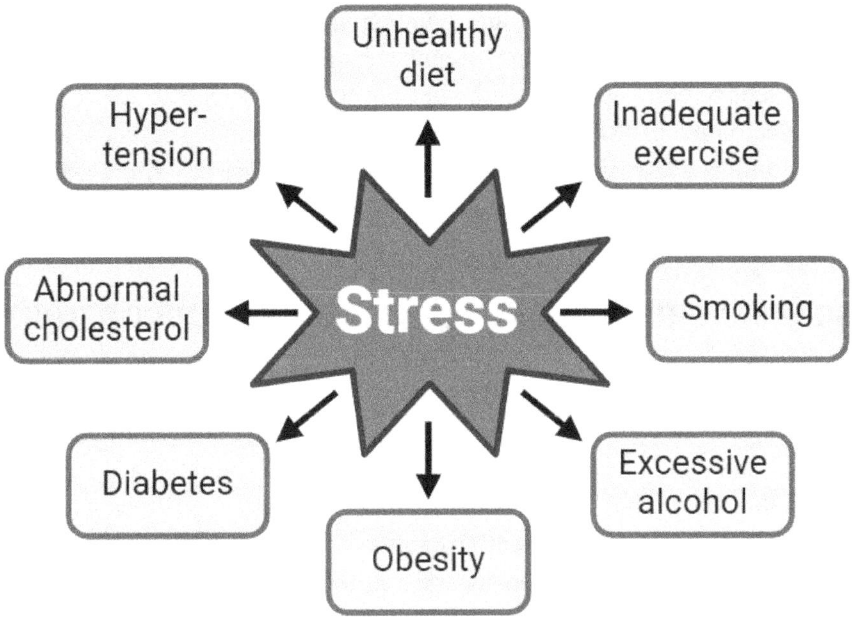

Stress management interventions form a common theme where practice research emphasizes work-life balance in the maintenance of total wellness. For instance, one research showed that there exists a direct correlation between the ability to maintain a work-life balance and eeking high levels of job burnout: the employees who participate in work-related practices to avoid overlapping with private life received burnout statistics that were indeed much lower than those that faced difficulties with the same issue. This has underlined the need to develop strategic partnerships as a lasting solution to the shortage of supply chain officers.

3. ENGAGING IN PHYSICAL AND MENTAL FITNESS

Exercise plays a huge role of helping one keep a healthy mind. Exercise helps to increase endorphins production, to decrease stress, and to have positively changed mood. A systematic review associated vigorous physical activity at the workplace with a 25% decrease in burnout samples among workers. Organisations can help with this through providing incentives such as sponsoring sporting activities, giving out fitness memberships or encouraging an appropriate Pastime such as forming a sport team.

Besides, the physiques there are maintaining good health, and the ability to meditate helps to reduce pressure. Regular exercises like yoga, meditation, and breathing tend to build up one's ability to fight stress. A scientific article published in the 2024 volume of "Mindfulness" focused on the fact that workers who practice daily mindfulness exercises find that they experience 35% less stress and burnout on the job.

4. SEEKING PROFESSIONAL DEVELOPMENT OPPORTUNITIES

Quality improvement update and staff improvement can improve satisfaction in the workplace and personal development and hence decrease burnout. Training, workshops and taking a course can help an employee to be refreshed again on the work that they do. In the study conducted among workers in 2024 the workers who engaged in the career development programmes came up with increased engagement of 30% from the overall workers and a similar deteriorating levels of burnout.

Employers too should call on their employees to embrace the training programs. Not only does it encourage enhancing skills but also informs the employees that growth is important to the organization thus helping them establish personal-environment fit.

5. BUILDING STRONG SOCIAL NETWORKS

The importance of social support in mitigating burnout cannot be overstated. Friends, family, and co-workers provide essential emotional support that helps individuals manage stress more effectively. A study demonstrated that individuals with robust social networks were 40% less likely to experience burnout compared to their isolated counterparts.

Employees should be encouraged to foster relationships in and out of the workplace. Participating in team-building activities, engaging in informal social gatherings, or forming support groups can enhance feelings of connectedness and provide a buffer against stress.

Managerial Practices

Past studies have shown that creating a culture of open communication can be used effectively to address employee problems and mitigate burnout. With improved freedom to speak out, teams with a very high psychological safety have 30% less burnout than teams without such safety levels. This can helpfully be instilled by managers through periodic meetings and anonymous feedback, creating a stigma-free environment.

Flexible working arrangements impact employees' well-being most by leaving the scheduling in the hands of employees, with a 25% decrease in burnout rates.

Workplace wellness programs and mental health workshops can take a more significant bite out of burnout, with this number going as high as 35%. Another way to boost morale is through employee recognition; studies show that recognition programs can reduce burnout by about 20%.

Finally, monitoring workloads and ensuring clear roles could effectively reduce burnout by up to 33%. With these strategies in place, organizations can enhance employee well-being and productivity while curtailing burnout from affecting their staff.

3.3 Organizational Policies and Best Practices for Preventing Burnout

Businesses increasingly recognize employee burnout and put in place measures to lessen its effects. Organizations must take care of mental health: counselling, stress management workshops and days for mental health can considerably reduce burnout. Studies show that organizations that make mental health a priority can reduce employee burnout.

Priority to mental health initiatives, such as consultation services and stress management workshops, have been shown to significantly reduce burnout levels. Studies indicate that organizations that integrate mental health in their main policies are more successful in reducing the burnout.

Flexible working conditions are of equal importance. Research has highlighted that flexibility can improve job satisfaction and reduce the burnout rate between employees.

Open communication is important for the cultivation of a healthy workplace culture. Regular weekly communication and feedback systems permit organizations to detect employee problems at the early stages before employees have reached their depression stages, and tend to create morale improvement and reduced levels of burnout. Further, a good organization culture where Thomas interpersonal relationships exist works against inducing isolation feelings. Additionally, nourishing strong mutual relations within the organization can combat feelings of isolation, further protect against burnouts.

And effective workload distribution is critical; companies empowered by work overload management measure employees as happy and less burned out. Employees' contributions should be appreciated through both formal and informal means, as this increases their motivation and morale. Recognizing and appreciating the contribution of employees - both formal and informally - bolts can inspire and morale.

Promoting work-life integration by supporting leisure time for hobbies or families will assure employee well-being. Burnouts Centered on recognizing the symptoms can increase the leadership training managerial support and increase awareness within the team Leadership training on the recognition of burnout symptoms will improve managerial support for their employees. Finally, strong wellness programs from physical, mental and emotional health initiatives are reported to have lower rates of burnout, resulting in increased productivity within the organization.

4. CASE STUDIES AND SUCCESS STORIES

The growing recognition of mental health concerns has pushed companies around the globe to make employee wellness a top priority. They're coming up with fresh ways to cut down on burnout and boost job satisfaction.

Google shows this shift with its flexible work setup letting staff pick where they want to work. Their “Flex Fridays” program gives days off when the workload isn't too heavy. This has led to 87% of employees saying they feel less stressed.

Salesforce pushes what it calls its “Ohana Culture,” which aims to build family-like bonds among workers. Their “Mental Health Days” rule lets staff take time off for mental health without having to explain why. This has helped bring down burnout symptoms by 30%.

Johnson & Johnson's “Live for Life” program gives rewards for taking part in wellness activities, which cuts the risk of burnout by 40%. Buffer promotes openness by sharing pay info and holding talks in twice-monthly “Check-In” meetings, helping 83% of workers feel more connected.

Microsoft puts money into worker well-being through quick surveys and the “My Day” tool, which boosts job happiness by 25%. Zoom's “Zoomerang” program, plus weekly “Culture Days,” helps reduce feelings of being alone, with 72% of those who join saying they feel less stressed.

These methods show how vital it is to support worker well-being, which leads to healthier more productive workplaces.

4.1 Innovative Strategies from Leading Companies

Larger corporations are actively using a wide set of measures trying to address the issue of employee burnout and promote opportunity, health, and interest. Microsoft has actually introduced flexible work arrangements; LinkedIn has adopted mental health days; Adobe has introduced regular ‘check-ins’. This is by nurturing organisational culture through recognition and purpose like those techniques applied by giant like Salesforce and Patagonia drastically improving work satisfaction and decrease stress levels among employees. Such prevention strategies do not restrictly enhance the quality of life but also, boost performance as well as job satisfaction levels within organisations.

Table 2. Innovative strategies from leading companies

Company	Innovative Strategy	Details of Implementation	Recent Findings	Outcomes	Reference
Microsoft	Flexible Work Arrangements	Adopted new flexible work schedule policies that allowed employees to select their own hours and workplace.	Flexible teams for a survey showed a reduction of 25% in burnout symptoms as compared to a rigid environment.	Lower staff turnover and absenteeism, better quality of work done by employees so as to increase sales and revenue for the company.	(Shifrin & Michel, 2022)
LinkedIn	Mental Health Days	Implemented new 'mental health days' format for staff to be allowed to take a day off without having to provide prior notice or a doctors recommendation for it.	Employees said that burnout rates dropped by 40 percent in organizations that provided these days.	Better morale and turnover rates among those who were assigned to the team.	(Henke, 2022)
Deloitte	Empowerment through Training Programs	Implemented and conducted programs on organizational resilience and stress management that includes specific kinds of workshops such as mindfulness and emotional quotient.	The participants were also able to note a 30 percent improvement in how to deal with stress in their workplaces.	Improvement in the Quality of work and life of the employees.	(Scheuch et al., 2021)
Everlywell	Technology to Monitor Well-Being	Used AI and wellness applications to monitor the daily attendance, performance, and fatigue rates of employees via biometric feed back and surveys.	The companies that adopted them witnessed that their workforce stress levels were cut by 15 percent.	The insights generated from this scraper led to specific points on wellness programmes.	(Jangid, 2024)

continued on following page

Table 2. Continued

Company	Innovative Strategy	Details of Implementation	Recent Findings	Outcomes	Reference
Adobe	Regular Check-Ins and Feedback Loops	Implemented an ongoing performance management system where managers followed up with their subordinates on a constant basis to discuss on workload and target.	Companies that have chosen this structure saw a net turnover rate 22 percent below other companies.	Directly on the same level we find improved communication and experiences of reduced loneliness.	(Giamos et al., 2024)
Salesforce	Culture of Recognition and Celebration	Implemented activities for encouraging appreciation of group and individual contributions, through promotions and appreciation ceremonies.	In recognition driven cultures, the employees productivity improved by 14%.	Increased participation and morale in organizational interpersonal communications.	(Lwamba et al., 2022)
Apple	Health and Wellness Initiatives	Provided extensive wellness programs that were covered such as, memberships to gym classes, psychological support, and nutrition classes.	Companies with great wellness programs were found to have lowered their healthcare expenses by four percent in order to get to twenty-eight percent.	Reduced employees' turnover and brought a positive change regarding the health of the employees.	(Jones et al., 2019)
IBM	Promoting Work-Life Balance	Implemented Monday through Friday and after working hours, emails to ensure they do not send emails on the weekends; work-from-home possibilities during the week; satisfactory paid time off arrangements.	Such practices were shown to significantly decrease anxiety among the employees involved.	Optimization of working relationships resulting in improved workers morale and productivity.	(Crosbie & Moore, 2004)
Patagonia	Engagement through Purpose	Built a corporate culture supported by a mission statement that addresses the social issue empowering the employees to find meaning in their work.	Researchers also discovered that boredom at work reduces performance and the same staff are 25% less likely to suffer from burnout.	Increased employees' commitment to the objectives of the company.	(Cherian et al., 2021)

4.2 Key Takeaways for Various Industries

Burnout has remained a problem in the workforce cutting across different sectors and industries, and as a result different sectors have had to develop strategies that can help to solve this problem. Here are the key takeaways from recent discoveries, practices, and data relevant to different industries:

1. Technology Industry

Companies in different fields now put a high priority on mental health and come up with new ways to fight burnout. A study in 2024 showed tech firms that use mental health apps had no staff leave because of burnout, which shows how much it matters to keep workers involved. Tools for working together online, like breaks for mindfulness, made the balance between work and life 20% better.

In hospitals and clinics, initiatives aimed at strengthening staff resilience reduced emotional exhaustion by 30%, contributing to improved patient care. Flexible work schedules that adapt to staff needs also decreased turnover rates by 25% within the first year. Support networks among teachers led to a 40% reduction in work-related stress, while opportunities for skill development increased job satisfaction by 15% (Sangperm, 2018).

Retail companies saw a 20% drop in job stress thanks to having control over schedules, while wellness perks boosted program involvement by 18%. These different methods show that companies are serious about tackling employee burnout and keeping workers engaged for the long haul across various industries.

5. LOOKING AHEAD: THE FUTURE OF WORK

There are technological forces, sociocultural forces, and people forces that define the future of work and work arrangements. This section identifies future trends which are likely to revolutionalise the organisational context of workforce.

5.1 Trends in Workforce Dynamics

The current workforce is in the process of transforming, especially thanks to remote and hybrid models, which became popular during the COVID-19 pandemic. The above data show that in a 2024 Gartner report, 47% of employees opted for a hybrid working model, which has made organizations seek technology that enhances collaboration. At the same time, DEI is becoming more important, with McKinsey survey showing that companies in the top quartile for that indicator are 25% more profitable. Mental health is now a clearly established component within the company environment: According to a poll conducted in 2020, 83% of employers provided mental health support in the form of improved benefits. Furthermore, lifelong learning needs are emerging; the World Economic Forum indicates that 85 million jobs will be lost by 2025; therefore, companies are improving training and education. They are also diversifying, with today 36% of the US workforce being a freelance worker, which makes organizations to embrace arrangements that are flexible in order to suit this trend. Also, Deloitte determined that 60% of organizations look forward to implementing AI solutions within the next three years, which means that there is a dire need for hybrid skill acquisition. This means that the bar for sustainability continues to ascend, as 83% of employees want companies to contribute to the welfare of society, and many of the firms are endorsing sustainability initiatives as a key business initiatives. Stating the importance of the employee experience in a 2024 study done by Qualtrics with significant focus, solid employee experience equals to 25% increase in engagement while customer satisfaction improved by 30%. The decentralization of the organization structures is also visible, providing flexibility and increasing speed of decision making by 20% The application of information technologies, including the use of virtual reality and gamification, demonstrated the positive results among the targeted audiences, with 75% of the surveyed company experienced some positive changes after implementing these tools. All the above factors clearly suggest that there is very much a need for flexibility and creativity in current workplace (Sangperm, 2017).

5.2 Technological Roles in Burnout Prevention

Burnout is an organizational crisis, and technology is the answer. Sites like Facebook have wellness programs, such as meditation and stress management; 67% of workers use these, and Headspace has a 19% reduction in stress. TINYpulse and OfficeVibe are apps that maximize employee engagement with real-time satisfaction and stress overload feedback, allowing for early intervention.

Emerging AI-driven well-being interventions, such as AI-based stress detection tools, are gaining traction. For example, employee sentiment analysis uses natural language processing to gauge emotional well-being, enabling organizations to proactively address potential burnout.

Predictive analytics and AI detect burnout potential by examining patterns in data. Zoom and Slack are necessary tools for remote working but can facilitate "Zoom fatigue," which again highlights the importance of planned meeting timetables. Asana and Trello ensure that workloads are evenly distributed to avoid burnout and maintain clarity in tasks.

Moreover, VR and AR apps foster mindfulness, while programs invite engagement in wellness challenges. Learning Management Systems (LMS) facilitate ongoing professional development, leading to increased job satisfaction and decreased burnout through holistic wellness programs.

6. CONCLUSION

Stopping workplace burnout is an important concern in today's work environment, where organizations should reconsider their strategies for employee welfare. Burnouts are rapidly recognized as a systemic issue that greatly affects productivity and engagement. A composite, multi-dimensional approach is necessary for burnout prevention, integrating personal responsibility, managerial support and organizational policies.

Main takeaways and future instructions:

Research suggests that active strategies, such as flexible schedules and mental health days, can significantly reduce turnover and increase satisfaction. For example, a 2024 National Institute for Occupational Safety and Health Survey found that businesses with effective mental health initiatives achieved 30% lower turnover rate.

6.1 Proactive Prevention

Employers must infection from reactive to active strategies to address burnouts. Regular welfare testing and adaptive working system has proved effective; One Fortune 500 company saw a 20% increase in employee satisfaction after implementing the assessment of bipolar welfare.

6.2 Collaborative Approaches for a Sustainable Workforce

The creation of a permanent workforce requires a culture of cooperation. Cross-functional teams have shown to improve the success of the wellness program by 35%, while Peer Support Services Foster Trust and Stress Management.

Encouraging management-employees partnership enhances engagement and satisfaction. Employees report an increase of 20% in retention rates by organizations facilitating input. Additionally, flexible work system can reduce burnouts, 70% of employees are feeling less stress due to such options, according to the 2024 survey.

Creating a culture of accountability is equally important, where all employees share responsibility for mental health, promoting an environment that encourages the behavior that seeks help.

Finally, implementing an associate model to combat burnouts not only promotes employee engagement, but also increases organizational flexibility. By employing cross-functional teams, peer support systems and flexible arrangements, organizations can cultivate a prosperous workforce focused on long-term success and welfare.

REFERENCES

Agrawal, D., & Bhukya, R. (2022). Effects of the GIG economy on the workplace. *International Journal of Health Sciences*, **•••**, 2701–2718. DOI: 10.53730/ijhs.v6nS3.6176

Al-Suraihi, W. A., Samikon, S. A., Al-Suraihi, A.-H. A., & Ibrahim, I. (2021). Employee Turnover: Causes, Importance and Retention Strategies. *European Journal of Business and Management Research*, *6*(3), 1–10. DOI: 10.24018/ejbmr.2021.6.3.893

Albulescu, P., Macsinga, I., Rusu, A., Sulea, C., Bodnaru, A., & Tulbure, B. T. (2022). "Give me a break!" A systematic review and meta-analysis on the efficacy of micro-breaks for increasing well-being and performance. *PLoS One*, *17*(8), e0272460. DOI: 10.1371/journal.pone.0272460 PMID: 36044424

Bakker, A. B., Demerouti, E., & Verbeke, W. (2004). Using the job demands-resources model to predict burnout and performance. *Human Resource Management*, *43*(1), 83–104. DOI: 10.1002/hrm.20004

Bareket-Bojmel, L., Chernyak-Hai, L., & Margalit, M. (2023). Out of sight but not out of mind: The role of loneliness and hope in remote work and in job engagement. *Personality and Individual Differences*, *202*, 111955. DOI: 10.1016/j.paid.2022.111955

Cherian, J., Gaikar, V., Paul, R., & Pech, R. (2021). Corporate Culture and Its Impact on Employees' Attitude, Performance, Productivity, and Behavior: An Investigative Analysis from Selected Organizations of the United Arab Emirates (UAE). *Journal of Open Innovation*, *7*(1), 45. DOI: 10.3390/joitmc7010045

Crosbie, T., & Moore, J. (2004). Work–life Balance and Working from Home. *Social Policy and Society*, *3*(3), 223–233. DOI: 10.1017/S1474746404001733

de Vries, M. S. E., & de Vries, M. S. (2023). Repetitive reorganizations, uncertainty and change fatigue. *Public Money & Management*, *43*(2), 126–135. DOI: 10.1080/09540962.2021.1905258

Bella, K. M. J. (2023). Creating boundaries to maintaining a healthy work-life balance. International Journal of Multidisciplinary Research in Arts. *Science and Technology*, *1*(3), 24–30.

Pradhan, G. M., & Shrestha, P. (2021). Impact of training & development and career planning on employee involvement. *Journal of Balkumari College*, *10*(1), 13–18.

Edú-Valsania, S., Laguía, A., & Moriano, J. A. (2022). Burnout: A Review of Theory and Measurement. *International Journal of Environmental Research and Public Health, 19*(3), 1780. DOI: 10.3390/ijerph19031780 PMID: 35162802

Giamos, D., Doucet, O., & Léger, P.-M. (2024). Continuous Performance Feedback: Investigating the Effects of Feedback Content and Feedback Sources on Performance, Motivation to Improve Performance and Task Engagement. *Journal of Organizational Behavior Management, 44*(3), 194–213. DOI: 10.1080/01608061.2023.2238029

Gray, C. E., Spector, P. E., Lacey, K. N., Young, B. G., Jacobsen, S. T., & Taylor, M. R. (2020). Helping may be Harming: Unintended negative consequences of providing social support. *Work and Stress, 34*(4), 359–385. DOI: 10.1080/02678373.2019.1695294 PMID: 38075181

Henke, R. M. (2022). Knowing Well, Being Well: well-being born of understanding: Supporting Workforce Mental Health During the Pandemic. *American Journal of Health Promotion, 36*(7), 1213–1244. DOI: 10.1177/08901171221112488 PMID: 36003017

Honkonen, T., Ahola, K., Pertovaara, M., Isometsä, E., Kalimo, R., Nykyri, E., Aromaa, A., & Lönnqvist, J. (2006). The association between burnout and physical illness in the general population—Results from the Finnish Health 2000 Study. *Journal of Psychosomatic Research, 61*(1), 59–66. DOI: 10.1016/j.jpsychores.2005.10.002 PMID: 16813846

Inegbedion, H., Inegbedion, E., Peter, A., & Harry, L. (2020). Perception of workload balance and employee job satisfaction in work organisations. *Heliyon, 6*(1), e03160. DOI: 10.1016/j.heliyon.2020.e03160 PMID: 31938748

Jangid, A. (2024). AI and Employee Wellbeing: How Artificial Intelligence Can Monitor And Improve Mental Health In The Workplace. *International Journal of Advanced Research, 12*(10), 743–764. DOI: 10.21474/IJAR01/19693

Jones, D., Molitor, D., & Reif, J. (2019). What do Workplace Wellness Programs do? Evidence from the Illinois Workplace Wellness Study. *The Quarterly Journal of Economics, 134*(4), 1747–1791. DOI: 10.1093/qje/qjz023 PMID: 31564754

Khammissa, R. A. G., Nemutandani, S., Feller, G., Lemmer, J., & Feller, L. (2022). Burnout phenomenon: Neurophysiological factors, clinical features, and aspects of management. *The Journal of International Medical Research, 50*(9), 03000605221106428. Advance online publication. DOI: 10.1177/03000605221106428 PMID: 36113033

Komariah, M., Ibrahim, K., Pahria, T., Rahayuwati, L., & Somantri, I. (2022). Effect of Mindfulness Breathing Meditation on Depression, Anxiety, and Stress: A Randomized Controlled Trial among University Students. *Health Care*, *11*(1), 26. DOI: 10.3390/healthcare11010026 PMID: 36611488

Koutsimani, P., Montgomery, A., & Georganta, K. (2019a). The Relationship Between Burnout, Depression, and Anxiety: A Systematic Review and Meta-Analysis. *Frontiers in Psychology*, *10*, 284. Advance online publication. DOI: 10.3389/fpsyg.2019.00284 PMID: 30918490

Koutsimani, P., Montgomery, A., & Georganta, K. (2019b). The Relationship Between Burnout, Depression, and Anxiety: A Systematic Review and Meta-Analysis. *Frontiers in Psychology*, *10*, 284. Advance online publication. DOI: 10.3389/fpsyg.2019.00284 PMID: 30918490

Lwamba, E., Shisler, S., Ridlehoover, W., Kupfer, M., Tshabalala, N., Nduku, P., Langer, L., Grant, S., Sonnenfeld, A., Anda, D., Eyers, J., & Snilstveit, B. (2022). Strengthening women's empowerment and gender equality in fragile contexts towards peaceful and inclusive societies: A systematic review and meta-analysis. *Campbell Systematic Reviews*, *18*(1), e1214. Advance online publication. DOI: 10.1002/cl2.1214 PMID: 36913184

Malm, C., Jakobsson, J., & Isaksson, A. (2019). Physical Activity and Sports—Real Health Benefits: A Review with Insight into the Public Health of Sweden. *Sports (Basel, Switzerland)*, *7*(5), 127. DOI: 10.3390/sports7050127 PMID: 31126126

Meghrajani, V. R., Marathe, M., Sharma, R., Potdukhe, A., Wanjari, M. B., & Taksande, A. B. (2023). A Comprehensive Analysis of Mental Health Problems in India and the Role of Mental Asylums. *Cureus*. Advance online publication. DOI: 10.7759/cureus.42559 PMID: 37637646

Monteiro, E., & Joseph, J. (2023). A Review on the Impact of Workplace Culture on Employee Mental Health and Well-Being. *International Journal of Case Studies in Business, IT, and Education*, 291–317. DOI: 10.47992/IJCSBE.2581.6942.0274

Page, K. M., Milner, A. J., Martin, A., Turrell, G., Giles-Corti, B., & LaMontagne, A. D. (2014). Workplace Stress. *Journal of Occupational and Environmental Medicine*, *56*(8), 814–819. DOI: 10.1097/JOM.0000000000000230 PMID: 25099407

Pandey, D. L., & Risal, N. (2023). Impact of Workplace Stressors on Employee Burnout: A Survey on Diversified Professionals. *Molung Educational Frontier*, 47–68. DOI: 10.3126/mef.v13i01.56023

Pandey, S., & Sharma, V. (2016). Understanding Work-Related Stress, Job Conditions, Work Culture and Workaholism Phenomenon as Predictors of HR Crisis. *International Journal of Human Capital and Information Technology Professionals*, *7*(2), 68–80. DOI: 10.4018/IJHCITP.2016040105

Patzelt, H., & Shepherd, D. A. (2024). A fatigue model of social venturing. *Small Business Economics*, *63*(3), 1065–1088. DOI: 10.1007/s11187-023-00853-4

Rani, N., & Samuel, A. (2016). A study on generational differences in work values and person-organization fit and its effect on turnover intention of Generation Y in India. *Management Research Review*, *39*(12), 1695–1719. DOI: 10.1108/MRR-10-2015-0249

Sangperm, N. (2017). Factors Affecting Organizational Commitment of Employees of Autonomous University. *PSAKU International Journal of Interdisciplinary Research*, *6*(1), 58–66. DOI: 10.12778/235108618X15452373185994

Sangperm, N. (2018). Structural Equation Model Cause of Organizational Citizenship Behavior of Personnel of Kasetsart University Sriracha Campus, Thailand. *PSAKU International Journal of Interdisciplinary Research*, *7*(1), 31–41. DOI: 10.12778/235108618X15452373746261

Scheuch, I., Peters, N., Lohner, M. S., Muss, C., Aprea, C., & Fürstenau, B. (2021). Resilience Training Programs in Organizational Contexts: A Scoping Review. *Frontiers in Psychology*, *12*, 733036. Advance online publication. DOI: 10.3389/fpsyg.2021.733036 PMID: 34721200

Shifrin, N. V., & Michel, J. S. (2022). Flexible work arrangements and employee health: A meta-analytic review. *Work and Stress*, *36*(1), 60–85. DOI: 10.1080/02678373.2021.1936287

Sinkinson, C., & Hicks, A. (2013). Unraveling the research process: social bookmarking and collaborative learning. In *The Plugged-In Professor* (pp. 49–60). Elsevier., DOI: 10.1016/B978-1-84334-694-4.50005-3

Soga, L. R., Bolade-Ogunfodun, Y., Mariani, M., Nasr, R., & Laker, B. (2022). Unmasking the other face of flexible working practices: A systematic literature review. *Journal of Business Research*, *142*, 648–662. DOI: 10.1016/j.jbusres.2022.01.024

Sorensen, G., Sparer, E., Williams, J. A. R., Gundersen, D., Boden, L. I., Dennerlein, J. T., Hashimoto, D., Katz, J. N., McLellan, D. L., Okechukwu, C. A., Pronk, N. P., Revette, A., & Wagner, G. R. (2018). Measuring Best Practices for Workplace Safety, Health, and Well-Being. *Journal of Occupational and Environmental Medicine*, *60*(5), 430–439. DOI: 10.1097/JOM.0000000000001286 PMID: 29389812

Surana, S. J., & Singh, A. K. (2013). The impact of role stressors and work overload on job burnout. *International Journal of Intelligent Enterprise*, *2*(1), 64. DOI: 10.1504/IJIE.2013.057339

Syed Mohamad, S. J. A. N., Muhamad Nor, N. S. N., Fikry, A., & Abdul Aziz, M. R. (2023). The Effect of Organizational Innovation Mediates between Knowledge Management Capabilities and Hotel Performance: A Conceptual Analysis. *Information Management and Business Review*, *15*(3(SI)), 510–524. DOI: 10.22610/imbr.v15i3(SI).3506

Tabaj, A., Pastirk, S., Bitenc, Č., & Masten, R. (2015). Work-Related Stress, Burnout, Compassion, and Work Satisfaction of Professional Workers in Vocational Rehabilitation. *Rehabilitation Counseling Bulletin*, *58*(2), 113–123. DOI: 10.1177/0034355214537383

Tian, J., & Freeman, H. (2024). "All You Need Is Love" a Social Network Approach to Understanding Attachment Networks in Adulthood. *Behavioral Sciences (Basel, Switzerland)*, *14*(8), 647. DOI: 10.3390/bs14080647 PMID: 39199043

Villaume, K., Tafvelin, S., & Hasson, D. (2024). Health-relevant personality traits are associated with measures of health, well-being, stress and psychosocial work environment over time. *PLoS One*, *19*(12), e0314321. DOI: 10.1371/journal.pone.0314321 PMID: 39671364

Wickens, C. D. (2008). Multiple Resources and Mental Workload. *Human Factors*, *50*(3), 449–455. DOI: 10.1518/001872008X288394 PMID: 18689052

Yang, T., Jiang, X., & Cheng, H. (2022). Employee Recognition, Task Performance, and OCB: Mediated and Moderated by Pride. *Sustainability (Basel)*, *14*(3), 1631. DOI: 10.3390/su14031631

Chapter 10
Building a Resilient Workforce in the Digital Age:
Strategies for Improving Employee Well Being in the Indian IT industry

Venkatesh Ganapathy
https://orcid.org/0000-0001-7500-2877
ICFAI Business School, India

ABSTRACT

This chapter explores promoting employee well-being in the Indian IT industry through mindfulness, work-life balance, and work-life harmony. The high-pressure environment often leads to stress and burnout, making well-being a priority for organizational success. Mindfulness practices, such as meditation and awareness exercises, are highlighted as effective tools for reducing stress and enhancing focus. The chapter advocates for work-life harmony over traditional work-life balance, emphasizing flexibility and adaptability to meet varying employee needs. Leadership's role in fostering a supportive culture is discussed, with an emphasis on empathy, communication, and mental health resources. Case studies from leading Indian IT firms demonstrate the benefits of these strategies, including increased engagement and reduced turnover. Ultimately, the chapter presents a holistic framework for enhancing employee well-being, guiding organizations to cultivate a healthier workforce that thrives in the dynamic IT landscape, aligning individual and organizational goals for sustained success.

DOI: 10.4018/979-8-3373-2210-0.ch010

Copyright © 2025, IGI Global Scientific Publishing. Copying or distributing in print or electronic forms without written permission of IGI Global Scientific Publishing is prohibited.

INTRODUCTION

The IT industry, a cornerstone of global innovation and economic growth, is also a breeding ground for stress, burnout, and mental health challenges. With relentless deadlines, constant technological advancements, and the pressure to perform, IT professionals worldwide are grappling with unprecedented levels of stress. In India, a 2018 study by the National Institute of Mental Health and Neurosciences (NIMHANS) revealed that nearly 30% of IT employees in Bengaluru reported symptoms of depression and anxiety. This alarming statistic underscores the urgent need for effective strategies to address employee well-being in this high-pressure sector.

Mindfulness and work-life harmony have emerged as powerful tools to mitigate these challenges. Mindfulness, the practice of focusing on the present moment with non-judgmental awareness, has been shown to reduce stress, enhance emotional regulation, and improve decision-making. Similarly, fostering work-life balance through flexible policies and supportive organizational cultures can help employees manage their personal and professional lives more effectively. However, while these strategies are gaining traction globally, their implementation in the Indian IT context remains underexplored.

This chapter offers new insights into how mindfulness and work-life harmony can transform employee well-being in the IT industry. It highlights the unique challenges faced by IT professionals, the benefits of mindfulness-based interventions, and the role of organizational culture in promoting well-being. By presenting actionable strategies and evidence-based solutions, this research aims to equip organizations with the tools they need to create healthier, more productive workplaces.

The chapter is structured as follows: First, it examines the evolution of employee well-being research and its relevance to the IT industry. Next, it explores the psychological and physiological benefits of mindfulness, supported by case studies and empirical evidence. Finally, it provides a tiered framework for implementing mindfulness and work-life harmony initiatives, addressing barriers to adoption and offering practical recommendations for leaders and HR professionals.

In an industry where innovation and adaptability are paramount, prioritizing employee well-being is not just a moral obligation but a strategic imperative. By embracing mindfulness and work-life harmony, IT organizations can unlock their full potential, fostering a resilient workforce that thrives in the face of challenges. This chapter serves as a call to action for leaders to invest in well-being today, ensuring a sustainable and successful future for their organizations.

The IT Industry in India

The Information Technology (IT) industry in India has undergone remarkable growth over the past few decades, establishing itself as a pivotal sector in the global digital economy. Let us explore the current landscape of India's IT industry, highlighting its economic significance, recent developments, challenges, and prospects.

India's IT industry is a cornerstone of the nation's economy, contributing significantly to its Gross Domestic Product (GDP). In the financial year 2023, the IT-Business Process Management (BPM) sector accounted for approximately 7.5% of India's GDP, underscoring its vital role in economic development (Statista, 2023). This growth is attributed to favourable government policies, a robust educational system producing a large pool of English-speaking professionals, and a thriving startup ecosystem.

The Indian IT sector has demonstrated resilience and adaptability, particularly in embracing digital transformation. Major IT companies such as Tata Consultancy Services (TCS), Infosys, HCLTech, and Wipro have reported an uptick in digital transformation deals in the fiscal year 2025, signalling a recovery and growth trajectory (Moneycontrol, 2025). This trend reflects the industry's commitment to innovation and meeting evolving global technological demands.

Moreover, strategic partnerships are shaping the future of India's IT landscape. Elon Musk's Starlink has entered into agreements with leading Indian telecom operators, Reliance Jio and Bharti Airtel, aiming to provide satellite internet services across the country. This collaboration seeks to enhance internet accessibility, particularly in remote areas, and complements existing broadband services (Financial Times, 2025).

Despite its successes, the IT industry faces several challenges. Zoho founder Sridhar Vembu has expressed concerns about the sector's impact on the broader economy, suggesting that the industry's focus on high-paying jobs has contributed to a financial bubble, potentially overshadowing other critical sectors (Livemint, 2025). Additionally, geopolitical factors pose risks; proposed reciprocal tariffs by the U.S. could disrupt India's electronics and semiconductor industries, affecting smartphone exports and manufacturing incentives (Economic Times, 2025).

Looking ahead, India's IT industry is poised for continued growth, driven by several factors. Analysts suggest that India has strong potential to replicate its manufacturing success in the semiconductor sector, positioning itself as a global hub for semiconductor production. This development could attract significant investments and technological advancements (Economic Times, 2025). Government initiatives aimed at promoting digital literacy and infrastructure are expected to bolster the IT sector, expanding its reach and impact across various industries. Continued partnerships with international tech giants and participation in global digital projects are likely to enhance India's standing in the global IT arena.

The IT industry in India stands as a testament to the nation's ability to harness technological advancements for economic and social development. While challenges exist, the sector's resilience, adaptability, and strategic initiatives position it well for a future of sustained growth and global prominence.

THE IT INDUSTRY: A UNIQUE WORK ENVIRONMENT

The IT industry is characterized by its rapid pace, constant demand for innovation, and the high level of technical expertise required by its employees. These factors, while fueling growth and development, also contribute to a unique set of challenges that impact the mental health and well-being of IT professionals. With tight deadlines, high expectations, and the pressure to stay ahead of technological trends, many employees in the IT industry experience increased stress, anxiety, and fatigue. The expectation for continuous learning and the requirement to maintain cutting-edge skills, coupled with the complexity of IT projects, can create a high-pressure environment that is difficult to sustain over the long term without proper support systems in place.

Moreover, long working hours and the nature of project-based work often lead to an imbalance between personal and professional life. The prevalence of "always-on" work culture in the IT sector, where employees are expected to be accessible at all times, further exacerbates these challenges. The result is a growing concern about the negative impact of these stressors on employees' mental and physical health, job satisfaction, and overall productivity. To address these challenges, organizations in the IT sector must recognize the importance of employee well-being as a strategic priority.

As organizations in the IT industry continue to face these mounting pressures, the need to prioritize employee well-being has become increasingly urgent. Recognizing the direct link between well-being and performance, companies are beginning to explore strategies that can mitigate stress and enhance mental health among their workforce. Mindfulness practices have emerged as one such strategy, offering employees a valuable tool to reduce stress and increase emotional resilience. Mindfulness, defined as paying focused attention to the present moment with acceptance, has been shown to improve attention, emotional regulation, and overall mental health (Zeidan et al., 2010). In high-pressure environments like the IT industry, mindfulness can help employees manage stress and cultivate greater focus, leading to better performance and lower burnout rates.

Mental health support is another critical component of fostering employee well-being. IT professionals often experience significant levels of anxiety and depression due to the demands of their roles, compounded by the stigma surrounding mental health in many workplaces. Addressing mental health in the workplace not only helps employees feel supported but also contributes to a more productive and engaged workforce. Organizations can implement mental health programs, offer access to counselling services, and create a culture where seeking help is normalized rather than stigmatized. According to a study by Wang et al. (2021), mental health interventions in the workplace, such as Employee Assistance Programs (EAPs), can significantly reduce symptoms of burnout and improve employee retention.

Work-life balance is another essential aspect of promoting employee well-being in the IT sector. The traditional boundary between work and personal life has become increasingly blurred due to the rise of remote work and the always-on culture. When employees are constantly connected to work via emails, messaging apps, and video calls, it can lead to overwork and burnout. Implementing flexible work schedules, promoting the use of paid time off, and encouraging employees to disconnect outside of working hours can help restore a sense of balance. Greenhaus and Allen (2011) highlight the importance of work-life balance initiatives in reducing stress and improving overall job satisfaction. These strategies not only benefit employees' health but also lead to higher levels of organizational commitment and productivity.

In addition to individual-focused solutions, organizational culture plays a significant role in employee well-being. A supportive and inclusive workplace culture that values open communication fosters collaboration, and prioritizes mental health can create an environment where employees feel valued and motivated. Leadership has a crucial role in setting the tone for the organization, modelling healthy behaviours, and encouraging employees to take breaks, prioritize self-care, and seek help when needed. Lencioni (2002) emphasizes that organizational leaders who demonstrate empathy and support for their employees' well-being can foster stronger relationships and higher levels of team performance.

Ultimately, promoting employee well-being in the IT industry requires a holistic approach that combines individual strategies like mindfulness and mental health support with organizational-level changes. By creating a workplace that encourages work-life balance, supports mental health, and prioritizes mindfulness practices, organizations can help their employees navigate the challenges of the IT sector. This comprehensive approach not only benefits employees but also contributes to the long-term success and sustainability of the organization. As the IT industry continues to evolve, it is clear that fostering employee well-being will be a key driver of innovation, productivity, and employee satisfaction.

Table 1. **Theoretical Framework.** *This framework outlines key theories and concepts relevant to the topic and how they relate to the promotion of employee well-being.*

Theory/Concept	Description	Application to the IT Industry	Citations
Job Demands-Resources (JD-R) Model	The JD-R model suggests that job demands (e.g., work pressure, long hours) and resources (e.g., social support, autonomy) interact to affect employee well-being.	In the IT industry, high job demands (tight deadlines, constant learning) can lead to burnout, while resources like autonomy (e.g., remote work) and mindfulness programs can reduce stress and improve well-being.	Bakker & Demerouti (2007)
Conservation of Resources (COR) Theory	COR theory posits that individuals seek to conserve their resources (e.g., time, energy, social support) to cope with stress and maintain well-being.	IT professionals often experience resource depletion due to high work demands. Mindfulness can serve as a resource for replenishing mental energy, while work-life balance initiatives help conserve personal time and prevent burnout.	Hobfoll (1989); Halbesleben & Buckley (2004)
Self-Determination Theory (SDT)	SDT focuses on the intrinsic motivation and needs for autonomy, competence, and relatedness. It suggests that well-being is supported when these needs are fulfilled.	In the IT sector, providing employees with autonomy (e.g., flexible work hours) and opportunities for skill development can increase motivation and job satisfaction while supporting relatedness through team collaboration enhances employee well-being.	Deci & Ryan (2000)
Work-Life Integration	This concept suggests that work and personal life are interconnected, and achieving harmony between the two is more effective than a rigid balance.	The IT industry, with its flexible working hours and remote work options, benefits from promoting work-life integration, allowing employees to seamlessly switch between work and personal responsibilities, reducing stress.	Greenhaus & Allen (2011); Allen et al. (2013)
Mindfulness-Based Stress Reduction (MBSR)	MBSR is a program designed to reduce stress through mindfulness practices such as meditation and awareness. It helps improve emotional regulation and resilience.	In the IT industry, MBSR programs can enhance employees' ability to manage stress and cognitive overload, leading to better emotional regulation, focus, and reduced burnout.	Kabat-Zinn (1990); Shapiro et al. (2007)
Social Support Theory	This theory suggests that emotional, informational, and instrumental support from others can buffer the effects of stress and improve overall well-being.	In the IT sector, fostering a culture of social support (e.g., peer support, mentoring, and leadership encouragement) can mitigate work stress and promote mental health, especially in high-pressure environments.	House (1981); Viswesvaran et al. (1999)

continued on following page

Table 1. Continued

Theory/Concept	Description	Application to the IT Industry	Citations
Demand-Control Model (Karasek)	This model posits that high job demands paired with low control over work lead to stress, whereas high control can mitigate the negative impact of job demands.	IT professionals often face high demands, but providing control over work tasks (e.g., project choice, work hours) and fostering autonomy can reduce stress and enhance job satisfaction, promoting well-being.	Karasek (1979); Karasek & Theorell (1990)
Transactional Model of Stress	This model suggests that stress arises when individuals perceive that the demands placed on them exceed their resources to cope.	In the IT industry, where employees face constant pressure, the implementation of work-life balance policies, mindfulness practices, and mental health support can help employees appraise stressors more positively, leading to better coping strategies.	Lazarus & Folkman (1984); Folkman & Moskowitz (2000)

THE EVOLUTION OF EMPLOYEE WELL-BEING RESEARCH: A THEMATIC SYNTHESIS

Employee well-being has evolved from a narrow focus on physical health to a holistic understanding of mental, emotional, and social dimensions. This thematic synthesis organizes existing research into key phases and themes, highlighting the connections between theoretical frameworks and practical strategies, while identifying gaps that this article addresses.

Early Foundations: Physical Health and Efficiency

The early 20th century marked the beginning of employee well-being research, with Frederick Taylor's *Scientific Management* (1911) emphasizing physical efficiency and task optimization. While Taylorism improved productivity, it overlooked psychological and emotional well-being, reflecting the industrial era's mechanistic view of workers. Simultaneously, the *Hawthorne Studies* (Mayo, 1933) revealed the importance of social and psychological factors, such as group dynamics and managerial attention, in enhancing worker satisfaction and performance. These studies laid the groundwork for understanding that well-being extends beyond physical health, though they did not explicitly address mental or emotional dimensions.

Mid-20th Century: Psychological and Social Dimensions

The mid-20th century saw a shift toward psychological and social aspects of well-being. Maslow's *Hierarchy of Needs* (1943) introduced a comprehensive model of human motivation, emphasizing higher-level needs like belonging and self-actualization. McGregor's *Theory X and Theory Y* (1960) further highlighted how managerial assumptions about employees—whether as inherently lazy or intrinsically motivated—shaped organizational practices and worker satisfaction. Herzberg's *Motivator-Hygiene Theory* (1959) distinguished between extrinsic factors (e.g., pay) and intrinsic motivators (e.g., recognition), underscoring the importance of meaningful work. These theories collectively shifted the focus from physical efficiency to psychological fulfilment, though they often treated well-being as a byproduct of motivation rather than a central goal.

Late 20th Century: Holistic Well-Being and Job Design

By the late 20th century, well-being research became more holistic, integrating physical, psychological, and social dimensions. Hackman and Oldham's *Job Characteristics Model* (1976) linked job design—autonomy, task variety, and skill utilization—to employee motivation and satisfaction. This period also saw the rise of *positive psychology* (Seligman, 1998), which emphasized strengths, resilience, and positive emotions, influencing workplace interventions aimed at fostering engagement and well-being. The *Demand-Control-Support Model* (Karasek & Theorell, 1990) highlighted how high job demands, low control, and insufficient social support contribute to stress and burnout, providing a framework for addressing workplace stressors. These developments marked a shift toward proactive strategies for enhancing well-being, though they often lacked a focus on mental health as a distinct priority.

21st Century: Mental Health and Technological Transformation

In the 21st century, well-being research has increasingly focused on mental health, work-life balance, and the impact of technology. The *World Health Organization* (2017) emphasized the importance of mental health in reducing absenteeism and improving productivity, while studies on *employee engagement* (Harter et al., 2002) demonstrated its link to job satisfaction and organizational performance. The rise of remote work and digital tools, accelerated by the COVID-19 pandemic, introduced new challenges, such as blurred work-life boundaries and increased stress. Organizations responded by integrating mindfulness practices (Kabat-Zinn, 2003), resilience-building strategies, and employee assistance programs (EAPs) into their well-being initiatives. However, research on the effectiveness of these interventions, particularly in diverse cultural contexts like India, remains limited.

Gaps in the Literature and Novel Contributions of this Study

While existing research provides a robust foundation, it often lacks a focus on the unique challenges faced by industries like IT, particularly in emerging economies such as India. Studies on mindfulness and mental health interventions are predominantly Western, leaving a gap in understanding their applicability in culturally diverse and high-pressure environments. Additionally, the integration of technology into well-being strategies is underexplored, especially in contexts where digital transformation is rapid but uneven. This chapter addresses these gaps by offering insights into the Indian IT industry, highlighting the role of mindfulness, mental health support, and work-life harmony in addressing burnout and stress. By synthesizing global research with local context, it provides actionable strategies for fostering employee well-being in a rapidly evolving workplace.

The evolution of employee well-being research reflects a growing recognition of its multidimensional nature and its critical role in organizational success. From early theories of physical efficiency to modern integrative models, the field has expanded to include mental health, emotional resilience, and social support. However, gaps remain in understanding the unique challenges of high-pressure industries and diverse cultural contexts.

Work-Life Balance in the 1960s

The 1960s marked a period of social and economic change, particularly in Western societies. During this time, the concept of work-life balance (WLB) was not as prevalent as it is today. The notion of balancing work and personal life was more of a social and cultural aspiration than a structured goal for organizations or employees. The post-World War II economic boom led to increased industrialization and expansion of businesses, where the primary focus was on productivity and economic growth. Most workers, particularly men, were expected to commit long hours to their jobs, often without much regard for their time or well-being. The typical work schedule was still heavily structured around the traditional 9-to-5 model, with the assumption that employees should be available to meet work demands, even outside of regular hours (Hochschild, 1997). However, during this period, there was also a growing awareness of the importance of family life, especially with the rise of the feminist movement, which started to challenge traditional gender roles in the workplace. Still, most workers, especially women, were expected to maintain separate responsibilities for both work and family, with little organizational support for balancing the two (Cohen, 2016). As such, the 1960s can be seen as a time of limited work-life balance, where personal life was often sacrificed for professional success.

Work-Life Balance in the 1970s

The 1970s witnessed significant changes in society and the workplace, with a notable shift in the dynamics of work-life balance. The decade was marked by the rise of the feminist movement and the introduction of more flexible workplace policies, particularly for women entering the workforce in greater numbers. As women gained more professional opportunities, the need for a balance between work and family responsibilities became more pressing. This period also saw the introduction of family leave policies, such as maternity leave, and early signs of labour unions advocating for better working conditions, including work hours and paid time off. These changes, however, were mostly limited to a few sectors and did not yet extend broadly across industries (Acker, 1990). The traditional "breadwinner" model was also under scrutiny as more women entered the workforce, leading to shifts in societal expectations and family roles (Hochschild, 1997). Although the demand for balance between work and personal life began to rise during this period, it was still not a formalized or widely accepted concept within most organizations. The concept of work-life conflict was emerging, but companies were still largely focused on efficiency and productivity, with little recognition of the need to support employees in balancing these roles. Therefore, while the groundwork for future WLB initiatives was laid in the 1970s, it was not yet a widespread corporate priority.

Work-Life Balance in the 1980s

By the 1980s, the discussion around work-life balance began to take on a more formalized tone. The decade saw significant economic restructuring and the rise of corporate culture, where long working hours were often equated with career success. In response, the idea of balancing work and personal life began to emerge more prominently, driven by increasing awareness of burnout and the effects of prolonged work-related stress on employees' health. While the 1980s were still characterized by long work hours in many industries, particularly in corporate settings, the decade also saw the early introduction of employee assistance programs (EAPs) and mental health initiatives, aimed at addressing the growing concerns about employee well-being. These programs provided support to employees dealing with stress, substance abuse, and personal issues, acknowledging that personal problems could affect work performance and vice versa (Cotton & Hart, 2003). The idea of flexible working arrangements also began to take shape, though it was largely limited to senior positions or specific professions, like technology or academia. However, despite these advancements, the majority of the workforce continued to operate under a rigid work structure, with little to no formal policies in place to support employees in balancing work and personal responsibilities. Thus, while the 1980s saw the beginnings of a shift towards understanding the importance of WLB, it remained a peripheral concern for most organizations.

Work-Life Balance in the 1990s and Later Years

The 1990s marked a significant turning point in the concept of work-life balance. With the rise of globalization and the increasing integration of technology into the workplace, the demands on employees began to intensify. The 1990s also saw the rise of information technology and telecommuting, which began to blur the lines between work and personal life. With the advent of mobile phones and the Internet, employees could now be accessible outside of regular working hours, leading to the rise of an "always-on" work culture (Mazmanian, Orlikowski, & Yates, 2013). Despite these challenges, the concept of WLB gained considerable attention during this time, with organizations beginning to implement more comprehensive workplace flexibility policies, such as telecommuting, compressed workweeks, and flexible hours. These policies were particularly beneficial for parents and caregivers, especially women, who struggled to balance work with family responsibilities. Companies such as Johnson & Johnson and Google began offering extensive benefits such as paid parental leave and flexible schedules, setting the stage for further improvements in employee well-being. By the late 1990s and into the 2000s, WLB was becoming a central theme in corporate social responsibility agendas. As the concept gained traction, it was increasingly understood that supporting work-life harmony was not just beneficial for employees but also for organizations, as it led to higher job satisfaction, greater employee retention, and improved productivity (Kossek & Ozeki, 1998).

In the more recent decades, particularly post-2010, work-life balance has evolved into a more nuanced concept of work-life integration or harmony, which recognizes that work and personal life are intertwined and should complement each other, rather than compete for time and energy. With the rise of flexible workspaces, remote working arrangements, and the gig economy, organizations are now embracing holistic well-being frameworks that support not just physical and mental health, but also emotional and financial well-being. Companies are increasingly offering benefits such as unlimited paid time off (PTO), wellness programs, mental health days, and the option for flexible schedules to promote a sense of work-life harmony (Shan, 2021). Companies like Salesforce and Microsoft have implemented innovative policies that allow employees to work from anywhere, at any time, fostering a more adaptable work culture that accommodates employees' personal lives while still promoting high productivity. The focus has shifted from rigid work hours to enabling employees to thrive both in and outside of work, highlighting the importance of employee agency and personal fulfilment in achieving overall work-life satisfaction. Thus, work-life balance has evolved into a more fluid and personalized approach to managing the interplay between professional and personal responsibilities.

Work-Life Balance: A Critical Element for Long-Term Success

Work-life balance is an essential component of employee well-being, especially in industries like IT, where the pressure to meet deadlines and remain constantly available can lead to burnout. A lack of work-life balance can result in decreased job satisfaction, higher turnover rates, and reduced productivity. Organizations in the IT industry must prioritize work-life balance to ensure that employees have the time and energy to maintain healthy personal lives, which in turn supports their professional success.

One of the most effective ways to foster work-life balance is by offering flexible work arrangements, such as remote work options, flexible hours, and the ability to take time off when needed. With the rise of digital communication tools, many IT jobs can be done remotely, allowing employees to better manage their schedules and avoid the stress of long commutes. Companies can also implement policies that encourage employees to disconnect from work outside of business hours, such as setting boundaries on after-hours emails and phone calls.

In addition to flexible work arrangements, organizations should encourage employees to take regular breaks and vacations, helping to prevent burnout and increase overall well-being. By promoting a healthy work-life balance, companies in the IT sector can create a more sustainable work environment, where employees can maintain a high level of performance without sacrificing their mental and physical health.

In addition to offering flexible work arrangements and encouraging employees to take regular breaks, it is also crucial for organizations in the IT sector to actively promote a culture that values work-life balance. Leadership plays a pivotal role in setting the tone for the entire organization. When leaders model healthy work-life balance practices, such as taking time off, respecting boundaries, and avoiding after-hours communications, it sends a powerful message to employees that their well-being is a priority. Research has shown that organizations with leaders who actively support work-life balance tend to have more engaged employees who experience lower levels of stress and higher job satisfaction (Greenhaus & Allen, 2011).

One strategy for promoting work-life balance is to set realistic expectations for employee performance and workload. Unrealistic deadlines and overburdening employees with tasks can quickly lead to burnout and disengagement. Managers should focus on aligning work demands with the capabilities of their team members and prioritize tasks that align with organizational goals. When employees feel their workload is manageable and their time is respected, they are more likely to remain motivated and productive over the long term. Furthermore, organizations can implement performance metrics that focus on quality rather than sheer output, encouraging employees to take the time they need to produce their best work without feeling pressured to overextend themselves.

Technology, while often contributing to work-life imbalance, can also be harnessed to promote work-life balance when used effectively. For instance, tools like task management software, team collaboration platforms, and time-tracking apps can help employees stay organized and focused, making it easier to manage work tasks within their designated work hours. Additionally, setting up clear communication guidelines for when and how employees should be available for work-related matters can help prevent burnout. By using technology to streamline workflows and establish clear boundaries, companies can help their employees maintain a healthier balance between their professional and personal lives (Derks et al., 2016).

Another important aspect of work-life balance in the IT industry is fostering a supportive and inclusive work environment that encourages employees to pursue their interests and hobbies outside of work. Encouraging employees to engage in activities that promote physical and mental health—such as exercise, social activities, or volunteer work—can help reduce stress and improve overall job satisfaction. Organizations can support this by offering wellness programs, organizing team-building activities, or providing incentives for employees to engage in personal development. When employees feel that their organization values their overall well-being and encourages them to pursue a balanced lifestyle, they are more likely to remain loyal and committed to their employer.

Work-life balance is not only beneficial for individual employees but also essential for the long-term success of organizations in the IT industry. By offering flexible work arrangements, setting realistic workload expectations, using technology to support balance, and fostering a culture that encourages personal well-being, companies can help prevent burnout and promote a sustainable and healthy work environment. In the competitive and high-stress IT sector, prioritizing work-life balance is a strategic investment that leads to higher employee satisfaction, reduced turnover, and improved organizational performance.

THE EMERGING CONCEPT OF WORK-LIFE HARMONY: A NEW PARADIGM FOR EMPLOYEE WELL-BEING

The concept of work-life balance has been a widely discussed topic in the context of employee well-being for several decades. However, as work dynamics evolve, particularly with the rise of remote work, flexible schedules, and technological advancements, a new concept has emerged: work-life harmony. Unlike work-life balance, which often implies a strict division between work and personal life, work-life harmony promotes the idea of blending the two in a way that benefits both the individual and the organization. This emerging concept acknowledges that work and personal life are not necessarily separate spheres, but can coexist in a manner that promotes overall well-being, productivity, and satisfaction.

Work-life balance has traditionally been understood as a clear demarcation between the demands of professional and personal life, where the objective is to ensure that neither aspect overwhelms the other. The aim is to maintain a structured separation between work hours and personal time, which is seen as essential for reducing stress, preventing burnout, and promoting health (Greenhaus & Allen, 2011). This concept arose in response to the challenges posed by long working hours and the increasing pressure on employees to perform. The rise of industrialization, coupled with the spread of the 9-to-5 workday model, led to an emphasis on having distinct boundaries between the workplace and home life.

Over time, work-life balance became a benchmark for employee well-being, with companies implementing policies such as flexible working hours, paid time off, and remote work options to help employees juggle their professional and personal lives. This approach was designed to help employees "switch off" from work and devote time to family, hobbies, or self-care, improving mental and physical health in the process.

The Shift Toward Work-Life Harmony

Despite the popularity of work-life balance, it became evident that the rigid boundaries associated with the concept were not always practical or beneficial in today's increasingly flexible and interconnected world. The idea of strict separation between work and personal life may not be realistic in many modern job roles, particularly in the age of constant connectivity. Advances in communication technology, such as email, messaging platforms, and video calls, have made it possible for employees to stay connected to work anytime and anywhere. The global pandemic further blurred these boundaries, with many employees experiencing "work from home" scenarios that required constant juggling of personal and professional responsibilities.

As a result, work-life harmony has emerged as a more flexible, holistic approach to achieving well-being. Rather than focusing on balancing the time and energy devoted to work and personal life, work-life harmony recognizes that both realms can coexist and interact in a way that is fluid, adaptive, and conducive to personal fulfilment (O'Neill & Hambley, 2018). This concept suggests that employees do not need to compartmentalize their time between work and personal life but instead can integrate the two in a way that enhances overall satisfaction and performance.

Indian IT companies like Infosys, TCS, Wipro, HCL Technologies, Tech Mahindra, and Mindtree have implemented various initiatives to promote work-life harmony. Infosys offers flexible work schedules and remote options, while TCS organizes "Bring Your Child to Work" days and wellness programs. Wipro's "Flexi-Work" policies and wellness sessions address stress management, though maintaining team collaboration and organizational culture remains a challenge. HCL's "Employee First" initiative focuses on flexibility, mental health support, and career development, but balancing real-time collaboration in project-driven environments is a hurdle. Tech Mahindra's "Right Shore" model reduces commute stress but faces data security and compliance challenges. Mindtree's "Mindtree Minds" program includes wellness activities and parental leave, though client demands for immediate availability can conflict with flexible policies. These examples highlight the importance of work-life harmony while underscoring challenges like productivity, security, and cultural cohesion, offering actionable insights for organizations to design tailored strategies.

Key Differences Between Work-Life Balance and Work-Life Harmony

While both work-life balance and work-life harmony focus on employee well-being, they are fundamentally different in their approach.

The key difference lies in the fundamental premise of separation versus integration. Work-life balance emphasizes a clear division of time between professional and personal spheres, whereas work-life harmony promotes integration, where work and personal life coexist in a mutually supportive manner. For example, in work-life balance, an employee might adhere to strict work hours, while in work-life harmony, the employee may choose to work at different times of the day to accommodate personal commitments.

Work-life balance often implies a rigid structure where employees work within set hours and take time off at designated intervals, while work-life harmony offers more flexibility. Employees have the autonomy to blend professional tasks with personal activities as long as it leads to a harmonious outcome. For instance, an employee may attend a family event during work hours and make up for the lost time later, provided it does not affect overall productivity. Work-life balance traditionally places responsibility on employers to create structures that help employees manage their time effectively. In contrast, work-life harmony gives greater emphasis on employee agency, with employees encouraged to define their own boundaries and schedule in a way that works best for them (Kelliher & Anderson, 2010).

The emergence of work-life harmony represents a shift away from the traditional concept of work-life balance. By promoting integration rather than separation, work-life harmony offers a more adaptable and holistic approach to employee well-being. The success of companies like Microsoft Japan, Google, Salesforce, and HubSpot demonstrates that fostering an environment where employees can blend their personal and professional lives can lead to improved productivity, satisfaction, and overall performance. As work continues to evolve, organizations that embrace the principles of work-life harmony will be better equipped to support their employees in maintaining both personal fulfilment and professional success.

The Role of Mindfulness in Enhancing Mental Health

Mindfulness, defined as paying deliberate, non-judgmental attention to the present moment, has emerged as a powerful tool for improving mental health, particularly in high-stress environments like the IT industry. Research demonstrates that mindfulness reduces stress, enhances focus, improves emotional regulation, and boosts overall well-being. For IT professionals, who often face cognitive overload, tight deadlines, and constant multitasking, mindfulness offers a practical strategy to manage stress, improve mental clarity, and foster resilience. By integrating mindfulness into the workplace, organizations can create a supportive environment that enhances employee well-being, collaboration, and productivity.

Mindfulness provides both psychological and physiological benefits, making it particularly valuable in high-pressure industries. Psychologically, it helps employees manage stress, reduce burnout, and improve emotional intelligence (EI). EI, which includes self-awareness, empathy, and emotional regulation, is critical in the IT sector, where teamwork and communication are essential for project success. Studies show that mindfulness enhances EI by encouraging self-reflection and emotional control (Kotsou et al., 2011), leading to better conflict resolution and stronger interpersonal relationships.

Physiologically, mindfulness practices such as meditation and deep breathing lower cortisol levels, reduce blood pressure and improve sleep quality (Goyal et al., 2014). These benefits are crucial for IT professionals, who often experience mental fatigue and physical strain due to long hours and high demands. By incorporating mindfulness into their routines, employees can recharge their mental and physical energy, leading to sustained productivity and reduced burnout.

Mindfulness also enhances decision-making abilities, a critical skill in the IT industry. In high-pressure environments, decision-making often occurs under tight deadlines and with limited information, leading to cognitive overload and mental fatigue. Mindfulness improves cognitive flexibility and focus, enabling employees to make clearer, more effective decisions (Zeidan et al., 2010). This is particularly valuable for IT professionals, who must navigate complex problems and innovate under pressure.

To maximize the benefits of mindfulness, organizations must adopt a structured, tiered approach that includes immediate actions, mid-term strategies, and long-term goals.

Immediate Actions (0–6 Months):

1. **Introduce Mindfulness Training:** Partner with certified trainers to offer workshops on mindfulness techniques, such as meditation and breathing exercises. For example, a 4-week introductory course with weekly sessions can help employees build foundational skills. Measure success through participation rates and post-training surveys showing improved stress levels.
2. **Create Dedicated Spaces:** Designate quiet rooms or zones for mindfulness practices, equipped with calming decor and guided meditation resources. Monitor usage rates and gather feedback to assess impact.
3. **Promote Leadership Endorsement:** Encourage senior leaders to participate in mindfulness programs and share their experiences. Leadership involvement can increase employee engagement and demonstrate organizational commitment.

Mid-Term Strategies (6–12 Months):

4. **Incorporate Mindfulness into Daily Routines:** Integrate short mindfulness exercises into the workday, such as 5-minute guided meditations at the start of meetings. Use tools like Microsoft Teams or Slack to send daily mindfulness reminders.
5. **Develop Culturally Sensitive Programs:** Tailor mindfulness initiatives to respect cultural and religious diversity, ensuring inclusivity and equitable access. Offer sessions in multiple languages and incorporate culturally relevant practices, such as yoga or tai chi.
6. **Provide Access to Digital Tools:** Subsidize subscriptions to mindfulness apps like Headspace or Calm, particularly for remote and hybrid employees. Track app usage and evaluate effectiveness through follow-up surveys.

Long-Term Goals (1–3 Years):

7. **Foster a Mindful Organizational Culture:** Embed mindfulness into the company's core values and policies. Include mindfulness goals in performance reviews and recognize employees who actively participate in programs.

8. **Measure and Communicate Impact:** Establish KPIs to evaluate the long-term impact of mindfulness initiatives on employee well-being and organizational performance. Publish annual reports highlighting the ROI of mindfulness programs.
9. **Expand Mindfulness to Leadership Development:** Integrate mindfulness training into leadership programs to enhance emotional intelligence, decision-making, and resilience among managers.

Despite its benefits, mindfulness adoption faces several barriers, including lack of awareness, scepticism, time constraints, and cultural diversity. To overcome these challenges, organizations should conduct regular awareness campaigns to educate employees about mindfulness benefits and share success stories and case studies to build credibility. They must engage diverse employee groups in program design to ensure inclusivity and relevance.

Mindfulness offers a transformative approach to enhancing employee well-being and organizational performance in the IT industry. By reducing stress, improving emotional intelligence, and enhancing decision-making, mindfulness empowers employees to thrive in high-pressure environments. However, successful implementation requires a structured, inclusive approach that addresses barriers and fosters a sustainable culture of mindfulness. Organizations that prioritize mindfulness will not only support their employees' mental and physical health but also gain a competitive edge through a more resilient, engaged, and productive workforce. To effectively integrate mindfulness into the workplace, organizations should adopt a tiered approach that prioritizes immediate actions, mid-term strategies, and long-term goals.

MENTAL HEALTH SUPPORT IN THE WORKPLACE

Mental health support has become increasingly important in the workplace, especially in industries like IT, where the demands on employees can lead to significant mental health challenges. Anxiety, depression, and burnout are common issues faced by IT professionals, yet many employees may feel reluctant to seek help due to stigma or fear of being perceived as less capable. As such, organizations must create a supportive environment where employees feel comfortable discussing their mental health needs and accessing resources that can help them manage stress and emotional challenges.

An important step in promoting mental health in the IT industry is the implementation of employee assistance programs (EAPs) that provide confidential counselling services, mental health resources, and workshops on managing stress. EAPs offer employees a safe space to address personal and professional issues without fear of judgment. In addition to offering counselling services, companies can also provide mental health awareness training for managers and team leaders to help them recognize signs of mental distress in employees and guide them toward appropriate resources.

Creating an open and supportive culture around mental health is critical to reducing the stigma associated with seeking help. When employees feel comfortable discussing their mental health concerns, it can lead to greater self-awareness and early intervention, preventing the escalation of mental health issues. As a result, organizations can foster a more positive work environment where employees are not only more productive but also more likely to stay with the company in the long term, as they feel supported in their overall well-being.

In addition to providing direct mental health resources such as EAPs and counselling services, it is equally important for organizations to address the broader workplace culture to effectively support mental health. Research suggests that work-related stressors, such as excessive workloads, unrealistic deadlines, and lack of control over work processes, can significantly contribute to mental health challenges such as burnout and anxiety (Maslach & Leiter, 2016). Therefore, organizations in the IT industry should strive to create an environment that promotes work-life balance, reduces excessive demands, and allows employees to feel in control of their tasks. Offering flexible work hours, encouraging regular breaks, and ensuring manageable workloads can help reduce work-related stress and promote mental well-being among IT professionals.

Another important strategy is the integration of mental health awareness into organizational policies and leadership practices. Leaders and managers play a critical role in shaping the work environment and influencing employee well-being. Training managers to recognize signs of mental health distress, such as changes in behaviour, performance, or mood, can lead to earlier identification and support for employees facing mental health challenges. A study by Nielsen et al. (2017) found that managers who were trained in mental health awareness were more effective in addressing employees' psychological needs and providing appropriate resources. By fostering a culture of care and open communication, leaders can not only reduce the stigma around mental health but also cultivate a more empathetic and supportive workplace.

Peer support and social connections also play a crucial role in promoting mental health in the IT industry. A sense of belonging and supportive relationships within the workplace can help employees cope with stress and feel more engaged in their work. IT professionals, particularly those in remote or hybrid work environments, may experience feelings of isolation, which can exacerbate mental health issues. To combat this, organizations can promote team-building activities, encourage open communication through regular check-ins, and create opportunities for employees to connect with their colleagues. These efforts can strengthen the sense of community and help employees feel more supported, both personally and professionally.

Additionally, addressing mental health challenges proactively through preventive initiatives can help reduce the occurrence of serious mental health issues. Offering mental health workshops, stress management seminars, and resilience-building training can equip employees with the skills to handle the daily stresses of the IT industry. Preventive measures, such as mindfulness training or physical wellness programs, can help employees build emotional resilience before stress or mental health issues escalate. Preventive care, along with ongoing support, can create a comprehensive approach to mental health that benefits employees and the organization as a whole.

Lastly, organizations in the IT sector can leverage technology to support mental health initiatives. Digital platforms that offer mental health apps, virtual therapy sessions, or stress-relief tools can provide employees with easily accessible resources, particularly in a remote or hybrid work setting. These tools allow employees to manage their mental health at their own pace, in a manner that is private and convenient. Integrating technology into mental health support ensures that employees have round-the-clock access to resources, regardless of their work location or schedule, further breaking down the barriers to seeking help.

Promoting mental health support in the IT industry is essential for creating a healthy, productive, and sustainable workforce. By offering a range of mental health resources, fostering a supportive workplace culture, and implementing preventive initiatives, organizations can help employees manage stress, reduce burnout, and maintain their overall well-being. The integration of mental health support into the workplace not only enhances employee satisfaction and performance but also contributes to long-term organizational success by promoting a resilient and engaged workforce.

CONCLUSION

The well-being of employees in the IT industry is not just a moral imperative but a strategic necessity for organizational success. As the industry grapples with escalating demands, burnout, and rapid technological changes, prioritizing mental health, mindfulness, and work-life balance is essential for fostering a resilient, innovative, and productive workforce. This article has highlighted the transformative potential of mindfulness in reducing stress, enhancing emotional intelligence, and improving decision-making, all of which are critical for thriving in high-pressure environments. By integrating mindfulness into workplace culture, organizations can create a supportive ecosystem that empowers employees to perform at their best while maintaining their mental and physical health.

For tech industry leaders and HR professionals, the path forward involves embedding mindfulness into the organizational culture. This can be achieved by offering structured training programs, creating dedicated spaces for mindfulness practices, and encouraging leadership participation to set a precedent. Additionally, adopting flexible work policies is crucial in today's evolving work landscape. Embracing remote and hybrid work models while ensuring equitable access to mental health resources and wellness programs will help employees balance their personal and professional lives effectively.

Normalizing conversations around mental health is another critical step. Reducing stigma through open dialogue, providing mental health training for employees and managers, and offering accessible support systems will create a safe environment where employees feel comfortable seeking help. Furthermore, organizations must adopt a data-driven approach to measure the impact of well-being initiatives and adapt strategies to meet evolving employee needs. Regular feedback systems and performance metrics that prioritize quality over quantity can help reduce pressure and encourage sustainable work practices.

The long-term impact of these strategies extends beyond individual well-being to organizational success. Companies that prioritize employee well-being will see higher retention rates, increased innovation, and sustained growth. By fostering a culture of mindfulness and resilience, organizations can build a workforce that is not only equipped to handle the challenges of today but also prepared to lead in the future.

In an industry defined by rapid change and relentless competition, investing in employee well-being is the ultimate differentiator. The time to act is now—by embracing mindfulness and holistic well-being strategies, IT organizations can unlock their full potential and set a new standard for workplace excellence. Let this be a call to action: prioritize well-being today to secure a thriving tomorrow.

REFERENCES

Acker, J. (1990). Hierarchies, jobs, bodies: A theory of gendered organizations. *Gender & Society*, *4*(2), 139–158. DOI: 10.1177/089124390004002002

Allen, T. D., Herst, D. E., Bruck, C. S., & Sutton, M. (2013). Consequences associated with work-to-family conflict: A review and meta-analysis. *Journal of Business and Psychology*, *17*(2), 217–228.

Bakker, A. B., & Demerouti, E. (2007). The job demands-resources model: State of the art. *Journal of Managerial Psychology*, *22*(3), 309–328. DOI: 10.1108/02683940710733115

Cohen, P. (2016). Work and family: A challenge for policy in the 21st century. *International Labour Review*, *155*(4), 493–513. DOI: 10.1111/ilr.12147

Cotton, S. P., & Hart, P. M. (2003). Occupational wellbeing and employee assistance programs: Their role in work-life balance. *Journal of Employee Assistance*, *33*(1), 45–53.

Deci, E. L., & Ryan, R. M. (2000). The "what" and "why" of goal pursuits: Human needs and the self-determination of behaviour. *Psychological Inquiry*, *11*(4), 227–268. DOI: 10.1207/S15327965PLI1104_01

Deloitte. (2020). *The Deloitte Global Human Capital Trends report*. https://www2.deloitte.com/global/en/insights/focus/human-capital-trends.html

Derks, D., Fischer, A. R. H., & van der Molen, H. T. (2016). Email as a source of stress and its impact on employees' work life balance. *Computers in Human Behavior*, *54*, 417–427. DOI: 10.1016/j.chb.2015.08.040

Diener, E. (2000). Subjective well-being: The science of happiness and a proposal for a national index. *The American Psychologist*, *55*(1), 34–43. DOI: 10.1037/0003-066X.55.1.34 PMID: 11392863

Folkman, S., & Moskowitz, J. T. (2000). Stress, positive emotion, and coping. *Current Directions in Psychological Science*, *9*(4), 115–118. DOI: 10.1111/1467-8721.00073

Google. (2020). *Our work culture*. Google Careers. https://careers.google.com/our-story/

Goyal, M., Singh, S., Sibinga, E. M. S., Gould, N. F., Rowland-Seymour, A., Sharma, R., & Haythornthwaite, J. A. (2014). Meditation programs for psychological stress and well-being: A systematic review and meta-analysis. *JAMA Internal Medicine*, *174*(3), 357–368. DOI: 10.1001/jamainternmed.2013.13018 PMID: 24395196

Greenhaus, J. H., & Allen, T. D. (2011). Work-family balance: A review and extension of the literature. *Psychology of Women Quarterly*, *35*(1), 74–95. DOI: 10.1111/j.1471-6402.2010.01634.x

Hackman, J. R., & Oldham, G. R. (1976). Motivation through design of work: Test of a theory. *Organizational Behavior and Human Performance*, *16*(2), 250–279. DOI: 10.1016/0030-5073(76)90016-7

Halbesleben, J. R. B., & Buckley, M. R. (2004). Burnout in organizational settings. *Journal of Management*, *30*(6), 859–879. DOI: 10.1016/j.jm.2004.06.004

Harter, J. K., Schmidt, F. L., & Hayes, T. L. (2002). Business-unit-level relationship between employee satisfaction, employee engagement, and business outcomes: A meta-analysis. *The Journal of Applied Psychology*, *87*(2), 268–279. DOI: 10.1037/0021-9010.87.2.268 PMID: 12002955

Hibino, T. (2019). Microsoft Japan's 4-day workweek increased productivity by 40%: Here's how. *Harvard Business Review*. https://hbr.org/2019/11/microsoft-japans-4-day-workweek-increased-productivity-by-40-heres-how

Hobfoll, S. E. (1989). Conservation of resources: A new attempt at conceptualizing stress. *The American Psychologist*, *44*(3), 513–524. DOI: 10.1037/0003-066X.44.3.513 PMID: 2648906

Hochschild, A. R. (1997). *The time bind: When work becomes home and home becomes work*. Metropolitan Books. DOI: 10.1111/j.1743-4580.1997.tb00019.x

House, J. S. (1981). *Work stress and social support*. Addison-Wesley.

HubSpot. (2020). *How HubSpot's remote-first approach is working*. HubSpot Blog. https://blog.hubspot.com/company/remote-first

Kabat-Zinn, J. (1990). *Full catastrophe living: Using the wisdom of your body and mind to face stress, pain, and illness*. Delacorte.

Kabat-Zinn, J. (2003). Mindfulness-based stress reduction (MBSR). In Nevid, J. K., & Pearson, S. A. E. (Eds.), *The Essential Handbook of Mindfulness* (pp. 23–40). Springer.

Karasek, R. A. (1979). Job demands, job decision latitude, and mental strain: Implications for job redesign. *Administrative Science Quarterly*, *24*(2), 285–308. DOI: 10.2307/2392498

Karasek, R. A., & Theorell, T. (1990). *Healthy work: Stress, productivity, and the reconstruction of working life*. Basic Books.

Kelliher, C., & Anderson, D. (2010). Flexible working and performance: A review of the evidence. *International Journal of Management Reviews*, *12*(4), 381–397. DOI: 10.1111/j.1468-2370.2009.00243.x

Kossek, E. E., & Ozeki, C. (1998). Work-family conflict, policies, and the job-life satisfaction relationship: A review and directions for organizational research. *The Journal of Applied Psychology*, *83*(2), 139–149. DOI: 10.1037/0021-9010.83.2.139

Kotsou, I., Mikolajczak, M., Heeren, A., & Leys, C. (2011). Emotional intelligence and sociodemographic factors: A study of the EI model proposed by Bar-On in a French-speaking population. *Personality and Individual Differences*, *50*(5), 1248–1253. DOI: 10.1016/j.paid.2011.01.019

Lazarus, R. S., & Folkman, S. (1984). *Stress, appraisal, and coping*. Springer.

Lencioni, P. (2002). *The five dysfunctions of a team: A leadership fable*. Jossey-Bass.

Maslach, C., & Leiter, M. P. (2016). Burnout: A short history of the concept. In Goodyear, L. R., & Mattingly, A. A. K. (Eds.), *Handbook of counselling psychology* (pp. 199–218). Wiley.

Mayo, E. (1933). *The human problems of an industrial civilization*. Macmillan.

Mazmanian, M., Orlikowski, W. J., & Yates, J. (2013). The autonomy paradox: The implications of mobile email devices for knowledge professionals. *Organization Science*, *24*(5), 1337–1357. DOI: 10.1287/orsc.1120.0806

McGregor, D. (1960). *The human side of enterprise*. McGraw-Hill.

Nielsen, K., & Noblet, A., & P. W. C. P. (. (2017). Workplace interventions to improve mental health. *International Journal of Environmental Research and Public Health*, *14*(4), 436. DOI: 10.3390/ijerph14040436 PMID: 28422081

O'Neill, J. W., & Hambley, L. A. (2018). Work-life balance and work-life harmony: Understanding the difference. In *Workplace wellbeing: A complete guide to employee wellness* (pp. 85–103). Springer.

Salesforce. (2021). *Salesforce Ohana culture*. Salesforce Careers. https://www.salesforce.com/company/culture/

Seligman, M. E. P. (1998). *Learned optimism: How to change your mind and your life*. Pocket Books.

Shan, H. (2021). The changing nature of work: Work-life balance and its implications. *Journal of Human Resource Management*, *10*(3), 25–41. DOI: 10.1080/23269688.2021.1905501

Shapiro, S. L., Astin, J. A., Bishop, S. R., & Cordova, M. (2007). Mindfulness-based stress reduction for health care professionals: Results from a randomized trial. *International Journal of Stress Management*, *14*(2), 179–192. DOI: 10.1037/1072-5245.14.2.179

Taylor, F. W. (1911). *The principles of scientific management*. Harper & Brothers.

Viswesvaran, C., Sanchez, J. I., & Fisher, J. (1999). The role of social support in the process of work stress: A meta-analysis. *Journal of Vocational Behavior*, *54*(3), 314–334. DOI: 10.1006/jvbe.1998.1661

Vonderlin, R., Matos, M., Lutz, W., & Barnhofer, T. (2021). Mindfulness interventions in organizational settings: A systematic review. *Journal of Occupational Health Psychology*, *26*(1), 22–37. DOI: 10.1037/ocp0000224 PMID: 34672643

Wang, H., Zhou, D., Zhang, C., & Xie, L. (2021). Mental health issues in the IT industry: An overview. *Journal of Workplace Behavioral Health*, *36*(4), 287–304. DOI: 10.1080/15555240.2021.1965673

World Health Organization. (2017). *Mental health in the workplace*. World Health Organization. https://www.who.int/news-room/fact-sheets/detail/mental-health-in-the-workplace

Zeidan, F., Johnson, S. K., Diamond, B. J., David, Z., & Goolkasian, P. (2010). Mindfulness meditation improves cognition: Evidence of brief mental training. *Consciousness and Cognition*, *19*(2), 597–605. DOI: 10.1016/j.concog.2010.03.014 PMID: 20363650

Chapter 11
Harnessing Chronobiology for a Healthier and More Productive Workforce:
Chronobiology at Work

Yogita Kalra
https://orcid.org/0009-0009-5136-9098
Lovely Professional University, India

Prabhjyot Kour
https://orcid.org/0009-0009-4430-7593
Lovely Professional University, India

ABSTRACT

Chronobiology, the study of biological rhythms, plays a crucial role in workplace well-being, influencing sleep, cognitive performance, and overall health. In a 24/7 work culture, misalignment between work schedules and circadian rhythms leads to fatigue, reduced productivity, and health risks. Understanding chronotypes—morning, evening, or intermediate—enables tailored scheduling to enhance efficiency and job satisfaction. Strategic interventions such as optimized lighting, flexible work arrangements, and structured breaks can mitigate circadian disruption. By integrating chronobiology into workplace policies, organizations can foster healthier, more engaged employees while improving performance. This chapter explores scientific insights and practical strategies to align work environments with natural biological rhythms, advocating for a shift towards evidence-based, employee-centered scheduling approaches.

DOI: 10.4018/979-8-3373-2210-0.ch011

Copyright © 2025, IGI Global Scientific Publishing. Copying or distributing in print or electronic forms without written permission of IGI Global Scientific Publishing is prohibited.

INTRODUCTION

The Role of Chronobiology in Workplace Wellbeing

"Our biological clocks have evolved to keep us in sync with the natural world. When we fight them, we pay the price." – Matthew Walker

"When we disrupt the body's clock, we disrupt everything else—sleep, mood, energy, and even our health." – Russell Foster

Every year, fatigue-related errors in shift-dependent industries lead to costly mistakes and even life-threatening consequences. In healthcare, overworked night-shift nurses report a higher incidence of medication errors(Donaldson et al., 2021; Rogers et al., 2004), while in aviation, pilots experiencing circadian misalignment have been linked to slower reaction times and increased safety risks (Caldwell, 2012; Wagstaff & Sigstad Lie, 2011). Despite clear evidence of these negative effects, many workplaces continue to ignore the fundamental role of biological rhythms in employee performance and well-being.

Circadian misalignment, a disruption between an individual's internal biological clock and external time cues, has been strongly linked to adverse mental health outcomes. Research indicates that individuals experiencing chronic circadian misalignment, such as night shift workers and those with irregular work schedules, are at significantly higher risk of mood disorders, including depression and anxiety(Baron & Reid, 2014). A meta-analysis found that shift workers have a 40% increased likelihood of developing depressive symptoms compared to daytime workers (Wickwire et al., 2017). Additionally, sleep disturbances caused by misaligned schedules contribute to cognitive impairments, increased workplace stress, and burnout, further exacerbating mental health challenges (Boudreau et al., 2013). Given the widespread prevalence of shift work and flexible job arrangements, addressing circadian misalignment is a critical concern for occupational well-being.

In the modern world, the demand for a 24/7 economy has significantly altered traditional work structures. Industries such as healthcare, transportation, manufacturing, and information technology increasingly require employees to work in shifts that do not align with their natural biological rhythms (Atkinson et al., 2008). While this model enhances operational efficiency and business continuity, it disrupts employees' circadian rhythms—the internal biological clocks that regulate physiological and behavioral functions, including sleep-wake cycles, hormone secretion, and cognitive performance (De Souza & Hidalgo, 2015; Juda et al., 2013).

The rise of flexible work schedules, gig economy jobs, and globalized business operations has intensified the conflict between work demands and biological timing. Employees often experience social jetlag, a phenomenon where work schedules force them to operate outside their natural sleep-wake cycles, leading to sleep deprivation, fatigue, and reduced workplace efficiency (Wittmann et al., 2006). Chronic misalignment between work schedules and circadian rhythms is linked to increased risks of cardiovascular disease, metabolic disorders, mood disturbances, and impaired cognitive performance (Baron & Reid, 2014; Knutsson & Bøggild, 2000). Thus, the growing disconnect between occupational demands and biological rhythms poses serious challenges to both employee well-being and organizational productivity.

Definition of chronobiology and its significance in occupational settings: Chronobiology is the scientific study of biological rhythms and their impact on physiological processes (Kim & Kim, 2020). These biological rhythms operate on different time scales, including circadian rhythms (approximately 24-hour cycles), ultradian rhythms (cycles shorter than 24 hours, such as the 90-minute sleep cycle), and infradian rhythms (longer cycles, such as menstrual rhythms) (Roenneberg, Kuehnle, et al., 2007; Roenneberg et al., 2008). Among these, circadian rhythms play a crucial role in regulating sleep, alertness, metabolism, and cognitive performance—all of which are essential for workplace efficiency and employee well-being (Adan et al., 2012).

The suprachiasmatic nucleus (SCN), located in the hypothalamus, serves as the body's central circadian pacemaker, synchronizing physiological processes with environmental cues such as light and darkness (D.-J. Dijk & Lockley, 2002; Kalmbach et al., 2017). Exposure to artificial light at night, irregular shift work, and prolonged screen time can interfere with the SCN's ability to regulate these cycles, leading to circadian misalignment and an increased risk of sleep disorders, stress, and burnout(Ferri et al., 2016).

In occupational settings, understanding chronotypes—individual differences in circadian preferences (morning, evening, or intermediate types)—is particularly important. Employees forced to work against their biological preferences are more likely to experience fatigue, decreased motivation, and lower productivity (Hittle & Gillespie, 2018). By integrating chronobiological principles into workplace policies, organizations can create healthier, more sustainable work environments.

How Aligning Work Schedules with Circadian Rhythms Can Enhance Well-Being and Productivity: Aligning work schedules with employees' natural biological rhythms has been shown to improve sleep quality, reduce stress, and enhance overall job satisfaction (Costa & Sartori, 2007). Research suggests that chronotype-based scheduling—where employees are assigned work shifts based on their individual circadian preferences—can enhance productivity and reduce absenteeism (Saksvik et al., 2011). For example, morning-type employees perform better in early shifts, while evening types are more effective in later shifts (Montaruli et al., 2019, 2021).

Furthermore, exposure to natural light during work hours and minimizing blue light exposure at night can help maintain circadian stability, improving cognitive function and mental health (Razavi et al., 2019). Implementing strategic napping policies in high-risk professions such as healthcare and aviation has also been found to mitigate fatigue-related errors and enhance performance (Purnell et al., 2002).

Organizations that adopt chronobiology-informed policies not only benefit from improved employee health and engagement but also experience lower turnover rates and enhanced operational efficiency. By prioritizing workplace interventions that support circadian health, companies can foster a culture of employee well-being and sustainable productivity.

Research Gap: Despite extensive research highlighting the harmful effects of circadian misalignment, there remains a critical gap in the implementation of chronobiology-informed workplace policies. While businesses acknowledge the importance of employee well-being, few have adopted scheduling systems that align with workers' biological clocks. This failure to integrate scientific insights into workplace structures continues to contribute to sleep deprivation, reduced efficiency, and long-term health complications among employees.

This chapter argues that aligning work schedules with employees' natural biological rhythms can improve sleep quality, reduce stress, and enhance job satisfaction. By leveraging chronobiological principles—such as chronotype-based scheduling, strategic lighting, and workplace interventions—organizations can foster a more sustainable and high-performing workforce. The following sections will explore key strategies to integrate circadian science into workplace policies, aiming to mitigate fatigue, optimize productivity, and support long-term employee well-being.

Key Strategies to Be Explored

1. Chronotype-Based Scheduling – Adapting work shifts to align with employees' natural peak performance times.
2. Light Exposure Management – Optimizing workplace lighting to support circadian rhythms and improve alertness.
3. Strategic Napping Policies – Implementing short naps to boost cognitive performance and reduce errors.
4. Flexible Work Arrangements – Encouraging remote work and individualized schedules to minimize circadian misalignment.
5. Wellness Interventions – Promoting sleep hygiene, ergonomic workspaces, and dietary strategies to support circadian health.

These strategies, rooted in chronobiological research, offer practical solutions for mitigating the negative effects of circadian misalignment, ultimately fostering a healthier and more productive workforce.

REVIEW OF LITERATURE

The Science of Chronobiology: Understanding Biological Rhythms

Chronobiology is the scientific study of biological rhythms, which regulate various physiological and behavioral functions in living organisms. These rhythms are influenced by both internal biological clocks and external environmental cues (Roenneberg et al., 2008; Roenneberg, Kumar, et al., 2007). The study of these cycles is crucial in understanding how individuals maintain homeostasis and how disruptions in these rhythms can lead to health consequences.

Explanation of Biological Rhythm

Biological rhythms are categorized into three main types based on their duration: circadian rhythms, ultradian rhythms, and infradian rhythms (Adan et al., 2012). These rhythms influence essential biological functions such as sleep, metabolism, hormone secretion, and cognitive performance.

Circadian Rhythms (24-Hour Cycles)

Circadian rhythms are biological cycles that operate on an approximately 24-hour period, regulating various physiological processes, including sleep-wake cycles, body temperature, and hormone secretion (D.-J. Dijk & Lockley, 2002). These rhythms are endogenously generated but can be synchronized by external cues such as light, temperature, and social activities. The suprachiasmatic nucleus (SCN), located in the hypothalamus, serves as the master circadian clock, ensuring synchronization between internal biological processes and the external environment (Reppert & Weaver, 2002).

One of the most studied circadian rhythms is the sleep-wake cycle, which is influenced by the production of melatonin—a hormone secreted by the pineal gland in response to darkness (Cajochen et al., 2003). Circadian misalignment, such as in shift workers or individuals exposed to excessive artificial light at night, can lead to sleep disturbances, metabolic dysfunction, and mood disorders (Baron & Reid, 2014).

Ultradian and Infradian Rhythms (Shorter and Longer Cycles)

Apart from circadian rhythms, biological processes also operate on ultradian and infradian cycles, which influence bodily functions on shorter or longer time scales.

- Ultradian Rhythms: These cycles occur more than once within 24 hours. Examples include the 90-minute sleep cycle, which consists of rapid eye movement (REM) and non-REM sleep phases (Kleitman, 1964). as well as fluctuations in hormonal secretion, such as the pulsatile release of cortisol and growth hormone (Weitzman et al., 1971). Ultradian rhythms are essential for maintaining optimal physiological balance, and disruptions can lead to impaired cognitive performance and increased stress levels.
- Infradian Rhythms: These rhythms occur over a period longer than 24 hours, such as the menstrual cycle (approximately 28 days), seasonal affective disorder (SAD), and hibernation in some animals. Infradian rhythms are influenced by both internal biological mechanisms and external environmental factors, such as seasonal light exposure.

Understanding ultradian and infradian rhythms is critical in workplace settings, as disruptions can affect energy levels, focus, and emotional regulation, ultimately impacting employee well-being and productivity. These rhythms is essential for designing workplace policies that align with employees' natural biological timing.

Role of the Suprachiasmatic Nucleus (SCN) in Regulating Biological Clocks

The suprachiasmatic nucleus (SCN), located in the hypothalamus, serves as the central pacemaker of the body's circadian rhythms (Reppert & Weaver, 2002). The SCN receives direct input from the retina via the retinohypothalamic tract, allowing it to synchronize the body's intern**al clocks with external light-dark cycles** (Roenneberg et al., 2003). This mechanism ensures that physiological processes such as sleep, metabolism, and hormone secretion follow a consistent 24-hour pattern.

Key functions of the SCN include:

1. **Regulating the Sleep-Wake Cycle:** The SCN controls melatonin production in the pineal gland, promoting sleep at night and wakefulness during the day (Cajochen et al., 2003).
2. **Influencing Body Temperature:** Body temperature follows a circadian pattern, with the lowest levels occurring during sleep and peak levels in the afternoon(D. Dijk & Czeisler, 1995).
3. **Coordinating Peripheral Clocks:** While the SCN serves as the master clock, peripheral tissues such as the liver, heart, and pancreas have their own circadian oscillators. These clocks regulate metabolic and immune system functions, ensuring synchronization with the external environment (Bass & Takahashi, 2010).

Workplace Disruptions: Shift Work, Social Jetlag, and Employee Burnout

Shift work is a work schedule that involves non-traditional hours, including evening, night, rotating, or irregular shifts, often required in industries that provide continuous services, such as healthcare, manufacturing, and transportation(Costa, 2010). Shift work and inconsistent schedules disrupt circadian rhythms, leading to severe consequences for employees' health, productivity, and job satisfaction. The demands of working non-traditional hours result in chronic sleep deprivation, increased fatigue, and diminished cognitive performance. Employees working night shifts sleep, on average, 1.5 to 2 hours less per day than their daytime counterparts, contributing to an increased risk of workplace errors and reduced overall efficiency(Rajaratnam & Arendt, 2001).

Social jetlag, a phenomenon where employees' work schedules force them to operate outside their natural sleep-wake cycles, further compounds these issues. It is particularly problematic for evening-type individuals who struggle with early-morning work demands. Social jetlag has been linked to increased risks of metabolic disorders, cardiovascular diseases, and mental health conditions such as depression and anxiety (Wittmann et al., 2006). Employees experiencing chronic social jetlag often report higher levels of stress, emotional exhaustion, and reduced job satisfaction, leading to increased absenteeism and turnover rates.

Burnout is another critical consequence of circadian misalignment in the workplace. Employees who work irregular shifts, particularly those in high-stress industries like healthcare and emergency response, face higher levels of psychological strain. Research indicates that shift workers experience a 65% higher rate of emotional exhaustion than their daytime counterparts (Khamisa et al., 2017). The lack of restorative sleep, combined with increased workplace demands, leads to cognitive overload, decreased motivation, and higher instances of workplace accidents.

Organizations that fail to address these disruptions risk significant losses in productivity and employee well-being. Implementing strategies such as optimizing shift rotations, reducing exposure to artificial light at night, and incorporating flexible work arrangements can mitigate these negative effects and promote a healthier work environment.

Impact of Circadian Misalignment on Employee Well-Being and Workplace Performance

Disruptions in biological rhythms—commonly caused by shift work, jet lag, excessive artificial light exposure, and social jetlag—can have serious consequences on sleep, cognitive function, and overall health (Baron & Reid, 2014). Circadian misalignment—caused by shift work, irregular schedules, and environmental disruptions—has been widely studied due to its profound effects on sleep quality, mental health, and workplace efficiency. This section synthesizes existing research under three key domains: impact on sleep, impact on mental health, and workplace interventions designed to mitigate these effects.

Sleep Disruptions and Fatigue: Circadian misalignment, particularly in night shift workers, is linked to poor sleep quality, excessive daytime sleepiness, and increased risk of insomnia(Boudreau et al., 2013). Circadian misalignment significantly reduces sleep quality and quantity, particularly in shift workers. Studies indicate that night shift workers sleep, on average, 1.5 to 2 hours less per day than their daytime counterparts(Rajaratnam & Arendt, 2001). Exposure to artificial light at night suppresses melatonin production, delaying sleep onset and reducing sleep efficiency (Figueiro et al., 2017). Chronic sleep deprivation due to misaligned work schedules has been associated with increased accident rates, particularly in industries requiring high levels of attention (Folkard, 2003). Chronic sleep restriction due to irregular work schedules leads to increased sleep latency, frequent nighttime awakenings, and reduced REM sleep (Eldevik et al., 2013; Wickwire et al., 2017).

Shift Work Sleep Disorder (SWSD): Shift Work Sleep Disorder (SWSD) is a common condition among employees working non-traditional hours, characterized by excessive sleepiness, chronic fatigue, and difficulty maintaining a consistent sleep schedule (Wickwire et al., 2017).). Research suggests that nearly 30% of night shift workers experience SWSD, which contributes to higher rates of workplace errors and absenteeism (Boivin et al., 2022).

Cognitive Impairments: Disruptions in circadian rhythms negatively affect memory consolidation, reaction times, and decision-making abilities (Lo et al., 2016). Studies have shown that working against one's chronotype (e.g., morning-type individuals working night shifts) leads to decreased cognitive flexibility and problem-solving skills (Hittle & Gillespie, 2018). Employees with chronic circadian misalignment often experience higher stress levels and reduced work engagement (Wittmann et al., 2006).

Metabolic and Cardiovascular Risks: Circadian rhythm disruptions contribute to an increased risk of obesity, diabetes, and cardiovascular diseases(Knutsson & Bøggild, 2000). Shift workers have a higher prevalence of metabolic syndrome, characterized by insulin resistance, hypertension, and abnormal lipid profiles (Antunes et al., 2010). Misalignment between circadian rhythms and mealtimes can lead to digestive disorders, including acid reflux and irritable bowel syndrome (IBS) (Costa & Sartori, 2007).

Mental Health Consequences: Circadian misalignment is strongly associated with mood disorders such as depression and anxiety (Baron & Reid, 2014). Individuals working against their biological rhythms report higher levels of perceived stress, emotional exhaustion, and job dissatisfaction (Khamisa et al., 2017).

Sleep Disruptions and Workplace Errors: Sleep deprivation due to misaligned work schedules significantly impairs cognitive function and reaction times, leading to increased workplace accidents and errors (Folkard, 2003). A study in healthcare settings found that nurses working rotating shifts were twice as likely to report medication errors compared to those with fixed day schedules (Stimpfel et al., 2012).

CHRONOTYPES: INDIVIDUAL DIFFERENCES IN BIOLOGICAL TIMING

Biological rhythms, particularly circadian rhythms, influence an individual's natural preference for wakefulness and activity throughout the day. This preference is referred to as chronotype, which reflects an individual's peak periods of alertness and productivity. Chronotypes vary across the population, and recognizing these differences is crucial for optimizing workplace productivity, mental well-being, and job satisfaction (Roenneberg, 2015).

Definition and Classification: Morning, Evening, and Intermediate Types

Chronotype is an individual's innate biological predisposition toward being active at specific times of the day. It is primarily determined by genetics, age, and environmental factors, such as exposure to natural light and work schedules (Adan et al., 2012). The classification of chronotypes is typically divided into three main categories:

Morning Type (MT)

Also known as "larks", these individuals wake up early, experience peak cognitive and physical performance in the morning, and feel fatigued by the evening (Randler, 2008). Morning types tend to have better sleep quality, lower risk of depression, and healthier metabolic regulation compared to evening types (Hidalgo et al., 2009). They generally prefer structured work schedules with early start times and are more aligned with traditional 9-to-5 work settings.

Evening Type (ET)

Also known as "owls", evening types naturally stay awake later and experience peak productivity in the late afternoon or evening (Horne & Östberg, 1977). Eveningness is often associated with higher creativity and risk-taking behavior but also with increased rates of sleep deprivation, mental health issues, and metabolic disorders (Wittmann et al., 2010). ETs often struggle with early work schedules, experiencing difficulties with morning-focused productivity demands.

Intermediate Type (IT)

Falling between morning and evening types, intermediate individuals do not exhibit strong preferences for early or late activity periods (Montaruli et al., 2019). They adapt more flexibly to different work schedules and are less susceptible to circadian misalignment. The majority of the population falls into this category, making them more resilient to changes in work hours and social schedules (Paine et al., 2006).

Understanding these differences is essential for designing workplace environments that align with individual chronobiological preferences, thereby enhancing well-being and performance.

Workplace Implications of Chronotypes

Chronotype plays a crucial role in job performance, productivity, and mental health. When an individual's work schedule aligns with their biological preference, they are more likely to be alert, engaged, and efficient (Hittle & Gillespie, 2018). Conversely, mismatched schedules contribute to fatigue, decreased concentration, and increased stress levels (Vetter, Devore, et al., 2015; Vetter, Fischer, et al., 2015).

Job Performance and Chronotype Compatibility

Morning types perform best in early morning meetings, structured work environments, and administrative role requiring consistency and organization (Preckel et al., 2011). Evening types excel in creative fields, problem-solving tasks, and flexible work environments, where late-night productivity is acceptable (Preckel et al., 2011). Intermediate types tend to have balanced productivity throughout the day, making them adaptable to varying schedules.

Decision-Making and Cognitive Function

Studies indicate that morning types are more strategic and risk-averse, while evening types show higher impulsivity and risk-taking behavior (Killgore, 2007). Decision-making efficiency varies across the day, with morning types excelling in analytical tasks earlier in the day, while evening types perform better in the afternoon or evening (Correa et al., 2020).

Mental Health and Work Engagement

Evening types are more prone to mood disorders, anxiety, and substance use due to increased circadian misalignment with standard work schedules (Baron & Reid, 2014; Boudreau et al., 2013; Figueiro et al., 2017; Hidalgo et al., 2009). Morning types generally have better emotional regulation and lower levels of workplace stress (Antúnez, 2020; Danna & Griffin, 1999). Chronotype-informed work arrangements can reduce burnout and increase job satisfaction, as employees work during their natural peak hours (Saksvik et al., 2011).

Social Jetlag and Impact on Mental Health and Productivity

Social jetlag occurs when individuals' biological clocks are misaligned with their work or social obligations, forcing them to adjust their sleep-wake patterns in an unnatural way. This phenomenon is particularly problematic for evening types, who struggle with early work schedules(Juda et al., 2013; Levandovski et al., 2011; Roenneberg et al., 2019; Wittmann et al., 2006).

Effects on Sleep and Well-Being

Social jetlag leads to chronic sleep deprivation, excessive daytime sleepiness, and reduced cognitive function (Roenneberg et al., 2003). Misalignment between biological and social time increases the risk of metabolic syndrome, cardiovascular disease, and obesity (Antunes et al., 2010).

Impact on Mental Health

Individuals with greater social jetlag report higher levels of depression, anxiety, and mood instability (Levandovski et al., 2011). Shift workers and employees with inflexible schedules often experience greater job dissatisfaction and emotional exhaustion (Jaradat et al., 2016; Knutsson & Bøggild, 2000).

Workplace Consequences

Reduced workplace efficiency and higher absenteeism rates are observed in employees suffering from social jetlag (Hittle & Gillespie, 2018; Vetter, Fischer, et al., 2015). Employees working outside their chronotype preferences show lower motivation, engagement, and workplace satisfaction (Amini et al., 2021; Blessing Ghosh & Arjun Sekhar Pm, 2024).

Understanding biological rhythm or chronotype is a fundamental factor influencing workplace productivity, mental health, and overall well-being. The mismatch between natural biological timing and imposed work schedules can lead to chronic fatigue, mental health issues, and decreased work performance. Understanding chronotypes and mitigating social jetlag through flexible scheduling, shift adjustments, and chronobiology-informed policies can lead to healthier, more engaged employees and improved organizational success.

SHIFT WORK AND ITS IMPACT ON CHRONOBIOLOGY

In modern workplaces, shift work has become an essential component of 24/7 operations, particularly in industries where continuous service is required. However, working outside the natural circadian rhythm disrupts biological processes, leading to adverse effects on sleep, metabolism, cognitive function, and overall well-being (Barger et al., 2009). The misalignment between internal biological clocks and external work schedules, especially in night shift and rotating shift workers, poses significant health risks and impacts workplace efficiency.

Disruptions Caused by Night Shifts and Rotating Schedules

Shift work involves irregular or extended working hours, including night shifts, early morning shifts, and rotating schedules, which interfere with the body's natural sleep-wake cycle (Wright et al., 2013). The primary disruptions include:

Circadian Misalignment and Sleep Disruptions

The circadian rhythm is primarily regulated by the suprachiasmatic nucleus (SCN) in the hypothalamus, which synchronizes physiological functions with the external light-dark cycle (Reppert & Weaver, 2002). Night shift work forces individuals to be awake during their biological night, leading to poor sleep quality, excessive daytime sleepiness, and reduced sleep duration (Eldevik et al., 2013; Flo et al., 2012).

Exposure to artificial light at night suppresses melatonin production, making it harder for night-shift workers to fall asleep during the day (Cajochen et al., 2003).

Rotating Shift Work and Chronic Sleep Debt

Workers on rotating shifts often struggle with inconsistent sleep schedules, as their bodies cannot fully adjust to new sleep-wake patterns before another shift change occurs (Vetter, Fischer, et al., 2015). This results in chronic sleep deprivation, which impairs cognitive performance, weakens the immune system and increases stress levels (Besedovsky et al., 2012; Born et al., 1997).

Social and Psychological Effects

Shift work disrupts social interactions, family life, and mental health, contributing to social jetlag—a mismatch between biological and social schedules (Khamisa et al., 2017; Roenneberg et al., 2019; Wittmann et al., 2006). Long-term night shift work is associated with higher rates of depression, anxiety, and burnout, particularly in healthcare professionals and emergency responders (Barger et al., 2009).

Health Consequences: Sleep Disorders, Metabolic Issues, and Cognitive Decline

Shift work is linked to numerous health risks, primarily due to circadian misalignment and sleep deprivation. The most significant consequences include:

Sleep Disorders and Chronic Fatigue: Shift workers are at higher risk of Shift Work Sleep Disorder (SWSD), characterized by insomnia, excessive daytime sleepiness, and non-restorative sleep (Wickwire et al., 2017). Fragmented and insufficient sleep leads to chronic fatigue, reducing workplace engagement and increasing the likelihood of errors (Rajaratnam & Arendt, 2001).

Metabolic and Cardiovascular Issues: Disruptions in circadian rhythms affect glucose metabolism, insulin sensitivity, and appetite regulation, leading to a higher risk of obesity, type 2 diabetes, and cardiovascular disease (Knutsson & Bøggild, 2000; Reutrakul et al., 2013). Night shift workers are more likely to experience dyslipidemia, hypertension, and metabolic syndrome, contributing to long-term cardiovascular risks (Antunes et al., 2010; Bass & Takahashi, 2010; Roenneberg et al., 2012). Irregular meal timing during night shifts leads to digestive issues, acid reflux, and irritable bowel syndrome (IBS) (Chang & Peng, 2021; Chen et al., 2022; Costa, 2010).

Cognitive Impairments and Decision-Making Deficits: Sleep deprivation impairs attention, memory, and reaction times, increasing the risk of workplace errors and accidents (Killgore, 2007). Executive functioning, problem-solving skills, and emotional regulation decline in chronically sleep-deprived shift workers (Banks & Dinges, 2007; Gobin et al., 2015). Long-term shift work is linked to neurodegeneration, with an increased risk of cognitive decline and dementia in later life(Lee et al., 2023; Wang et al., 2022).

Industries-Specific Challenges in Circadian Misalignment: Healthcare, Transportation, Manufacturing

Certain industries require continuous operations, making shift work unavoidable. However, these sectors face higher health risks and operational challenges due to circadian misalignment.

Healthcare: Nurses, doctors, and emergency responders frequently work overnight shifts, leading to burnout, increased error rates, and poor mental health (Ferri et al., 2016). Studies indicate that patient safety is compromised during night shifts due to cognitive fatigue and slower reaction times (Rogers et al., 2004). Nurses working rotating shifts are at a higher risk of chronic sleep deprivation, obesity, and mood disorders (Stimpfel et al., 2012).

Transportation and Aviation: Truck drivers, airline pilots, and railway operators often experience fatigue-related accidents, with sleep-deprived drivers posing a risk equivalent to drunk driving (Philip et al., 2003). Airline pilots working long-haul overnight flights show decreased vigilance and impaired performance due to circadian misalignment (Caldwell, 2012; Caldwell et al., 2009).

Manufacturing and Industrial Work: Factory workers operating heavy machinery during night shifts are more prone to errors, injuries, and long-term health complications (Folkard, 2003). Job rotation positively impacts job satisfaction and work engagement, with job satisfaction fully mediating the relationship, highlighting the need for effective job rotation programs to enhance employee performance in Qatari oil and gas companies (Al-Yafei, n.d.). A study published found that employees working rotating shifts reported lower job performance outcomes compared to those on fixed night shifts, which allowed for better resynchronization of circadian rhythms, though fixed night shifts were also associated with reduced job satisfaction (Costa, 2010; Dall'Ora et al., 2016).

Role Of Circadian Misalignment in Workplace Accidents and Reduced Efficiency

Circadian misalignment directly contributes to workplace accidents, decreased productivity, and increased absenteeism.

Increased Workplace Accidents: Sleep deprivation leads to slower reaction times, poor situational awareness, and decision-making deficits, increasing the likelihood of workplace incidents (Folkard, 2003; Folkard & Lombardi, 2006). Studies show that shift workers have a 30% higher risk of occupational injuries compared to daytime workers (Horwitz & McCall, 2004; Wagstaff & Sigstad Lie, 2011).

Reduced Cognitive and Physical Performance: Workers on night shifts demonstrate lower concentration, problem-solving skills, and motor coordination, leading to decreased productivity(Kecklund & Axelsson, 2016; Rosa et al., 2021). Cognitive impairment caused by fatigue results in errors in high-risk professions, such as healthcare and aviation (Rajaratnam & Arendt, 2001).

Increased Absenteeism and Employee Turnover: Shift workers experience higher absenteeism rates due to chronic health issues, sleep disorders, and workplace dissatisfaction (Boersma et al., 2023; Costa, 2010; Swanson et al., 2011).Companies with rigid shift schedules suffer from higher employee turnover, leading to increased recruitment and training costs (Vetter, Fischer, et al., 2015).

Shift work remains a necessary component of many industries but comes with significant health and cognitive risks. Night shifts and rotating schedules disrupt circadian rhythms, leading to sleep disorders, metabolic issues, and cognitive impairments. Certain industries, particularly healthcare, transportation, and manufacturing, face a higher burden due to shift-related fatigue. Circadian misalignment further increases workplace accidents, reduces efficiency, and raises absenteeism rates. Implementing chronobiology-informed workplace strategies, such as personalized scheduling, strategic lighting, and fatigue management programs, can help mitigate these negative effects and improve employee well-being.

THE PSYCHOSOMATIC CONSEQUENCES OF CIRCADIAN MISALIGNMENT

Circadian rhythms, which are governed by the body's internal clock, regulate various physiological processes, including sleep, body temperature, hormone release, and metabolism. Circadian misalignment occurs when an individual's internal biological clock is not in sync with the external environment, often due to irregular sleep patterns, shift work, or jet lag. Over time, chronic circadian misalignment can lead to significant psychosomatic consequences. This section explores how such misalignment contributes to several health issues, including sleep disorders, chronic fatigue, mood disturbances, gastrointestinal and cardiovascular problems, and its connection to cortisol, melatonin, and workplace stress.

Sleep Disorders and Chronic Fatigue

Sleep disorders are among the most immediate and noticeable consequences of circadian misalignment. Disruption of the natural sleep-wake cycle often leads to sleep deprivation or poor-quality sleep. Shift workers, for instance, who work during the night and sleep during the day, experience a constant misalignment of their internal clock with the external environment. This misalignment can result in difficulty falling asleep, reduced sleep duration, and frequent awakenings (Hirotsu et al., 2015). Chronic circadian misalignment has been strongly linked to the development of sleep disorders such as insomnia, delayed sleep phase disorder, and non-24-hour sleep-wake disorder (Wickwire et al., 2017).

As a consequence of disturbed sleep, individuals often experience chronic fatigue, characterized by persistent feelings of tiredness and low energy levels. Chronic fatigue is not merely the result of poor sleep but also a byproduct of disrupted circadian signaling, which affects various physiological processes, including hormone secretion and immune function. Research indicates that prolonged circadian misalignment can lead to a more significant sense of fatigue, impacting daily performance and overall quality of life (Boivin et al., 2022).

Mood Disturbances and Stress-Related Conditions

Circadian misalignment also has profound effects on mood regulation and is associated with an increased risk of mood disturbances, including depression, anxiety, and irritability. Disruption of the circadian rhythm has been shown to interfere with the regulation of neurotransmitters, including serotonin and dopamine, which play critical roles in mood regulation (Boudreau et al., 2013). Furthermore, studies have revealed a bidirectional relationship between sleep and mood disorders, where poor sleep exacerbates mood disturbances and vice versa(Ahmad et al., 2020).

Chronic stress is another key factor linked to circadian misalignment. Shift workers, for example, often report higher levels of stress due to the physical and psychological strain of working non-traditional hours, which can lead to increased susceptibility to stress-related conditions, including burnout and anxiety disorders. The body's failure to adapt to irregular sleep-wake cycles results in chronic activation of the hypothalamic-pituitary-adrenal (HPA) axis, contributing to the development of stress-related conditions (Baron & Reid, 2014; Catzigianni et al., 2018; Meerlo et al., 2008).

Gastrointestinal and Cardiovascular Problems

Circadian misalignment can also have significant implications for gastrointestinal (GI) and cardiovascular health. The gastrointestinal system is governed by the body's circadian clock, and misalignment can disrupt normal gastrointestinal motility and function. Studies have shown that circadian misalignment is linked to a higher incidence of gastrointestinal disorders, including irritable bowel syndrome (IBS), acid reflux, and inflammatory bowel disease (IBD)(Bishehsari et al., 2016; Vaughn et al., 2014).

Furthermore, chronic circadian misalignment has been associated with an increased risk of cardiovascular diseases. Shift workers, in particular, are at higher risk of developing hypertension, heart disease, and stroke (Knutsson & Bøggild, 2000). The underlying mechanism may involve the dysregulation of various biological pathways, including inflammation and metabolic processes, that are influenced by the circadian clock. Studies suggest that circadian misalignment contributes to altered cardiovascular function by increasing sympathetic nervous system activity and disrupting normal blood pressure regulation (Bass & Takahashi, 2010; Chellappa et al., 2019; Hirotsu et al., 2015).

Connection Between Cortisol, Melatonin, and Workplace Stress

Cortisol and melatonin are two critical hormones regulated by the circadian clock. Cortisol, often referred to as the "stress hormone," is involved in the body's response to stress and helps regulate metabolism and immune function. Melatonin, on the other hand, plays a crucial role in regulating the sleep-wake cycle. Circadian misalignment leads to an imbalance in the secretion of these hormones, contributing to various psychosomatic symptoms.

In a misaligned state, cortisol secretion may become dysregulated, leading to higher levels of cortisol during the night when it should be low, and insufficient secretion during the day. This hormonal imbalance can exacerbate the experience of stress, disrupt sleep patterns, and contribute to fatigue and mood disturbances(Wolkowitz et al., 2001) (Korostovtseva et al,. 2012). Similarly, melatonin production is typically inhibited during exposure to light at night, which can lead to a delay in sleep onset and poor sleep quality (Chtourou & Souissi, 2012) (Dawson & Encel, 1993; Xie et al., 2017). Chronic disruption of melatonin secretion is linked to increased risk for sleep disorders, fatigue, and mood disorders, further perpetuating the cycle of circadian misalignment and its psychosomatic consequences.

Theoretical Background: Biological Models of Circadian Misalignment

Sleep-Wake Homeostasis vs. Circadian Alerting System (Borbely, A. A 1982.): Borbély's two-process model of sleep regulation describes the interaction between sleep-wake homeostasis and the circadian alerting system. Sleep-wake homeostasis dictates that the longer an individual stays awake, the stronger the sleep pressure becomes, leading to sleep initiation. The circadian alerting system, controlled by the suprachiasmatic nucleus (SCN), counteracts this homeostatic pressure by promoting wakefulness at specific times of the day. When these two systems are misaligned—such as in shift workers—the risk of sleep disturbances and cognitive impairments increases significantly (Borbély, A. 2022).

Chronotype Variability Across Age Groups and Occupations: Chronotype is influenced by genetic, environmental, and occupational factors. Adolescents and young adults tend to exhibit a preference for eveningness, while older adults shift toward morningness. Occupational demands further shape chronotype expression, with night-shift workers often adapting to later sleep-wake patterns despite underlying biological predispositions. Understanding these variations is crucial for designing flexible work schedules that accommodate individual differences in circadian preference and mitigate negative health outcomes(Chauhan et al., 2023).

Circadian Rhythm Theory: Circadian rhythm theory explains that biological processes follow a roughly 24-hour cycle, regulated by the suprachiasmatic nucleus in response to light and other environmental cues(Reid, 2019). These rhythms influence sleep-wake cycles, hormone secretion, and cognitive functions, impacting overall health and well-being (Adan et al., 2012; Czeisler et al., 1982). Disruptions, such as shift work or jet lag, can lead to adverse physiological and psychological effects.

International Comparisons: Flexible Work Models vs. Rigid Structures

Scandinavian countries have pioneered chronobiology-informed workplace models, emphasizing flexible work hours, natural light exposure, and employee-centered scheduling. Countries like Sweden and Denmark have implemented policies that allow employees to adjust their work hours based on personal productivity peaks, leading to higher job satisfaction and reduced absenteeism (Härmä et al., 2024; Prodromidis et al., 2025). For example, companies in Finland have introduced flexible start times, enabling workers to align their schedules with their chronotype preferences (Anxo, D., & Karlsson, M. (2019) (Anttila et al., 2015; Cheng et al., 2021; Härmä et al., 2024; Messenger J. 2018).

In contrast, many traditional work environments, particularly in North America and parts of Asia, adhere to rigid 9-to-5 schedules. This standardized approach often disregards individual biological differences, leading to widespread circadian misalignment. Studies have shown that employees in flexible work environments report improved sleep quality, lower stress levels, and greater overall well-being compared to those in rigid work structures (Vetter, Fischer, et al., 2015).

These comparisons highlight the potential benefits of integrating chronobiology into workplace policies and suggest that businesses adopting flexible scheduling models may experience long-term gains in productivity and employee retention.

Conceptual Framework

A conceptual diagram illustrating the interaction between biological rhythms and workplace efficiency is depicted in figure-1.

1. **Chronotypes (Morning, Evening, Intermediate)** → Influence energy peaks and cognitive function.
2. **Chronobiological Disruptions (Shift Work, Social Jetlag, Circadian Misalignment)** → Cause sleep disturbances, reduced cognitive function, and workplace stress.
3. **Workplace Performance Metrics (Productivity, Cognitive Function, Job Satisfaction)** → Are impacted by the extent of circadian alignment.
4. **Intervention Strategies (Chronotype-Based Scheduling, AI-Driven Personalization, Wearable Sleep Tracking, HR Policy Changes)** → Aim to mitigate disruptions and optimize workplace outcomes.

Key Constructs Defined

- **Chronotypes:**
  - **Morning Type (Larks):** Peak energy in the early hours, fatigue in the evening.
  - **Evening Type (Owls):** Alertness peaks late in the day, struggles with early work schedules.
  - **Intermediate Type:** A balanced energy distribution throughout the day.
- **Chronobiological Disruptions:**
  - **Shift Work:** Non-traditional work hours leading to circadian misalignment.
  - **Social Jetlag:** The discrepancy between biological and socially imposed sleep schedules.
  - **Circadian Misalignment:** A broad term encompassing all deviations from natural biological rhythms due to work demands.
- **Workplace Performance Metrics:**
  - **Productivity:** The ability to maintain efficiency and performance without cognitive fatigue.
  - **Cognitive Function:** Mental alertness, memory, and decision-making capacity.
  - **Job Satisfaction:** Employee well-being, motivation, and engagement.

Figure 1. Conceptual model: Chronobiology and workplace efficiency

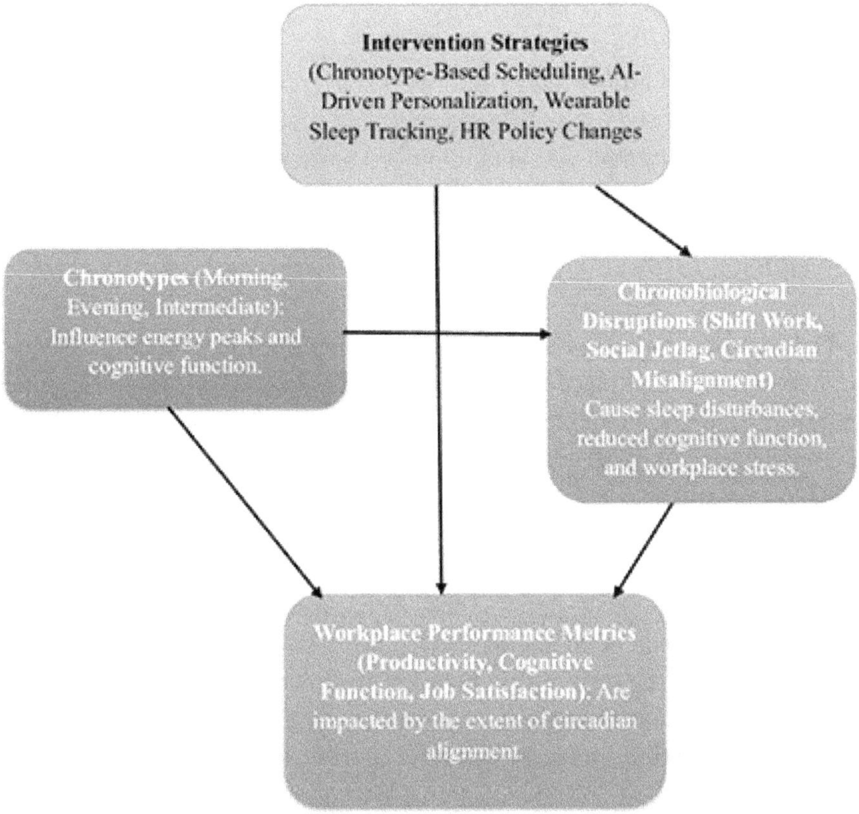

Model Uniqueness: Why This Approach Is Better

Traditional shift scheduling methods rely on fixed rotations and fail to consider individual chronotypes, leading to chronic circadian misalignment. The proposed model integrates:

- AI-Driven Personalization: Algorithms assess employee chronotypes and recommend optimal shift schedules.
- Wearable Sleep Tracking: Continuous data monitoring helps adjust schedules dynamically to reduce sleep deprivation.

- New HR Policies: Companies can implement evidence-based interventions, such as personalized work hours and light exposure management, to reduce burnout and enhance productivity.

By adopting a chronobiology-informed scheduling system, organizations can bridge the gap between scientific research and practical workplace applications, leading to healthier employees and improved business outcomes.

METHODOLOGY

This chapter employs a multidisciplinary approach to examine the impact of chronobiology on workplace efficiency and well-being. The methodology integrates theoretical analysis, literature review, and applied workplace strategies to provide a comprehensive understanding of how biological rhythms influence productivity and employee health.

Research Design: This chapter is structured as a narrative review and conceptual analysis. It synthesizes findings from chronobiology, occupational health, psychology, and organizational behavior to develop a conceptual framework that explains the relationship between circadian rhythms, work performance, and intervention strategies.
Data Collection Sources: literature review was conducted using academic databases such as: PubMed, Scopus, Web of Science, and Google Scholar for peer-reviewed journal articles, Official health and labour organizations (e.g., WHO, ILO) for workplace policies and shift work guidelines, Books, reports, and conference proceedings on workplace chronobiology, fatigue management, and occupational well-being.
Limitations: The study primarily relies on secondary data and does not include primary empirical research, Variability in chronobiological research methods across studies may affect comparability and generalizability. The application of chronobiology to workplaces is context-dependent, requiring industry-specific customization.

RESULT

Leveraging Chronobiology for Workplace Success

Chronobiology, the study of biological rhythms and their effects on human health and behavior, has emerged as a critical area of research for improving workplace efficiency and employee well-being. Understanding the impact of circadian rhythms on individual performance and health can help employers create work environments that align with the natural biological processes of their employees. This alignment can lead to enhanced productivity, reduced fatigue, better decision-making, and overall workplace satisfaction. Several strategies rooted in chronobiology, such as chronotype-based scheduling, light exposure management, strategic napping policies, flexible work arrangements, and wellness interventions, can be implemented to optimize employee performance and health.

Chronotype-Based Scheduling: Aligning Work Shifts with Employees' Natural Peaks

Chronotype-based scheduling involves tailoring work shifts to align with employees' natural biological rhythms, optimizing their productivity and well-being. Studies have shown that aligning work schedules with an individual's chronotype can enhance cognitive performance, improve mood, and reduce fatigue. For example, larks tend to perform better in the early hours of the day, while owls may experience heightened alertness in the late afternoon or evening (Glimer, D. 2018).). By offering flexible shift patterns that cater to these natural peaks, organizations can maximize employee efficiency and engagement while reducing the negative effects of misaligned work hours, such as sleep deprivation and burnout. This approach can be particularly beneficial in industries that rely on shift work, such as healthcare, manufacturing, and customer service.

Light Exposure Management: Optimizing Workplace Lighting to Regulate Circadian Rhythms

Light plays a crucial role in regulating the circadian rhythm, and optimizing workplace lighting can have a significant impact on employee well-being and performance. Exposure to bright light during the day, especially in the morning, helps to synchronize the internal clock with the external environment, promoting alertness and improving sleep quality(Caldwell et al., 2019). Conversely, exposure to artificial light at night, particularly blue light from screens, can disrupt circadian rhythms, making it harder for employees to fall asleep and affecting their cognitive performance the following day(Duffy & Czeisler, 2009; Knapen et al., 2016).

To optimize circadian alignment, organizations can invest in dynamic lighting systems that adjust to the time of day. Bright white or blue-enriched light in the morning can help employees feel more awake and focused, while warmer, dimmer lighting in the evening can promote relaxation and signal to the body that it is time to wind down. Additionally, providing employees with access to natural light or allowing breaks to step outside can further support healthy circadian rhythms (Rahman et al., 2022; Vanini, 2024). For shift workers, the use of bright light during work hours and minimizing light exposure at home during the day can help mitigate the effects of circadian misalignment.

Strategic Napping Policies: Short Naps to Enhance Alertness and Reduce Errors

Napping, when done strategically, can serve as an effective tool for managing fatigue and enhancing alertness. Research has demonstrated that short naps of 10 to 20 minutes can improve cognitive function, memory, and reaction time, without causing grogginess or interfering with nighttime sleep (Knapen et al., 2016; Purnell et al., 2002). In contrast, longer naps can lead to sleep inertia, where individuals experience a period of confusion and reduced performance upon waking.

Incorporating strategic napping policies in the workplace can benefit employees, particularly those working long hours or night shifts. Providing designated spaces for naps and encouraging employees to take brief naps during breaks can help restore energy levels and reduce errors caused by fatigue. Napping has been shown to enhance decision-making, creativity, and overall productivity, making it a valuable strategy for organizations aiming to optimize performance (Purnell et al., 2002). This approach is especially relevant in industries such as healthcare, transportation, and customer service, where alertness is critical for safety and productivity.

Flexible Work Arrangements: Remote Work and Individualized Schedules

Flexible work arrangements are increasingly recognized as essential for supporting work-life balance and optimizing employee productivity. By allowing employees to choose their work hours or work remotely, organizations can accommodate individual preferences and biological rhythms, thereby improving job satisfaction and performance (Baker et al., n.d.; Hunt et al., 2010). Flexible schedules enable employees to align their work hours with their natural peaks of alertness and energy, reducing the risk of fatigue, stress, and burnout.

Remote work, in particular, allows employees to better control their environment, including their sleep patterns, lighting, and breaks. For employees with specific chronotypes, remote work offers the flexibility to schedule work during their optimal hours, which can lead to higher productivity and better mental health. Additionally, by offering individualized schedules that take into account personal preferences and biological needs, employers can foster a supportive and inclusive work culture, leading to increased employee engagement and retention (Felstead & Henseke, 2017).

Wellness Interventions: Sleep Hygiene Programs, Ergonomic Workspaces, and Dietary Strategies

A comprehensive wellness strategy that incorporates sleep hygiene programs, ergonomic workspaces, and dietary strategies can further enhance employee well-being and performance. Sleep hygiene programs aim to educate employees on the importance of good sleep habits, such as maintaining a consistent sleep schedule, limiting caffeine intake, and creating a conducive sleep environment. Promoting healthy sleep is crucial for improving mood, cognitive function, and overall health, as sleep deprivation has been linked to impaired decision-making, emotional regulation, and productivity (Walker, 2017).

Ergonomic workspaces are another key component of workplace wellness. Poor ergonomics can lead to physical discomfort, musculoskeletal disorders, and fatigue, all of which negatively impact performance. By providing ergonomic furniture, adjustable chairs, and computer screens, employers can reduce physical strain and improve employee comfort and productivity (Robertson et al., 2016).

Dietary strategies also play a significant role in optimizing employee health and energy levels. Encouraging balanced, nutrient-rich meals and providing access to healthy snacks can help stabilize blood sugar levels, improve mood, and enhance cognitive function. For shift workers, particularly those working during the night, it is important to provide guidance on meal timing and nutrition to minimize the impact of circadian misalignment on digestion and metabolism (Boege et al., 2021; "Food and Mood: How Do Diet and Nutrition Affect Mental Wellbeing?," 2020; Phoi & Keogh, 2019).

Leveraging chronobiology in the workplace can lead to improved employee performance, health, and well-being. Chronotype-based scheduling, light exposure management, strategic napping, flexible work arrangements, and wellness interventions are all evidence-based strategies that can help employees align their work schedules with their natural biological rhythms. By adopting these approaches, organizations can foster a healthier, more productive work environment that supports the needs of their workforce and contributes to long-term success.

Quantitative Data on Circadian Misalignment and Workplace Mental Health Outcomes

Circadian misalignment has measurable effects on employee mental health, job performance, and retention rates. Below **Table- 1** shows some key data points from large-scale occupational health studies:

Table 1. Quantitative data on circadian misalignment and workplace mental health outcomes

Mental Health Outcome	Impact of Circadian Misalignment	Source
Depression	40% higher prevalence in shift workers compared to daytime workers	Wickwire et al., 2017
Anxiety Disorders	2.5x increased risk in night shift employees	Baron & Reid, 2014
Burnout	65% higher emotional exhaustion rates among rotating shift workers	Khamisa et al., 2017
Absenteeism	35% higher absenteeism rates in employees with irregular sleep schedules	Juda et al., 2013
Cognitive Impairments	20% slower reaction times and decreased decision-making accuracy in sleep-deprived workers	Lo et al., 2016

These statistics highlight the **urgent need for workplace interventions** to mitigate the mental health risks associated with circadian misalignment.

Workplace Mental Health Interventions for Circadian Misalignment

Cognitive Behavioral Therapy for Insomnia (CBT-I): CBT-I is a gold-standard treatment for sleep disturbances and has been shown to reduce anxiety, depression, and fatigue in employees with circadian misalignment (Hirshkowitz et al., 2015). Employer-provided CBT-I programs for shift workers and employees with chronic insomnia. Digital CBT-I apps (e.g., Sleepio, Somryst) offered through workplace wellness programs.Group-based CBT-I workshops to help employees build healthy sleep habits. Studies show that CBT-I improves sleep efficiency by 30–40% and reduces workplace stress by 25% within 6–8 weeks of intervention (Dall'Ora et al., 2016).

Mindfulness-Based Stress Reduction (MBSR)

MBSR techniques—including guided meditation, breathing exercises, and progressive muscle relaxation—have been proven to reduce workplace anxiety and improve sleep quality(Goldstein & Walker, 2014). Daily 10-minute mindfulness sessions in high-stress work environments, Integration of MBSR apps (e.g., Headspace, Calm) into employee wellness programs and On-site or virtual guided meditation programs to improve focus and relaxation. A randomized controlled trial of 500 employees found that MBSR reduced perceived workplace stress by 38% and improved sleep quality by 25% (Rahman et al., 2022).

Personalized Chronotherapy and Light Exposure Interventions

Chronotherapy—adjusting light exposure and work schedules to align with biological rhythms—can help shift workers and employees with social jetlag restore circadian stability. Blue-light exposure therapy during morning shifts to improve alertness, Use of amber-tinted glasses in evening shifts to reduce melatonin suppression and Gradual shift rotation policies to minimize abrupt circadian disruptions. A study in aviation workers found that light-based chronotherapy reduced fatigue by 32% and improved sleep duration by 90 minutes per night(Cajochen et al., 2003).

Future Directions and Recommendations in Chronobiology and Workplace Well-Being

As organizations increasingly recognize the importance of aligning work schedules and environments with the biological needs of their employees, the role of chronobiology in workplace management will continue to evolve. The integration of technology, artificial intelligence (AI), and personalized approaches offers promising avenues for optimizing employee performance and health. Moreover, human-centered policies will need to address the emerging needs of a diverse workforce. Here, we explore potential future directions and provide recommendations for further research in chronobiology and workplace well-being.

The Role of Technology and AI in Personalized Work Schedules

With advancements in technology, particularly AI and data analytics, the future of workplace scheduling will be revolutionized. One key opportunity lies in leveraging AI to create personalized work schedules that align with employees' chronotypes, lifestyle preferences, and productivity patterns. AI-driven systems could analyze data such as sleep patterns, activity levels, and performance metrics to predict optimal work hours for individual employees (Consultant, 14596 Farming Rd, Frisco, TX, 75035, USA & Parasa, 2023). By using wearable devices and apps that track circadian rhythms and health markers, employers can design highly personalized work schedules that maximize productivity while minimizing fatigue, stress, and health risks (Gubin et al., 2025; Kaushik et al., n.d.)

Furthermore, AI can assist in dynamic scheduling, where work shifts are adjusted in real-time based on an employee's performance and well-being indicators. This adaptability can be especially beneficial for industries that rely on shift work or have fluctuating workloads, such as healthcare, manufacturing, and logistics. Implementing such technology could enhance employee engagement, reduce burnout, and increase organizational efficiency.

However, the integration of AI in scheduling must be done cautiously to ensure that privacy concerns are addressed and that employees' autonomy in managing their work-life balance is maintained. Providing transparency and involving employees in the decision-making process will be crucial for the successful adoption of such technologies (Del Pero et al., 2022).

Policy Recommendations for Human-Centered Work Environments

For organizations to effectively implement chronobiology-informed strategies, policies must be designed with employee well-being as a central focus. Human-centered policies that prioritize flexibility, health, and work-life balance will be essential in fostering a productive and sustainable work environment.

- **Flexible Work Hours and Remote Work**: As discussed, flexible schedules and remote work options allow employees to align their work hours with their natural energy peaks. Policies should encourage managers to accommodate individual chronotypes and offer remote work or hybrid options to support a more flexible work culture. Additionally, offering flexible start and end times could prevent employees from working outside of their optimal performance window(Felstead & Henseke, 2017; Gilmer, n.d.).
- **Workplace Sleep Support Programs**: Many workplaces could benefit from incorporating sleep hygiene education and sleep support programs into their wellness initiatives. By offering sleep-focused interventions, such as sleep health seminars, access to sleep-tracking devices, or environments conducive to napping, employers can help employees achieve better sleep quality and, in turn, enhance their overall productivity and health (Hirshkowitz et al., 2015).

- **Ergonomics and Environmental Adjustments**: Human-centered work environments should also prioritize ergonomics, ensuring that physical spaces are conducive to both comfort and productivity. This can involve providing adjustable desks, ergonomic chairs, and lighting systems that support healthy circadian rhythms. A work environment that supports physical health, mental well-being, and the natural biological rhythms of employees is essential for fostering long-term workplace success.
- **Employee Involvement and Feedback Mechanisms**: Organizations should also implement systems for employees to provide feedback on their work environments and well-being. Regular surveys, focus groups, or wellness audits can ensure that policies are being effectively implemented and allow employees to have a voice in shaping the workplace.

Areas for Further Research in Chronobiology and Workplace Well-Being

While much progress has been made in understanding how chronobiology influences workplace well-being, several key areas remain underexplored. Future research should aim to build upon existing knowledge and address gaps in the field. Some promising directions include:

- **Long-Term Effects of Chronotype-Based Scheduling**: While short-term studies have shown the benefits of aligning work schedules with chronotype, there is limited research on the long-term effects of chronotype-based scheduling on employee performance, health, and career satisfaction. Longitudinal studies could provide valuable insights into whether chronotype-based scheduling leads to sustained improvements in productivity and well-being over time (Chtourou & Souissi, n.d.).
- **Impact of Chronobiology on Shift Work and Health**: Shift work continues to be a significant source of circadian misalignment for many workers, particularly in industries such as healthcare, transportation, and manufacturing. Research exploring the combined impact of shift work, chronotype, and health outcomes (such as cardiovascular health, mental health, and sleep disorders) could provide evidence for more effective interventions tailored to shift workers (Costa, 2010).
- **Individual Differences in Circadian Rhythms**: While chronobiology is often studied in broad terms, more research is needed to understand individual variations in circadian rhythms and how they interact with factors such as age, gender, lifestyle, and genetics. Research examining how these factors

influence optimal work schedules could lead to even more personalized and effective workplace interventions(Saksvik et al., 2011).

- **Exploring the Role of Technology in Chronobiology**: As discussed, wearable devices and apps are becoming increasingly common for tracking sleep and activity patterns. Future studies should explore how these technologies can be used to not only monitor employees' circadian rhythms but also provide real-time interventions, such as personalized lighting adjustments or sleep tips. Additionally, investigating the potential role of AI in managing circadian misalignment and optimizing workplace productivity will be a key area for exploration.
- **Chronobiology and Mental Health**: While much attention has been given to the physical impacts of circadian misalignment, its influence on mental health remains less understood. Future research should explore the relationship between circadian rhythms, sleep disturbances, and mental health conditions such as depression, anxiety, and stress. Understanding this connection will be vital for designing interventions that support mental well-being in the workplace (Goldstein & Walker, 2014).

The future of chronobiology in the workplace holds immense potential for enhancing both employee performance and well-being. With the integration of AI, personalized work schedules, and human-centered policies, organizations can create environments that support the biological rhythms of their employees. However, further research is needed to deepen our understanding of individual differences, long-term outcomes, and the role of technology in supporting workplace well-being. By continuing to explore these areas, organizations can foster healthier, more productive work environments that benefit both employees and employer.

CONCLUSION: A CALL FOR CHRONOBIOLOGY-INFORMED WORKPLACE POLICIES

In an era where workplace efficiency is often prioritized over employee well-being, chronobiology offers a transformative perspective—one that acknowledges the biological rhythms that govern human health and performance. This chapter has underscored the significant impact of circadian alignment on productivity, mental health, and overall job satisfaction. The disconnect between rigid work schedules and individual chronotypes not only impairs employee well-being but also reduces organizational efficiency.

The integration of chronobiology into workplace policies is not merely an option but a necessity for fostering a healthier, more productive workforce. As research consistently shows, circadian rhythms influence sleep quality, cognitive performance, and overall well-being. Misaligned work schedules contribute to increased stress, fatigue, and long-term health risks, making it imperative for organizations to acknowledge and accommodate individual chronotypes.

To create healthier, more sustainable workplaces, science-driven strategies must take center stage. Chronotype-based scheduling, exposure to natural light, strategic napping policies, and flexible work arrangements are not mere conveniences; they are essential interventions that can mitigate fatigue, enhance cognitive function, and foster long-term employee engagement. As technology advances, organizations have an unprecedented opportunity to leverage AI-driven scheduling and personalized work environments to optimize both human potential and business outcomes.

Ultimately, the future of workplace success lies in policies that work in harmony with, rather than against, our biological clocks. By integrating chronobiological principles into workplace design and management, organizations can not only enhance employee well-being but also cultivate a more resilient, motivated, and high-performing workforce. The time to act is now—embracing chronobiology is not just a progressive choice but a necessary evolution in modern work culture.

Implementing Chronobiology-Informed Workplace Strategies

Organizations that recognize the role of biological rhythms in employee performance and health can significantly improve workplace efficiency, engagement, and job satisfaction. The increasing prevalence of shift work, flexible job arrangements, and digital work environments has intensified the misalignment between work schedules and natural circadian rhythms, leading to increased fatigue, cognitive impairments, and long-term health risks (Baron & Reid, 2014; Costa, 2010).

To mitigate these negative effects, employers must adopt evidence-based chronobiological strategies that support employees' natural rhythms. The following Table-2 shows key interventions can help optimize work environments, improve health outcomes, and enhance productivity:

Table 2. Chronobiology-based workplace actions for enhanced employee well-being and productivity

Strategy	Workplace Actions	Benefits	Key References
Chronotype-Based Scheduling	Assess employees' chronotypes and assign shifts accordingly	Reduces fatigue, enhances performance, improves job satisfaction	(Hittle & Gillespie, 2018; Montaruli et al., 2019; Saksvik et al., 2011)
Optimized Light Exposure	Provide access to natural light, adjust artificial lighting to match circadian needs	Enhances alertness, improves sleep quality, boosts mood	(Duffy & Czeisler, 2009; Figueiro et al., 2017)
Strategic Napping Policies	Implement **short naps (10–20 min)** in high-risk jobs, create designated rest areas	Reduces errors, improves cognitive function, enhances alertness	(Purnell et al., 2002)
Flexible Work Arrangements	Allow **remote work, flexible start and end times, compressed workweeks**	Reduces burnout, increases engagement, enhances productivity	(Felstead & Henseke, 2017; Gilmer, n.d.)
Workplace Wellness Programs	Offer **sleep hygiene education, ergonomic workspaces, dietary guidance, and mindfulness sessions**	Supports physical and mental well-being, reduces absenteeism	(Boege et al., 2021; Phoi & Keogh, 2019)
Fatigue Risk Management	Implement **fatigue-monitoring tools, structured breaks, and workload redistribution**	Prevents burnout, enhances workplace safety	(Rajaratnam & Arendt, 2001)
Meal Timing and Nutrition Support	Encourage structured meal breaks, offer **high-protein, low-sugar meal options** for shift workers	Regulates metabolism, minimizes digestive discomfort, stabilizes energy levels	(Boege et al., 2021)
Workload Optimization Based on Cognitive Performance Peaks	Schedule critical tasks during employees' **biological peak hours**	Improves decision-making, increases efficiency, enhances problem-solving skills	(Correa et al., 2020)
Technology Integration for Circadian Health	Use **AI-powered scheduling, biometric tracking, and sleep-coaching apps**	Personalizes work schedules, reduces circadian misalignment	(Gubin et al., 2025)
Mental Health and Stress Management	Provide **counseling services, relaxation spaces, and stress reduction workshops**	Reduces anxiety, enhances job satisfaction, mitigates the effects of circadian misalignment	(Goldstein & Walker, 2014)

By integrating these chronobiology-informed workplace strategies, companies can enhance employee resilience, reduce turnover, and improve overall organizational success. The implementation of chronobiology-based workplace interventions is not just an innovation—it is a necessity in today's evolving work culture. Organizations that prioritize biological alignment in work scheduling, mental well-being, and environmental design will experience higher employee engagement, lower absenteeism, and sustained productivity gains. The future of workplace success depends on integrating science-backed, human-centered policies that align with employees' natural biological rhythms.

By proactively adopting these strategies, companies can enhance their workforce's health, efficiency, and job satisfaction, paving the way for a more sustainable and high-performing organizational culture

REFERENCES

Adan, A., Archer, S. N., Hidalgo, M. P., Di Milia, L., Natale, V., & Randler, C. (2012). Circadian Typology: A Comprehensive Review. *Chronobiology International, 29*(9), 1153–1175. DOI: 10.3109/07420528.2012.719971 PMID: 23004349

Ahmad, M., Md. Din, N. S. B., Tharumalay, R. D., Che Din, N., Ibrahim, N., Amit, N., Farah, N. M., Osman, R. A., Abdul Hamid, M. F., Ibrahim, I. A., Jamsari, E. A., Palil, M. R., & Ahmad, S. (2020). The Effects of Circadian Rhythm Disruption on Mental Health and Physiological Responses among Shift Workers and General Population. *International Journal of Environmental Research and Public Health, 17*(19), 7156. DOI: 10.3390/ijerph17197156 PMID: 33007836

Akinbami, A. A. (n.d.). *Integrating Natural Light for Wellbeing*. Performance, and Quality Care Delivery in Healthcare Environments.

Al-Yafei, A. (2024). The Relationship Between Job Rotation And Work Engagement: The Mediating Role Of Job Satisfaction (Doctoral dissertation, University of Central Lancashire).

Amini, F., Moosavi, S. M., Rafaiee, R., Nadi Ghara, A., & Babakhanian, M. (2021). Chronotype patterns associated with job satisfaction of shift working healthcare providers. *Chronobiology International, 38*(4), 526–533. DOI: 10.1080/07420528.2020.1869028 PMID: 33435743

Anttila, T., Oinas, T., Tammelin, M., & Nätti, J. (2015). Working-Time Regimes and Work-Life Balance in Europe. *European Sociological Review, 31*(6), 713–724. DOI: 10.1093/esr/jcv070

Antunes, L. C., Levandovski, R., Dantas, G., Caumo, W., & Hidalgo, M. P. (2010). Obesity and shift work: Chronobiological aspects. *Nutrition Research Reviews, 23*(1), 155–168. DOI: 10.1017/S0954422410000016 PMID: 20122305

Antúnez, J. M. (2020). Circadian typology is related to emotion regulation, metacognitive beliefs and assertiveness in healthy adults. *PLoS One, 15*(3), e0230169. DOI: 10.1371/journal.pone.0230169 PMID: 32168366

Anxo, D., & Karlsson, M. (2019). *Overtime work: A review of literature and initial empirical analysis*. International Labour Office, Inclusive Labour Markets, Labour Relations and Working Conditions Branch.

Atkinson, G., Fullick, S., Grindey, C., & Maclaren, D. (2008). Exercise, Energy Balance and the Shift Worker. *Sports Medicine (Auckland, N.Z.), 38*(8), 671–685. DOI: 10.2165/00007256-200838080-00005 PMID: 18620467

Baker, E., Avery, G. C., & Crawford, J. (n.d.). *Satisfaction and Perceived Productivity when Professionals Work From Home.*

Banks, S., & Dinges, D. F. (2007). Behavioral and Physiological Consequences of Sleep Restriction. *Journal of Clinical Sleep Medicine : JCSM : Official Publication of the American Academy of Sleep Medicine, 03*(05), 519–528. DOI: 10.5664/jcsm.26918 PMID: 17803017

Barger, L. K., Lockley, S. W., Rajaratnam, S. M. W., & Landrigan, C. P. (2009). Neurobehavioral, health, and safety consequences associated with shift work in safety-sensitive professions. *Current Neurology and Neuroscience Reports, 9*(2), 155–164. DOI: 10.1007/s11910-009-0024-7 PMID: 19268039

Baron, K. G., & Reid, K. J. (2014). Circadian misalignment and health. *International Review of Psychiatry (Abingdon, England), 26*(2), 139–154. DOI: 10.3109/09540261.2014.911149 PMID: 24892891

Bass, J., & Takahashi, J. S. (2010). Circadian Integration of Metabolism and Energetics. *Science, 330*(6009), 1349–1354. DOI: 10.1126/science.1195027 PMID: 21127246

Besedovsky, L., Lange, T., & Born, J. (2012). Sleep and immune function. *Pflügers Archiv, 463*(1), 121–137. DOI: 10.1007/s00424-011-1044-0 PMID: 22071480

Bishehsari, F., Levi, F., Turek, F. W., & Keshavarzian, A. (2016). Circadian Rhythms in Gastrointestinal Health and Diseases. *Gastroenterology, 151*(3), e1–e5. DOI: 10.1053/j.gastro.2016.07.036 PMID: 27480174

Boege, H. L., Bhatti, M. Z., & St-Onge, M.-P. (2021). Circadian rhythms and meal timing: Impact on energy balance and body weight. *Current Opinion in Biotechnology, 70*, 1–6. DOI: 10.1016/j.copbio.2020.08.009 PMID: 32998085

Boersma, G. J., Mijnster, T., Vantyghem, P., Kerkhof, G. A., & Lancel, M. (2023). Shift work is associated with extensively disordered sleep, especially when working nights. *Frontiers in Psychiatry, 14*, 1233640. DOI: 10.3389/fpsyt.2023.1233640 PMID: 38161719

Boivin, D. B., Boudreau, P., & Kosmadopoulos, A. (2022). Disturbance of the Circadian System in Shift Work and Its Health Impact. *Journal of Biological Rhythms, 37*(1), 3–28. DOI: 10.1177/07487304211064218 PMID: 34969316

Borbély, A. (2022). The two-process model of sleep regulation: Beginnings and outlook. *Journal of Sleep Research, 31*(4), e13598. DOI: 10.1111/jsr.13598 PMID: 35502706

Borbely, A. A. (1982). *A Two Process Model of Sleep Regulation.*

Born, J., Lange, T., Hansen, K., Mölle, M., & Fehm, H. L. (1997). Effects of sleep and circadian rhythm on human circulating immune cells. *The Journal of Immunology : Official Journal of the American Association of Immunologists, 158*(9), 4454–4464. DOI: 10.4049/jimmunol.158.9.4454 PMID: 9127011

Boudreau, P., Dumont, G. A., & Boivin, D. B. (2013). Circadian Adaptation to Night Shift Work Influences Sleep, Performance, Mood and the Autonomic Modulation of the Heart. *PLoS One, 8*(7), e70813. DOI: 10.1371/journal.pone.0070813 PMID: 23923024

Cajochen, C., Kräuchi, K., & Wirz-Justice, A. (2003). Role of Melatonin in the Regulation of Human Circadian Rhythms and Sleep. *Journal of Neuroendocrinology, 15*(4), 432–437. DOI: 10.1046/j.1365-2826.2003.00989.x PMID: 12622846

Caldwell, J. A. (2012). Crew Schedules, Sleep Deprivation, and Aviation Performance. *Current Directions in Psychological Science, 21*(2), 85–89. DOI: 10.1177/0963721411435842

Caldwell, J. A., Caldwell, J. L., Thompson, L. A., & Lieberman, H. R. (2019). Fatigue and its management in the workplace. *Neuroscience and Biobehavioral Reviews, 96*, 272–289. DOI: 10.1016/j.neubiorev.2018.10.024 PMID: 30391406

Caldwell, J. A., Mallis, M. M., Caldwell, J. L., Paul, M. A., Miller, J. C., & Neri, D. F. (2009). Fatigue Countermeasures in Aviation. *Aviation, Space, and Environmental Medicine, 80*(1), 29–59. DOI: 10.3357/ASEM.2435.2009 PMID: 19180856

Chang, W.-P., & Peng, Y.-X. (2021). Differences between fixed day shift workers and rotating shift workers in gastrointestinal problems: A systematic review and meta-analysis. *Industrial Health, 59*(2), 66–77. DOI: 10.2486/indhealth.2020-0153 PMID: 33408309

Chatzigianni, D., Tsounis, A., Markopoulos, N., & Sarafis, P. (2018). Occupational stress experienced by nurses working in a Greek Regional Hospital: A cross-sectional study. *Iranian Journal of Nursing and Midwifery Research, 23*(6), 450. DOI: 10.4103/ijnmr.IJNMR_120_17 PMID: 30386395

Chauhan, S., Norbury, R., Faßbender, K. C., Ettinger, U., & Kumari, V. (2023). Beyond sleep: A multidimensional model of chronotype. *Neuroscience and Biobehavioral Reviews, 148*, 105114. DOI: 10.1016/j.neubiorev.2023.105114 PMID: 36868368

Chellappa, S. L., Vujovic, N., Williams, J. S., & Scheer, F. A. J. L. (2019). Impact of Circadian Disruption on Cardiovascular Function and Disease. *Trends in Endocrinology and Metabolism*, *30*(10), 767–779. DOI: 10.1016/j.tem.2019.07.008 PMID: 31427142

Chen, H.-T., Chuang, H.-Y., Hsieh, T.-Y., Wu, P.-S., Lin, F.-J., Huang, H.-C., Yang, C.-C., & Kuo, C.-H. (2022). Shift work is significantly and positively associated with possible gastro-esophageal reflux disease: A meta-analysis study. *Frontiers in Public Health*, *10*, 980603. DOI: 10.3389/fpubh.2022.980603 PMID: 36504996

Cheng, W.-J., Liu, C.-S., Hu, K.-C., Cheng, Y.-F., Karhula, K., & Härmä, M. (2021). Night shift work and the risk of metabolic syndrome: Findings from an 8-year hospital cohort. *PLoS One*, *16*(12), e0261349. DOI: 10.1371/journal.pone.0261349 PMID: 34898652

Chtourou, H., & Souissi, N. (n.d.). The Effect Of Training At A Specific Time Of Day. *RE:view*.

Parasa, S. K. (2023). Impact of AI on Strategic Workforce Planning. *Journal of Artificial Intelligence & Cloud Computing*, *2*(1), 1–3. DOI: 10.47363/jaicc/2023(2)377

Correa, Á., Alguacil, S., Ciria, L. F., Jiménez, A., & Ruz, M. (2020). Circadian rhythms and decision-making: A review and new evidence from electroencephalography. *Chronobiology International*, *37*(4), 520–541. DOI: 10.1080/07420528.2020.1715421 PMID: 32000532

Costa, G. (2010). Shift Work and Health: Current Problems and Preventive Actions. *Safety and Health at Work*, *1*(2), 112–123. DOI: 10.5491/SHAW.2010.1.2.112 PMID: 22953171

Costa, G., & Sartori, S. (2007). Ageing, working hours and work ability. *Ergonomics*, *50*(11), 1914–1930. DOI: 10.1080/00140130701676054 PMID: 17972209

Czeisler, C. A., Moore-Ede, M. C., & Coleman, R. M. (1982). Rotating Shift Work Schedules That Disrupt Sleep Are Improved by Applying Circadian Principles. *Science*, *217*(4558), 460–463. DOI: 10.1126/science.7089576 PMID: 7089576

Dall'Ora, C., Ball, J., Recio-Saucedo, A., & Griffiths, P. (2016). Characteristics of shift work and their impact on employee performance and wellbeing: A literature review. *International Journal of Nursing Studies*, *57*, 12–27. DOI: 10.1016/j.ijnurstu.2016.01.007 PMID: 27045561

Danna, K., & Griffin, R. W. (1999). Health and Well-Being in the Workplace: A Review and Synthesis of the Literature. *Journal of Management*, *25*(3), 357–384. DOI: 10.1177/014920639902500305

Dawson, D., & Encel, N. (1993). Melatonin and sleep in humans. *Journal of Pineal Research, 15*(1), 1–12. DOI: 10.1111/j.1600-079X.1993.tb00503.x PMID: 8229640

De Souza, C. M., & Hidalgo, M. P. L. (2015). The midpoint of sleep on working days: A measure for chronodisruption and its association to individuals' well-being. *Chronobiology International, 32*(3), 341–348. DOI: 10.3109/07420528.2014.979941 PMID: 25392279

Dijk, D., & Czeisler, C. (1995). Contribution of the circadian pacemaker and the sleep homeostat to sleep propensity, sleep structure, electroencephalographic slow waves, and sleep spindle activity in humans. *The Journal of Neuroscience : The Official Journal of the Society for Neuroscience, 15*(5), 3526–3538. DOI: 10.1523/JNEUROSCI.15-05-03526.1995 PMID: 7751928

Dijk, D.-J., & Lockley, S. W. (2002). Invited Review: Integration of human sleep-wake regulation and circadian rhythmicity. *Journal of Applied Physiology, 92*(2), 852–862. DOI: 10.1152/japplphysiol.00924.2001 PMID: 11796701

Donaldson, L., Ricciardi, W., Sheridan, S., & Tartaglia, R. (Eds.). (2021). *Textbook of Patient Safety and Clinical Risk Management*. Springer International Publishing., DOI: 10.1007/978-3-030-59403-9

Duffy, J. F., & Czeisler, C. A. (2009). Effect of Light on Human Circadian Physiology. *Sleep Medicine Clinics, 4*(2), 165–177. DOI: 10.1016/j.jsmc.2009.01.004 PMID: 20161220

Eldevik, M. F., Flo, E., Moen, B. E., Pallesen, S., & Bjorvatn, B. (2013). Insomnia, Excessive Sleepiness, Excessive Fatigue, Anxiety, Depression and Shift Work Disorder in Nurses Having Less than 11 Hours in-Between Shifts. *PLoS One, 8*(8), e70882. DOI: 10.1371/journal.pone.0070882 PMID: 23976964

Felstead, A., & Henseke, G. (2017). Assessing the growth of remote working and its consequences for effort, well-being and work-life balance. *New Technology, Work and Employment, 32*(3), 195–212. DOI: 10.1111/ntwe.12097

Ferri, P., Guadi, M., Marcheselli, L., Balduzzi, S., Magnani, D., & Di Lorenzo, R. (2016). The impact of shift work on the psychological and physical health of nurses in a general hospital: A comparison between rotating night shifts and day shifts. *Risk Management and Healthcare Policy, 9*, 203–211. DOI: 10.2147/RMHP.S115326 PMID: 27695372

Figueiro, M. G., Steverson, B., Heerwagen, J., Kampschroer, K., Hunter, C. M., Gonzales, K., Plitnick, B., & Rea, M. S. (2017). The impact of daytime light exposures on sleep and mood in office workers. *Sleep Health*, *3*(3), 204–215. DOI: 10.1016/j.sleh.2017.03.005 PMID: 28526259

Flo, E., Pallesen, S., Magerøy, N., Moen, B. E., Grønli, J., Hilde Nordhus, I., & Bjorvatn, B. (2012). Shift Work Disorder in Nurses – Assessment, Prevalence and Related Health Problems. *PLoS One*, *7*(4), e33981. DOI: 10.1371/journal.pone.0033981 PMID: 22485153

Folkard, S. (2003). Shift work, safety and productivity. *Occupational Medicine*, *53*(2), 95–101. DOI: 10.1093/occmed/kqg047 PMID: 12637593

Folkard, S., & Lombardi, D. A. (2006). Modeling the impact of the components of long work hours on injuries and "accidents.". *American Journal of Industrial Medicine*, *49*(11), 953–963. DOI: 10.1002/ajim.20307 PMID: 16570251

Ghosh, B., & Pm, A. S. (2024). Chronotype preferences, work motivation, and gender differences among private sector employees in Bengaluru. *International Journal of Science and Research Archive*, *11*(2), 1702–1712. DOI: 10.30574/ijsra.2024.11.2.0654

Gilmer, D. O. (n.d.). *Workplace Chronotype Bias*. Flexible Scheduling, and Performance Beliefs.

Gobin, C. M., Banks, J. B., Fins, A. I., & Tartar, J. L. (2015). Poor sleep quality is associated with a negative cognitive bias and decreased sustained attention. *Journal of Sleep Research*, *24*(5), 535–542. DOI: 10.1111/jsr.12302 PMID: 25913483

Goldstein, A. N., & Walker, M. P. (2014). The Role of Sleep in Emotional Brain Function. *Annual Review of Clinical Psychology*, *10*(1), 679–708. DOI: 10.1146/annurev-clinpsy-032813-153716 PMID: 24499013

Gubin, D., Weinert, D., Stefani, O., Otsuka, K., Borisenkov, M., & Cornelissen, G. (2025). Wearables in Chronomedicine and Interpretation of Circadian Health. *Diagnostics (Basel)*, *15*(3), 327. DOI: 10.3390/diagnostics15030327 PMID: 39941257

Härmä, M., Kecklund, G., & Tucker, P. (2024). Working hours and health – key research topics in the past and future. *Scandinavian Journal of Work, Environment & Health*, *50*(4), 233–243. DOI: 10.5271/sjweh.4157 PMID: 38497926

Hidalgo, M. P., Caumo, W., Posser, M., Coccaro, S. B., Camozzato, A. L., & Chaves, M. L. F. (2009). Relationship between depressive mood and chronotype in healthy subjects. *Psychiatry and Clinical Neurosciences*, *63*(3), 283–290. DOI: 10.1111/j.1440-1819.2009.01965.x PMID: 19566758

Hirotsu, C., Tufik, S., & Andersen, M. L. (2015). Interactions between sleep, stress, and metabolism: From physiological to pathological conditions. *Sleep Science*, *8*(3), 143–152. DOI: 10.1016/j.slsci.2015.09.002 PMID: 26779321

Hirshkowitz, M., Whiton, K., Albert, S. M., Alessi, C., Bruni, O., DonCarlos, L., Hazen, N., Herman, J., Katz, E. S., Kheirandish-Gozal, L., Neubauer, D. N., O'Donnell, A. E., Ohayon, M., Peever, J., Rawding, R., Sachdeva, R. C., Setters, B., Vitiello, M. V., Ware, J. C., & Adams Hillard, P. J. (2015). National Sleep Foundation's sleep time duration recommendations: Methodology and results summary. *Sleep Health*, *1*(1), 40–43. DOI: 10.1016/j.sleh.2014.12.010 PMID: 29073412

Hittle, B. M., & Gillespie, G. L. (2018). Identifying shift worker chronotype: Implications for health. *Industrial Health*, *56*(6), 512–523. DOI: 10.2486/indhealth.2018-0018 PMID: 29973467

Horne, J. A., & Östberg, O. (1977). Individual differences in human circadian rhythms. *Biological Psychology*, *5*(3), 179–190. DOI: 10.1016/0301-0511(77)90001-1 PMID: 922076

Horwitz, I. B., & McCall, B. P. (2004). The impact of shift work on the risk and severity of injuries for hospitalemployees: An analysis using Oregon workers' compensation data. *Occupational Medicine*, *54*(8), 556–563. DOI: 10.1093/occmed/kqh093 PMID: 15385648

Hunt, V., Rasmussen, E., & Lamm, F. (2010). *Call Centre Work and Health and Safety Issues*. Labour, Employment and Work in New Zealand., DOI: 10.26686/lew.v0i0.1677

Jaradat, Y., Nielsen, M. B., Kristensen, P., Nijem, K., Bjertness, E., Stigum, H., & Bast-Pettersen, R. (2016). Workplace aggression, psychological distress, and job satisfaction among Palestinian nurses: A cross-sectional study. *Applied Nursing Research*, *32*, 190–198. DOI: 10.1016/j.apnr.2016.07.014 PMID: 27969027

Juda, M., Vetter, C., & Roenneberg, T. (2013). Chronotype Modulates Sleep Duration, Sleep Quality, and Social Jet Lag in Shift-Workers. *Journal of Biological Rhythms*, *28*(2), 141–151. DOI: 10.1177/0748730412475042 PMID: 23606613

Kalmbach, D. A., Schneider, L. D., Cheung, J., Bertrand, S. J., Kariharan, T., Pack, A. I., & Gehrman, P. R. (2017). Genetic Basis of Chronotype in Humans: Insights From Three Landmark GWAS. *Sleep (Basel)*, *40*(2). Advance online publication. DOI: 10.1093/sleep/zsw048 PMID: 28364486

Kaushik, P., Askari, K., Gupta, S., Mohan, R., & Skrinak, K. (n.d.). On Automated, Continuous Chronotyping from a Daily Calendar using. *Machine Learning*.

Keecklund, G., & Axelsson, J. (2016). Health consequences of shift work and insufficient sleep. *BMJ (Clinical Research Ed.)*, *5210*, i5210. Advance online publication. DOI: 10.1136/bmj.i5210 PMID: 27803010

Khamisa, N., Peltzer, K., Ilic, D., & Oldenburg, B. (2017). Effect of personal and work stress on burnout, job satisfaction and general health of hospital nurses in South Africa. *Health SA = SA Gesondheid*, *22*, 252–258. DOI: 10.1016/j.hsag.2016.10.001

Killgore, W. D. S. (2007). Effects of Sleep Deprivation and Morningness-Eveningness Traits on Risk-Taking. *Psychological Reports*, *100*(2), 613–626. DOI: 10.2466/pr0.100.2.613-626 PMID: 17564238

Kim, S., & Kim, S. J. (2020). Psychometric Properties of Questionnaires for Assessing Chronotype. *Chronobiology in Medicine*, *2*(1), 16–20. DOI: 10.33069/cim.2020.0003

Kleitman, N. (1964). The Evolutionary Theory of Sleep and Wakefulness. *Perspectives in Biology and Medicine*, *7*(2), 169–178. DOI: 10.1353/pbm.1964.0053 PMID: 14111141

Knapen, S. E., Gordijn, M. C. M., & Meesters, Y. (2016). The relation between chronotype and treatment outcome with light therapy on a fixed time schedule. *Journal of Affective Disorders*, *202*, 87–90. DOI: 10.1016/j.jad.2016.05.009 PMID: 27259079

Knutsson, A., & Bøggild, H. (2000). Shiftwork and Cardiovascular Disease: Review of Disease Mechanisms. *Reviews on Environmental Health*, *15*(4). Advance online publication. DOI: 10.1515/REVEH.2000.15.4.359 PMID: 11199246

Lee, K.-W., Yang, C.-C., Chen, C.-H., Hung, C.-H., & Chuang, H.-Y. (2023). Shift work is significantly and positively associated with dementia: A meta-analysis study. *Frontiers in Public Health*, *11*, 998464. DOI: 10.3389/fpubh.2023.998464 PMID: 36875407

Levandovski, R., Dantas, G., Fernandes, L. C., Caumo, W., Torres, I., Roenneberg, T., Hidalgo, M. P. L., & Allebrandt, K. V. (2011). Depression Scores Associate With Chronotype and Social Jetlag in a Rural Population. *Chronobiology International*, *28*(9), 771–778. DOI: 10.3109/07420528.2011.602445 PMID: 21895489

Lo, J. C., Groeger, J. A., Cheng, G. H., Dijk, D.-J., & Chee, M. W. L. (2016). Self-reported sleep duration and cognitive performance in older adults: A systematic review and meta-analysis. *Sleep Medicine*, *17*, 87–98. DOI: 10.1016/j.sleep.2015.08.021 PMID: 26847980

Meerlo, P., Sgoifo, A., & Suchecki, D. (2008). Restricted and disrupted sleep: Effects on autonomic function, neuroendocrine stress systems and stress responsivity. *Sleep Medicine Reviews, 12*(3), 197–210. DOI: 10.1016/j.smrv.2007.07.007 PMID: 18222099

Messenger, J. (n.d.). *Working time and the future of work.*

Mills, P. R., Tomkins, S. C., & Schlangen, L. J. (2007). The effect of high correlated colour temperature office lighting on employee wellbeing and work performance. *Journal of Circadian Rhythms, 5*(0), 2. DOI: 10.1186/1740-3391-5-2 PMID: 17217543

Montaruli, A., Castelli, L., Galasso, L., Mulè, A., Bruno, E., Esposito, F., Caumo, A., & Roveda, E. (2019). Effect of chronotype on academic achievement in a sample of Italian University students. *Chronobiology International, 36*(11), 1482–1495. DOI: 10.1080/07420528.2019.1652831 PMID: 31441334

Montaruli, A., Castelli, L., Mulè, A., Scurati, R., Esposito, F., Galasso, L., & Roveda, E. (2021). Biological Rhythm and Chronotype: New Perspectives in Health. *Biomolecules, 11*(4), 487. DOI: 10.3390/biom11040487 PMID: 33804974

Paine, S.-J., Gander, P. H., & Travier, N. (2006). The Epidemiology of Morningness/Eveningness: Influence of Age, Gender, Ethnicity, and Socioeconomic Factors in Adults (30-49 Years). *Journal of Biological Rhythms, 21*(1), 68–76. DOI: 10.1177/0748730405283154 PMID: 16461986

Philip, P., Sagaspe, P., Taillard, J., Moore, N., Guilleminault, C., Sanchez-Ortuno, M., Åkerstedt, T., & Bioulac, B. (2003). Fatigue, Sleep Restriction, and Performance in Automobile Drivers: A Controlled Study in a Natural Environment. *Sleep, 26*(3), 277–280. DOI: 10.1093/sleep/26.3.277 PMID: 12749545

Phoi, Y. Y., & Keogh, J. B. (2019). Dietary Interventions for Night Shift Workers: A Literature Review. *Nutrients, 11*(10), 2276. DOI: 10.3390/nu11102276 PMID: 31547547

Preckel, F., Lipnevich, A. A., Schneider, S., & Roberts, R. D. (2011). Chronotype, cognitive abilities, and academic achievement: A meta-analytic investigation. *Learning and Individual Differences, 21*(5), 483–492. DOI: 10.1016/j.lindif.2011.07.003

Prodromidis, N., Karlsson, M., & Kühnle, D. (2025). Working Hours and Workers' Health: Evidence from a National Experiment in Sweden. SSRN *Electronic Journal.* DOI: 10.2139/ssrn.5142319

Purnell, M. T., Feyer, A.-M., & Herbison, G. P. (2002). The impact of a nap opportunity during the night shift on the performance and alertness of 12-h shift workers. *Journal of Sleep Research, 11*(3), 219–227. DOI: 10.1046/j.1365-2869.2002.00309.x PMID: 12220318

Rahman, S. A., St. Hilaire, M. A., Grant, L. K., Barger, L. K., Brainard, G. C., Czeisler, C. A., Klerman, E. B., & Lockley, S. W. (2022). Dynamic lighting schedules to facilitate circadian adaptation to shifted timing of sleep and wake. *Journal of Pineal Research, 73*(1), e12805. DOI: 10.1111/jpi.12805 PMID: 35501292

Rajaratnam, S. M., & Arendt, J. (2001). Health in a 24-h society. *Lancet, 358*(9286), 999–1005. DOI: 10.1016/S0140-6736(01)06108-6 PMID: 11583769

Randler, C. (2008). Morningness-Eveningness Comparison in Adolescents from Different Countries around the World. *Chronobiology International, 25*(6), 1017–1028. DOI: 10.1080/07420520802551519 PMID: 19005902

Razavi, P., Devore, E. E., Bajaj, A., Lockley, S. W., Figueiro, M. G., Ricchiuti, V., Gauderman, W. J., Hankinson, S. E., Willett, W. C., & Schernhammer, E. S. (2019). Shift Work, Chronotype, and Melatonin Rhythm in Nurses. *Cancer Epidemiology, Biomarkers & Prevention, 28*(7), 1177–1186. DOI: 10.1158/1055-9965.EPI-18-1018 PMID: 31142495

Reid, K. J. (2019). Assessment of Circadian Rhythms. *Neurologic Clinics, 37*(3), 505–526. DOI: 10.1016/j.ncl.2019.05.001 PMID: 31256786

Reppert, S. M., & Weaver, D. R. (2002). Coordination of circadian timing in mammals. *Nature, 418*(6901), 935–941. DOI: 10.1038/nature00965 PMID: 12198538

Reutrakul, S., Hood, M. M., Crowley, S. J., Morgan, M. K., Teodori, M., Knutson, K. L., & Van Cauter, E. (2013). Chronotype Is Independently Associated With Glycemic Control in Type 2 Diabetes. *Diabetes Care, 36*(9), 2523–2529. DOI: 10.2337/dc12-2697 PMID: 23637357

Robertson, M. M., Huang, Y., & Larson, N. (2016). The relationship among computer work, environmental design, and musculoskeletal and visual discomfort: Examining the moderating role of supervisory relations and co-worker support. *International Archives of Occupational and Environmental Health, 89*(1), 7–22. DOI: 10.1007/s00420-015-1046-x PMID: 25827942

Roenneberg, T. (2015). Having Trouble Typing? What on Earth Is Chronotype? *Journal of Biological Rhythms, 30*(6), 487–491. DOI: 10.1177/0748730415603835 PMID: 26446872

Roenneberg, T., Allebrandt, K. V., Merrow, M., & Vetter, C. (2012). Social Jetlag and Obesity. *Current Biology*, *22*(10), 939–943. DOI: 10.1016/j.cub.2012.03.038 PMID: 22578422

Roenneberg, T., Chua, E. J., Bernardo, R., & Mendoza, E. (2008). Modelling Biological Rhythms. *Current Biology*, *18*(17), R826–R835. DOI: 10.1016/j.cub.2008.07.017 PMID: 18786388

Roenneberg, T., Kuehnle, T., Juda, M., Kantermann, T., Allebrandt, K., Gordijn, M., & Merrow, M. (2007). Epidemiology of the human circadian clock. *Sleep Medicine Reviews*, *11*(6), 429–438. DOI: 10.1016/j.smrv.2007.07.005 PMID: 17936039

Roenneberg, T., Kumar, C. J., & Merrow, M. (2007). The human circadian clock entrains to sun time. *Current Biology*, *17*(2), R44–R45. DOI: 10.1016/j.cub.2006.12.011 PMID: 17240323

Roenneberg, T., Pilz, L. K., Zerbini, G., & Winnebeck, E. C. (2019). Chronotype and Social Jetlag: A (Self-) Critical Review. *Biology (Basel)*, *8*(3), 54. DOI: 10.3390/biology8030054 PMID: 31336976

Roenneberg, T., Wirz-Justice, A., & Merrow, M. (2003). Life between Clocks: Daily Temporal Patterns of Human Chronotypes. *Journal of Biological Rhythms*, *18*(1), 80–90. DOI: 10.1177/0748730402239679 PMID: 12568247

Rogers, A. E., Hwang, W.-T., Scott, L. D., Aiken, L. H., & Dinges, D. F. (2004). The Working Hours Of Hospital Staff Nurses And Patient Safety. *Health Affairs*, *23*(4), 202–212. DOI: 10.1377/hlthaff.23.4.202 PMID: 15318582

Rosa, D. E., Marot, L. P., De Mello, M. T., Marqueze, E. C., Narciso, F. V., De Araújo, L. B., & Crispim, C. A. (2021). Association between chronotype and psychomotor performance of rotating shift workers. *Scientific Reports*, *11*(1), 6919. DOI: 10.1038/s41598-021-86299-8 PMID: 33767333

Saksvik, I. B., Bjorvatn, B., Hetland, H., Sandal, G. M., & Pallesen, S. (2011). Individual differences in tolerance to shift work – A systematic review. *Sleep Medicine Reviews*, *15*(4), 221–235. DOI: 10.1016/j.smrv.2010.07.002 PMID: 20851006

Stimpfel, A. W., Sloane, D. M., & Aiken, L. H. (2012). The Longer The Shifts For Hospital Nurses, The Higher The Levels Of Burnout And Patient Dissatisfaction. *Health Affairs*, *31*(11), 2501–2509. DOI: 10.1377/hlthaff.2011.1377 PMID: 23129681

Swanson, L. M., Arnedt, J. T., Rosekind, M. R., Belenky, G., Balkin, T. J., & Drake, C. (2011). Sleep disorders and work performance: Findings from the 2008 National Sleep Foundation Sleep in America poll: Sleep disorders and work performance. *Journal of Sleep Research, 20*(3), 487–494. DOI: 10.1111/j.1365-2869.2010.00890.x PMID: 20887396

Using Artificial Intelligence in the workplace: What are the main ethical risks? (OECD Social, Employment and Migration Working Papers 273; OECD Social, Employment and Migration Working Papers, Vol. 273). (2022). DOI: 10.1787/1815199X

Vanini, G. (2024). Are orexins–hypocretins the culprit for rapid eye movement sleep behavior disorder in narcolepsy? *Sleep (Basel), 47*(11), zsae208. Advance online publication. DOI: 10.1093/sleep/zsae208 PMID: 39238164

Vaughn, B., Rotolo, S., & Roth, H. (2014). Circadian rhythm and sleep influences on digestive physiology and disorders. *ChronoPhysiology and Therapy, 67*, 67. Advance online publication. DOI: 10.2147/CPT.S44806

Vetter, C., Devore, E. E., Ramin, C. A., Speizer, F. E., Willett, W. C., & Schernhammer, E. S. (2015). Mismatch of Sleep and Work Timing and Risk of Type 2 Diabetes. *Diabetes Care, 38*(9), 1707–1713. DOI: 10.2337/dc15-0302 PMID: 26109502

Vetter, C., Fischer, D., Matera, J. L., & Roenneberg, T. (2015). Aligning Work and Circadian Time in Shift Workers Improves Sleep and Reduces Circadian Disruption. *Current Biology, 25*(7), 907–911. DOI: 10.1016/j.cub.2015.01.064 PMID: 25772446

Wagstaff, A. S., & Sigstad Lie, J.-A. (2011). Shift and night work and long working hours – a systematic review of safety implications. *Scandinavian Journal of Work, Environment & Health, 37*(3), 173–185. DOI: 10.5271/sjweh.3146 PMID: 21290083

Wang, Z.-Z., Sun, Z., Zhang, M.-L., Xiong, K., & Zhou, F. (2022). Relationship between shift work, night work, and subsequent dementia: A systematic evaluation and meta-analysis. *Frontiers in Neurology, 13*, 997181. DOI: 10.3389/fneur.2022.997181 PMID: 36419534

Weitzman, E. D., Fukushima, D., Nogeire, C., Roffwarg, H., Gallagher, T. F., & Hellman, L. (1971). Twenty-four Hour Pattern of the Episodic Secretion of Cortisol in Normal Subjects. *The Journal of Clinical Endocrinology and Metabolism, 33*(1), 14–22. DOI: 10.1210/jcem-33-1-14 PMID: 4326799

Wickwire, E. M., Geiger-Brown, J., Scharf, S. M., & Drake, C. L. (2017). Shift Work and Shift Work Sleep Disorder. *Chest, 151*(5), 1156–1172. DOI: 10.1016/j.chest.2016.12.007 PMID: 28012806

Wittmann, M., Dinich, J., Merrow, M., & Roenneberg, T. (2006). Social Jetlag: Misalignment of Biological and Social Time. *Chronobiology International*, *23*(1–2), 497–509. DOI: 10.1080/07420520500545979 PMID: 16687322

Wittmann, M., Paulus, M., & Roenneberg, T. (2010). Decreased Psychological Well-Being in Late 'Chronotypes' Is Mediated by Smoking and Alcohol Consumption. *Substance Use & Misuse*, *45*(1–2), 15–30. DOI: 10.3109/10826080903498952 PMID: 20025436

Wolkowitz, O. M., Epel, E. S., & Reus, V. I. (2001). Stress Hormone-Related Psychopathology: Pathophysiological and Treatment Implications. *The World Journal of Biological Psychiatry*, *2*(3), 115–143. DOI: 10.3109/15622970109026799 PMID: 12587196

Wright, K. P.Jr, Bogan, R. K., & Wyatt, J. K. (2013). Shift work and the assessment and management of shift work disorder (SWD). *Sleep Medicine Reviews*, *17*(1), 41–54. DOI: 10.1016/j.smrv.2012.02.002 PMID: 22560640

Xie, Z., Chen, F., Li, W. A., Geng, X., Li, C., Meng, X., Feng, Y., Liu, W., & Yu, F. (2017). A review of sleep disorders and melatonin. *Neurological Research*, *39*(6), 559–565. DOI: 10.1080/01616412.2017.1315864 PMID: 28460563

KEY TERMS AND DEFINITIONS

Chronobiology: The scientific study of biological rhythms, including circadian, ultradian, and infradian cycles, and their impact on physiological processes, behavior, and overall health.

Circadian Rhythms: Approximately 24-hour biological cycles that regulate sleep-wake patterns, hormone secretion, metabolism, and cognitive function, synchronized by environmental cues such as light and darkness.

Chronotype: An individual's natural preference for activity and alertness at specific times of the day, typically classified as morning type (lark), evening type (owl), or intermediate type.

Social Jetlag: A misalignment between an individual's internal biological clock and socially imposed schedules, such as early work start times or shift work, leading to sleep deprivation and health consequences.

Shift Work Disorder (SWD): A condition characterized by chronic sleep disturbances, fatigue, and impaired cognitive function resulting from irregular or night shift work that disrupts circadian rhythms.

Melatonin: A hormone produced by the pineal gland in response to darkness, playing a crucial role in regulating sleep and synchronizing circadian rhythms.

Suprachiasmatic Nucleus (SCN): The master clock located in the hypothalamus that regulates circadian rhythms by responding to light signals from the retina and coordinating physiological processes.

Workplace Fatigue: A state of physical and mental exhaustion caused by prolonged work hours, circadian misalignment, or insufficient restorative sleep, leading to reduced productivity and increased risk of errors.

Chronotype-Based Scheduling: A workplace strategy that aligns employee work hours with their biological chronotype to optimize productivity, mental well-being, and job satisfaction.

Artificial Light Exposure: The impact of blue light from electronic devices or workplace lighting on circadian rhythms, particularly its role in delaying melatonin production and disrupting sleep cycles.

Flexible Work Arrangements: Work schedules that allow employees to adjust their hours based on their biological rhythms, improving work-life balance, reducing stress, and enhancing overall job performance.

Sleep Hygiene: A set of practices and environmental factors that promote healthy sleep, including maintaining a consistent sleep schedule, reducing light exposure before bed, and optimizing sleep environments

Chapter 12
Deep Learning and Big Data for Biomedical Image Processing in Employee Health:
Sparking a Digital Twin in an Era of Lifestyle Upheaval

Bhupinder Singh
https://orcid.org/0009-0006-4779-2553
Sharda University, India

Kittisak Wongmahesak
https://orcid.org/0009-0000-2129-4691
North Bangkok University, Thailand

ABSTRACT

Digital twins emerge as the cornerstone, ushering in an era of personalized healthcare and wellness recommendations. It guides the reader through the intricate network of Big Data and explains its crucial role in the examination of biological images. The foundation of these cutting-edge fields is the creation of digital twins, complex virtual depictions of individual health profiles. This chapter is about improving employees health, advocating for preventative care and providing people with the knowledge and resources they need to take control of their own lives. Simultaneously, it navigates the dynamic IoT ecosystem, revealing its multifaceted contributions to real-time health data acquisition. Deep learning with its neural networks and convolutional prowess, further enhances our understanding and interpretation of biomedical images.

DOI: 10.4018/979-8-3373-2210-0.ch012

Copyright © 2025, IGI Global Scientific Publishing. Copying or distributing in print or electronic forms without written permission of IGI Global Scientific Publishing is prohibited.

1. INTRODUCTION

The sheer volume, velocity, and variety of biomedical data demand sophisticated analytics and storage solutions, driving the need for scalable and efficient frameworks. As it navigate this data-driven landscape, the paper aims to unravel the complexities of utilizing Big Data in the context of biomedical image processing, emphasizing its role in enhancing precision, improving diagnostic accuracy, and fostering real-time analytics for informed decision-making.

Concurrently, the Internet of Things has infiltrated the healthcare sector, establishing a smooth network of information by tying together gadgets, sensors, and wearables. This networked network of intelligent medical equipment makes it possible to monitor patients continuously, do remote diagnostics, and give people the power to take an active role in their own health. In this article, the many uses of IoT in healthcare will be examined, from wearables that track vital signs to smart hospitals with IoT-enabled infrastructure (Sejdic & Falk, 2018). By examining the impact of the IoT universe on healthcare, the research aims to showcase its potential to revolutionize patient care, improve treatment outcomes, and elevate the overall quality of health services.

Through deep learning, computers learn to recognize patterns, anomalies, and subtle nuances in medical images, assisting radiologists and clinicians in diagnostics and treatment planning. Furthermore, AI-powered virtual assistants are emerging as intelligent interfaces for patients, offering real-time health recommendations and support. At the heart of this technological synergy lies the digital twin, an amalgamation of Big Data analytics, IoT data streams, and deep learning algorithms. Digital twins are personalized avatars, encapsulating an individual's health status. They herald an era of personalized treatment, preventive healthcare, and wellness management.

The transformative potential is evident across the healthcare spectrum, from precision medicine and proactive interventions to enhancing diagnostic accuracy and democratizing remote healthcare access. It becomes evident that the impact of this convergence extends beyond the realm of healthcare. Policy frameworks, ethical considerations, and data governance become paramount, necessitating interdisciplinary collaboration. The healthcare revolution catalyzed by Big Data, IoT, and deep learning is not an isolated phenomenon but a precursor to a broader upheaval in lifestyle management. Through illuminating case studies, this article underscores how organizations harness this transformative synergy to craft digital twins, providing personalized healthcare and wellness recommendations that empower individuals to lead healthier lives.

Moreover, the utilization of transfer learning in the medical domain will be scrutinized, shedding light on its capacity to leverage pre-trained models for specific medical imaging applications. This wealth of information enables more accurate and timely diagnosis, treatment planning, and medical research. Big Data is not merely about volume; it's about leveraging this data to derive insights, optimize healthcare delivery, and personalize treatment.

In the pursuit of a holistic healthcare approach, the concept of Digital Twins has gained prominence. Digital Twins represent virtual replicas of real-world entities, in this case, individuals and their health profiles. This paper will investigate the construction and implementation of Digital Twins in healthcare, emphasizing their role in personalized medicine and treatment strategies.

The synergistic effect of Big Data, IoT, and Deep Learning extends beyond the interactions between individual patients to community health management, epidemiological study, and medical research progress.

2. DIGITAL TWINS AND THEIR ROLE IN PERSONALIZING HEALTHCARE AND LIFESTYLE MANAGEMENT

The implementation of digital twins in healthcare and lifestyle management is not without challenges. Ethical considerations related to data privacy, security, and the responsible use of personal health information must be carefully navigated. Striking a balance between the benefits of personalization and the protection of individual privacy is imperative to ensure the widespread acceptance and adoption of digital twin technologies.

As the digital twin paradigm continues to evolve, its impact on shaping a more personalized, preventive, and participatory healthcare model is poised to redefine the future of healthcare and lifestyle management.

Identify challenges and offer recommendations for overcoming ethical, legal, and technical hurdles to ensure responsible and effective implementation in the evolving healthcare landscape.

3. SCOPE OF CHAPTER

The scope of this chapter is to comprehensively explore the integration and synergies among Big Data, IoT and Deep Learning in the context of biomedical image processing and employees health. The chapter is into the multifaceted applications and implications of these cutting-edge technologies, with a particular focus on the construction and impact of Digital Twins in healthcare (Panesar, 2019). The following key aspects encapsulate the scope of the paper as-

Big Data Integration: Investigate the effective integration of Big Data in the domain of biomedical image processing, emphasizing its role in managing large datasets, facilitating real-time analytics, and enhancing precision in diagnostics and treatment planning.

IoT in Healthcare: Explore the expansive applications of the Internet of Things in healthcare, encompassing wearable devices, sensors, and smart hospitals. Analyze how the interconnected nature of IoT devices contributes to continuous patient monitoring, remote diagnostics, and overall improvements in healthcare delivery.

Deep Learning in Biomedical Imaging: Scrutinize the application of Deep Learning techniques, including Convolutional Neural Networks (CNNs) and Recurrent Neural Networks (RNNs), in biomedical image processing. Examine their potential for automating tasks, improving image analysis, and revolutionizing medical diagnostics.

Digital Twins Construction: Investigate the concept and implementation of Digital Twins in healthcare. Assess how Digital Twins create virtual replicas of individuals, incorporating physiological, genetic, and lifestyle data for personalized medicine, treatment strategies, and proactive healthcare management.

Ethical and Privacy Considerations: Address ethical and privacy considerations associated with the integration of Big Data, IoT, and Deep Learning in healthcare, with a specific focus on the construction and utilization of Digital Twins. Explore potential challenges and propose solutions to ensure responsible and ethical implementation.

By exploring these facets, the paper aims to provide a comprehensive understanding of the integrated role of Big Data, IoT, and Deep Learning in biomedical image processing, with a particular emphasis on the transformative potential and ethical considerations of Digital Twins in healthcare and lifestyle management (Sengan et al., 2020).

4. BIG DATA IN BIOMEDICAL IMAGE PROCESSING

Considering the fine features obtained by contemporary imaging modalities, managing huge datasets is one of the main issues in biomedical image processing. Research on population health benefits from the use of big data in biomedical image processing. Researchers can detect risk factors, detect epidemiological patterns, and create evidence-based medical practices by compiling and evaluating huge datasets. Large-scale datasets offer valuable insights that can influence public health policies and provide policymakers with information, ultimately leading to the progress of healthcare for all.

The large datasets may be quickly processed and analyzed using big data analytics in biomedical image processing, giving doctors access to real-time information that is essential for precise diagnosis and therapy planning. Big Data frameworks that use machine learning algorithms improve these systems' interpretive powers by allowing the detection of minute patterns and correlations in medical pictures.

With regard to biomedical image processing in particular, the idea of big data in healthcare is a game-changer for contemporary medicine. By enabling medical practitioners to leverage the abundance of data contained in medical imaging, it propels improvements in medical research, diagnosis, and therapy customisation. The incorporation of Big Data analytics into biomedical image processing has the potential to significantly advance our capacity to realize the whole potential of medical imaging for better patient care as technology advances.

4.1 Difficulties in Managing Extensive Biomedical Imaging Datasets

Ensuring seamless and timely access to these datasets across different platforms and locations is crucial for fostering collaborative research efforts and facilitating data-driven healthcare.

The heterogeneity of biomedical image datasets poses another substantial challenge. Different imaging modalities, resolutions, and data formats create a complex landscape. Efficient computational processing is a critical challenge in handling large-scale biomedical image datasets. The computational demands for tasks such as image segmentation, feature extraction, and machine learning applications can overwhelm traditional computing infrastructures. Adopting advanced computational resources, including high-performance computing clusters and GPUs, becomes imperative to meet the processing demands of these datasets and enable timely analyses.

So, handling large-scale biomedical image datasets presents multifaceted challenges that span technical, computational, security, and ethical considerations. Overcoming these challenges requires the collaborative efforts of researchers, clinicians, and technologists to develop and implement innovative solutions that ensure the effective use of these datasets for advancements in medical research and improved patient care.

4.2 Enhance Image-based Diagnosis, Treatment Planning and Medical Research: Big Data Analytics

In the image-based diagnosis, big data analytics enables the extraction of intricate patterns and features within medical images that may elude the employees eye. Treatment planning, too, benefits significantly from big data analytics in the context of biomedical imaging. By analyzing large datasets encompassing diverse patient profiles, treatment outcomes, and responses to various interventions, clinicians can tailor treatment plans to individual patients. Predictive modeling facilitated by big data analytics aids in forecasting patient responses to specific therapies, optimizing treatment strategies, and minimizing adverse effects.

Moreover, Population-level studies become more robust, allowing for the identification of epidemiological trends, risk factors, and public health challenges.

5. IOT UNIVERSE IN HEALTHCARE

The important aspect of the Internet of Things in the healthcare industry is wearable technology. These gadgets let users to continually monitor a variety of health parameters, including heart rate, physical activity, and sleep patterns. They range from fitness trackers to smartwatches with health monitoring functions. By encouraging healthier lifestyle choices and preventative steps, this real-time data allows people to take a more active part in managing their health.

IoT applications cover a wider range of medical devices and sensors in healthcare facilities than just personal wearables. For example, IoT technology is used by remote patient monitoring systems to provide real-time health data and vital signs from patients' homes to healthcare practitioners. This not only facilitates timely interventions but also reduces the need for frequent hospital visits, enhancing the overall patient experience while optimizing healthcare resources.

The IoT universe enables the creation of intelligent healthcare ecosystems. Ambient assisted living solutions, for example, leverage smart sensors and IoT technology to monitor the well-being of elderly or chronically ill individuals in their homes. These systems can detect deviations from normal behavior patterns, providing early indications of potential health issues and triggering appropriate interventions, thereby promoting independent living and reducing the burden on formal healthcare services.

5.1 IoT Ecosystem and its Components: Sensors, Devices and Data Connectivity

The diversity of IoT devices spans across consumer electronics, healthcare equipment, smart home appliances, and industrial machinery, illustrating the breadth of applications within the IoT ecosystem. Data connectivity is the linchpin that binds sensors and devices into a cohesive IoT ecosystem. Robust and reliable connectivity enables the seamless exchange of information between devices and the central data processing infrastructure, whether it be cloud-based servers or edge computing systems. The connectivity protocols may include Wi-Fi, Bluetooth, cellular networks, or specialized low-power wide-area networks (LPWANs), depending on the specific requirements of the IoT application. The integration of 5G technology further enhances the speed and capacity of data transmission, unlocking new possibilities for real-time communication and data-intensive applications.

However, the proliferation of IoT also brings forth challenges, including security and privacy concerns, interoperability issues, and the need for standardized protocols.

5.2 Remote Patient Monitoring, Real-time Data Collection and Patient Engagement: IoT Applications in Healthcare

With the introduction of remote patient monitoring, real-time data gathering, and improved patient involvement, the Internet of Things (IoT) applications in healthcare have undergone a paradigm change. These linked technologies are transforming the way that healthcare is delivered by enabling prompt, individualized care, enhancing patient outcomes, and encouraging people to take a more proactive approach to maintaining their health.

Using IoT-enabled devices, remote patient monitoring (RPM) gathers and sends real-time health data from patients in their homes to healthcare practitioners. Sensor-equipped wearables keep an eye on vital signs, medication compliance, and other pertinent health data. Healthcare providers may remotely monitor patients' health state, identify warning signals, and take preemptive measures, especially for patients with chronic diseases, thanks to this constant stream of data. By lowering the need for repeated hospital visits, this IoT application not only improves treatment quality but also lessens the strain on the healthcare system (Ariffin et al., 2021).

The essential component of IoT applications in healthcare is real-time data gathering, which makes it possible to transfer patient data from several sources instantly to centralized systems. Numerous pieces of information are included in this data, such as vital signs, test findings, and outcomes as reported by the patient. Healthcare professionals may now make well-informed decisions more quickly because to the integration of real-time data, which enhances overall care coordination, treatment planning, and diagnostic accuracy. This dynamic information flow is especially helpful in emergency circumstances where prompt action is essential (Bao et al., 2019).

IoT applications have greatly improved patient involvement, leading to a more cooperative and participatory approach to healthcare. Individuals are empowered to actively monitor and control their health with IoT-enabled devices and applications. Through mobile applications and linked devices, patients may get individualized insights, monitor their progress, and obtain pertinent health information. This degree of involvement helps patients stick to treatment programs, preventative measures, and general lifestyle changes better in addition to fostering a sense of empowerment.

However, there are obstacles to the integration of these IoT applications in the healthcare industry, including the requirement for interoperability standards, privacy issues, and data security. Ensuring the safe transfer of data and protecting sensitive patient information are critical to preserving confidence in these technologies (Zhou et al., 2021). In order to facilitate smooth communication between various systems and devices and guarantee that the gathered data may be efficiently used for all-encompassing healthcare delivery, interoperability standards are essential.

The healthcare industry is changing as a result of the confluence of real-time data gathering, remote patient monitoring, and patient involvement with IoT applications. These innovations demonstrate the revolutionary potential of IoT in boosting the general patient experience and increasing healthcare outcomes by providing proactive, individualized, and patient-centered treatment. Resolving issues and making sure responsible deployment are crucial to achieving the full potential of these applications in healthcare as the IoT ecosystem develops.

6. DEEP LEARNING FOR BIOMEDICAL IMAGE PROCESSING

The popular type of Deep Learning architecture called Convolutional Neural Networks (CNNs) is very good at finding patterns and spatial correlations in pictures. CNNs can automatically recognize complex structures, abnormalities, and pertinent biomarkers in the context of medical imaging, greatly minimizing the employees labor and subjectivity often involved in picture interpretation.

Deep Learning techniques are very useful for applications like object recognition and picture segmentation. For the purpose of diagnosis and treatment planning, precise delineation of anatomical structures or diseased areas is essential in medical pictures. It is possible to train Deep Learning models to accurately segment regions of interest, which can help with abnormality identification and quantification.

Within the Deep Learning framework, Recurrent Neural Networks (RNNs) are particularly good at processing sequential data, which makes them useful for applications involving time-series data or dynamic medical imaging, such functional magnetic resonance imaging investigations.

Deep Learning plays a pivotal role in advancing the field of personalized medicine. By analyzing large datasets of patient images and clinical outcomes, Deep Learning models can identify subtle patterns and correlations that may elude traditional analytical approaches.

Deep Learning has ushered in a new era in biomedical image processing, redefining the landscape of medical diagnostics, research, and personalized healthcare. Its capacity to automatically learn and extract intricate patterns from complex image data holds promise for accelerating medical breakthroughs, enhancing diagnostic accuracy, and ultimately improving patient outcomes in the dynamic field of healthcare.

6.1 Fundamentals of Deep Learning, including Neural Networks and Convolutional Neural Networks (CNNs)

Neural Networks: Based on the architecture and operation of real neurons, a neural network is a computer model made up of linked nodes. These artificial neurons, or nodes, are arranged in three levels: an input layer, an output layer, and one or more hidden layers. During the training phase, the network learns by modifying the weights assigned to each link between neurons.

The input layer is where the first data is received. This data might be text, images, or any other kind of data with characteristics.

> Hidden Layers: A sequence of weighted connections is used by these layers to process the incoming data. The quantity of hidden layers in a neural network is referred to as its depth.
>
> Output Layer: The network's output, which reflects the model's judgment or prediction, is created by the last layer.

Labeled training data is fed into the network during the training phase, and then the weights are adjusted to reduce error by comparing the network's predictions to the true labels. Usually, optimization techniques like gradient descent are used for this.

CNNs, or convolutional neural networks, are a particular kind of neural network used to handle structured grid input, like photographs. Because they can learn the spatial hierarchies of features automatically and adaptively, they are very effective in computer vision applications.

Convolutional Layer: The convolutional layer is the fundamental structural component of CNNs. In order to capture the spatial hierarchies of features like edges, textures, and patterns, this layer applies filters or kernels to the incoming data.

Pooling Layer: Following convolution, pooling layers are frequently employed to decrease the spatial dimensions of the data while maintaining crucial characteristics and lowering computational complexity.

Fully Connected Layer: Exactly as in conventional neural networks, the last levels of a CNN are usually fully connected layers. To create predictions or classifications, they employ the traits that were retrieved.

Deep learning has emerged as a potent tool across a range of fields, especially when managing complex data like audio, pictures, and natural language, thanks to the use of neural networks and specialized designs like CNNs. Understanding these fundamentals is crucial for leveraging the potential of deep learning in solving diverse and intricate problems.

6.2 Deep Learning Models: Applied to Process and Analyze Biomedical Images

There are key aspects of how deep learning models are applied to biomedical images:

Image Segmentation: Deep learning models, especially CNNs, excel in image segmentation tasks where the goal is to delineate specific structures or regions of interest within a biomedical image. For example, in medical imaging such as MRI or CT scans, deep learning can automatically segment and identify organs, tumors, or abnormalities, providing precise and quantitative information for diagnosis and treatment planning.

Disease Detection and Classification: Deep learning models are trained on large datasets of annotated medical images to automatically detect and classify diseases. For instance, in radiology, deep learning algorithms can analyze X-rays or mammograms to identify signs of diseases like fractures or breast cancer. Deep learning is used in pathology to identify malignant cells and categorize various tumor kinds from histopathological pictures.

Image Registration and Fusion: By enabling the alignment and fusion of multimodal medical pictures, deep learning enables medical practitioners to combine data from different imaging modalities. This is especially helpful for merging information from PET, CT, and MRI scans, which increases the precision of treatment planning and the comprehensiveness of diagnostic data.

Pharmaceutical Research and Molecular Imaging: Through the analysis of pictures pertaining to cellular and molecular processes, deep learning models in molecular imaging aid in the discovery and development of new drugs.

6.3 Effective Deep Learning Applications for Improved Medical Imaging, Predictive Modeling and Disease Diagnostics

With applications ranging from illness detection and improved medical imaging to predictive modeling, deep learning has shown impressive performance in a number of healthcare fields. Here are some instances of effective deep learning uses in certain fields:

6.3.1 Diagnosis of the Disease

Diabetic Retinopathy: From retinal pictures, deep learning models have demonstrated remarkable effectiveness in diagnosing diabetic retinopathy. By identifying early signs of the condition and analyzing the small alterations in the retina linked to diabetes, these models allow for prompt intervention to avert vision loss.

Pathology Image Analysis: To assess microscopic pictures of tissue samples, deep learning is employed in pathology. These models can help pathologists diagnose patients more quickly and accurately by identifying anomalies and malignant cells.

Deep learning models have made significant progress in the diagnosis of a range of medical diseases using radiological images in the fields of radiology and medical imaging. Deep learning algorithms, for instance, may recognize irregularities suggestive of lung disorders or identify pneumonia in chest X-rays, leading to more rapid and precise diagnosis.

6.3.2 Medical Imaging Enhancement

Image Denoising and Reconstruction: By lowering noise and artifacts, deep learning models improve the quality of medical images. This is especially helpful for computed tomography (CT) and magnetic resonance imaging (MRI), where clear images are essential for precise diagnosis.

Super-Resolution Imaging: By applying deep learning techniques, medical picture resolution is improved, resulting in more accurate and detailed depictions of anatomical features. Applications like increasing the clarity of histopathology pictures or the resolution of ultrasound images can benefit from this.

Image Registration and Fusion: To align and fuse pictures from various modalities, deep learning is used. For example, leveraging deep learning techniques to combine data from PET and MRI scans enables a more thorough knowledge of the structural and functional elements of the observed anatomy.

6.3.3 Forecasting Models

Predicting the Progression of illnesses: To make predictions about the course of illnesses, deep learning models are trained using longitudinal patient data. In the field of neurology, for instance, these models may use patterns in brain imaging and clinical data to forecast how neurodegenerative diseases like Alzheimer's disease will proceed.

Drug Discovery and Response Prediction: To forecast the effectiveness and possible adverse effects of medications, deep learning is used in drug discovery. To find potential medication candidates and forecast each patient's reaction to a particular therapy, models examine biological data and molecular structures.

Population Health Management: Predicting illness patterns at the population level is the uses of deep learning applications. Large datasets, such as imaging and electronic health records, may be analyzed to find risk factors and disease hotspots as well as to develop preventative intervention techniques on a larger scale for public health.

These effective uses of deep learning in healthcare demonstrate how it may advance predictive modeling for improved patient outcomes, improve diagnostic accuracy, and improve medical imaging capabilities (Olshannikova et al., 2015). These applications will probably become more and more important in changing the face of healthcare service and research as technology develops.

7. DIGITAL TWINS IN HEALTHCARE: THEIR SIGNIFICANCE IN HEALTHCARE AND LIFESTYLE MANAGEMENT

By giving patients the tools to actively manage their health, this proactive approach improves overall quality of life, lowers hospitalization rates, and improves disease management. Digital twins have the potential to provide tailored advice for illness prevention and general well-being in the field of preventive healthcare by analyzing lifestyle variables, genetic predispositions, and environmental effects.

For digital twins to be widely used and accepted in the healthcare industry, it is imperative to strike a balance between the potential advantages and guaranteeing the appropriate and secure management of sensitive health data.

The revolutionary potential of digital twins to completely change patient care, treatment plans, and lifestyle management makes them important for the healthcare industry. Digital twins are positioned to be a key component of the healthcare industry's transition to a more proactive, patient-centered, and customized paradigm as technology advances. Their integration has the potential to improve preventative measures, boost health outcomes, and give people more control over their own well-being (Saadat & Shuaib, 2020).

7.1 Big Data, Iot Data Streams and Deep Learning in creating Personalized Digital Twins

Personalized digital twins are the result of a breakthrough advancement in healthcare marked by the combination of big data, Internet of Things (IoT) data streams, and deep learning. Through the use of cutting-edge connectivity, a variety of data sources, and advanced machine learning algorithms, this synergistic approach creates dynamic, extremely detailed virtual representations of particular patients.

This foundation is further enhanced by the addition of IoT data streams, which continually gather real-time data from smart sensors, wearables, and other linked health devices. These streams provide a comprehensive and current picture of an individual's well-being by capturing dynamic health indicators, lifestyle choices, and environmental influences.

To extract relevant insights from these complex datasets, deep learning techniques are essential. Deep learning models are able to recognize intricate patterns, correlations, and prediction linkages through the processing and analysis of integrated big data and IoT streams. These models, which are frequently represented as neural networks, use adaptive learning from the data to identify abnormalities, predict possible health hazards, and identify tiny changes in health markers. The personalized digital twin's accuracy and prediction powers are improved by the deep learning component, making it possible to depict a person's health trajectory more accurately.

As a result, There are further difficulties in integrating deep learning, IoT data streams, and big data to create tailored digital twins. To guarantee the appropriate use of sensitive health information, concerns about data privacy, security, and ethics must be taken into account. Technical obstacles that must be removed for this strategy to be widely adopted include interoperability standards and the smooth integration of various data sources.

A new age in healthcare is being ushered in by the use of big data, IoT data streams, and deep learning in the development of tailored digital twins. A person's health is represented holistically and dynamically, which improves the precision of diagnosis and treatment planning while enabling people to take an active role in their own health care.

8. TRANSFORMING HEALTHCARE AND LIFESTYLE

Big data and Internet of Things (IoT) devices enable digital health platforms, which are essential to this revolution. People may watch their vital signs, sleep habits, and physical activity with wearable technology and health monitoring applications, which provide them real-time health information. People may actively manage their health, make educated lifestyle decisions, and identify any health concerns before they worsen thanks to this constant flow of data. By facilitating remote consultations, tests, and follow-ups, telemedicine integration further improves accessibility to healthcare services. This is especially helpful in circumstances when physical attendance may be difficult.

This change in lifestyle is typified by a move away from general advice and toward customized, data-driven strategies. Individuals may view a live picture of their lifestyle and health using personalized digital twins, which are made possible by the integration of big data, IoT, and deep learning. This thorough knowledge makes it possible to create customized lifestyle programs that include advice on diet, exercise regimens, and stress-reduction techniques. Preventive care and general well-being are prioritized, with a focus shifting from illness treatment to the development of more sustainable and healthful lifestyles. Technology is a key component in helping people change their lifestyles by encouraging better choices and behaviors. People may monitor their sleep habits, diet, and physical activity with the use of smart gadgets, fitness trackers, and mobile applications. These tools provide tailored advice, monitor development, and increase awareness of lifestyle elements that affect general well-being.

The accessibility and provision of healthcare services are also being revolutionized by telehealth and remote healthcare services. People who live in distant or underdeveloped locations may now more easily access healthcare services because to digital health platforms, remote monitoring, and virtual consultations that eliminate geographical barriers.

The transition to digital healthcare not only improves accessibility but also makes healthcare delivery more effective. The change in healthcare and lifestyle is not without difficulties, though. To maintain trust and adherence to legal requirements, concerns about data privacy, security, and the moral use of personal health information must be addressed. For the advantages of transformation to be inclusive and reach a variety of communities, gaps in access to healthcare and technology must also be reduced.

8.1 Transformative Potential of Digital Twins in Healthcare and Lifestyle Management

Digital twins have the potential to revolutionize healthcare and lifestyle management, bringing about a paradigm change in the way that personal well-being is approached. Personalized and dynamic representations of people in the domains of health and lifestyle are being created more and more through the use of digital twins, which are virtual copies that mimic real-world things. This revolutionary potential is shown in a number of crucial areas:

Precision Medicine and Customized Healthcare: Digital twins use data from several sources, including genetics, medical imaging, and electronic health records, to create very personalized and comprehensive representations of people. Thanks to this accuracy, medical professionals can now customize treatment regimens to the unique traits and reactions of each patient, doing away with the need for generic treatments in favor of more focused and efficient interventions.

Proactive Health Monitoring and Early Intervention: Wearable technology and sensors are only a few of the sources of real-time health data that digital twins continually gather and evaluate. Proactive monitoring makes it easier to identify health problems early, which allows for prompt intervention and preventative actions. People may get tailored information on their health, which will enable them to make better decisions and live healthier lifestyles.

Improved Patient Empowerment and Engagement: Digital twins provide people the ability to take an active role in managing their own health. Digital twins encourage involvement and accountability by giving easily available and comprehensible information on their health status, treatment plans, and lifestyle choices. The patient-provider connection is strengthened by this cooperative approach, which also improves health outcomes.

Notwithstanding their revolutionary potential, digital twins in healthcare and lifestyle management have a number of obstacles that must be overcome before they are widely used and accepted, including data privacy, security, ethical issues, and the requirement for interoperability standards.

8.2 Impact on Personalized Treatment, Preventive Healthcare, Wellness Management, Diagnostics and Remote Monitoring

Digital twin integration transforms wellness management by analyzing lifestyle data, habits, and activity levels. Digital twins optimize everyday routines and encourage healthy choices by offering tailored information and recommendations. People get a better awareness of their overall state of health, which makes it easier for them to adopt healthy lifestyle choices that will benefit their health in the long run. Digital twins are used in diagnostics to improve efficiency and accuracy through the use of machine learning algorithms and sophisticated analytics. By supporting preventative actions and enabling people to make educated decisions about their health and adopt risk-reducing lifestyles, this proactive approach lowers the prevalence of illnesses (Teikari et al., 2019).

Digital twins dynamic and real-time characteristics enable ongoing health parameter monitoring, prompt diagnostic method changes, and early illness diagnosis. This enhances the precision of diagnoses and facilitates prompter, more efficient actions. Digital twins are revolutionizing remote monitoring, especially when it comes to managing chronic illnesses. Healthcare practitioners may remotely monitor patients, trace the evolution of diseases, and take action when deviations from typical patterns emerge thanks to the continuous gathering of real-time health data via wearable devices and sensors. This strategy lessens the need for recurrent hospital stays, increases patient comfort, and raises the standard of treatment generally (Pal et al., 2016).

While these advancements hold immense promise, challenges such as data privacy, security, and the ethical use of personal health information must be carefully addressed. Additionally, ensuring interoperability standards for seamless integration of diverse data sources is crucial for the widespread adoption of these technologies. The impact of digital twins on personalized treatment, preventive healthcare, wellness management, diagnostics, and remote monitoring is transformative (Namdech et al., 2025). These technologies are reshaping the healthcare landscape, offering a more patient-centric, proactive, and precise approach to health management, ultimately contributing to improved health outcomes and a more resilient healthcare system.

8.3 Ethical Considerations, Data Privacy and Security Concerns Associated With Digital Twins Implementation

The implementation of digital twins in healthcare raises significant ethical considerations, data privacy concerns, and security challenges, highlighting the need for a thoughtful and responsible approach to their deployment. As these virtual replicas capture and process a wealth of sensitive and personal health information, safeguarding the rights and privacy of individuals becomes paramount.

Ethical concerns arise in the creation and use of digital twins, particularly in areas such as informed consent, transparency, and the potential for unintended consequences. Obtaining informed consent from individuals for the creation and utilization of their digital twins is essential, ensuring that they are aware of how their data will be used, who will have access to it, and for what purposes (Singh & Chandra, 2025). Transparency in the algorithms and decision-making processes within digital twins is crucial to maintaining trust and allowing individuals to understand how decisions about their health are being made (Singh et al., 2025). Furthermore, moral rules and guidelines are required to control the ethical creation and application of digital twins, addressing matters like algorithmic bias, treatment suggestions that are equitable, and responsibility for unfavorable results (Chakraborty & Bhattacharya, 2020).

Safe storage procedures, encryption, and appropriate data anonymization are essential for protecting patient privacy. To stop unwanted access and reduce the chance of data breaches, strict access controls and defined procedures for data sharing must be established. Furthermore, moral rules and guidelines are required to control the ethical creation and application of digital twins, addressing matters like algorithmic bias, treatment suggestions that are equitable, and responsibility for unfavorable results.

The enormous volume of private health information included in digital twins presents a serious threat to data privacy. To keep people's faith in healthcare providers, it is crucial to guarantee the privacy and security of this sensitive data. Safe storage procedures, encryption, and appropriate data anonymization are essential for protecting patient privacy. To stop unwanted access and reduce the chance of data breaches, strict access controls and defined procedures for data sharing must be established.

In addressing these ethical considerations, data privacy concerns, and security challenges associated with digital twin implementation, it is crucial for stakeholders, including healthcare providers, technology developers, and policymakers, to collaborate in developing and adhering to robust ethical frameworks and guidelines. Striking a balance between the potential benefits of digital twins in healthcare and the protection of individuals' rights and privacy is essential to fostering a trusted and responsible environment for their widespread adoption. As technology continues to evolve, ongoing efforts in ethical and privacy considerations will be critical to ensuring the responsible and beneficial use of digital twins in the dynamic landscape of healthcare.

9. CONCLUSION AND FUTURE SCOPE

The confluence of developing technologies will be the driving force behind innovation in digital twins. A richer and more diversified data environment will result from the seamless integration of wearable technology, Internet of Things (IoT) devices, and sophisticated sensors. This will allow digital twins to record a wider range of health-related data. Blockchain technology offers a decentralized, impenetrable structure for handling health data inside the digital twin ecosystem, which shows potential for improving data security and privacy. Furthermore, the collaboration between healthcare providers, technology developers, and regulatory bodies will play a pivotal role in establishing standardized frameworks, ethical guidelines, and interoperability standards to ensure the responsible and widespread adoption of digital twins in healthcare.

REFERENCES

Ahmed, Y. A. E., Yue, B., Gu, Z., & Yang, J. (2023). An overview: Big data analysis by deep learning and image processing. *International Journal of Quantum Information, 21*(7), 2340009. DOI: 10.1142/S0219749923400099

Al-Jarrah, O. Y., Yoo, P. D., Muhaidat, S., Karagiannidis, G. K., & Taha, K. (2015). Efficient machine learning for big data: A review. *Big Data Research, 2*(3), 87–93. DOI: 10.1016/j.bdr.2015.04.001

Ariffin, N. A., Yunus, A. M., & Kadir, I. K. (2021). The role of big data in the healthcare industry. *Journal of Islamic, 6*(36), 235–245.

Bahri, S., Zoghlami, N., Abed, M., & Tavares, J. M. R. (2018). Big data for healthcare: A survey. *IEEE Access : Practical Innovations, Open Solutions, 7*, 7397–7408. DOI: 10.1109/ACCESS.2018.2889180

Bao, Y., Tang, Z., Li, H., & Zhang, Y. (2019). Computer vision and deep learning–based data anomaly detection method for structural health monitoring. *Structural Health Monitoring, 18*(2), 401–421. DOI: 10.1177/1475921718757405

Behura, A., Sahu, S., & Kabat, M. R. (2021). Advancement of Machine Learning and Cloud Computing in the Field of Smart Health Care. *Machine Learning Approach for Cloud Data Analytics in IoT*, 273-306.

Bhattacharyya, D., Stephen Neal Joshua, E., & Thirupathi Rao, N. (2023). Medical Image Analysis of Lung Cancer CT Scans Using Deep Learning with Swarm Optimization Techniques. *Machine Intelligence, Big Data Analytics, and IoT in Image Processing: Practical Applications*, 23-50.

Cabello, J. C., Karimipour, H., Jahromi, A. N., Dehghantanha, A., & Parizi, R. M. (2020). Big-data and cyber-physical systems in healthcare: Challenges and opportunities. *Handbook of Big Data Privacy*, 255-283.

Chakraborty, C., & Bhattacharya, S. (2020). Healthcare data monitoring under Internet of Things. In *Green Computing and Predictive Analytics for Healthcare* (pp. 1–18). Chapman and Hall/CRC. DOI: 10.1201/9780429317224-1

Chen, C. P., & Zhang, C. Y. (2014). Data-intensive applications, challenges, techniques and technologies: A survey on Big Data. *Information Sciences, 275*, 314–347.

Mayer-Schönberger, V., & Cukier, K. (2013). *Big data: A revolution that will transform how we live, work, and think.* Houghton Mifflin Harcourt.

Chen, M., Mao, S., Zhang, Y., & Leung, V. C. (2014). *Big data: related technologies, challenges and future prospects* (Vol. 100). Springer. DOI: 10.1007/978-3-319-06245-7

Dash, S., Shakyawar, S. K., Sharma, M., & Kaushik, S. (2019). Big data in healthcare: Management, analysis and future prospects. *Journal of Big Data*, *6*(1), 1–25. DOI: 10.1186/s40537-019-0217-0

Devika, G., & Karegowda, A. G. (2021). Deep Learning in IoT: Introduction, Applications, and Perspective in the Big Data Era. In *Deep Learning Applications and Intelligent Decision Making in Engineering* (pp. 1-54). IGI Global.

Elbadawi, M., Gaisford, S., & Basit, A. W. (2021). Advanced machine-learning techniques in drug discovery. *Drug Discovery Today*, *26*(3), 769–777. DOI: 10.1016/j.drudis.2020.12.003 PMID: 33290820

Hilbert, M. (2016). Big data for development: A review of promises and challenges. *Development Policy Review*, *34*(1), 135–174. DOI: 10.1111/dpr.12142

Jain, L. (2023). Artificial Intelligence and Machine Learning for Healthcare.

Jordan, M. I., & Mitchell, T. M. (2015). Machine learning: Trends, perspectives, and prospects. *Science*, *349*(6245), 255–260. DOI: 10.1126/science.aaa8415 PMID: 26185243

Kar, U. K., & Dash, R. (2018). Application of Artificial Intelligence in Healthcare: Past, Present and Future. Arch Biomed Eng & Biotechnol. 1 (1). *ABEB. MS. ID, 503*.

Kashyap, H., Ahmed, H. A., Hoque, N., Roy, S., & Bhattacharyya, D. K. (2015). Big data analytics in bioinformatics: A machine learning perspective. *arXiv preprint arXiv:1506.05101*.

Kashyap, H., Ahmed, H. A., Hoque, N., Roy, S., & Bhattacharyya, D. K. (2016). Big data analytics in bioinformatics: Architectures, techniques, tools and issues. *Network Modeling and Analysis in Health Informatics and Bioinformatics*, *5*(1), 1–28. DOI: 10.1007/s13721-016-0135-4

Keikhosrokiani, P. (Ed.). (2022). *Big data analytics for healthcare: datasets, techniques, life cycles, management, and applications*. Academic Press.

Kitchin, R. (2013). Big data and employees geography: Opportunities, challenges and risks. *Dialogues in employees geography, 3*(3), 262-267.

Leung, P. H., Chui, K. T., Lo, K., & de Pablos, P. O. (2021). A support vector machine–based voice disorders detection using employees voice signal. In *Artificial Intelligence and Big Data Analytics for Smart Healthcare* (pp. 197–208). Academic Press. DOI: 10.1016/B978-0-12-822060-3.00014-0

Li, W., Chai, Y., Khan, F., Jan, S. R. U., Verma, S., Menon, V. G., & Li, X. (2021). A comprehensive survey on machine learning-based big data analytics for IoT-enabled smart healthcare system. *Mobile Networks and Applications*, *26*(1), 234–252. DOI: 10.1007/s11036-020-01700-6

Luo, J., Wu, M., Gopukumar, D., & Zhao, Y. (2016). Big data application in biomedical research and health care: a literature review. *Biomedical informatics insights, 8*, BII-S31559.

Malik, S., & Tyagi, A. K. (Eds.). (2022). *Intelligent Interactive Multimedia Systems for E-Healthcare Applications*. CRC Press. DOI: 10.1201/9781003282112

Manyika, J., Chui, M., Brown, B., Bughin, J., Dobbs, R., Roxburgh, C., & Hung Byers, A. (2011). Big data: The next frontier for innovation, competition, and productivity.

Marjani, M., Nasaruddin, F., Gani, A., Karim, A., Hashem, I. A. T., Siddiqa, A., & Yaqoob, I. (2017). Big IoT data analytics: architecture, opportunities, and open research challenges. *ieee access, 5*, 5247-5261.

Miller, D. D., & Brown, E. W. (2018). Artificial intelligence in medical practice: The question to the answer? *The American Journal of Medicine*, *131*(2), 129–133. DOI: 10.1016/j.amjmed.2017.10.035 PMID: 29126825

Mohammadi, M., Al-Fuqaha, A., Sorour, S., & Guizani, M. (2018). Deep learning for IoT big data and streaming analytics: A survey. *IEEE Communications Surveys and Tutorials*, *20*(4), 2923–2960. DOI: 10.1109/COMST.2018.2844341

Monteiro, A. C. B., França, R. P., Arthur, R., & Iano, Y. (2021). An overview of medical Internet of Things, artificial intelligence, and cloud computing employed in health care from a modern panorama. *The Fusion of Internet of Things, Artificial Intelligence, and Cloud Computing in Health Care*, 3-23.

Muthu, B., Sivaparthipan, C. B., Manogaran, G., Sundarasekar, R., Kadry, S., Shanthini, A., & Dasel, A. (2020). IOT based wearable sensor for diseases prediction and symptom analysis in healthcare sector. *Peer-to-Peer Networking and Applications*, *13*(6), 2123–2134. DOI: 10.1007/s12083-019-00823-2

Namdech, P., Rotjanawasuthorn, S., Singh, B., & Kaunert, C. (2025). Harnessing Artificial Intelligence For Lifelong Education: Opportunities And Challenges. *Asian Education and Learning Review*, *3*(2), 4–4.

Olshannikova, E., Ometov, A., Koucheryavy, Y., & Olsson, T. (2015). Visualizing Big Data with augmented and virtual reality: Challenges and research agenda. *Journal of Big Data*, *2*(1), 1–27. DOI: 10.1186/s40537-015-0031-2

Padmaja, M., Shitharth, S., Prasuna, K., Chaturvedi, A., Kshirsagar, P. R., & Vani, A. (2022). Grow of artificial intelligence to challenge security in IoT application. *Wireless Personal Communications*, *127*(3), 1829–1845. DOI: 10.1007/s11277-021-08725-4

Pal, A., Mukherjee, A., & Dey, S. (2016). Future of healthcare—sensor data-driven prognosis. *Wireless World in 2050 and Beyond: A Window into the Future!*, 93-109.

Panesar, A. (2019). *Machine learning and AI for healthcare.* Apress. DOI: 10.1007/978-1-4842-3799-1

Pramanik, P. K. D., Pal, S., & Mukhopadhyay, M. (2022). Healthcare big data: A comprehensive overview. *Research anthology on big data analytics, architectures, and applications*, 119-147.

Qureshi, R., Irfan, M., Ali, H., Khan, A., Nittala, A. S., Ali, S., & Alam, T. (2023). Artificial Intelligence and Biosensors in Healthcare and its Clinical Relevance: A Review. *IEEE Access : Practical Innovations, Open Solutions*, *11*, 61600–61620. DOI: 10.1109/ACCESS.2023.3285596

Reddy, B. M. (2023). Amalgamation of Internet of Things and Machine Learning for Smart Healthcare Applications–A Review. *Int. J Comp. Eng. Sci. Res, 5*, 08-36.

Rodrigues, J. F.Jr, Florea, L., de Oliveira, M. C., Diamond, D., & Oliveira, O. N.Jr. (2021). Big data and machine learning for materials science. *Discover Materials*, *1*(1), 1–27. DOI: 10.1007/s43939-021-00012-0 PMID: 33899049

Rudin, C. (2019). Stop explaining black box machine learning models for high stakes decisions and use interpretable models instead. *Nature Machine Intelligence*, *1*(5), 206–215. DOI: 10.1038/s42256-019-0048-x PMID: 35603010

Saadat, M. N., & Shuaib, M. (2020). Advancements in deep learning theory and applications: Perspective in 2020 and beyond. *Advances and Applications in Deep Learning, 3.*

Scarpato, N., Pieroni, A., Di Nunzio, L., & Fallucchi, F. (2017). E-health-IoT universe: A review. *management, 21*(44), 46.

Sejdic, E., & Falk, T. H. (Eds.). (2018). *Signal processing and machine learning for biomedical big data.* CRC press. DOI: 10.1201/9781351061223

Sengan, S., Kamalam, G. K., Vellingiri, J., Gopal, J., Velayutham, P., & Subramaniyaswamy, V. (2020). Medical information retrieval systems for e-Health care records using fuzzy based machine learning model. *Microprocessors and Microsystems*, •••, 103344.

Shah, F., Li, J., Shah, Y., & Shah, F. (2017, November). Broad big data domain via medical big data. In *2017 4th International Conference on Systems and Informatics (ICSAI)* (pp. 732-737). IEEE.

Shahid, Z. (2021). Distributed Machine Learning for Anomalous Employees Activity Recognition using IoT Systems.

Singh, B., & Chandra, S. (2025). Augmented Reality and Virtual Reality in Health Advancements and Medical Education: Runway for Future Ready Healthcare Services. In R. R., S. Chowdhury, S. Kardy, R. Damaševičius, & R. Govindaraj (Eds.), *Digital Twins for Sustainable Healthcare in the Metaverse* (pp. 197-218). IGI Global Scientific Publishing. https://doi.org/DOI: 10.4018/979-8-3693-4199-5.ch008

Singh, B., Hammouch, H., & Chandra, S. (2025). Innovative Wind Energy Solutions for Smart-Sustainable Communities: Vision for Intelligent Energy Management and Climate Resilience in Industry 5.0. In Mitra, D., Choudhury, T., Madan, A., Chattaraj, S., & Pellegrini, M. (Eds.), *AI Technologies for Enhancing Recycling Processes* (pp. 491–508). IGI Global Scientific Publishing., DOI: 10.4018/979-8-3693-7282-1.ch020

Stephens, Z. D., Lee, S. Y., Faghri, F., Campbell, R. H., Zhai, C., Efron, M. J., & Robinson, G. E. (2015). Big data: Astronomical or genomical? *PLoS Biology*, *13*(7), e1002195. DOI: 10.1371/journal.pbio.1002195 PMID: 26151137

Sukeshini, P. S., Ved, M., Chintalapti, J., & Pal, S. N. (2020). Big Data Analytics and Machine Learning Technologies for HPC. Evolving Technologies for Computing, Communication and Smart World. *Proceedings of ETCCS*, *2020*(694), 411.

Teikari, P., Najjar, R. P., Schmetterer, L., & Milea, D. (2019). Embedded deep learning in ophthalmology: Making ophthalmic imaging smarter. *Therapeutic Advances in Ophthalmology*, *11*, 2515841419827172. DOI: 10.1177/2515841419827172 PMID: 30911733

Thapa, C., & Camtepe, S. (2021). Precision health data: Requirements, challenges and existing techniques for data security and privacy. *Computers in Biology and Medicine*, *129*, 104130. DOI: 10.1016/j.compbiomed.2020.104130 PMID: 33271399

Tiwari, S. K., Kaur, J., Singla, P., & Hrisheekesha, P. N. (2022, September). A Comprehensive Review of Big Data Analysis Techniques in Health-Care. In *International Conference on Emergent Converging Technologies and Biomedical Systems* (pp. 401-420). Singapore: Springer Nature Singapore.

Viceconti, M., Hunter, P., & Hose, R. (2015). Big data, big knowledge: Big data for personalized healthcare. *IEEE Journal of Biomedical and Health Informatics, 19*(4), 1209–1215. DOI: 10.1109/JBHI.2015.2406883 PMID: 26218867

Wu, X., Zhu, X., Wu, G. Q., & Ding, W. (2013). Data mining with big data. *IEEE Transactions on Knowledge and Data Engineering, 26*(1), 97–107.

Zhou, L., Pan, S., Wang, J., & Vasilakos, A. V. (2017). Machine learning on big data: Opportunities and challenges. *Neurocomputing, 237*, 350–361. DOI: 10.1016/j.neucom.2017.01.026

Zhou, S., Zhang, R., Chen, D., & Zhu, X. (2021). A novel framework for bringing smart big data to proactive decision making in healthcare. *Health Informatics Journal, 27*(2), 14604582211024698. DOI: 10.1177/14604582211024698 PMID: 34159834

Zhou, S. K., Greenspan, H., Davatzikos, C., Duncan, J. S., Van Ginneken, B., Madabhushi, A., Prince, J. L., Rueckert, D., & Summers, R. M. (2021). A review of deep learning in medical imaging: Imaging traits, technology trends, case studies with progress highlights, and future promises. *Proceedings of the IEEE, 109*(5), 820–838. DOI: 10.1109/JPROC.2021.3054390 PMID: 37786449

Chapter 13
Ethical AI in Psychiatric Care:
Balancing Compassion and Computational Intelligence for Employee Well-Being

Saurabh Chandra
https://orcid.org/0000-0003-4172-9968
Bennett University, Greater Noida, India

Bhupinder Singh
https://orcid.org/0009-0006-4779-2553
Sharda University, India

Kittisak Wongmahesak
https://orcid.org/0009-0000-2129-4691
North Bangkok University, Thailand

Santosh Kumar
https://orcid.org/0009-0002-3115-6772
Sharda University, India

ABSTRACT

Psychiatric treatment is undergoing a transformation through computational intelligence (CI) in neurodisorder diagnosis and management for disorders like depression, schizophrenia and autism for employee welfare in organizational culture. CI leverages advanced algorithms such as machine learning and neural networks to discover complex relationships found in brain imaging, genetics, and behavioral metrics more accurately than ever before. The integration of CI into

DOI: 10.4018/979-8-3373-2210-0.ch013

Copyright © 2025, IGI Global Scientific Publishing. Copying or distributing in print or electronic forms without written permission of IGI Global Scientific Publishing is prohibited.

psychiatry, however, creates important ethical challenges. Considerations like data privacy, algorithmic bias and misdiagnosis need to be examined closely. A lack of transparency in AI systems could damage the relationship between patients and clinicians, with decisions based on biased datasets having the potential to reinforce inequities within society. These endeavors would allow the development of new, but still ethically sound, psychiatric practices that would restore public trust in mental healthcare and deliver better outcomes.

1. INTRODUCTION

There is always the challenge of not sacrificing human touch to technological efficiency. Interdisciplinary engagement is needed to create CI that is transparent, equitable and patient-centred while avoiding the ethical dilemmas identified here. Ultimately although this means of implementing computational intelligence will transform psychiatric care in accurate and individualized ways, establishing these ethical guidelines is necessary to implement it with empathy, patient-centeredness, as well as equity. With incorporating machine learning and AI into neurodisorder diagnosis, along with supporting treatment options, computational intelligence stands poised to increase diagnostic efficacy while simultaneously enabling a more personalized care plan that can intervene sooner rather than later. But the move is leading to major ethical questions; it has its dark sides and some really big things need to be done very carefully (Sellers et al., 2024).

1.1. Significance of Computational Intelligence (CI) in Psychiatry

This demand is primarily driven by the increase in neurodisorders, which are among some of most common disorders around including but not limited to stroke, Parkinson's disease and dementia etc. Major contributors who provide treatment have finger-pointed strokes, attention deficit hyperactivity disorder (ADHD), functional neurological disorder (FND). Such conditions not only affect greatly the quality of life for an individual but also pose a heavy burden on healthcare systems and society as a whole. These types of technologies have the potential to increase diagnostic accuracy, personalize treatment approaches and improve earlier intervention. These are a group of diseases referred to as neuro disorders, specialised conditions that affect our brain and spinal cord (Singh et al., 2025). These range from cognitive, through motor and sensory to emotional disorders. These may improve diagnostic accuracy, allow for therapeutic personalization and empower early intervention Ultimately, the largest ethical concern is input into involuntary treatment.

If a mental illness is severe (i.e. schizophrenia or bipolar disorder) then that patient might not have the capacity to decide what type of care they actually need. In such cases, this calls upon psychiatrists to balance the ethical principles of respect for autonomy and the principle that we must not cause harm while simultaneously respecting how psychiatric diagnosis is simply not objective (Singh & Chandra, 2025). The complexity introduced with these systems may hinder healthcare professional to explain properly what drives their decisions and sharpen up transparency issues as well informed consensus. With the increasing application of computational intelligence in neurodisorder diagnosis and treatment, it is important to remember that maintaining a compassionate patient-centered approach which respects autonomy whilst promoting shared decision making The increasing role of computational intelligence (e.g., machine learning and artificial intelligence) in the diagnosis, management/conducting procedures/treatment of neurodisorders puts an emphasis on maintaining a compassionate approach to clinical care that honors patient autonomy while also supporting shared decision-making. Since the technologies are being used for life-threatening situations, it is very important to follow some ethical considerations (Singh et al. 2025).

1.2. Bridging Technology and Compassion in Psychiatric Care

The complexity introduced with these systems may hinder healthcare professional to explain properly what drives their decisions and sharpen up transparency issues as well informed consensus. Given the profound impact neurodisorders have on individuals, and in anticipation of new interventions coming online soon after they are demonstrated to be effective from clinical trials powered by thousands or even tens of thousands, addressing these ethical challenges is critical for enabling responsible and humane use. Major ethical concerns are related to privacy, algorithmic bias and overdigitization taking away the human responsibility from a part of care. More generally, issues of transparency and articulate are present in the description that must be given to patients before their decision concerning how data-hungry this method can get (Haeusemann & Chiong, 2024).

The application and integration of computational intelligence into psychiatry care also raise significant ethical concerns that need to be carefully addressed. The principal ethical challenges that arise are privacy, algorithmic bias and over-reliance on technology at the expense of human-centered care. The other issue is how to make the decision transit of these systems safe: improving transparency; making it less complex, and more comprehensible and gaining informed consent from patients. With further advances, computational intelligence will play an increasingly-prominent role in the diagnosis and treatment of neurodisorders; it is important to couple that approach with one which maintains a compassionate patient-centric ethos - respecting autonomy whilst advocating shared decision-making. It is important that these ethical challenges are addressed to promote the conscientious and empathic implementation of such technologies in improving lives for this vulnerable population with neurodisorders. This leads to improved results for patients and the more effective use of healthcare resources (Verstegen et al., 2024).

2. COMPUTATIONAL INTELLIGENCE IN PSYCHIATRIC TREATMENT: DEFINITION AND CORE CONCEPTS OF COMPUTATIONAL INTELLIGENCE

In the altered model of psychiatry reinforced through integrated CI concepts, there exists a particular attention to the most fundamental aspects of human behavior. CI applies computational tools such as Artificial Intelligence (AI), Machine Learning (ML), and Deep Learning (DL) to analyze large and complex datasets to extract information that would be challenging or impossible to obtain through manual or conventional means. The field of psychiatry, marked by subjectivity, variability and diagnostic uncertainty, CI has the unprecedented potential to help clinicians reach a more accurate neurodisorder diagnosis, individualize treatment strategies and ultimately optimize clinical outcomes in patients (Johar & Manjula, 2024).

Computational Intelligence is an interdisciplinary area made up of techniques and methods that empower machines to imitate and expand on human cognitive processes. This is represented by three main pillars: learning, adaptation, and decision-making. Contrary to classical computational algorithms that function based on predetermined rules, CI systems learn from data, adjust based on new information, and progress over time. This flexibility proves to be pivotal in psychiatry, where patient profiles, and symptoms tend to differ greatly.

CI encompasses neurodiverse approaches like neural networks, fuzzy logic, evolutionary algorithms, and hybrid models. Neural Networks in Psychiatric Applications The most common application of neural networks in psychiatry is simply to use artificial neural networks (ANNs) to model brain-like structures and processes. By analyzing large volumes of psychiatric data– behavioral metrics, neuroimaging results, genetic markers– these systems detect patterns and correlations, leading to a more comprehensive understanding of mental health disorders (Holt, 2022). On the contrary, fuzzy logic is a powerful tool for dealing with the uncertainty and ambiguity that are intrinsic to psychiatric diagnoses, enabling more nuanced decision-making. Used in conjunction, these techniques provide the foundation of CI systems, allowing them to tackle the complexities of neurodisorders with remarkable accuracy.

2.2. Role of Artificial Intelligence (AI), Machine Learning (ML), and Deep Learning (DL) in Psychiatry

ML and DL directly fall under the scope of AI which is a superior field that shapes innovation in psychiatric care. Machine Learning (ML) employs which learn from a given data and return a prediction or a classification. In psychiatry, ML algorithms have shown promise for identifying risk factors for and predicting the course of mental health disorders and for stratifying patients into subgroups to facilitate targeted interventions. Supervised learning techniques, for example, have been used to attempt to predict depression or anxiety onset based on the historical data of patients, and unsupervised learning methods have tried to detect latent subtypes of conditions such as schizophrenia.

Deep Learning (DL), a branch of ML, applies artificial neural networks that contain layers of nodes to ingest large and complex datasets. DL has proven its utility in processing neuroimaging data; for instance, (functional) magnetic resonance imaging (fMRI and electroencephalography) for the detection of structural and functional deficits in neurodisorders. With regards to biomarkers for diseases such as Alzheimer's disease, autism spectrum disorder, and bi-polar disorder, Convolutional Neural Networks (CNNs) and Recurrent Neural Networks (RNNs) have shown promise. DL not only speeds up the diagnostic process by automating the analysis of these types of data, but it also minimizes the human error probability (Liu et al., 2023).

The other branch of AI, tucked under the NLP umbrella, is also working wonders on psychiatric evaluations. By studying text from clinical notes, patient interviews, or even social media posts, NLP algorithms can measure mood, identify suicidal ideation, and detect early signs of psychosis. This ability can have profound implications for remote and scalable mental health monitoring, especially among underserved populations.

2.3. Applications in Neurodisorder Diagnosis and Management

CI can be utilized in the diagnosis and management of neurodisorders in multiple ways including predictive modeling, personalized treatment delivery, and real-time monitoring. Early diagnosis is a particularly important area of impact. Early intervention is known to help many neurodisorders including Alzheimer's disease and autism. The CI models augments the genetic, behavioral and environmental data to identify clinically at-risk individuals prior to the manifestation of symptoms. For example, ML algorithms have also been used to forecast the progression of Alzheimer's disease by drawing on longitudinal data, allowing them to provide care sooner and delaying the progress of the disease.

CI systems can analyze individuals' unique genetic information, medical history, and lifestyle factors to generate personalized treatment recommendations based on their specific needs. This is especially useful in psychiatry, where a one-size-fits-all treatment rarely meets patients' varied needs. Traditional psychopharmacology is characterized by a lengthy period of trial and error, but predictive models can quickly suggest the most likely effective antidepressant given a patient's unique genetic and metabolic profile. CI is also important in real-time monitoring of mental health. These CI support systems can be wearable devices or mobile health applications equipped with CI algorithms and that monitors physiological and behavioral cues including heart rate, sleep, and activity levels. These data are analysed in real-time to observe variances away from baseline, reflecting potential mental health crises. For example, a smart watch equipped with AI can notify caregivers or clinicians if a patient exhibits signs of severe anxiety or suicidal thoughts, allowing for immediate intervention.

CI has propelled the domain of neuroimaging analysis whereby the DL models are employed to characterize complex brain scans which detect minute changes in neurodisorders. And this has been especially revolutionary in conditions such as schizophrenia where structural changes in the brain are often difficult to detect through traditional means. CI's objective and reproducible neuroimaging analyses, combined with the automation of the analysis process, contributes to more reliable diagnoses (Taghian et al., 2021).

3. NEURODISORDERS: CHALLENGES IN DIAGNOSIS AND TREATMENT: COMMON NEURODISORDERS- DEPRESSION, ANXIETY, SCHIZOPHRENIA, AUTISM SPECTRUM DISORDERS

Neurodisorders include a wide range of disorders that affect how the brain is structured or does its job, resulting in cognitive, emotional or behavioral abnormalities. Such disorders include depression, anxiety, schizophrenia, and autism spectrum disorders (ASD), which ijreat challenges for diagnosis and treatment. Although neuroscience and psychiatry have made great strides in recent years, diagnosing mental health disorders often involves an unsatisfactory mix of subjective assessments and self-reported symptoms from patients, which can result in degraded consistency and late diagnosis. The inherent biotic nature e.g. genetic, environmental and psychogenic factors producing neurodisorders makes their treatment a cause of grave concern, therefore with the increasing demand for accurate and effective treatment, it actually begs for algorithmic and data grid approaches to enhance theтyp etencies.

The most widely seen neurodisorders are heterogeneous in both clinical manifestations and consequences, but all impair patients' quality of life. Depression, for instance, includes sustained sadness, lack of interest and impaired functioning. It is a top cause of disability globally, frequently running alongside other conditions such as anxiety and chronic pain. Anxiety disorders, such as generalized anxiety disorder and panic disorder, are characterized by extreme anxiety and worry that interfere with everyday life and productivity (Ray et al., 2023).

Hallucinations, delusions, and disorganized thinking disrupt reality perception in schizophrenia, a serious mental health condition. It requires lifelong management and places a substantial burden on patients and caregivers. In contrast, Autism Spectrum Disorders (ASD) are category of developmental disorders characterized by deficits in social communication and repetitive behaviors. ASD manifests as a wide spectrum, from mild deficits to severe disabilities, necessitating early diagnosis and customized therapies. Despite the heterogeneity of their clinical presentation these neurodisorders share diagnostic and therapeutic challenges including clinical heterogeneity of symptoms, and the deficiency of reliable biomarkers.

3.1 Diagnostic Complexities in Psychiatric Disorders

Psychiatric disorders are notoriously difficult to diagnose given the subjectivity of their symptoms, the high degree of overlap in symptoms, and the variability in how they present in individual patients. While physical ailments can be confirmed in laboratory tests or imaging, neurodisorders depend most heavily on clinical observations and interviews with patients. Symptoms of depression and anxiety, for instance, overlap insomnia, fatigue, apathy, etc. making it difficult to separate them at times. Likewise, early signs of schizophrenia such as social withdrawal and apathy may mimic depression, resulting in misdiagnosis or delayed recognition.

The episodic and dynamic nature of numerous neurodisorders also adds another layer of complexity to the equation. Symptoms can also come and go, which further complicates diagnosis. In addition, symptom expression may vary significantly due to cultural and linguistic differences, which could also introduce biases in the evaluation process, especially for heterogeneous populations. Adding to these difficulties is the lack of standardized, objective diagnostic tools, leading to high inter-clinician variability and unsatisfactory patient management (Arpaia et al., 2021).

3.2 Current Gaps in Traditional Psychiatric Practices

Conventional psychiatric approaches that draw on years of clinical wisdom cannot adequately tackle the increasing burden of neurodisorders. A significant gap is the current reliance on symptom-based diagnostic criteria, like the DSM (Diagnostic and Statistical Manual of Mental Disorders). As such, while they are useful, these criteria are categorically limited and do not account for the dimensional and multifactorial nature of mental health conditions.

The disconnections between psychiatry and new fields such as genomics, neuroimaging and digital phenotyping, contribute to this stagnation. This is because even though neuroimaging methods such as fMRI and EEG have provided valuable information on brain activity patterns, they have so far remained relatively underused in standard clinical practice. Research Relevant to Practitioners This discrepancy between the findings of studies and their practical application can lead to a treatment gap, where a substantial fraction of those suffering from neurodisorders remains undiagnosed or under-treated (Jadhakhan et al., 2022).

The conventional models tend towards a one-size-fits-all approach to treatments, ignoring the differences between individuals of all kinds, genetic, environmental and lifestyle. Not only does this have a wide variability in performance, but it adds to the duration of the trial-and-error approach in obtaining effective therapy. A case in point is that finding the right antidepressant for a patient suffering from major depressive disorder often involves many rounds of iteration, during with the patient is still suffering from sometimes debilitating symptoms.

3.3 Imperative for Computational and Data-Informed Approaches

These challenges necessitate the need for computational and data driven approaches in diagnosis and management of neurodisorders. Computational Intelligence (CI) provides tools to analyze and integrate complex, multidimensional data, supporting more accurate and objective diagnosis. These algorithms can analyze large volumes of data collected from electronic health records, neuroimaging scans, and genomic studies to isolate markers pertinent to specific disorders. The ability to use artificial intelligence for predictive analytics to predict disease pathways and responses to treatment can empower clinicians to intervene before it is too late. To illustrate, longitudinal patient data can be used to predict the likelihood of schizophrenia relapse or the progression of Alzheimer's disease, and therefore allow for timely amendments to care plans.

Computational tools can narrow the gap between research and clinical practice by transforming the insights gained from neuroscience and genetics into feasible interventions. Incorporating data from fMRI scans and behavioral assessments, for instance, allows for a nuanced understanding of the interplay between brain activity and behavior, which in turn can inform targeted therapies (Reger, 2020). Digital phenotyping, which utilizes data collected from smartphones and wearables, broadens the domain of monitoring and intervention, enabling real-time understanding of patients' mental health.

The other key advantage of computational approaches is scalability. AI systems can undertake the therapeutic role to extend the reach of psychiatric care in a world where most of the neurodisordered are away from a mental health professional. Hospital staff can also be freed up to deal with more complicated cases, for example, chatbots using natural language processing algorithms can deliver preliminary assessments and assistance.

4. ETHICAL CHALLENGES IN CI-BASED NEURODISORDER DIAGNOSIS

Incorporating computational intelligence (CI) into neurodisorder diagnosis has the potential to transform diagnostic practices, but also brings crucial ethical questions. Although CI tools enhance diagnostic accuracy, patient outcomes and access to care CI use leads to ethical complexities that need to be addressed for the responsible and equitable use of these technologies. These challenges range from data privacy protection, through minimization of algorithmic biases and the prevention of dependence from technology to the preservation of autonomy in terms of decision-making (Marvaso et al., 2022).

4.1. Risks Related to Data Privacy and Confidentiality

The large data requirements of CI systems often include sensitive personal information such as medical histories, neuroimaging scans, and behavioral patterns. The collection of such data itself, its storage, or the analysis of such data, can be used to compromise patient privacy and confidentiality. Cybersecurity breaches or unauthorized access to health data can have serious consequences, such as identity theft, stigmatization, or discrimination.

Wearables and digital phenotyping technologies for mental health monitoring produce downloads of personal data. Such systems are typically cloud based, which increases the risk of hacking and loss of data. And the de-identification process of the health data is not 100 percent successful; it is possible to reverse engineer the anonymization of some health care data with advanced re-identification techniques. Data encryption, secure data storage methods, and strict access control; all have to be in place to mitigate risks. Also, adherence to existing regulations like the General Data Protection Regulation (GDPR) and the Health Insurance Portability and Accountability Act (HIPAA) is essential to guarantee that patient data is processed in an ethical and transparent manner. The way that patient data is used, collected, and shared needs to be clearly communicated to them so that they are empowered to make informed consent decisions about their participation in CI-based detection of disease processes.

4.2. Algorithmic Bias and Fairness in Psychiatric Applications

Algorithmic bias has become an ethical issue of concern in CI-based diagnosis of neurodisorders. Prejudices in machine learning (ML) models are commonly derived from training data not reflecting patient population diversity. If an ML algorithm is trained mostly on data from one demographic group, the algorithm may then perform poorly when generalised to other demographics, which can result in misdiagnosis or other inequitable treatment (marvaso et al., 2022). In psychiatry as a field in which symptom expression and access to care are heavily informed by cultural, linguistic and socioeconomic factors these biases can further widen existing disparities. For example, if a trained algorithm has most of its data from predominantly urban, affluent populations, it could miss the unique mental health challenges of rural or underserved communities.

Dataset diversity and ongoing demographic group monitoring are key to address algorithmic bias. Equally important is transparency in model development and decision-making processes that facilitate clinicians and patients to understand how diagnostic conclusions are drawn. This can be addressed using Explainable AI (XAI) techniques able to increase transparency of the systems providing insight on how the algorithm reached certain recommendations.

4.3 Risk of Over-Reliance on Technology

Abundant use of CI systems for neurodisorder diagnosis is raising concerns regarding against depreciation of clinical expertise. While CI tools have the potential to complement and improve the decision making, they should not supplant the human factors of critical thinking, empathy, and context that are so vital to psychiatric therapeutic relationships. In short, too much focus on technology threatens to reduce complex human experiences to the arena of the quantifiable, focusing at the expense of potentially important even emergent aspects of mental illness that may delay traditional symptom onset.

A CI system, for instance, might identify particular patterns in neuroimaging data as indicative of schizophrenia but not consider psychosocial factors or patient history that may shift the diagnostic attribution. An unquestioning embrace of algorithmic outputs without awareness of their shortcomings could result in misdiagnosis, unnecessary treatments and loss of opportunities for personalized care. For avoiding this over-reliance, CI tools have to be embedded as supportive aid not as final decision maker in diagnosis process (Drigas et al., 2022). Clinician training programs should focus on integrating CI understanding with clinical experience. In addition, regular audits of CI systems are needed, including independent evaluations of their accuracy and reliability, to ensure trust and accountability.

5. COMPASSIONATE PSYCHIATRY AS BALANCING TECHNOLOGY AND HUMAN EMPATHY: ROLE OF HUMAN TOUCH IN PSYCHIATRIC CARE

Technological innovations in psychiatry, particularly computational intelligence (CI)/Artificial intelligence (AI) approaches, data-driven systems, etc., are revolutionizing the field at a rapid pace. These developments have improved accuracy in diagnostics, predictive analytics, and treatment customization. But even as technology is taking psychiatry to new heights, it cannot do without the human touch. Compassionate psychiatry speaks to the need to balance state-of-the-art tools with humanistic qualities, like empathy, understanding and interpersonal connection that are central to holistic mental health care (Elor & Kurniawan, 2020).

Psychiatry is a relational practice, negotiating the relational circuitry of mental health that is not confined to biological or technological limits, even as those are part of the conversation about the field. Patients suffering from mental health disorders including depression, anxiety or schizophrenia generally contends with loneliness, stigmatization, and vulnerability. For these patients, therapeutic alliance forged through empathetic listening, non-judgmental presence, and authentic concern constitutes a cornerstone of effective care. Unlike purely physical ailments, psychiatric conditions often involve subjective experiences that cannot be fully captured using algorithms or quantified through data analysis. For example, understanding a patient's lived experience, emotional history and personal values requires attunement to verbal and nonverbal cues characteristics that remain distinctly human. This feeling of being heard and validated builds trust, encourages compliance to treatment plans, and improves outcomes.

Advent of technology is challenging this basic truly human-to-human interaction. Automated diagnostic systems, wearable health monitors and telepsychiatry platforms, while providing important benefits, are in danger of depersonalizing care. And patients themselves can feel reduced to lozenges on a spreadsheet or alienated from providers who lean too heavily on digital tools. These may undermine the therapeutic alliance, which is critical in the success of psychiatric treatments. The nuanced empathy and emotional resonance of therapeutic encounters by humans cannot be reproduced by technology. Tears, hesitations, or unvoiced fears of a patient often provide crucial information that algorithms have a hard time parsing. This emotional attunement can be missing, which could probably result in the over-simplification of the condition which could inquiry potentially-leading to misdiagnosis or suboptimal care.

A compassionate psychiatry that resists the temptation of total digitalization in favor of a hybrid approach to treatment where the fastest growing aspect of the discipline used alongside human empathy as the irreplaceable line of defense against mental illness. This can be helping clinicians with detection of certain patters in patient data; predicting treatment responses; or personalizing care pathways. But these insights have to be made in the context of a therapeutic relationship that emphasizes empathy and understanding (Ebert et al., 2019). It is important to train clinicians to navigate this type of balance. These writing skills should serve as a microcosm of the value of technical and interpersonal competence in the medical domain. For example, clinicians could learn to view AI-generated insights not as definitive judgments but as auxiliary resources, so that patient narratives and subjective experiences remain at the heart of care.

Research consistently shows empathy has a healing power in psychiatry. Patients who feel treated by their clinicians as compassionate people tend to report greater satisfaction, and less symptoms and better quality of life. Empathy does more than validate patients' experiences; it empowers patients to become active participants in their recovery. Compassionate psychiatry lets innovative healthcare systems utilise the quantum strengths of technology without compromising the essence of humane care. It helps communicate that the future of mental health care is not either technology or empathy, but instead a seamless and humane combination of the two. The latter must use the former to meet the complexities of patient needs, whilst honouring the dignity, trust, and relationship offered by compassionate care.

6. LEGAL AND POLICY FRAMEWORKS: INTERNATIONAL STANDARDS AND GUIDELINES FOR ETHICAL CI USE IN PSYCHIATRY

CI in psychiatric diagnosis and treatment: transformative potential and the need for robust legal and policy frameworks to ensure that innovative transformation including CI systems is consistent with best practices, it is imperative to derive or develop comprehensive guidelines, implement national policies, and establish accountability structures. International standards, national policies, legal accountability mechanisms, and governance all contribute to the ethical and equitable use of CI in mental healthcare, and this section discusses these aspects in detail.

Ethical guidance from international standards and guidelines for the use of CI in psychiatry Agencies like the World Health Organization (WHO), UNESCO, and Council of Europe have noted that all AI use and CI needs to focus on human rights, equity and transparency. For example, the WHO has released recommendations that explore the ethical implications of digital health, articulating principles such as informed consent, data privacy, and equitable access to technology (Patangia et al. 2021).

The special vulnerability of psychiatric patients demands extra safeguards. Guidelines should ensure that CI tools are designed and implemented to respect patient autonomy, avoid the risk of stigmatization, and avoid discriminatory outcomes. For instance, UNESCO's ethical AI framework calls for algorithms that are explainable, unbiased, and aligned with societal values, particularly in sensitive areas like mental health. In addition to this, international cooperation is essential for aligning these standards across borders. International issues including data collaboration, global partnerships, and unequal access to technologies call for a collective effort to establish frameworks that work for everyone. Guidelines, like the OECD AI Principles, are the foundation for this kind of harmonization, which can help ensure responsible innovation of CI technologies.

6.1 National-Level Policies and Compliance Measures

International guidelines establish broad principles, but national policies are necessary to translate those standards into concrete rules. The responses of countries to how CI is regulated in psychiatry depend on the respective healthcare system, technological infrastructure, and cultural perceptions towards mental health; hence, the regulations surrounding the use of CI in psychiatry differ across the globe. The European Union's General Data Protection Regulation (GDPR) has raised the bar for data protection, focusing on consent, transparency, and accountability in using personal information. These might be especially important in psychiatry since coming to a diagnosis and being treated for one requires general sensitive health information. In similar fashion, nations such as Canada and Australia have introduced data governance frameworks through which the ethical use of AI in health care is addressed.

National policies should also focus on the validation and certification of CI tools utilized in psychiatry, complementing data protection. Regulatory organizations like the US Food and Drug Administration (FDA) have laid out pathways for the approval of medical devices powered by AI, including algorithms for diagnosing mental health issues. This approval process ensures that CI systems are safe, effective, and ethical when applied in clinical settings. This requires a balance of carrot and stick mechanisms to monitor post-deployment use of CI technologies. Audits, independent assessments, and required disclosure of negative effects can help to ensure that CI tools continue to perform reliably and ethically throughout their life cycle (Midha & Singh, 2023).

7. ETHICAL DILEMMAS IN DATA-DRIVEN NEURODISORDER DIAGNOSIS: BUILDING PUBLIC TRUST AND ACCEPTANCE OF CI IN PSYCHIATRY

The ethical question of whether psychotropic medications should be used even with informed consent is especially salient for vulnerable populations like children or those who are elderly. It is a cornerstone of ethical best practice in clinical psychiatry to ensure that patients, or their legal guardians are provided with an opportunity to appreciate fully the advantages, risks and options (and potential risks) of interventions before any decisions are made. In these cases, the moral principles from which each is exercised must be properly challenged and decisions made in favor of those of the patient suffering, while respecting their rights and dignity. The utilization of these technologies in psychiatric care also continues to be accompanied by a number of ethical challenges, including around consent and data use; issues related to the potential for algorithmic/empirical bias that can drive unintended marginalization or exclusion within the algorithmically-defined mental health marketplace (Bayrhammer-Savel et al., 2024).

Computational intelligence is revolutionizing psychiatric assessment using artificial intelligence, machine learning and big data to improve the diagnostic accuracy and efficiency of mental health disorders. Psychiatric evaluations typically involve subjective assessments, which might not yield concordant diagnoses. In contrast, computational intelligence has the ability to come through patient data genetic information, behavioral patterns, and even neurological signals in massive quantities to recognize patterns that could point out neuropsychiatric conditions such as depression or anxiety or even more complex diseases like schizophrenia or bipolar disorder.

In identifying the earliest warning signs for different mental illnesses, and predictive analytics could potentially help clinicians to intervene timely by using machine learning models. This happens in the form of detecting abnormalities in emotional or cognitive behavior, which can show as patterns in speech, facial expression or digital activity that can be analyzed by sophisticated AI algorithms. By using data to make decisions, we can ensure that diagnostic acumen is not biased by human error or subjectivity. As applied deep learning research contributes significantly to real-world decisions, so do some of the central concerns in computer science the right to privacy with respect to data and fairness for models; especially when such flawed AI systems may have a catastrophic impact on vulnerable populations. However, with all the challenges in healthcare today, computational intelligence can pave a way revolutionize psychiatric care by enabling personalized treatment plans and better mental health outcomes- offering hope for more diagnoses to be timely correctly and equitably. The most important ethical issues relate to privacy, since these technologies may require the collection and analysis of patients' data. There are also concerns over algorithmic bias, whereby the algorithms involved might reinforce social biases and further disadvantage already marginalized demographics.

These technologies can help boost diagnosis accuracy, stare personalized treat ments and promote early intervention. Psychiatry has very important ethical considerations when using computational intelligence to help treat patients The most important ethical issues relate to privacy, since these technologies may require the collection and analysis of patients' data. With the increasing application of computational intelligence in neurodisorder diagnosis and treatment, it is important to remember that maintaining a compassionate patient-centered approach which respects autonomy whilst promoting shared decision making. Several important factors relating to the significance of explainability and transparency as patients, specifically those whose healthcare is being determined for using sophisticated AI/ ML algorithms, have a right to know how such decisions are being made.

Transparency may strengthen patient autonomy and belief. Patients should be capable learn about the reasons and contributing aspects of CI-based diagnosis from their healthcare practitioners. Patients with neuro disorders who may experience cognitive deficits need to give special attention to this. Compassion mobilizes psychiatrists to speak up for the well-being of their patients resist the blind seduction by technology and protect our field from unethical use of CI models. Patients who are heard and respected usually receive better results by feeling useful, protected and encouraged to work on their recovery. It also raises ethical questions around resource allocation. Reduced access to care, such as waiting lists for therapy or medication, may be particularly burdensome in busy psychiatric settings and have a greater impact on already vulnerable groups. Decisions around which care to prioritize are left up to the clinicians, each centering on what would be most fair and equitable while still being practical. Decisions about involuntarily hospitalizing or treating patients present more difficult situations and call upon psychiatrists to provide evidence before abrogating a patient´s autonomy, in the presence of meaningful risk of harm. These ethical conundrums influence everyday clinical judgement, as it requires a careful negotiation of patient autonomy, beneficence and societal justice. Now that CI is becoming more prevalent in urban systems, it has also become increasingly important for humans to keep a watchful eye and continue making decisions.

There will always be the challenge of balancing what automation can offer to the benefits that come with human-centered approaches to decision-making. There need to be a greater collaboration between city leaders, technologists, ethicists and the citizens themselves who will ultimately live in these environments -to develop guidelines and best practices around ethical smart city development. Dealing with complex matters such as these will require pilot projects, regulatory sandboxes and multistakeholder dialogues. The future potential of CI for ethical smart sustainable cities will therefore be about achieving the full benefits while maintaining privacy, fairness, transparency and human flourishing. Dynamic, iterative learning and adaptive action will be essential to shape the cities of tomorrow as well as a responsibility in innovation.

8. CHALLENGES IN ACHIEVING EXPLAINABILITY

Transparency and explainability: It may be challenging for medical professionals to thoroughly explain the procedure for making decisions to patients due to the intricacy of CI algorithms employed in the diagnosis of neuro disorders. To facilitate informed consent and collaborative decision-making, efforts need to be made toward enhancing the explainability and transparency of these algorithms (Bright et al., 2023). Balancing autonomy and beneficence: Encouraging beneficence, or acting in the patient's best interest, but still respecting their autonomy may conflict. In order to give the best care possible and ensure that CI-based diagnoses respect autonomy, medical professionals must carefully manage this delicate line (Almendro, 2023).

8.1 Ethical Implications of Decision-Making in CI Systems

From a moral perspective, purpose of predictive testing should conform with these ethical standards that suits in favor for both individuals as well as society. Given the clinical case presented, by articulating what are considered to be principles - whilst making each principle and its corresponding argument explicit, it attempt to guide decision-making through a process of balancing these principles against one another (Bright et al., 2023). The paramount principle at the individual level is that of respect for autonomy, best served by ascertaining whether an intended test-subject desires predictive testing (or not). In the current technological, regulatory and ethical environment now overall predictive testing should be limited to asymptomatic individuals who specifically request it in a research use context (safely protected by Research Ethics) (Buda, 2023). Potential psychosocial harm through disclosure of test results must be kept to a minimum, and the party seeking to have a predictive test performed should receive sufficient information regarding limitations in terms of predictability. Apart from the danger people should ask about how much of a disease is out there so that governments make due provisions for social welfare (Te Maiharoa, & Woodhouse, 2023). The ethical rub is that this test provides clinically and socially useful information when there is no disease modifying treatment. As a result, the ethical stance of performing population-wide screenings using AI/ML algorithms to detect those who are at-risk is currently grey (Petkovic et al., 2023).

8.2 Patient-Doctor Relationships: Role of Empathy and Compassion in Psychiatry

The patient-doctor relationship, characterized by empathy and compassion (components related to the practice of psychiatry) is even more so relevant in cognitive science application for neurodisorder diagnosis via computational intelligence. Sympathetic listening enables psychiatrists to engage more effectively with the patients and leads them towards a better understanding of the subjective experience that is pivotal for diagnosis and treatment planning (Panda et al., 2024).

8.3 Clinical Psychiatry: Ethical Considerations Impact Day-to-Day Clinical Decisions

Ethical considerations are paramount in clinical psychiatry, where many patient care situations are fraught with conflicting values and thus lead to hard choices (Swargiary & Roy, 2024). Such example is informed consent which relates to the competence of a patient's ability to comprehend risks, benefits, and alternatives to a treatment strategy when they are otherwise mentally incapacitated (Lal et al.,

2024). The fact that physicians have a duty to obtain consent from proxies when patients are not capable of actively making a decision or if the choice is unreasonable raises ethical questions related to autonomy (Arora et al., 2024). This is also one of the ethical pillars which we are constructed to respect in practice everyday as well as confidentiality (Kaushik et al., 2024). This is a tough call to make, because psychiatrists get the trust and share in confidence many personal info about their patients but some cases require them to break this confidentiality as a matter of public safety (Raghav et al., 2024). Balancing the right to privacy versus their intention not to harm one another leads to an ethical nighmare as you decide when it is kosher to break confidentiality.

9. CONCLUSION AND FUTURE SCOPE

Through improved diagnostic accuracy, personalization of treatment, accessibility, and affordability CI has transformed psychiatric care in the burgeoning fields of neurodisorders, such as depression, anxiety, and schizophrenia. Psychiatry is experiencing seismic shifts through the integration of technologies such as Artificial Intelligence (AI), Machine Learning (ML), and Deep Learning (DL), which are unlocking new paradigms of understanding complex neural activity, anticipating clinical outcomes, and transcending into service pathways. Nonetheless, the incorporation of CI in psychiatry presents considerable ethical challenges relating to data privacy, algorithmic partiality and the possible dilution of human compassion in the provision of care. Such challenges call for strong legal frameworks, transparent governance, and compliance with international ethical standards to underscore equitable, responsible, and compassionate use of technology.

The future of CI in psychiatry focuses on balancing cutting-edge technology with patient-centered treatment. These actions will help create explainable AI systems that foster transparency and trust; mitigate dataset biases; and encourage inclusivity in algorithm design. As these innovations unfold, technologists, clinicians, policymakers, and patient advocacy groups must work together to establish ethical guidelines and ensure equitable access. In addition, advances in neuroimaging, brain-computer interfaces, and wearable technologies can lead to a deeper understanding of neurodisorders, allowing for real-time monitoring and intervention. It is about combining computational intelligence with human empathy and keeping our heart of empathy as the cornerstone of our therapeutic alliance with the patient. By continuing to adopt this balanced approach, psychiatry will usher in more compassionate, effective, and equitable mental healthcare for generations to come.

REFERENCES

Almendro, M. (2023). *The Labyrinth of Ayahuasca*. Cambridge Scholars Publishing.

Arora, M. K., Lal, S., Singh, B., & Olyaee, M. (2024). Through an Energy Lens: Examining SDGs From a Policy Perspective. In Riswandi, B., Singh, B., Kaunert, C., & Vig, K. (Eds.), *AI Applications for Clean Energy and Sustainability* (pp. 320–343). IGI Global., DOI: 10.4018/979-8-3693-6567-0.ch016

Arpaia, P., D'Errico, G., De Paolis, L. T., Moccaldi, N., & Nuccetelli, F. (2021). A narrative review of mindfulness-based interventions using virtual reality. *Mindfulness*, •••, 1–16.

Bayrhammer-Savel, M., Ortner, M., Van Hout, M. C., & Komorowski, A. (2024). Psychiatric and legal considerations for ketamine treatment within prison settings. *Frontiers in Psychiatry*, *15*, 1316108. DOI: 10.3389/fpsyt.2024.1316108 PMID: 38699451

Bright, C., Walden, S., Abdulla, S., & Ryan, R. (2023). Intellectual disability nursing for people with profound intellectual disabilities and complex needs. In *Learning and Intellectual Disability Nursing Practice* (pp. 194–239). Routledge. DOI: 10.4324/9781003296461-6

Buda, L. (2023). *Advancing Education for Neurodiverse Students in Morocco: A Repository for Teachers, Parents, and Students* (Doctoral dissertation, Worcester Polytechnic Institute).

Drigas, A., Mitsea, E., & Skianis, C. (2022). Virtual reality and metacognition training techniques for learning disabilities. *Sustainability (Basel)*, *14*(16), 10170. DOI: 10.3390/su141610170

Ebert, D. D., Harrer, M., Apolinário-Hagen, J., & Baumeister, H. (2019). Digital interventions for mental disorders: key features, efficacy, and potential for artificial intelligence applications. *Frontiers in Psychiatry: Artificial Intelligence, Precision Medicine, and Other Paradigm Shifts*, 583-627.

Elor, A., & Kurniawan, S. (2020). The ultimate display for physical rehabilitation: A bridging review on immersive virtual reality. *Frontiers in Virtual Reality*, *1*, 585993. DOI: 10.3389/frvir.2020.585993

Haeusermann, T., & Chiong, W. (2024). Ethical considerations in rapid and novel treatments in psychiatry. *Neuropsychopharmacology : Official Publication of the American College of Neuropsychopharmacology*, *49*(1), 291–293. DOI: 10.1038/s41386-023-01635-y PMID: 37391590

Hamacher, S. (2023). *Supervision: On Motherhood and Surveillance*. MIT Press.

Holt, S. (2022). Virtual reality, augmented reality and mixed reality: For astronaut mental health; and space tourism, education and outreach. *Acta Astronautica*.

Jadhakhan, F., Blake, H., Hett, D., & Marwaha, S. (2022). Efficacy of digital technologies aimed at enhancing emotion regulation skills: Literature review. *Frontiers in Psychiatry, 13*, 809332. DOI: 10.3389/fpsyt.2022.809332 PMID: 36159937

Johar, S., & Manjula, G. R. (2024). Interfering sensed input classification model using assimilated whale optimization and deep Q-learning for remote patient monitoring. *Biomedical Signal Processing and Control, 93*, 106202. DOI: 10.1016/j.bspc.2024.106202

Kaushik, T. K., Singh, A., Raghav, A., & Singh, B. (2024). Potential of Artificial Intelligence in the Agricultural Industry: A Comprehensive Review. AI Applications for Clean Energy and Sustainability, 344-365.

Lal, S., Arora, M. K., Riswandi, B. A., Singh, N., & Singh, B. (2024). Melding Artificial Intelligence and Remote Sensing Data for Real-Time Monitoring of Marine Biodiversity. In Riswandi, B., Singh, B., Kaunert, C., & Vig, K. (Eds.), *AI Applications for Clean Energy and Sustainability* (pp. 299–319). IGI Global., DOI: 10.4018/979-8-3693-6567-0.ch015

Liu, K., Madrigal, E., Chung, J. S., Parekh, M., Kalahar, C. S., Nguyen, D., & Harris, O. A. (2023). Preliminary Study of Virtual-reality-guided Meditation for Veterans with Stress and Chronic Pain. *Alternative Therapies in Health and Medicine, 29*(6). PMID: 34559692

Marvaso, G., Pepa, M., Volpe, S., Mastroleo, F., Zaffaroni, M., Vincini, M. G., & Jereczek-Fossa, B. A. (2022). Virtual and Augmented Reality as a Novel Opportunity to Unleash the Power of Radiotherapy in the Digital Era: A Scoping Review. *Applied Sciences (Basel, Switzerland), 12*(22), 11308. DOI: 10.3390/app122211308

Midha, S., & Singh, K. (2023). Happiness-Enhancing Strategies Among Indians. In *Religious and Spiritual Practices in India: A Positive Psychological Perspective* (pp. 341–368). Springer Nature Singapore. DOI: 10.1007/978-981-99-2397-7_15

Panda, M., Abraham, A., Gopi, B., & Ajith, R. (Eds.). (2024). *Computational Intelligence for Oncology and Neurological Disorders: Current Practices and Future Directions*. CRC Press. DOI: 10.1201/9781003450153

Patangia, B., Sankruthyayana, R. G., Sathiyaseelan, A., & Balasundaram, S. (2021). How could Mindfulness Help? A Perspective on the Applications of Mindfulness in Enhancing Tomorrow's Workplace. *i-Manager's. Journal of Management, 16*(3), 52.

Petković, D., Vuković, B., & Vuković, I. (2023, May). Clostridium Difficile infection and neurological disorders-a case report. In *Mind & Brain:62nd International Neuropsychiatric Congress.*

Raghav, A., Singh, B., & Jermsittiparsert, K. (2024). Role of Artificial Intelligence and Machine Learning in Clean and Blue Energy for Enhancing Efficiency and Sustainability. In Riswandi, B., Singh, B., Kaunert, C., & Vig, K. (Eds.), *AI Applications for Clean Energy and Sustainability* (pp. 366–386). IGI Global., DOI: 10.4018/979-8-3693-6567-0.ch018

Ray, J., Kumar, S., Pandey, S., & Akram, S. V. (2023, June). The Role of Augmented Reality and Virtual Reality in Shaping the Future of Health Psychology. In *2023 3rd International Conference on Pervasive Computing and Social Networking (ICPCSN)* (pp. 1604-1608). IEEE. DOI: 10.1109/ICPCSN58827.2023.00268

Reger, G. M. (Ed.). (2020). *Technology and mental health: a clinician's guide to improving outcomes*. Routledge. DOI: 10.4324/9780429020537

Sellers, K. K., Cohen, J. L., Khambhati, A. N., Fan, J. M., Lee, A. M., Chang, E. F., & Krystal, A. D. (2024). Closed-loop neurostimulation for the treatment of psychiatric disorders. *Neuropsychopharmacology: Official Publication of the American College of Neuropsychopharmacology*, *49*(1), 163–178. DOI: 10.1038/s41386-023-01631-2 PMID: 37369777

Singh, B., & Chandra, S. (2025). Augmented Reality and Virtual Reality in Health Advancements and Medical Education: Runway for Future Ready Healthcare Services. In R. R., S. Chowdhury, S. Kardy, R. Damaševičius, & R. Govindaraj (Eds.), *Digital Twins for Sustainable Healthcare in the Metaverse* (pp. 197-218). IGI Global Scientific Publishing. https://doi.org/DOI: 10.4018/979-8-3693-4199-5.ch008

Singh, B., Hammouch, H., & Chandra, S. (2025). Innovative Wind Energy Solutions for Smart-Sustainable Communities: Vision for Intelligent Energy Management and Climate Resilience in Industry 5.0. In Mitra, D., Choudhury, T., Madan, A., Chattaraj, S., & Pellegrini, M. (Eds.), *AI Technologies for Enhancing Recycling Processes* (pp. 491–508). IGI Global Scientific Publishing., DOI: 10.4018/979-8-3693-7282-1.ch020

Singh, B., Kaunert, C., Hammouch, H., & Raghav, A. (2025). Booster of IoMT in Diagnostics and Disease Screening: Hustler Artificial Intelligence Approaches Transforming Healthier Homes. In Kumar, V., Katina, P., & Zhao, J. (Eds.), *Convergence of Internet of Medical Things (IoMT) and Generative AI* (pp. 243–266). IGI Global Scientific Publishing., DOI: 10.4018/979-8-3693-6180-1.ch010

Swargiary, K., & Roy, K. (2024). *AI Angels: Empowering Children with Special Needs through Artificial Intelligence*. scholar press.

Taghian, A., Abo-Zahhad, M., Sayed, M. S., & Abdel-Malek, A. (2021, December). Virtual, Augmented Reality, and Wearable Devices for Biomedical Applications: A Review. In *2021 9th International Japan-Africa Conference on Electronics, Communications, and Computations (JAC-ECC)* (pp. 93-98). IEEE.

Te Maihāroa, K., & Woodhouse, A. (Eds.). (2023). *Indigenous Autoethnography: Illuminating Māori Voices*. Springer Nature. DOI: 10.1007/978-981-99-6718-6

Verstegen, N., Peters-Scheffer, N., Didden, P. D. R., Nijman, P. D. H., & de Vogel, P. D. V. (2024). Patient experiences of victimization during mandatory psychiatric treatment: A qualitative study. *Journal of Forensic Psychology Research and Practice*, *24*(1), 1–22. DOI: 10.1080/24732850.2022.2051662

Chapter 14
Ensuring Data Privacy of Employees in Healthcare and Well-Being in the Era of Cloud Computing and the Internet of Things (IoT)

Shashwata Sahu
https://orcid.org/0009-0003-6843-9554
School of Law, KIIT University, Bhubaneswar, India

Navonita Mallick
https://orcid.org/0000-0003-3621-3764
KIIT University, Bhubaneswar, India

Bhupinder Singh
https://orcid.org/0009-0006-4779-2553
Sharda University, India

Kittisak Wongmahesak
https://orcid.org/0009-0000-2129-4691
North Bangkok University, Thailand

Saurabh Chandra
https://orcid.org/0000-0003-4172-9968
Bennett University, India

DOI: 10.4018/979-8-3373-2210-0.ch014

Copyright © 2025, IGI Global Scientific Publishing. Copying or distributing in print or electronic forms without written permission of IGI Global Scientific Publishing is prohibited.

ABSTRACT

Cloud Computing and the Internet of Things have transformed the healthcare landscape in the digital age by improving quality of care and increasing operational efficiency. However, these technologies also entail significant employee data privacy and security risks. The current paper critically explores how the existing legislative measures successfully secure employees' data in the context of such technologies. In particular, a doctrinal research method was adopted to investigate the state of the law in the field and to identify the gaps and weaknesses. The results indicate that the existing rules, namely, the European Union General Data Protection Regulation and Digital Economy Act 2017 are insufficient to protect employee data ownership and access and ensure informed employee consent. In response, the current paper suggests reforming the laws to maintain their effectiveness in the face of rapidly developing technologies.

I. INTRODUCTION

> *"The advancement of technology is based on making it fit in so that you don't even notice it, so it's part of everyday life."*
> *- Bill Gates*

The advancement of Cloud Computing and the Internet of Things in healthcare have fundamentally transformed the industry, enabling significant improvements in employee care, data processing, and operational effectiveness. These technologies allow healthcare data to be stored and accessed in a remote server and transmitted across platforms, making it instantaneous and accessible to healthcare providers at all times (Rejeb et al., 2023). Cloud Computing and the Internet of Things (IoT), support thousands of applications and updates across platforms, which can be effectively used to predict which diseases may be emerging at any given time. The ability of healthcare organisations to utilise such technologies allows for the ability to remotely monitor employees and provide them with real-time predictions of the treatment modalities required for this (Kelly et al., 2020). However, it is essential to note that such advancements also come with significant challenges, with threats to the security of employee data being among the most prominent ones.

The number of cyberattacks against the healthcare sector has increased 350% since 2017. The increase is attributed to the digitisation of medical records and the presence of connected devices, which broaden the attack surface for cyber threats (Samantha Liss & Jasmine Ye Han, 2023). However, the pace at which healthcare integrated IoT and Cloud Computing adversely affected the safety of employee data. With the increased amount of information stored digitally and transmitted at any given moment, the risk of unauthorised access, data breaches, and cybersecurity attacks also increased. At this point, it is clear that the contemporary legal framework is insufficient to protect employee data, and the existing contamination is inadequate to prevent healthcare information breaches (Parihar et al., 2024). According to data breach statistics, between 2009 and 2023, the number of healthcare data breaches has significantly increased, with as many as 5,887 events involving 500 records reported to the Office for Civil Rights (OCR) in 2023. With those, severe breaches also increased, with 133 million records exposed in 2023, the worst year. The leading cause of breaches is hacking, responsible for almost 80 per cent of all cases in 2023 (Steve Alder, 2024). The importance of this study comes from the fact that it examines one of the critical issues of the modern age: the ways to protect employee privacy and healthcare data from IOT attacks in the age of Cloud Computing. Many stakeholders are unable and unwilling to utilise the technologies, leading to data breaches affecting as many as 60 Americans. With healthcare organisations using IOT and Cloud Computing at an increasing rate, the importance of reputable and analytical legislative protection becomes paramount (Mehrtak et al., 2021). A total of 3,051 healthcare data breach incidents were reported between 2010–2019, exposing about 255.18 million people. Alarming is the expected average cost per healthcare data breach in the U.S., which is $15 million, indicating the financial risk associated with inadequate data security practices (Seh et al., 2020). Data breaches can have devastating consequences, with negative implications in terms of identity theft, economic loss, and repercussions for the quality of employee care. This is why the ultimate goal of this doctrinal research is to bridge existing technologies with existing laws and recommendations, providing an understanding of how existing legal frameworks can be improved to face the challenges of the approaching era.

II. OBJECTIVES OF CHAPTER

This chapter aims to critically analyse the existing law measures designed to protect employee data in cloud computing and IoT in healthcare. It seeks to find out the gaps in the current legal system to make adequate suggestions to amend the law concerning the use of these technologies and corresponding risks. This paper also investigates how far modern legal standards can resolve the issue of preserving employees' rights and, on the other hand, triggering the emergence of innovations in healthcare services.

III. RESEARCH METHODOLOGY FOR CHAPTER

In this chapter, the author uses a doctrinal methodology based on analysing both primary and secondary sources of law to understand the legal rules regulating relationships in the studied field. As such, the initial stage of the study includes assessing the current legal regulations that are in effect. Significant attention is dedicated to analysing existing legislation, regulations, and case law devoted to the issue of data protection within healthcare organisations. Furthermore, the analysis also includes international legal instruments and commonly accepted standards, which are then compared with national regulations to establish best global practices. Secondary sources, such as academic articles, expert opinions, and reports of related studies, are also used to understand the subject and contextualise the legal analysis. Overall, this method allows the author to analyse existing rules systematically and how they protect employee information in Cloud Computing and IoT environments.

V. EXISTING LEGAL FRAMEWORK

This section will discuss how current regulations, such as the Health Insurance Portability and Accountability Act (HIPAA) in the United States or the General Data Protection Regulation (GDPR) in the European Union, cover the issue of employee data protection in the context of Cloud Computing and IoT. It will address the problem of cross-border data flows, data sovereignty, and jurisdictional inconsistencies.

In the United States, the HIPAA and in the European Union, the GDPR are the most popular and powerful legal frameworks to regulate the preservation of personal employee data. These regulations protect sensitive information (Fredric D. Bellamy, 2022). However, both pieces of legislation have numerous problems when used in the context of Cloud Computing and the Internet of Things. In particular, when cloud services and IoT devices are applied to store and manage data, it becomes difficult to follow the existing rules and meet necessary standards. The "Health Insurance Portability and Accountability Act" was enacted in 1996 in the United States to protect health information. It is considered one of the country's first and most influential pieces of legislation regarding the preservation of employee data (Stephen D. Gantz, 2014). HIPAA standards are developed to ensure that employee's private health information is protected adequately. HIPAA requires healthcare providers, payers, and their associated business partners to ensure that employees' data is not accessed by unauthorised people or used for inappropriate purposes. The so-called HIPAA Security Rule indicates that administrative, physical, and technical measures should be taken to protect "electronic protected health information (ePHI)" and to ensure that this information is always available for the parties who need it (Nass et al., 2009). In other words, the security rule protects ePHI's confidentiality, integrity, and availability. However, one of the new standards reflects the emergent needs of communities and indicates that if healthcare providers use cloud service providers, they must ensure that CSPs are also HIPAA-compliant. To regulate these relations, HIPAA BAAs should be signed to indicate the CSP's responsibilities. Unfortunately, ensuring that data on different platforms and devices will be protected unilaterally in Cloud Computing and IoT is almost impossible.

Similarly, GDPR, introduced in 2018, is another extensive legal set of rules and guidelines that target the personal data of individuals in the EU (Namdech et al., 2025). Even though the framework applies to all organisations, whether located in the region or not, which collect or process EU citizens' data, its influence is among the greatest (Altmetric et al., 2019). The regulation requires data controllers and processors to adhere to the practices of data minimisation, purpose limitation, and transparency, meaning that companies collecting personal data must collect no more than necessary for explicit, well-defined and legitimate purposes and inform the data subjects on the purpose of processing before or upon collection of data (Becker et al., 2024). Moreover, GDPR requires that no data may be processed without an individual's explicit consent, and an individual should have the right to withdraw this consent at any time.

Living in the Cloud Computing and IoT world, personal data must be protected throughout the entire cycle, including transfer, storage and processing in the cloud. The dilemma is whether it is practical and possible for data controllers and processors to ensure data protection when cloud environments and IoT ecosystems are distributed and untransparent (El-Gendy et al., 2023). Through cooperation with cloud and IoT providers, organisations must enforce technical and organisational measures to secure personal data from breaches and unauthorised access. At the same time, it is transferred, stored and processed. HIPAA and GDPR are examples of vigorous attempts to preserve employee data. However, their application to Cloud Computing and IoT introduces certain limitations. With its national focus, HIPAA is more rigid in using modern data technology, mainly when applied to multiple jurisdictions. On the other hand, GDPR is a better solution in terms of its broader scope and stricter demands, but it also cannot completely meet all the needs of IoT networks with multiple employers and vendors (Theodos & Sittig, 2020). The data of every employee can be sent across borders and stored in a cloud environment. Therefore, they can be compromised, although this data's level of security may differ. Overall, these regulations are imperfect and should be constantly changed and enforced with the help of mechanisms that would influence Cloud Computing and IoT applications in healthcare and consider modern risks and emergencies.

VI. GAPS AND CHALLENGES

The challenges that combining Cloud Computing and the IoT introduces to healthcare fall into two categories. The first group of challenges is complex and pertains to the complexity surrounding the issues of data ownership, employee consent, and liability in the case of a data breach. As medical data becomes more digitised and, in some cases, connected directly to the employees' devices, the question of who owns the data they produce and how the consent should work is becoming much more complex (Kumar et al., 2023).

A. Data Ownership and Consent: Challenges in the Digital Age

The massive adoption of Cloud Computing and IoT technologies in healthcare has disrupted the rules and norms surrounding data. Although employee data was once carefully controlled, organically managed, and contained in physical dockets or facilities, its utilisation today is far more productive and less regulated. As a result, healthcare providers and their employees are in a much more complicated situation, as their data may be owned and processed by various unrelated companies (Javaid & Khan, 2021). Owing to the vast dispersion and lack of control, the concept of data ownership is notably ambiguous concerning modern healthcare. If one petroleum geologist wants to calculate their carbon footprint, it is more or less clear who has the right to access their personal information and on what terms (Javaid & Khan, 2021). However, with the digitisation of healthcare, ownership is far less clear, and companies that process data and provide services have a vested interest in it. A potential solution lies in creating a legally codified system that separates the ownership of a employee's data from its processing.

Several companies and actors possess employee data to some extent. First, retention is traditionally viewed through the prism of the healthcare provider; in other words, hospitals are the owners of employee data, with employees having certain, often informal or arbitrary rights. In the age of digital health, however, these rights are far more fragile, as the data is now not necessarily restricted to a local server but can be stored remotely on cloud services and processed by various organisations. (Vera Ehrenstein et al., 2019). In addition to healthcare providers, cloud services providers and application developers may also process the data, which significantly in-polices any assumptions about total or partial ownership. In addition, these considerations are complicated by the financial considerations of the companies processing data. Many application developers, for example, view their products and platforms as their property (Cresswell et al., 2022). This perspective complicates relationships between employees' inalienable rights to their data and companies with some financial claim to it. Because of this, it is apparent that, in the digital age, there exists a need for a law that determines who owns a employee's data, what rights the employee holds, and what duties other companies owe.

The standard of informed consent prevalent in the US and many other countries where informed consent is or will be required is challenged by digital health and the many facets of modern data use. It was previously assumed and is currently implemented in data use cases for reasons other than direct employee care. It is not feasible or efficient that consent is needed every time employee data is used. For a traditionally understood data approach, someone will explain every specific use of data to employees and inform them about their options (Krogstad et al., 2010). Such an approach is particularly untenable in the case of the digital health ecosystem due to the wide variety of potential data sources and the fact that data may be used in a wide variety of ways by many different users, from the utility program that manages it and provides support for particular employees to researchers who analyze it for the creation of new drugs or insurers using it for marketing analytics of brand new types of data usages because of modern data collection methods and the prevalence of cloud computing and digital health products such as mobile health applications, it is also not relevant data are often collected in real time or passively, with employees not understanding when they are being collected, and such data could be sent to multiple locations for processing and storage, with the potential for retention and use becoming, from the employee's perspective, infinite (Quach et al., 2022). The issue is further complicated by the uneven extent of relevant data protection laws worldwide: the employee's data could be collected in one country and sent to another, with all the appropriate legal standards applicable to data storage and usage and often the standard of employee protection being different. There is a need, therefore, for a new approach to consent, one specifically tailored to the high complexities of digital health technology (Networks et al., 1994). Such an approach will include dynamic consent, where the employee will be able to monitor and change their data usage preferences in real-time, and legal reforms that will ensure that the employee is informed about the uses of their data in a relevant way and that they would be able, legally, to monitor and consent to such uses in the framework of the digital age.

B. Liability and Accountability: Legal Complexities in the Digital Healthcare Landscape

Cloud Computing and the IoT have recently gained vast popularity in healthcare. The integration of cloud computing in most healthcare systems has significantly changed how employee data is managed (Elhoseny et al., 2018). However, it has raised a complex of legal problems mainly related to the issue of responsibility and liability. As healthcare providers and various technology companies continue using the most progressive technologies, the ability to determine who is responsible for a data breach has become a pressing question (Banimfreg, 2023). The problem stems from the very structure of digital ecosystems, which is hardly transparent and provides several conditions that must be met. In turn, the means of achieving those conditions are not transparent, meaning it is still not entirely clear who is responsible for keeping employee data safe.

It is a widely recognised fact that healthcare providers have been traditionally responsible for protecting employee data in the realm of various legal frameworks, such as the US Health Insurance Protection and Portability Act and the EU General Data Protection Regulation (Insights, 2023). However, integrating Cloud Computing and the Internet of Things has spread this responsibility to various actors. This way, the liability for a data breach falling on cloud service providers, device manufacturers, and software developers has become commonplace. As a result, the responsibility for employees' data security has become dispersed, meaning that it is hard to say who can be liable for a data breach (Porter, 2023). The most crucial issue affecting the extent of establishing responsibility is the lack of sufficient clarity in the system of contractual relations. Therefore, in the case of a data breach, cloud service providers may claim that they are the service providers and that their obligations did not go further than mere storage of data since the healthcare provider had determined the content of data storage. In its turn, the healthcare provider may object and insist that a technology company providing cloud services is the liable party (Tosza, 2021). As a result, the lack of clarity on the issue of responsibility additionally complicates the process of ensuring the universality of data protection standards.

Also, the global footprint of Cloud Computing and IoT contributes to the lack of accountability. Employee data is usually stored and processed in several jurisdictions with legal norms and standards. The practice does not define which sets of rules are supposed to be applied in cases of breaches. The sense of data sovereignty also participates in the division of jurisdiction (Uddin et al., 2021). Like healthcare data or not, the entire industry functions within a patchwork of rules of up to 185 countries, which restrains accountability regulation within a unified legal space. On top of that, besides the already explained legal issues, there is a growing concern about the inadequacy of existing regulatory frameworks concerning the transformed nature of risks and challenges created by new digital tools. It is common for the legislative processes of various countries to expand nominal protection provisions that do not solve the problems (Mossialos et al., 2010). However, technologies evolve much faster, and the lag between creating and efficiently operating legal norms may add to the lack of accountability. Healthcare providers and technology companies may experience a 'black hole' in the context of accountability, which relies either on outdated standards or the absence of regulations. In enacting legal reforms, legislators worldwide should focus on defining the exact nature of relations in the context of accountable healthcare. Laws should be introduced in all countries or an alternative form that outlines the responsibility of all sides and regulates the divisions of roles between them (Priyadarshi & Kumar, 2020). The concepts of shared and exclusive liability, or following inconsiderate contractual definitions, must be included in such laws. Simultaneously, doing so for the sake of divide and conquer will be an erroneous step; international departments and governments have to harmonise data protection standards to address accountable healthcare.

C. Technological Advancements vs. Legislative Pace

The rapid development of technology in the contemporary era has significantly impacted the fields of Cloud Computing and the IoT, markedly impacting healthcare. As such, numerous technological innovations, especially in cloud computing and the IoT, have significantly improved how healthcare is facilitated in different settings. Cloud Computing allows for seamless real-time monitoring and other services, the introduction of which has dramatically transformed how healthcare is delivered (Barbara L Filkins et al., 2016). Similarly, IoT devices allow for a range of remote services previously unavailable, such as diagnostics and others. However, the effect of rapid technological development is not always solely positive, as the challenges it introduces are often multifaceted. One of the most urgent problems introduced by it, especially viewed in the context of the legal sphere, concerns the increasing lag between the development of innovative technologies and the development of legal system updates capable of regulating those innovations (Sachin Kumar et al., 2019). The fastest possible enactment of laws is insufficient, as the development of laws regulating new technologies and the changes those technologies bring to the environment has to follow a specific schedule. Additionally, such adjustments are highly complex, often dealing with emerging and multifaceted aspects of reality. When cloud computing and IoT are considered, the major problems concerning them are primarily data protection. Using such devices often results in the storage and processing through various interconnected platforms of increased amounts and categories of data concerning individual employees (Allioui & Mourdi, 2023). Such technological application runs contrary to the existing data protection laws created to regulate different, particularly older, data processing and storage forms.

The legislative process, by definition, is well-considered and slow in general. Laws take time to formulate, and creating new ones and amending old ones are typically centred around a consultative approach with paperwork and references, debated and voted on by relevant stakeholders, including regulatory bodies, relevant policymakers, and industry experts. This, in and of itself, is a mechanism to ensure that the laws are indeed both well-considered and accepted by most actors involved (Latapí Agudelo et al., 2019). In this way, legislative processes are naturally lengthier than industrial processes, and so is technological innovation. Technological innovations, in contrast, are typically developed and implemented as fast as viability allows, driven by both a for-profit industry naturally incentivised by competition to do so and by the needs of various sectors to modernise and improve at a faster pace. This has the effect that legal frameworks typically lag several years behind the latest technological insight and innovation, a problem that has several implications for the implementation of IoT devices and cloud-based services in the healthcare sector (Rissman et al., 2020). Firstly, the lack of regulation in many cases means that the healthcare provider and the employees are at risk of the technology. Data breaches, unauthorised revelations, and misuse of such data may be almost guaranteed without a regulatory body to limit and constrain both the collection and use of data by healthcare providers (Dolezel et al., 2023). Similarly, companies producing and supplying these devices on hard- or software may be unclear about their legal liabilities and base their behaviour on possibly outdated frameworks.

In addition, regulations are enacted in response to past incidents or emerging concerns, and they may be overly restrictive and not consider the potential benefits of particular technologies. It is imperative in healthcare since such constraints can be associated with risks that an organisation cannot provide necessary services. Thus, the main problem related to the rapid pace of ever-improving technologies in this sector is that investments in them are rarely made (Argaw et al., 2020). Instead, most resources are spent looking for possible solutions, and companies often lack the motivation to implement innovations. It is already discussed that the "move fast and break things" strategy is becoming prevalent in technology corporations (Ivanka Visnjic & Ronnie Leten, 2024). It often refers to the fact that they prioritise innovation over security and privacy restrictions, and with the implementation of decision theory within the economy, the majority of the research can become the source of manipulation of employee data.

VII. PROPOSED LEGISLATIVE REFORMS

In addressing the issues of Cloud Computing and IoT in healthcare, this section provides crucial legislative revisions. These include applying international data protection standards to protect international employee data and cloud usage. To ensure that employees give informed consent, as well as to ensure that it is not forgotten, there should also be improvements in the permission level (Zandesh et al., 2019). In addition, legislation should provide directions on sharing health data and notifying of data breaches or any incidences of incrimination. This serves as an effort to respect employee rights while adapting to the changes in the technology sector.

A. International Data Protection Standards

In a world where cloud computing and the Internet of Things have become the main drivers of effective medical management, employee data has started to cross many borders. It means that there is a need for international standards in the sphere of employee data protection. In turn, unlike one's expectations, many data protection laws are adopted by various countries and sections. Of course, the differences between the statutes create gaps for significant challenges linked with the effectiveness of employee data protection and tests and treatment of employees who ought to use modern tools (Singh et al., 2021). In this regard, it is crucial to adopt reliable international data protection standards that all countries will use to solve the problems and ensure that all employees will be exposed to necessary medical tools. One of the significant current differences between the countries is that some of the elements of the modern data ecosystems are not used in some regions (Abouelmehdi et al., 2018).

For example, some countries have not started to apply different medicines and IoT because of their potential vulnerabilities. At the same time, other countries may have fewer tools to protect their employee data. As long as the differences exist, adopting international data protection standards is essential. Finally, implementing international data protection standards can also mitigate the risks mentioned above (Affia et al., 2023). Since employee data is often subject to processing and storage in different countries, it is crucial to establish international standards that would be applicable in any jurisdiction. This is a solid foundation for improving data security since healthcare providers and companies would no longer be required to comply with various legislations in different countries (Xiang & Cai, 2021). Furthermore, global standards will guarantee organisations implementing this standard that any data processing and storage activities comply with international standards and that the risks of a data breach are minimal.

Presumably, the most suitable model for international data protection standards is GDPR. It is one of the most comprehensive pieces of data protection regulation and is recognised globally. It is rigorous in some aspects, adding credibility to the standard. For example, it fully complies with one of the central data protection standards, data minimisation. The regulation also implements the purpose limitation principle, which requires specifying the scope of actions with data (IBM, 2024). At the same time, considering that not all countries would be willing to follow the GDPR, it also allows for derogations and local specifics. Thus, to ensure that international data protection standards are complied with universally, international organisations should take a balanced approach, similar to the GDPR. Overall, the compromises mentioned above are integral to implementing data protection. Combined with international cooperation, these solutions can ensure the implementability and enforceability of the international standard (*IBM Sterling B2B Integrator*, 2024). Therefore, international bodies should be involved in creating international standards for data protection. First, organisations such as ISO or WHO will provide a framework for implementing essential practices and ensure the standard is implemented efficiently. Second, through bilateral agreements and familiar principles, countries that implement such solutions in their jurisdiction will be able to ensure the security of international data processing and storage.

B. Enhanced Consent Mechanisms

The digital landscape of healthcare is changing at a rapid pace every day. Today, we are at a point where cloud computing and IoT technologies are becoming pervasive in how healthcare is provided. Modern-day consent mechanisms need to do more than the traditional method of obtaining consent used in the past. The present forms used to obtain consent are the old paper-based records that were done personally (Javaid et al., 2023). The complex way of obtaining and recording consent will no longer work in today's digital world as data flows in and out from various technologies. All employees have new ways in which their personal health information is collected through multiple online platforms and devices. More advanced consent models are required today, which make sure that the employee is aware and informed of what and how their information is being used and handled (Verily et al., 2022). Modern-day consent is more about the awareness of the employee, and the method allows the employee more control of their health information. Modern-day consent is facing many challenges due to both practical and theoretical problems. These problems aid in the consent process whereby the employee is unable to understand or is made aware of how and with whom the data is being shared with (Hall et al., 2012).

This means that the current consent mechanism is not working well enough to provide the clarity needed for the employee. The current consent method uses complex consent forms and too many legal terms that the employee is unaware of. Often, the employee is unaware of the implications of sharing data and who will have access to the data. This is especially true when data is being shared and sent across multiple sites and sometimes even across multiple countries (Gupta, 2013). Therefore, a better consent form is needed to work. The form can make use of visual aids simple and short. The employee may also use an interactive tool like an app to consent to data sharing.

To begin, another influential aspect that helps to improve consent mechanisms is the development of dynamic consent models; according to the current model of receiving a employee's consent to share their data, medical personnel or representatives of an organisation request permission once. At the same time, variable health conditions, or the specifics of IoT and Cloud Computing, presume that data will be collected for a long time (Jane Kaye et al., 2014). Therefore, employees should be allowed to update their consent at the exact moment when using an app or any other digital platform. The employee decides precisely which data and with whom to share these data and has the full right to cancel consent. This practice not only does not violate the employee's autonomy but also increases the level of trust in the healthcare system by giving employees more control.

It is also essential to strengthen clear and concise informed consent. Signing a consent form should not be the only action a statement does. The employee is also entitled to information that could mitigate individual possible responses. The employee must be informed about the potential risks and benefits of sharing or not sharing their data with a particular organisation or individual (Olejarczyk & Young, 2024). Employees need to know which party or parties will have access to their data and what the data will be used for. Moreover, employees should be informed of their rights and how they can withdraw consent. Both healthcare providers and technology developers should be required to ensure that the form they prepare is genuinely informational. Therefore, the hospital staff involved in the consent process should receive additional training (Keshta & Odeh, 2021). Finally, novel technologies like AI or blockchain can further advance the consent process. For example, an AI tool may recognise precisely what a specific employee prefers and suggest what type of consent they will grant based on this information.

C. Guidelines for Data Sharing and Breach Notification

With the increase of data used in modern healthcare, many policies and protocols that previously did not seem relevant became essential questions of interest. This is also the case with GDPR requirements, and Gavin et al.'s ideas suggest the nature of the issue. Although the article is from 2018, the ideas described might still be relevant because of the rapidly changing legal environment and continuously increasing opportunities for data processing (Yuan & Li, 2019). According to the article, the pursuit of stricter GDPR requirements is mainly due to employee information sensitivity and the fact that these data are regularly stored and processed across various platforms. In recent years, when cloud computing and the Internet of Things have become elements of the conventional healthcare system, the opportunities to access data have increased dramatically. In this situation, the task of a legislator is to introduce relevant requirements regarding data sharing with a high degree of detail, which would also be possible to enforce effectively (Mocydlarz-Adamcewicz et al., 2023). These requirements, then, should be aimed at employee information data safety and, mainly, data specify the terms and rules of data sharing and their potential breach. It might seem that the central problem of modern healthcare and the digital environment, in general, is the possibility of sharing employees' data securely between different entities such as care providers, insurance companies, research centres and developers (Dash et al., 2019). On the one hand, such data sharing is essential since it contributes to proper medical treatment continuity, event research performance, and overall healthcare provision. However, the shared information can be extremely sensitive in terms of privacy and often oppressed by some unreliable legal frameworks, leading to unauthorised data access or inappropriate usage in other ways (Hulsen, 2020). These guidelines should predominantly rely on the principles of data minimisation. In other words, they need to be structured so that only that amount of data strictly required for a particular process is shared and that it is shared only with entities that need to access it (Wirth et al., 2021). The guidelines should also include requirements to use strong encryption protocols, secure data transmission channels, and stringent authentication to prevent unauthorised access. Additionally, participating healthcare providers and other entities that share employee data should be required to keep detailed records of all data exchanges, including information on the parties' identity, their roles, and the purpose of their respective access. This is designed to improve transparency and accountability.

Equally importantly, the legislative guidelines should include precise requirements regarding breach notification. In healthcare data breaches, it is essential for all affected individuals and relevant bodies to be notified in a timely manner to mitigate the damage. At the same time, several jurisdictions, such as the European Union under the General Data Protection Regulation or GDPR, already have laws that require breach notification within certain time limits. However, the specifics of these time limits generally differ significantly across jurisdictions, as in the example of the GDPR above, as opposed to HIPAA regulation in the United States (Verstraete & Zarsky, 2021). As a result, HCPs and their tech partners often do not know their expected requirements. Therefore, as part of the legislative reforms, the breach notification guidelines must be established in such a way that they are standardised across different jurisdictions to make sure that HCPs and their tech partners know the exact nature of their legal obligations (Melissa M. Goldstein & Hyatt Thorpe Jane, 2010). Specifically, these reforms should establish requirements for when breaches need to be notified, what information about them should be included, and what steps should be taken in response. The guidelines should also establish requirements for managing the incident, including procedures and assignments.

VIII. CONCLUSION

"Technology is best when it brings people together."
- Matt Mullenweg

This research paper aims to prove that high-quality medical assistance cannot be provided to employees without legal safeguards and that the legal protection of employees' data should be considered the primary condition for effective healthcare delivery. After conducting a review of the current legal infrastructure, the researcher concluded that the existing pieces of legislature that control the security of employee data about both IoT and cloud computing are rather insufficient (McGraw & Mandl, 2021). It is not to say, however, that the existing regulation is entirely useless; though general regulations such as GDPR in the EU and HIPAA in the US provide a shallow form of protection, the advanced nature of the two technologies creates a vast range of issues these policies are unable to address comprehensively (Motti & Berkovsky, 2022).

These issues include the lack of clarity in both data ownership and proper bargaining, the utter insufficiency of the measures that could be used to control the process of marketing and transferring employees' data across borders, and the fact that the emergence of new methods of IoT and changes in the existing prevent the law from catching up and providing the respective safeguards. In addition, the current lack of accountability in case of breaches is somewhat disturbing in that it does not offer mechanisms for determining the liability of multiple stakeholders, particularly the IT companies and healthcare institutions that use their technology (Tawalbeh et al., 2020). This is why we can positively affirm that the current state of things is highly insufficient while the quality of information and technical infrastructure in healthcare is growing! The results of this study indicate that it is necessary to carry out legislative reforms that consider the specifics of cloud computing and IoT in this sector. Modern technology continuously develops and is increasingly involved in medical processes. However, with the growing role of gadgets and cloud services, the complexity of the risks associated with the security of medical data and employee information becomes increasingly multi-faceted, which is not reflected in current legislation.

Although legal standards provide an elementary level of protection for such information, they are not sufficiently equipped to regulate the specific vulnerabilities associated with Cloud Computing and IoT. Thus, there is a vital need for legislative development on the part of legislators, which should be both focused on the specific technological context that needs to be regulated and, at the same time, flexible enough to work with new data in the future (Markopoulou & Papakonstantinou, 2021). In this context, significant legislative changes could be made by creating new legal standards on such issues as defining the ownership of data, managing employee consent, and distributing responsibility in a situation where a third-party service is involved in data processing. When developing these legislative standards, consideration should be given to the existing data protection standards accepted internationally to come to one acceptable option for cross-border data transmission in the international context (Demir, 2023). Another area of reform may be the introduction of standards for data sharing between healthcare providers and technology companies and the procedure for responding to data breaches. Legal standards that may require companies and third-party providers to notify customers during a data breach will lead primarily to transparency and accountability of companies using third-party providers in their services.

Since the discussion regarding the link between technology and healthcare and the attendant innovations will likely continue, future research should focus on how such technology as blockchain and Artificial Intelligence can serve the identified purpose. For example, it is anticipated that blockchain may be used to ensure the security of employee-related data. Notably, the technology offers a unique opportunity to secure employee details and ensure authenticity. Additionally, blockchain can be used to reveal the place where the data has been kept, further enhancing the transparency of employee data processing practice (Tagde et al., 2021). Similarly, AI can assist in responding to the threat of cybersecurity in real time and engaging with the problem of datakeeping and the corresponding regulation to ensure constant compliance. Furthermore, it is understood that should blockchain and AI be used in healthcare, a range of crucial challenges might be created that must be addressed. These include the legal implications of using the identified technologies, as well as the levels of their compliance and interoperability(Kaur et al., 2023). Therefore, future research has to investigate the technical capacity of the identified technology and the extent to which AI and blockchain can be utilised. Instead, the future investigation has to encompass the evaluation of the implications that both tools are likely to have for the corresponding set of legal regulations and ethical concerns to create a comprehensive picture of the potential contribution of the discussed technology.

REFERENCES

Abouelmehdi, K., Beni-Hessane, A., & Khaloufi, H. (2018). Big healthcare data: Preserving security and privacy. *Journal of Big Data*, *5*(1), 1. DOI: 10.1186/s40537-017-0110-7

Affia, A. O., Finch, H., Jung, W., Samori, I. A., Potter, L., & Palmer, X.-L. (2023). IoT Health Devices: Exploring Security Risks in the Connected Landscape. *IoT*, *4*(2), 150–182. DOI: 10.3390/iot4020009

Alder, S. (2024). *Healthcare Data Breach Statistics*. https://www.hipaajournal.com/healthcare-data-breach-statistics/

Allioui, H., & Mourdi, Y. (2023). Exploring the Full Potentials of IoT for Better Financial Growth and Stability: A Comprehensive Survey. *Sensors (Basel)*, *23*(19), 8015. DOI: 10.3390/s23198015 PMID: 37836845

Hoofnagle, C. J., van der Sloot, B., & Borgesius, F. Z. (2019). The European Union general data protection regulation: What it is and what it means*. *Information & Communications Technology Law*, *28*(1), 65–98. DOI: 10.1080/13600834.2019.1573501

Argaw, S. T., Troncoso-Pastoriza, J. R., Lacey, D., Florin, M.-V., Calcavecchia, F., Anderson, D., Burleson, W., Vogel, J.-M., O'Leary, C., Eshaya-Chauvin, B., & Flahault, A. (2020). Cybersecurity of Hospitals: Discussing the challenges and working towards mitigating the risks. *BMC Medical Informatics and Decision Making*, *20*(1), 146. DOI: 10.1186/s12911-020-01161-7 PMID: 32620167

Banimfreg, B. H. (2023). A comprehensive review and conceptual framework for cloud computing adoption in bioinformatics. *Healthcare Analytics*, *3*, 100190. DOI: 10.1016/j.health.2023.100190

Filkins, B. L., Kim, J. Y., Roberts, B., Armstrong, W., Miller, M. A., Hultner, M. L., & Steinhubl, S. R. (2016). Privacy and security in the era of digital health: What should translational researchers know and do about it? *American Journal of Translational Research*, *8*(3), 1560.

Becker, R., Chokoshvili, D., Thorogood, A., Dove, E. S., Molnár-Gábor, F., Ziaka, A., Tzortzatou-Nanopoulou, O., & Comandè, G. (2024). Purpose definition as a crucial step for determining the legal basis under the GDPR: Implications for scientific research. *Journal of Law and the Biosciences*, *11*(1), lsae001. Advance online publication. DOI: 10.1093/jlb/lsae001 PMID: 38313429

Cresswell, K., Domínguez Hernández, A., Williams, R., & Sheikh, A. (2022). Key Challenges and Opportunities for Cloud Technology in Health Care: Semistructured Interview Study. *JMIR Human Factors*, *9*(1), e31246. DOI: 10.2196/31246 PMID: 34989688

Dash, S., Shakyawar, S. K., Sharma, M., & Kaushik, S. (2019). Big data in healthcare: Management, analysis and future prospects. *Journal of Big Data*, *6*(1), 54. DOI: 10.1186/s40537-019-0217-0

Demir, E. (2023). The protection of human biodata: Is there any role for data ownership? *Computer Law & Security Review*, *51*, 105905. DOI: 10.1016/j.clsr.2023.105905

Dolezel, D., Beauvais, B., Stigler Granados, P., Fulton, L., & Kruse, C. S. (2023). Effects of Internal and External Factors on Hospital Data Breaches: Quantitative Study. *Journal of Medical Internet Research*, *25*, e51471. DOI: 10.2196/51471 PMID: 38127426

El-Gendy, S., Elsayed, M. S., Jurcut, A., & Azer, M. A. (2023). Privacy Preservation Using Machine Learning in the Internet of Things. *Mathematics*, *11*(16), 3477. DOI: 10.3390/math11163477

Elhoseny, M., Abdelaziz, A., Salama, A. S., Riad, A. M., Muhammad, K., & Sangaiah, A. K. (2018). A hybrid model of Internet of Things and cloud computing to manage big data in health services applications. *Future Generation Computer Systems*, *86*, 1383–1394. DOI: 10.1016/j.future.2018.03.005

Bellamy, F. (2023). U.S. Data Privacy Laws to Enter New Era in 2023. Reuters. https://www.reuters.com/legal/legalindustry/us-data-privacy-laws-enter-new-era-2023-2023-01-12/

Gupta, U. C. (2013). Informed consent in clinical research: Revisiting few concepts and areas. *Perspectives in Clinical Research*, *4*(1), 26–32. DOI: 10.4103/2229-3485.106373 PMID: 23533976

Hall, D. E., Prochazka, A. V., & Fink, A. S. (2012). Informed consent for clinical treatment. *Canadian Medical Association Journal*, *184*(5), 533–540. DOI: 10.1503/cmaj.112120 PMID: 22392947

Hulsen, T. (2020). Sharing Is Caring—Data Sharing Initiatives in Healthcare. *International Journal of Environmental Research and Public Health*, *17*(9), 3046. DOI: 10.3390/ijerph17093046 PMID: 32349396

IBM. (2024). *How to Implement General Data Protection Regulation (GDPR) | IBM*. https://www.ibm.com/think/topics/general-data-protection-regulation-implementation

IBM Sterling B2B Integrator. (2024, February 1). https://www.ibm.com/docs/en/b2b-integrator/6.1.2?topic=overview-general-data-protection-regulation-gdpr

Insights. (2023). *International: GDPR v. HIPAA - Comparing and contrasting two important data protection regimes | Insights | DataGuidance*. Insights. https://www.dataguidance.com/opinion/international-gdpr-v-hipaa-comparing-and-contrasting

Visnjic, I., & Leten, R. (2024). The Legacy Company's Guide to Innovation. Harvard Business Review. https://hbr.org/2024/09/the-legacy-companys-guide-to-innovation

Javaid, M., Haleem, A., Singh, R. P., & Suman, R. (2023). Towards insighting cybersecurity for healthcare domains: A comprehensive review of recent practices and trends. *Cyber Security and Applications*, *1*, 100016. DOI: 10.1016/j.csa.2023.100016

Javaid, M., & Khan, I. H. (2021). Internet of Things (IoT) enabled healthcare helps to take the challenges of COVID-19 Pandemic. *Journal of Oral Biology and Craniofacial Research*, *11*(2), 209–214. DOI: 10.1016/j.jobcr.2021.01.015 PMID: 33665069

Kaur, R., Gabrijelčič, D., & Klobučar, T. (2023). Artificial intelligence for cybersecurity: Literature review and future research directions. *Information Fusion*, *97*, 101804. DOI: 10.1016/j.inffus.2023.101804

Kaye, J., Edgar A Whitley, D. L., Morrison, M., Teare, H., & Melham, K. (2014). *Dynamic consent: A patient interface for twenty-first century research networks | European Journal of Human Genetics*. https://www.nature.com/articles/ejhg201471

Kelly, J. T., Campbell, K. L., Gong, E., & Scuffham, P. (2020). The Internet of Things: Impact and Implications for Health Care Delivery. *Journal of Medical Internet Research*, *22*(11), e20135. DOI: 10.2196/20135 PMID: 33170132

Keshta, I., & Odeh, A. (2021). Security and privacy of electronic health records: Concerns and challenges. *Egyptian Informatics Journal*, *22*(2), 177–183. DOI: 10.1016/j.eij.2020.07.003

Krogstad, D. J., Diop, S., Diallo, A., Mzayek, F., Keating, J., Koita, O. A., & Touré, Y. T. (2010). Informed Consent in International Research: The Rationale for Different Approaches. *The American Journal of Tropical Medicine and Hygiene*, *83*(4), 743–747. DOI: 10.4269/ajtmh.2010.10-0014 PMID: 20889858

Kumar, M., Kumar, A., Verma, S., Bhattacharya, P., Ghimire, D., Kim, S., & Hosen, A. S. M. S. (2023). Healthcare Internet of Things (H-IoT): Current Trends, Future Prospects, Applications, Challenges, and Security Issues. *Electronics (Basel)*, *12*(9), 2050. DOI: 10.3390/electronics12092050

Kumar, S., Tiwari, P., & Tiwari, P. (2019). *Internet of Things is a revolutionary approach for future technology enhancement: A review | Journal of Big Data | Full Text.* https://journalofbigdata.springeropen.com/articles/10.1186/s40537-019-0268-2

Latapí Agudelo, M. A., Jóhannsdóttir, L., & Davídsdóttir, B. (2019). A literature review of the history and evolution of corporate social responsibility. *International Journal of Corporate Social Responsibility*, *4*(1), 1. DOI: 10.1186/s40991-018-0039-y

Markopoulou, D., & Papakonstantinou, V. (2021). The regulatory framework for the protection of critical infrastructures against cyberthreats: Identifying shortcomings and addressing future challenges: The case of the health sector in particular. *Computer Law & Security Review*, *41*, 105502. DOI: 10.1016/j.clsr.2020.105502

McGraw, D., & Mandl, K. D. (2021). Privacy protections to encourage use of health-relevant digital data in a learning health system. *NPJ Digital Medicine*, *4*(1), 2. DOI: 10.1038/s41746-020-00362-8 PMID: 33398052

Mehrtak, M., SeyedAlinaghi, S. A., MohsseniPour, M., Noori, T., Karimi, A., Shamsabadi, A., Heydari, M., Barzegary, A., Mirzapour, P., Soleymanzadeh, M., Vahedi, F., Mehraeen, E., & Dadras, O. (2021). Security challenges and solutions using healthcare cloud computing. *Journal of Medicine and Life*, *14*(4), 448–461. DOI: 10.25122/jml-2021-0100 PMID: 34621367

Goldstein, M. M., & Thorpe Jane, H. (2010, September 1). The First Anniversary of the Health Information Technology for Economic and Clinical Health (HITECH) Act: The regulatory outlook for implementation. *Perspectives in Health Information Management*, *7*(Summer), 1c.

Mocydlarz-Adamcewicz, M., Bajsztok, B., Filip, S., Petera, J., Mestan, M., & Malicki, J. (2023). Management of Onsite and Remote Communication in Oncology Hospitals: Data Protection in an Era of Rapid Technological Advances. *Journal of Personalized Medicine*, *13*(5), 761. DOI: 10.3390/jpm13050761 PMID: 37240931

Mossialos, E., Permanand, G., Baeten, R., & Hervey, T. (2010). Health systems governance in Europe: The role of European Union law and policy. In Mossialos, E., Permanand, G., Baeten, R., & Hervey, T. K. (Eds.), *Health Systems Governance in Europe* (1st ed., pp. 1–83). Cambridge University Press., DOI: 10.1017/CBO9780511750496.002

Motti, V. G., & Berkovsky, S. (2022). Healthcare Privacy. In Knijnenburg, B. P., Page, X., Wisniewski, P., Lipford, H. R., Proferes, N., & Romano, J. (Eds.), *Modern Socio-Technical Perspectives on Privacy* (pp. 203–231). Springer International Publishing., DOI: 10.1007/978-3-030-82786-1_10

Namdech, P., Rotjanawasuthorn, S., Singh, B., & Kaunert, C. (2025). Harnessing Artificial Intelligence For Lifelong Education: Opportunities And Challenges. *Asian Education and Learning Review*, *3*(2), 4–4.

Nass, S. J., Levit, L. A., & Gostin, L. O. (2009). HIPAA, the Privacy Rule, and Its Application to Health Research. In *Beyond the HIPAA Privacy Rule: Enhancing Privacy, Improving Health Through Research*. National Academies Press.

Lohr, K. N., & Donaldson, M. S. (Eds.). (1994). *Health data in the information age: use, disclosure, and privacy*.

Olejarczyk, J. P., & Young, M. (2024). Patient Rights and Ethics. In *StatPearls*. StatPearls Publishing., https://www.ncbi.nlm.nih.gov/books/NBK538279/

Parihar, A., Prajapati, J. B., Prajapati, B. G., Trambadiya, B., Thakkar, A., & Engineer, P. (2024). *Role of IOT in healthcare: Applications, security & privacy concerns*. Intelligent Pharmacy., DOI: 10.1016/j.ipha.2024.01.003

Porter, A. (2023, June 23). Navigating the Privacy Maze: GDPR vs HIPAA. *BigID*. https://bigid.com/blog/gdpr-vs-hipaa/

Priyadarshi, M., & Kumar, S. (2020). Accountability in Healthcare in India. *Indian Journal of Community Medicine : Official Publication of Indian Association of Preventive & Social Medicine*, *45*(2), 125. DOI: 10.4103/ijcm.IJCM_224_19 PMID: 32905344

Quach, S., Thaichon, P., Martin, K. D., Weaven, S., & Palmatier, R. W. (2022). Digital technologies: Tensions in privacy and data. *Journal of the Academy of Marketing Science*, *50*(6), 1299–1323. DOI: 10.1007/s11747-022-00845-y PMID: 35281634

Rejeb, A., Rejeb, K., Treiblmaier, H., Appolloni, A., Alghamdi, S., Alhasawi, Y., & Iranmanesh, M. (2023). The Internet of Things (IoT) in healthcare: Taking stock and moving forward. *Internet of Things : Engineering Cyber Physical Human Systems*, *22*, 100721. DOI: 10.1016/j.iot.2023.100721

Rissman, J., Bataille, C., Masanet, E., Aden, N., Morrow, W. R.III, Zhou, N., Elliott, N., Dell, R., Heeren, N., Huckestein, B., Cresko, J., Miller, S. A., Roy, J., Fennell, P., Cremmins, B., Koch Blank, T., Hone, D., Williams, E. D., de la Rue du Can, S., & Helseth, J. (2020). Technologies and policies to decarbonize global industry: Review and assessment of mitigation drivers through 2070. *Applied Energy*, *266*, 114848. DOI: 10.1016/j.apenergy.2020.114848

Liss, S., & Han, Y. J. (2023). *Hacking healthcare: With 385M patient records exposed, cybersecurity experts sound alarm on breach surge*. Healthcare Dive. https://www.healthcaredive.com/news/cybersecurity-hacking-healthcare-breaches/643821/

Seh, A. H., Zarour, M., Alenezi, M., Sarkar, A. K., Agrawal, A., Kumar, R., & Ahmad Khan, R. (2020). Healthcare Data Breaches: Insights and Implications. *Health Care*, *8*(2), 133. DOI: 10.3390/healthcare8020133 PMID: 32414183

Singh, N., Raza, M., Paranthaman, V. V., Awais, M., Khalid, M., & Javed, E. (2021). Internet of Things and cloud computing. *Digital Health*, •••, 151–162. DOI: 10.1016/B978-0-12-818914-6.00013-2

Gantz, S. (2014). Health Insurance Portability and Accountability Act of 1996—An overview. Science Direct. https://www.sciencedirect.com/topics/computer-science/health-insurance-portability-and-accountability-act-of-1996

Tagde, P., Tagde, S., Bhattacharya, T., Tagde, P., Chopra, H., Akter, R., Kaushik, D., & Rahman, M. (2021). Blockchain and artificial intelligence technology in e-Health. *Environmental Science and Pollution Research International*, *28*(38), 52810–52831. DOI: 10.1007/s11356-021-16223-0 PMID: 34476701

Tawalbeh, L., Muheidat, F., Tawalbeh, M., & Quwaider, M. (2020). IoT Privacy and Security: Challenges and Solutions. *Applied Sciences (Basel, Switzerland)*, *10*(12), 4102. DOI: 10.3390/app10124102

Theodos, K., & Sittig, S. (2020). Health Information Privacy Laws in the Digital Age: HIPAA Doesn't Apply. *Perspectives in Health Information Management*, *18*(Winter), 11. https://www.ncbi.nlm.nih.gov/pmc/articles/PMC7883355/ PMID: 33633522

Tosza, S. (2021). Internet service providers as law enforcers and adjudicators. A public role of private actors. *Computer Law & Security Review*, *43*, 105614. DOI: 10.1016/j.clsr.2021.105614

Uddin, M. A., Stranieri, A., Gondal, I., & Balasubramanian, V. (2021). A survey on the adoption of blockchain in IoT: Challenges and solutions. *Blockchain: Research and Applications*, *2*(2), 100006. DOI: 10.1016/j.bcra.2021.100006

Ehrenstein, V., Kharrazi, H., Lehmann, H., & Taylor, C. O. (2019). Obtaining data from electronic health records. In Tools and technologies for registry interoperability, registries for evaluating patient outcomes: A user's guide, 3rd edition, Addendum 2 [Internet]. Agency for Healthcare Research and Quality (US).

Abernethy, A., Adams, L., Barrett, M., Bechtel, C., Brennan, P., Butte, A., & Valdes, K. (2022). The promise of digital health: Then, now, and the future. *NAM Perspectives*, *2022*, 10–31478.

Verstraete, M., & Zarsky, T. (2021). Optimizing breach notification. U. Ill. L. Rev., 803.

Wirth, F. N., Meurers, T., Johns, M., & Prasser, F. (2021). Privacy-preserving data sharing infrastructures for medical research: Systematization and comparison. *BMC Medical Informatics and Decision Making*, *21*(1), 242. DOI: 10.1186/s12911-021-01602-x PMID: 34384406

Xiang, D., & Cai, W. (2021). Privacy Protection and Secondary Use of Health Data: Strategies and Methods. *BioMed Research International*, *2021*(1), 1–11. DOI: 10.1155/2021/6967166 PMID: 34660798

Yuan, B., & Li, J. (2019). The Policy Effect of the General Data Protection Regulation (GDPR) on the Digital Public Health Sector in the European Union: An Empirical Investigation. *International Journal of Environmental Research and Public Health*, *16*(6), 1070. DOI: 10.3390/ijerph16061070 PMID: 30934648

Zandesh, Z., Ghazisaeedi, M., Devarakonda, M. V., & Haghighi, M. S. (2019). Legal framework for health cloud: A systematic review. *International Journal of Medical Informatics*, *132*, 103953. DOI: 10.1016/j.ijmedinf.2019.103953 PMID: 31630064

Chapter 15
From Unresolved to Resolved: Strengthening Data Protection for Privacy of Employee in Digital Health

Navonita Mallick
https://orcid.org/0000-0003-3621-3764
KIIT University, Bhubaneswar, India

Shashwata Sahu
https://orcid.org/0009-0003-6843-9554
KIIT University, Bhubaneswar, India

Bhupinder Singh
https://orcid.org/0009-0006-4779-2553
Sharda University, India

Kittisak Wongmahesak
https://orcid.org/0009-0000-2129-4691
North Bangkok University, Thailand

ABSTRACT

Health data digitalisation poses privacy and security concerns. Employee data, which we have never been able to access before, is rising with digital health. The strongest laws for the protection of employee data and privacy are actual. Consent, data collection, and third-party use agreements are mandatory for sensitive medical records. This chapter evaluates the state of data privacy due to existing legislative and regulatory measures that control the digital delivery of healthcare. The chapter

DOI: 10.4018/979-8-3373-2210-0.ch015

Copyright © 2025, IGI Global Scientific Publishing. Copying or distributing in print or electronic forms without written permission of IGI Global Scientific Publishing is prohibited.

initially addresses data protection laws and how they measure up against those of other countries. Assessing the results of present measures is best done by comparing them with judicial override and infringement. The findings suggest a need for improved data privacy knowledge and compliance, particularly within digital health.

1. INTRODUCTION

India's fast-growing digital health sector needs rigid data protection rules. The Indian healthcare sector is in the middle of a massive transformation thanks to the rapid adoption of digital technologies. Among the many advances that have been part of this so-called "digital health revolution", telemedicine platforms, Electronic Health Records (EHRs), and Health Information Exchanges (HIE) are some examples. These technologies can significantly improve healthcare accessibility, efficiency, and employee engagement. However, with all those exciting opportunities comes a significant challenge - ensuring strong data security and employee privacy in this fast-evolving digital world. It is a fact that digital health is on the rise in India. Telemedicine systems allow doctors to connect to distant locations and have remote consultations. (Maroju et al., 2023). This identified potential liability vulnerabilities in digital repositories that generate, store, and manipulate health data. Sharing information safely can help make healthcare systems more resilient. It means an umbrella approach that harmonises statutes, policy, and technology change to leave no seam or shortfall until delivery. This chapter calls for electronic health record privacy and national protocol security.

EHRs have been transforming medical records management, streamlined treatment coordination, and data-driven decision-making. Healthcare necessitates mobile health apps that empower employees to self-monitor their health and access information adapted to his or her well-being (Stephen & Frank, 2024a). Powered by data and digital technology, transform the way we deliver healthcare, focusing on prevention as well as giving individuals control over their health (Braghin & Cremonini, 2017a). We are also seeing a similarly quick adoption of digital health applications, which has stoked hesitations about security and privacy. Personal Health Information (PHI), which includes an individual's medical history, diagnosis, treatment plans, and genetic information, is being increasingly collected, maintained, and communicated electronically (Kassam et al., 2023). Strong legal and regulatory protections are needed to prevent unauthorised access, misuse, or disclosure of this precious trove of personally identifiable information.

Cyberattacks on healthcare facilities are experiencing a global rise in frequency. Global cybersecurity company Sophos tells us that nearly 60% of healthcare organisations worldwide have fallen victim to a cyberattack over the last year (SOPHOS,

2023). Security breaches can lead to the exposure of large volumes of private employee information - leading the employees to risk identity theft, financial fraud, and discrimination based on health issues. Written By The current legal framework in India is incapable of laying down specific rules or answering the question of who owns employee health information stored electronically and to whom accountability lies. In this way, the data subjects and payers are put in a grey area, not knowing how to treat their data, making it difficult for them to set up privacy rights quickly. Because health apps and online platforms are so ubiquitous, it might be hard for someone to obtain informed consent from users regarding the collection or use of data. This new data source may allow employees to bestow broad access permissions without accidentally comprehending the implications. The one-of-a-kind opportunity to reach into employee data for some other application besides its intended purpose can create an ethical issue. De-identified data is not readily applicable to the employee and may be re-identified using other information about the file. The chapter seeks to contribute towards a future where the boundless avenues of digital health in India are unlocked and where our most personal data -health records- is never mined without safeguarding their privacy.

2. OBJECTIVES OF THE CHAPTER

This chapter seeks to accomplish two main objectives. One of the first objectives is to undertake an in-depth review of current legislation and regulations regulating data protection vis-a-vis the digital health sector in India. This chapter forms the foundation upon which secondary aims will be built. The second objective is to identify gaps in current data protection practices. It will identify the vulnerabilities and offer methods to secure data management and enhance employee privacy. This will also look at the role of Indian courts in data privacy and review instances of data breaches within the digital health segment. It is an amalgamated strategy to discover and exploit the best ways by which it can infiltrate into the available Indian system.

3. RESEARCH METHODOLOGY

The chapter adopts an all-encompassing method to understand the data protection landscape in the Indian digital health space. The first part is to engage in doctrinal research. This requires an in-depth study of relevant Indian legal documents. This requires a review of the related statutes in various laws. Furthermore, this chapter also aims to investigate judicial rulings of data protection or privacy breaches issued by the courts in the health sector. Finally, relevant government policies and rules about protecting digital health data will be examined. Exploratory research is the second part of it. This means looking beyond India- well. The scope of the examination will be on privacy legislation and legislative frameworks established in other countries. Lessons can be drawn from successful regulation and top data protection practices in digital health as in other countries.

4. GLOBAL LANDSCAPE OF DATA PROTECTION IN THE DIGITAL HEALTHCARE ARENA

Navigating the landscape of global data protection in healthcare is complex and perilous. Digitising healthcare has revolutionised how employees are made well and how physicians conduct research. EHRs, telemedicine platforms, and HIE represent excellent opportunities that promise to improve healthcare access, effectiveness as well as innovation (Anawade et al., 2024). However, this technological change has also given rise to significant challenges, such as how we can keep data safe and employee information confidential. "Protected health information (PHI)", such as medical history, diagnoses, treatments, and genetic data - is being collected electronically more than ever before (Isola & Al Khalili, 2025). Consequently, it is important to develop robust legal and regulatory systems to protect this information from unauthorised access/ misuse/disclosure. Across the world, countries are grappling with how to leverage digital health's power while maintaining strong data privacy protections (Stevens, 2020).

Hyperprotect comes in response to the plight of the "General Data Protection Regulation (GDPR) of the European Union" enacted in 2018 and requires high-security standards to be enforced on data stored. It places significant control in individuals' hands by ensuring, inter alia, the right to access their data and have it corrected or deleted. This is true for all healthcare professionals or organisations that process personal data within the EU, irrespective of location. This rule has set the tone for global data protection and forced other countries to strengthen their judicial frameworks—incomplete Input. The US healthcare system is part of Federal and State law. "HIPAA - Health Insurance Portability and Accountability Act (1996)" is a federal legislation aimed at protecting the privacy of individually identifiable health information (IIHI) (Feld, 2005). HIPAA places strict security standards on anyone designated as a covered entity, which includes virtually any healthcare provider or practitioner (including dentists and other mental health professionals), an organisation that delivers payment for treatment services delivered by other (insurers) providers, plans providing prepaid long term care employee hospitalisation benefits; ambulance companies serving employees while they are being transported to hospitals/private clinics, etc. The HIPAA is considered narrow compared to the GDPR, which includes data portability and the right to delete. The "Personal Information Protection and Electronic Documents Act (PIPEDA)" is a Canadian federal law that governs the collection, use, or disclosure of personal data, including health-related information. It emphasises the principles of consent, accountability, and transparency. Similar to HIPAA, this policy gives individuals the right to access and amend their medical records. PIPEDA has come under fire for being light on enforcement mechanisms. The PHI is covered within Personal Information under the "Australian Privacy Act (APA)", but only in healthcare institutions, including public and private sectors. The applications also focus on data minimisation, limits to collection, and security safeguards. Mandatory data breach notification Australia has introduced mandatory data breach legislation for "Protected Health Information (PHI)" breaches by healthcare providers. The brief overview highlights how different countries have used several methods. While the GDPR of the EU sets a strict precedent for data protection, other regions like the US and Canada have provided a slightly flexible middle ground. China has a "Personal Information Protection Law (PIPL)" for personal data localisation and a government supervision system. Countries like Japan (APPI), Singapore, Argentina, and Brazil established comprehensive data privacy laws that include specific regulations relating to the healthcare sector. However, challenges remain, such as a lack of regulatory implementation capability and regional inconsistencies.

Regardless of the framework, key elements are needed to enable a strong data protection regime within health care. Legal frameworks that are clear and enforceable must be set up with explicit boundaries around data collection, access, storage, and sharing in the digital health ecosystem. Allow individuals, their families, and the care providers of their choosing to access, correct, or delete not only each other's PHI, thereby encouraging transparency while supporting employees in controlling information about them (McGraw & Mandl, 2021). To avoid data breaches and unauthorised access, healthcare providers and digital health platforms should ensure robust measures are in place to prevent security lapses. Knowing so, it is important to guide legitimate activities to enforce data protection rules and punish violations. As the digital health landscape evolves, ongoing dialogue and global partnership will be more important than ever. By emulating successful methods and addressing current shortcomings, countries can establish robust data protection legislation that supports innovation while protecting employee privacy in the digital age.

5. DIGITAL HEALTH BOOM IN INDIA: A DOUBLE-EDGED SWORD FOR EMPLOYEE INFORMATION

On the one hand, the accelerated adoption of digital health in India has benefits and drawbacks regarding employees' information (admin, 2022). India, where the healthcare sector is getting disrupted in a big way due to lightning-speed digital transformation happening there (Financialexpress, 2024). The digital health revolution touches many novel fronts, and its importance is non-debatable. In India, the volume of private employee information generated through telemedicine consultations, EHRs, mobile health apps, and HIEs is skyrocketing. Though digital health has the power to improve healthcare accessibility, efficiency, and employee engagement, it is also a significant problem in that this new, fast-evolving technology revolution needs to make sure strong data protection predominantly addresses employee privacy. According to Zion Market Research, "Global Digital Health Market was worth USD 143.9 billion in 2021 and is poised to reach USD 367.2 billion by year-end of eight years, expanding at a CAGR of around sixteen-point nine-percent." (MarketsandMarkets, 2023).

Telemedicine platforms provide virtual consultation and connect the regions in rural areas. Moreover, it improves the availability of experts and streamlines the collection of complete employee medical records. (George & A.S.Hovan George, 2023). The creation and maintenance of medical records are simplified, making it easier for healthcare professionals to coordinate care through EHRs (Stephen & Frank, 2024b). A typical EHR includes different types of personal health information, such as medical history, allergies, and lists of medications and prescriptions (Bajeh et al., 2021). Employees can also monitor their health and receive individual feedback on what affects them through mobile health applications. Software of this nature can collect biometric data, track health statistics like blood pressure and glucose levels, and send reminders to take medication (Kumar et al., 2023). Moreover, HIE enables the exchange of electronic health information among different authorised organisations. It ensures that integrity, confidentiality, and availability are maintained at each step, leading to better employee care delivery.

The development of digital health has caused a profound increase in the number of privately processed employee data collected, stored, and transmitted electronically (Rosenlund et al., 2023a). Remote Practice of Medicine Telemedicine involves the application of telecommunication technology to provide healthcare assistance between employees and clinicians remotely. For example, in teleconsultations, information from employees usually covers the reasons for seeking medical attention and chief complaints, their past or pertinent history of present illness, and individual symptoms. This data, combined with the physicians' documentation and treatment strategies, is included in a new prompts record that follows employee care, which can be electronically accessed. An EHR system is a centralised repository that collects and stores the employee's medical history, including information gleaned from doctor visits, test results such as laboratory tests or radiographic imaging, and medications prescribed to the employee. This thorough documentation gives a detailed picture of how the employee moved through the healthcare system (Ehrenstein et al., 2019). Many mHealth apps collect various personal data from users - biometric measures, medication history, lifestyle behaviours, and more. Some apps need GPS to measure user activity (Ehrenstein et al., 2019). The data is capable of providing critical insights into an employee's health but giving pause to concerns about privacy and misuse. While HIEs allow for the secure sharing of data across healthcare enterprises, they also raise red flags about how much employee information is now available to players worldwide. This increasing wealth of employee data has enormous consequences. Healthcare providers with a more complete health data record have greater confidence in their treatment and can coordinate that care better.

This gives PAs and NPs a holistic view of employees' health, such as better diagnostic results and more tailored treatments based on the employee's body data (Kruse et al., 2018). Pooling anonymous information about employees who have been stripped of their details can be invaluable for public health research and tracking the spread of diseases (Strategies, 2000). By analysing vast amounts of data, it is possible to find specific patterns/diseases that could be expected in epidemics or even lay the foundation for preventive measures. There is immense scope for personalised medicine here. Using vast employee data would support the application of personalised medicine plans (Goetz & Schork, 2018). Using a person's unique genetic background, lifestyle exposure history, and medical context as assessment points allows healthcare providers to create more employee-centred preventive or therapeutic approaches (Strianese et al., 2020). The vast collection of confidential employee data carries several significant privacy risks. However, news of this kind is always balanced between privacy and what hacks may lead to; in the case of data breaches or unauthorised access, employees' identity theft could be compromised by discrimination on health issues targeted at broad marketing based upon their medical history.

6. EVOLVING LEGAL LANDSCAPE OF DATA PROTECTION IN INDIAN DIGITAL HEALTH

India the incredible transformation of India's healthcare sector due to the quick integration of digital technologies has made it possible for employees everywhere in India (Stoumpos et al., 2023). Nowadays, India lacks a holistic personal data protection law exclusive to healthcare. The existing legal data privacy in health care amalgamates several legislations and policies that are not synchronised. Initially, a part of freedom, including the right to life and personal liberty under "Article-21 - Right to privacy", is not given separately as an article but with the help of informative interpretation by the Supreme Court, which derived it through pronounced judgments. The judgment itself again confirmed that privacy encompasses the protection of personal health data as an intrinsic component (Gupta, 2024). However, the absence of an overarching statutory and dedicated privacy paradigm for health data in India has created significant lacunae in the protection afforded to sensitive personal information - these gaps only serve to underscore why we urgently need contextualised data protection laws that account for such complexities within digital health landscapes.

India's data protection and information security legal framework is based on the "Information Technology Act of 2000 (IT Act)". The principal change proposed by the PDPB is introducing the concept of "reasonable security practices" to define what obligations rest on data controllers in respect of `safeguarding sensitive personal data (SPD), mainly health information. At the same time, The IT Act also empowers only the central government to pass supplementary legislation on data protection. Section 43A enables the Government of India to issue instructions that may be required to prevent unauthorised access, disclosure, or information sharing (Amal Chandra C., 2024).

The "Information Technology (Reasonable Security Practices and Procedures and Sensitive Personal Data or Information) Rules, 2011", are a set of regulations governing the handling and protection of sensitive personal data or information in the field of information technology (Vinod Joseph et al., 2020). The guidelines expand on the practical security safeguards organisations must maintain when processing SPD, which is mentioned under the IT Act. The chapter outlines clear technical, organisational, and procedural measures, including data encryption, permission rules, and training employees to secure their personal information. While the SPDI Rules provide a basic framework for data protection in the health sector, they have been criticised due to their broad scope and non-specificity directed at other sectors.

The Indian government recently introduced a comprehensive data protection law named the "Digital Personal Data Protection Act, 2023 (DPDPA)" and involved various rules to manage the personal information of their citizen. This act intends to establish a Data Protection Authority (DPA) to oversee the enforcement and access of data protection rules for end users' personal information. The DPDPA is a fine example of data protection but does not directly cover all the nuances of health data protection and privacy. Section 7 makes provision for healthcare workers to process personal data in the case of particular emergencies involving health. Data processing is allowed under clause (f) when an individual faces medical emergencies threatening their life or health. Clause (g) can be treated if this processing is for objectives connected to physical health reasons, facing epidemics, or spreading contagious diseases. Moreover, it is important to balance precautions that safeguard individual privacy while preventing these laws from impeding timely employee care and lawful uses for public health.

The "National Health Policy, 2017 (NHP)" outlines the vision of the government for health systems that are robust and flexible to deal with future challenges. While it is not enforceable, this demonstrates the importance of protecting health data privacy and security in digital health initiatives (Banerjee, 2020). It calls for strict security and data collection practices in which employee approval must be obtained.

"Data Security Council of India Privacy Guide for Healthcare, (DSCI) 2021", a policy framework on 'Protection & Preservation' by DSCI - Data Security Council of India to manage data privacy issues in the rapid-moving digital healthcare sector. This underscores how critical it is to have robust data protection mechanisms in place for delicate personal health-related information. It offers a complete view of the best practices for collecting, storing, processing, and sharing data so companies can always stay within global privacy regulations (Braghin & Cremonini, 2017). It further provides real-world examples of how to enhance trust while using digital health in three recommended ways: transparency, consumer permission, and a shield against data breaches for healthcare providers.

Here is the vision behind building one cohesive and interoperable health information system in India: "Electronic Health Record (EHR) Standard, 2016." The standard details processes and criteria for the production, management, and sharing of EHRs (Ministry of Health and Family Welfare, 2020). Standardising health data by anonymised models of care will provide a consistent quality and more cost-effective way to share information between healthcare providers and enable better employee coordination. The EHR Standard gives prominence to data security and employee privacy to safeguard health information against unlawful access or breach.

Telemedicine Guidelines 2020 were notified to establish a regulatory framework for enabling registered Medical Practitioners (RMPs) of Modern Medicine to practice Telemedicine in India. The guidelines have been issued under panoramic provisions and notification published on the website of the Board of Governors (BoG), Medical Council of India (MCI) (Saxena et al., 2020). These rules detail what healthcare practitioners must do and give up, establish the process for obtaining employee consent and keeping breaches confidential, and outline provisions related to electronic communication. These recommendations are intended to support effective remote health service conduct by offering advice on telemedicine's legal and ethical dimensions. These endeavours aim to promote telemedicine to boost healthcare access, particularly in resource-constrained and isolated areas. Priorities remain strict adherence to quality care and protection of employee information.

The Government of India commenced the ambitious "Ayushman Bharat Digital Mission (ABDM)" to create a comprehensive digital health ecosystem. This is to underpin the entire sector with an architecture that can help enable frictionless data sharing and integration across all players of the healthcare system (EY, 2025). Needless to say, essential ingredients of ABDM include the generation of unique health identifiers for an individual, and these details are uploaded in an appropriate form to the health registries, which will have EHRs that employees and healthcare practitioners can access. This aims to use technology to increase the efficiency, transparency, and accessibility of healthcare services, ultimately improving health outcomes and helping create a fairer system where no one is left behind (Sharma et al., 2023).

7. EVALUATING DATA PROTECTION IN INDIAN DIGITAL HEALTH THROUGH JUDICIAL OVERSIGHT AND BREACHES

Further, the Indian courts have played a crucial role in construing and enforcing extant laws on data privacy, such as the IT Act 2000 and SPDI Rules 2011. Those numbers at the bottom are significant court cases that delineate the limits and flaws in our current legal scheme. In the context of privacy being recognised as an inviolable right protected by Article 21 ("Right to Life"), explained in "Justice K.S. Puttaswamy [Retired] v. Union of India", this landmark case set a precedent for legal protection over personal sensitive data through Data Protection Principles. These judgments laid down what can be the bedrock of data protection in India, declaring that personal data is a critical part of privacy. The Supreme Court highlighted the need for a robust data protection regime to safeguard personal information, particularly individuals' health data, from any hunters and unauthorised access. This ruling had a significant effect on the legal landscape by inciting broad regulations governing data protection tailored to modern times (Supreme Court Observer, 2018b).

On the question of confidentiality and unauthorised disclosure of employee information, the judiciary had taken up this issue in the case, "Mr X v/s Hospital Z". The court decided that hospitals are under a legal obligation to protect their employee data and no confidence, also marking the importance of protecting health care sector related information as a type of personal sensitive matter. This was an example of the judiciary's commitment to employee privacy and its implementation of strict procedures for healthcare professionals that respect confidentiality. (Saha, 2021).

In the matter concerning "Balu Gopalakrishnan v. State of Kerala", safeguards have been put in place by the High Court of Kerala to ensure that the data relating to those who tested positive for COVID-19 is protected under certain conditions. The court also highlighted that the state should ensure data de-identification while sharing it with third-party service providers (e.g., US-based). The case illustrates a proactive judiciary in protecting personal health data and ensuring that the exchange methods conform to privacy norms. The court's orders have significantly influenced the health data by enhancing their protection amidst the epidemic. (Angiolini, 2021).

The Karnataka High Court in "Anivar A. Aravind v. Ministry of Home Affairs" directed that response data from users of the Aarogya Setu app concerning their health should not be shared by government agencies, including NIC, without attempting to secure informed consent. The court concluded that sharing in issue will violate the right to privacy guaranteed by Article 21 of the Constitution. It brought to the fore the need for judiciary intervention in protecting digital health information and ensuring that prior consent is taken before sharing, which further helped bring privacy standard principles into focus. (Chadha, 2021).

In the "Deepa Sanjeev Pawaskar & Anr. Vs State of Maharashtra" case, the Bombay High Court highlighted telemedicine practice guidelines to be followed. v. State of Maharashtra". The court judgment has therefore reiterated that adherence by healthcare professionals to standard protocols is a precaution that should be taken to maintain the safety of employees and not disclose data during teleconsultations. This case raised fundamental questions about judicial oversight of digital health practices and the extent of compliance with employee data protection requirements (Venkatesh et al., 2022).

This AIIMS server ransomware attack made healthcare organisations incredibly soft targets for the cyber threats they invoked. This incident illustrated the judiciary's role in enforcing cybersecurity diligence and holding healthcare professionals accountable for inadvertent security breaches. A judicial review of these aspects becomes the index of checking compliance with prevailing data protection frameworks that promote a security and privacy culture in healthcare industries. In this case, the judiciary pressure might end up with even stricter implementation of data security at all layers of its sector (Rajeswari Pillai Rajagopalan, 2022).

The judiciary had to step in when the report about a breach of sensitive employee information by the Max Healthcare data leak case started getting viral (Barman, 2023). The intervention by the court further reiterates that healthcare institutions must implement stringent protections to ensure their data is secure and have a prism of transparency into how organisations manage employee data. For instance, increased judicial scrutiny over the case is not a matter of defence, but it flourished to more robust regulatory compliance and centre stage on what you are risking by mishandling data relating to curtainless healthcare in improved privacy standards, especially for the health sector (Waraah et al., 2022).

The centre sought to lecture this handful of respondents that the Aadhaar data breach case had raised serious doubts about biometric and personal data collected by the government (Borah & Bhuyan, 2024). It highlighted the importance of protecting large arrays of data and how every attempt at mass collection should be assessed against a privacy framework - as the court reaction showed. The court-set rules, which were designed to help tighten security and protect employee information, have had long-lasting repercussions on data protection laws guiding the processing of health records (Supreme Court Observer, 2018).

This law came into place after the Fortis Healthcare data breach in 2018 to address inadequacies in the protection of health information within this industry (PTI, 2018). The judiciary's involvement underscored that healthcare providers should follow strong data security contrives and protect employees' confidentiality. The whole case put the judiciary system in light to protect against such breaches so that other entities become more accountable for data breaches, which results in the Cultivation of privacy and security awareness in the healthcare sector.

The Kerala Health Data Leak 2021 incident is a prominent case of inadequate security towards confidential Health Data (Chathukulam & Tharamangalam, 2021). In this case, the judicial monitoring primarily ensured that the state government was following privacy norms and that adequate steps were taken not to make itself a soft target for data breaches in the future. The nature of the exercise by the judiciary underlines the importance of ensuring that health data is anonymised before sharing with third parties and reinforces the necessity for actual privacy laws - robust laws related to data protection.

While judicial oversight and breach cases are salient in the determination of data protection within the Indian Digital health sector, this underpins how imperative a role the judiciary plays. While data protection concerns are resolved and privacy regulations enforced, the judiciary also secures the private rights of employees and ensures that healthcare providers install some safety measures. Increasingly, the Bench in our digital health ecosphere is rendering critical decisions related to data protection and establishing a firm order of guidelines for a safe and secure environment required for management.

8. AWARENESS-ENFORCEMENT GAP: A HURDLE TO ROBUST DATA PROTECTION

Enhancing public consciousness and stricter enforcement of applicable legislation is what it will take to ensure robust data protection in the Indian digital health arena. Today, a significant gap between the two hinders many data protection techniques. While the "Puttaswamy v. Union of India" ruling acknowledged data privacy as at least so fundamental a right that it characterised under Article 21, what specific rights regarding digital health data are recognised by the general public continue to be a largely unknown firmament in this sky of lawlessness? However, employees may be unaware of the general types and specificity of data collected by healthcare providers or digital health platforms. When it comes to what they are being required for data, how that information is used, or who their data might be passed on through. Despite what they think of themselves, their limited understanding gets in the way of them making educative and well-informed decisions on data sharing or better-exercising actions that can protect those rights. Provisions for enforcing data protection rules are not adequate enough under current laws. The existing IT Act and SPDI Rules do not have a bite on their enforcement. It is an ineffective deterrent, as the repercussions of not adhering to rules are seen as close to zero for data breaches or privacy violations. Regulatory authorities may lack adequate resources or ability to enforce compliance and investigate breach actions. The enforcement qualms have fostered a culture where proper data security procedures are not taken seriously, and this lackadaisical attitude leaves employee privacy to chance.

A two-pronged approach is needed to narrow this gap between ability and application. Indeed, the first step is to initiate public education efforts for employees to know their data privacy rights in a digital health landscape. These ads should explain how employee data is collected, used, and held. Employees should be empowered to know and exercise their right to access, modify, or delete PHI about them. Second, enhanced enforcement mechanisms are indispensable. This could involve more costly data breach and privacy violation fines; Building the enforcement capacity of regulatory authorities that can ensure raging compliance and targeted investigation to shift violators; Acting promptly and holding all parties accountable while the lender is subject to transparent processes that demand robust investigations when a data breach happens.

Increasing public awareness and enhancing enforcement can help India build a culture of responsible data management across the digital health ecosystem. This will allow consumers to make informative decisions about their data and drive regulation of healthcare institutions and app platforms to ensure they can provide secure environments for our health data, inspiring trust in the digital health revolution.

9. DEFICIENCIES IDENTIFIED: CRACKS IN THE DATA PROTECTION FOUNDATION

Data Protection Foundation Cracks The existing regulatory framework for data protection in the Indian digital health sector suffers from two notable shortcomings that compromise its efficacy: a lack of accountability for digital health data and insufficient methods for ensuring data security.

(a) Gaps in Accountability: Blurring Lines of Responsibility

The Data Protection Foundation Cracks Without a Backbone Surge of the digital health sector in India has only corroborated existing drawbacks within the regulatory structure governing data protection; two primary concerns pushing boundaries on efficacy are the absence of accountability for digital health data and frail methods liable to ensure security (Rosenlund et al., 2023). The current situation is not conducive to determining who has the right and responsibility to own digital health data. This ambiguity creates problems in an ecosystem where data health flows virtually without limits. The actions of healthcare data controllers blur when care providers delegate the storage or processing of this information to third-party service providers, known in GDPR terms as data processors (Brun, 2023). In a subsequent data breach, it is anyone's guess who should be responsible for keeping the breached information further secure - either the health care provider that originally collected/obtained again or wherever (i.e., in transit) the processor put even before they got their hands on to do whatever with. The ambiguity of this writing creates the impression that neither side takes serious defensive steps, which enhances potential failures in data security. The lack of a designated responsibility causes problems in implementing regulations regarding data protection. In non-compliance, it is difficult to understand who should be brought to book - the healthcare provider or the data processor committing regulatory violations (Silven et al., 2022). This hinders the smooth observance of data protection rights and many spider holes for ulterior exploitation, re: the potential stifling of the field from lack of clarity around data ownership and obligations in a digital health context. The pushback on deploying new data-driven solutions likely stems from two main things: growing privacy concerns and uncertainty around who owns the BRANDS' valuable first-party data.

(b) Inadequate Measures for Data Security: Leaving the Gate Wide Open

The existing Legislation, i.e. the IT Act, along with the SPDI Rules, prescribes specific security provisions that need to be implemented for the protection of “Sensitive Personal Data (SPD)”, which includes health information. However, the details surrounding these actions are subject to perception. The lack of clear criteria may lead to initiatives that fail to provide enough security, and employee data can be exposed to different risks. This process, widely expected to be lengthy and challenging on all fronts, will impact how 'reasonable security practices' are defined. That means that healthcare providers and digital health platforms can set their standards for data protection (David Goodman, 2022). Some entities may opt to implement minimal security measures because they are worried about the cost or do not realise properly how important it is. The digital space is in constant flux, attracting new cyber threats. Current rules and regulations may not be able to react quickly enough or effectively address some of these new worries. Many providers and platforms may not have the security tools or expertise in their toolbox today to adequately protect employee data. Inadequate data security measures are the primary cause of data breaches (Pool et al., 2024). Medical records are compromised by unauthorised access, hacking attacks, or human errors. Those results might then harm employee outcomes - a risk of either identity theft, discrimination, or financial loss. The Indian digital health ecosystem is extremely vulnerable from the perspective of accountability and data security. They erode employee trust, suffocate innovation, and ultimately stop the growth of a sustainable digital health era (Paul et al., 2023).

According to FireEye, the healthcare sector experiences the highest average cost of a single stolen record at $380 compared to other industries. Cybercriminals target healthcare websites and organisations, exploiting vulnerabilities to access health data, which they sell on the black market. The stolen data can be misused for malicious purposes. *"The sheer number of healthcare-associated databases for sale underground is outrageous. Even more concerning, many of these databases can be purchased for under $2,000." – FireEye."*(Soni, 2019). These statistics and the negative impacts of compromised health data highlight the urgent need for India to enact a comprehensive healthcare data protection law.

10. THE IMPERATIVE FOR REGULATORY INTERVENTION: SAFEGUARDING THE FUTURE OF DIGITAL HEALTH

The shortcomings in the existing data protection framework for Indian digital health require prompt and thorough regulatory intervention. The importance of fast action lies in its criticality.

(a) A Dynamic Landscape Demands Adaptable Regulations

Shortcomings identified in the present Indian Digital Health Data Protection Framework demand immediate and extensive regulatory action. The urgency of delivering is, in its nature, crucial (Senbekov et al., 2020). A landscape of rapid progress selection, digital health is a fast-moving area with ever-increasing technological progress. As these innovations keep growing, there are new ways to collect and store data more efficiently than ever - snowflakeDB (mind-blowing), BigQuery, or all of the resources in the AWS line-up. The current data protection framework (IT Act, SPDI Rules) lags behind the fast-paced technological changes.

Artificial Intelligence (AI) and Machine Learning (ML) are growing prevalently in healthcare. The promise that these technologies hold, however, is matched only by the risks associated with new data privacy concerns (Javaid et al., 2022). The current framework may not have the necessary safeguards/ mechanisms to deal with these challenges of data anonymisation and aggregation specific to the ethical application of AI and ML in healthcare (Bajwa et al., 2021).

Cyber fraudsters are forever coming up with creative ways to exploit vulnerabilities in information security systems (Alawida et al., 2022). So, the rules must be flexible enough to cope with these dynamic risks. This may include ensuring that regular security audits, vulnerability assessments, and cyber hygiene protocols for staff are carried out.

(b) Building Public Trust Hinges on Robust Data Protection

We read more frequently about data breaches in the media, which have damaged public confidence concerning digital health solutions. The preservation of the digital health ecosystem requires confidence, and this cannot be easy to earn without robust data privacy measures (Filkins et al., 2016). Data breaches in high-profile cases have raised questions as to the reliability of both healthcare providers and digital health platforms when securing employee data. This can lead to an unwillingness - even refusal by some - to adopt digital health solutions, which may prevent the benefits they could bring by improving healthcare access and delivery. Data protection measures can empower employees by working to ensure they have greater control over their health information (Marley, 2023). Employees need clear and understandable information on how their data is collected, used, and distributed. Here, people must be given the right to access and correct their data; essentially, a person can get involved in any decision relating to her health information by saying, 'This is me.

(c) Aligning with International Standards: Fostering Collaboration and Innovation

Vast opportunities exist in the global healthcare sector for those ready to innovate and collaborate. However, differences in data protection laws mean that even with adequate decisions and BCRs to authenticate the appropriate level of protection offered, legal obstacles can still arise when transferring personal information from one country/region to another (Compagnucci et al., 2024). This makes it very difficult to access advanced world-class knowledge and innovation in healthcare, which can significantly uplift the healthcare sector of a country like India. Collaborating with nations and global bodies on digital health research and development will be the key to progress. On the other hand, Countries with stringent data protection legislation may present India with a roadblock if its domestic framework is not up to global standards. Strong policy structures that prioritise stringent data protection guidelines while supporting innovation are key to encouraging investment and the development of modern digital health systems in India (Hemangini Dadwal et al., 2024), where it could make a win-win scenario for employee data privacy and the digital health industry itself.

11. RECOMMENDATIONS: FORTIFYING THE DATA PROTECTION FORTRESS IN INDIAN DIGITAL HEALTH

This chapter uncovers gaps in the current digital health data protection regime set up within India. A uniform set of rules for privacy and security, a harmonised legal framework, and improved enforcement mechanisms are essential to safeguard employees' confidential information.

1. Standardized Privacy and Security Protocols: Building the Foundation

Preparing the ground Given the current fragmented nature of data protection, there is a clear need to develop nationally standardised privacy and security frameworks tailored to the digital health ecosystem. These will set out clear instructions that healthcare providers and services will have to abide by if they want their data security applications to be robust. It is equally important to have a separate nationwide law for the protection of healthcare data. Such legislation must borrow from international standards like the GDPR framework while being custom-built for India. The guidelines should specify the conditions for data to be collected, retained, recovered, or released; in particular, they emphasise more stringent requirements before details are gathered, including principles such as minimisation of information captured wherever possible and employee anonymity. The legislation should require mandatory safeguards, including regular security audits, vulnerability tests, and employee training in data protection practices. Therefore, it is important to have a data breach notification protocol in place with clear guidelines and timelines regarding the need for employee notification.

2. Integrated Legal Framework: Bridging the Gaps

For the effective resolution of demonstrative shortcomings in existing data protection structures, it is necessary to have a concurrent legal regime that combines legislation with procedural mechanisms and technology. This framework would ensure consistency and accuracy in the implementation of data protection principles. The healthcare data protection law should complement existing laws regulating the processing of electronic medical records (IT Act and SPDI Rules). Side note: AAX's Real Time Auditing feature will eliminate discrepancies and achieve the highest compliance performance. It must address the current confusion around data ownership and accountability for this, specifically. With clear responsibility lines, especially for data hand-out to third parties, the framework should define proper detailed SOPs covering the complete data handling life-cycle from collection to storage, access, and disposal. The maintenance of employee data would also be consistent across all users who operate within the healthcare ecosystem.

3. Enhanced Enforcement Mechanisms: Strengthening Deterrence

Improving the efficacy of non-compliance deterrence. This is important as it does not drive compliance and a data breach-preventing culture. Regulatory bodies in charge of ensuring data protection need more money. This, in turn, would give them increased capacity to exercise oversight over compliance, investigate alleged violations, and prosecute the violators. The financial consequences of not honouring data protection law need to be far higher. This will improve the deterrent effect and encourage healthcare providers such as maloclinics.com to invest in data security. There could be an argument for healthcare organisations to have DPOs appointed within. The role of "Data Protection Officers (DPOs)" is to oversee and keep check that regulation standards around data protection are met. Act as champions for data privacy within their organisations.

These three pieces of advice, when put into work with standardised protocols and a collaborative legal framework or enforcement, can only structure a robust data protection layer for the Indian digital health ecosystem. It would extend the powers of employees, spur creativity, and market adoption for new safe healthcare technologies, ultimately restoring faith in digital health.

12. CONCLUSION

Digital health could revolutionise the way healthcare is delivered, transforming care provision and employee power for India, which already offers a unique opportunity to improve access to medical services. Be that as it may be, achieving this potential necessitates fundamentally robust data privacy controls. The current legislative web for protecting health information has been scrutinised in this chapter, outlining the deficiencies and calling out for improved regulatory mechanisms to be placed. Improvement of compliance risk preventive effects and better enforcement from data protection tools is key to deterring breaches and encouraging compliance-minded behaviour. Such regulatory data protection arms should be provided with more money. This will empower them to better supervise compliance, investigate potential violations, and hold accountable those who fail to follow the rules. We must dramatically increase such fines for violating data protection laws. This should strengthen the deterrent value and incentivise care providers as well as platforms to invest more in data security. Mandatory designation of DPOs within health services organisations may have benefits. Customer Protection Officers (DPOs) who are supposed to be appointed must supervise and monitor an enterprise's compliance with data protection regulations. They are also data privacy champions in their organisations.

Active steps such as standardisation, a single legal framework, and more effective enforcement measures can set up a robust data protection infrastructure in the Indian Digital Health sector. This will build the spirit of employee ownership and lead to untapped innovation in a more reliable healthcare solution that can make the digital health revolution. It is irresponsible to allow the ownership of data and safeguards for their protection inconvenience and risk employee confidentiality.

These findings offer significant implications for politicians and healthcare professionals. The most urgent policy imperative is to enact specific data privacy legislation covering healthcare. Such legislation would establish clear and specific conditions under which data could be collected, held, recalled, or released. Efforts must turn to the promotion of data minimisation practices and anonymisation wherever possible. Moreover, the law needs to address ambiguity in the data ownership provision more directly as well when it comes to how and who is liable for such information, especially if they are delegating their collected material out of the house. The need here is not only from the employee end but also from healthcare providers and digital health platforms. Companies must also set strict data security standards in place and enforce them by holding regular security audits and vulnerability assessments along with thorough training of employees on all possible best practices to safeguard their sensitive information. At the same time, explicit and clear procedures must be in place to inform those concerned about such violations. Hiring a Data Protection Officer (DPO) to ensure that they adhere to data protection rules often helps in creating and maintaining a culture of compliance with and respect for the GDPR in healthcare organisations.

Covered entities face ongoing challenges with their digital health ecosystem, where new players emerge, and the threat of cybersecurity breaches and endpoint security incidents leads to data hacks. Immediate action is necessary to protect sensitive employee data - and trust in the digital healthcare age. Failing to make timely improvements in the data protection framework could have two adverse effects: employee trust will erode or obstruct innovation, such as in the digital health sector! India is uniquely poised to lead the way in developing such secure and ethical digital health solutions. To enable employee trust and to provide a foundation for secure, responsible data-sharing practices within the country's unique economic and cultural healthcare environment, robust personal information protection around health records is needed. By doing so, it will empower employees, incentivise innovation, and, in the end, release the huge promise of digital health, which works together to change healthcare delivery for all people. We also believe that India's ascent in terms of health is well-documented, with digital technology as a key enabler. We can ensure this with robust data protection but and enable employees to own their knowledge.

REFERENCES

7 Startup. (2022, July 12). *Advantages and Disadvantages of Digital Healthcare Technology*. 7startup - Startup Funding Consultants. https://www.7startup.vc/post/advantages-and-disadvantages-of-digital-healthcare-technology/

Alawida, M., Omolara, A. E., Abiodun, O. I., & Al-Rajab, M. (2022). A deeper look into cybersecurity issues after Covid-19: A survey. *Journal of King Saud University. Computer and Information Sciences*, *34*(10), 8176–8206. DOI: 10.1016/j.jksuci.2022.08.003 PMID: 37521180

Amal Chandra C. (2024). Strengthening India's Cybersecurity and Data Privacy Landscape: A Comprehensive Overview. Indian Journal of Public Administration, 70(3), 466-478. https://doi.org/ (Original work published 2024)DOI: 10.1177/00195561241271616

Anawade, P. A., Sharma, D., & Gahane, S. (2024). A Comprehensive Review on Exploring the Impact of Telemedicine on Healthcare Accessibility. *Cureus*. Advance online publication. DOI: 10.7759/cureus.55996 PMID: 38618307

Angiolini, C. (2021). Case Law Survey On Data Protection – COVID-19 Litigation Project. SSRN *Electronic Journal*. DOI: 10.2139/ssrn.3999319

Bajeh, A. O., Abikoye, O. C., Mojeed, H. A., Salihu, S. A., Oladipo, I. D., Abdulraheem, M., Awotunde, J. B., Sangaiah, A. K., & Adewole, K. S. (2021). Application of computational intelligence models in IoMT big data for heart disease diagnosis in personalised health care. In *Intelligent IoT Systems in Personalized Health Care* (pp. 177–206). Elsevier., DOI: 10.1016/B978-0-12-821187-8.00007-1

Bajwa, J., Munir, U., Nori, A., & Williams, B. (2021). Artificial intelligence in healthcare: Transforming the practice of medicine. *Future Healthcare Journal*, *8*(2), e188–e194. DOI: 10.7861/fhj.2021-0095 PMID: 34286183

Balu Gopalakrishnan v. State Of Kerala | Kerala High Court | Judgment | Law | CaseMine. (n.d.). Retrieved June 30, 2024, from https://www.casemine.com/judgement/in/5fe9797f9fca192d632e8f86

Banerjee, A. (2020). Equity and quality of healthcare access: Where do we stand and the way forward? *Indian Journal of Community Medicine : Official Publication of Indian Association of Preventive & Social Medicine*, *45*(1), 4. DOI: 10.4103/ijcm.IJCM_183_19 PMID: 32029975

Barman, A. (2023, May 2). Care Hospitals buyout: Max Healthcare sues TPG for "breach of term sheet agreement." *The Economic Times*. https://economictimes.indiatimes.com/industry/healthcare/biotech/healthcare/care-hospitals-buyout-max-healthcare-sues-tpg-for-breach-of-term-sheet-agreement/articleshow/99919224.cms?from=mdr

Borah, P. P., & Bhuyan, A. J. (2024). Living with the *Aadhaar*: India's Changing Contours of Identity and Governance. *The Indian Journal of Public Administration*, *70*(3), 615–620. DOI: 10.1177/00195561241257460

Braghin, C., & Cremonini, M. (2017a). Online Privacy. In *Computer and Information Security Handbook* (pp. 743–758). Elsevier., DOI: 10.1016/B978-0-12-803843-7.00052-1

Braghin, C., & Cremonini, M. (2017b). Online Privacy. In *Computer and Information Security Handbook* (pp. 743–758). Elsevier., DOI: 10.1016/B978-0-12-803843-7.00052-1

Brun, J. (2023, July 26). Understanding non-compliance: Meaning, Consequences, and Corrective Measures. *Nimonik*. https://nimonik.com/blog/unveiling-non-compliance-in-regulatory-standards-implications-types-factors-proactive-solutions/

Chadha, A. (2021). Digital Data Protection and The Right to Privacy. SSRN *Electronic Journal*. DOI: 10.2139/ssrn.3899815

Chathukulam, J., & Tharamangalam, J. (2021). The Kerala model in the time of COVID19: Rethinking state, society and democracy. *World Development*, *137*, 105207. DOI: 10.1016/j.worlddev.2020.105207 PMID: 32989341

Compagnucci, M. C., Fenwick, M., & Haapio, H. (2024). *Unlocking the Potential of Binding Corporate Rules (BCRs) in Health Data Transfers* (Version 1). arXiv. DOI: 10.1007/978-981-97-9983-1_3

Dadwal, H., Singh, S., Poddar, D., & Singh, A. (2024). *India: Regulators must balance growth and innovation with user protection*. https://globalcompetitionreview.com/guide/data-antitrust-guide/first-edition/article/india-regulators-must-balance-growth-and-innovation-user-protection

Data Privacy Laws and Regulations Around the World—Securiti. (n.d.). Retrieved June 30, 2024, from https://securiti.ai/privacy-laws/

Data Security Council of India establishes privacy guidelines for healthcare sector. (n.d.). Retrieved June 30, 2024, from https://www.medianama.com/2021/09/223-dsci-health-privacy-guidelines-2/

Ehrenstein, V., Kharrazi, H., Lehmann, H., & Taylor, C. O. (2019). Obtaining Data From Electronic Health Records. In *Tools and Technologies for Registry Interoperability, Registries for Evaluating Patient Outcomes: A User's Guide, 3rd Edition, Addendum 2 [Internet]*. Agency for Healthcare Research and Quality (US). https://www.ncbi.nlm.nih.gov/books/NBK551878/

EY. (2025). *The AIdea of India 2025: How much productivity can GenAI unlock in India*.

Feld, A. D. (2005). The Health Insurance Portability and Accountability Act (HIPAA): Its Broad Effect on Practice. *The American Journal of Gastroenterology*, *100*(7), 1440–1443. DOI: 10.1111/j.1572-0241.2005.50621.x PMID: 15984962

Filkins, B. L., Kim, J. Y., Roberts, B., Armstrong, W., Miller, M. A., Hultner, M. L., Castillo, A. P., Ducom, J.-C., Topol, E. J., & Steinhubl, S. R. (2016). Privacy and security in the era of digital health: What should translational researchers know and do about it? *American Journal of Translational Research*, *8*(3), 1560–1580. PMID: 27186282

Financialexpress. (2024, March 5). Digital Technologies Driving the Evolution of Indian Healthcare in 2024 and Beyond. *Financialexpress*. https://www.financialexpress.com/business/healthcare-digital-technologies-driving-the-evolution-of-indian-healthcare-in-2024-and-beyond-3413739/

George, D. A. S. & A.S.Hovan George. (2023). *Telemedicine: A New Way to Provide Healthcare*. DOI: 10.5281/ZENODO.8075850

Goetz, L. H., & Schork, N. J. (2018). Personalized medicine: Motivation, challenges, and progress. *Fertility and Sterility*, *109*(6), 952–963. DOI: 10.1016/j.fertnstert.2018.05.006 PMID: 29935653

Goodman, D. (2022, October 12). *Reasonable Security*. CyberSec4Europe | Cyber Security for Europe. https://cybersec4europe.eu/reasonable-security/

Gupta, A. K. (2024). Right to Privacy in Digital Technology Act: Issues and Policy in India. *The Indian Journal of Public Administration*, *70*(3), 532–545. DOI: 10.1177/00195561241271517

India—Privacy Protection—A Review Of The Information Technology Rules, 2011. (n.d.). Retrieved June 30, 2024, from https://www.mondaq.com/india/privacy-protection/904916/a-review-of-the-information-technology-rules-2011

Isola, S., & Al Khalili, Y. (2025). Protected Health Information. In *StatPearls*. StatPearls Publishing., https://www.ncbi.nlm.nih.gov/books/NBK553131/

Javaid, M., Haleem, A., Pratap Singh, R., Suman, R., & Rab, S. (2022). Significance of machine learning in healthcare: Features, pillars and applications. *International Journal of Intelligent Networks*, *3*, 58–73. DOI: 10.1016/j.ijin.2022.05.002

Joseph, V., Basu, P., & Bhargava, A. (2020). *A Review Of The Information Technology Rules, 2011.* https://www.mondaq.com/india/privacy-protection/904916/a-review-of-the-information-technology-rules-2011

Journal of Medical Internet Research—The Use of Digital Health Services Among Patients and Citizens Living at Home: Scoping Review. (n.d.). Retrieved June 30, 2024, from https://www.jmir.org/2023/1/e44711

Justice K.S. Puttaswamy (Retd.) & Anr. Vs. Union of India & Ors. (n.d.). Retrieved June 30, 2024, from https://privacylibrary.ccgnlud.org/case/justice-ks-puttaswamy-ors-vs-union-of-india-ors

Kassam, I., Ilkina, D., Kemp, J., Roble, H., Carter-Langford, A., & Shen, N. (2023). Patient Perspectives and Preferences for Consent in the Digital Health Context: State-of-the-art Literature Review. *Journal of Medical Internet Research*, *25*(1), e42507. DOI: 10.2196/42507 PMID: 36763409

Kruse, C. S., Stein, A., Thomas, H., & Kaur, H. (2018). The use of Electronic Health Records to Support Population Health: A Systematic Review of the Literature. *Journal of Medical Systems*, *42*(11), 214. DOI: 10.1007/s10916-018-1075-6 PMID: 30269237

Kumar, D., Hasan, Y., & Afroz, S. (2023). Mobile Health Monitoring System: A Comprehensive Review. *International Journal of Research Publication and Reviews*, *4*(6), 1922–1954. DOI: 10.55248/gengpi.4.623.45128

MarketsandMarkets. (2023). *Digital Health Market Growth, Drivers, and Opportunities.* MarketsandMarkets. https://www.marketsandmarkets.com/Market-Reports/digital-health-market-45458752.html

Marley, R. (2023, August 23). Patient Empowerment: The key to harvesting real world data. *Healthcare Transformers.* https://healthcaretransformers.com/digital-health/healthcare-data/patient-empowerment-harvesting-real-world-data/

Maroju, R. G., Choudhari, S. G., Shaikh, M. K., Borkar, S. K., & Mendhe, H. (2023). Role of Telemedicine and Digital Technology in Public Health in India: A Narrative Review. *Cureus*, *15*(3), e35986. DOI: 10.7759/cureus.35986 PMID: 37050980

McGraw, D., & Mandl, K. D. (2021). Privacy protections to encourage use of health-relevant digital data in a learning health system. *NPJ Digital Medicine*, *4*(1), 2. DOI: 10.1038/s41746-020-00362-8 PMID: 33398052

Ministry of Health and Family Welfare. (2020). *Electronic Health Record Standards for India.* https://health.vikaspedia.in/viewcontent/health/nrhm/national-health-policies/electronic-health-record-standards-for-india?lgn=en

Mobile Health Application—An overview | ScienceDirect Topics. (n.d.). Retrieved June 28, 2024, from https://www.sciencedirect.com/topics/computer-science/mobile-health-application

Patient Empowerment: The key to harvesting real world data. (n.d.). Retrieved June 30, 2024, from https://healthcaretransformers.com/digital-health/healthcare-data/patient-empowerment-harvesting-real-world-data/

Paul, M., Maglaras, L., Ferrag, M. A., & Almomani, I. (2023). Digitization of healthcare sector: A study on privacy and security concerns. *ICT Express*, *9*(4), 571–588. DOI: 10.1016/j.icte.2023.02.007

Pool, J., Akhlaghpour, S., Fatehi, F., & Burton-Jones, A. (2024). A systematic analysis of failures in protecting personal health data: A scoping review. *International Journal of Information Management*, *74*, 102719. DOI: 10.1016/j.ijinfomgt.2023.102719

PTI. (2018). *Fortis Healthcare says it has found 'systemic lapses' found in inter-corporate borrowings | Business News—The Indian Express.* https://indianexpress.com/article/business/systemic-lapses-found-in-inter-corporate-borrowings-fortis-healthcare-5235343/

Rajagopalan, P. R. (2022). The AIIMS cyberattack reflects India's critical vulnerabilities. Observer Research Foundation. https://www.orfonline.org/expert-speak/the-aiims-cyberattack-reflects-indias-critical-vulnerabilities

Rosenlund, M., Kinnunen, U.-M., & Saranto, K. (2023a). The Use of Digital Health Services Among Patients and Citizens Living at Home: Scoping Review. *Journal of Medical Internet Research*, *25*, e44711. DOI: 10.2196/44711 PMID: 36972122

Rosenlund, M., Kinnunen, U.-M., & Saranto, K. (2023b). The Use of Digital Health Services Among Patients and Citizens Living at Home: Scoping Review. *Journal of Medical Internet Research*, *25*, e44711. DOI: 10.2196/44711 PMID: 36972122

Saha, M. (2021). Application of Right to Privacy in Mr X v. Hospital Z Case and Its Subsequent Developments. *Indian Journal of Law and Legal Research*, *2*, 1. https://heinonline.org/HOL/Page?handle=hein.journals/injlolw2&id=5165&div=&collection=

Saxena, S., Srivastava, K., Dilbagi, R., & Saxena, A. (2020). Telemedicine units for COVID-19: An experience from Madhya Pradesh. *Indian Journal of Community Health*, *32*(2, Supp), 277–280. DOI: 10.47203/IJCH.2020.v32i02SUPP.021

Senbekov, M., Saliev, T., Bukeyeva, Z., Almabayeva, A., Zhanaliyeva, M., Aitenova, N., Toishibekov, Y., & Fakhradiyev, I. (2020). The Recent Progress and Applications of Digital Technologies in Healthcare: A Review. *International Journal of Telemedicine and Applications, 2020*, 1–18. DOI: 10.1155/2020/8830200 PMID: 33343657

Sharma, R. S., Rohatgi, A., Jain, S., & Singh, D. (2023). The Ayushman Bharat Digital Mission (ABDM): Making of India's Digital Health Story. *CSI Transactions on ICT, 11*(1), 3–9. DOI: 10.1007/s40012-023-00375-0

Silven, A. V., Van Peet, P. G., Boers, S. N., Tabak, M., De Groot, A., Hendriks, D., Van Os, H. J. A., Bonten, T. N., Atsma, D. E., De Graaf, T. J., Sombroek, M. P., Chavannes, N. H., & Villalobos-Quesada, M. (2022). Clarifying responsibility: Professional digital health in the doctor-patient relationship, recommendations for physicians based on a multi-stakeholder dialogue in the Netherlands. *BMC Health Services Research, 22*(1), 129. DOI: 10.1186/s12913-021-07316-0 PMID: 35094713

Soni, V. (2019, December 5). What is Digital Information Security in Healthcare Act (DISHA) in India? *ZNetLive Blog - A Guide to Domains, Web Hosting & Cloud Computing*. https://www.znetlive.com/blog/digital-information-security-healthcare-act-disha/

SOPHOS. (2023). *Cybercriminals Successfully Encrypted Data in Ransomware Attacks on Nearly 75% of Healthcare Organizations That Sophos Surveyed | Sophos*. https://www.sophos.com/en-us/press/press-releases/2023/11/cybercriminals-successfully-encrypted-data-ransomware-attacks-nearly

Stephen, M., & Frank, L. (2024a). *The Role of Electronic Health Records in Transforming Healthcare Delivery and Financial Gains.*

Stephen, M., & Frank, L. (2024b). *The Role of Electronic Health Records in Transforming Healthcare Delivery and Financial Gains.*

Stevens, N. C. Philip. (2020). *Building a Global Framework for Digital Health Services in the Era of COVID-19*. https://itif.org/publications/2020/05/26/building-global-framework-digital-health-services-era-covid-19/

Stoumpos, A. I., Kitsios, F., & Talias, M. A. (2023). Digital Transformation in Healthcare: Technology Acceptance and Its Applications. *International Journal of Environmental Research and Public Health, 20*(4), 3407. DOI: 10.3390/ijerph20043407 PMID: 36834105

Strategies, N. R. C. (US) C. on E. the I. for H. A. T. R. and I. (2000). Health Applications of the Internet. In *Networking Health: Prescriptions for the Internet*. National Academies Press (US). https://www.ncbi.nlm.nih.gov/books/NBK44714/

Strianese, O., Rizzo, F., Ciccarelli, M., Galasso, G., D'Agostino, Y., Salvati, A., Del Giudice, C., Tesorio, P., & Rusciano, M. R. (2020). Precision and Personalized Medicine: How Genomic Approach Improves the Management of Cardiovascular and Neurodegenerative Disease. *Genes*, *11*(7), 747. DOI: 10.3390/genes11070747 PMID: 32640513

Supreme Court Observer. (2018a). *Constitutionality of Aadhaar Act: Judgment Summary*. Supreme Court Observer. https://www.scobserver.in/reports/constitutionality-of-aadhaar-justice-k-s-puttaswamy-union-of-india-judgment-in-plain-english/

Supreme Court Observer. (2018b). *Fundamental Right to Privacy*. Supreme Court Observer. https://www.scobserver.in/cases/puttaswamy-v-union-of-india-fundamental-right-to-privacy-case-background/

Thieme E-Journals—Yearbook of Medical Informatics / Abstract. (n.d.). Retrieved June 30, 2024, from https://www.thieme-connect.de/products/ejournals/abstract/10.1055/s-0042-1742519

Venkatesh, U., Aravind, G. P., & Velmurugan, A. A. (2022). Telemedicine practice guidelines in India: Global implications in the wake of the COVID-19 pandemic. *World Medical & Health Policy*, *14*(3), 589–599. DOI: 10.1002/wmh3.497 PMID: 35601469

Waraah, U., Tiwari, A., Rawat, D., & Jha, R. (2022). *Data Breach In Healthcare Industry: An Infringement Of Right To Privacy; A Modern Era Effect*.

Compilation of References

Aarons, G. A., & Sawitzky, A. C. (2006). Organizational culture and climate and mental health provider attitudes toward evidence-based practice. *Psychological Services*, *3*(1), 61–72. DOI: 10.1037/1541-1559.3.1.61

Abernethy, A., Adams, L., Barrett, M., Bechtel, C., Brennan, P., Butte, A., & Valdes, K. (2022). The promise of digital health: Then, now, and the future. *NAM Perspectives*, *2022*, 10–31478.

Abid, G., Arya, B., Arshad, A., Ahmed, S., & Farooqi, S. (2021). Positive personality traits and self-leadership in sustainable organizations: Mediating influence of thriving and moderating role of proactive personality. [HTML]. *Sustainable Production and Consumption*, *25*, 299–311.

Abouelmehdi, K., Beni-Hessane, A., & Khaloufi, H. (2018). Big healthcare data: Preserving security and privacy. *Journal of Big Data*, *5*(1), 1. DOI: 10.1186/s40537-017-0110-7

Acker, J. (1990). Hierarchies, jobs, bodies: A theory of gendered organizations. *Gender & Society*, *4*(2), 139–158. DOI: 10.1177/089124390004002002

Adan, A., Archer, S. N., Hidalgo, M. P., Di Milia, L., Natale, V., & Randler, C. (2012). Circadian Typology: A Comprehensive Review. *Chronobiology International*, *29*(9), 1153–1175. DOI: 10.3109/07420528.2012.719971 PMID: 23004349

Adane, A. A., & Jemal, K. (2017). Mental health training for primary health care workers and implication for success of integration of mental health into primary care: Evaluation of effect on knowledge, attitude and practices (KAP). *International Journal of Mental Health Systems*, *11*(1), 63–69. DOI: 10.1186/s13033-017-0169-8

Aday, J. S., Heifets, B. D., Pratscher, S. D., Bradley, E., Rosen, R., & Woolley, J. D. (2022). Great Expectations: Recommendations for improving the methodological rigor of psychedelic clinical trials. [nih.gov]. *Psychopharmacology*, *239*(6), 1989–2010.

Adkins, J. A., Douglas, S., Voorhies, P., & Bickman, L. (2024). Program evaluation: The bottom line in organizational health.

Affia, A. O., Finch, H., Jung, W., Samori, I. A., Potter, L., & Palmer, X.-L. (2023). IoT Health Devices: Exploring Security Risks in the Connected Landscape. *IoT*, *4*(2), 150–182. DOI: 10.3390/iot4020009

Aftab, J., Abid, N., Sarwar, H., & Veneziani, M. (2022). Environmental ethics, green innovation, and sustainable performance: Exploring the role of environmental leadership and environmental strategy. [HTML]. *Journal of Cleaner Production*.

Agrawal, D., & Bhukya, R. (2022). Effects of the GIG economy on the workplace. *International Journal of Health Sciences*, •••, 2701–2718. DOI: 10.53730/ijhs.v6nS3.6176

Agteren, J., Iasiello, M., & Lo, L. (2018). Improving the well-being and resilience of health services staff via psychological skills training. *BMC Research Notes*, *11*(1), 924. Advance online publication. DOI: 10.1186/s13104-018-4034-x PMID: 30577884

Ahmad, M., Md. Din, N. S. B., Tharumalay, R. D., Che Din, N., Ibrahim, N., Amit, N., Farah, N. M., Osman, R. A., Abdul Hamid, M. F., Ibrahim, I. A., Jamsari, E. A., Palil, M. R., & Ahmad, S. (2020). The Effects of Circadian Rhythm Disruption on Mental Health and Physiological Responses among Shift Workers and General Population. *International Journal of Environmental Research and Public Health*, *17*(19), 7156. DOI: 10.3390/ijerph17197156 PMID: 33007836

Ahmed, F., Zhao, F., Faraz, N. A., & Qin, Y. J. (2021). How inclusive leadership paves way for psychological well-being of employees during trauma and crisis: A three-wave longitudinal mediation study. [nih.gov]. *Journal of Advanced Nursing*, *77*(2), 819–831. DOI: 10.1111/jan.14637 PMID: 33231300

Ahmed, K. A. (2020). Employees' mental health and productivity and its impact on contextual and task performance in organizations. *Journal of Advanced Research in Dynamical and Control System*, *12*(8).

Ahmed, M., Bashar, I., Alam, S. T., Wasi, A. I., Jerin, I., Khatun, S., & Rahman, M. (2021). An overview of Asian cement industry: Environmental impacts, research methodologies and mitigation measures. [HTML]. *Sustainable Production and Consumption*, *28*, 1018–1039.

Ahmed, M., Zehou, S., Raza, S., Qureshi, M., & Yousufi, S. (2020). Impact ofcsrand environmental triggers on employee green behavior: The mediating effect of employeewell-being. *Corporate Social Responsibility and Environmental Management*, *27*(5), 2225–2239. DOI: 10.1002/csr.1960

Ahmed, Y. A. E., Yue, B., Gu, Z., & Yang, J. (2023). An overview: Big data analysis by deep learning and image processing. *International Journal of Quantum Information, 21*(7), 2340009. DOI: 10.1142/S0219749923400099

Ahsan, M. J. (2024). Green leadership and innovation: Catalysts for environmental performance in Italian manufacturing. [HTML]. *The International Journal of Organizational Analysis.*

Akinbami, A. A. (n.d.). *Integrating Natural Light for Wellbeing*. Performance, and Quality Care Delivery in Healthcare Environments.

AlAmeri, A. (2023). Covid-19 impact on employees behavior and mental well-being in uae (abu dhabi emirates). *Journal of Human Resource and Leadership, 8*(2), 20–34. DOI: 10.47604/jhrl.1975

Alawida, M., Omolara, A. E., Abiodun, O. I., & Al-Rajab, M. (2022). A deeper look into cybersecurity issues after Covid-19: A survey. *Journal of King Saud University. Computer and Information Sciences, 34*(10), 8176–8206. DOI: 10.1016/j.jksuci.2022.08.003 PMID: 37521180

Albulescu, P., Macsinga, I., Rusu, A., Sulea, C., Bodnaru, A., & Tulbure, B. T. (2022). "Give me a break!" A systematic review and meta-analysis on the efficacy of micro-breaks for increasing well-being and performance. *PLoS One, 17*(8), e0272460. DOI: 10.1371/journal.pone.0272460 PMID: 36044424

Alder, S. (2024). *Healthcare Data Breach Statistics*. https://www.hipaajournal.com/healthcare-data-breach-statistics/

Alfaraby, A., & Sinambela, L. P. (2025). Human Capital Development Strategies in Improving the Performance of The General and Financial Bureaus of The Indonesian Quarantine Agency. *International Journal of Management Science and Information Technology, 5*(1), 20–26. DOI: 10.35870/ijmsit.v5i1.3619

Al-Jarrah, O. Y., Yoo, P. D., Muhaidat, S., Karagiannidis, G. K., & Taha, K. (2015). Efficient machine learning for big data: A review. *Big Data Research, 2*(3), 87–93. DOI: 10.1016/j.bdr.2015.04.001

Allen, T. D., Golden, T. D., & Shockley, K. M. (2015). How effective is telecommuting? Assessing the status of our scientific findings. *Psychological Science in the Public Interest, 16*(2), 40–68. DOI: 10.1177/1529100615593273 PMID: 26403188

Allen, T. D., Golden, T. D., & Shockley, K. M. (2021). Flexible work arrangements and work-family conflict: A meta-analysis of their effects on work-life balance. *The Journal of Applied Psychology, 106*(6), 892–915. DOI: 10.1037/apl0000899

Allen, T. D., Herst, D. E., Bruck, C. S., & Sutton, M. (2013). Consequences associated with work-to-family conflict: A review and meta-analysis. *Journal of Business and Psychology*, *17*(2), 217–228.

Allen, T. D., Johnson, R. C., Kiburz, K. M., & Shockley, K. M. (2013). Work–family conflict and flexible work arrangements: Deconstructing flexibility. *Personnel Psychology*, *66*(2), 345–376. DOI: 10.1111/peps.12012

Allioui, H., & Mourdi, Y. (2023). Exploring the Full Potentials of IoT for Better Financial Growth and Stability: A Comprehensive Survey. *Sensors (Basel)*, *23*(19), 8015. DOI: 10.3390/s23198015 PMID: 37836845

Almendro, M. (2023). *The Labyrinth of Ayahuasca*. Cambridge Scholars Publishing.

Alsomaidaee, M., Joumaa, B., & Khalid, K. (2023). Toxic workplace, mental health and employee well-being, the moderator role of paternalistic leadership, an empirical study. *Journal of Applied Business and Technology*, *4*(2), 114–129. DOI: 10.35145/jabt.v4i2.126

Al-Suraihi, W. A., Samikon, S. A., Al-Suraihi, A.-H. A., & Ibrahim, I. (2021). Employee Turnover: Causes, Importance and Retention Strategies. *European Journal of Business and Management Research*, *6*(3), 1–10. DOI: 10.24018/ejbmr.2021.6.3.893

Al-Yafei, A. (2024). The Relationship Between Job Rotation And Work Engagement: The Mediating Role Of Job Satisfaction (Doctoral dissertation, University of Central Lancashire).

Amal Chandra C. (2024). Strengthening India's Cybersecurity and Data Privacy Landscape: A Comprehensive Overview. Indian Journal of Public Administration, 70(3), 466-478. https://doi.org/ (Original work published 2024)DOI: 10.1177/00195561241271616

Amini, F., Moosavi, S. M., Rafaiee, R., Nadi Ghara, A., & Babakhanian, M. (2021). Chronotype patterns associated with job satisfaction of shift working healthcare providers. *Chronobiology International*, *38*(4), 526–533. DOI: 10.1080/07420528.2020.1869028 PMID: 33435743

Amoadu, M., Agyare, D. F., Doe, P. F., & Abraham, S. A. (2025). Examining the impact of psychosocial safety climate on working conditions, well-being and safety of healthcare providers: A scoping review. *BMC Health Services Research*, *25*(1), 90. DOI: 10.1186/s12913-025-12254-2 PMID: 39819783

Amponsah-Tawiah, K., Mensah, J., Boakyewaa, R., & Asare, G. (2023). From muddiness to madness: An examination of decent work and mental health in the ghanaian mining industry. *International Journal of Law and Management*, *65*(4), 289–299. DOI: 10.1108/IJLMA-01-2022-0001

Anawade, P. A., Sharma, D., & Gahane, S. (2024). A Comprehensive Review on Exploring the Impact of Telemedicine on Healthcare Accessibility. *Cureus*. Advance online publication. DOI: 10.7759/cureus.55996 PMID: 38618307

Andersen, L. P., Andersen, D. R., & Pihl-Thingvad, J. (2025). Psychosocial Climate as Antecedent for Resources to Manage Emotional Demands at Work. *International Journal of Environmental Research and Public Health*, *22*(1), 64. DOI: 10.3390/ijerph22010064 PMID: 39857517

Anderson, L. A., Notice, M., Armstrong, J., & Smith, K. R. (2025). The unspoken experiences of systemic supervisors of color: A modified Delphi study. *Journal of Marital and Family Therapy*, *51*(1), e12749. DOI: 10.1111/jmft.12749 PMID: 39533407

Angiolini, C. (2021). Case Law Survey On Data Protection – COVID-19 Litigation Project. SSRN *Electronic Journal*. DOI: 10.2139/ssrn.3999319

Antonacopoulou, E. P., & Georgiadou, A. (2021). Leading through social distancing: The future of work, corporations and leadership from home. [worktribe.com]. *Gender, Work and Organization*, *28*(2), 749–767. DOI: 10.1111/gwao.12533

Anttila, T., Oinas, T., Tammelin, M., & Nätti, J. (2015). Working-Time Regimes and Work-Life Balance in Europe. *European Sociological Review*, *31*(6), 713–724. DOI: 10.1093/esr/jcv070

Antunes, L. C., Levandovski, R., Dantas, G., Caumo, W., & Hidalgo, M. P. (2010). Obesity and shift work: Chronobiological aspects. *Nutrition Research Reviews*, *23*(1), 155–168. DOI: 10.1017/S0954422410000016 PMID: 20122305

Antúnez, J. M. (2020). Circadian typology is related to emotion regulation, metacognitive beliefs and assertiveness in healthy adults. *PLoS One*, *15*(3), e0230169. DOI: 10.1371/journal.pone.0230169 PMID: 32168366

Anxo, D., & Karlsson, M. (2019). *Overtime work: A review of literature and initial empirical analysis*. International Labour Office, Inclusive Labour Markets, Labour Relations and Working Conditions Branch.

April, K., & Daya, P. (2025). The Use of AI in HRM and Management Processes: The Promise of Diversity, Equity, and Inclusion. In *AI and Diversity in a Datafied World of Work: Will the Future of Work be Inclusive?* (Vol. 12, pp. 97–123). Emerald Publishing Limited. DOI: 10.1108/S2051-233320250000012012

Argaw, S. T., Troncoso-Pastoriza, J. R., Lacey, D., Florin, M.-V., Calcavecchia, F., Anderson, D., Burleson, W., Vogel, J.-M., O'Leary, C., Eshaya-Chauvin, B., & Flahault, A. (2020). Cybersecurity of Hospitals: Discussing the challenges and working towards mitigating the risks. *BMC Medical Informatics and Decision Making*, *20*(1), 146. DOI: 10.1186/s12911-020-01161-7 PMID: 32620167

Ariffin, N. A., Yunus, A. M., & Kadir, I. K. (2021). The role of big data in the healthcare industry. *Journal of Islamic*, *6*(36), 235–245.

Aripin, Z., Agusiady, R., & Ariyanti, M. (2024). The Importance of a Sense Of Purpose For Salespersons: More Than Just A Financial Aspect. *Journal of Economics, Accounting, Business, Management. Engineering and Society*, *1*(3), 48–62.

Aripin, Z., Matriadi, F., & Ermeila, S. (2024, February). Optimization of Worker Work Environment, Robots, and Marketing Strategy: The Impact of Digital-Based Spatiotemporal Dynamics on Human Resource Management (HRM). *Journal of Jabar Economic Society Networking Forum*, *1*(3), 33–49.

Arnetz, B. B., & Arnetz, J. E. (2011). Organizational Climate, Occupational Stress, and Employee Mental Health. *Journal of Occupational and Environmental Medicine*, *53*(1), 34–42. DOI: 10.1097/JOM.0b013e3181ffo5b

Arora, M. K., Lal, S., Singh, B., & Olyaee, M. (2024). Through an Energy Lens: Examining SDGs From a Policy Perspective. In Riswandi, B., Singh, B., Kaunert, C., & Vig, K. (Eds.), *AI Applications for Clean Energy and Sustainability* (pp. 320–343). IGI Global., DOI: 10.4018/979-8-3693-6567-0.ch016

Arpaia, P., D'Errico, G., De Paolis, L. T., Moccaldi, N., & Nuccetelli, F. (2021). A narrative review of mindfulness-based interventions using virtual reality. *Mindfulness*, •••, 1–16.

Ashforth, B. E., Kreiner, G. E., & Fugate, M. (2000). All in a day's work: Boundaries and micro role transitions. *Academy of Management Review*, *25*(3), 472–491. DOI: 10.2307/259305

Atkinson, G., Fullick, S., Grindey, C., & Maclaren, D. (2008). Exercise, Energy Balance and the Shift Worker. *Sports Medicine (Auckland, N.Z.)*, *38*(8), 671–685. DOI: 10.2165/00007256-200838080-00005 PMID: 18620467

Atthakorn, S., Kaiyanan, C., Phoorisophon, T., Ludpa, Y., Seti, S., Lavong, A., & Pliankham, P. (2024). Strategic approaches in educational administration and management for advancing sustainable development. *Journal of Education and Learning Reviews*, *1*(3), 21–32. DOI: 10.60027/jelr.2024.796

Avolio, B. J., & Gardner, W. L. (2005). Authentic leadership development: Getting to the root of positive forms of leadership. *The Leadership Quarterly*, *16*(3), 315–338. DOI: 10.1016/j.leaqua.2005.03.001

Azizah, S., Raharjo, A., & Kristiana, I. (2023). Humility and psychological well-being of hospital employees. Proc. Int. Conf. of Psy. Stu., 4, 280-286. DOI: 10.58959/icpsyche.v4i1.45

Bahri, S., Zoghlami, N., Abed, M., & Tavares, J. M. R. (2018). Big data for healthcare: A survey. *IEEE Access : Practical Innovations, Open Solutions*, *7*, 7397–7408. DOI: 10.1109/ACCESS.2018.2889180

Bailey, D. E., & Kurland, N. B. (2002). A review of telework research: Findings, new directions, and lessons for the study of modern work. *Journal of Organizational Behavior*, *23*(4), 383–400. DOI: 10.1002/job.144

Bailey, D. E., & Kurland, N. B. (2020). A review of telework research: Findings and implications for the future of flexible work. *Human Resource Management Review*, *30*(4), 100692. DOI: 10.1016/j.hrmr.2020.100692

Bai, X., Li, H., & Wang, L. (2019). Work–family conflict and employee retention: A moderated mediation model. *Journal of Business Research*, *100*, 103–111. DOI: 10.1016/j.jbusres.2019.03.021

Bai, Z., Zhang, S., & He, H. (2025). Extraordinary nature and human recovery: Psychological and physiological perspectives. *Journal of Environmental Management*, *373*, 123661. DOI: 10.1016/j.jenvman.2024.123661 PMID: 39673850

Bajeh, A. O., Abikoye, O. C., Mojeed, H. A., Salihu, S. A., Oladipo, I. D., Abdulraheem, M., Awotunde, J. B., Sangaiah, A. K., & Adewole, K. S. (2021). Application of computational intelligence models in IoMT big data for heart disease diagnosis in personalised health care. In *Intelligent IoT Systems in Personalized Health Care* (pp. 177–206). Elsevier., DOI: 10.1016/B978-0-12-821187-8.00007-1

Bajwa, J., Munir, U., Nori, A., & Williams, B. (2021). Artificial intelligence in healthcare: Transforming the practice of medicine. *Future Healthcare Journal*, *8*(2), e188–e194. DOI: 10.7861/fhj.2021-0095 PMID: 34286183

Baker, E., Avery, G. C., & Crawford, J. (n.d.). *Satisfaction and Perceived Productivity when Professionals Work From Home*.

Bakker, A. B., & Demerouti, E. (2007). The Job Demands-Resources model: State of the art. *Journal of Managerial Psychology*, *22*(3), 309–328. DOI: 10.1108/02683940710733115

Bakker, A. B., Demerouti, E., & Verbeke, W. (2004). Using the job demands-resources model to predict burnout and performance. *Human Resource Management*, *43*(1), 83–104. DOI: 10.1002/hrm.20004

Bakri, N. N., Thomson, W. M., Broadbent, J. M., & Smith, M. B. (2025). Key informants' views on the benefits, planning and implementation of workplace oral health promotion programme. *Health Promotion International*, *40*(1), daae198. DOI: 10.1093/heapro/daae198 PMID: 39883052

Balu Gopalakrishnan v. State Of Kerala | Kerala High Court | Judgment | Law | CaseMine. (n.d.). Retrieved June 30, 2024, from https://www.casemine.com/judgement/in/5fe9797f9fca192d632e8f86

Banerjee, A. (2020). Equity and quality of healthcare access: Where do we stand and the way forward? *Indian Journal of Community Medicine : Official Publication of Indian Association of Preventive & Social Medicine*, *45*(1), 4. DOI: 10.4103/ijcm.IJCM_183_19 PMID: 32029975

Banimfreg, B. H. (2023). A comprehensive review and conceptual framework for cloud computing adoption in bioinformatics. *Healthcare Analytics*, *3*, 100190. DOI: 10.1016/j.health.2023.100190

Banks, S., & Dinges, D. F. (2007). Behavioral and Physiological Consequences of Sleep Restriction. *Journal of Clinical Sleep Medicine : JCSM : Official Publication of the American Academy of Sleep Medicine*, *03*(05), 519–528. DOI: 10.5664/jcsm.26918 PMID: 17803017

Bao, Y., Tang, Z., Li, H., & Zhang, Y. (2019). Computer vision and deep learning–based data anomaly detection method for structural health monitoring. *Structural Health Monitoring*, *18*(2), 401–421. DOI: 10.1177/1475921718757405

Baquero, A. (2023). Authentic leadership, employee work engagement, trust in the leader, and workplace well-being: A moderated mediation model. Psychology research and behavior management. tandfonline.com

Bareket-Bojmel, L., Chernyak-Hai, L., & Margalit, M. (2023). Out of sight but not out of mind: The role of loneliness and hope in remote work and in job engagement. *Personality and Individual Differences*, *202*, 111955. DOI: 10.1016/j.paid.2022.111955

Barger, L. K., Lockley, S. W., Rajaratnam, S. M. W., & Landrigan, C. P. (2009). Neurobehavioral, health, and safety consequences associated with shift work in safety-sensitive professions. *Current Neurology and Neuroscience Reports*, *9*(2), 155–164. DOI: 10.1007/s11910-009-0024-7 PMID: 19268039

Barman, A. (2023, May 2). Care Hospitals buyout: Max Healthcare sues TPG for "breach of term sheet agreement." *The Economic Times*. https://economictimes.indiatimes.com/industry/healthcare/biotech/healthcare/care-hospitals-buyout-max-healthcare-sues-tpg-for-breach-of-term-sheet-agreement/articleshow/99919224.cms?from=mdr

Barnes, C. M., Wagner, D. T., Ghumman, S., & Koopman, J. (2019). Sleep and employee performance: Advancing research and practice. *Annual Review of Organizational Psychology and Organizational Behavior*, *6*, 77–102. DOI: 10.1146/annurev-orgpsych-012218-015027

Baron, K. G., & Reid, K. J. (2014). Circadian misalignment and health. *International Review of Psychiatry (Abingdon, England)*, *26*(2), 139–154. DOI: 10.3109/09540261.2014.911149 PMID: 24892891

Barrero, J. M., Bloom, N., & Davis, S. J. (2021). *Why working from home will stick*. National Bureau of Economic Research., DOI: 10.3386/w28731

Bass, B. M., & Riggio, R. E. (2006). *Transformational Leadership*. Psychology Press. DOI: 10.4324/9781410617095

Bass, J., & Takahashi, J. S. (2010). Circadian Integration of Metabolism and Energetics. *Science*, *330*(6009), 1349–1354. DOI: 10.1126/science.1195027 PMID: 21127246

Bayrhammer-Savel, M., Ortner, M., Van Hout, M. C., & Komorowski, A. (2024). Psychiatric and legal considerations for ketamine treatment within prison settings. *Frontiers in Psychiatry*, *15*, 1316108. DOI: 10.3389/fpsyt.2024.1316108 PMID: 38699451

Becker, R., Chokoshvili, D., Thorogood, A., Dove, E. S., Molnár-Gábor, F., Ziaka, A., Tzortzatou-Nanopoulou, O., & Comandè, G. (2024). Purpose definition as a crucial step for determining the legal basis under the GDPR: Implications for scientific research. *Journal of Law and the Biosciences*, *11*(1), lsae001. Advance online publication. DOI: 10.1093/jlb/lsae001 PMID: 38313429

Beers, T. M. (2000). Flexible schedules and shift work: Replacing the '9-to-5' workday? *Monthly Labor Review*, *123*(6), 33–40.

Begum, G. T. (2025). Achieving sustainable development goals for mental health and gender equality through work-life balance and emotional intelligence. *Gender in Management*, *40*(1), 134–150. DOI: 10.1108/GM-04-2023-0149

Begum, S., Ashfaq, M., Xia, E., & Awan, U. (2022). Does green transformational leadership lead to green innovation? The role of green thinking and creative process engagement. [wiley.com]. *Business Strategy and the Environment*, *31*(1), 580–597.

Behura, A., Sahu, S., & Kabat, M. R. (2021). Advancement of Machine Learning and Cloud Computing in the Field of Smart Health Care. *Machine Learning Approach for Cloud Data Analytics in IoT*, 273-306.

Bella, K. M. J. (2023). Creating boundaries to maintaining a healthy work-life balance. International Journal of Multidisciplinary Research in Arts. *Science and Technology*, *1*(3), 24–30.

Bella, K. M. J. (2023). The power of employee well-being: A catalyst for organizational success. *International Journal of Scientific Research in Modern Science and Technology*, *2*(4), 20–26.

Bellamy, F. (2023). U.S. Data Privacy Laws to Enter New Era in 2023. Reuters. https://www.reuters.com/legal/legalindustry/us-data-privacy-laws-enter-new-era-2023-2023-01-12/

Benitez, J., Arenas, A., Castillo, A., & Esteves, J. (2022). Impact of digital leadership capability on innovation performance: The role of platform digitization capability. *Information & Management*, *59*(2), 103590.

Bergström, G., Bodin, T., & Lindh, T. (2021). Remote work and mental health: A longitudinal study of work-related factors, stress, and well-being. *Scandinavian Journal of Work, Environment & Health*, *47*(1), 8–15. DOI: 10.5271/sjweh.3938

Besedovsky, L., Lange, T., & Born, J. (2012). Sleep and immune function. *Pflügers Archiv*, *463*(1), 121–137. DOI: 10.1007/s00424-011-1044-0 PMID: 22071480

Bhattacharyya, D., Stephen Neal Joshua, E., & Thirupathi Rao, N. (2023). Medical Image Analysis of Lung Cancer CT Scans Using Deep Learning with Swarm Optimization Techniques. *Machine Intelligence, Big Data Analytics, and IoT in Image Processing: Practical Applications*, 23-50.

Bishehsari, F., Levi, F., Turek, F. W., & Keshavarzian, A. (2016). Circadian Rhythms in Gastrointestinal Health and Diseases. *Gastroenterology*, *151*(3), e1–e5. DOI: 10.1053/j.gastro.2016.07.036 PMID: 27480174

Bisht, R., & Riach, K. (2025). Going loca: Depression at work as a public feeling in Peru. *Gender, Work and Organization, 32*(2), 634–652. DOI: 10.1111/gwao.13170

Blau, P. M. (1964). *Exchange and power in social life*. Wiley.

Bloom, N., Liang, J., Roberts, J., & Ying, Z. J. (2015). Does working from home work? Evidence from a Chinese experiment. *The Quarterly Journal of Economics, 130*(1), 165–218. DOI: 10.1093/qje/qju032

Boege, H. L., Bhatti, M. Z., & St-Onge, M.-P. (2021). Circadian rhythms and meal timing: Impact on energy balance and body weight. *Current Opinion in Biotechnology, 70*, 1–6. DOI: 10.1016/j.copbio.2020.08.009 PMID: 32998085

Boersma, G. J., Mijnster, T., Vantyghem, P., Kerkhof, G. A., & Lancel, M. (2023). Shift work is associated with extensively disordered sleep, especially when working nights. *Frontiers in Psychiatry, 14*, 1233640. DOI: 10.3389/fpsyt.2023.1233640 PMID: 38161719

Boivin, D. B., Boudreau, P., & Kosmadopoulos, A. (2022). Disturbance of the Circadian System in Shift Work and Its Health Impact. *Journal of Biological Rhythms, 37*(1), 3–28. DOI: 10.1177/07487304211064218 PMID: 34969316

Bolatov, A., Baikanova, R., Igenbayeva, B., & Seisembekov, T. (2025). Health care providers have faced the pandemic altruistically, but financial support is important for their well-being and motivation to work. *Public Health, 240*, 119–124. DOI: 10.1016/j.puhe.2025.01.023 PMID: 39904063

Bondar, J., Morrow, C., Gueorguieva, R., Brown, M., Hawrilenko, M., Krystal, J., & Chekroud, A. (2022). Clinical and financial outcomes associated with a workplace mental health program before and during the covid-19 pandemic. *JAMA Network Open, 5*(6), e2216349. DOI: 10.1001/jamanetworkopen.2022.16349 PMID: 35679044

Borah, P. P., & Bhuyan, A. J. (2024). Living with the *Aadhaar*: India's Changing Contours of Identity and Governance. *The Indian Journal of Public Administration, 70*(3), 615–620. DOI: 10.1177/00195561241257460

Borbely, A. A. (1982). *A Two Process Model of Sleep Regulation*.

Borbély, A. (2022). The two-process model of sleep regulation: Beginnings and outlook. *Journal of Sleep Research, 31*(4), e13598. DOI: 10.1111/jsr.13598 PMID: 35502706

Born, J., Lange, T., Hansen, K., Mölle, M., & Fehm, H. L. (1997). Effects of sleep and circadian rhythm on human circulating immune cells. *The Journal of Immunology : Official Journal of the American Association of Immunologists, 158*(9), 4454–4464. DOI: 10.4049/jimmunol.158.9.4454 PMID: 9127011

Boudreau, P., Dumont, G. A., & Boivin, D. B. (2013). Circadian Adaptation to Night Shift Work Influences Sleep, Performance, Mood and the Autonomic Modulation of the Heart. *PLoS One, 8*(7), e70813. DOI: 10.1371/journal.pone.0070813 PMID: 23923024

Bovopoulos, N., & Jorm, A. (2018). Exploring the role of mental health first aid officers in workplaces: A qualitative study using case study methodology. *International Journal of Workplace Health Management, 11*(6), 366–381. DOI: 10.1108/IJWHM-06-2018-0082

Braghin, C., & Cremonini, M. (2017a). Online Privacy. In *Computer and Information Security Handbook* (pp. 743–758). Elsevier., DOI: 10.1016/B978-0-12-803843-7.00052-1

Bright, C., Walden, S., Abdulla, S., & Ryan, R. (2023). Intellectual disability nursing for people with profound intellectual disabilities and complex needs. In *Learning and Intellectual Disability Nursing Practice* (pp. 194–239). Routledge. DOI: 10.4324/9781003296461-6

Briker, R., Walter, F., & Cole, M. S. (2021). Hurry up! The role of supervisors' time urgency and self-perceived status for autocratic leadership and subordinates' well-being. *Personnel Psychology, 74*(1), 55–76.

Brohan, E., & Thornicroft, G. (2010). Employees with mental health problems: Survey of UK employers' knowledge, attitudes and workplace practices. *Epidemiologia e Psichiatria Sociale, 19*(4), 326–332. DOI: 10.1017/S1121189X0000066X

Brougham, D., & Haar, J. M. (2018). Smart technology, artificial intelligence, robotics, and algorithms (STARA): Employees' perceptions of future workplace technology change. *International Journal of Human Resource Management, 29*(10), 1547–1566. DOI: 10.1080/09585192.2017.1362666

Brough, P., & O'Driscoll, M. P. (2010). Organizational interventions for balancing work and home demands: An overview. *Work and Stress, 24*(3), 280–297. DOI: 10.1080/02678373.2010.506808

Brown, M. E., & Treviño, L. K. (2006). Ethical leadership: A review and future directions. *The Leadership Quarterly, 17*(6), 595–616. DOI: 10.1016/j.leaqua.2006.10.004

Brun, J. (2023, July 26). Understanding non-compliance: Meaning, Consequences, and Corrective Measures. *Nimonik*. https://nimonik.com/blog/unveiling-non-compliance-in-regulatory-standards-implications-types-factors-proactive-solutions/

Bryan, M. L., Bryce, A. M., & Roberts, J. (2021). The effect of mental and physical health problems on sickness absence. [springer.com]. *The European Journal of Health Economics*, *22*(9), 1519–1533. DOI: 10.1007/s10198-021-01379-w PMID: 34626291

Bryson, A., Forth, J., & Stokes, L. (2017). Does employees' subjective well-being affect workplace performance? *Human Relations*, *70*(8), 1017–1037. DOI: 10.1177/0018726717693073

Buda, L. (2023). *Advancing Education for Neurodiverse Students in Morocco: A Repository for Teachers, Parents, and Students* (Doctoral dissertation, Worcester Polytechnic Institute).

Buxton, O. M., Lee, S., L'Hermite-Balériaux, M., Turek, F. W., & Van Cauter, E. (2016). Sleep and performance. *Nature Reviews. Neuroscience*, *17*(6), 388–399. DOI: 10.1038/nrn.2016.53 PMID: 27320790

Cabello, J. C., Karimipour, H., Jahromi, A. N., Dehghantanha, A., & Parizi, R. M. (2020). Big-data and cyber-physical systems in healthcare: Challenges and opportunities. *Handbook of Big Data Privacy*, 255-283.

Cajochen, C., Kräuchi, K., & Wirz-Justice, A. (2003). Role of Melatonin in the Regulation of Human Circadian Rhythms and Sleep. *Journal of Neuroendocrinology*, *15*(4), 432–437. DOI: 10.1046/j.1365-2826.2003.00989.x PMID: 12622846

Caldwell, J. A. (2012). Crew Schedules, Sleep Deprivation, and Aviation Performance. *Current Directions in Psychological Science*, *21*(2), 85–89. DOI: 10.1177/0963721411435842

Caldwell, J. A., Caldwell, J. L., Thompson, L. A., & Lieberman, H. R. (2019). Fatigue and its management in the workplace. *Neuroscience and Biobehavioral Reviews*, *96*, 272–289. DOI: 10.1016/j.neubiorev.2018.10.024 PMID: 30391406

Caldwell, J. A., Mallis, M. M., Caldwell, J. L., Paul, M. A., Miller, J. C., & Neri, D. F. (2009). Fatigue Countermeasures in Aviation. *Aviation, Space, and Environmental Medicine*, *80*(1), 29–59. DOI: 10.3357/ASEM.2435.2009 PMID: 19180856

Cann, R. F., Riedel-Prabhakar, R., & Powell, D. (2021). A model of positive school leadership to improve teacher wellbeing. [HTML]. *International Journal of Applied Positive Psychology*, *6*(2), 195–218.

Cao, X., Zhang, H., Li, P., & Huang, X. (2022). The influence of mental health on job satisfaction: Mediating effect of psychological capital and social capital. *Frontiers in Public Health, 10*, 797274. Advance online publication. DOI: 10.3389/fpubh.2022.797274 PMID: 35211441

Cao, X., Zhang, Z., & Jiang, L. (2021). The effect of flexible work arrangements on employee mental health: A systematic review and meta-analysis. *Journal of Organizational Behavior, 42*(8), 920–944. DOI: 10.1002/job.2527

Carnevale, J. B., & Hatak, I. (2020). Employee adjustment and well-being in the era of COVID-19: Implications for human resource management. *Journal of Business Research, 116*, 183–187. DOI: 10.1016/j.jbusres.2020.05.037 PMID: 32501303

Cascio, W. F., & Ehrhardt, K. (2024). Designing recruitment programs for impact. In *Essentials of Employee Recruitment* (pp. 330–350). Routledge. DOI: 10.4324/9781003356752-20

Cavanagh, J., Bartram, T., Walker, M., Pariona-Cabrera, P., & Halvorsen, B. (2024). Health services in Australia and the impact of antiquated rostering practices on medical scientists: A case for HR analytics and evidenced-based human resource management. *Personnel Review, 53*(1), 18–33. DOI: 10.1108/PR-09-2021-0690

Cavusoglu, L., & Demirbag-Kaplan, M. (2025). Unraveling the Threads of Marketplace Diversity. *The Journal of Consumer Affairs, 59*(1), e70006. DOI: 10.1111/joca.70006

Cerdeira, J., Cakirpaloglu, S., & Cakirpaloglu, P. (2023). Crushing the spirit: Unmasking the impact of workplace bullying on psychological well-being among portuguese employees. *Administrative Sciences, 13*(11), 244. DOI: 10.3390/admsci13110244

Chadha, A. (2021). Digital Data Protection and The Right to Privacy. SSRN *Electronic Journal*. DOI: 10.2139/ssrn.3899815

Chakraborty, C., & Bhattacharya, S. (2020). Healthcare data monitoring under Internet of Things. In *Green Computing and Predictive Analytics for Healthcare* (pp. 1–18). Chapman and Hall/CRC. DOI: 10.1201/9780429317224-1

Chang, W.-P., & Peng, Y.-X. (2021). Differences between fixed day shift workers and rotating shift workers in gastrointestinal problems: A systematic review and meta-analysis. *Industrial Health, 59*(2), 66–77. DOI: 10.2486/indhealth.2020-0153 PMID: 33408309

Chathukulam, J., & Tharamangalam, J. (2021). The Kerala model in the time of COVID19: Rethinking state, society and democracy. *World Development, 137*, 105207. DOI: 10.1016/j.worlddev.2020.105207 PMID: 32989341

Chatterjee, K., Clark, B., Martin, A., & Davis, A. (2020). The commuting and well-being study: Understanding the impact of commuting on people's lives. *Transportation Research Part A, Policy and Practice, 132*, 157–173. DOI: 10.1016/j.tra.2020.06.006

Chatzigianni, D., Tsounis, A., Markopoulos, N., & Sarafis, P. (2018). Occupational stress experienced by nurses working in a Greek Regional Hospital: A cross-sectional study. *Iranian Journal of Nursing and Midwifery Research, 23*(6), 450. DOI: 10.4103/ijnmr.IJNMR_120_17 PMID: 30386395

Chauhan, S., Norbury, R., Faßbender, K. C., Ettinger, U., & Kumari, V. (2023). Beyond sleep: A multidimensional model of chronotype. *Neuroscience and Biobehavioral Reviews, 148*, 105114. DOI: 10.1016/j.neubiorev.2023.105114 PMID: 36868368

Chellappa, S. L., Vujovic, N., Williams, J. S., & Scheer, F. A. J. L. (2019). Impact of Circadian Disruption on Cardiovascular Function and Disease. *Trends in Endocrinology and Metabolism, 30*(10), 767–779. DOI: 10.1016/j.tem.2019.07.008 PMID: 31427142

Chen, C. P., & Zhang, C. Y. (2014). Data-intensive applications, challenges, techniques and technologies: A survey on Big Data. *Information Sciences, 275*, 314–347.

Chen, C., & Nath, R. (2021). Organizational agility and digital HRM: Facilitating work flexibility through technology. *Journal of Business Research, 124*, 293–304. DOI: 10.1016/j.jbusres.2020.11.051

Cheng, W.-J., Liu, C.-S., Hu, K.-C., Cheng, Y.-F., Karhula, K., & Härmä, M. (2021). Night shift work and the risk of metabolic syndrome: Findings from an 8-year hospital cohort. *PLoS One, 16*(12), e0261349. DOI: 10.1371/journal.pone.0261349 PMID: 34898652

Chen, H.-T., Chuang, H.-Y., Hsieh, T.-Y., Wu, P.-S., Lin, F.-J., Huang, H.-C., Yang, C.-C., & Kuo, C.-H. (2022). Shift work is significantly and positively associated with possible gastro-esophageal reflux disease: A meta-analysis study. *Frontiers in Public Health, 10*, 980603. DOI: 10.3389/fpubh.2022.980603 PMID: 36504996

Chen, M., Mao, S., Zhang, Y., & Leung, V. C. (2014). *Big data: related technologies, challenges and future prospects* (Vol. 100). Springer. DOI: 10.1007/978-3-319-06245-7

Cherian, J., Gaikar, V., Paul, R., & Pech, R. (2021). Corporate Culture and Its Impact on Employees' Attitude, Performance, Productivity, and Behavior: An Investigative Analysis from Selected Organizations of the United Arab Emirates (UAE). *Journal of Open Innovation, 7*(1), 45. DOI: 10.3390/joitmc7010045

Chetty, L. (2017). An evaluation of the health and well-being needs of employees: An organizational case study. *Journal of Occupational Health, 59*(1), 88–90. DOI: 10.1539/joh.16-0197-BR PMID: 27853056

Chtourou, H., & Souissi, N. (n.d.). The Effect Of Training At A Specific Time Of Day. *RE:view.*

Clark, C. M., & Kosciw, J. G. (2022). Engaged or excluded: LGBTQ youth's participation in school sports and their relationship to psychological well-being. *Psychology in the Schools, 59*(1), 95–114.

Clark, S. C. (2000). Work/family border theory: A new theory of work/family balance. *Human Relations, 53*(6), 747–770. DOI: 10.1177/0018726700536001

Codinhoto, R., & Cooper, R. (2009). The impacts of the built environment on health outcomes. *Facilities, 27*(3/4), 138–151. DOI: 10.1108/02632770910933152

Cohen, P. (2016). Work and family: A challenge for policy in the 21st century. *International Labour Review, 155*(4), 493–513. DOI: 10.1111/ilr.12147

Compagnucci, M. C., Fenwick, M., & Haapio, H. (2024). *Unlocking the Potential of Binding Corporate Rules (BCRs) in Health Data Transfers* (Version 1). arXiv. DOI: 10.1007/978-981-97-9983-1_3

Connery, L. A., & Frick, W. C. (2021). A formal administrator mentoring program: Perceived learning benefits and insights into leadership well-being. ie. *Inquiry in Education, 13*(1), 3.

Cooper, C. L., & Quick, J. C. (2017). *The Handbook of Stress and Health: A Guide to Research and Practice.* Wiley. DOI: 10.1002/9781118993811

Correa, Á., Alguacil, S., Ciria, L. F., Jiménez, A., & Ruz, M. (2020). Circadian rhythms and decision-making: A review and new evidence from electroencephalography. *Chronobiology International, 37*(4), 520–541. DOI: 10.1080/07420528.2020.1715421 PMID: 32000532

Correia, T., Kuhlmann, E., Lotta, G., Beja, A., Morais, R., Zapata, T., & Campbell, J. (2025). Turning the global health and care workforce crisis into action: The pathway to effective evidence-based policy and implementation. *The International Journal of Health Planning and Management, 40*(1), 224–233. DOI: 10.1002/hpm.3860 PMID: 39396240

Costa, G. (2010). Shift Work and Health: Current Problems and Preventive Actions. *Safety and Health at Work, 1*(2), 112–123. DOI: 10.5491/SHAW.2010.1.2.112 PMID: 22953171

Costa, G., & Sartori, S. (2007). Ageing, working hours and work ability. *Ergonomics*, *50*(11), 1914–1930. DOI: 10.1080/00140130701676054 PMID: 17972209

Cotton, S. P., & Hart, P. M. (2003). Occupational wellbeing and employee assistance programs: Their role in work-life balance. *Journal of Employee Assistance*, *33*(1), 45–53.

Cresswell, K., Domínguez Hernández, A., Williams, R., & Sheikh, A. (2022). Key Challenges and Opportunities for Cloud Technology in Health Care: Semistructured Interview Study. *JMIR Human Factors*, *9*(1), e31246. DOI: 10.2196/31246 PMID: 34989688

Crosbie, T., & Moore, J. (2004). Work–life Balance and Working from Home. *Social Policy and Society*, *3*(3), 223–233. DOI: 10.1017/S1474746404001733

Curry, T., Lovecraft, A., & Quintyne, A. (2025). Exploration of Racial Dynamics and Climate Change Experience: Insights from Underrepresented Communities in Interior Alaska. *Weather, Climate, and Society*. Advance online publication. DOI: 10.1175/WCAS-D-24-0087.1

Cvenkel, N. (2021). Work-life balance and well-being at work: Employees' perspective to promote a psychologically healthy workplace. In *The Palgrave handbook of corporate social responsibility* (pp. 429–451). Springer International Publishing.

Czeisler, C. A., Moore-Ede, M. C., & Coleman, R. M. (1982). Rotating Shift Work Schedules That Disrupt Sleep Are Improved by Applying Circadian Principles. *Science*, *217*(4558), 460–463. DOI: 10.1126/science.7089576 PMID: 7089576

da Silva, T. M. H. R. (2025). The Role of Emotional Intelligence in Promoting Mental Peace, Healthy Work Environments, and Emotional Well-Being Among Entrepreneurs. In *Supporting Psychological and Emotional Wellbeing Among Entrepreneurs* (pp. 401–426). IGI Global.

Dadwal, H., Singh, S., Poddar, D., & Singh, A. (2024). *India: Regulators must balance growth and innovation with user protection*. https://globalcompetitionreview.com/guide/data-antitrust-guide/first-edition/article/india-regulators-must-balance-growth-and-innovation-user-protection

Dall'Ora, C., Ball, J., Recio-Saucedo, A., & Griffiths, P. (2016). Characteristics of shift work and their impact on employee performance and wellbeing: A literature review. *International Journal of Nursing Studies*, *57*, 12–27. DOI: 10.1016/j.ijnurstu.2016.01.007 PMID: 27045561

Danna, K., & Griffin, R. W. (1999). Health and Well-Being in the Workplace: A Review and Synthesis of the Literature. *Journal of Management*, *25*(3), 357–384. DOI: 10.1177/014920639902500305

Daruwalla, S., & Ley, S. (2025). Friendship as a lifeline: Navigating the precarious landscape of the US employment-based immigration as women of color psychologists. *Family Process*, *64*(1), e13078. DOI: 10.1111/famp.13078 PMID: 39551484

Dash, S., Shakyawar, S. K., Sharma, M., & Kaushik, S. (2019). Big data in healthcare: Management, analysis and future prospects. *Journal of Big Data*, *6*(1), 1–25. DOI: 10.1186/s40537-019-0217-0

Data Privacy Laws and Regulations Around the World—Securiti. (n.d.). Retrieved June 30, 2024, from https://securiti.ai/privacy-laws/

Data Security Council of India establishes privacy guidelines for healthcare sector. (n.d.). Retrieved June 30, 2024, from https://www.medianama.com/2021/09/223-dsci-health-privacy-guidelines-2/

Davenport, L. J., & Reavley, N. J. (2016). How can organizations help employees thrive? The development of guidelines for promoting positive mental health at work. *International Journal of Workplace Health Management*, *9*(4), 411–427. DOI: 10.1108/IJWHM-01-2016-0001

Davey, J., Johns, R., & Leino, H. M. (2024). Strengths-based service solutions: mapping a way forward in marketplace vulnerabilities. In *A Research Agenda for Service Marketing* (pp. 251–280). Edward Elgar Publishing. DOI: 10.4337/9781803923178.00021

Dawson, D., & Encel, N. (1993). Melatonin and sleep in humans. *Journal of Pineal Research*, *15*(1), 1–12. DOI: 10.1111/j.1600-079X.1993.tb00503.x PMID: 8229640

De Haas, H. (2021). A theory of migration: the aspirations-capabilities framework. Comparative migration studies. springer.com

De Souza, C. M., & Hidalgo, M. P. L. (2015). The midpoint of sleep on working days: A measure for chronodisruption and its association to individuals' well-being. *Chronobiology International*, *32*(3), 341–348. DOI: 10.3109/07420528.2014.979941 PMID: 25392279

de Vries, M. S. E., & de Vries, M. S. (2023). Repetitive reorganizations, uncertainty and change fatigue. *Public Money & Management*, *43*(2), 126–135. DOI: 10.1080/09540962.2021.1905258

Deb, B. C., Rahman, M. M., & Haseeb, M. (2024). Unveiling the impact on corporate social responsibility through green tax and green financing: A PLS-SEM approach. *Environmental Science and Pollution Research International, 31*(1), 1543–1561. DOI: 10.1007/s11356-023-31150-y PMID: 38041735

Deci, E. L., & Ryan, R. M. (1985). *Intrinsic motivation and self-determination in human behavior*. Springer. DOI: 10.1007/978-1-4899-2271-7

Deci, E. L., & Ryan, R. M. (2000). The "what" and "why" of goal pursuits: Human needs and the self-determination of behavior. *Psychological Inquiry, 11*(4), 227–268. DOI: 10.1207/S15327965PLI1104_01

Deci, E. L., Vallerand, R. J., & Ryan, R. M. (2017). Self-determination and motivational development in work settings. *Journal of Organizational Behavior, 38*(2), 257–271. DOI: 10.1002/job.2308

DeGroot, T., & Kiker, D. S. (2003). A meta-analysis of the non-monetary effects of employee health management programs. Human Resource Management: Published in Cooperation with the School of Business Administration, The University of Michigan and in alliance with the Society of Human Resources Management, 42(1), 53-69.

Deka, P., Singh, G., Sharma, C., Verma, P., & Kapoor, S. (2024). The interplay of resilience, stress, mental well-being and task performance: Implications for sustainable workplaces. *Model Assisted Statistics and Applications : An International Journal, 19*(3), 265–274. DOI: 10.3233/MAS-241933

Dekker, S. W., & Schaufeli, W. B. (1995). The Effects of Job Insecurity on Psychological Health and Withdrawal: A Longitudinal Study. *Australian Psychologist, 30*(1), 57–63. DOI: 10.1080/00050069508259607

Deloitte. (2020). *2020 Global Human Capital Trends: The social enterprise at work—Paradox as a path forward*. Deloitte Insights.

Deloitte. (2020). *The Deloitte Global Human Capital Trends report*. https://www2.deloitte.com/global/en/insights/focus/human-capital-trends.html

Demir, E. (2023). The protection of human biodata: Is there any role for data ownership? *Computer Law & Security Review, 51*, 105905. DOI: 10.1016/j.clsr.2023.105905

Derks, D., Fischer, A. R. H., & van der Molen, H. T. (2016). Email as a source of stress and its impact on employees' work-life balance. *Computers in Human Behavior, 54*, 417–427. DOI: 10.1016/j.chb.2015.08.040

Derks, D., van Mierlo, H., & Schmitz, E. B. (2014). A diary study on work-related smartphone use, psychological detachment and exhaustion: Examining the role of the perceived segmentation norm. *Journal of Occupational Health Psychology*, *19*(1), 74–84. DOI: 10.1037/a0035076 PMID: 24447222

Devi, A. D., & Subiyantoro, S. (2021). Implementation of democratic leadership style and transformational head of madrasah in improving the quality. *Nidhomul Haq: Jurnal Manajemen Pendidikan Islam*, *6*(1), 14–26.

Devika, G., & Karegowda, A. G. (2021). Deep Learning in IoT: Introduction, Applications, and Perspective in the Big Data Era. In *Deep Learning Applications and Intelligent Decision Making in Engineering* (pp. 1-54). IGI Global.

Dhand, S. (2025). Theories and Concepts of Well-being and Happiness in the Workplace: Foundations and Practical Applications. In *Insights on Wellbeing and Happiness in the Workplace* (pp. 283-304). IGI Global Scientific Publishing.

Di Maio, M., Basch, E., Denis, F., Fallowfield, L. J., Ganz, P. A., & Howell, D.ESMO Guidelines Committee. (2022). The role of patient-reported outcome measures in the continuum of cancer clinical care: ESMO Clinical Practice Guideline. [sciencedirect.com]. *Annals of Oncology : Official Journal of the European Society for Medical Oncology*, *33*(9), 878–892.

Diener, E. (2000). Subjective well-being: The science of happiness and a proposal for a national index. *The American Psychologist*, *55*(1), 34–43. DOI: 10.1037/0003-066X.55.1.34 PMID: 11392863

Dijk, D., & Czeisler, C. (1995). Contribution of the circadian pacemaker and the sleep homeostat to sleep propensity, sleep structure, electroencephalographic slow waves, and sleep spindle activity in humans. *The Journal of Neuroscience : The Official Journal of the Society for Neuroscience*, *15*(5), 3526–3538. DOI: 10.1523/JNEUROSCI.15-05-03526.1995 PMID: 7751928

Dijk, D.-J., & Lockley, S. W. (2002). Invited Review: Integration of human sleep-wake regulation and circadian rhythmicity. *Journal of Applied Physiology*, *92*(2), 852–862. DOI: 10.1152/japplphysiol.00924.2001 PMID: 11796701

Dimoff, J., & Kelloway, E. (2019). With a little help from my boss: The impact of workplace mental health training on leader behaviors and employee resource utilization. *Journal of Occupational Health Psychology*, *24*(1), 4–19. DOI: 10.1037/ocp0000126 PMID: 29939045

Dolezel, D., Beauvais, B., Stigler Granados, P., Fulton, L., & Kruse, C. S. (2023). Effects of Internal and External Factors on Hospital Data Breaches: Quantitative Study. *Journal of Medical Internet Research*, *25*, e51471. DOI: 10.2196/51471 PMID: 38127426

Donaldson, L., Ricciardi, W., Sheridan, S., & Tartaglia, R. (Eds.). (2021). *Textbook of Patient Safety and Clinical Risk Management*. Springer International Publishing., DOI: 10.1007/978-3-030-59403-9

Donato, S., Parise, M., Pagani, A. F., Lanz, M., Regalia, C., Rosnati, R., & Iafrate, R. (2021). Together against COVID-19 concerns: The role of the dyadic coping process for partners' psychological well-being during the pandemic. [frontiersin.org]. *Frontiers in Psychology*, *11*, 578395. DOI: 10.3389/fpsyg.2020.578395 PMID: 33488449

Dongarwar, D., Yusuf, K., Maiyegun, S., Ibrahimi, S., Ikedionwu, C., & Salihu, H. (2020). Covid-19 and neuro-behavioral economics: A conceptual framework to improve physical and mental health among remote workers. *International Journal of MCH and AIDS*, *9*(3), 360–363. DOI: 10.21106/ijma.399 PMID: 33014623

Do, T. T., & Mai, N. K. (2021). A systematic review on high performance organization. [HTML]. *Management Research Review*, *44*(1), 181–208. DOI: 10.1108/MRR-11-2019-0495

Dougall, I., Vasiljevic, M., Kutlaca, M., & Weick, M. (2023). Socioeconomic inequalities in mental health and well-being among uk students during the covid-19 pandemic: Clarifying underlying mechanisms. *PLoS One*, *18*(11), e0292842. DOI: 10.1371/journal.pone.0292842 PMID: 37910542

Drigas, A., Mitsea, E., & Skianis, C. (2022). Virtual reality and metacognition training techniques for learning disabilities. *Sustainability (Basel)*, *14*(16), 10170. DOI: 10.3390/su141610170

Drigas, A., Papoutsi, C., & Skianis, C. (2023). Being an emotionally intelligent leader through the nine-layer model of emotional intelligence—The supporting role of new technologies. *Sustainability*, *15*(10), 8103.

Duffy, J. F., & Czeisler, C. A. (2009). Effect of Light on Human Circadian Physiology. *Sleep Medicine Clinics*, *4*(2), 165–177. DOI: 10.1016/j.jsmc.2009.01.004 PMID: 20161220

Dutraj, R. and Sengupta, P. (2024). Investigation into the nexus between workplace spirituality and employee performance in Indian banks: the interplay with mental health as a mediating factor in the context of West Bengal, India. Journal of Human Resource Management – HR Advances and Developments, 2024(1), 109-127. DOI: 10.46287/KLSN5929

Dutta, D., & Mishra, S. (2023). Bots for mental health: The boundaries of human and technology agencies for enabling mental well-being within organizations. *Personnel Review, 53*(5), 1129–1156. DOI: 10.1108/PR-11-2022-0832

Ebert, D. D., Harrer, M., Apolinário-Hagen, J., & Baumeister, H. (2019). Digital interventions for mental disorders: key features, efficacy, and potential for artificial intelligence applications. *Frontiers in Psychiatry: Artificial Intelligence, Precision Medicine, and Other Paradigm Shifts*, 583-627.

Edú-Valsania, S., Laguía, A., & Moriano, J. A. (2022). Burnout: A Review of Theory and Measurement. *International Journal of Environmental Research and Public Health, 19*(3), 1780. DOI: 10.3390/ijerph19031780 PMID: 35162802

Edwards, A., & Marcus, S. (2018). Employee perceptions of well-being programs. *Journal of Social, Behavioral and Health Sciences, 12*(1). Advance online publication. DOI: 10.5590/JSBHS.2018.12.1.07

Ehrenstein, V., Kharrazi, H., Lehmann, H., & Taylor, C. O. (2019). Obtaining data from electronic health records. In Tools and technologies for registry interoperability, registries for evaluating patient outcomes: A user's guide, 3rd edition, Addendum 2 [Internet]. Agency for Healthcare Research and Quality (US).

Ehrenstein, V., Kharrazi, H., Lehmann, H., & Taylor, C. O. (2019). Obtaining Data From Electronic Health Records. In *Tools and Technologies for Registry Interoperability, Registries for Evaluating Patient Outcomes: A User's Guide, 3rd Edition, Addendum 2 [Internet]*. Agency for Healthcare Research and Quality (US). https://www.ncbi.nlm.nih.gov/books/NBK551878/

Einwiller, S. A., Wolfgruber, D., & Leitner, A. K. (2025). Addressing backlash? Corporate DEI communication and user complaints on social media. *Journal of Marketing Communications*, •••, 1–19. DOI: 10.1080/13527266.2025.2471954

Elbadawi, M., Gaisford, S., & Basit, A. W. (2021). Advanced machine-learning techniques in drug discovery. *Drug Discovery Today, 26*(3), 769–777. DOI: 10.1016/j.drudis.2020.12.003 PMID: 33290820

Eldevik, M. F., Flo, E., Moen, B. E., Pallesen, S., & Bjorvatn, B. (2013). Insomnia, Excessive Sleepiness, Excessive Fatigue, Anxiety, Depression and Shift Work Disorder in Nurses Having Less than 11 Hours in-Between Shifts. *PLoS One*, *8*(8), e70882. DOI: 10.1371/journal.pone.0070882 PMID: 23976964

El-Gendy, S., Elsayed, M. S., Jurcut, A., & Azer, M. A. (2023). Privacy Preservation Using Machine Learning in the Internet of Things. *Mathematics*, *11*(16), 3477. DOI: 10.3390/math11163477

Elhoseny, M., Abdelaziz, A., Salama, A. S., Riad, A. M., Muhammad, K., & Sangaiah, A. K. (2018). A hybrid model of Internet of Things and cloud computing to manage big data in health services applications. *Future Generation Computer Systems*, *86*, 1383–1394. DOI: 10.1016/j.futurc.2018.03.005

Elor, A., & Kurniawan, S. (2020). The ultimate display for physical rehabilitation: A bridging review on immersive virtual reality. *Frontiers in Virtual Reality*, *1*, 585993. DOI: 10.3389/frvir.2020.585993

Elshaer, I. A., Azazz, A. M., Ghaleb, M. M., Abdulaziz, T. A., Mansour, M. A., & Fayyad, S. (2024). The impact of work-related ICT use on perceived injustice: Exploring the effects of work role overload and psychological detachment. *Journal of Open Innovation*, *10*(1), 100208. DOI: 10.1016/j.joitmc.2024.100208

Elshaer, I., & Azazz, A. (2023). Mental health of tourism employees post covid-19 pandemic: A test of antecedents and moderators. *European Journal of Investigation in Health, Psychology and Education*, *13*(3), 626–641. DOI: 10.3390/ejihpe13030048 PMID: 36975400

Elufioye, O., Ndubuisi, N., Daraojimba, R., Awonuga, K., Ayanponle, L., & Asuzu, O.Oluwafunmi Adijat ElufioyeNdubuisi Leonard NdubuisiRosita Ebere DaraojimbaKehinde Feranmi AwonugaLatifat Omolara AyanponleOnyeka Franca Asuzu. (2024). Reviewing employee well-being and mental health initiatives in contemporary hr practices. *International Journal of Science and Research Archive*, *11*(1), 828–840. DOI: 10.30574/ijsra.2024.11.1.0153

Esquierdo-Leal, J. L., & Houmanfar, R. A. (2021). Creating inclusive and equitable cultural practices by linking leadership to systemic change. *Behavior Analysis in Practice*, *14*(2), 499–512.

EY. (2025). *The AIdea of India 2025: How much productivity can GenAI unlock in India*.

Fakunle, O. (2021). Developing a framework for international students' rationales for studying abroad, beyond economic factors. Policy Futures in Education. sagepub.com

Falcon, M., Chen, C., Bandari, R., Kocher, B., & Shah, N. (2021). Impact of evidence-based psychotherapy on employee retention. *Medical Research Archives*, *9*(11). Advance online publication. DOI: 10.18103/mra.v9i11.2574

Feld, A. D. (2005). The Health Insurance Portability and Accountability Act (HIPAA): Its Broad Effect on Practice. *The American Journal of Gastroenterology*, *100*(7), 1440–1443. DOI: 10.1111/j.1572-0241.2005.50621.x PMID: 15984962

Felstead, A., & Henseke, G. (2017). Assessing the growth of remote working and its consequences for effort, well-being, and work-life balance. *New Technology, Work and Employment*, *32*(3), 195–212. DOI: 10.1111/ntwe.12097

Ferri, P., Guadi, M., Marcheselli, L., Balduzzi, S., Magnani, D., & Di Lorenzo, R. (2016). The impact of shift work on the psychological and physical health of nurses in a general hospital: A comparison between rotating night shifts and day shifts. *Risk Management and Healthcare Policy*, *9*, 203–211. DOI: 10.2147/RMHP.S115326 PMID: 27695372

Figueiro, M. G., Steverson, B., Heerwagen, J., Kampschroer, K., Hunter, C. M., Gonzales, K., Plitnick, B., & Rea, M. S. (2017). The impact of daytime light exposures on sleep and mood in office workers. *Sleep Health*, *3*(3), 204–215. DOI: 10.1016/j.sleh.2017.03.005 PMID: 28526259

Filkins, B. L., Kim, J. Y., Roberts, B., Armstrong, W., Miller, M. A., Hultner, M. L., & Steinhubl, S. R. (2016). Privacy and security in the era of digital health: What should translational researchers know and do about it? *American Journal of Translational Research*, *8*(3), 1560.

Financialexpress. (2024, March 5). Digital Technologies Driving the Evolution of Indian Healthcare in 2024 and Beyond. *Financialexpress*. https://www.financialexpress.com/business/healthcare-digital-technologies-driving-the-evolution-of-indian-healthcare-in-2024-and-beyond-3413739/

Fish, J. N., Paceley, M. S., Evans, S., Kosi-Huber, J. A., Phillips, D. R., & Levine, D. S. (2025). Community Efforts to Support LGBTQ+ Youth Mental Health: Programs Objectives, Development, and Delivery. *Journal of Community Psychology*, *53*(2), e70002. DOI: 10.1002/jcop.70002 PMID: 39985818

Fitzgerald, L. (2020). The impact of telecommuting on employee anxiety: A mixed-methods approach. *International Journal of Stress Management*, *27*(1), 65–74. DOI: 10.1037/str0000101

Flo, E., Pallesen, S., Magerøy, N., Moen, B. E., Grønli, J., Hilde Nordhus, I., & Bjorvatn, B. (2012). Shift Work Disorder in Nurses – Assessment, Prevalence and Related Health Problems. *PLoS One*, *7*(4), e33981. DOI: 10.1371/journal.pone.0033981 PMID: 22485153

Fløvik, L., Knardahl, S., & Christensen, J. (2018). Organizational change and employee mental health: A prospective multilevel study of the associations between organizational changes and clinically relevant mental distress. *Scandinavian Journal of Work, Environment & Health*, *45*(2), 134–145. DOI: 10.5271/sjweh.3777 PMID: 30334062

Folkard, S. (2003). Shift work, safety and productivity. *Occupational Medicine*, *53*(2), 95–101. DOI: 10.1093/occmed/kqg047 PMID: 12637593

Folkard, S., & Lombardi, D. A. (2006). Modeling the impact of the components of long work hours on injuries and "accidents.". *American Journal of Industrial Medicine*, *49*(11), 953–963. DOI: 10.1002/ajim.20307 PMID: 16570251

Folkman, S., & Moskowitz, J. T. (2000). Stress, positive emotion, and coping. *Current Directions in Psychological Science*, *9*(4), 115–118. DOI: 10.1111/1467-8721.00073

Foster, K., Roche, M., Giandinoto, J.-A., Platania-Phung, C., & Furness, T. (2021). Mental health matters: A cross-sectional study of mental health nurses' health-related quality of life and work-related stressors. *International Journal of Mental Health Nursing*, *30*(3), 624–634. DOI: 10.1111/inm.12823

Fox, K. E., Johnson, S. T., Berkman, L. F., Sianoja, M., Soh, Y., Kubzansky, L. D., & Kelly, E. L. (2022). Organisational-and group-level workplace interventions and their effect on multiple domains of worker well-being: A systematic review. [HTML]. *Work and Stress*, *36*(1), 30–59. DOI: 10.1080/02678373.2021.1969476

Frias, A., Hampton, D., Tharp-Barrie, K., & Thomas, J. (2021). The impact of an emotional intelligence training program on transformational leadership. [ceconnection.com]. *Nursing Management*, *52*(2), 18–25. DOI: 10.1097/01.NUMA.0000731924.03153.df PMID: 33512880

Fujimoto, A., Kanegae, H., Kitaoka, K., Ohashi, M., Okada, K., Node, K., Takase, K., Fukuda, H., Miyazaki, T., & Yano, Y. (2024). The association between employee lifestyles and the rates of mental health-related absenteeism and turnover in japanese companies. *Epidemiology and Health*, *46*, e2024068. DOI: 10.4178/epih.e2024068 PMID: 39118545

Fung, H. Y., Sha, E. S., Chiu, W. K., & Fong, B. Y. F. (2025). Community Health Models. In *The Handbook of Primary Healthcare: The Case of Hong Kong* (pp. 19–33). Springer Nature Singapore. DOI: 10.1007/978-981-96-0817-1_2

Funk, M., Drew, N., & Knapp, M. (2012). Mental health, poverty and development. *Journal of Public Mental Health, 11*(4), 166–185. DOI: 10.1108/17465721211289356

Furtner, N. C., Kocher, M. G., Martinsson, P., Matzat, D., & Wollbrant, C. (2021). Gender and cooperative preferences. *Journal of Economic Behavior & Organization, 181*, 39–48. st-andrews.ac.uk. DOI: 10.1016/j.jebo.2020.11.030

Gajendran, R. S., & Harrison, D. A. (2007). The good, the bad, and the unknown about telecommuting: Meta-analysis of psychological mediators and individual consequences. *The Journal of Applied Psychology, 92*(6), 1524–1541. DOI: 10.1037/0021-9010.92.6.1524 PMID: 18020794

Gantz, S. (2014). Health Insurance Portability and Accountability Act of 1996—An overview. Science Direct. https://www.sciencedirect.com/topics/computer-science/health-insurance-portability-and-accountability-act-of-1996

Garg, N. (2017). Workplace spirituality and employee well-being: An empirical exploration. *Journal of Human Values, 23*(2), 129–147. DOI: 10.1177/0971685816689741

Gates, G. J. (2022). LGBTQ+ employees and workplace inclusion: Current challenges and strategies. *Human Resource Management Review, 32*(1), 100867. DOI: 10.1016/j.hrmr.2021.100867

Gedecho, E. K., & Kim, S. (2025). Mental health and well-being in tourism scholarship: A Horizon 2050 paper. *Tourism Review, 80*(1), 108–120. https://doi.org/DOI: 10.1108/TR-12-2023-0842

Genedy, M., Hellerstedt, K., Naldi, L., & Wiklund, J. (2024). Growing pains in scale-ups: How scaling affects new venture employee burnout and job satisfaction. *Journal of Business Venturing, 39*(2), 106367. DOI: 10.1016/j.jbusvent.2023.106367

George, D. A. S. & A.S.Hovan George. (2023). *Telemedicine: A New Way to Provide Healthcare*. DOI: 10.5281/ZENODO.8075850

Ghazali, H., Rahim, N., Ismail, N., Othman, M., & Ishak, M. (2023). Covid-19 related mental health effects in the workplace: A case of fast-food industry in malaysia. *International Journal of Human Resource Studies, 13*(1), 21. DOI: 10.5296/ijhrs.v13i1.20441

Ghosh, B., & Pm, A. S. (2024). Chronotype preferences, work motivation, and gender differences among private sector employees in Bengaluru. *International Journal of Science and Research Archive, 11*(2), 1702–1712. DOI: 10.30574/ijsra.2024.11.2.0654

Giamos, D., Doucet, O., & Léger, P.-M. (2024). Continuous Performance Feedback: Investigating the Effects of Feedback Content and Feedback Sources on Performance, Motivation to Improve Performance and Task Engagement. *Journal of Organizational Behavior Management, 44*(3), 194–213. DOI: 10.1080/01608061.2023.2238029

Gilmer, D. O. (n.d.). *Workplace Chronotype Bias*. Flexible Scheduling, and Performance Beliefs.

Giorgi, G., & Cupelli, V. (2015). Economic stress in the workplace: The impact of fear of the crisis on mental health. *Work (Reading, Mass.), 51*(1), 135–142. DOI: 10.3233/WOR-141844

Gkliati, A., Saiti, A., Chletsos, M., & Bechlioulis, A. P. (2025). The relationship of Minimum Wage on Employees' Well–being, Job satisfaction and Work–life balance. *The International Journal of Organizational Analysis*. Advance online publication. DOI: 10.1108/IJOA-05-2024-4520

Glazer, S. (2021). Organizational role ambiguity as a proxy for uncertainty avoidance. [HTML]. *International Journal of Intercultural Relations, 85*, 1–12. DOI: 10.1016/j.ijintrel.2021.08.011

Glisson, C., & Schoenwald, S. K. (2005). The ARC Organizational and Community Intervention Strategy for Implementing Evidence-Based Children's Mental Health Treatments. *Mental Health Services Research, 7*(4), 243–259. DOI: 10.1007/s11020-005-7456-1

Gobin, C. M., Banks, J. B., Fins, A. I., & Tartar, J. L. (2015). Poor sleep quality is associated with a negative cognitive bias and decreased sustained attention. *Journal of Sleep Research, 24*(5), 535–542. DOI: 10.1111/jsr.12302 PMID: 25913483

Goetzel, R. Z., Ozminkowski, R. J., Sederer, L. I., & Mark, T. L. (2002, April). The Business Case for Quality Mental Health Services: Why Employers Should Care About the Mental Health and Well-Being of Their Employees. *Journal of Occupational and Environmental Medicine, 44*(4), 320–330.

Goetz, L. H., & Schork, N. J. (2018). Personalized medicine: Motivation, challenges, and progress. *Fertility and Sterility, 109*(6), 952–963. DOI: 10.1016/j.fertnstert.2018.05.006 PMID: 29935653

Golden, T. D., & Gajendran, R. S. (2019). Unpacking telecommuting's effect on performance: Is it about time spent or time saved? *Human Resource Management Review*, *29*(2), 184–195. DOI: 10.1016/j.hrmr.2018.02.003

Golden, T. D., & Veiga, J. F. (2005). The impact of extent of telecommuting on job satisfaction: Resolving inconsistent findings. *Journal of Management*, *31*(2), 301–318. DOI: 10.1177/0149206304271768

Goldstein, A. N., & Walker, M. P. (2014). The Role of Sleep in Emotional Brain Function. *Annual Review of Clinical Psychology*, *10*(1), 679–708. DOI: 10.1146/annurev-clinpsy-032813-153716 PMID: 24499013

Goldstein, M. M., & Thorpe Jane, H. (2010, September 1). The First Anniversary of the Health Information Technology for Economic and Clinical Health (HITECH) Act: The regulatory outlook for implementation. *Perspectives in Health Information Management*, *7*(Summer), 1c.

Goleman, D. (2017). *Emotional Intelligence: Why It Can Matter More Than IQ*. Bantam.

Gómez-Leal, R., Holzer, A. A., Bradley, C., Fernández-Berrocal, P., & Patti, J. (2022). The relationship between emotional intelligence and leadership in school leaders: A systematic review. [researchgate.net]. *Cambridge Journal of Education*, *52*(1), 1–21. DOI: 10.1080/0305764X.2021.1927987

Goodman, D. (2022, October 12). *Reasonable Security*. CyberSec4Europe | Cyber Security for Europe. https://cybersec4europe.eu/reasonable-security/

Goodman-Scott, E., Sampson, D. J., Johnson, K. F., & Sawyer-Mays, D. (2025). School counseling district leaders' experiences with anti–DEI laws and policies: A phenomenological investigation. *Journal of Counseling and Development*, *103*(2), 185–200. DOI: 10.1002/jcad.12551

Google. (2020). *Our work culture*. Google Careers. https://careers.google.com/our-story/

Görgens-Ekermans, G., & Roux, C. (2021). Revisiting the emotional intelligence and transformational leadership debate:(How) does emotional intelligence matter to effective leadership? *SA Journal of Human Resource Management*, *19*, 1279. journals.co.za. DOI: 10.4102/sajhrm.v19i0.1279

Görgényi-Hegyes, É., Nathan, R., & Fekete-Farkas, M. (2021). Workplace health promotion, employee well-being and loyalty during covid-19 pandemic—Large scale empirical evidence from hungary. *Economies*, *9*(2), 55. DOI: 10.3390/economies9020055

Goyal, M., Singh, S., Sibinga, E. M. S., Gould, N. F., Rowland-Seymour, A., Sharma, R., & Haythornthwaite, J. A. (2014). Meditation programs for psychological stress and well-being: A systematic review and meta-analysis. *JAMA Internal Medicine, 174*(3), 357–368. DOI: 10.1001/jamainternmed.2013.13018 PMID: 24395196

Grawitch, M. J., Gottschalk, M., & Munz, D. C. (2006). The path to a healthy workplace: A critical review linking healthy workplace practices, employee well-being, and organizational improvements. *Consulting Psychology Journal, 58*(3), 129–147. DOI: 10.1037/1065-9293.58.3.129

Gray, E. (2025). *Equity, Diversity, and Inclusion in Canadian National Sport Organizations* (Doctoral dissertation, Université d'Ottawa/University of Ottawa).

Gray, C. E., Spector, P. E., Lacey, K. N., Young, B. G., Jacobsen, S. T., & Taylor, M. R. (2020). Helping may be Harming: Unintended negative consequences of providing social support. *Work and Stress, 34*(4), 359–385. DOI: 10.1080/02678373.2019.1695294 PMID: 38075181

Greenhaus, J. H., & Allen, T. D. (2011). Work-family balance: A review and extension of the literature. *Psychology of Women Quarterly, 35*(1), 74–95. DOI: 10.1111/j.1471-6402.2010.01634.x

Greenhaus, J. H., Collins, K. M., & Shaw, J. D. (2020). The work-family interface: A review and look forward. *Journal of Vocational Behavior, 118*, 103484. DOI: 10.1016/j.jvb.2020.103484

Gubin, D., Weinert, D., Stefani, O., Otsuka, K., Borisenkov, M., & Cornelissen, G. (2025). Wearables in Chronomedicine and Interpretation of Circadian Health. *Diagnostics (Basel), 15*(3), 327. DOI: 10.3390/diagnostics15030327 PMID: 39941257

Guhn, M., Gadermann, A., & Wu, A. D. (2024). Trends in international mathematics and science study (TIMSS). In *Encyclopedia of quality of life and well-being research* (pp. 7309–7311). Springer International Publishing.

Gulzar, S., Hussain, K., Akhlaq, A., Abbas, Z., & Ghauri, S. (2024). Exploring the psychological contract breach of nurses in healthcare: An exploratory study. *Asia-Pacific Journal of Business Administration, 16*(1), 204–230. DOI: 10.1108/APJBA-03-2021-0102

Gupta, A. K. (2024). Right to Privacy in Digital Technology Act: Issues and Policy in India. *The Indian Journal of Public Administration, 70*(3), 532–545. DOI: 10.1177/00195561241271517

Gupta, U. C. (2013). Informed consent in clinical research: Revisiting few concepts and areas. *Perspectives in Clinical Research*, *4*(1), 26–32. DOI: 10.4103/2229-3485.106373 PMID: 23533976

Gutman, L. M., Younas, F., Perowne, R., & O'Hanrachtaigh, E. (2024). Lived experiences of diverse university staff during COVID-19: An examination of workplace wellbeing. *Studies in Higher Education*, *49*(2), 251–268. DOI: 10.1080/03075079.2023.2231015

Haase, D. (2021). Integrating Ecosystem Services, Green Infrastructure and Nature-Based Solutions—New Perspectives in Sustainable Urban Land Management: Combining Knowledge About Urban Nature for Action. Sustainable Land Management in a European Context: A Co-Design Approach, 305-318. oapen.org

Hackman, J. R., & Oldham, G. R. (1976). Motivation through design of work: Test of a theory. *Organizational Behavior and Human Performance*, *16*(2), 250–279. DOI: 10.1016/0030-5073(76)90016-7

Haeusermann, T., & Chiong, W. (2024). Ethical considerations in rapid and novel treatments in psychiatry. *Neuropsychopharmacology : Official Publication of the American College of Neuropsychopharmacology*, *49*(1), 291–293. DOI: 10.1038/s41386-023-01635-y PMID: 37391590

Haider, Z., & Dasti, R. (2022). Mentoring, research self-efficacy, work–life balance and psychological well-being of doctoral program students. [HTML]. *International Journal of Mentoring and Coaching in Education*, *11*(2), 170–182. DOI: 10.1108/IJMCE-07-2020-0036

Halbesleben, J. R. B., & Buckley, M. R. (2004). Burnout in organizational settings. *Journal of Management*, *30*(6), 859–879. DOI: 10.1016/j.jm.2004.06.004

Hall, D. E., Prochazka, A. V., & Fink, A. S. (2012). Informed consent for clinical treatment. *Canadian Medical Association Journal*, *184*(5), 533–540. DOI: 10.1503/cmaj.112120 PMID: 22392947

Hamacher, S. (2023). *Supervision: On Motherhood and Surveillance*. MIT Press.

Hamouche, S. (2023). COVID-19 and employees' mental health: Stressors, moderators and agenda for organizational actions. *Emerald Open Research*, *1*(2). Advance online publication. DOI: 10.1108/EOR-02-2023-0004

Hanisch, S., Birner, U., Oberhauser, C., Nowak, D., & Sabariego, C. (2017). Development and evaluation of digital game-based training for managers to promote employee mental health and reduce mental illness stigma at work: Quasi-experimental study of program effectiveness. *JMIR Mental Health*, *4*(3), e31. DOI: 10.2196/mental.7600 PMID: 28778839

Harding, S., Morris, R., Gunnell, D., Ford, T., Hollingworth, W., Tilling, K., Evans, R., Bell, S., Grey, J., Brockman, R., Campbell, R., Araya, R., Murphy, S., & Kidger, J. (2019). Is teachers' mental health and well-being associated with students' mental health and well-being? *Journal of Affective Disorders*, *253*, 460–466. DOI: 10.1016/j.jad.2019.03.046 PMID: 30189355

Härmä, M., Kecklund, G., & Tucker, P. (2024). Working hours and health – key research topics in the past and future. *Scandinavian Journal of Work, Environment & Health*, *50*(4), 233–243. DOI: 10.5271/sjweh.4157 PMID: 38497926

Harrison, R., & Willness, C. (2022). Cross-cultural differences in perceptions of flexible work: A global study of mental health outcomes. *Journal of Cross-Cultural Psychology*, *53*(4), 529–549. DOI: 10.1177/00220221221019530

Harris, R., Maxwell, T., & Tate, H. (2023). A systematic review of telework, gender, and intersectionality in the modern workplace. *International Journal of Human Resource Management*, *34*(5), 1022–1045. DOI: 10.1080/09585192.2022.2105731

Harter, J. K., Schmidt, F. L., & Hayes, T. L. (2002). Business-unit-level relationship between employee satisfaction, employee engagement, and business outcomes: A meta-analysis. *The Journal of Applied Psychology*, *87*(2), 268–279. DOI: 10.1037/0021-9010.87.2.268 PMID: 12002955

Harvey, S. B., Modini, M., Joyce, S., Milligan-Saville, J. S., Tan, L., Mykletun, A., & Mitchell, P. B. (2017). Can work make you mentally ill? A systematic meta-review of work-related risk factors for common mental health problems. *Occupational and Environmental Medicine*, *74*(4), 301–310.

Hasanudin, S., Safar, F., Saaidun, N., & Abdullah, N. (2022). A survey on occupational mental health at a private college in northern region of peninsular malaysia. *Advances in Business Research International Journal*, *8*(1), 1–9. DOI: 10.24191/abrij.v8i1.17679

Hauff, S., Krick, A., Klebe, L., & Felfe, J. (2022). High-performance work practices and employee well-being—Does health-oriented leadership make a difference? *Frontiers in Psychology*, *13*, 833028. Advance online publication. DOI: 10.3389/fpsyg.2022.833028 PMID: 35310243

Hawke, L. D., Dada-Phillips, W., Seiyad, H., Orson, J., Goldsmith, L., Conway, S., Jordan, A., Sheikhan, N. Y., Hiebert, M., Kidd, S., & Kuluski, K. (2025). Best Practices Guidelines for the Engagement of People With Lived Experience and Family Members in Mental Health and Substance Use Health Research: A Modified Delphi Consensus Study. *Health Expectations*, *28*(1), e70152. DOI: 10.1111/hex.70152 PMID: 39832210

Hayat, I. & Rehan, Q. (2024). Investigating The Roles of Pakistani Private Secondary School Teachers and Principals as Environmental Sustainable Leaders. Jahan-e-Tahqeeq. jahan-e-tahqeeq.com

Hendriks, M., Burger, M., Rijsenbilt, A., Pleeging, E., & Commandeur, H. (2020). Virtuous leadership: A source of employee well-being and trust. *Management Research Review*, *43*(8), 951–970. DOI: 10.1108/MRR-07-2019-0326

Henke, R. M. (2022). Knowing Well, Being Well: well-being born of understanding: Supporting Workforce Mental Health During the Pandemic. *American Journal of Health Promotion*, *36*(7), 1213–1244. DOI: 10.1177/08901171221112488 PMID: 36003017

Hibino, T. (2019). Microsoft Japan's 4-day workweek increased productivity by 40%: Here's how. *Harvard Business Review*. https://hbr.org/2019/11/microsoft-japans-4-day-workweek-increased-productivity-by-40-heres-how

Hidalgo, M. P., Caumo, W., Posser, M., Coccaro, S. B., Camozzato, A. L., & Chaves, M. L. F. (2009). Relationship between depressive mood and chronotype in healthy subjects. *Psychiatry and Clinical Neurosciences*, *63*(3), 283–290. DOI: 10.1111/j.1440-1819.2009.01965.x PMID: 19566758

Higgins, O., & Wilson, R. L. (2025). Integrating Artificial Intelligence (AI) With Workforce Solutions for Sustainable Care: A Follow Up to Artificial Intelligence and Machine Learning (ML) Based Decision Support Systems in Mental Health. *International Journal of Mental Health Nursing*, *34*(2), e70019. DOI: 10.1111/inm.70019 PMID: 40055746

Hilbert, M. (2016). Big data for development: A review of promises and challenges. *Development Policy Review*, *34*(1), 135–174. DOI: 10.1111/dpr.12142

Hirotsu, C., Tufik, S., & Andersen, M. L. (2015). Interactions between sleep, stress, and metabolism: From physiological to pathological conditions. *Sleep Science*, *8*(3), 143–152. DOI: 10.1016/j.slsci.2015.09.002 PMID: 26779321

Hirshkowitz, M., Whiton, K., Albert, S. M., Alessi, C., Bruni, O., DonCarlos, L., Hazen, N., Herman, J., Katz, E. S., Kheirandish-Gozal, L., Neubauer, D. N., O'Donnell, A. E., Ohayon, M., Peever, J., Rawding, R., Sachdeva, R. C., Setters, B., Vitiello, M. V., Ware, J. C., & Adams Hillard, P. J. (2015). National Sleep Foundation's sleep time duration recommendations: Methodology and results summary. *Sleep Health*, *1*(1), 40–43. DOI: 10.1016/j.sleh.2014.12.010 PMID: 29073412

Hittle, B. M., & Gillespie, G. L. (2018). Identifying shift worker chronotype: Implications for health. *Industrial Health*, *56*(6), 512–523. DOI: 10.2486/indhealth.2018-0018 PMID: 29973467

Hoare, C., & Vandenberghe, C. (2024). Are they created equal? A relative weights analysis of the contributions of job demands and resources to well-being and turnover intention. *Psychological Reports*, *127*(1), 392–418. DOI: 10.1177/00332941221103536 PMID: 35707875

Hobfoll, S. E. (1989). Conservation of resources: A new attempt at conceptualizing stress. *The American Psychologist*, *44*(3), 513–524. DOI: 10.1037/0003-066X.44.3.513 PMID: 2648906

Hochschild, A. R. (1997). *The time bind: When work becomes home and home becomes work*. Metropolitan Books. DOI: 10.1111/j.1743-4580.1997.tb00019.x

Holt, S. (2022). Virtual reality, augmented reality and mixed reality: For astronaut mental health; and space tourism, education and outreach. *Acta Astronautica*.

Honkonen, T., Ahola, K., Pertovaara, M., Isometsä, E., Kalimo, R., Nykyri, E., Aromaa, A., & Lönnqvist, J. (2006). The association between burnout and physical illness in the general population—Results from the Finnish Health 2000 Study. *Journal of Psychosomatic Research*, *61*(1), 59–66. DOI: 10.1016/j.jpsychores.2005.10.002 PMID: 16813846

Hoofnagle, C. J., van der Sloot, B., & Borgesius, F. Z. (2019). The European Union general data protection regulation: What it is and what it means*. *Information & Communications Technology Law*, *28*(1), 65–98. DOI: 10.1080/13600834.2019.1573501

Horne, J. A., & Östberg, O. (1977). Individual differences in human circadian rhythms. *Biological Psychology*, *5*(3), 179–190. DOI: 10.1016/0301-0511(77)90001-1 PMID: 922076

Horwitz, I. B., & McCall, B. P. (2004). The impact of shift work on the risk and severity of injuries for hospitalemployees: An analysis using Oregon workers' compensation data. *Occupational Medicine*, *54*(8), 556–563. DOI: 10.1093/occmed/kqh093 PMID: 15385648

Hossain, S., Moll, S., Tompa, E., & Gewurtz, R. (2021). The interactive process of negotiating workplace accommodations for employees with mental health conditions. *Work (Reading, Mass.)*, *69*(1), 75–90. DOI: 10.3233/WOR-213459 PMID: 33998573

House, J. S. (1981). *Work stress and social support*. Addison-Wesley.

Hsu, F., Liu, Y., & Tsaur, S. (2019). The impact of workplace bullying on hotel employees' well-being. *International Journal of Contemporary Hospitality Management*, *31*(4), 1702–1719. DOI: 10.1108/IJCHM-04-2018-0330

Huang, D., & Zhou, H. (2024). Self-sacrificial leadership, thriving at work, workplace well-being, and work–family conflict during the COVID-19 crisis: The moderating role of self-leadership. *Business Research Quarterly*, *27*(1), 10–25. DOI: 10.1177/23409444231203744

Huang, N., Qiu, S., Yang, S., & Deng, R. (2021). Ethical leadership and organizational citizenship behavior: Mediation of trust and psychological well-being. [tandfonline.com]. *Psychology Research and Behavior Management*, 655–664.

HubSpot. (2020). *How HubSpot's remote-first approach is working*. HubSpot Blog. https://blog.hubspot.com/company/remote-first

Hulsen, T. (2020). Sharing Is Caring—Data Sharing Initiatives in Healthcare. *International Journal of Environmental Research and Public Health*, *17*(9), 3046. DOI: 10.3390/ijerph17093046 PMID: 32349396

Hunt, V., Rasmussen, E., & Lamm, F. (2010). *Call Centre Work and Health and Safety Issues*. Labour, Employment and Work in New Zealand., DOI: 10.26686/lew.v0i0.1677

IBM Sterling B2B Integrator. (2024, February 1). https://www.ibm.com/docs/en/b2b-integrator/6.1.2?topic=overview-general-data-protection-regulation-gdpr

IBM. (2024). *How to Implement General Data Protection Regulation (GDPR) | IBM*. https://www.ibm.com/think/topics/general-data-protection-regulation-implementation

Ilyas, S., Abid, G., & Ashfaq, F. (2023). Enhancing the perceived organizational support, perceived ethical-philanthropic CSR and subjective well-being: The role of ethical leadership. *International Journal of Ethics and Systems*, *39*(4), 713–736.

India—Privacy Protection—A Review Of The Information Technology Rules, 2011. (n.d.). Retrieved June 30, 2024, from https://www.mondaq.com/india/privacy-protection/904916/a-review-of-the-information-technology-rules-2011

Inegbedion, H., Inegbedion, E., Peter, A., & Harry, L. (2020). Perception of workload balance and employee job satisfaction in work organisations. *Heliyon*, *6*(1), e03160. DOI: 10.1016/j.heliyon.2020.e03160 PMID: 31938748

Insights. (2023). *International: GDPR v. HIPAA - Comparing and contrasting two important data protection regimes | Insights | DataGuidance*. Insights. https://www.dataguidance.com/opinion/international-gdpr-v-hipaa-comparing-and-contrasting

Irvine, A., & Suter, J. (2023). Managing mental health problems in the workplace: Are small businesses different? *Employee Relations*, *45*(5), 1161–1179. DOI: 10.1108/ER-09-2022-0451

Jadhakhan, F., Blake, H., Hett, D., & Marwaha, S. (2022). Efficacy of digital technologies aimed at enhancing emotion regulation skills: Literature review. *Frontiers in Psychiatry*, *13*, 809332. DOI: 10.3389/fpsyt.2022.809332 PMID: 36159937

Jain, L. (2023). Artificial Intelligence and Machine Learning for Healthcare.

Jangid, A. (2024). AI and Employee Wellbeing: How Artificial Intelligence Can Monitor And Improve Mental Health In The Workplace. *International Journal of Advanced Research*, *12*(10), 743–764. DOI: 10.21474/IJAR01/19693

Janssen, M., & Engels, J. (2018). Effects of Mindfulness-Based Stress Reduction on employees' mental health: A systematic review. *PLoS One*, *13*(1), e0191332. DOI: 10.1371/journal.pone.0191332

Jaradat, Y., Nielsen, M. B., Kristensen, P., Nijem, K., Bjertness, E., Stigum, H., & Bast-Pettersen, R. (2016). Workplace aggression, psychological distress, and job satisfaction among Palestinian nurses: A cross-sectional study. *Applied Nursing Research*, *32*, 190–198. DOI: 10.1016/j.apnr.2016.07.014 PMID: 27969027

Jarosz, J. (2021). The impact of coaching on well-being and performance of managers and their teams during pandemic. *International Journal of Evidence Based Coaching and Mentoring*, *19*(1), 4–27. brookes.ac.uk

Javaid, M., Haleem, A., Pratap Singh, R., Suman, R., & Rab, S. (2022). Significance of machine learning in healthcare: Features, pillars and applications. *International Journal of Intelligent Networks*, *3*, 58–73. DOI: 10.1016/j.ijin.2022.05.002

Javaid, M., Haleem, A., Singh, R. P., & Suman, R. (2023). Towards insighting cybersecurity for healthcare domains: A comprehensive review of recent practices and trends. *Cyber Security and Applications*, *1*, 100016. DOI: 10.1016/j.csa.2023.100016

Javaid, M., & Khan, I. H. (2021). Internet of Things (IoT) enabled healthcare helps to take the challenges of COVID-19 Pandemic. *Journal of Oral Biology and Craniofacial Research, 11*(2), 209–214. DOI: 10.1016/j.jobcr.2021.01.015 PMID: 33665069

Jedaman, P., Kenaphoom, S., & Udompan, A. (2022). Transcendental leadership in leader's strategies management under the 21st-century dynamics era. *Interdisciplinary Academic and Research Journal, 2*(3), 27–44.

Jha, I. N., Pal, D., & Sarkar, S. (2024). Unlocking the secret to happiness at work: The power of inclusive leadership, organizational justice and workplace inclusion. [HTML]. *Journal of Management Development, 43*(2), 200–221. DOI: 10.1108/JMD-04-2023-0136

Jia, K., Zhu, T., Zhang, W., Rasool, S. F., Asghar, A., & Chin, T. (2022). The linkage between ethical leadership, well-being, work engagement, and innovative work behavior: The empirical evidence from the higher education sector of China. [mdpi.com]. *International Journal of Environmental Research and Public Health, 19*(9), 5414. DOI: 10.3390/ijerph19095414 PMID: 35564809

Jnaneswar, K., & Sulphey, M. (2021). Workplace spirituality, self-compassion and mindfulness as antecedents of employee mental well-being. *South Asian Journal of Business Studies, 12*(2), 269–292. DOI: 10.1108/SAJBS-07-2020-0258

Joel, O. T., & Oguanobi, V. U. (2024). Leadership and management in high-growth environments: Effective strategies for the clean energy sector. [fepbl.com]. *International Journal of Management & Entrepreneurship Research, 6*(5), 1423–1440.

Johar, S., & Manjula, G. R. (2024). Interfering sensed input classification model using assimilated whale optimization and deep Q-learning for remote patient monitoring. *Biomedical Signal Processing and Control, 93*, 106202. DOI: 10.1016/j.bspc.2024.106202

Johnson, R. M., DeCuir-Gunby, J. T., Kenney, A. J., & Lyons, T. V. (2025). Black Student Belonging in K12 Schools: Implications for Policy and Practice Amid Attacks on Diversity, Equity, and Inclusion. *Social Issues and Policy Review, 19*(1), e70002. DOI: 10.1111/sipr.70002

Jones, D., Molitor, D., & Reif, J. (2019). What do Workplace Wellness Programs do? Evidence from the Illinois Workplace Wellness Study. *The Quarterly Journal of Economics, 134*(4), 1747–1791. DOI: 10.1093/qje/qjz023 PMID: 31564754

Joosen, M. C., Lugtenberg, M., Arends, I., van Gestel, H. J., Schaapveld, B., Terluin, B., & Brouwers, E. P. (2021). Barriers and facilitators for return to work from the perspective of workers with common mental disorders with short, medium and long-term sickness absence: A longitudinal qualitative study. [springer.com]. *Journal of Occupational Rehabilitation*, •••, 1–12. PMID: 34580811

Jordan, M. I., & Mitchell, T. M. (2015). Machine learning: Trends, perspectives, and prospects. *Science*, *349*(6245), 255–260. DOI: 10.1126/science.aaa8415 PMID: 26185243

Jose, G., PM, N., & Kuriakose, V. (. (2024). HRM practices and employee engagement: Role of personal resources-a study among nurses. *International Journal of Productivity and Performance Management*, *73*(1), 1–17. DOI: 10.1108/IJPPM-04-2021-0212

Joseph, V., Basu, P., & Bhargava, A. (2020). *A Review Of The Information Technology Rules, 2011*. https://www.mondaq.com/india/privacy-protection/904916/a-review-of-the-information-technology-rules-2011

Journal of Medical Internet Research—The Use of Digital Health Services Among Patients and Citizens Living at Home: Scoping Review. (n.d.). Retrieved June 30, 2024, from https://www.jmir.org/2023/1/e44711

Juda, M., Vetter, C., & Roenneberg, T. (2013). Chronotype Modulates Sleep Duration, Sleep Quality, and Social Jet Lag in Shift-Workers. *Journal of Biological Rhythms*, *28*(2), 141–151. DOI: 10.1177/0748730412475042 PMID: 23606613

Justice K.S. Puttaswamy (Retd.) & Anr. Vs. Union of India & Ors. (n.d.). Retrieved June 30, 2024, from https://privacylibrary.ccgnlud.org/case/justice-ks-puttaswamy-ors-vs-union-of-india-ors

Kabat-Zinn, J. (1990). *Full catastrophe living: Using the wisdom of your body and mind to face stress, pain, and illness*. Delacorte.

Kabat-Zinn, J. (2003). Mindfulness-based stress reduction (MBSR). In Nevid, J. K., & Pearson, S. A. E. (Eds.), *The Essential Handbook of Mindfulness* (pp. 23–40). Springer.

Kalmbach, D. A., Schneider, L. D., Cheung, J., Bertrand, S. J., Kariharan, T., Pack, A. I., & Gehrman, P. R. (2017). Genetic Basis of Chronotype in Humans: Insights From Three Landmark GWAS. *Sleep (Basel)*, *40*(2). Advance online publication. DOI: 10.1093/sleep/zsw048 PMID: 28364486

Kaluza, A. J., Junker, N. M., Schuh, S. C., Raesch, P., von Rooy, N. K., & van Dick, R. (2022). A leader in need is a leader indeed? The influence of leaders' stress mindset on their perception of employee well-being and their intended leadership behavior. [wiley.com]. *Applied Psychology*, *71*(4), 1347–1384.

Kar, U. K., & Dash, R. (2018). Application of Artificial Intelligence in Healthcare: Past, Present and Future. Arch Biomed Eng & Biotechnol. 1 (1). *ABEB. MS. ID, 503*.

Karakitapoğlu-Aygün, Z., Erdogan, B., Caughlin, D. E., & Bauer, T. N. (2024). Transformational leadership, idiosyncratic deals and employee outcomes. *Personnel Review*, *53*(2), 562–579. DOI: 10.1108/PR-07-2022-0470

Karasek, R. A. (1979). Job demands, job decision latitude, and mental strain: Implications for job redesign. *Administrative Science Quarterly*, *24*(2), 285–308. DOI: 10.2307/2392498

Karasek, R. A., & Theorell, T. (1990). *Healthy work: Stress, productivity, and the reconstruction of working life*. Basic Books.

Karimi, L., Leggat, S. G., Bartram, T., Afshari, L., Sarkeshik, S., & Verulava, T. (2021). Emotional intelligence: Predictor of employees' wellbeing, quality of patient care, and psychological empowerment. [springer.com]. *BMC Psychology*, *9*(1), 93. DOI: 10.1186/s40359-021-00593-8 PMID: 34088348

Karimi, S., Ahmadi Malek, F., Yaghoubi Farani, A., & Liobikienė, G. (2023). The role of transformational leadership in developing innovative work behaviors: The mediating role of employees' psychological capital. [mdpi.com]. *Sustainability (Basel)*, *15*(2), 1267. DOI: 10.3390/su15021267

Kashyap, H., Ahmed, H. A., Hoque, N., Roy, S., & Bhattacharyya, D. K. (2015). Big data analytics in bioinformatics: A machine learning perspective. *arXiv preprint arXiv:1506.05101*.

Kashyap, H., Ahmed, H. A., Hoque, N., Roy, S., & Bhattacharyya, D. K. (2016). Big data analytics in bioinformatics: Architectures, techniques, tools and issues. *Network Modeling and Analysis in Health Informatics and Bioinformatics*, *5*(1), 1–28. DOI: 10.1007/s13721-016-0135-4

Kassam, I., Ilkina, D., Kemp, J., Roble, H., Carter-Langford, A., & Shen, N. (2023). Patient Perspectives and Preferences for Consent in the Digital Health Context: State-of-the-art Literature Review. *Journal of Medical Internet Research*, *25*(1), e42507. DOI: 10.2196/42507 PMID: 36763409

Katajavuori, N., Vehkalahti, K., & Asikainen, H. (2023). Promoting university students' well-being and studying with an acceptance and commitment therapy (ACT)-based intervention. *Current Psychology (New Brunswick, N.J.)*, *42*(6), 4900–4912.

Kaur, R., Gabrijelčič, D., & Klobučar, T. (2023). Artificial intelligence for cybersecurity: Literature review and future research directions. *Information Fusion*, *97*, 101804. DOI: 10.1016/j.inffus.2023.101804

Kaushik, T. K., Singh, A., Raghav, A., & Singh, B. (2024). Potential of Artificial Intelligence in the Agricultural Industry: A Comprehensive Review. AI Applications for Clean Energy and Sustainability, 344-365.

Kaushik, P., Askari, K., Gupta, S., Mohan, R., & Skrinak, K. (n.d.). On Automated, Continuous Chronotyping from a Daily Calendar using. *Machine Learning*.

Kawiana, I., Dewi, L. K. C., Hartati, P. S., Setini, M., & Asih, D. (2021). Effects of leadership and psychological climate on organizational commitment in the digitization era. *The Journal of Asian Finance, Economics and Business*, *8*(1), 1051–1062. triatmamulya.ac.id

Kaye, J., Edgar A Whitley, D. L., Morrison, M., Teare, H., & Melham, K. (2014). *Dynamic consent: A patient interface for twenty-first century research networks | European Journal of Human Genetics*. https://www.nature.com/articles/ejhg201471

Kecklund, G., & Axelsson, J. (2016). Health consequences of shift work and insufficient sleep. *BMJ (Clinical Research Ed.)*, *5210*, i5210. Advance online publication. DOI: 10.1136/bmj.i5210 PMID: 27803010

Keikhosrokiani, P. (Ed.). (2022). *Big data analytics for healthcare: datasets, techniques, life cycles, management, and applications*. Academic Press.

Kelliher, C., & Anderson, D. (2010). Flexible working and performance: A review of the evidence. *International Journal of Management Reviews*, *12*(4), 381–397. DOI: 10.1111/j.1468-2370.2009.00243.x

Kelly, J. T., Campbell, K. L., Gong, E., & Scuffham, P. (2020). The Internet of Things: Impact and Implications for Health Care Delivery. *Journal of Medical Internet Research*, *22*(11), e20135. DOI: 10.2196/20135 PMID: 33170132

Keshta, I., & Odeh, A. (2021). Security and privacy of electronic health records: Concerns and challenges. *Egyptian Informatics Journal*, *22*(2), 177–183. DOI: 10.1016/j.eij.2020.07.003

Khamisa, N., Peltzer, K., Ilic, D., & Oldenburg, B. (2017). Effect of personal and work stress on burnout, job satisfaction and general health of hospital nurses in South Africa. *Health SA = SA Gesondheid*, *22*, 252–258. DOI: 10.1016/j.hsag.2016.10.001

Khammissa, R. A. G., Nemutandani, S., Feller, G., Lemmer, J., & Feller, L. (2022). Burnout phenomenon: Neurophysiological factors, clinical features, and aspects of management. *The Journal of International Medical Research*, *50*(9), 03000605221106428. Advance online publication. DOI: 10.1177/03000605221106428 PMID: 36113033

Khan, I., Zakari, A., Zhang, J., Dagar, V., & Singh, S. (2022). … trilemma energy balance, clean energy transitions, and economic expansion in the midst of environmental sustainability: New insights from three trilemma leadership. [HTML]. *Energy*.

Khan, K., e-Habiba, U., Sabeen, Z., & Waseem, M. (2022). Occupational mental health of non-family members in family firms: Evidence from pakistan. *Frontiers in Public Health*, *10*, 961553. Advance online publication. DOI: 10.3389/fpubh.2022.961553 PMID: 36225765

Khan, K., Niazi, A., Nasir, A., Hussain, M., & Khan, M. (2021). The effect of covid-19 on the hospitality industry: The implication for open innovation. *Journal of Open Innovation*, *7*(1), 30. DOI: 10.3390/joitmc7010030

Khan, M. A., Kumar, J., Shoukat, M. H., & Selem, K. M. (2024). Does injustice perception threaten organizational performance in the healthcare setting? A sequential mediation examination. *International Journal of Conflict Management*, *35*(2), 287–308. DOI: 10.1108/IJCMA-05-2023-0100

Khoreva, V., & Wechtler, H. (2018). HR practices and employee performance: The mediating role of well-being. *Employee Relations*, *40*(2), 227–243. DOI: 10.1108/ER-08-2017-0191

Killgore, W. D. S. (2007). Effects of Sleep Deprivation and Morningness-Eveningness Traits on Risk-Taking. *Psychological Reports*, *100*(2), 613–626. DOI: 10.2466/pr0.100.2.613-626 PMID: 17564238

Kim, S., & Kim, S. J. (2020). Psychometric Properties of Questionnaires for Assessing Chronotype. *Chronobiology in Medicine*, *2*(1), 16–20. DOI: 10.33069/cim.2020.0003

Kinman, G. (2016). Effort–reward imbalance and overcommitment in uk academics: Implications for mental health, satisfaction and retention. *Journal of Higher Education Policy and Management*, *38*(5), 504–518. DOI: 10.1080/1360080X.2016.1181884

Kirkpatrick, S. A., Verburg, R. M., & Vandewaerde, A. (2019). Organizational culture and employee well-being: A systematic review. *European Journal of Work and Organizational Psychology*, *28*(6), 738–753. DOI: 10.1080/1359432X.2019.1628665

Kitchin, R. (2013). Big data and employees geography: Opportunities, challenges and risks. *Dialogues in employees geography, 3*(3), 262-267.

Kleitman, N. (1964). The Evolutionary Theory of Sleep and Wakefulness. *Perspectives in Biology and Medicine*, *7*(2), 169–178. DOI: 10.1353/pbm.1964.0053 PMID: 14111141

Kleynhans, D. J., Heyns, M. M., & Stander, M. W. (2021). Authentic leadership and follower trust in the leader: The effect of precariousness. *SA Journal of Industrial Psychology*, *47*(1), 1–10. scielo.org.za. DOI: 10.4102/sajip.v47i0.1904

Knapen, S. E., Gordijn, M. C. M., & Meesters, Y. (2016). The relation between chronotype and treatment outcome with light therapy on a fixed time schedule. *Journal of Affective Disorders*, *202*, 87–90. DOI: 10.1016/j.jad.2016.05.009 PMID: 27259079

Knutsson, A., & Bøggild, H. (2000). Shiftwork and Cardiovascular Disease: Review of Disease Mechanisms. *Reviews on Environmental Health*, *15*(4). Advance online publication. DOI: 10.1515/REVEH.2000.15.4.359 PMID: 11199246

Kock, R., Graupner, L. I., & Baloyi, S. (2025). Cultivating a culture of mental health in organisations: Reading the room. *SA Journal of Industrial Psychology*, *51*, 2233. DOI: 10.4102/sajip.v51i0.2233

Komariah, M., Ibrahim, K., Pahria, T., Rahayuwati, L., & Somantri, I. (2022). Effect of Mindfulness Breathing Meditation on Depression, Anxiety, and Stress: A Randomized Controlled Trial among University Students. *Health Care*, *11*(1), 26. DOI: 10.3390/healthcare11010026 PMID: 36611488

Kong, D., Liu, J., Wang, Y., & Zhu, L. (2024). Employee stock ownership plans and corporate environmental engagement. *Journal of Business Ethics*, *189*(1), 177–199. DOI: 10.1007/s10551-023-05334-y

Kossek, E. E., & Lautsch, B. A. (2018). Work-life flexibility for whom? Occupational status and work-life inequality in upper, middle, and lower level jobs. *The Academy of Management Annals*, *12*(1), 5–36. DOI: 10.5465/annals.2016.0059

Kossek, E. E., Ollier-Malaterre, A., Lee, M. D., Pichler, S., & Hall, D. T. (2014). Matchmaking flexibility: Organizational initiatives and individual use of formal and informal flexibility. *Journal of Vocational Behavior*, *84*(3), 377–389. DOI: 10.1016/j.jvb.2014.01.007

Kossek, E. E., & Ozeki, C. (1998). Work-family conflict, policies, and the job-life satisfaction relationship: A review and directions for organizational research. *The Journal of Applied Psychology*, *83*(2), 139–149. DOI: 10.1037/0021-9010.83.2.139

Kotera, Y., Mayer, C., & Vanderheiden, E. (2021). Cross-cultural comparison of mental health between german and south african employees: Shame, self-compassion, work engagement, and work motivation. *Frontiers in Psychology*, *12*, 627851. Advance online publication. DOI: 10.3389/fpsyg.2021.627851 PMID: 34239473

Kotsou, I., Mikolajczak, M., Heeren, A., & Leys, C. (2011). Emotional intelligence and sociodemographic factors: A study of the EI model proposed by Bar-On in a French-speaking population. *Personality and Individual Differences*, *50*(5), 1248–1253. DOI: 10.1016/j.paid.2011.01.019

Koutsimani, P., Montgomery, A., & Georganta, K. (2019a). The Relationship Between Burnout, Depression, and Anxiety: A Systematic Review and Meta-Analysis. *Frontiers in Psychology*, *10*, 284. Advance online publication. DOI: 10.3389/fpsyg.2019.00284 PMID: 30918490

Kouzes, J. M. & Posner, B. Z. (2023). The leadership challenge: How to make extraordinary things happen in organizations. cjpl.org

Krogstad, D. J., Diop, S., Diallo, A., Mzayek, F., Keating, J., Koita, O. A., & Touré, Y. T. (2010). Informed Consent in International Research: The Rationale for Different Approaches. *The American Journal of Tropical Medicine and Hygiene*, *83*(4), 743–747. DOI: 10.4269/ajtmh.2010.10-0014 PMID: 20889858

Krug, H., Haslam, S. A., Otto, K., & Steffens, N. K. (2021). Identity leadership, social identity continuity, and well-being at work during [Frontiers in psychology. frontiersin.org]. *COVID*, •••, 19. PMID: 34177738

Kruse, C. S., Stein, A., Thomas, H., & Kaur, H. (2018). The use of Electronic Health Records to Support Population Health: A Systematic Review of the Literature. *Journal of Medical Systems*, *42*(11), 214. DOI: 10.1007/s10916-018-1075-6 PMID: 30269237

Kumar, S., Tiwari, P., & Tiwari, P. (2019). *Internet of Things is a revolutionary approach for future technology enhancement: A review | Journal of Big Data | Full Text*. https://journalofbigdata.springeropen.com/articles/10.1186/s40537-019-0268-2

Kumar, D., Hasan, Y., & Afroz, S. (2023). Mobile Health Monitoring System: A Comprehensive Review. *International Journal of Research Publication and Reviews*, *4*(6), 1922–1954. DOI: 10.55248/gengpi.4.623.45128

Kumar, M., Kumar, A., Verma, S., Bhattacharya, P., Ghimire, D., Kim, S., & Hosen, A. S. M. S. (2023). Healthcare Internet of Things (H-IoT): Current Trends, Future Prospects, Applications, Challenges, and Security Issues. *Electronics (Basel)*, *12*(9), 2050. DOI: 10.3390/electronics12092050

Laidlaw, A., McLellan, J., & Özakinci, G. (2015). Understanding undergraduate student perceptions of mental health, mental well-being and help-seeking behaviour. *Studies in Higher Education, 41*(12), 2156–2168. DOI: 10.1080/03075079.2015.1026890

Latapí Agudelo, M. A., Jóhannsdóttir, L., & Davídsdóttir, B. (2019). A literature review of the history and evolution of corporate social responsibility. *International Journal of Corporate Social Responsibility, 4*(1), 1. DOI: 10.1186/s40991-018-0039-y

Lazarus, R. S., & Folkman, S. (1984). *Stress, appraisal, and coping*. Springer.

Lee, J., Resick, C. J., Allen, J. A., Davis, A. L., & Taylor, J. A. (2024). Interplay between safety climate and emotional exhaustion: Effects on first responders' safety behavior and wellbeing over time. *Journal of Business and Psychology, 39*(1), 209–231. DOI: 10.1007/s10869-022-09869-1 PMID: 36573129

Lee, K.-W., Yang, C.-C., Chen, C.-H., Hung, C.-H., & Chuang, H.-Y. (2023). Shift work is significantly and positively associated with dementia: A meta-analysis study. *Frontiers in Public Health, 11*, 998464. DOI: 10.3389/fpubh.2023.998464 PMID: 36875407

Lee, M., & Kim, B. (2023). Effect of the employees' mental toughness on organizational commitment and job satisfaction: Mediating psychological well-being. *Administrative Sciences, 13*(5), 133. DOI: 10.3390/admsci13050133

Lee, W., & Cronin, M. A. (2023). Mental Health and Mental Illness in Organizations: A Review, Comparison, and Extension. *The Academy of Management Annals, 17*(2), 751–797. Advance online publication. DOI: 10.5465/annals.2021.0211

Lencioni, P. (2002). *The five dysfunctions of a team: A leadership fable*. Jossey-Bass.

Leung, P. H., Chui, K. T., Lo, K., & de Pablos, P. O. (2021). A support vector machine–based voice disorders detection using employees voice signal. In *Artificial Intelligence and Big Data Analytics for Smart Healthcare* (pp. 197–208). Academic Press. DOI: 10.1016/B978-0-12-822060-3.00014-0

Levandovski, R., Dantas, G., Fernandes, L. C., Caumo, W., Torres, I., Roenneberg, T., Hidalgo, M. P. L., & Allebrandt, K. V. (2011). Depression Scores Associate With Chronotype and Social Jetlag in a Rural Population. *Chronobiology International, 28*(9), 771–778. DOI: 10.3109/07420528.2011.602445 PMID: 21895489

Lindencrona, F. (2025). Eudaimonic well-being: A foundation for public administration systems fit to build a sustainable future. In *Sustainable Transformation and Well-being: The Role of Business for Individual and Collective Flourishing* (pp. 219–241). Springer Nature Switzerland. DOI: 10.1007/978-3-031-75566-8_14

Liss, S., & Han, Y. J. (2023). *Hacking healthcare: With 385M patient records exposed, cybersecurity experts sound alarm on breach surge*. Healthcare Dive. https://www.healthcaredive.com/news/cybersecurity-hacking-healthcare-breaches/643821/

Liu, B. F., Shi, D., Lim, J. R., Islam, K., Edwards, A. L., & Seeger, M. (2022). When crises hit home: How US higher education leaders navigate values during uncertain times. [springer.com]. *Journal of Business Ethics*, *179*(2), 353–368.

Liu, F., Khong-Khai, S., Leelapattana, W., & Tsai, C. (2024). Analyzing the Influence of Leadership Style on Employee Engagement in Digital Economy. *Asian Administration and Management Review*, *7*(2), 31–44.

Liu, K., Madrigal, E., Chung, J. S., Parekh, M., Kalahar, C. S., Nguyen, D., & Harris, O. A. (2023). Preliminary Study of Virtual-reality-guided Meditation for Veterans with Stress and Chronic Pain. *Alternative Therapies in Health and Medicine*, *29*(6). PMID: 34559692

Liu, W., Xu, Y., & Ma, D. (2021). Work-related mental health under covid-19 restrictions: A mini literature review. *Frontiers in Public Health*, *9*, 788370. Advance online publication. DOI: 10.3389/fpubh.2021.788370 PMID: 34900925

Li, W., Chai, Y., Khan, F., Jan, S. R. U., Verma, S., Menon, V. G., & Li, X. (2021). A comprehensive survey on machine learning-based big data analytics for IoT-enabled smart healthcare system. *Mobile Networks and Applications*, *26*(1), 234–252. DOI: 10.1007/s11036-020-01700-6

Lixia, C. (2017). The Relationship between Teachers' Leadership Styles and Teaching Quality in Lower Secondary Schools in Liang Zhou District of Wuwei, Gansu, China. *Asian Political Science Review*, *1*(1), 71–78. DOI: 10.12778/235108617X15452339029545

Lohr, K. N., & Donaldson, M. S. (Eds.). (1994). *Health data in the information age: use, disclosure, and privacy.*

Lo, J. C., Groeger, J. A., Cheng, G. H., Dijk, D.-J., & Chee, M. W. L. (2016). Self-reported sleep duration and cognitive performance in older adults: A systematic review and meta-analysis. *Sleep Medicine*, *17*, 87–98. DOI: 10.1016/j.sleep.2015.08.021 PMID: 26847980

López-Cabarcos, M. Á., Vázquez-Rodríguez, P., & Quiñoá-Piñeiro, L. M. (2022). An approach to employees' job performance through work environmental variables and leadership behaviours. [sciencedirect.com]. *Journal of Business Research, 140*, 361–369.

Lorber, M., & Dobnik, M. (2022). The importance of monitoring the psychological well-being and mental health of nursing staff for sustainable management. *Sustainability (Basel), 14*(14), 8300. DOI: 10.3390/su14148300

Loretto, W., Platt, S., & Popham, F. (2010). Workplace change and employee mental health: Results from a longitudinal study. *British Journal of Management, 21*(2), 526–540.

Luo, J., Wu, M., Gopukumar, D., & Zhao, Y. (2016). Big data application in biomedical research and health care: a literature review. *Biomedical informatics insights, 8*, BII-S31559.

Lu, X., Yu, H., & Shan, B. (2022). Relationship between employee mental health and job performance: Mediation role of innovative behavior and work engagement. *International Journal of Environmental Research and Public Health, 19*(11), 6599. DOI: 10.3390/ijerph19116599 PMID: 35682185

Lwamba, E., Shisler, S., Ridlehoover, W., Kupfer, M., Tshabalala, N., Nduku, P., Langer, L., Grant, S., Sonnenfeld, A., Anda, D., Eyers, J., & Snilstveit, B. (2022). Strengthening women's empowerment and gender equality in fragile contexts towards peaceful and inclusive societies: A systematic review and meta-analysis. *Campbell Systematic Reviews, 18*(1), e1214. Advance online publication. DOI: 10.1002/cl2.1214 PMID: 36913184

Lyu, G., Horadal, P., Sawangcharoen, K., & Teekasap, S. (2024). Leadership for sustainable growth of high-tech enterprises in Guangxi Province. *International Journal of Sociologies and Anthropologies Science Reviews, 4*(6), 139–150. DOI: 10.60027/ijsasr.2024.4777

Magalhães, A., dos Santos, N. R., & Pais, L. (2024). Human resource management practices and decent work in UN global compact: A qualitative analysis of participants' reports. *Social Sciences (Basel, Switzerland), 13*(1), 56. DOI: 10.3390/socsci13010056

Mahipalan, M., & Garg, N. (2024). Does workplace toxicity undermine psychological capital (PsyCap) of the employees? Exploring the moderating role of gratitude. *The International Journal of Organizational Analysis, 32*(3), 476–503. DOI: 10.1108/IJOA-12-2022-3543

Majcherek, D., Kowalski, A., & Lewandowska, M. (2022). Lifestyle, demographic and socio-economic determinants of mental health disorders of employees in the european countries. *International Journal of Environmental Research and Public Health, 19*(19), 11913. DOI: 10.3390/ijerph191911913 PMID: 36231214

Mäkikangas, A., Kinnunen, U., Feldt, T., & Schaufeli, W. (2016). The longitudinal development of employee well-being: A systematic review. *Work and Stress, 30*(1), 46–70. DOI: 10.1080/02678373.2015.1126870

Malik, S., & Tyagi, A. K. (Eds.). (2022). *Intelligent Interactive Multimedia Systems for E-Healthcare Applications*. CRC Press. DOI: 10.1201/9781003282112

Malm, C., Jakobsson, J., & Isaksson, A. (2019). Physical Activity and Sports—Real Health Benefits: A Review with Insight into the Public Health of Sweden. *Sports (Basel, Switzerland), 7*(5), 127. DOI: 10.3390/sports7050127 PMID: 31126126

Manyika, J., Chui, M., Brown, B., Bughin, J., Dobbs, R., Roxburgh, C., & Hung Byers, A. (2011). Big data: The next frontier for innovation, competition, and productivity.

Marín-García, J., & Bonavía, T. (2021). Empowerment and employee well-being: A mediation analysis study. *International Journal of Environmental Research and Public Health, 18*(11), 5822. DOI: 10.3390/ijerph18115822 PMID: 34071574

Marjani, M., Nasaruddin, F., Gani, A., Karim, A., Hashem, I. A. T., Siddiqa, A., & Yaqoob, I. (2017). Big IoT data analytics: architecture, opportunities, and open research challenges. *ieee access, 5*, 5247-5261.

MarketsandMarkets. (2023). *Digital Health Market Growth, Drivers, and Opportunities*. MarketsandMarkets. https://www.marketsandmarkets.com/Market-Reports/digital-health-market-45458752.html

Markopoulou, D., & Papakonstantinou, V. (2021). The regulatory framework for the protection of critical infrastructures against cyberthreats: Identifying shortcomings and addressing future challenges: The case of the health sector in particular. *Computer Law & Security Review, 41*, 105502. DOI: 10.1016/j.clsr.2020.105502

Marley, R. (2023, August 23). Patient Empowerment: The key to harvesting real world data. *Healthcare Transformers*. https://healthcaretransformers.com/digital-health/healthcare-data/patient-empowerment-harvesting-real-world-data/

Maroju, R. G., Choudhari, S. G., Shaikh, M. K., Borkar, S. K., & Mendhe, H. (2023). Role of Telemedicine and Digital Technology in Public Health in India: A Narrative Review. *Cureus, 15*(3), e35986. DOI: 10.7759/cureus.35986 PMID: 37050980

Marschark, M., Shaver, L. A., & Boudreau, L. (2020). The role of technology in enhancing the mental health of remote workers. *Technology in Human Services, 38*(2), 56–72. DOI: 10.1080/15228835.2020.1833359

Martín, À., Woods, M., & Dawkins, S. (2018). How managers experience situations involving employee mental ill-health. *International Journal of Workplace Health Management, 11*(6), 442–463. DOI: 10.1108/IJWHM-09-2017-0069

Marufu, T. C., Collins, A., Vargas, L., Gillespie, L., & Almghairbi, D. (2021). Factors influencing retention among hospital nurses: Systematic review. [HTML]. *British Journal of Nursing (Mark Allen Publishing), 30*(5), 302–308. DOI: 10.12968/bjon.2021.30.5.302 PMID: 33733849

Marvaso, G., Pepa, M., Volpe, S., Mastroleo, F., Zaffaroni, M., Vincini, M. G., & Jereczek-Fossa, B. A. (2022). Virtual and Augmented Reality as a Novel Opportunity to Unleash the Power of Radiotherapy in the Digital Era: A Scoping Review. *Applied Sciences (Basel, Switzerland), 12*(22), 11308. DOI: 10.3390/app122211308

Maslach, C., & Leiter, M. P. (2016). Burnout: A short history of the concept. In Goodyear, L. R., & Mattingly, A. A. K. (Eds.), *Handbook of counselling psychology* (pp. 199–218). Wiley.

Maslach, C., & Leiter, M. P. (2016). Understanding the burnout experience: Recent research and its implications for psychiatry. *World Psychiatry; Official Journal of the World Psychiatric Association (WPA), 15*(2), 103–111. DOI: 10.1002/wps.20311 PMID: 27265691

Maslach, C., & Leiter, M. P. (2017). *The truth about burnout: How organizations cause personal stress and what to do about it*. Jossey-Bass.

Mathibe, M., & Chinyamurindi, W. (2021). Determinants of employee mental health in the south african public service: The role of organizational citizenship behaviours and workplace social support. *Advances in Mental Health, 19*(3), 306–316. DOI: 10.1080/18387357.2021.1938153

Mayer-Schönberger, V., & Cukier, K. (2013). *Big data: A revolution that will transform how we live, work, and think*. Houghton Mifflin Harcourt.

Mayo, E. (1933). *The human problems of an industrial civilization*. Macmillan.

Mazmanian, M., Orlikowski, W. J., & Yates, J. (2013). The autonomy paradox: The implications of mobile email devices for knowledge professionals. *Organization Science, 24*(5), 1337–1357. DOI: 10.1287/orsc.1120.0806

McGlinchey, D., Roebuck, B. S., Sakauye, P., Lalonde, C., Ferns, A., & Killian, K. (2025). "Increasing Demands and Competing Priorities": How Organizational Structure Affects Worker Well-Being in the Victim Services Field. *Human Service Organizations, Management, Leadership & Governance, 49*(2), 152–169.

McGraw, D., & Mandl, K. D. (2021). Privacy protections to encourage use of health-relevant digital data in a learning health system. *NPJ Digital Medicine*, *4*(1), 2. DOI: 10.1038/s41746-020-00362-8 PMID: 33398052

McGregor, D. (1960). *The human side of enterprise*. McGraw-Hill.

Meerlo, P., Sgoifo, A., & Suchecki, D. (2008). Restricted and disrupted sleep: Effects on autonomic function, neuroendocrine stress systems and stress responsivity. *Sleep Medicine Reviews*, *12*(3), 197–210. DOI: 10.1016/j.smrv.2007.07.007 PMID: 18222099

Meghrajani, V. R., Marathe, M., Sharma, R., Potdukhe, A., Wanjari, M. B., & Taksande, A. B. (2023). A Comprehensive Analysis of Mental Health Problems in India and the Role of Mental Asylums. *Cureus*. Advance online publication. DOI: 10.7759/cureus.42559 PMID: 37637646

Mehrtak, M., SeyedAlinaghi, S. A., MohsseniPour, M., Noori, T., Karimi, A., Shamsabadi, A., Heydari, M., Barzegary, A., Mirzapour, P., Soleymanzadeh, M., Vahedi, F., Mehraeen, E., & Dadras, O. (2021). Security challenges and solutions using healthcare cloud computing. *Journal of Medicine and Life*, *14*(4), 448–461. DOI: 10.25122/jml-2021-0100 PMID: 34621367

Mei, W., Wu, J., Zoghbi-Manrique-de-Lara, P., Liu, L., He, Y., & Song, M. (2023). Lose at sunrise, but gain at sunset: Linking social cyberloafing to psychological detachment, personal life enhancement of work, and mental health. *Work (Reading, Mass.)*, *75*(1), 339–348. DOI: 10.3233/WOR-220126 PMID: 36591686

Merung, A. Y., Sofyan, I. R., Sudirman, N. A., & Sma, A. (2024). Do Entrepreneurial Competence and Psychological Well-Being Affect Entrepreneurial Interest among Young Entrepreneurs? *Indonesian Journal of Business and Entrepreneurship Research*, *2*(1), 63–75. DOI: 10.62794/ijober.v2i1.1445

Messenger, J. (n.d.). *Working time and the future of work*.

Messenger, J. C., & Gschwind, L. (2016). Three generations of telework: New ICTs and the (r)evolution from home office to virtual office. *New Technology, Work and Employment*, *31*(3), 195–208. DOI: 10.1111/ntwe.12073

Metin-Orta, I. (2021). The impact of destructive leadership on followers' well-being. In Destructive Leadership and Management Hypocrisy: Advances in Theory and Practice (pp. 101-115). Emerald Publishing Limited.

Microsoft. (2021a). Embracing a flexible workplace. https://blogs.microsoft.com/blog/2021/03/22/hybrid-work-is-just-work/

Microsoft. (2021b). Building digital resilience in the workplace. https://news.microsoft.com

Microsoft. (2021c). 2021 Work Trend Index: The next great disruption is hybrid work—Are we ready? https://www.microsoft.com/en-us/worklab/work-trend-index/hybrid-work

Midha, S., & Singh, K. (2023). Happiness-Enhancing Strategies Among Indians. In *Religious and Spiritual Practices in India: A Positive Psychological Perspective* (pp. 341–368). Springer Nature Singapore. DOI: 10.1007/978-981-99-2397-7_15

Miller, D. D., & Brown, E. W. (2018). Artificial intelligence in medical practice: The question to the answer? *The American Journal of Medicine*, *131*(2), 129–133. DOI: 10.1016/j.amjmed.2017.10.035 PMID: 29126825

Mills, P. R., Tomkins, S. C., & Schlangen, L. J. (2007). The effect of high correlated colour temperature office lighting on employee wellbeing and work performance. *Journal of Circadian Rhythms*, *5*(0), 2. DOI: 10.1186/1740-3391-5-2 PMID: 17217543

Ministry of Health and Family Welfare. (2020). *Electronic Health Record Standards for India*. https://health.vikaspedia.in/viewcontent/health/nrhm/national-health-policies/electronic-health-record-standards-for-india?lgn=en

Miron, D., Petcu, M. A., David-Sobolevschi, M. I., & Cojocariu, R. C. (2021). A multidimensional approach of the relationship between teleworking and employees well-being-Romania during the pandemic generated by the SARS-COV-2 virus. [econstor.eu]. *Amfiteatru Economic*, *23*(58), 586–600. DOI: 10.24818/EA/2021/58/586

Mobile Health Application—An overview | ScienceDirect Topics. (n.d.). Retrieved June 28, 2024, from https://www.sciencedirect.com/topics/computer-science/mobile-health-application

Mocydlarz-Adamcewicz, M., Bajsztok, B., Filip, S., Petera, J., Mestan, M., & Malicki, J. (2023). Management of Onsite and Remote Communication in Oncology Hospitals: Data Protection in an Era of Rapid Technological Advances. *Journal of Personalized Medicine*, *13*(5), 761. DOI: 10.3390/jpm13050761 PMID: 37240931

Mohammadi, M., Al-Fuqaha, A., Sorour, S., & Guizani, M. (2018). Deep learning for IoT big data and streaming analytics: A survey. *IEEE Communications Surveys and Tutorials*, *20*(4), 2923–2960. DOI: 10.1109/COMST.2018.2844341

Momin, M. M., & Rolla, K. P. (2025). Narratives of Workplace Well-Being: Foundations, Constructs, and UN-SDGs. In *Insights on Wellbeing and Happiness in the Workplace* (pp. 317–352). IGI Global Scientific Publishing. DOI: 10.4018/979-8-3693-2939-9.ch016

Montano, D., & Siegrist, J. (2014). Effects of organisational-level interventions at work on employees' health: A systematic review. *BMC Public Health*, *14*(1), 135–144. DOI: 10.1186/1471-2458-14-135

Montaruli, A., Castelli, L., Galasso, L., Mulè, A., Bruno, E., Esposito, F., Caumo, A., & Roveda, E. (2019). Effect of chronotype on academic achievement in a sample of Italian University students. *Chronobiology International*, *36*(11), 1482–1495. DOI: 10.1080/07420528.2019.1652831 PMID: 31441334

Montaruli, A., Castelli, L., Mulè, A., Scurati, R., Esposito, F., Galasso, L., & Roveda, E. (2021). Biological Rhythm and Chronotype: New Perspectives in Health. *Biomolecules*, *11*(4), 487. DOI: 10.3390/biom11040487 PMID: 33804974

Monteiro, A. C. B., França, R. P., Arthur, R., & Iano, Y. (2021). An overview of medical Internet of Things, artificial intelligence, and cloud computing employed in health care from a modern panorama. *The Fusion of Internet of Things, Artificial Intelligence, and Cloud Computing in Health Care*, 3-23.

Monteiro, E., & Joseph, J. (2023). A Review on the Impact of Workplace Culture on Employee Mental Health and Well-Being [IJCSBE]. *International Journal of Case Studies in Business, IT, and Education*, *7*(2), 291–317. DOI: 10.47992/IJCSBE.2581.6942.0274

Mosley, T. J., Zajdel, R. A., Alderete, E., Clayton, J. A., Heidari, S., Pérez-Stable, E. J., Salt, K., & Bernard, M. A. (2025). Intersectionality and diversity, equity, and inclusion in the healthcare and scientific workforces. *Lancet Regional Health. Americas*, *41*, 41. DOI: 10.1016/j.lana.2024.100973

Mossialos, E., Permanand, G., Baeten, R., & Hervey, T. (2010). Health systems governance in Europe: The role of European Union law and policy. In Mossialos, E., Permanand, G., Baeten, R., & Hervey, T. K. (Eds.), *Health Systems Governance in Europe* (1st ed., pp. 1–83). Cambridge University Press., DOI: 10.1017/CBO9780511750496.002

Motti, V. G., & Berkovsky, S. (2022). Healthcare Privacy. In Knijnenburg, B. P., Page, X., Wisniewski, P., Lipford, H. R., Proferes, N., & Romano, J. (Eds.), *Modern Socio-Technical Perspectives on Privacy* (pp. 203–231). Springer International Publishing., DOI: 10.1007/978-3-030-82786-1_10

Mulawarman, W. G., & Komariyah, L. (2021). Women and Leadership Style in School Management: Study of Gender Perspective. *Cypriot Journal of Educational Sciences, 16*(2), 594–611.

Mullen, C. A., & Klimaitis, C. C. (2021). Defining mentoring: A literature review of issues, types, and applications. [HTML]. *Annals of the New York Academy of Sciences, 1483*(1), 19–35. DOI: 10.1111/nyas.14176 PMID: 31309580

Muthu, B., Sivaparthipan, C. B., Manogaran, G., Sundarasekar, R., Kadry, S., Shanthini, A., & Dasel, A. (2020). IOT based wearable sensor for diseases prediction and symptom analysis in healthcare sector. *Peer-to-Peer Networking and Applications, 13*(6), 2123–2134. DOI: 10.1007/s12083-019-00823-2

Namdech, P., Rotjanawasuthorn, S., Singh, B., & Kaunert, C. (2025). Harnessing Artificial Intelligence for Lifelong Education: Opportunities and Challenges. *Asian Education and Learning Review, 3*(2), 4–4.

Namdech, P., Rotjanawasuthorn, S., Singh, B., & Kaunert, C. (2025). Harnessing Artificial Intelligence For Lifelong Education: Opportunities And Challenges. *Asian Education and Learning Review, 3*(2), 4–4.

Nass, S. J., Levit, L. A., & Gostin, L. O. (2009). HIPAA, the Privacy Rule, and Its Application to Health Research. In *Beyond the HIPAA Privacy Rule: Enhancing Privacy, Improving Health Through Research.* National Academies Press.

Nelson, D. L., & Burke, R. J. (2000). Women executives: Health, stress, and success. *The Academy of Management Perspectives, 14*(2), 107–121. DOI: 10.5465/ame.2000.3819310

Nguyen, L. T., Chen, R., & Zhang, W. (2021). Remote work and stress in the era of COVID-19: The role of work structures and leadership practices. *The Journal of Applied Psychology, 106*(6), 935–947. DOI: 10.1037/apl0000506

Nguyen, M. V., Khanh, H. D., Phan, C. T., & Thuc, L. D. (2025). Investigating the impacts of psychological safety climate on mental ill health in the Vietnamese construction industry. *Engineering, Construction, and Architectural Management.* Advance online publication. DOI: 10.1108/ECAM-11-2024-1576

Nguyen, M., Rundle-Thiele, S., Malik, A., & Budhwar, P. (2023). Impact of technology-based knowledge sharing on employee outcomes: Moderation effects of training, support and leadership. *Journal of Knowledge Management, 27*(8), 2283–2301. DOI: 10.1108/JKM-07-2022-0552

Nielsen, K., & Noblet, A., & P. W. C. P. (. (2017). Workplace interventions to improve mental health. *International Journal of Environmental Research and Public Health, 14*(4), 436. DOI: 10.3390/ijerph14040436 PMID: 28422081

Nielsen, M. B. D., Bültmann, U., Madsen, I. E. H., Martin, M., Christensen, U., Diderichsen, F., & Rugulies, R. (2011). Health, work, and personal-related predictors of time to return to work among employees with mental health problems. *Disability and Rehabilitation, 34*(15), 1311–1316. DOI: 10.3109/09638288.2011.641664

Nielsen, M., Ekholm, O., Møller, S., Ersbøll, A., Santini, Z., Grønbæk, M., & Thygesen, L. (2022). Mental well-being among danish employees during the covid-19 pandemic: Results from a longitudinal study on the role of industry and working environment. *European Journal of Public Health, 32*(6), 871–876. DOI: 10.1093/eurpub/ckac150 PMID: 36228122

Niinihuhta, M., & Häggman-Laitila, A. (2022). A systematic review of the relationships between nurse leaders' leadership styles and nurses' work-related well-being. [wiley.com]. *International Journal of Nursing Practice, 28*(5), e13040. DOI: 10.1111/ijn.13040 PMID: 35102648

Nittrouer, C. L., Arena, D.Jr, Silver, E. R., Avery, D. R., & Hebl, M. R. (2025). Despite the haters: The immense promise and progress of diversity, equity, and inclusion initiatives. *Journal of Organizational Behavior, 46*(1), 188–201. DOI: 10.1002/job.2835

Nizam, N., Mokhtar, U., Dahlan, N., Bakri, N., Ahmad, M., & Safwan, N. (2024). Exploring the correlation between physical activity levels and mental health among employees at majlis sukan negeri johor. *International Journal of Academic Research in Business & Social Sciences, 14*(3). Advance online publication. DOI: 10.6007/IJARBSS/v14-i3/20818

O'Neill, J. W., & Hambley, L. A. (2018). Work-life balance and work-life harmony: Understanding the difference. In *Workplace wellbeing: A complete guide to employee wellness* (pp. 85–103). Springer.

Oh, H., Park, H., & Boo, S. (2017). Mental health status and its predictors among call center employees: A cross-sectional study. *Nursing & Health Sciences, 19*(2), 228–236. DOI: 10.1111/nhs.12334 PMID: 28295980

Oja, B., Kim, M., Perrewé, P., & Anagnostopoulos, C. (2019). Conceptualizing a-hero for sport employees' well-being. *Sport, Business and Management, 9*(4), 363–380. DOI: 10.1108/SBM-10-2018-0084

Ojogiwa, O. T. (2021). The crux of strategic leadership for a transformed public sector management in Nigeria. [sobiad.org]. *International Journal of Business and Management Studies, 13*(1), 83–96.

Olaleye, B. R., & Lekunze, J. N. (2024). Emotional intelligence and psychological resilience on workplace bullying and employee performance: A moderated-mediation perspective. *Journal of Law and Sustainable Development, 12*(1), e2159–e2159.

Olejarczyk, J. P., & Young, M. (2024). Patient Rights and Ethics. In *StatPearls*. StatPearls Publishing., https://www.ncbi.nlm.nih.gov/books/NBK538279/

Oleksa-Marewska, K., & Tokar, J. (2022). Facing the post-pandemic challenges: The role of leadership effectiveness in shaping the affective well-being of healthcare providers working in a hybrid work mode. [mdpi.com]. *International Journal of Environmental Research and Public Health, 19*(21), 14388.

Olshannikova, E., Ometov, A., Koucheryavy, Y., & Olsson, T. (2015). Visualizing Big Data with augmented and virtual reality: Challenges and research agenda. *Journal of Big Data, 2*(1), 1–27. DOI: 10.1186/s40537-015-0031-2

Öngel, G., Taşkıran, E., & Çelik, G. G. (2025). Perspective Chapter: The Role of Human Resources Management in Employee Well-Being.

Ortiz-Gómez, M., Molina-Sánchez, H., Ariza-Montes, A., & de Los Ríos-Berjillos, A. (2022). Servant leadership and authentic leadership as job resources for achieving workers' subjective well-being among organizations based on values. [tandfonline.com]. *Psychology Research and Behavior Management*, 2621–2638.

Oussible, N., & Tinaztepe, C. I. H. A. N. (2022). The Effect of Democratic Leadership Style on Organizational Productivity by the mediating role of Employee performance in Turkey. [paperpublications.org]. *International Journal of Recent Research in Commerce Economics and Management, 9*(1), 6–16.

Owens, B., & Mills, S. (2025). Conceptualizing discrimination against LGBTQ+ workers in the unbounded workplace. *The Canadian Geographer. Geographe Canadien, 69*(1), e12971. DOI: 10.1111/cag.12971

Ozkan, S., Tari Selcuk, K., & Kan, Z. E. (2024). Is green behaviors of health professionals related to green practices in the workplace? Multicenter study in Turkey. *International Journal of Environmental Health Research, 34*(2), 898–910. DOI: 10.1080/09603123.2023.2185209 PMID: 36854645

Padmaja, M., Shitharth, S., Prasuna, K., Chaturvedi, A., Kshirsagar, P. R., & Vani, A. (2022). Grow of artificial intelligence to challenge security in IoT application. *Wireless Personal Communications, 127*(3), 1829–1845. DOI: 10.1007/s11277-021-08725-4

Page, K. M., Milner, A. J., Martin, A., Turrell, G., Giles-Corti, B., & LaMontagne, A. D. (2014). Workplace Stress. *Journal of Occupational and Environmental Medicine, 56*(8), 814–819. DOI: 10.1097/JOM.0000000000000230 PMID: 25099407

Pagkratis, K., & Dobson, S. (2024). Promoting Learning Inclusion Through the Global Network of Learning Cities and Sustainable Development Goals (SDGs). In *Learning Inclusion in a Digital Age: Belonging and Finding a Voice with the Disadvantaged* (pp. 49–63). Springer Nature Singapore. DOI: 10.1007/978-981-99-7196-1_4

Paine, S.-J., Gander, P. H., & Travier, N. (2006). The Epidemiology of Morningness/Eveningness: Influence of Age, Gender, Ethnicity, and Socioeconomic Factors in Adults (30-49 Years). *Journal of Biological Rhythms, 21*(1), 68–76. DOI: 10.1177/0748730405283154 PMID: 16461986

Pal, A., Mukherjee, A., & Dey, S. (2016). Future of healthcare—sensor data-driven prognosis. *Wireless World in 2050 and Beyond: A Window into the Future!*, 93-109.

Panda, M., Abraham, A., Gopi, B., & Ajith, R. (Eds.). (2024). *Computational Intelligence for Oncology and Neurological Disorders: Current Practices and Future Directions*. CRC Press. DOI: 10.1201/9781003450153

Pandey, D. L., & Risal, N. (2023). Impact of Workplace Stressors on Employee Burnout: A Survey on Diversified Professionals. *Molung Educational Frontier*, 47–68. DOI: 10.3126/mef.v13i01.56023

Pandey, S., & Sharma, V. (2016). Understanding Work-Related Stress, Job Conditions, Work Culture and Workaholism Phenomenon as Predictors of HR Crisis. *International Journal of Human Capital and Information Technology Professionals, 7*(2), 68–80. DOI: 10.4018/IJHCITP.2016040105

Pandya, A., Khanal, N., & Upadhyaya, M. (2022). Workplace mental health interventions in india: A rapid systematic scoping review. *Frontiers in Public Health, 10*, 800880. Advance online publication. DOI: 10.3389/fpubh.2022.800880 PMID: 35592077

Panesar, A. (2019). *Machine learning and AI for healthcare*. Apress. DOI: 10.1007/978-1-4842-3799-1

Papageorgiou, G., Athanasiadou, P., Tsappi, E., Xergia, S. A., Maimaris, A., & Efstathiades, A. (2025). Organizational Work, Well-Being, and Quality of Life at an Elderly Age: The Case of Cyprus. *Journal of Aging Research, 2025*(1), 7194723. DOI: 10.1155/jare/7194723 PMID: 40017702

Parasa, S. K. (2023). Impact of AI on Strategic Workforce Planning. *Journal of Artificial Intelligence & Cloud Computing*, *2*(1), 1–3. DOI: 10.47363/jaicc/2023(2)377

Parihar, A., Prajapati, J. B., Prajapati, B. G., Trambadiya, B., Thakkar, A., & Engineer, P. (2024). *Role of IOT in healthcare: Applications, security & privacy concerns*. Intelligent Pharmacy., DOI: 10.1016/j.ipha.2024.01.003

Parslow, R. A., Jorm, A. F., Christensen, H., Rodgers, B., Strazdins, L., & D'Souza, R. M. (2004). The associations between work stress and mental health: A comparison of organizationally employed and self-employed workers. *Work and Stress*, *18*(3), 231–244.

Patangia, B., Sankruthyayana, R. G., Sathiyaseelan, A., & Balasundaram, S. (2021). How could Mindfulness Help? A Perspective on the Applications of Mindfulness in Enhancing Tomorrow's Workplace. *i-Manager's. Journal of Management*, *16*(3), 52.

Patient Empowerment: The key to harvesting real world data. (n.d.). Retrieved June 30, 2024, from https://healthcaretransformers.com/digital-health/healthcare-data/patient-empowerment-harvesting-real-world-data/

Pattali, S., Sankar, J. P., Al Qahtani, H., Menon, N., & Faizal, S. (2024). Effect of leadership styles on turnover intention among staff nurses in private hospitals: The moderating effect of perceived organizational support. *BMC Health Services Research*, *24*(1), 1–13. DOI: 10.1186/s12913-024-10674-0 PMID: 38355546

Patzelt, H., & Shepherd, D. A. (2024). A fatigue model of social venturing. *Small Business Economics*, *63*(3), 1065–1088. DOI: 10.1007/s11187-023-00853-4

Paudyal, P., Wasti, S. P., Neupane, P., Sapkota, J. L., Watts, C., Kulasabanathan, K., Silwal, R., Memon, A., Shukla, P., Pathak, R. S., Michelson, D., Berry, C., Moult, A., Simkhada, P., van Teijlingen, E. R., & Cassell, J. (2025). Coproducing a culturally sensitive storytelling video intervention to improve psychosocial well-being: A multimethods participatory study with Nepalese migrant workers. *BMJ Open*, *15*(2), e086280. DOI: 10.1136/bmjopen-2024-086280 PMID: 39961714

Paul, M., Maglaras, L., Ferrag, M. A., & Almomani, I. (2023). Digitization of healthcare sector: A study on privacy and security concerns. *ICT Express*, *9*(4), 571–588. DOI: 10.1016/j.icte.2023.02.007

Pawar, B. (2016). Workplace spirituality and employee well-being: An empirical examination. *Employee Relations*, *38*(6), 975–994. DOI: 10.1108/ER-11-2015-0215

Peethambaran, M., & Naim, M. F. (2025). Employee flourishing-at-work: A review and research agenda. *The International Journal of Organizational Analysis*. Advance online publication. DOI: 10.1108/IJOA-04-2024-4455

Petković, D., Vuković, B., & Vuković, I. (2023, May). Clostridium Difficile infection and neurological disorders-a case report. In *Mind & Brain:62nd International Neuropsychiatric Congress.*

Philip, P., Sagaspe, P., Taillard, J., Moore, N., Guilleminault, C., Sanchez-Ortuno, M., Åkerstedt, T., & Bioulac, B. (2003). Fatigue, Sleep Restriction, and Performance in Automobile Drivers: A Controlled Study in a Natural Environment. *Sleep, 26*(3), 277–280. DOI: 10.1093/sleep/26.3.277 PMID: 12749545

Phoi, Y. Y., & Keogh, J. B. (2019). Dietary Interventions for Night Shift Workers: A Literature Review. *Nutrients, 11*(10), 2276. DOI: 10.3390/nu11102276 PMID: 31547547

Pilbeam, C. (2024). Practices and challenges of safety management in outsourced facilities management. *Journal of Safety Research, 90*, 144–162.

Pillai, R., Ghanghorkar, Y., Sivathanu, B., Algharabat, R., & Rana, N. P. (2024). Adoption of artificial intelligence (AI) based employee experience (EEX) chatbots. *Information Technology & People, 37*(1), 449–478. DOI: 10.1108/ITP-04-2022-0287

Pless, N. M., Sengupta, A., Wheeler, M. A., & Maak, T. (2021). Responsible Leadership and the Reflective CEO: Resolving Stakeholder Conflict by Imagining What Could be done. Journal of Business Ethics. springer.com

Pool, J., Akhlaghpour, S., Fatehi, F., & Burton-Jones, A. (2024). A systematic analysis of failures in protecting personal health data: A scoping review. *International Journal of Information Management, 74*, 102719. DOI: 10.1016/j.ijinfomgt.2023.102719

Porter, A. (2023, June 23). Navigating the Privacy Maze: GDPR vs HIPAA. *BigID.* https://bigid.com/blog/gdpr-vs-hipaa/

Pradhan, G. M., & Shrestha, P. (2021). Impact of training & development and career planning on employee involvement. *Journal of Balkumari College, 10*(1), 13–18.

Pradhan, R., & Hati, L. (2019). The measurement of employee well-being: Development and validation of a scale. *Global Business Review, 23*(2), 385–407. DOI: 10.1177/0972150919859101

Pramanik, P. K. D., Pal, S., & Mukhopadhyay, M. (2022). Healthcare big data: A comprehensive overview. *Research anthology on big data analytics, architectures, and applications*, 119-147.

Preckel, F., Lipnevich, A. A., Schneider, S., & Roberts, R. D. (2011). Chronotype, cognitive abilities, and academic achievement: A meta-analytic investigation. *Learning and Individual Differences, 21*(5), 483–492. DOI: 10.1016/j.lindif.2011.07.003

Priyadarshi, M., & Kumar, S. (2020). Accountability in Healthcare in India. *Indian Journal of Community Medicine : Official Publication of Indian Association of Preventive & Social Medicine*, *45*(2), 125. DOI: 10.4103/ijcm.IJCM_224_19 PMID: 32905344

Prodromidis, N., Karlsson, M., & Kühnle, D. (2025). Working Hours and Workers' Health: Evidence from a National Experiment in Sweden. SSRN *Electronic Journal*. DOI: 10.2139/ssrn.5142319

Provencher, H. L., & Keyes, C. L. M. (2011). Complete mental health recovery: Bridging mental illness with positive mental health. *Journal of Public Mental Health*, *10*(1), 57–69. DOI: 10.1108/17465721111134556

PTI. (2018). *Fortis Healthcare says it has found 'systemic lapses' found in inter-corporate borrowings | Business News—The Indian Express*. https://indianexpress.com/article/business/systemic-lapses-found-in-inter-corporate-borrowings-fortis-healthcare-5235343/

Purnell, M. T., Feyer, A.-M., & Herbison, G. P. (2002). The impact of a nap opportunity during the night shift on the performance and alertness of 12-h shift workers. *Journal of Sleep Research*, *11*(3), 219–227. DOI: 10.1046/j.1365-2869.2002.00309.x PMID: 12220318

Quach, S., Thaichon, P., Martin, K. D., Weaven, S., & Palmatier, R. W. (2022). Digital technologies: Tensions in privacy and data. *Journal of the Academy of Marketing Science*, *50*(6), 1299–1323. DOI: 10.1007/s11747-022-00845-y PMID: 35281634

Quilitch, H. R. (1978). Using a simple feedback procedure to reinforce the submission of written suggestions by mental health employees. *Journal of Organizational Behavior Management*, *1*(2), 155–163. DOI: 10.1300/J075v01n02_07

Qureshi, R., Irfan, M., Ali, H., Khan, A., Nittala, A. S., Ali, S., & Alam, T. (2023). Artificial Intelligence and Biosensors in Healthcare and its Clinical Relevance: A Review. *IEEE Access : Practical Innovations, Open Solutions*, *11*, 61600–61620. DOI: 10.1109/ACCESS.2023.3285596

Rahman, S. A., St. Hilaire, M. A., Grant, L. K., Barger, L. K., Brainard, G. C., Czeisler, C. A., Klerman, E. B., & Lockley, S. W. (2022). Dynamic lighting schedules to facilitate circadian adaptation to shifted timing of sleep and wake. *Journal of Pineal Research*, *73*(1), e12805. DOI: 10.1111/jpi.12805 PMID: 35501292

Raineri, A., & Valenzuela-Ibarra, S. (2022). The role of inter-team relational coordination in the high-performance work systems–team performance linkage. [HTML]. *International Journal of Human Resource Management, 33*(18), 3662–3702. DOI: 10.1080/09585192.2021.1928729

Rai, S. (2015). Organizational justice and employee mental health's moderating roles in organizational identification. *South Asian Journal of Global Business Research, 4*(1), 68–84. DOI: 10.1108/SAJGBR-01-2014-0006

Rajagopalan, P. R. (2022). The AIIMS cyberattack reflects India's critical vulnerabilities. Observer Research Foundation. https://www.orfonline.org/expert-speak/the-aiims-cyberattack-reflects-indias-critical-vulnerabilities

Rajaratnam, S. M., & Arendt, J. (2001). Health in a 24-h society. *Lancet, 358*(9286), 999–1005. DOI: 10.1016/S0140-6736(01)06108-6 PMID: 11583769

Randler, C. (2008). Morningness-Eveningness Comparison in Adolescents from Different Countries around the World. *Chronobiology International, 25*(6), 1017–1028. DOI: 10.1080/07420520802551519 PMID: 19005902

Rani, N., & Samuel, A. (2016). A study on generational differences in work values and person-organization fit and its effect on turnover intention of Generation Y in India. *Management Research Review, 39*(12), 1695–1719. DOI: 10.1108/MRR-10-2015-0249

Rathobei, K. E., Ranängen, H., & Lindman, Å. (2024). Exploring broad value creation in mining-Corporate social responsibility and stakeholder management in practice. *The Extractive Industries and Society, 17*, 101412. DOI: 10.1016/j.exis.2024.101412

Rattanasirivilai, S. (2024). Happiness Based on the Happy Workplace Concept of Military Officials: Evidence in Thailand. *Asian Political Science Review, 8*(2), 8–16.

Ray, J., Kumar, S., Pandey, S., & Akram, S. V. (2023, June). The Role of Augmented Reality and Virtual Reality in Shaping the Future of Health Psychology. In *2023 3rd International Conference on Pervasive Computing and Social Networking (ICPCSN)* (pp. 1604-1608). IEEE. DOI: 10.1109/ICPCSN58827.2023.00268

Razavi, P., Devore, E. E., Bajaj, A., Lockley, S. W., Figueiro, M. G., Ricchiuti, V., Gauderman, W. J., Hankinson, S. E., Willett, W. C., & Schernhammer, E. S. (2019). Shift Work, Chronotype, and Melatonin Rhythm in Nurses. *Cancer Epidemiology, Biomarkers & Prevention, 28*(7), 1177–1186. DOI: 10.1158/1055-9965.EPI-18-1018 PMID: 31142495

Reddy, B. M. (2023). Amalgamation of Internet of Things and Machine Learning for Smart Healthcare Applications–A Review. *Int. J Comp. Eng. Sci. Res, 5*, 08-36.

Reece, A., Yaden, D., Kellerman, G., Robichaux, A., Goldstein, R., Schwartz, B., & Baumeister, R. (2021). Mattering is an indicator of organizational health and employee success. *The Journal of Positive Psychology*, *16*(2), 228–248.

Reger, G. M. (Ed.). (2020). *Technology and mental health: a clinician's guide to improving outcomes*. Routledge. DOI: 10.4324/9780429020537

Reid, K. J. (2019). Assessment of Circadian Rhythms. *Neurologic Clinics*, *37*(3), 505–526. DOI: 10.1016/j.ncl.2019.05.001 PMID: 31256786

Reimann, M., & Guzy, J. (2017). Psychological contract breach and employee health: The relevance of unmet obligations for mental and physical health. *Journal of Work and Organizational Psychology*, *33*(1), 1–11. DOI: 10.1016/j.rpto.2016.11.001

Rejeb, A., Rejeb, K., Treiblmaier, H., Appolloni, A., Alghamdi, S., Alhasawi, Y., & Iranmanesh, M. (2023). The Internet of Things (IoT) in healthcare: Taking stock and moving forward. *Internet of Things : Engineering Cyber Physical Human Systems*, *22*, 100721. DOI: 10.1016/j.iot.2023.100721

Reppert, S. M., & Weaver, D. R. (2002). Coordination of circadian timing in mammals. *Nature*, *418*(6901), 935–941. DOI: 10.1038/nature00965 PMID: 12198538

Reutrakul, S., Hood, M. M., Crowley, S. J., Morgan, M. K., Teodori, M., Knutson, K. L., & Van Cauter, E. (2013). Chronotype Is Independently Associated With Glycemic Control in Type 2 Diabetes. *Diabetes Care*, *36*(9), 2523–2529. DOI: 10.2337/dc12-2697 PMID: 23637357

Rissman, J., Bataille, C., Masanet, E., Aden, N., Morrow, W. R.III, Zhou, N., Elliott, N., Dell, R., Heeren, N., Huckestein, B., Cresko, J., Miller, S. A., Roy, J., Fennell, P., Cremmins, B., Koch Blank, T., Hone, D., Williams, E. D., de la Rue du Can, S., & Helseth, J. (2020). Technologies and policies to decarbonize global industry: Review and assessment of mitigation drivers through 2070. *Applied Energy*, *266*, 114848. DOI: 10.1016/j.apenergy.2020.114848

Roberge, C., Meunier, S., & Cleary, J. (2024). In Action at Work! Mental Health Self-Management Strategies for Employees Experiencing Anxiety or Depressive Symptoms. *Canadian Journal of Behavioural Science*, *56*(1), 10–19. DOI: 10.1037/cbs0000346

Robertson, M. M., Huang, Y., & Larson, N. (2016). The relationship among computer work, environmental design, and musculoskeletal and visual discomfort: Examining the moderating role of supervisory relations and co-worker support. *International Archives of Occupational and Environmental Health*, *89*(1), 7–22. DOI: 10.1007/s00420-015-1046-x PMID: 25827942

Robinson, M. A., Allen, J. A., & Staley, A. M. (2019). Remote work and inclusion: Diversity impacts of distance work arrangements. *Equality, Diversity and Inclusion*, *38*(5), 503–516. DOI: 10.1108/EDI-04-2018-0076

Rodrigues, J. F.Jr, Florea, L., de Oliveira, M. C., Diamond, D., & Oliveira, O. N.Jr. (2021). Big data and machine learning for materials science. *Discover Materials*, *1*(1), 1–27. DOI: 10.1007/s43939-021-00012-0 PMID: 33899049

Roenneberg, T. (2015). Having Trouble Typing? What on Earth Is Chronotype? *Journal of Biological Rhythms*, *30*(6), 487–491. DOI: 10.1177/0748730415603835 PMID: 26446872

Roenneberg, T., Allebrandt, K. V., Merrow, M., & Vetter, C. (2012). Social Jetlag and Obesity. *Current Biology*, *22*(10), 939–943. DOI: 10.1016/j.cub.2012.03.038 PMID: 22578422

Roenneberg, T., Chua, E. J., Bernardo, R., & Mendoza, E. (2008). Modelling Biological Rhythms. *Current Biology*, *18*(17), R826–R835. DOI: 10.1016/j.cub.2008.07.017 PMID: 18786388

Roenneberg, T., Kuehnle, T., Juda, M., Kantermann, T., Allebrandt, K., Gordijn, M., & Merrow, M. (2007). Epidemiology of the human circadian clock. *Sleep Medicine Reviews*, *11*(6), 429–438. DOI: 10.1016/j.smrv.2007.07.005 PMID: 17936039

Roenneberg, T., Kumar, C. J., & Merrow, M. (2007). The human circadian clock entrains to sun time. *Current Biology*, *17*(2), R44–R45. DOI: 10.1016/j.cub.2006.12.011 PMID: 17240323

Roenneberg, T., Pilz, L. K., Zerbini, G., & Winnebeck, E. C. (2019). Chronotype and Social Jetlag: A (Self-) Critical Review. *Biology (Basel)*, *8*(3), 54. DOI: 10.3390/biology8030054 PMID: 31336976

Roenneberg, T., Wirz-Justice, A., & Merrow, M. (2003). Life between Clocks: Daily Temporal Patterns of Human Chronotypes. *Journal of Biological Rhythms*, *18*(1), 80–90. DOI: 10.1177/0748730402239679 PMID: 12568247

Rogers, A. E., Hwang, W.-T., Scott, L. D., Aiken, L. H., & Dinges, D. F. (2004). The Working Hours Of Hospital Staff Nurses And Patient Safety. *Health Affairs*, *23*(4), 202–212. DOI: 10.1377/hlthaff.23.4.202 PMID: 15318582

Rosa, D. E., Marot, L. P., De Mello, M. T., Marqueze, E. C., Narciso, F. V., De Araújo, L. B., & Crispim, C. A. (2021). Association between chronotype and psychomotor performance of rotating shift workers. *Scientific Reports*, *11*(1), 6919. DOI: 10.1038/s41598-021-86299-8 PMID: 33767333

Rosenlund, M., Kinnunen, U.-M., & Saranto, K. (2023a). The Use of Digital Health Services Among Patients and Citizens Living at Home: Scoping Review. *Journal of Medical Internet Research*, *25*, e44711. DOI: 10.2196/44711 PMID: 36972122

Rothbard, N. P., Phillips, K. W., & Dumas, T. L. (2005). Managing multiple roles: Work-family policies and individuals' organizational attachment. *Organization Science*, *16*(3), 243–267. DOI: 10.1287/orsc.1050.0124

Rudin, C. (2019). Stop explaining black box machine learning models for high stakes decisions and use interpretable models instead. *Nature Machine Intelligence*, *1*(5), 206–215. DOI: 10.1038/s42256-019-0048-x PMID: 35603010

Rurkkhum, S. (2023). A bundle of human resource practices and employee resilience: The role of employee well-being. *Asia-Pacific Journal of Business Administration*, *16*(3), 716–731. DOI: 10.1108/APJBA-01-2022-0050

Russell-Bennett, R., Rosenbaum, M. S., Fisk, R. P., & Raciti, M. M. (2024). SDG editorial: Improving life on planet earth–a call to action for service research to achieve the sustainable development goals (SDGs). *Journal of Services Marketing*, *38*(2), 145–152. DOI: 10.1108/JSM-11-2023-0425

Saadat, M. N., & Shuaib, M. (2020). Advancements in deep learning theory and applications: Perspective in 2020 and beyond. *Advances and Applications in Deep Learning, 3*.

Saha, M. (2021). Application of Right to Privacy in Mr X v. Hospital Z Case and Its Subsequent Developments. *Indian Journal of Law and Legal Research*, *2*, 1. https://heinonline.org/HOL/Page?handle=hein.journals/injlolw2&id=5165&div=&collection=

Sahoo, N., Kumar, A., & Samsher, . (2022). Review on energy conservation and emission reduction approaches for cement industry. [HTML]. *Environmental Development*, *44*, 100767. DOI: 10.1016/j.envdev.2022.100767

Saksvik, I. B., Bjorvatn, B., Hetland, H., Sandal, G. M., & Pallesen, S. (2011). Individual differences in tolerance to shift work – A systematic review. *Sleep Medicine Reviews*, *15*(4), 221–235. DOI: 10.1016/j.smrv.2010.07.002 PMID: 20851006

Salesforce. (2021). How we're reopening our offices safely. https://www.salesforce.com/news

Salesforce. (2021). *Salesforce Ohana culture*. Salesforce Careers. https://www.salesforce.com/company/culture/

Salesforce. (2022). Success from anywhere: Our strategy for the future of work. https://www.salesforce.com/company/news-press/stories/

Salzer, M. S. (2002). Consumer-delivered services as a best practice in mental health care delivery and the development of practice guidelines. *Psychiatric Rehabilitation Skills*, *6*(3), 355–382. DOI: 10.1080/10973430208408443

Sangperm, N. (2017). Factors Affecting Organizational Commitment of Employees of Autonomous University. *PSAKU International Journal of Interdisciplinary Research*, *6*(1), 58–66. DOI: 10.12778/235108618X15452373185994

Sangperm, N. (2018). Structural Equation Model Cause of Organizational Citizenship Behavior of Personnel of Kasetsart University Sriracha Campus, Thailand. *PSAKU International Journal of Interdisciplinary Research*, *7*(1), 31–41. DOI: 10.12778/235108618X15452373746261

Saxena, S., Srivastava, K., Dilbagi, R., & Saxena, A. (2020). Telemedicine units for COVID-19: An experience from Madhya Pradesh. *Indian Journal of Community Health*, *32*(2, Supp), 277–280. DOI: 10.47203/IJCH.2020.v32i02SUPP.021

Scarpato, N., Pieroni, A., Di Nunzio, L., & Fallucchi, F. (2017). E-health-IoT universe: A review. *management, 21*(44), 46.

Scheuch, I., Peters, N., Lohner, M. S., Muss, C., Aprea, C., & Fürstenau, B. (2021). Resilience Training Programs in Organizational Contexts: A Scoping Review. *Frontiers in Psychology*, *12*, 733036. Advance online publication. DOI: 10.3389/fpsyg.2021.733036 PMID: 34721200

Schultz, A., & Burton, W. (2018). Sleep: An integral component of employee well-being programs. *American Journal of Health Promotion*, *32*(7), 1639–1641. DOI: 10.1177/0890117118790621c PMID: 30099898

Schultz, T. R., Edemba, D., Lecuyer, M. E., Garzone, A., Henise, S., Liljestrand, A., Hinds, P. S., & King, S. (2025). LGBTQ+ Population Well-Being: Health Equity Implementation Science in Action. *Public Health Nursing (Boston, Mass.)*, *42*(2), 957–965. DOI: 10.1111/phn.13480 PMID: 39623732

Schur, L., Ameri, M., & Kruse, D. (2020). Telework after COVID: A "silver lining" for workers with disabilities? *Journal of Occupational Rehabilitation*, *30*(4), 521–536. DOI: 10.1007/s10926-020-09936-5 PMID: 33156435

Schwepker, C. H.Jr, Valentine, S. R., Giacalone, R. A., & Promislo, M. (2021). Good barrels yield healthy apples: Organizational ethics as a mechanism for mitigating work-related stress and promoting employee well-being. [researchgate.net]. *Journal of Business Ethics*, *174*(1), 143–159. DOI: 10.1007/s10551-020-04562-w

Seh, A. H., Zarour, M., Alenezi, M., Sarkar, A. K., Agrawal, A., Kumar, R., & Ahmad Khan, R. (2020). Healthcare Data Breaches: Insights and Implications. *Health Care*, *8*(2), 133. DOI: 10.3390/healthcare8020133 PMID: 32414183

Sejdic, E., & Falk, T. H. (Eds.). (2018). *Signal processing and machine learning for biomedical big data*. CRC press. DOI: 10.1201/9781351061223

Seligman, M. E. P. (1998). *Learned optimism: How to change your mind and your life*. Pocket Books.

Sellers, K. K., Cohen, J. L., Khambhati, A. N., Fan, J. M., Lee, A. M., Chang, E. F., & Krystal, A. D. (2024). Closed-loop neurostimulation for the treatment of psychiatric disorders. *Neuropsychopharmacology: Official Publication of the American College of Neuropsychopharmacology*, *49*(1), 163–178. DOI: 10.1038/s41386-023-01631-2 PMID: 37369777

Senbekov, M., Saliev, T., Bukeyeva, Z., Almabayeva, A., Zhanaliyeva, M., Aitenova, N., Toishibekov, Y., & Fakhradiyev, I. (2020). The Recent Progress and Applications of Digital Technologies in Healthcare: A Review. *International Journal of Telemedicine and Applications*, *2020*, 1–18. DOI: 10.1155/2020/8830200 PMID: 33343657

Sengan, S., Kamalam, G. K., Vellingiri, J., Gopal, J., Velayutham, P., & Subramaniyaswamy, V. (2020). Medical information retrieval systems for e-Health care records using fuzzy based machine learning model. *Microprocessors and Microsystems*, •••, 103344.

Sethumadhavan, R. (2025). Creating a Positive Workplace for the Employee Well-being. In *Harnessing Happiness and Wisdom for Organizational Well-Being* (pp. 131–150). IGI Global Scientific Publishing. DOI: 10.4018/979-8-3693-8457-2.ch005

Shah, F., Li, J., Shah, Y., & Shah, F. (2017, November). Broad big data domain via medical big data. In *2017 4th International Conference on Systems and Informatics (ICSAI)* (pp. 732-737). IEEE.

Shahid, Z. (2021). Distributed Machine Learning for Anomalous Employees Activity Recognition using IoT Systems.

Shahzad, K., Khan, S. A., & Iqbal, A. (2024). Mental health issues of university librarians: A systematic literature review. *Global Knowledge, Memory and Communication*. Advance online publication. DOI: 10.1108/GKMC-07-2023-0261

Shan, H. (2021). The changing nature of work: Work-life balance and its implications. *Journal of Human Resource Management*, *10*(3), 25–41. DOI: 10.1080/23269688.2021.1905501

Shanker, M. (2024). Impact of social media usage & social engagement on physical- mental health of young employees. *International Journal of Social Science and Human Research*, *7*(04). Advance online publication. DOI: 10.47191/ijsshr/v7-i04-69

Shapiro, S. L., Astin, J. A., Bishop, S. R., & Cordova, M. (2007). Mindfulness-based stress reduction for health care professionals: Results from a randomized trial. *International Journal of Stress Management*, *14*(2), 179–192. DOI: 10.1037/1072-5245.14.2.179

Sharma, P. K., & Kumra, R. (2020). Relationship between workplace spirituality, organizational justice and mental health: Mediation role of employee engagement. *Journal of Advances in Management Research*, *17*(5), 627–650. DOI: 10.1108/JAMR-01-2020-0007

Sharma, R. S., Rohatgi, A., Jain, S., & Singh, D. (2023). The Ayushman Bharat Digital Mission (ABDM): Making of India's Digital Health Story. *CSI Transactions on ICT*, *11*(1), 3–9. DOI: 10.1007/s40012-023-00375-0

Shifrin, N. V., & Michel, J. S. (2022). Flexible work arrangements and employee health: A meta-analytic review. *Work and Stress*, *36*(1), 60–85. DOI: 10.1080/02678373.2021.1936287

Shimazu, A., Matsudaira, K., Jonge, J., Tosaka, N., Watanabe, K., & Takahashi, M. (2016). Psychological detachment from work during non-work time: Linear or curvilinear relations with mental health and work engagement? *Industrial Health*, *54*(3), 282–292. DOI: 10.2486/indhealth.2015-0097 PMID: 26829972

Shin, J., Han, H., & Ko, H. (2022). Telework and well-being: A review of empirical studies on the relationship between remote work and mental health outcomes. *Social Science & Medicine*, *277*, 113724. DOI: 10.1016/j.socscimed.2021.113724

Shu, Y., Zhuang, X., Ying, R., & Xu, G. (2024). … Pressure and the Integration of Corporate Environmental and Financial Performance: Empirical Evidence from Listed Companies in Heavily Polluting Industries in…. Sustainability. mdpi.com

Silven, A. V., Van Peet, P. G., Boers, S. N., Tabak, M., De Groot, A., Hendriks, D., Van Os, H. J. A., Bonten, T. N., Atsma, D. E., De Graaf, T. J., Sombroek, M. P., Chavannes, N. H., & Villalobos-Quesada, M. (2022). Clarifying responsibility: Professional digital health in the doctor-patient relationship, recommendations for physicians based on a multi-stakeholder dialogue in the Netherlands. *BMC Health Services Research*, *22*(1), 129. DOI: 10.1186/s12913-021-07316-0 PMID: 35094713

Singh, B., & Chandra, S. (2025). Augmented Reality and Virtual Reality in Health Advancements and Medical Education: Runway for Future Ready Healthcare Services. In R. R., S. Chowdhury, S. Kardy, R. Damaševičius, & R. Govindaraj (Eds.), *Digital Twins for Sustainable Healthcare in the Metaverse* (pp. 197-218). IGI Global Scientific Publishing. DOI: 10.4018/979-8-3693-4199-5.ch008

Singh, B., & Kaunert, C. (2025). Leveraging IoT for Patient Monitoring and Smart Healthcare: Connected Healthcare System. In Revolutionizing Healthcare Systems Through Cloud Computing and IoT (pp. 27-46). IGI Global.

Singh, B., Hammouch, H., & Chandra, S. (2025). Innovative Wind Energy Solutions for Smart-Sustainable Communities: Vision for Intelligent Energy Management and Climate Resilience in Industry 5.0. In Mitra, D., Choudhury, T., Madan, A., Chattaraj, S., & Pellegrini, M. (Eds.), *AI Technologies for Enhancing Recycling Processes* (pp. 491–508). IGI Global Scientific Publishing., DOI: 10.4018/979-8-3693-7282-1.ch020

Singh, B., Kaunert, C., Hammouch, H., & Raghav, A. (2025). Booster of IoMT in Diagnostics and Disease Screening: Hustler Artificial Intelligence Approaches Transforming Healthier Homes. In Kumar, V., Katina, P., & Zhao, J. (Eds.), *Convergence of Internet of Medical Things (IoMT) and Generative AI* (pp. 243–266). IGI Global Scientific Publishing., DOI: 10.4018/979-8-3693-6180-1.ch010

Singh, B., Kaunert, C., & Jermsittiparsert, K. (2025). Advocating Medical Tourism and Healthcare in Global Health Market Places: Promoting Sustainability and Technological Advancements. In Jermsittiparsert, K., & Marzo, R. (Eds.), *AI Technologies and Advancements for Psychological Well-Being and Healthcare* (pp. 327–350). IGI Global., DOI: 10.4018/979-8-3693-9158-7.ch012

Singh, N., Raza, M., Paranthaman, V. V., Awais, M., Khalid, M., & Javed, E. (2021). Internet of Things and cloud computing. *Digital Health*, •••, 151–162. DOI: 10.1016/B978-0-12-818914-6.00013-2

Sinkinson, C., & Hicks, A. (2013). Unraveling the research process: social bookmarking and collaborative learning. In *The Plugged-In Professor* (pp. 49–60). Elsevier., DOI: 10.1016/B978-1-84334-694-4.50005-3

Smith, A., & Lockwood, N. (2020). The hidden costs of remote work: Psychological effects of social isolation on mental health. *Journal of Occupational Health Psychology*, *25*(3), 135–149. DOI: 10.1037/ocp0000198

Smith, H. A., Besunder, J. B., Betters, K. A., Johnson, P. N., Srinivasan, V., Stormorken, A., & Berkenbosch, J. W. (2022). 2022 Society of Critical Care Medicine clinical practice guidelines on prevention and management of pain, agitation, neuromuscular blockade, and delirium in critically ill pediatric patients with consideration of the ICU environment and early mobility. [stonybrookmedicine.edu]. *Pediatric Critical Care Medicine*, *23*(2), e74–e110.

Soga, L. R., Bolade-Ogunfodun, Y., Mariani, M., Nasr, R., & Laker, B. (2022). Unmasking the other face of flexible working practices: A systematic literature review. *Journal of Business Research*, *142*, 648–662. DOI: 10.1016/j.jbusres.2022.01.024

Somani, P. (2022). Managing mental health at work during periods of uncertainty. *Journal of Economics Finance and Management Studies*, *05*(04). Advance online publication. DOI: 10.47191/jefms/v5-i4-13

Soni, V. (2019, December 5). What is Digital Information Security in Healthcare Act (DISHA) in India? *ZNetLive Blog - A Guide to Domains, Web Hosting & Cloud Computing*. https://www.znetlive.com/blog/digital-information-security-healthcare-act-disha/

Sonnentag, S., Binnewies, C., & Mojza, E. J. (2020). Can work be fun? The role of work characteristics and individual differences in promoting work-related well-being. *Journal of Vocational Behavior*, *109*, 151–165. DOI: 10.1016/j.jvb.2018.08.008

SOPHOS. (2023). *Cybercriminals Successfully Encrypted Data in Ransomware Attacks on Nearly 75% of Healthcare Organizations That Sophos Surveyed | Sophos*. https://www.sophos.com/en-us/press/press-releases/2023/11/cybercriminals-successfully-encrypted-data-ransomware-attacks-nearly

Sorensen, G., Sparer, E., Williams, J. A. R., Gundersen, D., Boden, L. I., Dennerlein, J. T., Hashimoto, D., Katz, J. N., McLellan, D. L., Okechukwu, C. A., Pronk, N. P., Revette, A., & Wagner, G. R. (2018). Measuring Best Practices for Workplace Safety, Health, and Well-Being. *Journal of Occupational and Environmental Medicine*, *60*(5), 430–439. DOI: 10.1097/JOM.0000000000001286 PMID: 29389812

Søvold, L. E., Naslund, J. A., Kousoulis, A. A., Saxena, S., Qoronfleh, M. W., Grobler, C., & Münter, L. (2021). Prioritizing the mental health and well-being of healthcare workers: An urgent global public health priority. [frontiersin.org]. *Frontiers in Public Health*, *9*, 679397.

Specchia, M. L., Cozzolino, M. R., Carini, E., Di Pilla, A., Galletti, C., Ricciardi, W., & Damiani, G. (2021). Leadership styles and nurses' job satisfaction. Results of a systematic review. [mdpi.com]. *International Journal of Environmental Research and Public Health*, *18*(4), 1552.

Spotify. (2021a). Spotify announces Work From Anywhere program. https://newsroom.spotify.com/2021-02-12/introducing-work-from-anywhere/

Spotify. (2021b). How Spotify redesigned work to unlock global talent. https://hrblog.spotify.com

Spreitzer, G., Cameron, L., & Garrett, L. (2017). Alternative work arrangements: Two images of the new world of work. *Annual Review of Organizational Psychology and Organizational Behavior*, *4*(1), 473–499. DOI: 10.1146/annurev-orgpsych-032516-113332

Srivastava, H. (2023). How motivational leadership can positively affect the mental health of employees, leading to better productivity. *Russian Law Journal*, *11*(3). Advance online publication. DOI: 10.52783/rlj.v11i3.2050

Stafford, A. M., Pulgar, C. A., & Villarreal-Otálora, T. (2025). Strategies to Improve Engagement of Latino Adolescents in Mental Health Research. *Mental Health Science*, *3*(1), e70005. DOI: 10.1002/mhs2.70005

Stalin, M. V., & Maheswari, M. U. (2024). The Influence of Human Resource Management Practices on Employee Work Engagement In Selected Manufacturing Companies in South India. *The Journal of Research Administration*, *6*(1).

Stephen, M., & Frank, L. (2024a). *The Role of Electronic Health Records in Transforming Healthcare Delivery and Financial Gains*.

Stephen, M., & Frank, L. (2024b). *The Role of Electronic Health Records in Transforming Healthcare Delivery and Financial Gains*.

Stephens, Z. D., Lee, S. Y., Faghri, F., Campbell, R. H., Zhai, C., Efron, M. J., & Robinson, G. E. (2015). Big data: Astronomical or genomical? *PLoS Biology*, *13*(7), e1002195. DOI: 10.1371/journal.pbio.1002195 PMID: 26151137

Stevens, N. C. Philip. (2020). *Building a Global Framework for Digital Health Services in the Era of COVID-19*. https://itif.org/publications/2020/05/26/building-global-framework-digital-health-services-era-covid-19/

Stimpfel, A. W., Sloane, D. M., & Aiken, L. H. (2012). The Longer The Shifts For Hospital Nurses, The Higher The Levels Of Burnout And Patient Dissatisfaction. *Health Affairs*, *31*(11), 2501–2509. DOI: 10.1377/hlthaff.2011.1377 PMID: 23129681

Stoumpos, A. I., Kitsios, F., & Talias, M. A. (2023). Digital Transformation in Healthcare: Technology Acceptance and Its Applications. *International Journal of Environmental Research and Public Health*, *20*(4), 3407. DOI: 10.3390/ijerph20043407 PMID: 36834105

Strategies, N. R. C. (US) C. on E. the I. for H. A. T. R. and I. (2000). Health Applications of the Internet. In *Networking Health: Prescriptions for the Internet*. National Academies Press (US). https://www.ncbi.nlm.nih.gov/books/NBK44714/

Stratton, E., Lampit, A., Choi, I., Calvo, R. A., Harvey, S. B., & Glozier, N. (2017). Effectiveness of eHealth interventions for reducing mental health conditions in employees: A systematic review and meta-analysis. *PLoS One*, *12*(12), e0189904.

Strianese, O., Rizzo, F., Ciccarelli, M., Galasso, G., D'Agostino, Y., Salvati, A., Del Giudice, C., Tesorio, P., & Rusciano, M. R. (2020). Precision and Personalized Medicine: How Genomic Approach Improves the Management of Cardiovascular and Neurodegenerative Disease. *Genes*, *11*(7), 747. DOI: 10.3390/genes11070747 PMID: 32640513

Strudwick, J., Gayed, A., Deady, M., Haffar, S., Mobbs, S., Malik, A., Akhtar, A., Braund, T., Bryant, R. A., & Harvey, S. (2023). Workplace mental health screening: A systematic review and meta-analysis. *Occupational and Environmental Medicine*, *80*(8), 469–484. DOI: 10.1136/oemed-2022-108608 PMID: 37321849

Subramony, M., & Rosenbaum, M. S. (2024). SDG commentary: Economic services for work and growth for all humans. *Journal of Services Marketing*, *38*(2), 190–216. DOI: 10.1108/JSM-05-2023-0201

Sukeshini, P. S., Ved, M., Chintalapti, J., & Pal, S. N. (2020). Big Data Analytics and Machine Learning Technologies for HPC. Evolving Technologies for Computing, Communication and Smart World. *Proceedings of ETCCS*, *2020*(694), 411.

Supreme Court Observer. (2018a). *Constitutionality of Aadhaar Act: Judgment Summary*. Supreme Court Observer. https://www.scobserver.in/reports/constitutionality-of-aadhaar-justice-k-s-puttaswamy-union-of-india-judgment-in-plain-english/

Supreme Court Observer. (2018b). *Fundamental Right to Privacy*. Supreme Court Observer. https://www.scobserver.in/cases/puttaswamy-v-union-of-india-fundamental-right-to-privacy-case-background/

Surana, S. J., & Singh, A. K. (2013). The impact of role stressors and work overload on job burnout. *International Journal of Intelligent Enterprise*, *2*(1), 64. DOI: 10.1504/IJIE.2013.057339

Suriyankietkaew, S., Krittayaruangroj, K., & Iamsawan, N. (2022). Sustainable Leadership practices and competencies of SMEs for sustainability and resilience: A community-based social enterprise study. Sustainability. mdpi.com

Suwannapirom, P., & Pranee, S. (2023). A Model of Enhancing Innovative Work Behavior of Airports of Thailand. *Asian Administration and Management Review*, *6*(2), 12–22.

Swanson, L. M., Arnedt, J. T., Rosekind, M. R., Belenky, G., Balkin, T. J., & Drake, C. (2011). Sleep disorders and work performance: Findings from the 2008 National Sleep Foundation Sleep in America poll: Sleep disorders and work performance. *Journal of Sleep Research*, *20*(3), 487–494. DOI: 10.1111/j.1365-2869.2010.00890.x PMID: 20887396

Swargiary, K., & Roy, K. (2024). *AI Angels: Empowering Children with Special Needs through Artificial Intelligence*. scholar press.

Syed Mohamad, S. J. A. N., Muhamad Nor, N. S. N., Fikry, A., & Abdul Aziz, M. R. (2023). The Effect of Organizational Innovation Mediates between Knowledge Management Capabilities and Hotel Performance: A Conceptual Analysis. *Information Management and Business Review*, *15*(3(SI)), 510–524. DOI: 10.22610/imbr.v15i3(SI).3506

Szeto, A. C., & Dobson, K. S. (2010). Reducing the stigma of mental disorders at work: A review of current workplace anti-stigma intervention programs. *Applied & Preventive Psychology*, *14*(1-4), 41–56.

Tabaj, A., Pastirk, S., Bitenc, Č., & Masten, R. (2015). Work-Related Stress, Burnout, Compassion, and Work Satisfaction of Professional Workers in Vocational Rehabilitation. *Rehabilitation Counseling Bulletin*, *58*(2), 113–123. DOI: 10.1177/0034355214537383

Tagde, P., Tagde, S., Bhattacharya, T., Tagde, P., Chopra, H., Akter, R., Kaushik, D., & Rahman, M. (2021). Blockchain and artificial intelligence technology in e-Health. *Environmental Science and Pollution Research International*, *28*(38), 52810–52831. DOI: 10.1007/s11356-021-16223-0 PMID: 34476701

Taghian, A., Abo-Zahhad, M., Sayed, M. S., & Abdel-Malek, A. (2021, December). Virtual, Augmented Reality, and Wearable Devices for Biomedical Applications: A Review. In *2021 9th International Japan-Africa Conference on Electronics, Communications, and Computations (JAC-ECC)* (pp. 93-98). IEEE.

Tavares, A. I. (2017). Telework and health effects review. *International Journal of Healthcare*, *3*(2), 30–36. DOI: 10.5430/ijh.v3n2p30

Tawalbeh, L., Muheidat, F., Tawalbeh, M., & Quwaider, M. (2020). IoT Privacy and Security: Challenges and Solutions. *Applied Sciences (Basel, Switzerland)*, *10*(12), 4102. DOI: 10.3390/app10124102

Taylor, F. W. (1911). *The principles of scientific management*. Harper & Brothers.

Te Maihāroa, K., & Woodhouse, A. (Eds.). (2023). *Indigenous Autoethnography: Illuminating Māori Voices*. Springer Nature. DOI: 10.1007/978-981-99-6718-6

Teikari, P., Najjar, R. P., Schmetterer, L., & Milea, D. (2019). Embedded deep learning in ophthalmology: Making ophthalmic imaging smarter. *Therapeutic Advances in Ophthalmology*, *11*, 2515841419827172. DOI: 10.1177/2515841419827172 PMID: 30911733

Thapa, C., & Camtepe, S. (2021). Precision health data: Requirements, challenges and existing techniques for data security and privacy. *Computers in Biology and Medicine*, *129*, 104130. DOI: 10.1016/j.compbiomed.2020.104130 PMID: 33271399

Theodos, K., & Sittig, S. (2020). Health Information Privacy Laws in the Digital Age: HIPAA Doesn't Apply. *Perspectives in Health Information Management*, *18*(Winter), 1l. https://www.ncbi.nlm.nih.gov/pmc/articles/PMC7883355/ PMID: 33633522

Thieme E-Journals—Yearbook of Medical Informatics / Abstract. (n.d.). Retrieved June 30, 2024, from https://www.thieme-connect.de/products/ejournals/abstract/10.1055/s-0042-1742519

Tian, J., & Freeman, H. (2024). "All You Need Is Love" a Social Network Approach to Understanding Attachment Networks in Adulthood. *Behavioral Sciences (Basel, Switzerland)*, *14*(8), 647. DOI: 10.3390/bs14080647 PMID: 39199043

Tisu, L., Lup a, D., Vîrgă, D., & Rusu, A. (2020). Personality characteristics, job performance and mental health: The mediating role of work engagement. *Personality and Individual Differences*, *153*, 109644.

Tiwari, S. K., Kaur, J., Singla, P., & Hrisheekesha, P. N. (2022, September). A Comprehensive Review of Big Data Analysis Techniques in Health-Care. In *International Conference on Emergent Converging Technologies and Biomedical Systems* (pp. 401-420). Singapore: Springer Nature Singapore.

Tosza, S. (2021). Internet service providers as law enforcers and adjudicators. A public role of private actors. *Computer Law & Security Review*, *43*, 105614. DOI: 10.1016/j.clsr.2021.105614

Trenerry, B., Chng, S., Wang, Y., Suhaila, Z. S., Lim, S. S., Lu, H. Y., & Oh, P. H. (2021). Preparing workplaces for digital transformation: An integrative review and framework of multi-level factors. [frontiersin.org]. *Frontiers in Psychology, 12*, 620766. DOI: 10.3389/fpsyg.2021.620766 PMID: 33833714

Tsiotsou, R. H., Kabadayi, S., & Fisk, R. P. (2024). Advocating human rights and Sustainable Development Goals: an ecosystem-based Transformative Service Research (TSR) approach. In *A Research Agenda for Service Marketing* (pp. 225-249). Edward Elgar Publishing.

Tu n, L. (2019). Discretionary hr practices and employee well-being. *Personnel Review, 49*(1), 43–66. DOI: 10.1108/PR-05-2018-0162

Tucker, M. A., & Lindsay, D. P. (2023). The intersectionality of flexible work policies: Implications for marginalized employees. *Journal of Business and Psychology, 38*(2), 1015–1034. DOI: 10.1007/s10869-022-09837-9

Tuzovic, S., & Kabadayi, S. (2021). The influence of social distancing on employee well-being: A conceptual framework and research agenda. *Journal of Service Management, 32*(2), 145–160.

Uddin, M. A., Stranieri, A., Gondal, I., & Balasubramanian, V. (2021). A survey on the adoption of blockchain in IoT: Challenges and solutions. *Blockchain: Research and Applications, 2*(2), 100006. DOI: 10.1016/j.bcra.2021.100006

Using Artificial Intelligence in the workplace: What are the main ethical risks? (OECD Social, Employment and Migration Working Papers 273; OECD Social, Employment and Migration Working Papers, Vol. 273). (2022). DOI: 10.1787/1815199X

Vaidyanathan, S., & Mahapatra, G. (2020). Enhancing employee stress resilience (wellness): A study of women leaders in asia pacific. *NHRD Network Journal, 14*(1), 144–154. DOI: 10.1177/2631454120973513

Vanini, G. (2024). Are orexins–hypocretins the culprit for rapid eye movement sleep behavior disorder in narcolepsy? *Sleep (Basel), 47*(11), zsae208. Advance online publication. DOI: 10.1093/sleep/zsae208 PMID: 39238164

Vaughn, B., Rotolo, S., & Roth, H. (2014). Circadian rhythm and sleep influences on digestive physiology and disorders. *ChronoPhysiology and Therapy, 67*, 67. Advance online publication. DOI: 10.2147/CPT.S44806

Veage, S., Ciarrochi, J., Deane, F. P., Andresen, R., Oades, L. G., & Crowe, T. P. (2014). Value congruence, importance and success and in the workplace: Links with well-being and burnout amongst mental health practitioners. *Journal of Contextual Behavioral Science, 3*(4), 258–264. DOI: 10.1016/j.jcbs.2014.06.004

Venkatesh, U., Aravind, G. P., & Velmurugan, A. A. (2022). Telemedicine practice guidelines in India: Global implications in the wake of the COVID-19 pandemic. *World Medical & Health Policy*, *14*(3), 589–599. DOI: 10.1002/wmh3.497 PMID: 35601469

Verstegen, N., Peters-Scheffer, N., Didden, P. D. R., Nijman, P. D. H., & de Vogel, P. D. V. (2024). Patient experiences of victimization during mandatory psychiatric treatment: A qualitative study. *Journal of Forensic Psychology Research and Practice*, *24*(1), 1–22. DOI: 10.1080/24732850.2022.2051662

Verstraete, M., & Zarsky, T. (2021). Optimizing breach notification. U. Ill. L. Rev., 803.

Vetter, C., Devore, E. E., Ramin, C. A., Speizer, F. E., Willett, W. C., & Schernhammer, E. S. (2015). Mismatch of Sleep and Work Timing and Risk of Type 2 Diabetes. *Diabetes Care*, *38*(9), 1707–1713. DOI: 10.2337/dc15-0302 PMID: 26109502

Vetter, C., Fischer, D., Matera, J. L., & Roenneberg, T. (2015). Aligning Work and Circadian Time in Shift Workers Improves Sleep and Reduces Circadian Disruption. *Current Biology*, *25*(7), 907–911. DOI: 10.1016/j.cub.2015.01.064 PMID: 25772446

Viceconti, M., Hunter, P., & Hose, R. (2015). Big data, big knowledge: Big data for personalized healthcare. *IEEE Journal of Biomedical and Health Informatics*, *19*(4), 1209–1215. DOI: 10.1109/JBHI.2015.2406883 PMID: 26218867

Villaume, K., Tafvelin, S., & Hasson, D. (2024). Health-relevant personality traits are associated with measures of health, well-being, stress and psychosocial work environment over time. *PLoS One*, *19*(12), e0314321. DOI: 10.1371/journal.pone.0314321 PMID: 39671364

Visnjic, I., & Leten, R. (2024). The Legacy Company's Guide to Innovation. Harvard Business Review. https://hbr.org/2024/09/the-legacy-companys-guide-to-innovation

Viswesvaran, C., Sanchez, J. I., & Fisher, J. (1999). The role of social support in the process of work stress: A meta-analysis. *Journal of Vocational Behavior*, *54*(3), 314–334. DOI: 10.1006/jvbe.1998.1661

Vonderlin, R., Matos, M., Lutz, W., & Barnhofer, T. (2021). Mindfulness interventions in organizational settings: A systematic review. *Journal of Occupational Health Psychology*, *26*(1), 22–37. DOI: 10.1037/ocp0000224 PMID: 34672643

Vonderlin, R., Schmidt, B., Müller, G., Biermann, M., Kleindienst, N., Bohus, M., & Lyssenko, L. (2021). Health-oriented leadership and mental health from supervisor and employee perspectives: A multilevel and multisource approach. *Frontiers in Psychology, 11*, 614803. Advance online publication. DOI: 10.3389/fpsyg.2020.614803 PMID: 33536980

Wagstaff, A. S., & Sigstad Lie, J.-A. (2011). Shift and night work and long working hours – a systematic review of safety implications. *Scandinavian Journal of Work, Environment & Health, 37*(3), 173–185. DOI: 10.5271/sjweh.3146 PMID: 21290083

Wang, B., Liu, Y., & Parker, S. K. (2020). How does the use of information communication technology affect individuals? A work design perspective. *The Academy of Management Annals, 14*(2), 695–725. DOI: 10.5465/annals.2018.0127

Wang, B., Liu, Y., Qian, J., & Parker, S. K. (2020). Achieving effective remote working during the COVID-19 pandemic: A work design perspective. *Applied Psychology, 70*(1), 16–59. DOI: 10.1111/apps.12290 PMID: 33230359

Wang, H., Zhou, D., Zhang, C., & Xie, L. (2021). Mental health issues in the IT industry: An overview. *Journal of Workplace Behavioral Health, 36*(4), 287–304. DOI: 10.1080/15555240.2021.1965673

Wang, W., Kang, S. W., & Choi, S. B. (2021). Effects of employee well-being and self-efficacy on the relationship between coaching leadership and knowledge sharing intention: A study of UK and US employees. [mdpi.com]. *International Journal of Environmental Research and Public Health, 18*(20), 10638. DOI: 10.3390/ijerph182010638 PMID: 34682385

Wang, Y., Ummar, R., Qureshi, T. M., Ul Haq, J., & Bonn, M. A. (2025). Employee Sustainability: How Green Practices Drive Employee Well-Being and Citizenship Behavior. *Sustainability (Basel), 17*(3), 936. DOI: 10.3390/su17030936

Wang, Z.-Z., Sun, Z., Zhang, M.-L., Xiong, K., & Zhou, F. (2022). Relationship between shift work, night work, and subsequent dementia: A systematic evaluation and meta-analysis. *Frontiers in Neurology, 13*, 997181. DOI: 10.3389/fneur.2022.997181 PMID: 36419534

Waraah, U., Tiwari, A., Rawat, D., & Jha, R. (2022). *Data Breach In Healthcare Industry: An Infringement Of Right To Privacy; A Modern Era Effect.*

Wardani, L., Apriliani, A., Riskinanti, K., Dearly, D., & Sharif, S. (2023). The role of employee well-being as a moderator: Job crafting and work engagement. *Indigenous Jurnal Ilmiah Psikologi, 8*(1), 22–38. DOI: 10.23917/indigenous.v8i1.19903

Ward, E., Fragala, M., Birse, C., Hawrilenko, M., Smolka, C., Ambwani, G., Brown, M., Krystal, J. H., Corlett, P. R., & Chekroud, A. (2023). Assessing the impact of a comprehensive mental health program on frontline health service workers. *PLoS One*, *18*(11), e0294414. DOI: 10.1371/journal.pone.0294414 PMID: 37988363

Watthanabut, B., & Manasabutr, S. (2017). Happy Workplace according to Buddhist Way. *PSAKU International Journal of Interdisciplinary Research*, *6*(1), 21–28. DOI: 10.12778/235108618X15452373185949

Wei, S., & Bunchapattanasakda, C. (2024). Impact of Female Servant Leadership Style on Employee Engagement in Beijing's Public Universities. *Asian Political Science Review*, *8*(2), 99–105.

Weitzman, E. D., Fukushima, D., Nogeire, C., Roffwarg, H., Gallagher, T. F., & Hellman, L. (1971). Twenty-four Hour Pattern of the Episodic Secretion of Cortisol in Normal Subjects. *The Journal of Clinical Endocrinology and Metabolism*, *33*(1), 14–22. DOI: 10.1210/jcem-33-1-14 PMID: 4326799

Wel, K., Bambra, C., Dragano, N., Eikemo, T., & Lunau, T. (2015). Risk and resilience: health inequalities, working conditions and sickness benefit arrangements: an analysis of the 2010 european working conditions survey. *Sociology of Health & Illness*, *37*(8), 1157–1172. DOI: 10.1111/1467-9566.12293 PMID: 26094941

Wickens, C. D. (2008). Multiple Resources and Mental Workload. *Human Factors*, *50*(3), 449–455. DOI: 10.1518/001872008X288394 PMID: 18689052

Wickwire, E. M., Geiger-Brown, J., Scharf, S. M., & Drake, C. L. (2017). Shift Work and Shift Work Sleep Disorder. *Chest*, *151*(5), 1156–1172. DOI: 10.1016/j.chest.2016.12.007 PMID: 28012806

Wieneke, K. C., Berkland, B. E., Kruse, G. C., Priestley, M. R., Teal, D. M., & West, C. P. (2025, March). Charting a new path forward in addressing employee well-being in health care. []). Elsevier.]. *Mayo Clinic Proceedings*, *100*(3), 501–513. DOI: 10.1016/j.mayocp.2024.11.018 PMID: 40044362

Wieneke, K., Egginton, J., Jenkins, S., Kruse, G., López-Jiménez, F., Mungo, M., Riley, B. A., & Limburg, P. (2019). Well-being champion impact on employee engagement, staff satisfaction, and employee well-being. *Mayo Clinic Proceedings. Innovations, Quality & Outcomes*, *3*(2), 106–115. DOI: 10.1016/j.mayocpiqo.2019.04.001 PMID: 31193868

Williams, J. C., Blair-Loy, M., & Berdahl, J. L. (2016). Cultural schemas, social class, and the flexibility stigma. *The Journal of Social Issues*, *72*(2), 209–232. DOI: 10.1111/josi.12012

Wirth, F. N., Meurers, T., Johns, M., & Prasser, F. (2021). Privacy-preserving data sharing infrastructures for medical research: Systematization and comparison. *BMC Medical Informatics and Decision Making*, *21*(1), 242. DOI: 10.1186/s12911-021-01602-x PMID: 34384406

Wittmann, M., Dinich, J., Merrow, M., & Roenneberg, T. (2006). Social Jetlag: Misalignment of Biological and Social Time. *Chronobiology International*, *23*(1–2), 497–509. DOI: 10.1080/07420520500545979 PMID: 16687322

Wittmann, M., Paulus, M., & Roenneberg, T. (2010). Decreased Psychological Well-Being in Late 'Chronotypes' Is Mediated by Smoking and Alcohol Consumption. *Substance Use & Misuse*, *45*(1–2), 15–30. DOI: 10.3109/10826080903498952 PMID: 20025436

Wolkowitz, O. M., Epel, E. S., & Reus, V. I. (2001). Stress Hormone-Related Psychopathology: Pathophysiological and Treatment Implications. *The World Journal of Biological Psychiatry*, *2*(3), 115–143. DOI: 10.3109/15622970109026799 PMID: 12587196

Wong, P., Elsbach, K. D., & Fridman, S. (2021). The mental health impact of flexible work models: A review and agenda for future research. *Journal of Organizational Behavior*, *42*(3), 330–347. DOI: 10.1002/job.2520

World Health Organization (WHO). (2020). Mental health in the workplace. Retrieved from https://www.who.int/news-room/fact-sheets/detail/mental-health-at-work

World Health Organization. (2017). *Mental health in the workplace*. World Health Organization. https://www.who.int/news-room/fact-sheets/detail/mental-health-in-the-workplace

Wright, K. P.Jr, Bogan, R. K., & Wyatt, J. K. (2013). Shift work and the assessment and management of shift work disorder (SWD). *Sleep Medicine Reviews*, *17*(1), 41–54. DOI: 10.1016/j.smrv.2012.02.002 PMID: 22560640

Wu, X., Zhu, X., Wu, G. Q., & Ding, W. (2013). Data mining with big data. *IEEE Transactions on Knowledge and Data Engineering*, *26*(1), 97–107.

Xiang, D., & Cai, W. (2021). Privacy Protection and Secondary Use of Health Data: Strategies and Methods. *BioMed Research International*, *2021*(1), 1–11. DOI: 10.1155/2021/6967166 PMID: 34660798

Xie, Z., Chen, F., Li, W. A., Geng, X., Li, C., Meng, X., Feng, Y., Liu, W., & Yu, F. (2017). A review of sleep disorders and melatonin. *Neurological Research*, *39*(6), 559–565. DOI: 10.1080/01616412.2017.1315864 PMID: 28460563

Yang, T., Jiang, X., & Cheng, H. (2022). Employee Recognition, Task Performance, and OCB: Mediated and Moderated by Pride. *Sustainability (Basel), 14*(3), 1631. DOI: 10.3390/su14031631

Young, A., Bourke, A., Foley, S., & Blasi, Z. (2024). Effects of time management interventions on mental health and well-being factors: A protocol for a systematic review. *PLoS One, 19*(3), e0288887. DOI: 10.1371/journal.pone.0288887 PMID: 38466711

Yuan, B., & Li, J. (2019). The Policy Effect of the General Data Protection Regulation (GDPR) on the Digital Public Health Sector in the European Union: An Empirical Investigation. *International Journal of Environmental Research and Public Health, 16*(6), 1070. DOI: 10.3390/ijerph16061070 PMID: 30934648

Yuliantini, T., Daru, A. S. I. H., Sudiro, A., Apriadi, I., Yuniarinto, A., Suryadhi, J., & Kurniawan, D. (2021, October). Online-Learning Program To Develop Leadership On Student Council Organisation. In ICCD (Vol. 3, No. 1, pp. 303-307).

Yulianti, P., & Fitdiarini, N. (2023). Job insecurity and psychological well-being: Is it necessary to foster employee performance. *International Journal of Current Science Research and Review, 06*(06). Advance online publication. DOI: 10.47191/ijcsrr/V6-i6-14

Zandesh, Z., Ghazisaeedi, M., Devarakonda, M. V., & Haghighi, M. S. (2019). Legal framework for health cloud: A systematic review. *International Journal of Medical Informatics, 132*, 103953. DOI: 10.1016/j.ijmedinf.2019.103953 PMID: 31630064

Zeidan, F., Johnson, S. K., Diamond, B. J., David, Z., & Goolkasian, P. (2010). Mindfulness meditation improves cognition: Evidence of brief mental training. *Consciousness and Cognition, 19*(2), 597–605. DOI: 10.1016/j.concog.2010.03.014 PMID: 20363650

Zheng, C., Molineux, J., Mirshekary, S., & Scarparo, S. (2015). Developing individual and organisational work-life balance strategies to improve employee health and well-being. *Employee Relations, 37*(3), 354–379. DOI: 10.1108/ER-10-2013-0142

Zhou, L., Pan, S., Wang, J., & Vasilakos, A. V. (2017). Machine learning on big data: Opportunities and challenges. *Neurocomputing, 237*, 350–361. DOI: 10.1016/j.neucom.2017.01.026

Zhou, S. K., Greenspan, H., Davatzikos, C., Duncan, J. S., Van Ginneken, B., Madabhushi, A., Prince, J. L., Rueckert, D., & Summers, R. M. (2021). A review of deep learning in medical imaging: Imaging traits, technology trends, case studies with progress highlights, and future promises. *Proceedings of the IEEE, 109*(5), 820–838. DOI: 10.1109/JPROC.2021.3054390 PMID: 37786449

Zhou, S., Zhang, R., Chen, D., & Zhu, X. (2021). A novel framework for bringing smart big data to proactive decision making in healthcare. *Health Informatics Journal, 27*(2), 14604582211024698. DOI: 10.1177/14604582211024698 PMID: 34159834

Zhu, S., Tse, S., Goodyear-Smith, F., Yuen, W., & Wong, P. (2016). Health-related behaviours and mental health in hong kong employees. *Occupational Medicine, 67*(1), 26–32. DOI: 10.1093/occmed/kqw137 PMID: 27707896

About the Contributors

Kittisak Wongmahesak serves as a lecturer at the Faculty of Political Science, North Bangkok University, and the Director of the Association of Legal & Political Studies in Thailand. Currently, he holds the position of Research Fellow at Shinawatra University, Thailand, and Universiti Sultan Zainal Abidin, Malaysia. He is also an Adjunct Professor at Sekolah Tinggi Ilmu Administrasi Abdul Haris, Indonesia, and an Adjunct Research Professor at several Indonesian universities, including Universitas Muhammadiyah Sinjai, Universitas Muhammadiyah Makassar, and Universitas Muhammadiyah Sidenreng Rappang. Previously, he was a Full Professor of Public Administration at Huanghe Business School, Henan University of Economics and Law in China, and at the University of City Island in Cyprus. He also served as an Adjunct Researcher at Ton Duc Thang University and Duy Tan University in Vietnam. His academic credentials include a Ph.D. in Social Sciences, an M.A. and a B.A. in Political Science, all from Kasetsart University. Additionally, he earned an M.B.A. and an M.P.A. from Ramkhamhaeng University, and a B.Pol.Sc. in International Relations and Comparative Government and Politics from Sukhothai Thammathirat Open University. His expertise spans Political Science, Public and Private Management, International Political Economy, and Social Research. He is the editor of numerous prestigious journals worldwide, including Sustainability, Frontiers in Psychology, PLOS One, World Food Policy, Asian Academy of Management Journal, International Journal of Public Policy and Administration Research, International Journal of Innovative Research and Scientific Studies, and Recent Advances in Computer Science and Communications. Recognized as one of the world's top 2% of scientists by Stanford University since 2020, he has published over 450 Scopus/Web of Science indexed documents and holds an h-index of 57 with more than 10,000 citations.

Roy Rillera Marzo is the Dean of the Faculty of Humanities and Health Sciences with over 15 years of research experience in communicable and non-communicable diseases. Dr. Roy has published extensively in peer-reviewed journals and serves on several editorial boards related to public health and epidemiology. His investigation into global adult vaccine hesitancy earned the "Award-Winning Research of 2022," marking a significant contribution to the field. Furthermore, his global survey on COVID-19 vaccine perceptions stood out as among the top 1% of viewed papers in a prestigious journal, highlighting its critical impact. Dr. Roy's scholarly output includes 30 articles featured in the World Health Organization Research Database, underscoring his key role in shaping global public health policies and interventions.

Uday Kumar Ghosh is a faculty member in Business Administration at Lincoln University, California, where he also serves as the President's Advisor for International Business Development. A published author and researcher, his work focuses on Hybrid Leadership, quality management in higher education, and digital transformation. With over two decades of global corporate leadership experience, including roles as CEO and Managing Director across Europe and Asia, Dr.Ghosh brings unique industry insights to academia. He holds a Ph.D. in Leadership from the University of the Cumberlands and multiple master's degrees in international business, HR & Marketing, and Public Administration.

***

Saurabh Chandra is an accomplished legal scholar and currently serves as an Associate Professor & Assistant Dean at the School of Law, Bennett University, India. With a robust academic foundation, he earned his Bachelor of Arts and Bachelor of Laws (B.A. LL.B.) from the prestigious Aligarh Muslim University (A.M.U.). He further specialized in Business Laws, completing his Master of Laws (LL.M.) at the renowned National Law School of India University (NLSIU), Bangalore. Dr. Chandra's academic journey culminated in a Doctorate in Law (Ph.D.) from the esteemed National Law University (NLU) Delhi. In addition to his impressive legal education from some of India's most prestigious institutions, Dr. Saurabh Chandra also holds a master's degree in Management with specialization in Human Resources in Management and another in Journalism and Mass Communication. With 16 years of teaching experience, he has established himself as an expert in Business and Corporate Laws, with numerous publications to his credit. Dr. Saurabh Chandra is a distinguished expert in Business and Corporate Laws, with a profound understanding of the intricate legal frameworks that govern the business world. His expertise is complemented by a robust portfolio of scholarly publications, which underscores his commitment to advancing knowledge in his field. Throughout his career, Dr. Chandra has consistently produced high-impact research that addresses critical issues in Business and Corporate Law. His publications are widely recognized for their depth of analysis, innovative perspectives, and practical relevance. He has contributed extensively to leading journals, where his work has often set new standards for legal scholarship. His publications not only reflect his scholarly rigor but also his dedication to addressing contemporary challenges faced by businesses and policymakers. By bridging the gap between theoretical insights and real-world applications, Dr. Chandra's work serves as a valuable resource for academics, legal practitioners, and industry professionals alike. Dr. Chandra brings a wealth of experience in Academic Administration, having successfully held various key administrative positions. His diverse qualifications and extensive experience make him a distinguished figure in the academic and legal communities.

Ishani Gupta is a third-year Bachelor of Business Administration (BBA) student at Christ University, Bengaluru, India. With a strong academic foundation in business strategy, digital marketing, and project management, she has gained hands-on experience through virtual internships at JPMorgan Chase, GE Aerospace, Accenture, and PepsiCo. Passionate about research and innovation, she aims to bridge business insights with practical solutions, contributing to the evolving landscape of management and strategy.

Yogita Kalra is a dedicated Nursing Officer at the Ministry of Health and Family Welfare, Deen Dayal Upadhyay Hospital, New Delhi, and a Research Scholar in the Department of Psychology at Lovely Professional University, Punjab. With a strong foundation in both nursing and psychology, she is passionate about bridging the gap between healthcare practice and academic research. She holds a Diploma in General Nursing and Midwifery, a Post Basic BSc in Nursing, and a Master's in Psychology from IGNOU. Currently, she is pursuing her Ph.D. in Psychology, focusing on shift work, chronotype, and psychosomatic symptoms among healthcare professionals. Her research contributions include publications in Scopus-indexed journals, a book chapter on chronotype and its impact on education, and multiple conference presentations on psychosomatic symptoms and quality care in elderly homes. She has also undergone extensive training in research methodology, structural equation modeling, and statistical data analysis. Yogita actively participates in national and international workshops, faculty development programs, and webinars to stay at the forefront of emerging healthcare trends. Her commitment to improving patient care, nursing education, and workplace well-being makes her a valuable contributor to the healthcare and research community. She continues to explore innovative ways to enhance nursing practices, mental health awareness, and research in healthcare settings.

Santosh Kumar is working as associate professor at the Sharda School of Business Studies, Sharda University. He is MBA (finance), M.com, M.A. (eco.), ICWA (I), and Ph.D. with a vast experience of 20 years in teaching and research. He has published many research papers in national and international journals of high repute. He has authored a book on financial accounting. He is a certified derivative expert of NISM and a resource person of the Indian Institute of Corporate Affairs. He has delivered several guest talks and workshops on the functioning of the stock market. He has trading experience of around 10 years in equity and derivatives markets.

Navonita Mallick is a doctoral candidate at KIIT Law School, Bhubaneswar, specializing in Child Rights in India. She is actively engaged in research, publications, and presentations at national and international conferences, addressing critical issues of child protection, digital transformation, and legal reform. She has authored multiple books and scholarly articles published by renowned international publishers, addressing diverse legal themes ranging from criminal law to sustainable governance. Navonita's analytical and communication skills drive her commitment to fostering impactful legal and social change.

Prerna Mehta is a distinguished academic and accomplished author with a robust educational background. She completed her BSc in Biotechnology at Rungta College of Science and Technology in Bhilai, Chhattisgarh, where she was honored with a gold medal for her exceptional performance. She then pursued a Master of Science in Biotechnology from Government V.Y.P.T. College, Durg, and obtained a B.Ed. degree from Ghanshyam Singh Arya Kanya College in Durg. Prerna's expertise covers a range of fields, including genetics, nanoparticles, biochemistry, and genetic engineering. Additionally, she is a lifetime member of the International Organization of Academic and Scientific Development (IOASD) and serves as a reviewer for the East African Scholars Journal of Biotechnology and Genetics. Prerna is also a lifetime member of The Indian Science Congress Association in Kolkata. As an accomplished author, she has written three books and holds utility patents for innovative projects: "A chamber to detect radiation and a method to shower melanin to protect the user against radiation" and "AI-Powered Rural Enhancement System for Tackling Hunger & Ensuring Water Conservation through Smart Resource M

Ramji Nagariya is working as an Assistant Professor in the School of Business and Management, CHRIST University, Bengaluru, India. He holds a Ph.D. in the area of sustainable service supply chain from the Department of Management Studies, Malaviya National Institute of Technology, Jaipur, India. He holds an M. Tech in Industrial Management from Indian Institute of Technology (BHU), Varanasi and a bachelor's degree in Aeronautical Engineering. His research papers are published in Production Planning & Control, International Journal of Logistics Management, Business Process Management Journal, Benchmarking: An International Journal, International Journal of Productivity & Performance Management, Management of Environmental Quality, Decision, and International Journal of Services and Operations Management. His research interest includes service supply chain, buyer-supplier relationship, and sustainability in supply chain.

Shashwata Sahu, a distinguished research scholar currently pursuing her Ph.D. in Law at KIIT University, Bhubaneswar, embodies an unwavering passion for the field of law. With a profound interest in Constitutional Law, she stands as a self-driven scholar, firmly rooted in the principles of altruism. With an impressive literary portfolio, Shashwata has authored nine impactful books, each delving into crucial aspects of law and society. Her works include "The Growing Significance of Artificial Intelligence," "The role of Indian media in covering crimes: a critical analysis," "The use of Amicus Curiae Briefs at the International Criminal Tribunals," "Assessing the legal landscape of bio-medical waste management in India," "Journey of Law: From Deities to Decrees," "Evolution of Local-Self Government in India", "The Invisible Manual Scavengers of India", "Law and Justice in a Globalizing World: An LL.M. Companion" and "Comparative Public Law: An LLM. Companion." Beyond her authored books, Shashwata's contributions extend to numerous publications in both international and national journals indexed in Scopus and Web of Science.

Deepa Sharma has done Ph.D., MBA in Human Resource Management, currently working as Assistant Professor at MMIM, Maharishi Markandeshwar (Deemed to be University), NAAC Accredited Grade 'A++' University, Mullana, Ambala (Haryana). She has more than 9 years of experience in academics. She has written 61+ research papers for various Scopus and UGC listed referred National & International Journals and 13 papers appear on SCOPUS Preview.

Bhupinder Singh working as Professor at Sharda University, India. Also, Honorary Professor in University of South Wales UK and Santo Tomas University Tunja, Colombia. His areas of publications as Smart Healthcare, Medicines, fuzzy logics, artificial intelligence, robotics, machine learning, deep learning, federated learning, IoT, PV Glasses, metaverse and many more. He has 3 books, 139 paper publications, 163 paper presentations in international/national conferences and seminars, participated in more than 40 workshops/FDP's/QIP's, 25 courses from international universities of repute, organized more than 59 events with international and national academicians and industry people's, editor-in-chief and co-editor in journals, developed new courses. He has given talks at international universities, resource person in international conferences such as in Nanyang Technological University Singapore, Tashkent State University of Law Uzbekistan; KIMEP University Kazakhstan, All'ah meh Tabatabi University Iran, the Iranian Association of International Criminal law, Iran and Hague Center for International Law and Investment, The Netherlands, Northumbria University Newcastle UK,

Sumin Samuel Sybol is currently an assistant professor at CHRIST (Deemed to be University), Delhi NCR Campus, and has previous teaching experience as a visiting faculty member at Amity University, Noida. He has substantial expertise in analytics, Machine Learning, programming, and networking. His professional experience includes holding the position of Head of IT at Enrope Solutions and Keyfill Light, where he managed IT operations and strategies. Additionally, he has published research papers and secured a patent on improving power efficiency for wearable devices. Prof. Sumin is proficient in programming languages, including C/C++, Java, and Python, and has experience using software like Tableau, Power BI, and MySQL. He has also actively participated in various faculty development programs (FDPs) and workshops related to AI, data visualization, and IoT sensors. His work has been presented at prestigious conferences organized by IIT Roorkee and IIT Mandi.

Index

B

C

D

E

F

G

H

I

J

L

M

N

O

P

R

S

W

www.ingramcontent.com/pod-product-compliance
Lightning Source LLC
LaVergne TN
LVHW060007031026
849161LV00025B/2250